Theories of Human Learning

Mrs. Gribbin's Cat

Seventh Edition

Both a serious academic text and an intriguing story, this seventh edition reflects a significant update in research, theory, and applications in all areas. It presents a comprehensive view of the historical development of learning theories from behaviorist through to cognitive models. The chapters also cover memory, motivation, social learning, machine learning, and artificial intelligence.

The author's highly entertaining style clarifies concepts, emphasizes practical applications, and presents a thought-provoking, narrator-based commentary. The stage is given to Mrs. Gribbin and her swashbuckling cat, who both lighten things up and supply much-needed detail. These two help to explore the importance of technology for simulating human cognitive processes and engage with current models of memory. They investigate developments in, and applications of, brain-based research and plunge into models in motivation theory, to name but a few of the adventures they embark upon in this textbook.

Guy R. Lefrançois is Honorary Professor in the Department of Educational Psychology at the University of Alberta, Canada. He has published over 50 titles, including a number of best-selling textbooks in their respective fields.

Theories of Human Learning

Mrs. Gribbin's Cat

Seventh Edition

GUY R. LEFRANÇOIS
University of Alberta

Shaftesbury Road, Cambridge CB2 8EA, United Kingdom

One Liberty Plaza, 20th Floor, New York, NY 10006, USA

477 Williamstown Road, Port Melbourne, VIC 3207, Australia

314–321, 3rd Floor, Plot 3, Splendor Forum, Jasola District Centre, New Delhi – 110025, India

103 Penang Road, #05–06/07, Visioncrest Commercial, Singapore 238467

Cambridge University Press is part of Cambridge University Press & Assessment, a department of the University of Cambridge.

We share the University's mission to contribute to society through the pursuit of education, learning and research at the highest international levels of excellence.

www.cambridge.org
Information on this title: www.cambridge.org/9781108484633

DOI: 10.1017/9781108696333

Fifth edition © 2006 Wadsworth, Cengage Learning
Sixth edition © 2012 Wadsworth, Cengage Learning
Seventh edition © Cambridge University Press & Assessment 2020

This publication is in copyright. Subject to statutory exception and to the provisions of relevant collective licensing agreements, no reproduction of any part may take place without the written permission of Cambridge University Press & Assessment.

Fifth edition 2006
Sixth edition 2012
Seventh edition 2020

A catalogue record for this publication is available from the British Library

ISBN 978-1-108-48463-3 Hardback
ISBN 978-1-108-73599-5 Paperback

Additional resources for this publication at www.cambridge.org/lefrancois7ed

Cambridge University Press & Assessment has no responsibility for the persistence or accuracy of URLs for external or third-party internet websites referred to in this publication and does not guarantee that any content on such websites is, or will remain, accurate or appropriate.

This book is dedicated to my grandmother, Emerilda Francœur, who taught me things I would never otherwise have known, with an honorable mention to Mrs. Gribbin's feline, Schrödinger.

(Editor's Note: This is Mrs. Gribbin's motto, thumbprint, seal, and signature – all of which she insisted are necessary to make a document true and binding. In English, this Latin motto – *fronti nulla fides* – means, more or less, "you can't judge a book by its cover.")

BRIEF CONTENTS

List of Illustrations	*page* xiii
List of Boxes	xviii
Preface: Read this First . . .	xix

Part I Science and Theory

1	**Human Learning**	3

Part II Mostly Behavioristic Theories

2	**Early Behaviorism: Pavlov, Watson, and Guthrie**	37
3	**The Effects of Behavior: Thorndike and Hull**	81
4	**Operant Conditioning: Skinner's Radical Behaviorism**	111
5	**Evolutionary Psychology: Learning, Biology, and the Brain**	154

Part III The Beginnings of Modern Cognitivism

6	**Transition to Modern Cognitivism: Hebb, Tolman, and the Gestaltists**	195

Part IV Mostly Cognitive Theories

7	**Three Cognitive Theories: Bruner, Piaget, and Vygotsky**	239
8	**Learning and Memory**	287
9	**Motivation and Emotions**	325

viii **Brief Contents**

10 Social Learning: Bandura's Social Cognitive Theory 366

11 Machine Learning and Artificial Intelligence: The Future? 394

Part V Summary

12 Summary, Synthesis, and Integration 425

Lefrançois's Epilogue 452
Glossary 456
References 496
Name Index 532
Subject Index 538

CONTENTS

List of Illustrations	*page* xiii
List of Boxes	xviii
Preface: Read this First ...	xix

Part I Science and Theory

1 Human Learning — 3
What Mrs. Gribbin Said: This Book — 4
The Psychology of Learning — 5
Scientific Theories — 9
Science and Psychological Theories — 15
Theories of Learning: A Brief Overview — 27
Preview of this Text — 29
Applications of Learning Theories — 33
Main Point Chapter Summary — 33

Part II Mostly Behavioristic Theories

2 Early Behaviorism: Pavlov, Watson, and Guthrie — 37
This Chapter — 38
Early Scientific Psychology — 39
Ivan P. Pavlov (1849–1936) — 42
John B. Watson (1878–1958) — 54
Edwin R. Guthrie (1886–1959) — 66
Evaluation of Early Behavioristic Theories — 78
Main Point Chapter Summary — 79

3 The Effects of Behavior: Thorndike and Hull — 81
This Chapter — 82
Edward L. Thorndike's Connectionism — 83
Animal Intelligence — 83
Clark L. Hull's Hypothetico-Deductive System — 95
Overview of Hull's System — 96

Contents

Educational Implications of Thorndike and Hull	108
Main Point Chapter Summary	109

4 Operant Conditioning: Skinner's Radical Behaviorism 111

This Chapter	112
Radical Behaviorism: An Antitheory?	113
Reinforcement and Punishment	120
Schedules of Reinforcement	125
Fading, Generalization, and Discrimination	139
Practical Applications of Operant Conditioning	141
Skinner's Position: An Appraisal	149
Main Point Chapter Summary	151

5 Evolutionary Psychology: Learning, Biology, and the Brain 154

This Chapter	155
Taste Aversion Learning	156
Evolutionary Psychology	164
A Transition	176
Learning and the Brain	178
Biofeedback and Neurofeedback	189
Main Point Chapter Summary	191

Part III The Beginnings of Modern Cognitivism

6 Transition to Modern Cognitivism: Hebb, Tolman, and the Gestaltists 195

This Chapter	196
Hebb's Theory	197
From Behaviorism to Cognitivism	213
Mechanistic Behaviorism	214
Tolman's Purposive Behaviorism	214
Gestalt Psychology	221
Metaphors in Psychology	232
Main Point Chapter Summary	234

Part IV Mostly Cognitive Theories

7 Three Cognitive Theories: Bruner, Piaget, and Vygotsky 239

This Chapter	240
Cognitive Psychology	241
Cognitivism Compared with Behaviorism	242

Contents xi

Bruner's Theory: Going Beyond the Information Given	244
Jean Piaget: A Developmental-Cognitive Position	258
Lev Vygotsky: Social/Cognitive Theory	276
Main Point Chapter Summary	285

8 Learning and Memory 287

This Chapter	288
Objectives	289
Memory Metaphors	289
Modal Model of Memory	294
Categories of Long-Term Memory	306
Physiology of Memory	311
Why We Forget	315
Learning and Remembering: Educational Applications	319
Main Point Chapter Summary	323

9 Motivation and Emotions 325

This Chapter	326
Motivation and Emotions	327
Reflexes, Instincts, and Imprinting	328
Psychological Hedonism	332
Drive Reduction and Incentives	332
Arousal Theory	338
Social Cognitive Views of Motivation	342
Applications and Implications of Motivation Theory	359
Main Point Chapter Summary	364

10 Social Learning: Bandura's Social Cognitive Theory 366

This Chapter	367
Social Learning	368
Overview of Bandura's Social Cognitive Theory	371
Operant Conditioning in Observational Learning	374
Cognitive Control in Bandura's Social Cognitive Theory	380
Applications of Bandura's Social Cognitive Theory	388
Bandura's Social Cognitive Theory: An Appraisal	391
Main Point Chapter Summary	392

11 Machine Learning and Artificial Intelligence: The Future? 394

This Chapter	395
The Computer and the Brain	396
Symbolic and Connectionist Models	400
Artificial Intelligence	410

xii **Contents**

Educational and Social Implications	419
A Field in Progress	421
Main Point Chapter Summary	421

Part V Summary

12 Summary, Synthesis, and Integration 425

This Chapter	426
Objectives	426
Two Major Approaches to Learning Theory	427
Summaries of Key Theories and Approaches	428
Synthesis and Appraisal	442
An Integration	446
A Last Word	449
Main Point Chapter Summary	450
Lefrançois's Epilogue	452
Glossary	456
References	496
Name Index	532
Subject Index	538

ILLUSTRATIONS

1.1 Evidence of learning is found in actual or potential changes in behavior as a result of experience. Lefrançois, G. R. (2018). *Psychology for Teaching* (2nd ed.). San Diego, CA: Bridgepoint Education, Fig. 5.1. Used by permission. *page* 9
1.2 The hallmark of scientific research is objectivity and replicability. 18
1.3 A simple experiment designed to test a hypothesis. 19
2.1 A graphic portrayal of Weber's law. As intensity of stimulation increases, proportionally greater increases in stimulation are required if they are to be just noticeable differences. 42
2.2 What Pavlov first noticed was that the sight of the handler alone was enough to cause many of his experimental dogs to salivate. 45
2.3 In his experiments, Pavlov often placed his dogs in a harness. H. E. Garrett, (1951), *Great experiments in psychology*. Appleton-Century-Crofts. 45
2.4 A simple illustration of classical conditioning. Adapted from Lefrançois, G. R. (2016). *Psychology: The Human Puzzle* (2nd ed.). San Diego, CA: Bridgepoint Education, Fig. 5.4. Used by permission. 46
2.5 Impact of variations in CS–US procedures. 50
2.6 A hypothetical learning curve. 51
2.7 A hypothetical representation of spontaneous recovery following extinction. 52
2.8 Illustration of how a dislike and fear of mathematics can be classically conditioned. From Lefrançois, G. R. (2018). *Psychology for Teaching* (2nd ed.). San Diego, CA: Bridgepoint Education, Fig. 5.2. Used by permission. 65
2.9 Guthrie's law of one-trial learning. 71
2.10 Guthrie's three ways of breaking habits applied to "breaking" a horse. 75
3.1 Thorndike's puzzle box. From "Animal intelligence: An experimental study of the associative processes in animals," by E. L. Thorndike, 1898, *Psychological Review Monograph Supplement*, *2*(8). Used by permission of the American Psychological Association. 84
3.2 The behavior of one cat in Thorndike's puzzle box. From "Animal intelligence: An experimental study of the associative processes in animals," by E. L. Thorndike, 1898, *Psychological Review Monograph Supplement*, *2*(8). Used by permission of the American Psychological Association. 85
3.3 Median lengths of 3,000 separate lines drawn by a single subject with eyes closed, over 12 sessions. Data from *Human learning* by E. L. Thorndike, p. 9 (table 1). Cambridge, MA: MIT Press, 1931. 92

xiv   **Illustrations**

3.4   The influence of two consecutive "Rights" or "Wrongs" on the next choice
       of possible word meanings. Data from *Human learning* by E. L. Thorndike,
       p. 44. Cambridge, MA: MIT Press, 1931.   93
3.5   A simplified representation of Hull's system.   99
3.6   A hypothetical habit-family hierarchy.   106
4.1   Skinner's investigations of operant conditioning looked at the relationships
       between variables under the control of the experimenter (independent variables)
       and the organism's behavior (dependent variables).   117
4.2   A classical (B) and an operant conditioning (A) explanation for changes in
       Mrs. Gribbin's fishing behaviors.   121
4.3   In the same way as there are two kinds of reinforcement (positive and negative),
       so too are there two kinds of punishment (presentation or castigation, and
       removal or penalty). Adapted from Lefrançois, G. R. (2018). *Psychology for
       Teaching* (2nd ed.). San Diego, CA: Bridgepoint Education, Fig. 5.7. Used by
       permission.   123
4.4   In operant conditioning, each type of schedule tends to generate a predictable
       pattern of responding.   127
4.5   A cumulative recording showing the responses of an untrained (naïve) rat on a
       continuous schedule of reinforcement. From *The Behavior of Organisms:
       An Experimental Analysis*, p. 67, by B. F. Skinner. Copyright © 1938 by
       Appleton-Century-Crofts. Reprinted courtesy of the B.F. Skinner Foundation.   129
4.6   A cumulative recording showing four typical extinction curves. From *The
       Behavior of Organisms: An Experimental Analysis*, p. 67, by B. F. Skinner.
       Copyright © 1938 by Appleton-Century-Crofts. Reprinted courtesy of the
       B.F. Skinner Foundation.   130
4.7   A cumulative recording showing initial extinction over a one-hour period
       (left half of the graph) and spontaneous recovery of the rat's bar-pressing
       responses over a second one-hour period. From *The Behavior of Organisms:
       An Experimental Analysis*, p. 67, by B. F. Skinner. Copyright © 1938 by
       Appleton-Century-Crofts. Reprinted courtesy of the B.F. Skinner Foundation.   131
4.8   Idealized graphs showing the effects of fixed interval and random ratio
       schedules of reinforcement on rate of responding. From Lefrançois, G. R.
       (2016). *Psychology: The Human Puzzle* (2nd ed.). San Diego, CA:
       Bridgepoint Education. Fig. 5.8. Used by permission.   133
4.9   Generalization involves responding to similarities and therefore making
       similar responses for different stimuli.   141
5.1   A classical conditioning explanation of taste aversion learning.   157
5.2   A representation of Kamin's study of blocking in classical conditioning.   161
5.3   In A, a lighted key is paired with food. In B, the pigeon pecks the
       lighted key even though doing so has nothing to do with obtaining food.   166
5.4   The desired outcome of this training procedure is explained by the
       principles of operant conditioning.   168

5.5	A sagittal (bisected front to back) view of the human brain.	180
5.6	The four lobes of the cerebral cortex.	184
6.1	Idealized representation of two neurons.	201
6.2	Cell assemblies consist of activity in a large number of related neurons.	204
6.3	Schematic representation of a phase sequence: a, b, c, d, and e can be thought of as cell assemblies.	204
6.4	Perception with incomplete data.	208
6.5	In the Tolman and Honzik blocked-path study, rats that had learned this maze almost invariably selected path 3 when path 1 was blocked at B. From Lefrançois, G. R. (2016). *Psychology: The Human Puzzle* (2nd ed.). San Diego, CA: Bridgepoint Education, Fig. 5.11. Used by permission.	217
6.6	In the Tolman, Ritchie, and Kalish study, rats learned a simple maze with an indirect path to the goal.	217
6.7	Closure is the tendency to perceive incomplete objects (or thoughts) as being complete.	225
6.8	An illustration of the Gestalt concept of continuity.	226
6.9	People have a tendency to perceive similar input as belonging together.	226
6.10	There is a tendency to perceive things that are close together as belonging together.	226
6.11	Leveling describes a tendency toward symmetry and toward reducing abnormalities and peculiarities.	227
6.12	Sharpening is evident in a tendency to emphasize the distinctiveness of a pattern.	227
6.13	Normalizing is the tendency to perceive (and remember) what is expected.	228
7.1	Schematic representation of a coding system. From Lefrançois, G. R. (2018). *Psychology for Teaching* (2nd ed.). San Diego, CA: Bridgepoint Education, Fig. 6.2. Used by permission.	251
7.2	Piaget defines intelligence in terms of the individual's interactions with the environment.	263
7.3	Material for a simple conservation of liquid experiment.	267
7.4	Some of the demonstrations Piaget devised to illustrate the main characteristics of children's thinking between the ages of 2 and 7. Adapted from Lefrançois, G. R. (2018). *Psychology for Teaching* (2nd ed.). San Diego, CA: Bridgepoint Education, Fig. 2.5. Used by permission.	268
7.5	Experimental procedures devised by Piaget to determine the presence or absence of the understanding of conservation in each of a variety of different areas such as volume, number, length, and liquid quantity. Adapted from Lefrançois, G. R. (2016). *Psychology: The Human Puzzle* (2nd ed.). San Diego, CA: Bridgepoint Education, Fig. 4.8. Used by permission.	269
7.6	A test of a child's understanding of seriation. Adapted from Lefrançois, G. R. (2018). *Psychology: The Human Puzzle* (2nd ed.). San Diego, CA: Bridgepoint Education, Fig. 4.9. Used by permission.	271

Illustrations

8.1 An idealized memory curve, similar to some generated by Ebbinghaus. 291

8.2 A widely used model of human memory. From Lefrançois, G. R. (2016). *Psychology: The Human Puzzle* (2nd ed.). San Diego, CA: Bridgepoint Education, Fig. 6.1. Used by permission. 294

8.3 Proportion of nonsense syllables recalled correctly when subjects were given no time for rehearsal, compared with those allowed to rehearse for 3 seconds. From Peterson, L. R. & Peterson, M. J. (1959) "Short-term retention of individual verbal items," In the *Journal of Experimental Psychology*, vol. 58, p. 197. Copyright © 1959 by the American Psychological Association. Reprinted by permission of the American Psychological Association. 298

8.4 A representation of Baddeley's model of working memory. Adapted from Lefrançois, G. R. (2016). *Psychology: The Human Puzzle* (2nd ed.). San Diego, CA: Bridgepoint Education, Fig. 6.3. Used by permission. 300

8.5 Accuracy of memory for recent and distant odors. Based on "Very Long-Term Memory for Odors: Retention of Odor–Name Associations," by W. P. Goldman and J. G. Seamon, 1992. In the *American Journal of Psychology*, 105, pp. 549–563 (Table 1, p. 553). © 1992 by the Board of Trustees of the University of Illinois. Reprinted by permission of University of Illinois Press. 303

8.6 Children's drawings of water lines. 304

8.7 A model of memory. From Lefrançois, G. R. (2016). *Psychology: The Human Puzzle* (2nd ed.). San Diego, CA: Bridgepoint Education, Fig. 6.5. Used by permission. 309

8.8 Node theory suggests that we remember abstractions (meanings, associations, and gists rather than specifics). 310

8.9 Summaries and interpretations of vast amounts of educational research have identified 10 distinct learning strategies. Based in part on Dunlosky, J., Rawson, K. A., Marsh, E. J., Nathan, M. J., & Willingham, D. T. (2013). Improving students' learning with effective learning techniques: Promising directions from cognitive and educational psychology. *Psychological Science in the Public Interest*, 14(1), 4–58; and on Brown, P. C., Roediger, H. L. III, & McDaniel, M. A. (2014). *Making it stick: The science of successful learning*. Cambridge, Mass.: The Belknap Press of Harvard University Press. 321

9.1 Under appropriate conditions, exposure to a releaser (a mother duck, for example) during the critical period (within a few hours of hatching) leads to imprinting, which is evident in the "following" behavior of the hatchling. 331

9.2 The drive-reduction model of motivation. From Lefrançois, G. R. (2018). *Psychology for Teaching* (2nd ed.). San Diego, CA: Bridgepoint Education, Figure 8.4. Used by permission. 333

9.3 Drives alone cannot explain behavior. 335

9.4 The hierarchy is shown in the form of a pyramid depicting lowest-level needs, such as the need for food and drink, at the bottom. From Maslow, Abraham H.; Frager, Robert D.; Fadiman, James. MOTIVATION AND PERSONALITY,

	3rd EDITION©1987. Printed and Electronically reproduced by permission of Pearson Education, Inc., New York: New York.	337
9.5	The Yerkes–Dodson law describes the relationship between behavioral performance and arousal level.	339
9.6	Everyone experiences conflicts (cognitive dissonance) between beliefs or desires and reality. From Lefrançois, G. R. (2016). *Psychology: The Human Puzzle* (2nd ed.). San Diego, CA: Bridgepoint Education, Fig. 8.5. Used by permission.	346
9.7	The overjustification hypothesis suggests that rewarding certain activities unexpectedly or excessively can undermine intrinsic motivation for those activities. Based on data from M. R. Lepper and D. Greene (1975), "Turning play into work: Effects of adult surveillance and extrinsic rewards on children's intrinsic motivation." In the *Journal of Personality and Social Psychology*, 31, 479–486.	348
9.8	Four important possible attributions for success and failure. From Lefrançois, G. R. (2018). *Psychology for Teaching* (2nd ed.). San Diego, CA: Bridgepoint Education, Fig. 8.6. Used by permission.	349
9.9	Relations between causal attributions and feelings associated with success and failure. Based on Bernard Weiner, "The Role of Affect in Rational (Attributional) Approaches to Human Motivation." In *Educational Researcher*, July/August 1980, pp. 4–11. Copyright © 1980. American Educational Research Association, Washington, D.C. Used by permission.	353
9.10	Keller's ARCS model of instruction design suggests ways in which teachers can design instruction to foster and maintain high levels of motivation among learners. From Lefrançois G. R. (2020). *Of Learning and Assessment* (2nd ed.). San Diego, CA: Bridgepoint Education, Fig. 3.9. Used by permission.	363
10.1	The four processes involved in observational learning. From A. Bandura, *Social Learning Theory*, © 1977, p. 23. Reprinted by permission of Prentice Hall, Inc., Englewood Cliffs, NJ.	374
10.2	Some of the results from Bandura, Ross, and Ross's study of children's interactions with a Bobo doll following exposure to models interacting aggressively or nonaggressively with the doll. From Lefrançois, G. R. (2018). *Psychology for Teaching* (2nd Ed.). San Diego, CA: Bridgepoint Education, Fig. 5.12. Used by permission.	378
10.3	Bandura's notion of triadic reciprocal determinism. From Lefrançois, G. R. (2016). *Psychology: The Human Puzzle*. San Diego, CA: Bridgepoint Education, Fig. 5.12. Used by permission.	387
11.1	Analogies between computer and human structures and functions.	398
11.2	A schematic representation of NETtalk, a neural network model.	408
12.1	Diagrammatic and symbolic representations of the key concepts of each of the preceding 11 chapters.	444

BOXES

2.1	Wilhelm Wundt (1832–1920)	40
2.2	Ivan Petrovich Pavlov (1849–1936)	43
2.3	John Broadus Watson (1878–1958)	55
2.4	Edwin R. Guthrie (1886–1959)	67
3.1	Edward Lee Thorndike (1874–1949)	86
3.2	Clark Leonard Hull (1884–1952)	96
4.1	Burrhus Frederic Skinner (1904–1990)	115
6.1	Donald Olding Hebb (1904–1985)	199
6.2	Edward Chace Tolman (1886–1959)	215
6.3	Kurt Koffka (1886–1941), Wolfgang Köhler (1887–1967), and Max Wertheimer (1880–1943)	222
7.1	Jerome Seymour Bruner (1915–2016)	245
7.2	Jean Piaget (1896–1980)	258
7.3	Lev Semenovich Vygotsky (1896–1934)	277
10.1	Albert Bandura (1925–)	369

PREFACE: READ THIS FIRST...

... not just because it's at the beginning of the book but because if you don't, you might wonder what the devil is going on.

Let me get right to the point: I didn't write this book. Truth is, the first edition was a report written and given to me by Kongor, a behavioral scientist from – well, it doesn't really matter in any case. That report, published in 1972, was titled *Psychological Theories and Human Learning: Kongor's Report.*

A decade later, readers began to complain that some of what Kongor had written was imprecise, irrelevant, inaccurate, or insulting. So, I was forced to prepare a second edition by myself. It was published in 1982.

Then, almost two decades after Kongor's visit, somebody named Kro crawled out of the muddy slough in front of my bush cabin, claiming he was here to update Kongor's original report, which he did. That was the third edition: *Psychological Theories and Human Learning: Kro's Report*, published in 1995.

A few years later, an Old Man barged uninvited into my living room, insisting he had updated, corrected, polished, and absolutely perfected all previous editions. That was the fourth edition: *Theories of Human Learning: What the Old Man Said.*

Only five years after that, late one Thursday afternoon, a disheveled Old Woman rode up to me on a unicycle. "Things change. Science doesn't stand still," she muttered, "so I'm gonna give you the next edition." That was *Theories of Human Learning: What the Old Woman Said.*

I thought that would be it. But no. In the middle of one of those sleepless nights when I worried they might be closing in, I received this message sent to my anonymous email address: "Outstanding new edition is ready," it said. "Come get it at the Palladium. Come alone. DO NOT BRING YOUR FRIENDS! (You know who!)." I went, met some guy who said he was a Professor, and ended up with the sixth edition (*Theories of Human Learning: What the Professor Said*) ... and more trouble I didn't need.

No matter where I hide, they find me. A few weeks ago, my phone rang in the middle of the night. Startled out of a weird dream about small donkeys, I staggered out of bed and fumbled around in the darkness, but by the time I found the phone, it had stopped ringing.

In the morning, I saw that a voicemail message had been left. That's where this all starts.

The voicemail, which I have kept because publishers (and readers) are often skeptical, barked in what sounded like a disgruntled woman's voice: "That learning book is completely out of date and lots of it is dead wrong and misleading so if you want to fix it, and you're still on the loose, be at Willy's Social House next Monday after dark." That's all it said, except for the very end which is where the voice laughs, sort of a cackling, croaking sound, and says that maybe I should wear a disguise even when it's dark. I don't need one any more, with the facial hair and everything.

It was a damp, gloomy night, that Monday, and when I didn't immediately see anyone near Willy's, I thought I might have been lured here, finally trapped, and I turned to flee. But then an old lady rose from the shadows and when I asked was it her who had called and who was she, she hesitated for an awkward time and then said yes, she was nobody else than she who had called and that if I needed to name her, Mrs. Gribbin would be okay, but she didn't sound convinced.[1]

Mrs. Gribbin brought me this manuscript. I wrote only this preface, the epilogue, some footnotes, and a few little bits here and there (always in italics). The rest, organized into 12 chapters, is what she read from a really battered old manuscript, often throwing in her own explanations and examples. She insisted that I record her words as she read them and that I also make handwritten notes. "For future generations," she said when I asked why.

I changed nothing of what she wrote; I am just a lowly clerk. When she spoke "off the record," she insisted that the recorder be turned off. If what she said in those circumstances seemed important, I put what I could remember or what I could decipher from my handwritten notes into footnotes.

Old lady Gribbin wanted it made perfectly clear that although she spoke all these words as she told me this book, they were certainly not all her words and thoughts. She asked that I explain very carefully that this is a revision – an updating and a correcting of the first six editions. She grumbled that many of the words and examples in this seventh edition are left over from those primitive earlier editions and that she could have done better if she had time to start from scratch.

The few comments I have permitted myself in this seventh edition serve only to tell something of this old lady, Mrs. Gribbin – to describe where she was and what she was doing at this moment or that. Very rarely, I asked questions. Sometimes, she responded; mostly, she didn't. When she did, I included what I remembered of her replies – but always only in footnotes.

WHAT'S NEW IN THE SEVENTH EDITION?

This seventh edition is a survey and interpretation of some of the important theories and findings in the psychology of learning. It includes a detailed examination of the main behavioristic and cognitive theories and an appraisal of each, together with a discussion of its most important practical applications, especially in education. Also, it looks at the most recent and useful models of memory, motivation, social/cognitive learning, and current brain-based research, and it explores recent and rapidly changing progress in the field of machine learning and artificial intelligence. Like its predecessors, this edition continues to emphasize relevance and practical implications of topics, clarity of presentation, and maintenance of high interest. The seventh edition reflects a significant updating of research, theory, and applications in all areas, including:

---

[1] I still don't know if Gribbin was her real name. That's the only name she ever gave me. I mostly just thought of her as the Old Lady, but to her face I always called her Mrs. Gribbin.

- highlighting recent developments in, and applications of, brain-based research;
- describing newer models in motivation theory and their implications;
- summarizing current models of memory and related implications for theories of learning;
- exploring the importance of technology for simulating human cognitive processes and suggesting new models of learning;
- examining the effects of *screen violence* on children and adults; and
- looking at what machines capable of deep learning and artificially intelligent behaviors might mean for the future.

There is also a tidbit of information about Schrödinger, a unique cat.

The book is written primarily for students of human learning, teachers, counselors, social workers, industrial psychologists, nurses, social psychologists, quantum physicists, numismatists, physicians, lawyers, dentists, engineers, housewives, spelunkers, farmers, judges, philatelists, fishermen, tree planters, glass blowers, plasma physicists, vagabonds, poets, stockbrokers, philosophers, retired types, environmental activists, grandmothers, and all others – more or less in that order.

ACKNOWLEDGMENTS

Mrs. Gribbin wanted me to pass on her appreciation to about 500 different people, all of whom she said deserved emoluments, credits, applause, and many wet kisses. I said there's no room, this isn't an encyclopedia. She said okay, but you have to say thank you to the publisher (Cambridge University Press), the acquisition editor (David Repetto), the assistant editor (Emily Watton), the content managers (Rosie Crawley and Nicola Chapman) and copy editor (Gary Smith) . . . your grandmother (Emerilda Francœur), the guy you borrowed the boat from, your office cleaning company – and then I said, whoa, that's enough, are you trying to get all 500 in? And she said no, but please thank the anonymous reviewers because they were so amazingly competent and clever.

The old lady Gribbin also wanted me to indicate that she's not responsible for any errors and misinterpretations that remain in this text. "If any errors creep in," she said, "it'll be the fault of reviewers, editors, and other publishing types." That, of course, is absolutely untrue. The old lady, Mrs. Gribbin, is fully responsible for any weaknesses and flaws in the book.

Guy R. Lefrançois

P.S. Many thanks to Claire, who succeeded in photographing Kro, and to Claire and Liam, who came closer than anyone to getting recognizable photos of the Old Man and the Old Woman. I took the photo of the Professor myself with my hidden, motion-activated, infrared wildlife camera. The only photo we have of Mrs. Gribbin is a screen shot from a security camera she inadvertently activated the night she apparently got lost and broke into my neighbor's kitchen (see page 455).

Part I

Science and Theory

1 Human Learning

CHAPTER OUTLINE

What Mrs. Gribbin Said: This Book	4
Objectives	5
The Psychology of Learning	5
Knowing and Consciousness	5
Defining Learning	7
Scientific Theories	9
Theories, Principles, Laws, and Beliefs	10
Common Misconceptions and Folk Beliefs	11
Purposes of Theories	13
Characteristics of Good Theories	13
Science and Psychological Theories	15
What Is Science?	16
Steps in the Scientific Method	16
Experiments	18
Evaluating Psychological Research	20
Participants in Psychological Research	24
Ethics in Animal Research	25
Humans as Research Participants	26
Theories of Learning: A Brief Overview	27
Structuralism and Functionalism	27
Classification of Learning Theories	28
Preview of this Text	29
Chapter 2. Early Behaviorism: Pavlov, Watson, and Guthrie	29
Chapter 3. The Effects of Behavior: Thorndike and Hull	29
Chapter 4. Operant Conditioning: Skinner's Radical Behaviorism	31
Chapter 5. Evolutionary Psychology: Learning, Biology, and the Brain	31
Chapter 6. Transition to Modern Cognitivism: Hebb, Tolman, and the Gestaltists	31
Chapter 7. Cognitive Theories: Bruner, Piaget, and Vygotsky	31
Chapter 8. Learning and Memory	32
Chapter 9. Motivation and Emotions	32
Chapter 10. Social Learning: Bandura's Social Cognitive Theory	32

Chapter 11. Machine Learning and Artificial Intelligence: The Future?	32
Chapter 12. Analysis, Synthesis, and Integration	32
Applications of Learning Theories	33
Main Point Chapter Summary	33

Often a man finds a theory that explains things and he builds atop that theory, finding all the right answers … only the basic theory is wrong. But that's the last thing he will want to admit.

Louis L'Amour, *Treasure Mountain*

Mrs. Gribbin moved into the bush cabin that very night. I tried to talk her out of it; I sometimes need a place to lay low for a few days. "Why don't you just give me the whole manuscript right now?" I asked. "Save you the trouble of reading it out to me page after page." But no, she wouldn't. She said there was stuff in it that she had to explain and we'd just do it one chapter at a time.

When I showed up in the morning she was sitting at the table, ragged yellow pages scattered everywhere. I tried to make small talk. The old lady grunted once or twice. The first intelligible thing she said was "Enough talking," as she waved a fistful of those dog-eared pages at me. "That old book of yours is hopelessly outdated and mistaken and missing all kinds of important stuff and … never mind. Just turn on your recorder and pay attention."

I pressed the little circle at the bottom left corner of the new digital recorder that I had bought just in case. Wisely, I had read the instructions.

The old lady started to talk. I couldn't always tell for sure when she was actually reading or just talking. This is what she said.

WHAT MRS. GRIBBIN SAID: THIS BOOK

This book, *she explained as she smoothed out a clutch of manuscript pages on her knees,* summarizes what psychologists know and believe about human learning. *I noticed, then, that the one-eyed cat, the one who had suddenly appeared at the bush cabin a couple of months ago and who had always been too wild to touch – only tame enough to feed if I kept my distance – had buried himself under the manuscript. Strangely, he was allowing Mrs. Gribbin to scratch his ears. Change of heart, I thought, reaching over gingerly to finally pet him. He growled and tried to bite me again. The old lady said, "That's not nice, Schrödinger," but her voice seemed to be saying, "Nice kitty."* [1] Among other things, this text presents a historical view of the development of psychological theories related to human learning, *the old lady continued.* It describes the major principles and the practical applications of each theory, and it evaluates each theory's main strengths and weaknesses.

---

[1] "Schrödinger?" I said. "That miserable cat doesn't have a name." "He's always been Schrödinger, no matter where he's been," she retorted. "Please don't interrupt again." I shut up.

Objectives

Tell your readers, *said Mrs. Gribbin*, that this first chapter is a bit of a preamble: It defines important terms and sets the stage for what comes later. Explain to them that after studying this chapter, they should know with stunning clarity:

- What is meant by the term *learning*.
- How theories are developed and can be evaluated.
- What terms such as *structuralism*, *functionalism*, *behaviorism*, and *cognitivism* mean.
- What the principal information-gathering methods are in psychology.
- What *placebos* and *nocebos* are and why they might be important in psychological research.

THE PSYCHOLOGY OF LEARNING

Let me begin at the beginning, *said the old lady*. **Psychology**[2] is the science that studies human behavior and thinking. It is often defined as the science that studies the mind and mental processes. Among other things, it looks at how experience affects thought and action; it explores the roles of biology and heredity; it examines consciousness and dreams; it traces how people develop from infants into adults; it investigates social influences; it explores the mysteries of the human brain. Basically, psychology tries to explain why people think, act, and feel as they do.

Of course, this book doesn't tackle all of psychology but is limited to psychological theories that deal with human learning and behavior – and animal learning, too, because studies of learning in animals are inextricably linked with the development of theories of human learning. So, it is important from the outset to know what learning is.

Knowing and Consciousness

What do we learn? What do we know? What is knowledge?

These questions define the branch of philosophy known as **epistemology**. Epistemology asks how we know the world. It also asks how we know that what we think is real actually is.

Some of the ancient Greek philosophers, such as Aristotle (384–322 BC), answered these questions by proposing the theory that whatever is out there in the world is copied onto the mind. The mind, simply defined, is the set of cognitive (intellectual) faculties involved in human consciousness – our ability to do things such as perceive, feel, think, remember, and imagine. What happens, Aristotle explained, is that the act of perceiving something results in a copy that we then somehow *know*. Thus, we can never know reality directly; all we know is indirect, resulting from our knowledge of copies of reality. We know not so much because of our senses, he argued, but more as a result of our reason. Thus, the educated person, whose

---

[2] Boldfaced terms are defined in the glossary at the end of the book, starting on page 456. Unlike most of the text, glossary items and many of the footnotes aren't Mrs. Gribbin's words but mine. (GRL)

mind is presumably better able to reason, knows reality more clearly than does the less educated person. "The roots of education are bitter," said Aristotle, "but the fruit is sweet."

Plato (427–348 BC), another well-known Greek philosopher who was actually Aristotle's teacher, believed that we know only ideas (he and Aristotle disagreed on the nature of ideas). Hence, the importance of educating people, of making them into thinkers and philosophers. "And may we not say," asked Plato, "that the most gifted minds, when they are ill-educated, become the worst?" (Plato, 1993, p. 491).[3]

But, asked other philosophers, how do we even know that there actually is a reality out there if all we have are copies in our minds. Maybe, some suggested, reality exists only in our minds, a belief sometimes referred to as *idealism* as opposed to *materialism*. Whereas materialism holds that everything that actually exists is physical (or material), idealism suggests that ideas are the only knowable reality.

These issues are at the core of a big issue in psychology: the **mind–body problem**. Simply stated, this problem asks about the relationship between the mind and the body. How can something purely physical, such as a cat, produce something purely mental, such as the idea of a cat? And how can the idea of a cat be translated into an act, such as that of looking for a cat?

French philosopher and mathematician René Descartes (1596–1650) presented one of the earliest and most influential resolutions for this problem, at the same time penning one of the most widely known and repeated phrases ever produced by any philosopher: *I think; therefore I am*. Descartes arrived at this insight by first pretending that everything he was thinking was not real – was simply like a dream. He writes:

> But immediately upon this I noticed that while I was trying to think everything false, it must needs be that I, who was thinking this, was something. And observing that this truth "I am thinking, therefore I exist" was so solid and secure that the most extravagant suppositions of the skeptics could not overthrow it, I judged that I need not scruple to accept it as the first principle. (Anscombe & Geach, 1954, pp. 31–32)

I think; therefore I am. The Latin form of this sentence, the language in which learned philosophers and scientists of Descartes's age wrote, is *Cogito, ergo sum*. As a result, this principle is commonly referred to as Descartes's *Cogito*. One very important conclusion that flows from this principle, said Descartes, is that all ideas must come from God because humans are clearly not perfect enough to generate them on their own (Vrooman, 1970). Hence, the mind and the body must be separate, insisted Descartes. Furthermore, the existence of ideas proves that what we think is out there actually *is* out there because God would surely never give us ideas that are false. Thus, ideas are pure and innate because they come from God. In contrast, the body is physical or material; its functioning is like the functioning of a machine.

It follows that there are two basic substances in the world, says Descartes: material and immaterial. The material includes things such as bodies, bats, and beverages, all of which actually exist in space and all of which can be compared to machines in their functioning. The

---

[3] In this text, references are cited in the style approved by the American Psychological Association (APA) – that is, the name of the author(s) is followed by the year of the relevant publication. The list of references at the end of the book provides complete information about the source.

immaterial includes the mind or, to use what Descartes considered an equivalent term, the *soul*. The soul is more closely related to God than to a machine. Thus, mind and body are fundamentally different and separate. This *Cartesian* (referring to Descartes) position is labeled **dualism**. Descartes is referred to as an *interactive dualist* because he believed that even though the mind and the body are separate (are dual, in other words), they are, in a sense, united in the brain. The brain allows the body to influence the mind and the mind to influence the body – hence, *interactive dualism*.

Descartes thought that communication between body and mind was accomplished by means of a small organ in the brain known as the **pineal gland**. Why the pineal gland? Because as far as Descartes knew, the pineal gland was the only structure in the brain that did not have a duplicate. Most other brain structures are duplicated in each of the brain's halves (called *hemispheres*; see Chapter 5 for a discussion of the anatomy and functions of the brain). We now know that Descartes was wrong about the functions of the pineal gland, which is mainly involved in regulating *melatonin*, the hormone that is involved in maintaining sleep patterns.

Descartes's speculations about the mind and the body underlined a very important problem for psychologists: What is consciousness? Put another way, how are physical sensations translated into our minds so we become aware of reality?

One way around this problem is simply to ignore mind or consciousness, which cannot be observed directly, and instead look for the laws that govern observable human behavior. In fact, this solution has been the basis for a great deal of early research and theorizing about learning.

Defining Learning

Ask someone what learning is, and the most likely answer will have something to do with the acquisition of information. If I tell you that the bird over there is a red-breasted nuthatch and the next time you see such a bird you correctly identify it as a red-breasted nuthatch, I might infer that you have learned something. In this case, the nature of the information that you have acquired is obvious. Also note that your behavior has changed as a result of experience. In this case, the specific experience of my telling you that this bird is a red-breasted nuthatch affects your response when you next see a bird of this species.[4]

Disposition

In many cases, what is acquired during learning is not so obvious. For example, if Mrs. Toch laughs sarcastically at Helen's attempts to pronounce "procrastinate," some of her other students might subsequently be far more hesitant to try to pronounce difficult words. They have learned to be wary. Put another way, there has been a change in their **disposition** – that is, in their inclination to do or not to do something – rather than observable changes in actual

---

[4] As Old Lady Gribbin spoke of red-breasted nuthatches, she pointed toward the window where you can see the feeding platform and, sure enough, a red-breasted nuthatch was just then retrieving a sunflower seed. I now knew she wasn't reading everything she was saying.

behavior. Changes in disposition have to do with **motivation**. Motivation looks at the causes of behavior; the conscious or unconscious forces that underlie our actions. Motivation is discussed in detail in Chapter 9.

Capability

Learning involves not only changes in disposition but also changes in **capability** – that is, changes in the skills or knowledge required to do something. Like changes in disposition, changes in capability are not always observed directly. For example, several of Mrs. Toch's students might well have learned how to pronounce "procrastinate" when she corrected Helen. But these changes may not be apparent unless these students are given the opportunity to manifest them. The inference that dispositions or capabilities have changed – in other words, that learning has occurred – will always be based on **performance**, which is the act of carrying out an action, of *behaving*.

Performance

Psychologists usually look for evidence of learning in the changes that occur in people's behaviors as a result of experience. But not all changes in behavior are examples of learning. If someone smacks you on the head or feeds you strange drugs, your behavior might change in bizarre ways. Hubert claimed this is what happened to him when, thinking there was a pair of small but lethal dragons in his closet, he ran madly down the street shouting for help. This was a striking change in Hubert's behavior, but to say that this change is an example of learning is to stretch the term beyond reasonable limits.

Behavior changes that are the temporary results of fatigue or drugs do not illustrate learning. Similarly, changes that are mainly biologically determined, such as physical growth or sexual maturation, or that result from injury or disease (especially of the brain and other parts of the nervous system) are not examples of learning.

The Definition

To summarize, **learning** is defined as all relatively permanent changes in potential for behaviors that result from experience but are not caused by fatigue, maturation, drugs, injury, or disease. Strictly speaking, of course, learning is not really the actual or potential changes that we observe. Rather, learning is what happens to the organism (human or nonhuman) as a result of experience. Changes in behavior are simply evidence that learning has occurred (see Figure 1.1).

Note that the definition specifies changes in *potential* for behavior rather than simply changes in behavior. Why? Because, as we saw, the permanent effects of experience are not always apparent. And this is true even among nonhuman animals. In a classic experiment, Buxton (1940) left rats in large mazes for several nights. These mazes had start boxes at their beginnings and goal boxes at their ends, but there was no food or other reward in the goal boxes. After these few nights in the

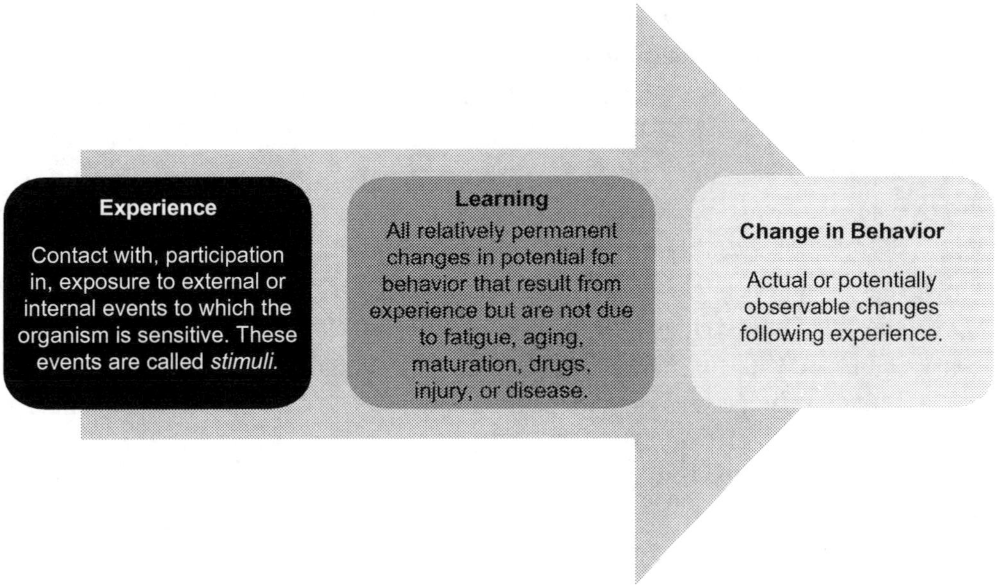

Scientific Theories

Figure 1.1 Evidence of learning is found in actual or potential changes in behavior as a result of experience. But learning itself is an invisible, internal neurological process. Lefrançois, G. R. (2018). *Psychology for Teaching* (2nd ed.). San Diego, CA: Bridgepoint Education, Fig. 5.1. Used by permission.

maze, there was no evidence that the rats had learned anything at all. Later, however, Buxton gave them a small taste of food in the goal boxes and then placed them in the start boxes. Now more than half of them ran directly to the goal boxes without making a single error! Clearly, the most clever of these rats had learned a lot during the first nights in the maze. But their learning was **latent** rather than actual (latent means dormant or hidden rather than apparent). That is, the rats' learning was not evident in their performance until there had also been a change in their *dispositions* – in this case, a change in their reasons for going to the goal box.

So, learning may involve changes in capability (in the capacity to do something) and also in disposition (in the inclination to perform). And evidence that learning has occurred may also depend on the opportunity to perform; hence, the need to define learning as a change in potential for behavior rather than simply as a change in behavior. For example, as you read this book, some astounding changes may occur in your capabilities. That these changes should mostly remain potential, becoming apparent only if you are given the opportunity to perform (on a test, for example), makes them no less real.

SCIENTIFIC THEORIES[5]

Behavior is a complicated thing; there are all sorts of factors involved in determining what you do (or don't do). The main task of the learning psychologist is to understand behavior and

---

[5] At this point, the old lady asked me whether I needed a break – should we continue later – but I said no, it was okay, and I didn't really think the reader would need a break yet. Well, they won't ask if they do, she said. That's the way students are. Besides, she continued, some of the brighter ones might be asking themselves some philosophical questions right now,

behavior change. And from understanding comes the ability to predict and sometimes to control, both of which are useful and important functions. For example, teachers' predictions about how well students are likely to perform are critical for decisions relating to assessment and instruction.

To understand something as complicated as behavior, psychologists need to simplify, to discover regularity and predictability, to invent metaphors (comparisons). Man looks for order where there is none, said Francis Bacon (perhaps not yet realizing that woman is as guilty of this as man). And Bacon may have been correct that humans would look for order even if there were none – that they seem to have a need to find order. But we have long assumed that there is considerable order in the world. This assumption has guided our research and colored our theories. Discovering this assumed regularity and trying to explain it is what theory building is all about.

Humans like to build theories. Years ago, they devised theories about the lights in the sky, about why babies look like their parents, about the shape of Earth – which some believe might be flat. Often, these theories were expressed as metaphors: The sun is a chariot racing across the sky; dreams are the adventures of souls walking in parallel worlds while the body sleeps. Modern scientific theories can also often be explained and understood as metaphors: The heart is a pump; the brain is a computer; the eye is a camera. In Chapters 6 and 11, we look in more detail at metaphors in psychology.

Theories, Principles, Laws, and Beliefs

A scientific **theory** is a collection of related statements whose main function is to summarize and explain observations. In a simplified sense, theory building works something like this: Theorists begin with certain assumptions (unproven beliefs) about human behavior, perhaps based partly on their observations of regularity or predictability in actions. As a result, they develop tentative explanations for what they observe. This leads them to believe that certain relationships exist – that *if this, then that*. These *if–then* statements, or educated predictions, are called **hypotheses**. Now the theorist gathers observations (data) to test the validity of the hypotheses. The most useful theories in scientific research are those that lead to testable hypotheses. Nontestable hypotheses have little place in scientific theories. Hypotheses that are supported by evidence permit theorists to make generalizations – statements that summarize relationships and become part of the theory. Some of these statements might take the form of *principles*; some might be expressed as *laws*; others might simply be *beliefs*.

so they should maybe take a break and try to answer them. When I asked her what these philosophical questions might be, she said free will and determinism. She explained that this was another of those really big issues in philosophy and in psychology. Determinism, she explained, is the belief that all behaviors result from identifiable causes – even if we don't know what these causes are – and that they don't result from the exercise of free will. Lots of philosophers think the two are incompatible, she said, meaning determinism and free will. She said that learning theorists pretty well have to assume that behavior is determined. That's one of the essential assumptions of science, she said, shaking her head and making her long braids fly wildly. I hadn't noticed them before. So, does that mean there's no free will? I asked, and she replied, well, that's the philosophical question. Then, she went back to her pages.

Principles are statements that relate to some predictability in nature or, more important for psychology, in behavior. For example, principles of learning describe specific factors that affect learning and remembering. A very general principle of learning, which we discuss in more detail in later chapters, might be worded as follows: Behaviors that are followed by certain agreeable consequences, such as food, sex, or praise, become more probable.

Theorists have long hoped that a few simple principles of this kind might explain vast chunks of human behavior. For example, this principle seems to be widely evident. It is apparent in the fact that birds come to winter feeders; that dogs that are fed, petted, or praised quickly learn to roll over if you want them to; that children who are rewarded for studying hard continue to study hard. But as we will see in Chapter 5, not all children study harder when they are praised or given high grades for so doing; not all dogs willingly roll over for a bone; and some birds shy away from the best stocked of winter feeders. By definition, principles are probabilistic and uncertain. Although they represent generally agreed-upon conclusions based on what seems solid evidence, they are nevertheless tentative. With new evidence, principles are subject to change.

Such is not the case with respect to laws. **Laws** are statements whose accuracy is beyond reasonable doubt. They are conclusions based on what seem to be undeniable observations and unquestionable logic. Unlike principles, laws are not ordinarily open to exceptions and doubt. For example, the statement $E = mc^2$ is a law. However, laws should not be confused with truth because any law can be refuted given sufficient contrary evidence. By definition, truth can never be found to be untrue.[6]

Beliefs describe statements that are more private and more personal than are principles or laws. For example, the notion that redheaded people are more prone to anger than are dark-haired people is a belief rather than a principle or a law. Note that, like principles and laws, beliefs attempt to describe general facts. Unfortunately, they are often treated as though they were as universal as principles (or even laws). Beliefs are often formed very early in life, and they are not always based on objective observation or reliable logic. Furthermore, they tend to be maintained even in the face of strong contradiction (Dagnall, Denovan, Drinkwater, Parker, & Clough, 2017). They act as a sort of filter through which people view and understand the world; beliefs guide thought and action.

Common Misconceptions and Folk Beliefs

All societies have developed large bodies of commonly held beliefs about human behavior. These beliefs are part of what Kelley (1992) calls **bubba psychology** (bubba means grand-mother in some Eastern European languages). Hence, the term indicates an intuitive sort of *folk psychology*, also sometimes labeled *implicit* or *naïve psychology*.[7] Folk, or bubba, psychology

---

[6] How about *fake truth* I interrupted. "Not possible," said Old Lady Gribbin emphatically. "That's an oxymoron. That's like saying 'All generalizations are false. Except this one.'" I noticed that the cat had left. I couldn't see him anywhere but I could not recall anyone opening the door. "Where's the cat?" I asked, but the old lady ignored my question.

[7] When I pointed out to Old Lady Gribbin that in this age of political correctness it isn't wise to single out identifiable groups (like grandmothers or maybe even monkeys) as examples of anything that might seem in any way negative, she shot back

should not be confused with **pop psychology**. Pop (or *popular*) psychology refers to widely disseminated and generally accepted beliefs and theories about human nature that are passed off as the results of sound academic research, but are instead based on simplistic and often inaccurate interpretations that are popularized (hence *pop*) through various media.

Many of the intuitive beliefs of folk psychology are correct. If they were not, people would constantly be surprised at what others say and do. Most people know enough about human behavior to be able to predict that, for example, those who are sad might cry, those who are overjoyed might smile and laugh, and those who are outraged might do outrageous things.

Quite often, though, the beliefs of folk psychology are wrong. For example, it might seem obvious that many people do not dream, that some women are more likely than others to give birth to sons, and that most people are altruistic enough to try to help someone being raped, mugged, or beaten. In fact, however, all normal people dream, although not all can remember doing so; it is the man's sperm and not the woman's ovum (egg) that determines the infant's sex; and some studies indicate that many people will not try to help a person or even an animal being raped, mugged, beaten, or even killed (for example, Arluke, 2012; Darley & Latané, 1968).

Misconceptions About Learning and the Brain

Because they are often misleading or flatly incorrect, personal beliefs can be very dangerous in science. Misconceptions, argue Bensley and Lilienfeld (2017), often interfere with learning and with clear, logical thinking.

Even educated and trained professionals are often victims of false beliefs. And so are students, many of whom approach their psychology courses with more than a handful of false beliefs that are stubbornly resistant to extinction. For example, we tend to believe that there is an average, normal way of thinking and learning – that we all think and learn in identical ways and that the task of learning research is to discover these ways of learning. In reality, things are not quite so simple. For example, there are important differences in people's **learning styles** – the preferred and customary approaches that different people use when trying to learn. The point is that learning is not a fixed process, unvarying in all learners. Not only is the human organism characterized by remarkable *plasticity* (that is, a striking ability to change), but it is also characterized by a variety of ways of thinking and learning.

Related to this, we tend to believe in the average individual. Thus, we think that six-year-olds are this way or that, that nine-year-olds are this or that other way, and that 50-year-olds are yet another way. But if we think about it, we know that there are profound individual differences among all 6-, 9-, and 50-year-olds: Each person is unique. The average learner (and the average child) is a mathematical invention that makes our study and our understanding easier. As we see throughout this text, most learning theories describe the *average* learner – a mythical, prototypical individual. But as we also see, most theories also try to account for individual differences.

that she wasn't real interested in being politically correct, that her people had long ago paid the price for telling the truth. "If the book isn't sufficiently politically correct," she said, using what I soon learned was a variation of one of her favorite expressions, "well bugger them." I was much taken aback and did not immediately think of asking who her people were.

Many also have serious misconceptions about the role and functioning of the brain. For example, there is a common belief that we use only about 10 per cent of our brains. But in fact, there's no evidence to support this belief (Cherry, 2018b). Many also believe that the right and left hemispheres have distinct and clearly separate functions. As we see in Chapter 5, that belief is incorrect. Although some functions tend to be localized more in one hemisphere than the other, most abilities are spread across both hemispheres. Furthermore, if one hemisphere is damaged, especially if the damage occurs early in life, the intact hemisphere often takes over activities that were previously localized in the damaged hemisphere.

Another common misconception is that the brain does not change and that no new neurons (nerve cells) form after birth. In fact, the brain changes throughout life. Neurons form new connections, strengthen or weaken existing connections, or lose connections. And while some neurons die, there is now evidence that some may divide. There is also evidence that new neurons may be formed in some parts of the brain (termed **neurogenesis**), including some that may be directly involved with higher thought processes (for example, Alam et al., 2018; Karadottir & Kuo, 2018).

Purposes of Theories

Clearly, however, not all personal beliefs are misconceptions. One of the things that theories do is provide a basis for judging the accuracy and usefulness of beliefs. The most important functions of a theory are to simplify and organize observations and to provide a basis for making predictions. In the end, the usefulness of a theory in psychology may depend a great deal on how accurately it predicts. Thus, a theory that tries to explain how humans learn through experience should provide a basis for predicting the most likely effects of different experiences. Similarly, such a theory should lead to suggestions for arranging experiences so that behavior will change in desired and happy ways.

In addition to their practical usefulness for predicting and controlling behavior, theories also suggest which facts (observations) are most important as well as which relationships among these facts are most meaningful (Thomas, 2005). However, theorists may have dramatically different ideas about what is important, so a large number of theories may emerge in the same area of investigation. And although these theories may be quite different, none will necessarily be totally incorrect, although some may be more useful than others. In the final analysis, a theory cannot easily be evaluated in terms of whether it is right or wrong. Instead, it must be judged mainly by its usefulness.

Characteristics of Good Theories

Good theories in psychology should not only be useful, but should also have other qualities (Kuhn, 1962; Thomas, 2005).

1. They should summarize and organize important facts (observations).
2. Theories depend on observations and should reflect them accurately. Observations are often based on scientific experiments; theories therefore need to demonstrate agreement with relevant experiments.

3. A good theory should be clear and understandable.

4. Theories should simplify; they should impose order where there might otherwise be complexity, confusion and chaos. Put another way, theories should be **parsimonious**. A parsimonious statement is the simplest and shortest statement that adequately covers the facts. The principle of parsimony, also termed **Occam's razor**, holds that where there are two competing theories that each explain or summarize a set of observations, the least complex is better. Accordingly, a parsimonious theory is one that describes all important relationships in the simplest but most accurate terms possible. Theories that are unnecessarily detailed and complex are said to lack parsimony.[8]

5. A theory should be useful for predicting as well as for explaining. In fact, one of the most important criteria of a good theory is that it should lead to predictions that are potentially false – that is, that are falsifiable. This is because a theory that does not lead to falsifiable predictions cannot be proven to be incorrect and therefore cannot be proven correct either.

6. Predictions and explanations based on a theory should have some usefulness in terms of application in the real world – for example, in education or in therapy or in the further development of theory.

7. Theories should be internally consistent rather than contradictory. Poorer theories sometimes lead to contradictory explanations and predictions. Such theories cannot easily be tested and are of limited usefulness.

8. Theories should not be based on a large number of **assumptions** (beliefs accepted as fact but essentially not verifiable). Theories that are based on many assumptions are difficult to evaluate. And if the assumptions on which they are based are invalid, the theories may be misleading. Still, scientific theories are generally based on the inescapable assumption of **determinism**; in other words, they are based on the assumption that behavior results from predictable relationships among identifiable causes and effects rather than from what might be termed *free will*.

9. Finally, a good theory should be thought-provoking as well as providing satisfying explanations. Theories that have the greatest impact on a field are often those that give rise as much to opposition as to support. Such theories typically lead to research designed to support, to refute, or to elaborate. They are said to have high **heuristic** value in the sense that they lead to new research and to new discoveries (heuristic is an adjective used to describe an approach to problem solving that leads to discovery or learning).

These criteria are summarized in Table 1.1 and illustrated with respect to Grandma Francœur's Fertilizer Theory.[9]

---

[8] Should you maybe explain this just a bit more, this business of parsimony and simplicity, I asked Old Lady Gribbin, and she laughed that same mocking, cackling laugh I had heard earlier. She said that our human preference for parsimony and simplicity seems highly revealing. Of what? I asked, and she laughed her sardonic laugh again. Of intellectual limitations, she answered. Of limitations evident in a widespread inability to understand chaos and an aversion to detail and complexity. You've lost me, I said, and she said, "That's my point."

[9] The grandma in question is my own grandmother. When I was younger, my cousins and I had a less polite word for what Mrs. Gribbin called Grandma Francœur's Fertilizer Theory. We called it grandma's **** theory. (**Bleeped by the editorial committee.**)

Table 1.1 **Criteria of a good theory, applied to Grandma Francœur's fertilizer theory. This theory holds, in part, that horse manure stimulates potatoes and carrots, that chicken droppings invigorate cabbages, and that dried cow dung excites flowers.**

Criteria of a good theory	Grandmother Francœur's Fertilizer Theory
Does it summarize and organize important facts?	Yes, if carrots, potatoes, and other plants behave as expected under specified conditions.
Does it agree with relevant scientific experiments?	"My experiments, yes, they were good experiments," insisted grandma. "They proved the power of the right dung."
Is it clear and understandable?	It's quite clear, except for the very stupid, who are seldom asked to judge theories.
Is it as parsimonious as it should be? Has Occam's razor pared it sufficiently?	That, of course, depends on who presents the theory. There are many wonderful details that would naturally be omitted in the most parsimonious presentation.
Is it useful for predicting as well as explaining?	Very. For example, knowing what fertilizers have been applied in the spring, the theory allows the gardener to predict and explain the final harvest. That the predictions are clearly falsifiable means that the theory can be tested directly.
Is it practically useful?	Clearly, yes, for those engaged in the growing of vegetable things.
Is it internally consistent?	Unfortunately, no, the theory is weak in this regard. For example, grandma has sometimes claimed that chicken droppings are better for potatoes than horse manure. Which, apparently, is horse manure.
Is it based on many unverifiable assumptions?	No. The assumptions upon which it's based could be verified – or falsified.
Is it satisfying and thought-provoking?	Oh, yes indeed!

SCIENCE AND PSYCHOLOGICAL THEORIES

Many of the most stubborn and widespread beliefs about human behavior, often based on what is termed **common sense** (what we think of as the *good judgment* or *natural wisdom* that all people share), are wrong; common sense doesn't always make sense. For example, there are far more astrologers than astronomers in North America. But there is no good evidence that the beliefs and predictions of astrology are the least bit valid. Similarly, more people believe in **paranormal phenomena** (such as telekinesis, ghosts, extrasensory perception, or mind-reading), a collection of phenomena that science hasn't been able to verify, than believe in evolution, a theory that has received enormous scientific support. Astrology and belief in the paranormal are part of what are often collectively labeled **pseudoscience** (based on widely held beliefs rather than on science) (Smith, 2010).

One of psychology's important tasks is to determine which beliefs about human behavior make sense. How can psychology accomplish this? The answer, in one word, is **science**.

What Is Science?

In one sense, science is a collection of information related to a field of study. For example, the science of physics is a collection of information relating to the nature and properties of matter, and the science of psychology is a collection of information relating to the nature and properties of human thought and behavior.

In another sense, science is a way of dealing with information. The scientific approach to information is evident in (a) an attitude toward the search for knowledge that emphasizes replicability, objectivity, precision, and consistency and (b) a collection of methods for gathering and analyzing observations, designed to ensure that conclusions are objective, accurate, and generalizable.

Science is psychology's most powerful tool for separating fact from fiction.

Steps in the Scientific Method

A useful way of looking at the meaning of the term *science* is to think of it as an attitude rather than simply as one of several bodies of knowledge or as a series of recipes for acquiring and systematizing knowledge. As an attitude, science insists on objectivity, precision, and replicability; it accepts as valid only those observations that have been collected in such a way that others can repeat them under similar circumstances.

This view of science leads to a clear set of methods for gathering information. These methods collectively compose what is often referred to as the *scientific method*. For more than 100 years now, the social sciences have used the scientific method to reduce uncertainty and to search for knowledge.

The scientific method can be simplified and described in terms of five steps.

1. Ask the Question

Do people who are most highly rewarded always work hardest? Is punishment effective in eliminating undesirable behavior? Are teenagers who make the greatest use of social media better adjusted than those who avoid them? Are they lonelier? Happier? More intelligent? Less intelligent? There is no shortage of questions in the study of learning and behavior. As a method, science makes no judgments about whether questions are trivial or important; it simply insists that they be clear.

And it absolutely refuses to jump to conclusions. There are certain procedures to be followed and certain logical steps to be taken first.

In practice, the researcher's first task after identifying a problem is to find out what is already known about it. Usually, this involves doing library research, conducting computer searches, or consulting other sources, such as experts and professionals in the field.

2. Develop a Hypothesis

Once the scientific researcher has uncovered relevant background information, the next step is to arrive at a tentative conclusion, or hypothesis, which is an educated guess that guides the research. It usually takes the form of a prediction or a statement of relationships. Hypotheses are often based on theories. By definition, they are unproven and falsifiable. As a result, the outcome of a scientific investigation can lead to the rejection of a hypothesis.

3. Collect Relevant Observations

The scientific study of any phenomenon always begins with observations. After all, observations are what science tries to explain and understand. Observations are the basis of all science.

Science suggests several different ways of gathering observations. The most powerful of these is the **experiment**, a carefully arranged and controlled set of circumstances under which an investigator can observe a phenomenon. Experiments sometimes use **surveys** (ways of collecting observations relating to the behaviors, the beliefs, the attitudes, and other characteristics of a sample representing some population). Surveys often use **questionnaires** (lists of predetermined questions to which participants respond), **interviews** (where investigators question individuals), or different kinds of tests and measurements (such as intelligence or personality tests or measures of weight and height). (We look at experiments in more detail shortly.)

4. Test the Hypothesis

The reason for gathering observations is to determine the validity of hypotheses. The whole point of the exercise is to answer the questions that inspired the research in the first place.

If conclusions are to be valid, observations must be accurate and meaningful. Science is very concerned that observations might just be chance occurrences. For this reason, researchers often use one or more of a number of special mathematical (*statistical*) procedures to separate chance events from those that are **significant**. Observations are deemed *significant* when they would be expected to occur only very rarely by chance. The assumption is that significant observations must have some identifiable, non-random cause.

5. Reach and Share a Conclusion

In scientific research, conclusions usually take the form of accepting or rejecting the hypotheses that have guided the investigation. Sometimes, of course, the results are unclear or are contrary to what is expected. Often, the results of research suggest another question or lead to another hypothesis rather than providing a definite and final answer. Thus, conclusions are often tentative. A series of unexpected observations and conclusions may lead to major changes in the theories upon which hypotheses are based.

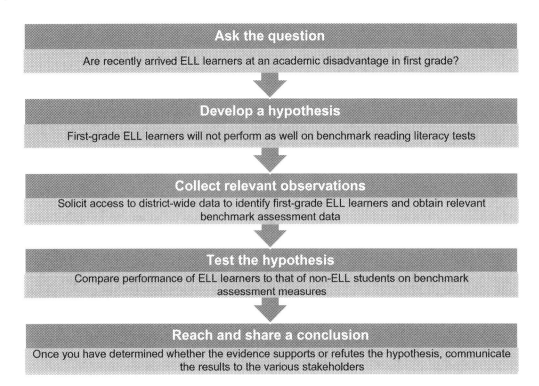

Figure 1.2 The hallmark of scientific research is objectivity and replicability. The five steps that commonly define the scientific method are designed with these goals in mind.

And if science is to progress, the results of its research must be shared. One fundamental principle of academic science is that its fruits belong to everyone. (See Figure 1.2 for a summary and illustration of the five steps characteristic of the scientific method.)

Experiments

The experiment is science's most powerful tool for avoiding bias and reliably determining the validity of hypotheses. An experiment is a situation in which the investigator systematically manipulates some aspect of the environment, termed a **variable** (a variable is any feature or quality of a person, animal, or thing that is subject to variation) to determine the effect of so doing on some important outcome. What is manipulated is the **independent variable**; the effect of this control or manipulation is reflected in the **dependent variable**.

As an example, consider the hypothesis that *Rewards for current learning have a positive effect on subsequent learning*. The first step in conducting an experiment to test this hypothesis is to define the abstract terms involved in such a way that they can be manipulated, controlled, and measured. Such definitions are labeled **operational definitions**. Operational definitions involve defining something in terms of precise actions (*operations*) that can be observed and therefore measured. Thus, the most common operational definitions refer to methods used to measure a variable. For example, hunger might be operationally defined in terms of number of hours without eating. Similarly "subsequent learning" in the hypothesis *Rewards for current learning have a positive effect on subsequent learning*, could be operationally defined in terms

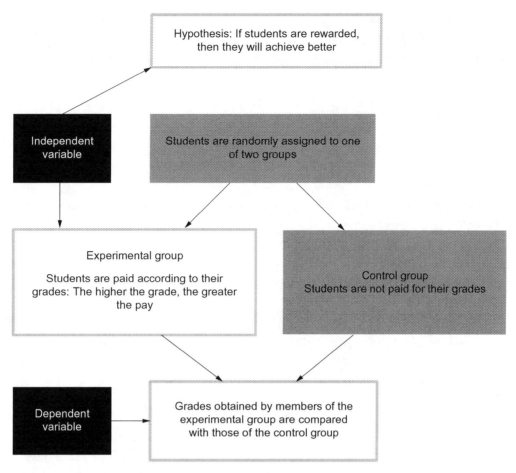

Figure 1.3 A simple experiment designed to test a hypothesis. Note that hypotheses can generally be worded as if–then statements. The *if* part of the statement is the independent variable (in this case, the payment students in the experimental group receive); the *then* part is the dependent variable (in this case, the grades obtained by members of the experimental group).

of performance on a test following a clearly defined learning experience. An operational definition of "rewards for current learning" might refer to objective, measurable outcomes, such as receiving money or prizes, being granted privileges, or being showered with verbal praise. Furthermore, operational definitions might specify several other details, such as whether the learner had prior expectations of being rewarded, and so on. Thus, a simple experiment designed to examine this hypothesis might consist of an arrangement whereby some learners are paid for their grades and others not; all are subsequently exposed to a learning experience, and the performance of the rewarded group is compared with that of the unrewarded group. In this case, the *independent variable* (that which is controlled by the experimenter) is the money reward; the *dependent variable* is the learner's subsequent performance (see Figure 1.3).

Identifying dependent and independent variables is a relatively simple matter when an experiment is phrased as an *if–then* statement. The objective of an experiment is to determine whether it is true that "if this, then that." The "if" part of the equation represents what is controlled or manipulated – hence, the *independent* variable(s); the "then" part represents the consequences or outcomes – hence, the *dependent* variable(s). Virtually any hypothesis can be phrased as an if–then statement. Thus, the previous example can be rephrased as follows: *If* a learner is consistently rewarded for performing well, *then* subsequent learning will improve.

Sampling and Comparison Groups

An important step in carrying out most experiments in psychology is to select participants for the experiment (sometimes referred to as *subjects*, a term which now seems less politically correct than *participant*, given its connotations of subservience). Clearly, experimenters are seldom able to conduct their investigations with the entire **population** in which they might be interested (a *population* is defined as the entire group of individuals to which the results of an experiment might be generalized; for example, all grade-five learners, all left-handed males, all three-year-olds). Instead, experimenters conduct their research with small groups (or sometimes with single individuals), termed a **sample**, selected from a larger population.

In an experiment, it is very important that participants be selected at **random** from the population to which the investigator wants to generalize. Random selection means that everybody has an equal chance of being a participant. Common, nonrandom ways of selecting participants are to have them volunteer or to select them from institutions or classrooms.

The problem with nonrandom selection of subjects is that systematic biases may be introduced. For example, people who volunteer for experiments may be more adventurous than those who don't and the investigator's conclusions might then be valid only for those who are adventurous. Similarly, students may be systematically different from nonstudents (and institutionalized people from those not in institutions) in interests, motivation, background, and other characteristics. As a result, conclusions based on studies that use nonrandom samples – often referred to as *samples of convenience* – may not be valid for the larger population.

Having selected participants, the investigator then assigns them randomly to one of two groups. As shown in Figure 1.3, these are labeled **experimental groups** or **control groups** (control groups are sometimes also called *comparison* or *no-treatment* groups). These two groups are as identical as possible, except that experimental group members are given some experimental treatment (such as being rewarded for grades), whereas members of the control group are not. Without a control group, it might be impossible for the investigator to know for certain that any changes observed after the experimental treatment are actually caused by the treatment and not by something else.

Evaluating Psychological Research

One important limitation in psychological investigations is that the observations with which psychology deals are not always undeniable facts. In some ways, observations in other sciences, such as chemistry or physics, are less open to doubt. Thus, it is a fact that apples fall when they become detached from trees. And if a lazy Newton happens to be sleeping below the tree directly under the apple, it will hit him on the head. Put another way, gravity is more than simply a *belief* or even a *principle*; it is a *law*. But that rewarding children for being good increases the probability of their behaving well is not so much a law as a principle. And as we see in Chapter 9, it is not always a very straightforward principle; there are circumstances under which rewarding children may have unexpected results. The characteristics of children are highly variable and complex; at least in some ways, apples are more predictable.[10]

Psychological investigations are also limited by the amount of control psychologists have over relevant variables. Two rats reared in identical cages and subjected to the same daily routines from birth may reasonably be assumed to have had highly comparable experiences. The same assumption cannot be made as confidently about two children who are raised in different homes. Because their parents, friends, siblings, relatives, and so many other important aspects of their worlds are different, their experiences will also have been very different. Psychological experimentation needs to take into account these and many other important differences among participants.

Consider the following illustration:

- **Problem:** To determine the relationship of sleep deprivation to problem-solving behavior.
- **Participants:** All students in a private school are selected for the study. They are randomly divided into two groups.
- **Hypothesis:** Sleep-deprived students will perform significantly more poorly on a problem-solving test.
- **Experimental treatment:** One group is allowed to sleep as usual; the other is kept awake all night. In the morning, the test is given to all students, and results for the two groups are compared.
- **Results:** The sleep-deprived group does significantly more poorly.

Is the conclusion that sleep deprivation is related to problem-solving ability warranted? The answer is a tentative yes, providing that a number of other relevant variables have also been controlled. For example, if the rested group were on average more or less intelligent, all male or female, or had had previous training in problem solving, these variables could also account for differences in test performance. It would then not be logical to conclude that sleep is the significant factor. But because participants were assigned at random to either of the two groups, there is a greater chance that they are similar on each of these important variables.

Random selection and assignment to groups is one way to match groups on important variables, and also to make sure that the sample is a good representation of the population. Another possibility is to try to match the groups directly, making sure that the composition of the groups is highly similar for variables such as intelligence, sex, previous training, and so on. In fact, however, it is usually impossible to identify and account for all potentially relevant variables in psychological experimentation. Investigators have to be aware that the outcomes of

---

[10] When I said to Old Lady Gribbin that this might not be entirely clear to everyone and that she made it sound as if we shouldn't place too much faith in the results of psychological investigations, she said no, not at all. She explained that it shouldn't be inferred from these comments that physical facts are more "factual" than psychological facts. Indeed, she said, in this chaotic and relativistic world, the word *fact*, be it physical or psychological, is a statistical concept of varying probability. The point, she concluded, is that it's relatively simple to observe an apple falling, but it's far more difficult to evaluate things like the effects of rewards, or children's attachment to their mothers, or how punishment affects dogs and cats and people, and on and on.

experiments might not always mean what they seem to mean. Science insists that investigators and consumers of research think critically. At the very least, says science, when interpreting and evaluating psychological research, ask the following questions:

Have I Committed the Nominal Fallacy?

Luria (1968) reports the case of S, whose memory was so remarkable that he could remember completely accurately the most trivial of details not just for minutes, hours, or days, but also for decades. He seemed never to forget even the most meaningless of sounds and the most nonsensical of words. "Yes, yes," he would say when Luria asked him to remember some jumbled paragraph or a complex table of digits he had been asked to learn years earlier. "Yes, this was a series you gave me once when we were in your apartment . . . . [Y]ou were wearing a gray suit and you look at me like this . . ." (Luria, 1968, p. 12).

Why did S remember so well? Do you suppose it was because he had what's popularly called a *photographic memory*? Or did he remember so well because he was a professional **mnemonist** – a professional memorizer?

Neither of these possibilities is correct. In fact, neither is even an explanation. S didn't remember because he was a mnemonist or because he had a photographic memory. These are just labels for someone with a good memory; they don't explain why the person is exceptionally good at remembering. All they do is *name* something; they say nothing about what underlies actual performance. The assumption that names are explanations is the **nominal fallacy**.

Nominal fallacies are quite common. For example, if you think some children have difficulty learning because they are mentally challenged or learning disabled, you are guilty of a nominal fallacy. To say that children have difficulty learning because they are learning disabled or mentally challenged is not to say anything at all about why they have difficulty.

Is the Sample Representative?

The samples on which conclusions are based have to be representative of the groups to which they are generalized. Investigators try to select *unbiased* samples (samples whose characteristics are much the same as those of the general population) by using random selection whenever possible. However, research is sometimes limited to *samples of convenience* – easily accessible groups, such as students of one school or one class, institutional inmates, or residents of a housing complex. In such cases, to ensure that a sample represents a larger population, it is necessary to compare the two on important variables such as age, sex, and educational background. If the sample is *biased* (different from the population), conclusions might apply only to the sample upon which they are based.

Can Subjects Be Believed?

Sometimes research runs into memory problems. How well can participants remember their fourth birthday? Do they remember the age at which they first became interested in politics?

Does a mother accurately recall when Johnnie took his first steps? When Sarah first said "mama"? Can you describe with absolute certainty what the thief was wearing? The color of her eyes?

Sometimes, the problem is one of honesty. Investigations that probe into highly personal areas are especially vulnerable to deliberate distortion. If there is something to be gained or lost by presenting a certain image, that too must be taken into account by the critical consumer of research.

Is There a Possibility of Subject Bias?

In a historic study, Roethlisberger and Dickson (1939) tried to increase the productivity of a group of workers at the Hawthorne Electric plant by changing aspects of their work environment. Over a series of experiments, the researchers did things such as increase or decrease the number of work periods, shorten or lengthen breaks, increase or decrease illumination, and provide or take away bonuses. Strangely, it did not matter what the experimenters did; production still increased. This phenomenon is now known as the **Hawthorne effect**. It seemed that subjects were simply responding to the knowledge they were being studied. Maybe they just wanted to please the investigator.

More recent research has shown that what is labeled the Hawthorne effect is not always apparent or very significant and that the concept is complex and not always very useful. As Paradis and Sutkin (2017) note following an investigation into the effect of observers on participant behavior, "Evidence of a Hawthorne Effect is scant, and amounts to little more than a good story" (p. 31). Nevertheless, it may still be an important factor in some psychological research. As Barnes (2010) discovered in his investigation of the Hawthorne effect in investigations in developing countries, participants in experiments are often anxious to please the investigator; consequently, their responses and behaviors may occasionally be misleading. To guard against this possibility, subjects are often not told that they are members of experimental groups or they are compared with others who also think they are part of the experiment but actually are not.

Is There a Possibility of Experimenter Bias?

Margaret Mead, the well-known anthropologist/sociologist, had a profound belief that cultures shape people. Her studies of isolated inhabitants of New Guinea uncovered three very different tribes (Mead, 1935). Among the cannibalistic Mundugummor, both men and women were ruthless and aggressive. She describes them as being "very *masculine*" by North American standards. In contrast, both sexes among the agricultural Arapesh seemed *feminine* in a traditional, 1935, sense (noncompetitive, nonaggressive, warm, and emotional). And in a third tribe, the Tchambuli, where the men spent most of their time adorning themselves and devising new dances while the women gathered food, there appeared to be a reversal of the sex roles that were common in early twentieth-century North America. This is striking evidence of the power of culture in shaping important characteristics such as masculinity and femininity, claimed Mead.

Not so, argues Freeman (1983). After six years of research in Samoa, where Mead had done much of her work on culture, Freeman found little evidence of cultural differences as striking as those described by Mead. Her observations and conclusions, he writes, were highly subjective and largely undocumented. Freeman suggests that Mead was so convinced of the importance of culture that her biases blinded her to contradictory evidence.

In the same way that subjects are sometimes not told whether they are members of the experimental or control group to guard against the possibility of subject bias and of the Hawthorne effect, so too are experimental observers often kept ignorant of who is an experimental subject and who is not. This is called a **single-blind procedure**.

A **double-blind procedure** is when neither subjects nor experimenters know which subjects received which treatment. For example, in educational or psychological research, tests might be scored and interpreted without the investigator knowing whether the testee is part of the experimental or the control group. Or in a medical investigation of the effectiveness of a new drug, neither the patients nor the examining physicians would know which patients have received the new drug and which have received an older drug or simply a **placebo** (a substance or treatment known to have no effects).

Interestingly, as research has shown repeatedly, placebos often do have a positive effect in a variety of situations, including psychotherapy (Tuchina et al., 2018); advertising that promises that particular brands are better than others, whether or not they are (Alves, Lopes, & Hernandez, 2017); and in medicine (Barbagallo et al., 2018). The **placebo effect** is generally attributed to the patient's belief in the effectiveness of the treatment. The opposite effect, labeled the **nocebo effect**, is evident where the patient's belief in the negative consequences of a substance or a treatment exacerbates those consequences. The nocebo effect is sometimes described as the *dark side* of the placebo effect. It is occasionally observed in situations where a patient is so convinced of the probable dire consequences of a diagnosis that those consequences actually become more likely (Mukherjee & Sahay, 2018; Webster, Weinman, & Rubin, 2018).

Participants in Psychological Research

Even psychologists who are mainly interested in human behavior often use animals as experimental subjects. For example, in well-known psychological investigations:

- Infant monkeys have been separated from their mothers at birth and reared in cages with inanimate wire models wearing bizarre-looking masks.
- Blowflies have had a nerve between their brains and their foreguts severed and have been observed to eat until they burst.
- Worms have been trained, ground up, and fed to other worms.
- Rats have been given electric shocks.
- Cats have been caged within sight and smell of presumably succulent but difficult to obtain morsels of fish.

These investigations have provided us with useful information about infant attachment, the mechanisms that control eating, the nature of memory, the relationship between negative consequences and learning, and the role of trial and error in problem solving. They serve as good examples of one of the advantages of using animals in psychological investigations: specifically, that many of the procedures sometimes used with animals cannot ethically be performed with humans.

Using animals rather than humans in psychological research has several other distinct advantages. For example, an animal's experiences can be controlled very carefully; that is seldom the case with human subjects. Also, most animals can reproduce many mature generations over a relatively short period, and of course, mates can be selected for them in accordance with the requirements of the investigation. This can be especially useful in studies of genetic influences. Humans reproduce more slowly, mature very gradually, and many stubbornly insist on choosing their own mates.

In many cases, results of animal studies can be generalized, at least tentatively, to humans. Still, there is always the possibility that conclusions based on animal research might not apply to people. And, ultimately, psychology is most interested in people.[11]

Ethics in Animal Research

In this age of greater sensibility, awareness, compassion, and political sensitivity, some of the procedures used in experiments such as those mentioned earlier are considered by many to be unacceptable on moral and ethical grounds. Some argue that even though the goal of science is to improve human welfare, this does not automatically justify causing pain and suffering to an animal (and often even sacrificing it). The use of animals rather than humans, some argue, reveals that animals are less valued than humans. Many believe that under no circumstances should animals be harmed in the interests of science (Joffe, Bara, Anton, & Nobis, 2016). Some, like Fenton (2018), suggest that what he considers to be *intensely social animals* such as, for example, chimpanzees, should be allowed to refuse to participate in research when their behavior indicates that they prefer not to. An increasing number think that not only should animals be protected from pain and suffering, but they are also entitled to pleasure and even happiness.

On the other side of this controversial and highly emotional issue are those who insist that the benefits that might ultimately be derived justify animal research under certain circumstances (Fahmy & Gaafar, 2016). Animal researchers must become more active in public education and more transparent in their research, suggest Yeates and Reed (2015), so the potential benefits of animal research become more apparent. They must also assume a more active role in explaining

---

[11] Here, Old Lady Gribbin stopped and asked me to turn off the recorder. She said this wasn't really part of the book, but she wanted to explain that throughout their history, many humans have gone to great lengths to demonstrate that they're fundamentally different from nonhuman animals, and many have devoted much time and effort to trying to discover exactly how it is that they're different. She said that some propose that it's the *soul* that separates the two; others suggest *language* or *consciousness*. Still others claim that some Maker made humans according to a self-likeness and that this accounts for a critical, basic difference. She pointed out that some psychologists argue that because humans and nonhumans are different, animals make poor subjects in investigations of human behavior; others argue that in some ways they're very similar, and because of the fact that certain experimental procedures are better performed with animals, it makes sense to use animals in psychological research.

Human Learning

the benefits of animal research and in demonstrating that research animals are humanely and ethically treated (Beverdorf, Roos, Hauser, Lennon, & Mehler, 2015).

The Association for the Study of Animal Behavior (*Animal Behaviour* 2012) as well as the American Psychological Association (APA, 2012, available online at www.apa.org/science/leadership/care/care-animal-guidelines.pdf) present a number of principles intended to guide the conduct of scientists doing research with animals. Among them are the following:

- The research should have a clear scientific purpose with positive potential benefits for humans or other animals.
- Animal care must comply with existing laws and regulations.
- All animal research must be supervised by a psychologist trained in the care of laboratory animals.
- Every effort must be made to minimize animal pain and suffering.
- Animals should be subjected to surgery, pain, and discomfort only when this is justified by the potential value of the research.
- If animals need to be killed, this should be done quickly and painlessly.

Humans as Research Participants

Human participants are seldom subjected to pain and suffering as obvious as that among monkeys whose participation requires that they develop experimentally induced ulcers, or rabbits who are exposed to allergenic cosmetics. But there are experimental treatments with humans that are psychologically stressful; some might even have lasting negative consequences. As a result, the APA has developed a set of guidelines governing the conduct of research with human participants (American Psychological Association, 2016).

In practice, almost all investigations conducted in North American schools and colleges, whether with animals or with humans, are subject to approval by ethical review committees. The purpose of these committees is to ensure adherence to appropriate ethical standards whose purpose is to protect participants. The APA's guidelines for research with human participants include the following:

- The investigator is responsible for evaluating the ethical acceptability of the research.
- Investigators need to determine whether participants are "at risk" or "at minimal risk."
- Before the investigation, all participants should be made fully aware of all aspects of the research that might affect their willingness to participate.
- When an investigation requires that participants be deceived, investigators need to (a) determine whether the potential benefits of the study justify the use of deception; (b) determine whether other approaches that do not involve deception might answer the same questions; (c) provide participants with a "sufficient" explanation as soon as possible.
- Informed consent is required of all participants. This means that participants (or their guardians if they are underage) need to understand the purpose of the research, its expected duration, the benefits that might accrue, and so on.
- Participants must be protected from physical and mental danger or discomfort. Procedures that might result in harm to participants may be used only when failure to use them might

have even more harmful consequences or where the potential benefits are very significant and all participants have given fully informed consent.

- Where there are harmful consequences to participants, the investigator is responsible for removing and correcting these.
- Information about participants is private and confidential unless otherwise agreed in advance.

The most important principle underlying these guidelines is that of *informed consent*. Not only do participants need to be made aware of the nature and purpose of the research, but they must be completely free not to participate. This is especially important where investigators are in a position of power over potential participants, as is usually the case for students or for residents in homes for the elderly.

THEORIES OF LEARNING: A BRIEF OVERVIEW

Because learning involves changes in behavior that result from experience, the psychology of learning is based on observations of behavior and behavior change. Not surprisingly, the terms **learning theory** and *behavior theory* are often synonymous in psychological literature.

Learning theories result from psychologists' attempts to organize the observations, hypotheses, hunches, laws, principles, and guesses that have been made about human behavior. Not surprisingly, the earliest learning theories were, in many ways, somewhat simpler than more recently developed theories. Theories have become increasingly complex with new findings and with the recognition that earlier theories do not account for all the facts. Still, the earliest theories continue to have a profound influence on current theories and research.

Structuralism and Functionalism

The earliest psychologists directed much of their effort toward understanding mental processes such as thinking, imagining, and feeling. These are processes that define consciousness (the **mind**, in other words). Most important among these early psychologists was Wilhelm Wundt in Germany and William James in the United States. Two schools of psychology resulted from their writings.

Structuralism, the approach associated with Wundt, directed its efforts toward breaking down mental processes into their most basic components. The goal of structuralism was to understand the elements – that is, the *structure* – of consciousness. Structuralism relied heavily on **introspection** (examining one's own feelings and motives and generalizing from these) as a way of discovering things about human learning and behavior. Recall that Descartes also used this approach. It's an approach that differs dramatically from the more objective methods of science that eventually came to dominate much of psychology.

Functionalism, the approach associated with James, was largely an American reaction to structuralism. Heavily influenced by the work of Charles Darwin, James tried to understand mental processes by looking at the *purposes* that drive behavior – that is, the *function* of behavior. Darwin's theories of natural selection suggested that all characteristics of a species serve some adaptive purpose; this explains why those characteristics have survived. In the same way, consciousness is assumed to have purpose often evident in behavior. Hence, functionalists believed very strongly that the mind could not be explained by looking at its elements (at its structure). Instead, they focused on the reasons (or *purposes*) for behavior. They viewed structuralism as far too mentalistic to be useful and were highly critical of that approach. Functionalism also used introspection as one of its principal research methods. However, James and his followers dealt far less with mentalistic concepts than did the structuralist school. In addition, they drew from Darwinian evolutionary theory in trying to explain behavior in terms of stimuli.

Although structuralism and functionalism used introspection to develop their ideas, both saw the need to make psychology more scientific. In fact, the establishment of a psychological laboratory in Leipzig, Germany, by Wundt in 1879 is considered to be the beginning of psychology *as a science*. Although Wundt and his followers continued to deal with *mentalistic* concepts such as consciousness, sensation, feeling, imagining, and perceiving, they attempted to use the more objective methods of science to study them.

Partly because of its excessive reliance on introspection and because of the highly subjective interests of the structuralist school, it didn't last much beyond the death of Edward Bradford Titchener, one of its main proponents in the United States. However, functionalism had a profound influence on the subsequent development of psychology. Its influence is especially evident in theories that are concerned mainly with behavior.

Classification of Learning Theories

By the early 1900s, psychologists (especially in the United States) had begun to reject subjective and difficult topics such as mind and thinking, choosing instead to concentrate on the more objective and observable aspects of behavior. This orientation eventually became known as **behaviorism**. It led to learning theories concerned mainly with objective events such as stimuli, responses, and rewards. *Stimuli* (conditions that lead to behavior) and *responses* (actual behavior), behavioristic theorists argued, are the only directly observable aspects of behavior; hence, they are the objective variables that can be used to develop a science of behavior. Behaviorism, explains Moore, "emphasized publicly observable stimuli (s) and responses (r), and spurned supposedly unobservable, centrally initiated processes like consciousness" (2010, p. 143). Its central belief is that human and animal behavior can be explained without appealing to mentalistic notions such as *mind* or *feelings*.

Behavioristic theories include those of Pavlov, Watson, and Guthrie (Chapter 2); Thorndike and Hull (Chapter 3); and Skinner (Chapter 4). Other theories that share many beliefs of the behaviorists but in which there is greater use of biological (Chapter 5) or mentalistic (Chapter 6) concepts serve as a transition to the second major division of theories – **cognitivism**.

Cognitive psychologists are interested in human mental activity and specifically in information processing, representation, and self-awareness. Gestalt theories, with their interest in perception and awareness, are important early examples of cognitive theories (Chapter 6). Other examples include Bruner, Piaget, and Vygotsky (Chapter 7). Current investigations of memory (Chapter 8), motivation (Chapter 9), and social learning (Chapter 10), are also unmistakably cognitive. More recent information-processing approaches, evident in computer models of thinking and in the development of *artificially intelligent* and *deep learning* systems (Chapter 11) are also primarily cognitive approaches. They may also herald the beginning of the next major shift in the development of learning theories (see Table 1.2).

The main importance of the distinction between behavioristic and cognitive approaches is that this simple classification of explanations of human learning makes it easier to understand, remember, and apply learning theories. However, be warned that behaviorism and cognitivism exist only as convenient labels for extremely complex theories. Even theories that might appear very different often share common ideas. Few are clear examples of only one theoretical approach.

PREVIEW OF THIS TEXT

Mrs. Gribbin got up and stretched at this point. She said we were about done with Chapter 1, but before going on to Chapter 2, she would present little previews of each of the remaining 11 chapters of the book. She said that each of these previews would contain questions that you are very likely to answer intelligently once you have mastered the content of this book. She explained that these previews are being offered as appetizers. She said that, like hors d'oeuvres, they might whet your appetite, satiate you completely if your appetite is extraordinarily tiny, or make you quite ill. She thought that some of you might choose to go directly to the main course, and she said there would be no dessert and probably no wine either, and she laughed so unexpectedly it startled me.

Chapter 2. Early Behaviorism: Pavlov, Watson, and Guthrie

They say Watson liked to impress his friends with his dog's intelligence. So, at dinner one night, he knelt with the dog and began to bark the way an intelligent dog might. The dog listened politely and then ate. The next night, Watson did the same thing again. He knelt and barked and howled while the dog again listened attentively and then ate its supper. Watson was trying to teach the dog to bark, not just in an ordinary way but intelligently, for its supper. The procedure, called *conditioning*, half-worked. At the end of two weeks, the dog still would not bark, but it absolutely refused to eat until Watson had knelt and barked. Why?

Chapter 3. The Effects of Behavior: Thorndike and Hull

Some professors complain that their students often go to sleep when they present their magnificent lectures on Hull. They think that the students are bored, but perhaps most of them are simply suffering from symbol shock.

What does this mean: $_sE_R = {_sH_R} \times D \times V \times K$?

Table 1.2 Major divisions in learning theory

	Variables of interest	Representative theorists
Early approaches		
Structuralism	The Mind Feelings Sensations Immediate experience "Elements of thought"	Wundt Titchener
Functionalism	The Mind Purpose of behavior Adjustment to the environment Stream of consciousness	James Dewey
Later approaches		
Behaviorism	Stimuli Responses Reinforcement Punishment Shaping Needs and drives	Thorndike Pavlov Guthrie Watson Skinner Hull
A transition: the beginnings of modern cognitivism	Evolutionary psychology Sociobiology Stimuli Responses Reinforcement Purpose Goals Expectation Representation	Rescorla–Wagner Wilson Hebb Tolman Koffka Köhler Wertheimer
Cognitivism	Representation Self-awareness Information processing Perceiving Organizing Decision making Problem solving Attention Memory culture language Artificial intelligence Models of memory and motivation Social learning theory Computer models Neural networks Information processing Deep learning	Bruner Piaget Vygotsky Bandura Artificially intelligent machines

Chapter 4. Operant Conditioning: Skinner's Radical Behaviorism

A bright psychologist once decided that he would show a rat how to eat. "Pshaw," his grandmother croaked, "rats already know how to eat." That's not what her grandson meant; he intended to teach this rat how to eat properly, using a tiny spoon, sitting at the table, chewing with its mouth closed. He also expected the rat eventually would learn to wipe its chops delicately on a napkin after an especially mouth-watering chew.

The psychologist tried and almost succeeded. Unfortunately, the rat and the grandmother both died of old age before the learning program was completed.

How was the rat trained?

Chapter 5. Evolutionary Psychology: Learning, Biology, and the Brain

When he was much younger and living with his grandmother, Lefrançois says he ate a lot of rabbits – dozens every winter.[12] But one night, when the stew was too old, the milk rancid, or the rabbit diseased, all who had been at dinner became violently ill shortly afterward. From then on, says he, he does not molest or eat rabbits – or even write about them.

Why?

Chapter 6. Transition to Modern Cognitivism: Hebb, Tolman, and the Gestaltists

A poverty-stricken graduate student in psychology, driven by hunger (for food and for knowledge), accepted a summer job at an isolated fire-lookout tower. They flew him to the tower by helicopter and left him, absolutely and very completely alone.

The second morning, his radio broke.

The sixth morning, the helicopter came back with a radio repair technician. But the student was gone. He had scribbled a note: "Can't take it. Going home." Home was only a 300-mile hike through black spruce forest and muskeg. He was never seen again.

Why? Not why was he never seen again, but why did he leave? Like most students, he wasn't unintelligent.

Chapter 7. Cognitive Theories: Bruner, Piaget, and Vygotsky

If I say to you "red hair, single blue eye, facial scar," do you simply see a thatch of reddish hair, a single eyeball with a blue iris, a length of surgical scar?

Or have you already built a face, added a nose and ears, drawn your scar from ear to jowl, and covered the other eye with an ominous black patch?

Could you help *going beyond the information given*?

---

[12] I was startled to think that Mrs. Gribbin appears to know my grandmother. I'm certain I had never seen the Old Lady Gribbin before this morning. But I have no doubt my grandmother told her something very much like this story because the important parts of it actually happened – although not exactly as described. (GRL).

Chapter 8. Learning and Memory

In a carefully guarded psychological laboratory at a large North American university, a small, bespectacled, shabbily dressed undergraduate student sits on a straight-backed kitchen chair. Her name is Miranda. In front of Miranda is a dish filled with curled, grayish pieces of food. She doesn't know what the food is, but when well salted and peppered, it is quite palatable. She has not been fed for 24 hours and is now busily eating.

Just before being given this meal, Miranda was given a simple problem in advanced calculus, which she failed miserably. Now, after eating four dishes of this food, she is expected to be able to solve the problem. Why? And do you really believe this one?

Chapter 9. Motivation and Emotions

Three radical student leaders are cleverly coerced into volunteering for a psychological investigation. They later discover that they will be required to write an essay strongly advocating a pro-Establishment, nonradical viewpoint. None of them dares refuse for fear of incurring the wrath of the psychology instructor. For their efforts, one student is paid $100, the second is paid $20, and the third is presented with a single $1 bill. The students are told that their essays are quite good and that the authorities would like to see them published. The money is ostensibly payment for publication rights. The students agree to allow their work to be published. A day later, a skilled interviewer uncovers how each of the participants really feels about the Establishment. A naïve bystander would almost certainly predict that the student who was paid $100 dollars would be most likely to feel better about the Establishment. But the bystander would be wrong. Why?

Chapter 10. Social Learning: Bandura's Social Cognitive Theory

Twelve-year-old Ronald, who has been a rule-abiding child all his short life, is allowed to spend the summer with his cousin Edward. One day shortly after returning home at the end of the summer, he smashes his thumb with a hammer while helping his dad

". @#!%**&," says Ronald with impressive conviction. His dad had never before heard Ronald say @#!%**&.

What might Ronald's saying @#!%**& suggest about Edward? What might it suggest about Ronald?

Chapter 11. Machine Learning and Artificial Intelligence: The Future?

Can machines think? How do they think and how deeply? What do they think? Can they deliberately lie?

Chapter 12. Analysis, Synthesis, and Integration

There are many different ways of learning, distinct outcomes of the learning process, and varied models of the learner. For example:

Is there a lesson for you here?

APPLICATIONS OF LEARNING THEORIES

As we saw, learning involves relatively permanent actual or potential changes in behavior as a result of experience. Learning theories are systematic attempts to explain these changes. Good learning theories allow us to explain behavior and to predict and perhaps to control it.

The business of education is to change behavior and at the same time to predict and control it. Predicting, controlling, and changing behavior is also the business of parenting, of therapy, of sales, and of many other human endeavors.

It follows that good learning theories should be practically useful for each of these undertakings. Accordingly, each chapter in this text contains one or more sections that deal specifically with the educational implications as well as with applications in other fields.

Main Point Chapter Summary

1. Psychology is the science that studies human behavior and thinking (the mind). Its roots lie in the branch of philosophy, *epistemology*, which deals with the nature of knowledge and of knowing. The mind–body problem asks about the relationship between the mind (consciousness) and the physical world (including the body).

2. Learning can be defined as relatively permanent changes in potential for behavior, usually involving changes in disposition (inclination to behave) and/or capability. These changes are the result of experience. Learning may not always be apparent unless there is an observable change in performance.

3. Theories are collections of related statements intended to summarize and explain important observations. These statements are seldom laws (verifiable beyond reasonable doubt), but more often take the form of principles (statements relating to some general predictability) and beliefs (more personal convictions, sometimes accurate and sometimes not; the basis of bubba [naïve or folk] psychology).

4. Misconceptions and folk beliefs are common in psychology. Important misconceptions relate to our tendency to view learning as a uniform process for all individuals rather than recognizing plasticity and individual differences. Also common are some misleading notions about the structure and function of the brain.

5. Learning theories are attempts to systematize and organize what is known about human learning. They are useful for explaining, predicting, and controlling behavior and they may lead to new information.

6. Good theories reflect the facts, agree with the results of good research, are clear and understandable, are parsimonious, are useful for predicting as well as explaining, are useful in practical ways, are internally consistent, are based on few unverifiable assumptions, and are satisfying and thought-provoking in that they lead to further research (have heuristic value).

7. Science refers to collections of related information (chemistry or physics, for example) as well as to an attitude toward the search for knowledge (it insists on objectivity, replicability, consistency) and a collection of methods to ensure objectivity (ask the question; make a hypothesis; collect relevant observations; test the hypothesis; reach and share a conclusion). It rejects beliefs based solely on intuition and common sense, as well as pseudoscientific beliefs.

8. Experiments involve systematically manipulating some aspect of the environment to determine the effect of so doing. They can be thought of as ways of testing if–then statements, where the *if* refers to independent variables that are manipulated to determine their effects on dependent variables (the *then*).

9. Psychological research should be subjected to critical questions such as: Does it provide an explanation or does it simply label (the nominal fallacy)? Is the sample representative? Is there a possibility that the subjects were dishonest or behaved as they did because they knew they were part of an experiment? Might the investigators have been influenced by their own wishes, beliefs, and expectations?

10. Findings based on animal studies have to be generalized to humans with caution. In addition, there are important ethical guidelines for research with animals and people.

11. Structuralism, associated with Wundt, is an early school of psychology that tried to understand consciousness by looking at basic elements of mental activity such as feelings and sensations (the structure of the mind). Functionalism, associated with James, was more concerned with the purpose (function) of mental activity and how it contributed to adaptation.

12. The two traditional divisions in theories of learning are behaviorism (deals mainly with the observable aspects of human functioning) and cognitivism (concerned more with topics such as perception, information processing, concept formation, awareness, and understanding).

Part II

Mostly Behavioristic Theories

2 Early Behaviorism

Pavlov, Watson, and Guthrie

CHAPTER OUTLINE

This Chapter	38
Objectives	38
Early Scientific Psychology	39
Psychophysics	39
Ivan P. Pavlov (1849–1936)	42
Classical (Pavlovian) Conditioning	44
Behavioristic Explanations for Learning: Contiguity and Reinforcement	49
Contingency and Contiguity	49
Biological Predispositions and Backward Conditioning	50
Findings in Classical Conditioning	51
Educational Implications of Pavlovian Conditioning	54
An Appraisal of Pavlov's Classical Conditioning	54
John B. Watson (1878–1958)	54
Behaviorism	57
Watson's Explanation of Learning	58
Conditioned Emotional Reactions	58
Transfer	60
Watson's Environmentalism	62
Higher Learning	63
Practical Applications of Watson's Behaviorism	63
An Appraisal of Watson's Behaviorism	65
Edwin R. Guthrie (1886–1959)	66
Guthrie's Law of One-Shot Learning	68
The Role of Repetition	69
Movement-Produced Stimuli	70
Habits	70
Extinction	71
Reward and Punishment	72
Practical Applications of Guthrie's Theory	72
An Appraisal of Guthrie's One-Shot Learning	77
Evaluation of Early Behavioristic Theories	78
Main Point Chapter Summary	79

Early Behaviorism

If we ever do end up acting just like rats or Pavlov's dogs, it will be largely because behaviorism has conditioned us to do so.

Richard Rosen

Mrs. Gribbin was already there when I arrived, although I couldn't tell how she had come. She had said that she wanted to catch a whitefish and that I should meet her at Pigeon Lake. "Do you like this car?" she asked when she saw me, waving a full-page magazine ad in front of me. I no longer recall the make or color of the car, but I remember something about the long-legged model draped over its hood.

"How about this one?" She spread out another colorful ad as I stumbled into the boat. This one showed another culturally approved female form with a different car. I wondered why she would show me this.

"I know you like both of them," she said somewhat aggressively, not giving me time to think of an intelligent response. "And I'll tell you why." She motioned for me to sit down, which I did.

I waited for her to tell me why, but she was silent as she carefully folded the ads, slipping them into her bag where, it seemed, there were many other similar ads. Now she began to pull on the oars, and the shore quickly receded until we were far out on the lake. She stopped then, baited her hook, dropped it into the dark water, and immediately pulled a ragged handful of pages from her pocket.

"You said you'd tell me why I like those two cars," I reminded her.

"Turn on the recorder," she answered, explaining that the beginning of an explanation would be found in this second chapter. I asked could I maybe fish too while she spoke, but she said no, that I should pay attention and that I should keep both hands free to take notes. "I'll catch enough," she added, and she began to read her manuscript.

THIS CHAPTER

The first chapter of *this* book, *she read*, defined important terms and concepts in the study of human learning and described different approaches to building theories. This chapter traces the early beginnings of behaviorism, which is an explicit concern with actual behavior in contrast to a concern with more mental things such as knowing and thinking. The chapter describes one of the simplest forms of learning: *classical conditioning*.

Objectives

Tell your readers, *said Old Lady Gribbin*, that after they finish this chapter, they may be overcome by an overwhelming urge to stop complete strangers on the street and explain to them:

- what classical conditioning is;
- the meanings of US, UR, CS, CR, extinction, spontaneous recovery, generalization, discrimination, transfer, and other things;
- how emotions might be learned;
- why models sell cars;

Early Scientific Psychology | 39

- similarities and differences among Pavlov, Watson, and Guthrie;
- how to treat a phobia;
- why it is so hard to teach a cow to sit up.

Also explain to them, *said Mrs. Gribbin*, that if they don't know these things when they finish, they shouldn't bother asking their grandmothers. Instead, write to Lefrançois, *she said.*[1]

EARLY SCIENTIFIC PSYCHOLOGY

Early psychologists relied heavily on introspection as a tool for investigating human behavior. After all, they had no access to the kinds of sophisticated instruments we now use to detect, measure, and analyze mental activity (for example, the brain-scanning devices discussed in Chapter 5 or the digital technology discussed in Chapter 11). Using *introspection*, the psychologist would systematically analyze and interpret personal thoughts and feelings, trying to arrive at an understanding that could then be generalized to others. Introspection – sometimes called *armchair research* – was the method Descartes used as he struggled to understand the meaning of reality, of knowledge, and of mind. It was also the method used by William James, widely recognized as the father of American psychology. As we saw in Chapter 1, James was a *functionalist*. He tried to understand human experience and consciousness as a whole, claiming that it could not meaningfully be chopped up into little bits like stimuli and responses or understood in terms of sensations or associations (as the *structuralists*, led by Wundt and Titchener, were trying to do). "A river or a stream are the metaphors by which it is most naturally described," he insisted – from which the common expression "stream of consciousness" comes (James, 1890 [1950], p. 239).

At the time that James was lecturing and writing in America, the structuralist movement was well under way in Europe. This movement was strongly influenced by biology and physiology. Although it relied heavily on the highly subjective method of introspection, it also attempted to apply a more scientific approach to the study of the mind. Among its methods were those of **psychophysics** – the measurement of physical stimuli and their effects.

Psychophysics

Imagine you are standing in a completely darkened room staring in the general direction of an unlit 100-watt light bulb that is controlled by a dimmer switch. As long as the light is off, you will not see it. And even if the light is turned on, if it is kept sufficiently low, you will still see nothing. In fact, you will continue to see nothing until light intensity has reached a sufficient minimum level, a *threshold*.

---

[1] I think this is just Mrs. Gribbin's strange attempt at humor. So, don't write unless you're sending gifts. Just ask your grandmother. (GRL)

Absolute Threshold

Early psychologists, such as Wilhelm Wundt and Gustav Theodor Fechner in Europe, and Edward Bradford Titchener, one of Wundt's students, in the United States were interested in questions such as these: What is the minimum amount of light the human eye can detect? The softest sound that can be heard? The lightest touch that can be felt? What they wanted to do through their psychophysical measurements is determine exactly the **absolute threshold** for each sense, where *absolute threshold* is defined as the least amount of stimulation required for a stimulus to be detected at least 50 percent of the time. (See the Wundt biography.)

It turns out that it is not possible to find a fixed absolute threshold for any given stimulus that applies to all people: There is no single level of light or sound or pressure that always leads to sensation for everyone, whereas all stimulation below this threshold goes undetected. We know that some people are more sensitive than others (have better hearing or better vision, for example). As a result, absolute thresholds vary for different individuals. But for any given individual, there is a lower limit below which a stimulus will never be detected and an upper limit above which it will always be detected. Between the two, there is a point at which it will be detected 50 percent of the time. This point is the *absolute threshold*, although it is more approximate than absolute.

BOX 2.1 Wilhelm Wundt (1832–1920)

Credit: Everett Collection/Superstock. Superstock # 4048-6194.

BOX 2.1 (cont.)

Wundt was one of four children born to a Lutheran minister and his wife in a small village that is now part of Mannheim, Germany; only he and one older brother survived childhood. He was reportedly a profoundly introverted boy whose only friend was somewhat older and mentally challenged. Wundt's upbringing was extremely strict; he was often locked, terrified, in dark closets when he had misbehaved.

Wundt's early school career was difficult and not very successful, but when he went to university, he became fascinated by the anatomy and mysteries of the brain and, almost overnight, became a scholar. At the age of 24, he obtained a medical degree and subsequently became an instructor in physiology.

He spent 17 years at Heidelberg University on the medical faculty, one year in Zurich as a professor of philosophy, and 42 years at Leipzig, where he founded the psychological laboratory that is generally associated with the beginning of psychology as a science. He was apparently a quiet, unassuming man who seldom left his laboratory or his home. He wrote almost constantly, producing more than 500 books and articles. Boring (1950) estimated that Wundt wrote an average of one published word every two minutes, day and night, for 68 years. His major textbook on psychology appeared in three volumes in its first edition: 553, 680, and 796 pages of very complex German (Diamond, 2001; Hunt, 2007; Rieber & Robinson, 2001).

Differential Threshold

Psychophysicists tried to measure not only absolute thresholds but also what they called the **differential threshold**, often referred to as the **just noticeable difference (JND)** – the least amount of *change* in the intensity of a stimulus that can actually be detected by an individual. You can tell the difference between weights of one and two pounds – as you can easily demonstrate if you hold a sack containing one pound of black beans in one hand and another containing two pounds of turnips in the other: The difference between the two is a *noticeable* difference. Fechner (1860 [1966]) and his brother-in-law, Max Weber, were interested in finding out the *least* amount of change in stimulation that would be noticeable – that is, the *differential threshold* or *JND*.

If you can tell the difference between one and two pounds, does that mean that the JND for weight is something less than one pound? No, explains Fechner. You can tell the difference between one and two pounds and perhaps between six and seven pounds, but you cannot so easily tell the difference between 10 and 11 pounds, much less between 99 and 100 pounds. In the same way, you can tell the difference between a 25-watt bulb and a 60-watt bulb – a difference of 35 watts. But you cannot discriminate between 1,000 watts of light and 1,100 watts. Even though the difference is almost three times greater in the second case, it is not a *noticeable* difference.

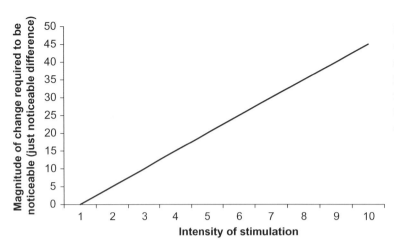

Figure 2.1 A graphic portrayal of Weber's law. As intensity of stimulation increases, proportionally greater increases in stimulation are required if they are to be just noticeable differences.

Just noticeable differences, said Fechner, are a constant proportion of a stimulus. For example, for lifted weights, the constant is about 1/30. This means that a weightlifter who normally lifts 300 pounds would probably not notice an addition of 5 pounds but would notice a difference of 10 pounds; one who lifts 600 pounds would require an addition of 20 pounds before noticing the difference (see Figure 2.1). Fechner labeled this conclusion **Weber's law**.

Unfortunately for psychophysics, Weber's constants are not very constant. That is partly because there is no average individual. The average is a very useful mathematical invention, but we are *individually different*. Thus, some people are more sensitive to stimulus changes and others less. Furthermore, people's sensitivity can vary from day to day or even from moment to moment, depending on fatigue and other factors. Nevertheless, Weber's law appears to be true as a general principle and continues to be widely investigated. For example, Bruno, Uccelli, Viviani, and de'Sperati (2016) report that Weber's law applies to visual perception of small objects; various researchers have found that it applies to size estimates of 'graspable' objects (Ganel, 2015); others have provided evidence that it accurately describes speed discrimination in young infants (Mohring, Libertus, & Bertin, 2012).

IVAN P. PAVLOV (1849–1936)

Fechner, Weber, Titchener, Wundt, and other early psychologists were as much physiologists and, often, philosophers, as psychologists. Another physiologist who had an enormous influence on the development of psychology throughout the world is the Russian Ivan Pavlov. (See Pavlov biography.)

The experiment for which Pavlov is most famous was the result of an almost accidental observation. Pavlov had been studying the role of various juices in digestion, one of these being saliva, and he had developed a procedure that allowed him to detect and measure salivation in the dogs he used in his experiments. In fact, in 1904, he was awarded a Nobel Prize in medicine and physiology for his work on digestion.

During this work, Pavlov happened to notice that some of the dogs in his laboratory began to salivate before they were fed. He also saw that this occurred only in dogs that had been in the laboratory for some time.

BOX 2.2 Ivan Petrovich Pavlov (1849–1936)

Credit: Bettmann / Getty Images. Getty UK 515177772

Pavlov was born to a poor village priest in Russia. He did rather poorly in elementary school; no one would have dreamt that he would one day win a Nobel Prize.

His early post-secondary education was at the Ryazan Ecclesiastic Seminary; the intention was clearly that, like his father, he would become a priest. But, says Windholz (1997), the young Pavlov was so influenced by Russian translations of Western scientific writings, and particularly with their Darwinian overtones, that he promptly abandoned his religious training and headed to the University of St. Petersburg. There, he specialized in animal physiology and in medicine.

After he received his medical degree, Pavlov went to Germany, where he studied physiology and medicine for another two years before returning to St. Petersburg to work as an assistant in a physiology laboratory. He was later appointed professor of pharmacology

Continued

BOX 2.2 (cont.)

and, at the age of 41, head of a physiology department. His work continued to deal almost exclusively with physiological topics, specifically with digestive processes. It was not until the age of 50 that he began to study classical conditioning, these studies lasting another 30 years. His international reputation was so great, says Windholz (1997), that he was one of the few Soviet scientists of his era who could openly criticize the Bolshevik regime and who could defend human rights with impunity. In 1923, when he was 74 years old, the famous scientist and Nobel Prize winner visited the United States. And in New York's Grand Central Station, Pavlov was mugged (Thomas, 1997, 2007).

To the end, Pavlov insisted he was a physiologist and not a psychologist (Samoilov & Zayas, 2007). In fact, he viewed psychology with such disdain that he fined any of his laboratory assistants who used psychological rather than physiological terms (Watson, 1971). But he wrote papers and provided theoretical explanations for psychological topics such as hypnosis and paranoia and made invaluable contributions to the early development of theories of learning (Windholz, 1996a, 1996b).

Classical (Pavlovian) Conditioning

In trying to find some scientific explanation for the salivation of his dogs before they were fed, Pavlov devised a series of now-famous experiments. In these experiments, he demonstrated that not only could the sight of food eventually bring about salivation in his dogs, but that almost any other distinctive stimulus could have the same effect if paired with food often enough. Ever the physiologist, Pavlov thought he had discovered "psychic secretions." What he had discovered, in fact, was **classical conditioning** (also referred to as *Pavlovian conditioning*). Classical conditioning describes how responses to previously neutral stimulation can be learned as a result of the repeated pairing of stimuli.

In his demonstration, Pavlov refers to the food as an **unconditioned stimulus (US)**. It is called a *stimulus* because it is an environmental event that affects the organism, and it is labeled unconditioned because it leads to a response (muscular or glandular reaction) without any learning taking place. The salivation in response to the food is called an **unconditioned response (UR)** because it is associated with an unconditioned stimulus. Hence, an unconditioned response is a response that occurs without any learning.[2]

What Pavlov showed is that if a US (food, for example) is paired with another stimulus often enough, this other stimulus will eventually lead to the response originally associated only with the US (in this case, salivation). For example, if a buzzer is sounded every time food is presented to a dog, the buzzer – called a **conditioned stimulus (CS)** – will eventually elicit

---

[2] In fact, said Old Lady Gribbin as an aside, Pavlov didn't really use the words "conditioned" and "unconditioned." He used "conditional" and "unconditional" – terms that make a lot more sense if you think about it. It's the translators who screwed it up, she grumbled.

Figure 2.2 What Pavlov first noticed was that the sight of the handler alone was enough to cause many of his experimental dogs to salivate. Through further experiments, he studied the learning processes involved. In these experiments, the stimulus food or a buzzer that is paired with the food, which are controlled by the experimenter, are independent variables. The dog's response (in this case, salivation) is a dependent variable.

Figure 2.3 In his experiments, Pavlov often placed his dogs in a harness like this one. Food powder (an independent variable controlled by the experimenter) can be placed either in the dog's mouth or in the dish. A tube is surgically inserted into the duct of the parotid gland so the amount of saliva produced (a dependent variable) can be measured as it drops down the tube, causing movement in a balancing mechanism at the other end of the tube. This movement is in turn recorded on a revolving drum. In the experiment illustrated here, the US (food) is paired with a CS (light shining in the window). H. E. Garrett, (1951), *Great experiments in psychology*. Appleton-Century-Crofts.

the response of salivation – now a **conditioned response (CR)**. Illustrations of this procedure are shown in Figures 2.2, 2.3, and 2.4.[3]

Recall from Chapter 1 that in an experiment the investigator manipulates (controls) some aspect of the environment to see what the effect of the manipulation will be. In Pavlov's demonstration of classical conditioning, the CS – perhaps a bell or a buzzer or maybe just the

---

[3] "So," said the old lady at this point, "do you now know why half-dressed human forms sell cars?" But according to my notes, she continued before I could answer. Chapter 10 provides an answer.

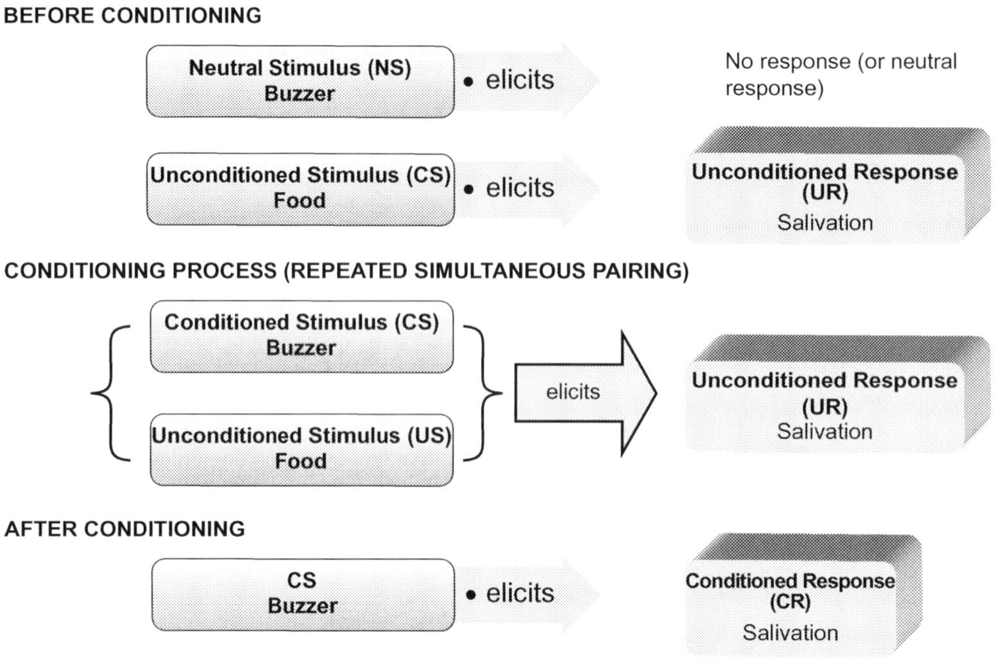

BEFORE CONDITIONING

Neutral Stimulus (NS) Buzzer • elicits → No response (or neutral response)

Unconditioned Stimulus (CS) Food • elicits → Unconditioned Response (UR) Salivation

CONDITIONING PROCESS (REPEATED SIMULTANEOUS PAIRING)

{ Conditioned Stimulus (CS) Buzzer / Unconditioned Stimulus (US) Food } elicits → Unconditioned Response (UR) Salivation

AFTER CONDITIONING

CS Buzzer • elicits → Conditioned Response (CR) Salivation

Figure 2.4 A simple illustration of classical conditioning. Food, an unconditioned stimulus, (US) elicits salivation in a dog, but a buzzer, a neutral stimulus (NS), does not. After successive pairings of food and buzzer, the buzzer alone, now a conditioned stimulus (CS; an independent variable), causes the dog to salivate, now a conditioned response (CR; a dependent variable). Adapted from Lefrançois, G. R. (2016). *Psychology: The Human Puzzle* (2nd. ed.). San Diego, CA: Bridgepoint Education, Fig. 5.4. Used by permission.

sight of the trainer – is controlled by the investigator. Hence, the CS is an *independent variable*. The response, which is affected by the independent variable – in this case, the CR – is a *dependent variable*. It is the *then* part of the if–then relationship that typically characterizes an experiment, whereas the CS represents the *if* part. The hypothesis in the Pavlovian classical conditioning experiment can be worded as follows: "If buzzer, then salivation."

Classical conditioning is sometimes referred to as *learning through stimulus substitution*. That is because the basic facts of classical conditioning are this: If a stimulus (or situation) that readily leads to a response is paired with a *neutral* stimulus often enough, the previously neutral stimulus becomes a *conditioned stimulus* that can eventually be *substituted* for the original stimulus. The CS will evoke a similar but weaker response.

Learning through classical conditioning is also sometimes referred to as *signal learning* because the CS serves as a signal for the occurrence of the US. For example, in the Pavlov demonstration, the buzzer is a signal that food will soon follow.

In classical conditioning, learning always begins with an unlearned response (UR) that can reliably be elicited by a specific stimulus (the US). This unlearned stimulus–response unit is called a **reflex**.

Human Reflexes

Reflexes are defined as simple, nonintentional, unlearned behaviors. In a sense, they are automatic, prewired stimulus–response units. The stimulus *food* reliably leads to salivation whether you intend to salivate or not. Your response is *reflexive*; that is, it is involuntary and largely uncontrollable. Similarly, when somebody strikes your patella, your knee jerks. In the same way, you blink if something potentially threatening approaches your eye.

Humans are born with a number of reflexes, many of which are very important for survival. The **sucking reflex**, evident in the fact that all normal infants suck when the mouth is appropriately stimulated, is clearly related to infant survival. So is the **Moro reflex**, although its relationship to survival is somewhat less obvious. The Moro reflex is the infant's startle reaction. It involves throwing out the arms and feet symmetrically and then pulling them back in. Some speculate that this reflexive response could have been important for tree-dwelling primate infants who might, as a result of this reflexive action when suddenly dropped by a careless mother, be lucky enough to catch a branch and save themselves. Table 2.1 lists a number of reflexes present in young infants. Some of these, like sucking and rooting, eventually become voluntary actions; others, like the toe grasp reflex and the palmar grasp, disappear within the first year; and a number, like the sneezing reflex, are present throughout life.

Most reflexive responses that can reliably be elicited by a stimulus can be classically conditioned in humans and in nonhuman animals. Thus, the knee-jerk reflex, the eye-blink

Table 2.1 **Some reflexive behaviors in newborn infants**

Reflex	Stimulus	Response
Sucking	Object in mouth or on lips	Sucks
Rooting (head turning)	Stroking the cheek or the corner of the mouth	Turns head toward side being stroked
Swallowing	Food in mouth	Swallows
Sneezing	Irritation in the nasal passages	Sneezes
Moro reflex	Sudden loud noise; loss of support	Throws arms and legs out symmetrically
Babinski reflex	Tickling the middle of the soles	Spreads and raises toes
Toe grasp	Tickling the soles just below the toes	Curls toes around object
Palmar grasp	Object placed in infant's hand	Grasps object tightly
Swimming reflex	Infant horizontal; supported by abdomen	Makes coordinated swimming movements
Stepping reflex	Infant vertical; feet lightly touching flat surface	Makes coordinated walking movements

reflex, and the pupillary reflex can all be conditioned to various stimuli. In addition, some glandular responses (such as salivation) and other internal reactions can be conditioned. The term **interoceptive conditioning** is used to describe the conditioning of actions involving glands or involuntary muscles. For example, blood vessel constriction or dilation, which is brought about by the external application of cold or hot packs, can be conditioned to a bell or a buzzer. So too can responses such as urination.

That urination can also be classically conditioned has led to some effective treatments for *incontinence* (lack of urinary control). For example, electrical stimulation can be applied in such a way as to stimulate urination, thus becoming a CS for urination. If this CS is paired with a signal such as a bell, a buzzer, or specific music, these can eventually serve as a US to bring about urination without the electrical stimulation (for example, Eriksen, Bergmann, & Mjølnerød, 1987; Godec, 1983).

Even internal responses such as body temperature, over which we normally have little control, are susceptible to classical conditioning. Keller (1969) describes a procedure in which subjects are asked to dip their right hands in pitchers of ice water. This causes an immediate drop in the temperature of that hand and, interestingly, also causes a more easily measured drop in the temperature of the other hand. If the hand is dipped in the ice water at regular intervals (three or four minutes) and each dip is preceded by a buzzer, after 20 or so pairings, the buzzer alone will cause a measurable drop in hand temperature.

Another type of response that can readily be classically conditioned involves **taste aversion** – a powerful disinclination to eat or drink something. Some taste aversions are hereditary; they prevent animals and people from eating very much of any bitter-tasting substances (which, incidentally, often taste bitter precisely because they are toxic). (Classical conditioning of taste aversions is discussed in more detail in Chapter 5.)

How easily a classically conditioned response is acquired is related to a number of factors. Not the least important is the distinctiveness of the CS. In fact, as Coleman (2007) points out, not all stimuli are equally effective as conditioning stimuli. Buzzers and other tones have been particularly good conditioning stimuli in animal experimentation because they can be highly distinctive stimuli.[4]

---

[4] When she finished this section, Old Lady Gribbin said she had another example but that I should pause my recording. When I asked why, she explained that she, personally, didn't give a rat's butt one way or another, but after reading some prerevision reviews, she had come to the conclusion that it might be wise to shield student readers from exposure to certain topics, especially in this age when the modern witch hunters have turned their sights on the politically incorrect – or even those who are just slightly politically unwise. So, I turned off the recorder. The Old Lady paused while she retrieved her hook and rebaited it. Then, she began to describe the details of a study by Letourneau and O'Donohue (1997). Unfortunately, my notes here are almost illegible because in the middle of the telling, the old lady caught a whitefish, and when I went to help her, my notebook got wet and the ink ran. What I recall is that in this study, 25 women aged 18–40 years were shown clips from erotic videos in a conditioning study where the videos were paired with an amber light and the women's sexual arousal was measured by using physiological measures such as *vaginal impulse amplitude* and *vaginal photoplethysmograph recordings*. Old Lady Gribbin didn't explain what those were. Different sorts of pairings of the light and the videos were used, she said, and the results apparently showed that sexual arousal can be classically conditioned so these women could later be "turned on" with a stupid amber light. "But there's no need to put that in the book," the old lady explained.

Behavioristic Explanations for Learning: Contiguity and Reinforcement

Basically, conditioning theory offers two different explanations for learning: **contiguity** and **reinforcement**. Contiguity, which is the simultaneous or nearly simultaneous occurrence of events, is the explanation used by Pavlov and also by theorists such as Watson, and Guthrie. These theorists believed that for behavior to change (that is, for learning to occur), it is sufficient that two events be paired, sometimes only once; sometimes more often.

Reinforcement is a more complex concept having to do with the *effects* of a stimulus. For example, one kind of reinforcement is positive reinforcement, in which an effect, like the satisfaction of hunger, leads to learning. Reinforcement is defined in more detail and illustrated in Chapter 3.

Contingency and Contiguity

Events are contiguous when they occur at the same time and place. But note that contiguity doesn't imply **contingency**. Events are said to be contingent when the occurrence of one depends on the occurrence of the other. Thus, event A is contingent on event B when the occurrence of A depends on the occurrence of B. For example, if being given a new car depends on selling X amount of CleanSoap, receiving the car is *contingent on* selling the soap. Pavlovian conditioning is based on contiguity rather than contingency. In contrast, reinforcement-based theories such as B.F. Skinner's operant conditioning use contingency as an explanatory principle. These theories are concerned with the *outcomes* of behavior rather than with the simultaneous occurrence of stimulus or response events.

Contiguity in classical conditioning does not always mean that the CS starts and ends at exactly the same time as the US. Actually, this arrangement – termed **simultaneous pairing** (or *simultaneous conditioning*) – isn't the most effective way of classically conditioning a response.

Far more effective is **delayed pairing** (or *delayed conditioning*), in which the CS is presented before the US and continues during presentation of the US. This is termed *delayed pairing* because of the time lag between the presentation of the CS and the beginning of the US.

In **trace pairing** (or *trace conditioning*), the CS starts and ends before the US, so that there is a very brief time lapse between the two. (With time lapses longer than half a second or so, trace conditioning is usually not very effective.)[5]

In **backward pairing** (or *backward conditioning*), the US has already been presented and removed before presentation of the CS.

In the classical Pavlovian demonstration, *simultaneous pairing* requires that the buzzer be sounded at the same time food powder is injected into the dog's mouth; *delayed pairing* would occur when the buzzer is turned on slightly before the food powder is injected into the dog's mouth and then the buzzer is turned off at the same time as the food injection ends; *trace pairing* would require that the buzzer be turned on and then off again before the injection of

---

[5] One exception in which conditioning can be effective even after a long lapse between the CS and the US, said the Old lady as an aside, is taste aversion learning. She promised that this topic will be discussed in Chapter 5. (GRL)

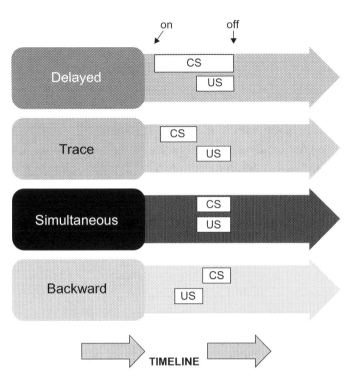

Figure 2.5 Impact of variations in CS–US procedures. The pairing sequences are shown here in the order of effectiveness. Conditioning takes place most quickly in the delayed sequence, when the conditioned stimulus (for example, the buzzer) is presented shortly before the unconditioned stimulus (food powder) and continues throughout the time the US is presented.

food powder; and in *backward pairing*, food powder is injected first and then, after a brief time lapse, the buzzer sounds. These four options are shown in Figure 2.5, in order from most to least effective.

Biological Predispositions and Backward Conditioning

Backward conditioning, or backward pairing – in which the CS follows the US – was long thought to be completely ineffective. In fact, in most circumstances, classical conditioning does not ordinarily occur with this arrangement. However, in an increasing number of experiments, investigators have succeeded in bringing about backward conditioning. For example, in one study, rats were conditioned to fear a plastic hedgehog by being shocked electrically (US) and afterward having a plastic hedgehog toy placed in their cages (CS). A significant number of rats responded with apparent fear when shown the plastic toy the following day (Keith-Lucas & Guttman, 1975).

The significance of this and of related studies is not so much that they establish that conditioning through backward pairing is possible but, rather, that they add to the growing evidence that biology makes some types of learning far easier than others for certain organisms. As is shown in Chapter 5, humans seem to be *prepared* to learn certain things, such as language, for example, or fear of heights or snakes or even insects. Similarly, young ducks and geese seem to be *prepared* to learn to follow the first moving object they see after hatching. In learning theory, this describes what is labeled **preparedness.**

In the same way as different organisms are prepared to learn certain things very easily, they also seem to be prepared *not* to learn certain other things, a situation described as

contrapreparedness. Contrapreparedness is evident in situations that require learning that is very difficult or even impossible to acquire. For example, humans seem to be *contraprepared* to learn the avoidance of sweet foods. Similarly, while rats are prepared to learn to fear hedgehogs, they are not prepared to learn language. In fact, as Griffin and Galef (2005) point out, preyed-upon animals are typically highly prepared to learn about predators. Even fish quickly and easily learn about new predators (Manassa, McCormick, Dixson, Ferrari, & Chivers 2014). Research suggests that backward conditioning is often involved in such learning. For example, that a warbler flies like the devil when a swiftly moving shadow sweeps by may well be because the shadow (a CS) has previously been preceded by signs of alarm among other warblers (a US). The discovery and elaboration of these biological constraints on learning constitute an important and growing area of psychological research and theorizing (see Chapter 5).

Findings in Classical Conditioning

During more than 20 years of detailed experimentation on classical conditioning, Pavlov and his students discovered a range of phenomena, many of which continue to be investigated.

Acquisition

For example, they found that acquisition, the formation of the stimulus–response association, typically requires a number of pairings of CS and US. After only one or two pairings, the CS alone does not ordinarily lead to a CR. But with increasing numbers of pairings, the CR occurs more frequently and more strongly. For example, in the salivation experiment, the amount of salivation in response to the CS increases until it reaches a peak, after which it levels off. Psychology researchers and students have plotted thousands of learning curves illustrating this. One is shown in Figure 2.6.

Learning curves are affected by the number of US–CS pairings and by the strength of the US. In general, the stronger the US (the bigger the steak; the louder the noise; the stronger the puff of air), the more quickly the CR will reach its peak.

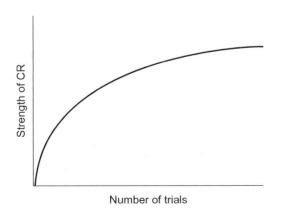

Figure 2.6 A hypothetical learning curve. The strength of the conditioned response increases rapidly at first and then levels off.

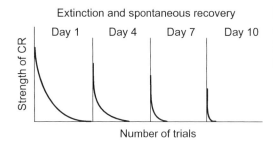

Figure 2.7 A hypothetical representation of spontaneous recovery following extinction. The strength of the CR is less following each extinction period; progressively fewer trials are required for extinction.

Extinction and Recovery

Another important Pavlovian finding is that classically conditioned associations are remarkably durable. A research dog conditioned to salivate to a tone and then allowed to do nothing but lazy-dog things for many weeks will soon begin to drool again (although perhaps in a more restrained way) when he is brought back into the laboratory and hears the familiar tone. Similarly, Marcel, who had several terrifying experiences with snakes as a young boy, would break into a cold sweat if you showed him a snake now, many years later, even if he has not seen a snake for many years.

But classically conditioned responses like the dog's salivating in response to a tone can be eliminated, a procedure that defines **extinction**. Extinction, as we see later in connection with Skinner's theory, is the disappearance of a behavior when it is not reinforced. In connection with Pavlov's theory of classical conditioning, extinction is what happens when a previously effective CS (like a snake for Marcel) no longer brings about a conditioned response (such as Marcel's fear response to the snake).[6]

One way to extinguish a conditioned response is to present the CS repeatedly without the US. For example, if the buzzer keeps buzzing but no food is presented, the dog will soon stop salivating. Interestingly, however, if the CS (the buzzer) is presented again later, the dog will again salivate, although at a lower intensity – a phenomenon called **spontaneous recovery**. To completely extinguish the response, it would be necessary to present the CS without the US again, and perhaps to repeat the procedure a number of times. Eventually, there would no longer be evidence of spontaneous recovery (see Figure 2.7).

Extinction of a fear such as Marcel's snake phobia is somewhat more complex but entirely possible using a therapeutic procedure developed by Wolpe (1958), called **systematic desensitization** (a form of what is called *counterconditioning*). Systematic desensitization is a procedure for replacing an undesirable response such as a specific phobia with a more desirable response, such as relaxation, through conditioning. In systematic desensitization, a patient would be trained in relaxation techniques and then exposed to a series of stimuli beginning

---

[6] "Enough," shouted Old Lady Gribbin holding up her hand in a rather firm signal that I should stop right there. I had just started to tell her that garter snakes den up here very close to the bush cabin. "I don't much care for snakes," she growled. "And I'm not the only one!" Then she referred me to an article she had read which I looked up. And sure enough, she and Marcel are not the only ones. This article reported that about half of the entire human population feels at least somewhat anxious about snakes. And somewhere around 2–3 percent meet the criteria for a clinical diagnosis of snake phobia (Polak, Sedlackova, Nacar, Landova, & Frynta, 2016).

with those least likely to bring about the fear reaction. This procedure has been used successfully to treat snake phobia (for example, Andersson et al., 2013).

Generalization and Discrimination

When a dog is conditioned to salivate to a given tone, it will then usually salivate in response to a wide range of tones. Similarly, a person conditioned to fear small birds will often react with fear to a wide assortment of birds. This phenomenon is referred to as **stimulus generalization**, defined as making the same or very similar responses to a range of related stimuli. For example, in a study where individuals with *social anxiety disorder* (high anxiety and fear in social situations) were conditioned to react with fear when presented with a photo of a human face paired with a loud scream and a fearful face, they generalized their fear to photos of other faces (Ahrens et al., 2016).

The opposite of stimulus generalization is seen when the individual makes *different* responses to related but distinctly different stimuli. This is called **stimulus discrimination.** Thus, dogs conditioned to salivate in response to a tone can also be conditioned not to respond to a second tone that varies in pitch only slightly from the original CS.

An intriguing demonstration of generalization and discrimination is provided in a pair of studies in which pigeons demonstrated that they could discriminate between good and bad children's paintings (Watanabe, 2010). In the first study, pigeons were taught to peck at paintings that had been judged "good" and not to peck at others judged "bad." When they were later presented with paintings they had never seen, they were far more likely to peck at those that a panel of experts had judged "good" than at those judged "bad." As Watanabe puts it, "[T]he results showed that pigeons could discriminate novel 'good' and 'bad' paintings" (2010, p. 75). And in the second study, pigeons were taught to discriminate between watercolor and pastel paintings. They were subsequently able to *generalize* what they had learned by identifying novel watercolor and pastel paintings.

Higher-Order Conditioning

A dog conditioned to respond to a tone will eventually salivate readily in response to that tone – and perhaps in response to other similar tones (stimulus generalization). If the tone is then paired repeatedly with another stimulus – say, a light – but the second stimulus (in this case, the light) is never paired with food, the dog may nevertheless subsequently salivate in response to the light. This is an example of what Pavlov labeled **second-order conditioning** (a form of what is labeled **higher-order conditioning**). Now, if the light is paired with yet another conditioning stimulus, such as a black square, the black square will eventually elicit salivation. This example of higher-order conditioning is sometimes labeled *third-order conditioning*.

As we see later, many behaviorists, including Skinner, used the concept of higher-order conditioning extensively in their theories. Higher-order conditioning expands the applicability of conditioning theories enormously. It provides an explanation for the observation that responses, stimuli, and reinforcers often become linked in very complex ways.

Educational Implications of Pavlovian Conditioning

Although we are often not aware of it, classical conditioning, especially of emotional responses, occurs in all schools pretty well at all times. It is at least partly through unconscious processes of classical conditioning that learners come to like or dislike school, teachers, and specific subjects.

To illustrate, we can assume that in the beginning, a given subject such as mathematics is a neutral stimulus. That is, it does not lead to a strong positive or negative emotional reaction in most students. It follows from what we know about classical conditioning that non-neutral stimuli that are repeatedly present when the learner is exposed to mathematics can serve as unconditioned stimuli. These unconditioned stimuli might be associated with positive reactions (a smiling, friendly teacher, a welcoming environment) or they might be associated with negative reactions (a stern, demanding teacher with an unpleasant voice; an uncomfortable desk; an unfriendly environment). After a while, mathematics may become a CS associated with either negative or positive reactions depending on the US with which it is repeatedly paired. Thus, it is entirely possible to teach mathematics while teaching students, through classical conditioning, to like or dislike mathematics (see Figure 2.8).

Among the most useful educational implications of Pavlov's classical conditioning are the following (Lefrançois, 2018):

- Teachers need to do whatever they can to maximize the frequency, distinctiveness, and potency of pleasant unconditioned stimuli in their classrooms.
- Teachers need to try to minimize the unpleasant aspects of classroom learning to reduce the number and potency of negative unconditioned stimuli in their classrooms.
- Teachers need to know what is being paired with what in their classrooms.

An Appraisal of Pavlov's Classical Conditioning

Pavlov's description of classical conditioning has served a crucial role in the early development of psychology. It is absolutely remarkable that the work done by this Russian physiologist, exemplified in a single classical study of a dog learning to salivate in response to a tone, should, more than a century later, still form an essential part of every introductory psychology course in most countries of the world. Bitterman (2006) notes that the basic concepts of classical conditioning have changed very little since Pavlov first described them. Moreover, many of the principles of classical conditioning (of generalization and extinction, for example) continue to be applied in clinical psychology, in education, in industry, and elsewhere.

JOHN B. WATSON (1878–1958)

Profoundly influenced by Pavlov's model of classical conditioning, a determined young rebel set out to revolutionize American psychology – and succeeded. His name was John Broadus Watson. (See Watson biography.)

BOX 2.3 John Broadus Watson (1878–1958)

Credit: Bettmann / Getty Images. Getty Images 515512132

The founder of American behaviorism, John B. Watson was born in Greenville, South Carolina, in 1878. His devoutly religious mother, who prayed that he would become a clergyman, named him after a Baptist minister, which explains the unusual middle name, *Broadus*. But Watson's highly unruly early years were a disappointment to his mother. He was apparently an aggressive boy and was arrested at least twice (once for fighting, another time for firing a gun within city limits). By his own admission, he was not an especially good student, although on one occasion, he was the only person who passed a Greek final exam. He later claimed he was able to do so because he spent the previous afternoon cramming and drinking an entire quart of Coca-Cola™[7] syrup (Murchison, 1936).

Watson took his graduate training at the University of Chicago, working his way through school with rather unusual employment as a rat caretaker. After he graduated, he lectured at the University of Chicago. Several years later, when he was only 29, he was offered a full professorship at Johns Hopkins. He moved rapidly through the ranks partly

Continued

---

[7] I said to Mrs. Gribbin that the symbol ™ was not really necessary, but she explained that she had no wish to subvert the natural order, or to become embroiled in some legal action for lack of social, political, or legal sensitivity and correctness. I think she might have been mocking me. That's the way she is.

BOX 2.3 (cont.)

because of the misfortunes of his department head, James Baldwin, who had been forced to resign after being caught in a police raid on a Baltimore brothel. Watson stepped easily into Baldwin's position, directing the development of psychology at Johns Hopkins and editing one of the most influential publications in psychology at that time: *Psychological Review*. At the age of 36, Watson became president of the American Psychological Association. By then, he had become one of the most powerful contemporary voices in psychology.

A few years later, Watson undertook the study for which he is most famous: the conditioning of Little Albert (described in the text). His assistant for this experiment was a young graduate student named Rosalie Rayner. Watson, who was then 42, began an affair with Rayner, which came to the attention of his wife.[8] She sued for divorce and, during the messy trial that followed, used love letters from Watson to Rayner (that she had stolen from Rayner's room) to underline Watson's depravity. The divorce settlement, remarkable for the 1920s, left Watson with less than one-third of his university salary (Buckley, 1994). The ensuing scandal led to Watson's being forced to resign from Johns Hopkins.

Watson then went to New York, married Miss Rayner on New Year's Eve of 1920, had two more children (he had already fathered two), and went to work in advertising with the J. Walter Thompson Company at more than four times his university salary.

During his time as an advertising executive and, later, as vice president of J. Walter Thompson Company, Watson wrote popular psychology articles for magazines such as *Harper's*, *McCall's*, *Liberty*, *Collier's*, and *Cosmopolitan*. With Rayner, he also wrote a book on infant and child care, advocating rigid and highly controlling approaches to dealing with children. These activities, for which he was well paid, did little to endear him to his former colleagues, who spent some time and effort criticizing Watson's articles and books. (Rayner also wrote popular articles, including one entitled "I Am the Mother of a Behaviorist's Sons," which appeared in *Parents Magazine* [Rayner, 1930].)

Watson never returned to academic life. But in 1958, just before he died, the American Psychological Association honored him for his outstanding contributions to psychology, presenting him with a gold medal. (Based in part on Benjafield, 1996; Buckley, 1994; Burnham, 1994; DiClemente & Hantula, 2000; Todd & Morris, 1994.)

---

[8] It was in reference to this passage and in reference to an earlier edition's mention of the widely reported but totally unsubstantiated rumor that Watson involved Rayner in a series of investigations of physiological changes during sex that one of the reviewers of that earlier edition exclaimed, "The discussion of Watson's sexual history is completely inappropriate in a textbook. Our purpose is to educate, not titillate" (Reviewer E, 1998). When I brought this to Old Lady Gribbin's attention, she snorted that there was no mention of Watson's unsubstantiated sex research in this seventh edition. And she explained that she had left out much of the interesting stuff on Watson's personal life, such as, for example, when Burnham interviewed different people who knew Watson and concluded, "[H]e may well have been one of the great lovers in all history" (Burnham, 1994, p. 69). Burnham based his conclusion on the fact that what people seemed to remember most clearly about Watson were his allegedly numerous romantic adventures. "I learned a great deal that I did not want to know, some of it of the most intimate nature," says Burnham (p. 70).

Behaviorism

In the early twentieth century, psychology was an intuitive and highly subjective discipline. Its early development was based largely on ideas developed by Wundt. Wundt saw psychology as a discipline whose principal methods of inquiry were contemplation and speculation (introspection) and whose most important questions had to do with consciousness. As Watson described it, most of the followers of psychology believed it to be "a study of the science of the phenomena of consciousness" (1914, p. 1). That, argued Watson, had been a mistake. He thought that because of this belief, there had been no significant discoveries in psychology since Wundt established his laboratory. It has now, said Watson, "been proved conclusively that the so-called introspective psychology of Germany was founded upon wrong hypotheses" (1930, p. 5). "The subject matter of human psychology," he insisted, "*is the behavior of the human being*" (p. 2; italics in the original). To make a science of this approach, it is essential that it be completely objective; that it concern itself only with actual behavior and not with such mentalistic things as thoughts and emotions. Because it would deal with observable behavior, the science would be called **behaviorism**.

In 1913, Watson wrote a brief article, now often referred to as *the behavioristic manifesto*, entitled "Psychology as the Behaviorist Views It." The opening sentence makes his position – and his antagonism to introspection – very clear: "Psychology as the behaviorist views it is a purely objective experimental branch of natural science. Its theoretical goal is the prediction and control of behavior. Introspection forms no essential part of its methods" (p. 158).

Watson firmly believed that consciousness, which is the basis of introspection, is an irrelevant concept, and he made no bones about saying so. He began a 1915 address to the American Psychological Association, of which he was then president, by saying: "Since the publication two years ago of my somewhat impolite papers against current methods in psychology I have felt it incumbent upon me before making further unpleasant remarks to suggest some method which we might begin to use in place of introspection" (Watson, 1916, p. 89). The methods he went on to describe are the methods of what is now known as *behaviorism*. Human actions, says Watson, can be understood through actual behaviors that can readily be observed and studied. Limiting psychology to actual behaviors, he insists, would do away with much of the contradiction that exists in psychology. In his words, "Consciousness is neither a definite nor a usable concept" (Watson, 1930, p. 2).

The term *behaviorism* has come to mean concern with the observable aspects of behavior. This orientation assumes that behavior consists of responses that can be observed and related to other observable events, such as conditions that precede and follow behavior. "Behaviorism is the scientific study of human behavior," wrote Watson. "Its real goal is to provide the basis for the prediction and control of human beings: Given the situation, to tell what the human being will do; given the man in action,[9] to be able to say why he is reacting in that way" (1928, p. 2). The ultimate goal of behaviorism is to derive laws to explain the relationships existing among antecedent conditions (stimuli), behavior (responses), and consequent conditions (reward,

---

[9] And, presumably, the woman too, the old lady muttered as an aside. Watson lived in a more chauvinistic, less politically correct age.

punishment, or neutral effects). Put simply – and in what Watson referred to as "technical language" – the behaviorist's job is "given the stimulus, to predict the response – given the response, to predict the stimulus" (Watson, 1928, p. 2).

Mills summarizes the basic beliefs and purposes of early behaviorism as follows:

> All (behaviorists) denied any intrinsic life to the mind, none believed that the mind was psychology's primary area of study, and all believed that introspection was a futile and misleading way of gathering psychological data.... All shared the faith that behaviorist doctrine could be applied directly to human beings and that experimentation with humans was a direct route to knowledge. Almost all also believed that psychological research would have direct social implications. (1998, p. 3)

Watson's Explanation of Learning

Watson's (1930) explanation for learning is based directly on Pavlov's model of classical conditioning. Humans are born with a number of reflexes, says Watson. These include physical and glandular reactions (such as salivating in response to food or blinking in response to a puff of air) and a handful of emotional responses such as fear and rage and love. Each of these reflexes can be brought about by a specific stimulus. For example, feelings of love might result from being stroked; fear, from being dropped suddenly; and anger, from being restrained or not fed. Pavlov's model of classical conditioning makes it clear, insists Watson, that any distinctive stimulus that is present at the time a reflexive response is brought about can serve as a CS. If this stimulus is present often enough, it will eventually become associated with the response.

Behaviorists tried to limit psychology to the study of actual, observable behaviors

Conditioned Emotional Reactions

It follows, says Watson, that emotional behavior, like all other behavior, is simply another example of classical conditioning. He assumed that individual differences are virtually nonexistent to begin with; that is, all people are born with the same emotional reflexes of fear, love, and rage. These reflexive responses initially occur only in response to certain specific stimuli such as loud noises, sudden loss of support, or fondling. Eventually, however, humans react emotionally to a variety of stimulation that previously had no emotional significance at all. Put another way, they acquire **conditioned emotional reactions (CERs)** – emotional reactions that are learned through conditioning rather than being purely reflexive.

Watson proposed to explain this important phenomenon of emotional learning by using classical conditioning. All later emotional reactions, he explained, result from the pairing of initially neutral stimuli with stimuli that are associated with emotional responses. To illustrate and validate this belief, assisted by his then-student Rosalie Rayner, he performed one of his most famous and controversial investigations: the study of Little Albert (Watson & Rayner, 1920).

Little Albert

The study of Little Albert is more a demonstration than an experiment; it involves a display of emotional conditioning rather than the systematic manipulation of an independent variable to investigate its effect on a dependent variable. In fact, note Paul and Blumenthal (1989), the original study is scientifically weak and has often been embellished by later writers.

The subject of this study was "Little Albert," an 11-month-old boy. At the beginning of the demonstration, Little Albert showed no fear of a great variety of objects and people. "Everything coming within twelve inches of him was reached for and manipulated," said Watson (1930, p. 159). And among the things he always reached for was a white rat that he had played with for weeks.

But Watson and Rayner quickly established that Albert, like most infants, would react with fear to a loud noise. "A steel bar about one inch in diameter and three feet long, when struck with a carpenter's hammer, produced the most marked kind of reaction," Watson informs us (1930, p. 159). And so began the study with Little Albert, at the age of 11 months, 3 days, sitting on his mattress, reaching for the white rat, his hand just touching it when – kaboom! – Watson pounded the bar "just behind his [Albert's] head," and poor Albert "jumped violently and fell forward, burying his face in the mattress." But Albert was a staunch little fellow; he didn't cry. In fact, he reached for the rat again. And again, Watson (or Rayner; the point is not clear from Watson's notes) banged on the steel bar just as Albert's hand touched the rat. This time, Albert began to whimper and, as Watson put it, "On account of his disturbed condition, no further tests were made for one week" (1930, p. 160).

A week later, the procedure was repeated, the rat and the loud sound being combined a total of five more times. Now Albert's behavior had changed dramatically. When the rat was presented alone, he no longer reached for it. In Watson's words, "The instant the rat was shown the baby began to cry. Almost instantly he turned sharply to the left, fell over, raised himself on all fours and began to crawl away so rapidly that he was caught with difficulty before he reached the edge of the mattress" (1930, p. 161).

Watson considered this demonstration extremely important to his theory. "Surely this is proof of the conditioned origin of a fear response," he argued. "It yields an explanatory principle that will account for the enormous complexity in the emotional behavior of adults" (1930, p. 161).

Transfer

The explanatory principle has two facets: (1) Emotional responses are conditioned to various stimuli as a result of pairings that occur between conditioned stimuli such as distinctive sounds, smells, sights, or tastes, and unconditioned stimuli such as those that produce fear or love or anger; and (2), emotional responses can spread to stimuli to which they have not been conditioned, but that resemble conditioned stimuli. This phenomenon, as we saw earlier, illustrates *stimulus generalization* or, as Watson put it, *transfer*.

These two principles are clearly illustrated in the Little Albert demonstration. First, after only seven separate pairings of the rat with the fearsome noise, Little Albert had become very frightened of the rat. And second, when Little Albert was tested again five days later (at the age of 11 months, 15 days), he was now afraid not only of the rat but also of a white rabbit, a seal coat, white cotton wool, a white-bearded Santa Claus mask, and Dr. Watson's hair – all objects with which he had previously played.[10]

This phenomenon, which Watson called **transfer**, or *spread*, is what Pavlov described as *stimulus generalization* – the making of similar responses for a variety of related stimuli. Stimulus generalization is what occurs when a dog that has been conditioned to salivate to a given tone also salivates in response to a variety of other tones. And this is precisely what happened when Little Albert, conditioned to fear a white rat, generalized the fear response to other similar stimuli, such as white beards and white cats.

Positive Emotions

The Little Albert study indicates that it is possible to condition negative emotional reactions by repeatedly pairing a stimulus ordinarily associated with some negative emotion with another distinctive stimulus. Similarly, it is also possible to condition positive emotional reactions to neutral stimuli. For example, it is highly probable that if the white rat had been paired with a dish of ice cream, a wet kiss, or a high-five, Little Albert might very soon have come to love white rats with some passion. Similarly, even after being conditioned to respond with fear to the presence of a white rat, it might still have been possible to condition a positive response to the rat – a procedure termed **counterconditioning**, which is still often used in therapy. Systematic desensitization, described earlier, is one form of counterconditioning. (Counterconditioning is illustrated later in this chapter in the section on Edwin Guthrie.)

It seems clear from the original article that Watson had intended to countercondition Little Albert so that he would then react positively to white rats and related objects (see Harris, 1979;

---

[10] Some of your whizz-bang smart students might want to write their term papers on the Little Albert story, said Old Lady Gribbin, motioning that I should turn off the recorder. She said that because this study makes such a good story, as Gilovich (1991) notes, it has been exaggerated and misrepresented by many textbook writers. Some have had Little Albert fearing cats, white gloves, his own mother, or a teddy bear. Others have insisted that Watson later cured Little Albert of his fear, which he didn't. Some even suggest that Little Albert was actually not the normal infant he was supposed to be, but that he was actually a neurologically impaired infant named Douglas Merritte who died early in life with *hydrocephalus* (Fridlund, Beck, Goldie, and Irons, 2012). Others disagree, insisting that Little Albert was a normal infant named Albert Barger. Who was the real Little Albert? That controversy continues, still unresolved. (See, for example, Digdon, Powell, and Smithson, 2014; Griggs, 2014, 2015; Powell, Digdon, Harris, and Smithson, 2014.)

Prytula, Oster & Davis, 1977). Unfortunately, the infant was Watson's subject only because he happened to be in a hospital at the time. And as luck would have it, he was released from the hospital the day before Watson was to have begun his counterconditioning procedures. That these procedures would probably have been successful was demonstrated four years later when Mary Cover Jones found a small boy, Peter, who had a profound fear of rabbits. She cured him of his fear through a classical conditioning procedure (Jones, 1974).[11]

The Controversy

Although the study of Little Albert is well known and widely cited as an example of emotional conditioning, it remains controversial for a number of reasons – apart from the fact that it has often been misreported and we don't even know for sure who Little Albert was or that he was a normal infant or whether he was severely neurologically impaired. First, only a single subject was used in the study, and many who have tried to replicate the findings have not been able to do so (Eysenck, 1982). Second, Watson seems to have been unclear about exactly what he did with Little Albert. Samelson (1980) found that in one published report, Watson complained that whenever Little Albert was upset, he would stick his thumb into his mouth and then calm down. In fact, as long as he had his thumb in his mouth, he showed no signs of the conditioned fear response, so when Watson and Rayner were trying to film the experiment, they continually had to pull Little Albert's thumb from his mouth. Samelson raises the interesting possibility that Little Albert could have been crying not because he was afraid of the rat but because they would not let him suck his thumb! And although Watson does not suggest it, it is conceivable that thumb sucking might also have been a classically conditioned response.

Transfer in Everyday Life

Although the preceding discussion of transfer and the Little Albert demonstration deal mainly with the learning of emotional responses, it is important to note that transfer (or *generalization*) applies to all areas of learning. As Sousa (2017) put it, "Transfer is the core of problem solving, creative thinking, and all other higher mental processes, inventions, and artistic products" (p. 153). That is because transfer is what happens when you use what you already know when trying to understand and acquire new learning, solve problems, or invent works of art.

That you respond correctly when I say, "Please give me half now; you can pay the rest tomorrow," presupposes that you can *transfer*, and therefore apply, some basic prior knowledge about what "half" means, as well as about the meanings of "now," "tomorrow," and "pay." This is an example of what is termed **positive transfer**, where previous learning helps the learner with new learning or with solving new problems.

---

[11] Advertisers are keenly aware of the power of emotional conditioning, Mrs. Gribbin said, again showing me the car ad with the picture of the striking model. Many people have a strong positive conditioned emotional reaction when they look at this ad. And that's exactly what the advertisers want. If you really like the model, you're going to really like the car without even knowing why. "Don't look so confused," she said, "we'll talk more about this in Chapter 10." I don't think I was confused.

Previous learning can also sometimes have a negative influence, illustrating what is termed **negative transfer**. For example, Lenora, a second-grader who writes all her little stories on her father's desktop computer without ever having had any instruction in keyboarding eventually develops her own "hunt and peck" techniques and becomes quite proficient at keyboarding. But when her fifth-grade teacher introduces a series of lessons on what are considered optimal keyboarding skills, she struggles mightily. Her self-taught keyboarding strategies now interfere with the new learning; she has developed a series of habits that need to be replaced.

Not surprisingly, teaching for positive transfer (also referred to as teaching for *generalization*), is one of the most important tasks of schools.

Watson's Environmentalism

A recurrent theme in psychological literature is the controversy over the nature and nurture question – the **nature–nurture controversy**: Are humans primarily a product of genetic makeup or are they molded and shaped mainly by the environment?

The chief spokesman for the nature position at the turn of the twentieth century was Francis Galton (1870), a cousin of Charles Darwin. He believed that genes are largely responsible for the differences that exist among people. Accordingly, he advocated that people should be selected and bred for desirable characteristics, such as intelligence and strength, in much the same way as horses are bred for speed, dogs for appearance and hunting instincts, and turkeys for breast size. This practice is termed **eugenics**.

The main spokesman for the environment (nurture) camp was none other than John Broadus Watson (1930). He was convinced that there are no individual differences at birth: What people become is a function of their experiences. "There is no such thing," claimed Watson, "as an inheritance of *capacity, talent, temperament, mental constitution and characteristics*" (1930, p. 94; italics in original).

When Watson arrived on the scene, John Locke, the philosopher, had already given scholars his **tabula rasa** doctrine. This is essentially a metaphor that views the mind as a *blank slate* (that's what *tabula rasa* means) upon which experience writes its message. Watson accepted this proclamation wholeheartedly. "Give me the child and my world to bring it up in," he wrote, "and I'll make it crawl or walk; I'll make it climb and use its hands in constructing buildings of stone or wood; I'll make it a thief, a gunman, or a dope fiend. The possibility of shaping in any direction is almost endless" (Watson, 1928, p. 35).

Some years later, Watson published another version of this same declaration in what may be his most widely quoted (and longest) sentence: "Give me a dozen healthy infants well-formed," he said, "and my own specified world to bring them up in and I'll guarantee to take any one at random and train him to become any type of specialist I might select – doctor, lawyer, artist, merchant-chief and yes, even beggar-man and thief, regardless of his talents, penchants, tendencies, abilities, vocations, and race of his ancestors" (1930, p. 104).[12]

---

[12] It's interesting, said Old Lady Gribbin, that everybody ends this quotation right here. Actually, Watson's very next printed words are highly revealing. "I am going beyond my facts," he writes, "and I admit it, but so have advocates of the contrary

The controversy surrounding the relative roles of experience and heredity in shaping human development is far from resolved. In fact, science does not clearly support one camp over the other. The clearest thinking regarding this controversy readily admits that neither genes nor the environment produce anything by themselves. The current emphasis in genetic research is on finding out how genes and contexts work together to bring about human development, and in identifying specific genes and discovering their role. As Durmaz et al. (2015) report, more than 1,800 genes associated with specific diseases have now been identified. A wide variety of genetic tests is now available. So too are an increasing number of new biotechnological interventions.[13]

Higher Learning

All learning, said Watson, is a matter of responses that are selected and sequenced. Even complex sequences of behavior result from a conditioning process whereby the most recent behavior is linked with a stimulus through a sort of chaining of sequences of responses. More complex learning simply requires the conditioning of more stimulus–response sequences eventually leading to what he called **habits** – regular and highly predictable sequences of behaviors learned through conditioning.

Even something as apparently complex as language begins as simple stimulus–response links, claimed Watson. Speech, he explained, involves actual movements of the vocal cords and the larynx as well as of the mouth, tongue, and lips. These movements are conditioned to occur in the presence of appropriate stimuli. As he put it, words are simply substitutes (through conditioning) for objects and situations. And thinking is nothing more complicated than subvocal speech. Watson believed that subvocal speech is accompanied by minute movements of the larynx, which he attempted to measure and describe. He referred to these movements as *implicit* rather than *explicit* behaviors.

Practical Applications of Watson's Behaviorism

Watson's unwavering conviction that experiences determine all that people do and know leads logically to the belief that all humans are basically equal – that the differences between the eminent and the unknown, the rich and the poor, the brave and the timid are simply a question

---

and they have been doing it for many thousands of years" (p. 104). He may not have been nearly as adamant in his beliefs as is often portrayed.

[13] Your really bright students, said Old Lady Gribbin (which I'm sure is most of them, she added, but I couldn't tell whether she was being sarcastic, although I don't think so) – your bright students, she said, might want to have a look at some of the amazing things that have been happening in genetics and computer technologies in the last several decades. With the complete mapping of the human genome, she explained, it's not at all unrealistic to think that within the foreseeable future, we will abandon our passports and drivers' licenses and government-issued identity cards. Instead, each of us will be carrying around with us a chip or disk or what-have-you containing our complete genome characteristics. Gene corrections, cloned organs, and gene enhancements will no doubt be widely available by then. Even today, there are several dozen companies that offer genetic testing and DNA analysis to anyone willing to pay a small fee. But, insisted the old lady, pointing her bony finger aggressively at me, you make sure they think about the ethical dilemmas that will surely arise. I told her I would.

of different experiences and opportunities. This inherently egalitarian view of the human condition has proven immensely popular. As Stagner (1988) notes, it fit remarkably well with the **Zeitgeist** – the spirit of the times.[14]

But the theory also lends itself to rigid prescriptions for child rearing and education, as well as for training and control in the military, in industry, and elsewhere. Not only does it fail to recognize differences among individuals, but it insists that people's behaviors can be controlled through the judicious and clever arrangements of stimulus and response events. Don't kiss and cuddle your children, Watson urged; shake their hands and then arrange their environments so that the behaviors you desire will be brought under the control of appropriate stimuli.

Attitudes and Emotions

As we saw in our discussion of the educational implications of Pavlov's theory, simple models of classical conditioning are very useful in explaining emotional learning. That is because many emotions appear to be learned as a result of an often-unconscious process of classical conditioning. For example, Figure 2.8 illustrates how something like a math phobia might be classically conditioned.

Behavior Modification

In the same way as a phobia might be acquired through classical conditioning, it might also be removed by using similar principles. The deliberate application of theories such as Watson's in efforts to change or control undesirable behavior is labeled **behavior modification**.

One example of the role of classical conditioning in learning (and unlearning) behaviors is provided by Bevins (2009) in his discussion of smoking (nicotine addiction). He argues that the effects of nicotine act as a US that may become associated with a variety of co-occurring stimuli (for example, situational cues such as the sight of a cigarette package, the smell of tobacco smoke, the sight of someone else smoking, media advertising, and so on). These co-occurring stimuli eventually become conditioned stimuli that give rise to the urge to smoke (now a conditioned response). One way to modify the smoker's behavior based on classical conditioning theory is to associate the act of smoking with negative (*aversive*) outcomes. One example is a behavioral therapy, labeled *rapid smoking*, where participants are compelled to smoke up to

---

[14] That's not really your Zeitgeist, Mrs. Gribbin said, motioning that I should pause my recording, explaining that what she was about to say wasn't really part of the book. She explained that true egalitarianism isn't part of our Zeitgeist at all. She said that one face of today's Zeitgeist, at least in the Western industrialized world, is that of *political correctness*. She said that although one aspect of political correctness means going out of your way not to say or do things that might be offensive, inappropriate, tactless, unfair, or demeaning, this doesn't imply egalitarianism at all. She said that political correctness is an insincere motive for treating people with respect and love and fairness and that it leads to paying lip service to egalitarian principles for purely selfish reasons. The fact is, she said, becoming progressively angrier and more agitated, that most societies in this increasingly and depressingly tribalistic world don't behave as though they actually believe that all people are initially equal (and, by extrapolation, equally valuable). She said many other cynical things about today's Zeitgeist, about isolationism and regionalism and xenophobia and . . . and then suddenly she said to be quiet because there was a fish nibbling at her hook, although I had not yet said anything. Then, she began to read from her pages once more, and I thought the fish must have moved away. I pressed the record icon once more.

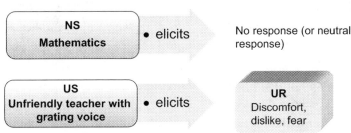

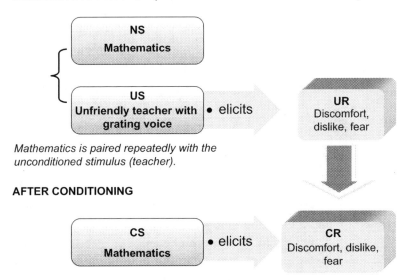

Figure 2.8 Illustration of how a dislike and fear of mathematics can be classically conditioned. From Lefrançois, G. R. (2018). *Psychology for Teaching* (2nd ed.). San Diego, CA: Bridgepoint Education, Fig. 5.2. Used by permission.

nine cigarettes in one session, inhaling as deeply as possible at six-second intervals. Rapid smoking usually results in dizziness, nausea, sore throat, and other unpleasant feelings. As a result rapid smoking leads to a strong negative reaction to cigarettes and has often proven effective in treating nicotine addiction (Brandon, 2001; Hajek & Stead, 2004). However, another study with individuals who habitually *rapid smoke* (in this case, smokers diagnosed with schizophrenia) indicates that attempts to modify their behavior through rapid smoking are generally not effective (Williams, Gandhi, Steinberg, & Benowitz, 2013). (Other behavior modification techniques are discussed in Chapter 4.)

An Appraisal of Watson's Behaviorism

Watson's theory, which became immensely popular in the United States, had a profound influence on childrearing and educational practices. It also had an enormous influence on the development of psychological thinking and theorizing in North America, leading to what is often referred to as *the behavioral revolution* (Pear, 2007). "By the early 1920s," writes Mills, "behaviorism had come to mean the doctrines of John B. Watson" (1998, p. 55). These doctrines were a form of psychology that dismissed mental and other abstract qualities as unworthy of study, while emphasizing the importance of social agents, especially of the mother, in shaping the child. Watson strongly advocated the application of this doctrine of behaviorism to produce humans with desirable characteristics.

As will become clearer when we consider the development of more recent psychological theories, much of what earlier theorists such as Watson and Pavlov believed has been greatly elaborated and qualified or simply no longer fits well with the spirit of contemporary times. Watson was surely guilty of exaggerating the role of learning in determining behavior and underemphasizing the role of heredity. In addition, it now seems clear that he tried to explain too much with a model that is overly simple for the enormous complexity of human beings. And it explicitly subscribes to the myth of the average. In effect, it views all individuals as pretty well identical, a view that does considerable violence to current knowledge and beliefs.

Watson appears to have been more of a spokesman for behaviorism than a rigorous researcher actively looking to discover new facts. Not surprisingly, some of Watson's early theorizing about emotional development has not stood the test of objective inquiry. Despite his attempts to deal only with objective variables, fear, rage, and love are emotional reactions that remain difficult to identify in young children.

Still, it remains true that many human behaviors are the result of classical conditioning: fear in response to the sound of a gunshot, although the sound of a shot has never hurt; salivating on seeing food (usually with more restraint than a dog); and countless other automatic responses that result from previous stimulus pairings.

Watson's contribution to the understanding of human behavior is difficult to assess, largely because the behaviorist approach for which he was clearly the strongest spokesman continues to exert a profound influence on contemporary psychological thinking. Among other things, he did much to make the science of psychology more rigorous and more objective, he popularized the notion that environmental experiences are potent forces in shaping behavior patterns, and he elaborated a learning model (classical conditioning) that explains at least some aspects of animal and human behaviors. In addition, he exerted a profound influence on the thinking of other psychologists such as Guthrie.

EDWIN R. GUTHRIE (1886–1959)

In retrospect, it is perhaps astounding that almost all learning textbooks still discuss someone who wrote as little as did Edwin Guthrie (a handful of books and articles), who had almost no students and followers (unlike most other well-known psychologists of that time, such as Pavlov, Watson, and Thorndike), and whose theory consisted of a single law with virtually no original experimental support. That one law of learning must be pretty big. (See the Guthrie biography.)

Like Watson, Guthrie believed that psychology should deal only with what is seen rather than with what has to be inferred. "Only the observable conditions under which learning occurs are of any use for a theory or for an understanding of learning," he insisted (1935, p. 143). But he did not share Watson's determination to revolutionize American psychology, overthrowing the mentalism of his predecessors and putting in its stead a completely objective experimental behaviorism. In fact, Guthrie performed only one experiment (Guthrie & Horton, 1946). In this experiment, a cat is placed in a cage from which it must escape to obtain food that is left a short distance outside the box. To escape, the cat has to engage in a series of new behaviors, leading to the unlatching of an escape door.[15]

BOX 2.4 Edwin R. Guthrie (1886–1959)

Credit: courtesy Special collections, University of Washington Libraries, neg. S-01540-A.

Edwin Guthrie was born on January 9, 1886, in Lincoln, Nebraska, the oldest of five children. His father owned a bicycle and piano shop, and his mother was a schoolteacher (Clarke, 2005). In 1886, this was rural ranch country, and it isn't surprising that when he later felt the need to illustrate his theory, many of his examples dealt with horses and dogs.

Guthrie received an arts degree from the University of Nebraska in 1907. Three years later, he received a master's degree with a major in philosophy, a minor in mathematics, and an additional minor, almost as an afterthought, in the fledgling discipline of psychology. Subsequently, he spent three years as a high-school teacher.

Continued

---

[15] When Schrödinger was Schrödinger's cat, said Old Lady Gribbin, he would have found this puzzle box offensively simple. He might have been both in and out of two of those boxes at the same time. He used to do it all the time. "What?" I asked. She ignored my question and just went right back to talking about Thorndike's cats. Was she losing it?

BOX 2.4 (cont.)

Guthrie then went to the University of Pennsylvania, where, in 1912, he obtained a Ph.D. in philosophy. Most of the remainder of his 42-year academic career was spent at the University of Washington. During the Second World War, he was a lieutenant in the US army, serving as a consultant to the War Department.

The philosopher Edgar Arthur Singer, who believed that many philosophical problems could be reduced to problems of behavior, strongly influenced Guthrie's shift to psychology. This shift occurred early in his professional career at the University of Washington. A contemporary of Watson's (he was only eight years younger), Guthrie was also profoundly influenced by Pavlov's classical conditioning. Mills (1998) reports that, unlike Watson, Guthrie had the advantage of having access to translations of Pavlov's work.[16]

The most important of Guthrie's writings is his book *The Psychology of Learning*, published in 1935 and revised in 1952. Clarke (2005) notes that Guthrie, in sharp contrast with his contemporaries, used an "irreverent" writing style filled with humor and anecdotes. Later, he also coauthored a book on educational psychology (Guthrie & Powers, 1950). He was widely recognized during his academic career, served as dean of graduate studies at the University of Washington, and was honored by the American Psychological Association (of which, like Watson, he was president for a time).

Guthrie's Law of One-Shot Learning

Most reasonably intelligent cats soon solve the problem and obtain the food. And the next time the cat is placed in the cage, it solves the problem even faster. Guthrie explains the cat's behavior the same way he explains all learning, by using a single, all-encompassing law of learning: "*A combination of stimuli which has accompanied a movement will on its recurrence tend to be followed by that movement*" (italics in original; 1935, p. 26).

What the Law Means

"This is a short and simple statement," claims Guthrie (1935, p. 26). He was only half right: It's short but only superficially simple. What the law says, in effect, is that when an organism does something on one occasion, it will tend to do exactly the same thing if the occasion repeats itself. Furthermore, claims Guthrie, the full strength of the "bond" between a stimulus and a response is reached during the first pairing; it will neither be weakened nor strengthened by practice. In behavioristic terms, if a stimulus leads to a specific response now, it will lead to the same response in the future. Thus, learning occurs and is complete in a single trial!

But this isn't true, you protest. He must have meant something else.

---

[16] Your brighter students might be fascinated to know that one of the philosophical questions that especially interested Guthrie, said the old lady, is what is known as Russell's paradox. That's the paradox that exists when I say "I'm a liar." The paradox resides in the fact that the statement can't be true. Nor can it be false. If the statement is true, then I'm not a liar because I have just now told the truth. Hence the statement is false. But if it's false, then, of course, I'm not a liar – so it's true. Another example of Russell's paradox is the statement "All generalizations are false except this one."

One-Shot Learning

Yes, it is true, says Guthrie. People and animals learn in one shot. What they learn is not a connection between two stimuli (as happens in Pavlovian classical conditioning, for example) but a connection between a stimulus and a response. If you do X in situation Y, you will do X again the next time you are in situation Y. To learn X, you do not need to repeat it over and over again nor does it need to be rewarded. If X has been performed once in response to Y, the link between X and Y is as strong as it will ever be.

So, if someone shouts "stop" and you immediately stop, does this mean that every time you hear someone shout "stop," you will come to a halt?

No, says Guthrie. Note the wording of the law, which is worth repeating at least once: *A combination of stimuli which has accompanied a movement will on its recurrence tend to be followed by that movement*. Guthrie uses the phrase *combination of stimuli* and the word *tend* because, as he puts it, "the outcome of any one stimulus or stimulus pattern cannot be predicted with certainty because there are other stimulus patterns present" (1935, p. 26). So, the answer is yes, you will *tend* to stop because that is the last thing you did when you were previously in this situation. But the answer is also no, you might not stop when you hear the command because the combination of stimuli may not be identical the second time. Any number of things might be different: You might be tired; the voice might be more plaintive or less insistent; there might be other voices in the background; you might be paying attention to something else; or your head might be in the refrigerator.

The Role of Repetition

Hence, the value of practice and repetition. What practice does is clear, says Guthrie: It provides an opportunity for making the same response in a wide variety of different situations. "An act is learned in the single occurrence," he insists. "The need for repetition comes from the need for executing the act in a variety of circumstances" (1935, p. 138). The more often an action has been practiced, the wider the range of combinations of stimuli to which it has been exposed and connected. Hence, it is more likely to be repeated in similar situations.

One-Shot Classical Conditioning

Does this mean that Pavlov's dog learned to salivate in response to a buzzer in a single trial? Yes, says Guthrie, even though Pavlov reported that in his earlier work, he sometimes needed as many as 50–100 pairings of CS and US before the CS reliably elicited salivation. According to Guthrie, the large number of trials was necessary because the conditions under which the learning was taking place were not perfectly controlled. As he put it, "[S]tanding in the loose harness the dog can shift his weight from one leg to another, turn his head, prick up his ears, yawn, stretch, in fact alter his whole pattern of proprioceptive stimulation, and a certain amount of his exteroceptive stimulation" (1935, p. 98). (**Proprioceptive stimulation** refers to internal sensations, such as those associated with movements of muscles; **exteroceptive stimulation** relates to sensations associated with external stimuli such as those involving the senses of vision, hearing, taste, and smell.) As a result, the learning required dozens of trials simply to ensure that the response would be associated with most of the various combinations of stimuli possible. That Pavlov was later able to condition salivation in dogs in as few as 10–20 trials simply reflects the fact that he was now better able to control stimulus conditions.

Movement-Produced Stimuli

To understand Guthrie's law of learning, which actually implies his entire theory, it is important to understand that a stimulus is not just one sensation but, rather, is a combination of numerous sensations. In Guthrie's words, learning involves associating a response to a combination of stimuli.

Similarly, for Guthrie, a response is not just a single final act; rather, it is a sequence of actions. To simplify, the sound of a bell leads to a number of alerting responses: turning the ears, moving the eyes, perhaps moving the head and neck, and so on. "Every such motion," says Guthrie, "is a stimulus to many sense organs in muscles, tendons, and joints, as well as the occasion for changing stimuli to eyes, ears, etc." (1935, p. 54). Guthrie labeled these stimuli **movement-produced stimuli (MPS)**. Movement-produced stimuli in turn give rise to other responses, which can also have an effect on muscles, glands, and tendons, thus giving rise to more stimuli.

Contiguity through MPS

Thus, the sequence between the initial presentation of a stimulus and the occurrence of a response is filled with a sequence of responses and the proprioceptive (internal) stimulation that results (MPS). Each of these responses and their corresponding MPS are in contiguity (occur at the same time). Thus, each becomes associated or learned. These learned associations are what guide behavior, claims Guthrie. "One movement starts another, then a third, a fourth, and so on" (1935, p. 54). And the entire sequence is learned because each individual MPS is present at the same time as the response occurs. One of the clearest examples of MPS is found in the learning of athletic skills. These skills often consist of long sequences (or chains) of responses. Each response in the sequence serves as a signal for the next response. Thus, like Watson, Guthrie believed that even very complex sequences of behavior result from the chaining of sequences of stimuli that are often internal (see Figure 2.9).

Habits

Learning, Guthrie insists, occurs in one trial. But this does not mean that a complex behavior can be learned in one trial. What it means is that each individual component of the vast number of stimulus–response associations that compose a complex act requires only a single pairing. However, a number of trials might be required before all have been associated as they need to be. When they are all linked so a particular combination of stimuli reliably leads to a particular combination of responses, what we have is a **habit** – a stereotyped, predictable pattern of responding.

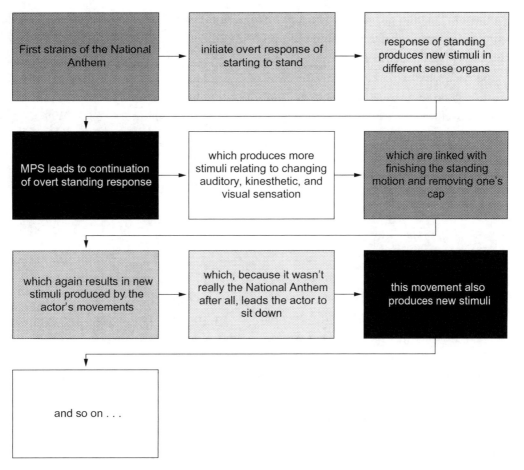

Figure 2.9 Guthrie's law of one-trial learning: "A combination of stimuli which has accompanied a movement will on its recurrence tend to be followed by that movement." According to the theory, each overt response is accompanied by a series of stimuli produced by the response (changes in the visual field, in bodily sensations, and so on). These movement-produced stimuli (MPS) lead to a continuation of the overt action – or to a change of response. Each MPS and each response in the chain is sequential and overlapping in time (hence, in contiguity). Thus, in Guthrie's theory, learning occurs through contiguity.

But humans are seldom completely predictable. They don't respond exactly the same way every time they are placed in the same situation. According to Guthrie, there are several possible explanations for this. One is that if responses to two stimuli are different, it is because the stimuli are not exactly identical; another is that, through one of a number of procedures, a new habit has replaced an old one. The old one is not forgotten: it is merely replaced.

Extinction

Guthrie (1935) tells the story of two young boys whose Friday afternoons were "made dreary" by the pastor's weekly visit during which they were required to unharness, groom, feed, and water that good man's horse. One day, they got the bright idea of retraining the horse. One of them stood behind the animal, shouted "Whoa," and, at the same time, jabbed it sharply with a pitchfork. It isn't clear, says Guthrie, how many times they did this nor does the story report exactly what happened later when the pastor drove his horse home and shouted "Whoa!" But apparently the boys were quite happy with the outcome.

The point, explains Guthrie, is not that the horse had forgotten how to stop; that is hardly likely. Rather, the old habit of stopping in response to the command "Whoa!" had been replaced by a different habit.

The best explanation for forgetting, says Guthrie, is not that associations are wiped out with the passage of time, but that time allows new learning to replace the old. It follows from the theory that whatever response was last performed in a stimulus situation will tend to be repeated again when that situation next arises.

Reward and Punishment

For this reason, reward is sometimes important in learning. According to Guthrie, reward doesn't do anything to strengthen the link between stimulus and response. But what it does is change the stimulus situation, thus preventing the animal (or person) from learning something different.

Punishment can also change a stimulus situation and serve, in Guthrie's words, to "sidetrack" a habit. The important point is that because learning depends on contiguity (that is, on the simultaneity of stimulus and response events) to be effective, punishment has to occur during the response or very soon afterward. And because punishment works by interrupting the unwanted habit, anything that grabs attention and brings about a different behavior will work. "Picking up a small child and tossing him or swinging him by the heels," writes Guthrie, "is just as effective in overcoming a balky fit as is a sound spanking" (1935, p. 141).

Practical Applications of Guthrie's Theory

Guthrie was very interested in making his theory highly practical. As a result, his writing is filled with examples of how learning and remembering can be improved.

What this "one-shot theory of contiguity learning" means from a practical viewpoint, says Guthrie, is that to bring behavior under control, it is necessary to arrange for the behavior to occur in the presence of stimulus conditions that you control. If you want a dog to come when you call it, he explains, you first have to get him to come to you either by holding up a bone, running away from him, pulling him toward you, or doing whatever else you suspect might entice the dog to approach. If you yell "Come," at the same time, an association may soon form between the command and the action.

Note that the dog has not learned a new response; he already knew how to run toward you. Here, as in all learning, what changes are associations between the response of running toward a person and a signal. What makes it easy to teach a dog to come, says Guthrie, is that this is something that dogs do, just as they fetch sticks, lie down, roll over, and so on. "We cannot teach cows to retrieve a stick because this is one of the things that cows do not do," claims Guthrie (1935, p. 45).[17]

Consistent with his theory, Guthrie maintains that responses are never forgotten; they are merely replaced by more recently learned responses. "Unlearning becomes merely a case of learning something else," he says (1935, p. 66). Hence, the best way of breaking a habit is to find the cues that initiate the habit and to practice another response to these same cues. For example, if you smoke, a wide range of stimulus conditions will have become associated with the action of smoking: finishing eating, drinking, watching television, meeting a friend who smokes, getting up in the morning. A general unconditioning of all these links is a long process, says Guthrie, which requires that the smoker attach other responses to the situations associated with the beginning of the smoking sequence.

Guthrie (1952) describes three specific techniques for sidetracking (breaking) habits: the *fatigue technique*, the *threshold technique*, and the *method of incompatible stimuli*. What each of these has in common is that it involves what Guthrie terms **inhibitory conditioning** – that is, the conditioning of a response that *inhibits* the habit to be broken.

The Fatigue Technique

Sometimes termed *flooding*, the **fatigue technique** involves presenting the stimulus repeatedly to elicit continued repetition of the undesired response. Eventually, the organism will become so fatigued that it can no longer perform the response; at that point, a different response will be emitted (even if that response is to do nothing). It follows from Guthrie's theory of one-shot learning that this new response – because it is the most recent reaction to that stimulus – will be repeated if the stimulus is presented again. In this way, the original undesirable habit has been broken.

The Threshold Technique

The **threshold technique** involves presenting the stimulus that forms part of the undesirable S–R (for stimulus–response) unit (habit), but presenting it so faintly that it is below the threshold required to elicit the undesirable response. If it doesn't elicit the undesirable behavior, then it will elicit another response, even if that is simply the response of not reacting. The stimulus is then presented with increasing intensity over a succession of trials, but the degree of increase is carefully kept so small that the undesirable response will never be elicited. By the time an intensity level is reached that would initially have stimulated the undesirable behavior, a different habit has been learned.

---

[17] It appears that Guthrie had never seen a cow sitting up, smoking cigars, and reading, said Old Lady Gribbin as an aside. She seemed dead serious.

The Method of Incompatible Stimuli

The **method of incompatible stimuli** involves presenting the stimulus when the unwanted response cannot occur. Because the undesirable reaction is prevented, a different response that is incompatible with it takes its place and eventually replaces the old habit entirely.

Horse Illustrations

Each of these techniques can be illustrated in the training of horses – a subject about which the Nebraska-raised Guthrie knew something (see Figure 2.10).

Most people will readily admit that a bucking horse has a bad habit – a bad S–R chain, as the behaviorists would say. The stimulus part of this habit is represented by various things, such as saddles and people that are put onto a horse's back leading it to react in an antisocial manner. The response part is represented by the antisocial activity, the bucking response. Guthrie's theory suggests three different techniques for modifying the horse's behavior.

The common "rodeo" technique of breaking a horse is simply to throw a saddle on its back and to ride the living %$^^&#**#**%&&^ and **&$^*@[18] out of it. When it gets sufficiently tired, it will stop responding in an undesirable way, and if the rider is still on its back, the horse may eventually begin to respond by standing, walking, or running. This is Guthrie's fatigue technique.

The threshold method is also commonly used for breaking horses. It breaks as many horses as the rodeo technique, but fewer riders. This method involves "gentling" the horse, usually beginning by placing a light blanket on its back and gradually increasing the weight and number of items on the horse's back over successive trials (that is, increasing the intensity of the stimulus). Given sufficient time and patience, a horse may be gentled (broken) in this fashion.

The third technique, incompatible stimuli, is also very effective with unruly horses. It involves presenting the stimulus (saddle and rider on the horse's back) when the response cannot occur. The incompatible stimulus usually involves tying the horse to a post ("snubbing short") so it cannot buck.

Human Illustrations

Each of Guthrie's three techniques can be applied to people. Of course, it is quite unacceptable to break a child in the same manner that a horse would be broken. But with due consideration for the humanity of children and without having to hold them up by their heels or toss them about, it is possible to remove certain bad habits that might be acquired even in the very best of homes. For example, consider the purely fictitious example of a small boy who habitually

---

[18] The old lady had originally filled this long space with some surprisingly colorful expressions. Editorial wisdom being what it is, those expressions have been deleted. Those of you who are old enough and strangely curious might try writing and begging for a copy of the original.

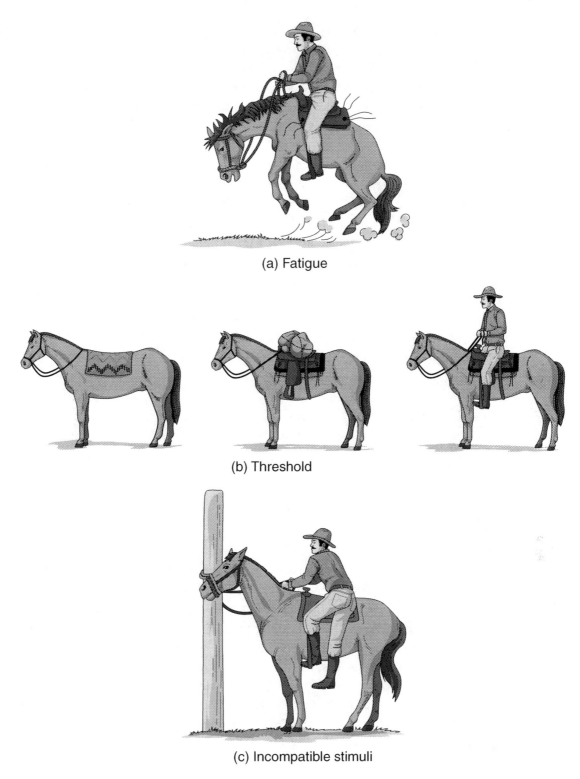

Figure 2.10 Guthrie's three ways of breaking habits applied to "breaking" a horse. In (a), the horse is "broken" in the traditional sense, being allowed to buck until fatigued. In (b), the horse is "gentled" by having progressively heavier weights placed on its back, beginning with a blanket and culminating with a saddle and rider. In (c), the horse is tied down so it can't buck when mounted. In all three instances, the tendency to buck when a foreign object is placed on the horse's back is eventually replaced by another response.

responds to the sight of his grandfather with intense fear, which he acquired because the old man once punished him with a short whip. In the manner of Jones and her subject, Peter, one can remove the boy's fear by having him eat something pleasant like ice cream while the grandfather stands quietly in the distance. Over succeeding trials, Grandpa can be invited to move a little closer each time but never close enough to bring about the old fear reaction (threshold method). Eventually, the fear response will be replaced by a more desirable behavior.

Guthrie's threshold technique is similar to Wolpe's (1958) **counterconditioning** (also called *systematic desensitization*), discussed earlier in connection with the treatment of snake phobia. When used to treat phobias, counterconditioning typically requires that the patient list all stimuli associated with the phobia. These are ranked hierarchically – beginning with the stimulus associated with the least amount of fear, progressing through other stimuli associated with increasing fear, and culminating with those associated with the most intense fear reaction. Following this first step, the therapist trains the patient in one or more of a variety of relaxation techniques. Therapy, which generally occurs over a number of sessions, then involves having the subject imagine or describe a situation low on the hierarchy of fear-producing stimuli. While this is happening, the patient is continually instructed to relax. The object of the procedure is to have the patient imagine fear-producing stimuli without feeling anxiety. Care is taken to ensure that the stimuli being imagined remain below the threshold for fear – in other words, that they don't lead to the phobic reaction (hence, the similarity to Guthrie's threshold method). In the end, if the therapy is successful, the undesirable fear reaction will have been replaced by a response that is essentially incompatible with it – a response of relaxation.

Cousin Renault

The fatigue method and the method of incompatible stimuli can also be used to correct various behavior and emotional problems, a fact of which cousin Renault is still painfully aware. The story is that his sweet tooth would have led him unerringly in the direction of juvenile criminality had it not been for his grandmother's cunning and resourcefulness. You see, Renault, as devious as any other fledgling criminal, had become so successful at pilfering doughnuts, pies, cakes, and other assorted delights from his grandmother's kitchen that the poor lady was quite at her wit's end. She had eventually realized that beating little Renault with her willow cane was not likely to teach him anything other than to dislike willow and to fear the old lady herself. And cleverly inserting vinegars, mustards, pickles, and other foul surprises in her pastries had done nothing but make him more cautious. Now, like a dog, he sniffed everything before he ate it. But eat it he did, almost as fast as the old lady baked.

At one point, the old lady considered the method of incompatible stimuli. "Make a muzzle for him," she told Frank, Renault's grandfather, "and he'll have to leave my baking alone." But the muzzle was never made; they both realized that Renault would learn little from wearing a muzzle, other than not to eat with a muzzle on. She considered the threshold method too, thinking that if Frank set up a huge fan that would blow her kitchen odors toward the barn, Renault might slowly learn to stop turning toward the kitchen like a ravenous wolf every time he passed by. "He goes toward the barn too," Frank reminded the grandmother.

So, as a last resort, they exposed Renault to the fatigue technique. The story has it that one June day, the grandmother started baking at dawn: pies and cakes; creamy tortes and almond cookies; chocolate wafers and sugar doughnuts; lemon meringues and cherry cupcakes. And Renault ate. Sitting on a straight-backed wooden chair, his grandfather encouraging him, he ate – jubilantly at first, then less gladly, and, finally, quite reluctantly. In the end, he said he was certain he could eat no more. But even then, he ate a little more because he had no choice. "Eat. You never have enough. You're going to sit there and eat everything." Renault no longer much likes desserts.

An Appraisal of Guthrie's One-Shot Learning

Guthrie's is a highly appealing and, in some ways, relatively simple theory. In fact, among its principal virtues are its clarity and its simplicity. True to his behaviorist orientation, he insisted that the psychologist should look not at mental states or at vague concepts such as reinforcement but, rather, at objective stimuli and responses. To understand behavior, argued Guthrie, it is essential to look at specific responses and the conditions under which they occur.

Guthrie's is also a highly practical theory. He went to great lengths to point out how stimulus and response events could be arranged to bring about learning through the formation of habits, and how those habits might be changed or replaced once they had been formed.

Although the simplicity of the theory is one of its main attractions, it is also one of its weaknesses. The theory lacks the sort of detail required to make clear what concepts such as habits, MPS, and, indeed, responses and stimuli are. In this theory, stimuli are what lead to responses; responses are what result from stimuli. Hence, these two variables, both of which are central to the theory, are defined only in terms of each other, explains Mills (1998).

EVALUATION OF EARLY BEHAVIORISTIC THEORIES

Pavlov, Watson, and Guthrie were mainly concerned with discovering and explaining regularities that underlie relationships among stimuli and responses. Among the important regularities that these theorists discovered were those now described as Pavlovian or classical conditioning.

But how good are these theories relative to the criteria discussed in Chapter 1 and illustrated in Table 1.1? For example, how well do they summarize and organize important facts, keeping in mind that facts are simply the observations on which theories are based? The answer is that they fit the facts reasonably well as the facts were known then. As is shown in later chapters, many observations had yet to be made. In addition, the "facts" explained by these theories are those that the theorists in question thought to be most in need of explanation, an observation that is true of virtually all psychological theories. That the theories did relatively little to explain "higher" mental processes, such as language, thought, problem solving, perception, and so on, is really not a valid criticism of the theories as theories. These theories were concerned with accounting for "behavior"; hence, the observations to which they paid attention – the "facts" they tried to explain – relate directly to observable behavior rather than to more mental events.

With respect to the other criteria, the theories fare quite well. They tend to be clear and understandable, they are relatively parsimonious, they are internally consistent, they explain and predict certain behaviors quite well, and their insistence on objectivity generally means that they are not based on many unverifiable assumptions.

These three early behavioristic theories have proven to be highly practical in a variety of applied situations, especially in education and therapy. Also, in many ways they serve as important precursors of contemporary theories. Their contributions to the subsequent development of learning theories can hardly be overestimated. In fact, the terms and concepts used today in investigations of classical conditioning are almost entirely terms and concepts first explored and labeled by Pavlov almost a century ago!

One of the weaknesses of the early behavioristic positions is that they largely ignored individual differences in ability and in preferred ways of learning (what are often labeled **learning styles** or *intellectual styles*). We now know that these differences can be important for learning and behavior (Zhang, 2017; Zhang & Sternberg, 2006).

Clearly, early behavioristic theories don't explain all of human learning. However, doing so was not every theorist's goal. Many theorists, such as Pavlov, were concerned mainly with investigating one or two interesting and important phenomena in detail. They believed that other phenomena (many of which might seem more important and more interesting) would eventually be understood – that science needs to progress in increments, beginning with simple concepts and progressing toward the more complex.

The explanations of these early behaviorists provide valuable insights into human and animal functioning. They should not be dismissed because of their failure to explain symbolic functioning or so-called higher mental processes. Instead, they should be viewed in light of their contribution to the development of a science that might not yet explain all human behavior but that explains more behavior increasingly clearly with each succeeding theoretical contribution.

Main Point Chapter Summary

1. Early psychologists such as Wundt, a *structuralist*, and William James, a *functionalist*, used introspection to try to understand human consciousness – although both thought psychology should be more scientific. James tried to understand human consciousness as a whole; Wundt and his followers (e.g., Titchener and Weber) tried to understand the elements that compose the *structure* of consciousness using objective measurements of physical stimuli and their effects (psychophysics – for example, absolute thresholds and JNDs).

2. Pavlov, a physiologist, is famous for his elaboration of classical conditioning, a procedure where a neutral (conditioned) stimulus (CS) is paired with an unconditioned stimulus (US) often enough that it can eventually substitute for it in bringing about a conditioned response (CR) like salivation on the part of Pavlov's dog in response to a tone. Classical conditioning explains learning on the basis of contiguity, the simultaneity of the stimuli that become associated, rather than on the basis of reinforcement.

3. Many emotional responses can be explained in terms of Pavlovian (classical) conditioning. Stimuli need not be perfectly simultaneous in classical conditioning; the pairing can also be delayed (CS before US but overlapping: most effective), trace (CS starts and ends before US), or backward (US occurs before the CS: least effective). Organisms seem predisposed to learn certain behaviors.

4. Acquisition depends on the number of CS–US pairings as well as on the strength of the US. CS–US bonds are remarkably durable but can be extinguished by repeatedly presenting the CS without the US. Spontaneous recovery normally occurs after a period following extinction. Subsequent extinction is faster. Extinction of unwanted behaviors (bedwetting, smoking, or phobias, for example) can sometimes be brought about through conditioning therapies. Stimulus generalization and discrimination are important features of classical conditioning.

5. Watson originated and preached behaviorism in North American psychology. His position was a carefully objective reaction to an earlier, more mentalistic psychological orientation. He based much of his theory on Pavlov's work.

6. Watson found classical conditioning useful for explaining the learning of emotional responses in people. Conditioned emotional reactions (CERs) of fear, love, hate, and so on, can often be traced to experiences where previously neutral stimuli are associated with emotion-producing stimuli. His best-known demonstration of emotional learning involves conditioning Little Albert to fear a white rat, a still-controversial demonstration that has been widely misreported and exaggerated.

7. A strong believer in the power of the environment in determining people's behavior, Watson is closely linked with his often-quoted claim that he would be able to make anything he wished out of a dozen healthy infants if he were given a free hand in determining their environments.

8. Guthrie's explanation of learning, referred to as a one-shot learning theory, is based on contiguity. He maintained that whatever response follows a stimulus is likely to follow that stimulus again when the stimulus is repeated. In addition, the strength of the bond between the stimulus and the response is fixed after the first pairing.

9. In Guthrie's system, practice is important because it permits an association to be formed between a behavior and a variety of stimulus complexes. Reinforcement is effective because it changes the situation, preventing the person (organism) from learning another response. Similarly, punishment works because it disrupts the learning sequence, forcing the individual to perform (and therefore learn) some other response.

10. The notion that stimuli and responses occur in temporal contiguity is made plausible by Guthrie's belief that external stimuli give rise to muscular and glandular responses that produce internal (proprioceptive) stimuli, termed *movement-produced stimuli* (MPS). These MPS are stimuli for other responses in the chain of response events maintained between the presentation of a stimulus and the occurrence of a final response.

11. Sequences of stimuli and responses define habits. These are never forgotten but may be replaced. Guthrie describes three ways of breaking habits: repeated presentation of a stimulus (fatigue technique); presenting the stimulus in gradually increasing increments, but always below the threshold for eliciting a response (threshold technique); and presenting the stimulus when the response cannot occur (method of incompatible stimuli).

12. It is fairer to evaluate these theories by their enormous contributions to the development of psychological theory rather than by their shortcomings.

3 The Effects of Behavior

Thorndike and Hull

CHAPTER OUTLINE

This Chapter	82
Objectives	83
Edward L. Thorndike's Connectionism	83
Animal Intelligence	83
Reinforcement and Contiguity: Two Explanations	86
Thorndike's Early Theory: Main Laws	87
Subsidiary Laws	90
Thorndike's Later Theory: Repealed Laws and New Emphases	91
An Appraisal of Thorndike's Connectionism	94
Clark L. Hull's Hypothetico-Deductive System	95
Overview of Hull's System	96
Main Components of Hull's System	97
Graphic Summary of Hull's System	98
Input Variables: Stimuli	98
Intervening Variables: Connectors	99
Output Variables: Responses	103
Hull's Summary Equation Illustrated	103
Fractional Antedating Goal Reactions	105
Habit-Family Hierarchies	106
Summary and Appraisal of Hull's System	107
Educational Implications of Thorndike and Hull	108
Main Point Chapter Summary	109

Just as the science and art of agriculture depend upon chemistry and botany, so the art of education depends upon physiology and psychology.

Edward L. Thorndike

Old Lady Gribbin motioned for me to turn off the recorder and said to shush and listen, Schrödinger, the one-eyed cat, was coming, and we could hear the dry grasses and the leaves rustling as he made his way through the willows below the bush cabin. Then, for a long time there was silence as though Schrödinger had paused. Earlier, we had watched as he crossed the beaver dam holding up one paw, limping uncertainly on three legs, his right ear torn, a splash of blood across his blind-side cheek, dark black on his orange fur, a streak of mud across his back as though the fight had just now ended and he hadn't yet had time to do his toilet.

He was a long time coming through the willows, and Old Lady Gribbin called him once using a strange name, sadly not recorded but I know it wasn't Schrödinger. The cat made no response and the Old Lady pulled her hat down low over her face against the morning sun and her eyes were lost in its shadow. She arranged her notes across her knees as though she were about to continue into the third chapter, but for a long time she said nothing.

And then the cat eased himself from the willows and ambled across the clearing, more strut than walk, using all four legs but stepping lightly on his right forepaw so we knew we hadn't dreamt his pain. His face was now fresh-cleaned, glistening where he had rubbed the smirch with wetted paw, his orange fur laid smooth, the mud all gone.

He arched his back and growled as he side-stepped around me. That's the way he is. Then he curled himself carefully against the old lady's leg and she asked did I think Schrödinger thought he'd fought a good fight? Did I think he'd deliberately stopped to clean his fur before presenting himself to us, careful that he not make a bad impression? Did I think it was his macho pride that made him strut so and pretend that, no, nothing hurt because he was a Real Cat?

But before I could answer, she said to turn on the recorder and she gathered her ragged notes once more.

THIS CHAPTER

This is sometimes called **anthropomorphism**, *said Mrs. Gribbin as she sorted through her tattered, handwritten pages,* this business of giving nonhuman animals or objects characteristics, such as motives and values, which belong solely to humans.

But who is to say that cats don't think? Who is to say what characteristics of emotion and intelligence are solely human and which might also belong to cats? These might seem to be simple questions, but they have no simple answers.

At about the time that scientific psychology was being born, Charles Darwin's highly influential *The Origin of Species* (1859 [1962]) seemed to suggest that humans are just another species of animal, evolved with certain distinctly different characteristics to be sure, but nevertheless basically animal. Did this mean that nonhuman animals might also possess capacities that had previously been considered beyond the abilities of "dumb" animals? Might they be intelligent in a human sense?

These questions interested Edward Thorndike, whose theory is discussed in the first part of this chapter. The second part of the chapter looks at the theory developed by Clark Hull. These theories are behaviorist: Both are mainly concerned with observable behaviors and with discovering the laws that govern relationships among behaviors (responses) and the conditions that lead to and follow behavior.

Objectives

Explain to your readers, *said Mrs. Gribbin*, that after they finish this chapter, they should be able to describe in words so simple and clear their grandmothers would be astounded:

- the difference between contiguity and reinforcement;
- the principal features of Thorndike's connectionism;
- Thorndike's laws of effect and readiness and the main subsidiary laws;
- changes in Thorndike's thinking after 1930;
- the nature of Hull's system;
- why fractional antedating goal responses are important in Hull's system;
- what is meant by a habit-family hierarchy;
- the relevance to learning theory of Darwin's theory of natural selection.

The old lady bent to scratch the injured cat; he purred loudly. I made that kiss-kiss sound people make to call cats, thinking he might come over and let me pet him. He didn't even look at me, just got up, walked across to the woodpile, and lay down in the shade of the splitting stump, staring out over the pond. The old lady continued to read and expound her notes.

EDWARD L. THORNDIKE'S CONNECTIONISM

So, do "dumb" animals possess human-like capacities of thought and reason? *she asked.* Maybe, *she continued.* Certainly, Darwin's writings contained numerous anecdotes illustrating what seemed to be animal intelligence – for example, describing how monkeys who cut themselves with a sharp object never make the same mistake twice or how monkeys who have been fed sugar lumps wrapped in paper and who are then given a wrapped sugar lump that also contains a wasp reason that they must from then on hold the wrapping to their ear and listen to see whether there might be a wasp inside.

People are anxious to find intelligence in animals, claims Edward Thorndike (1898). If a dog gets lost and then luckily finds its way home over a long distance, newspapers all run stories about how intelligent dogs are. But there are no stories about the hundreds of other dogs who go out for an evening neighborhood stroll, stupidly make a wrong turn, and never find their way home again.

Similarly, if a cat stretches upward on the refrigerator, seeming to reach toward the handle with its paw, people immediately assume that the cat has somehow figured out the connection between the handle and the door. Hogwash, says Thorndike. Anecdotes make a poor source of evidence for scientific theories. If psychology is to determine whether animals can actually reason out complex relationships in their solutions of day-to-day problems, researchers should carry out controlled experiments to this end.

ANIMAL INTELLIGENCE

And so Thorndike devised a number of what he called *puzzle boxes*. The most typical, shown in Figure 3.1, is designed so a cat locked in the box can escape only if it does three things: pull a

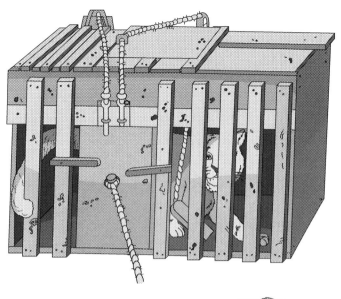

Figure 3.1 Thorndike's puzzle box. To get out of the box, the cat has to pull a string to release one of the door locks, step on the lever to release the second, and then flick one of the door latches. From "Animal intelligence: An experimental study of the associative processes in animals," by E. L. Thorndike, 1898, *Psychological Review Monograph Supplement, 2*(8). Used by permission of the American Psychological Association.

string to release one lock, step on a lever to release a second, and flip a latch upright to finally open the door. To make sure the cat is interested in getting out of the cage, some tidbit of food like a dead fish is placed not far away but beyond reach. Most cats have a number of ready-made solutions for this problem such as trying to squeeze between the bars, scratching and clawing at the door or at the floor, or meowing indignantly for help. Of course, the puzzle box is designed so none of these work.

Basically, the cat can solve this problem in two ways. One is to try a dozen different actions, or 100 or 200, until all three required actions have been performed and – voilà! – the door is open. This is the **trial and error** approach to solving problems.

The other approach to solving a problem is to sit back, look the situation over, think about possible courses of action, and suddenly – bang! – figure out what needs to be done. This defines **insight** as a problem-solving strategy. This strategy was demonstrated by the psychologist Wolfgang Köhler (whose theories are considered in Chapter 6) in an experiment similar to Thorndike's puzzle box demonstration, but using chimpanzees rather than cats. In a typical Köhler (1927) experiment, a caged chimpanzee is unable to reach a bunch of bananas hanging outside the cage until, in a sudden flash of *insight*, it occurs to the animal to use a stick or to pile boxes one on top of the other to reach them.

But Thorndike's cats did not act at all like Köhler's chimpanzees; instead, they used the first approach: *trial and error*. As Figure 3.2 shows, it didn't take them very long to get out of the cage – only about three minutes the first time. But after that, it seldom took them more than a minute.

The conclusion, says Thorndike, is that there is no easily demonstrated, high-level reasoning among cats – nor, indeed, among monkeys. As additional evidence that this is so, notes Thorndike, there appears to be no real imitation, based on understanding and ideas, among animals. That one dog should follow another through a field is not evidence that the dog that

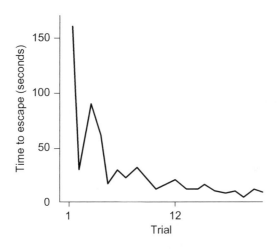

Figure 3.2 The behavior of one cat in Thorndike's puzzle box. The cat took almost three minutes to escape the first time but almost always less than one minute after the first successful escape. From "Animal intelligence: An experimental study of the associative processes in animals," by E. L. Thorndike, 1898, *Psychological Review Monograph Supplement*, 2(8). Used by permission of the American Psychological Association.

follows figures out mentally that it is wise to imitate a fellow dog. Rather, this is simply evidence of a natural behavior, or of a behavior learned through associations that have previously had satisfying consequences. Thorndike demonstrated repeatedly that a naïve cat, dog, or monkey can be allowed to witness a trained cat, dog, or monkey performing some behavior to escape from a puzzle box, but will not learn that behavior as a result (Thorndike, 1911).

It seems clear, concluded Thorndike, that cats don't learn by developing some special insight into a situation. Instead, they learn through trial and error. Simply put, in a given situation the organism makes a number of responses, one or more of which leads to a solution or, in Thorndike's words, to "a satisfying state of affairs." Subsequently, a connection is formed between the response and the situation. This connection is learned, or "stamped in" as Thorndike puts it.

And people, he insists, learn in the same way: "These simple, semi-mechanical phenomena ... which animal learning discloses, are the fundamentals of human learning also" (Thorndike, 1913b, p. 16).[1]

However, we should point out that Thorndike was not entirely correct about animals not learning though imitation. In fact, there is considerable research demonstrating that many animals do imitate each other and learn as a result (Subiaul, Renner, and Krajkowski, 2016). Even dogs are capable of imitating both the behavior of other dogs as well as some human actions (Fugazza, Pogany, & Miklosi, 2016; Miller, Rayburn-Reeves, & Zentall, 2009). And young rhesus macaques are highly skilled at imitating the facial gestures of other macaques (Ferrari et al., 2009). There is evidence that opportunities for early face-to-face interaction and imitation are important for the healthy social development of young monkeys (Sclafani, Paukner, Suomi, & Ferrari, 2015). Also, Dindo, Whiten, and de Waal (2009) showed that when capuchin monkeys are allowed to observe another monkey who has already mastered a

---

[1] Speaking of people, *said Old Lady Gribbin looking at me over her glasses and motioning toward the digital recorder so I would know that this was an aside and I should pause the recording and just take notes*, Thorndike seemed to consider humans fundamentally different from animals, although he remained unclear about what the differences were. He didn't believe that language and reason alone distinguished humans from other animals, *the old lady explained, reading a passage from Thorndike's* 1911 *book that she produced from her bag*: "I said a while ago that man was no more an animal with language than an elephant was a cow with a proboscis. We may safely add the statement that man is not an animal plus reason" (p. 127). But he did accept that humans can learn by associating ideas; he believed that this doesn't seem to happen among other animals.

The Effects of Behavior

complex behavior associated with obtaining food, they are far more likely to be successful in learning the same behavior.

Reinforcement and Contiguity: Two Explanations

How does this learning, or, using Thorndike's terms, "stamping in," occur?

Learning theories that look at the formation of connections or associations (conditioning theories) rely on one of two different explanations for learning: **contiguity** or **reinforcement**. A contiguity explanation says that an association is formed between stimuli or between stimuli and responses because they occur simultaneously or nearly simultaneously (*in contiguity*). The second alternative, reinforcement, maintains that learning occurs because of the consequences of the behavior – more specifically, because the behavior leads to positive consequences or the elimination of something negative (or both).

As we saw in Chapter 2, Ivan P. Pavlov, John B. Watson, and Edwin Guthrie used contiguity to explain learning. Pavlovian (classical) conditioning is based on the notion that the simultaneous presentation of two stimuli leads to the development of some sort of equivalence between them. For example, in the well-known Pavlovian demonstration, the buzzer becomes at least partly equivalent to food when it elicits a response similar to that elicited by food.

In Guthrie's theory, a link is formed between a stimulus and a response because they are simultaneous (in contiguity). To support this position, given the time lag between the presentation of most stimuli and their responses, Guthrie borrowed the concept of movement-produced stimuli (MPS) from what was known of the physiology of muscles and glands, where MPS are a series of internal (muscular, glandular, neural) stimuli and responses that occur between an overt stimulus and a response.

But Thorndike's theory goes beyond simple contiguity. Clearly, says Thorndike, contiguity is only part of the story. Surely, the cat would not learn to escape from the puzzle box were it not for the consequences of so doing.

BOX 3.1 Edward Lee Thorndike (1874–1949)

Like Pavlov, Thorndike was the son of a clergyman, a fact whose significance relates to the greater probability that the children of ministers and pastors would receive a college education. In fact, Thorndike learned to read before starting school at age five.

Thorndike's father was not only a clergyman, but had studied and practiced law earlier in his career, later becoming a noted preacher in Massachusetts. Thorndike's mother, Abigail Brewster Ladd, is described as extraordinarily intelligent. These parents, with the help of Abigail's mother, raised four highly gifted children. Their child rearing is reported to have been strict and to have emphasized hard work and good manners, and Edward Thorndike reportedly grew up to be extremely industrious and self-controlled. All three Thorndike brothers, Edward, Ashley, and Lynn, later taught at Columbia University and their sister, Mildred, was a high-school English teacher.

BOX 3.1 (cont.)

Thorndike began his academic career studying English at Wesleyan, this being the field of study pursued by his sister and one of his brothers. The other brother, Lynn, studied and taught medieval history. From Wesleyan, Thorndike then went to Harvard, where he took a class from William James and soon switched to psychology. While at Harvard, he raised chickens in the basement of William James's house, using them in studies of animal intelligence. Later, he transferred to Columbia, where he obtained a Ph.D. in psychology in 1898. His thesis on animal intelligence, published that same year, is still a classic (he was then 24). He tried to establish, through experimentation, that animals (specifically cats) learn through a gradual process of trial and error that eventually leads to the "stamping in" of the correct response. Much of his later career in psychology involved generalizing this observation to human learning and demonstrating how humans also learn through trial and error as a function of reward or punishment. Interestingly, Thorndike claimed never to have been very interested in animals or in animal research. "The motive for my first investigations of animal intelligence was chiefly to satisfy requirements for courses and degrees. Any other topic would probably have served me as well. I certainly had no special interest in animals . . .." (Thorndike, 1936 [1949], pp. 3–4).

Thorndike wrote extensively, publishing more than 78 books and in excess of 400 articles. His writing deals with a wide range of topics in education and psychology (it is said that all his course outlines eventually became books). He almost single-handedly defined and established educational psychology when, in 1913 and 1914, he published his three-volume book entitled *Educational Psychology* (Thorndike, 1913–1914); he changed the study of child development into an objective science; he established the use of tests and statistical methods in psychology and education; he was instrumental in the psychological testing movement in psychology; and he conducted literally hundreds of experiments on learning and transfer using human subjects. Like Watson, and Guthrie, he also served as president of the American Psychological Association. During his lifetime, he was widely honored not only in North America but also in Europe. (Based in part on Hunt, 2007; Joncich, 1968; Kincheloe & Horn, 2007; Woodworth, 1952).

Thorndike's Early Theory: Main Laws

Traditionally, psychologists have made two types of statements with respect to people and animals, notes Thorndike: those that have to do with consciousness and those that have to do with behavior. But, he cautions, statements about consciousness are uncertain and difficult, especially in animals and young children. And in adults, they are based mainly on introspection, which is a scientifically suspect approach. At least in part, argues Thorndike, psychology can be "as independent of introspection as physics is" (1911, p. 2). Hence, Thorndike emphasizes experimentation rather than introspection, and behavior rather than thought (although he did not consider himself a behaviorist but, rather, a *connectionist*).

For Thorndike, learning consists of the formation of bonds between stimuli and responses – bonds that take the form of neural connections (hence, the label **connectionism**). Learning, Thorndike explains, involves the *stamping in* of stimulus–response (S–R) connections; forgetting involves *stamping out* connections.

Thorndike's theory summarizes the effects of classical conditioning's three important variables (recency, frequency, and contiguity) in a single law: the **law of exercise**.

The Law of Exercise

The law of exercise states that bonds between stimuli and responses are strengthened through being exercised "frequently," "recently," and "vigorously" (Thorndike, 1913a). As we see later, this law played a very minor role in Thorndike's final system, but it had a tremendous influence on educational theory and practice in the early decades of the twentieth century. Although Thorndike did not invent the notion that practice and repetition improve learning (these ideas had long been the basis of formal education), his early belief in the effectiveness of "exercising" S–R connections did a great deal to encourage the repetitive "drill" approaches to learning that became increasingly popular in the 1930s and 1940s. Ironically, however, following later revisions of his theory, Thorndike would certainly not have recommended mere repetition and practice as an instructional process.

The Law of Effect

That is because Thorndike believed that whether a connection is stamped in or not depends far more on its consequences (its effects) than on how often it is exercised. Hence, Thorndike's most important law is the **law of effect** (Thorndike, 1913a). As Leslie (2006) notes, the law of effect explains how the organism *adapts* to the environment by modifying behavior as a result of its consequences. It is a law that continues to be widely investigated and applied in psychology (for example, Navakatikyan, Murrell, Bensemann, Davison, & Elliffe, 2013; Staddon, 2014).

Simply stated, the law of effect maintains that responses just before a satisfying state of affairs are more likely to be repeated. The converse also applies, although it is less important in explaining learning: Responses just before an annoying state of affairs are more likely not to be repeated. Thus, what Thorndike calls *satisfiers* and *annoyers* are critical to learning.

Whoa! Staunch behaviorists might object at this point: Terms such as *satisfying* and *annoying* are not very objective and not very behavioristic. These sound a lot like the sorts of mentalistic terms favored by psychologists given to introspection and contemplation and not at all like the kinds of terms that would appeal to experimentally inclined, more objective psychologists such as Thorndike or Watson.

But, responds Thorndike to his would-be critics, satisfiers and annoyers can be defined completely objectively. A satisfying state of affairs is simply one that the animal (or person) either does nothing to avoid or actively attempts to maintain. An annoying state of affairs is one that the animal (person) does nothing to preserve or attempts to end (Thorndike, 1913b). Note that the definition has nothing to do with the organism's feelings but only with behavior.

The law of effect is basically a description of what is often termed **instrumental learning**. Instrumental learning occurs when an organism performs a response that is *instrumental* in bringing about a satisfying state of affairs and a connection is then formed between the response and the stimulus preceding it.

One important aspect of this model of instrumental learning is the assumption that the connection is formed between the stimulus and the response rather than between the reward and the response.[2] B. F. Skinner's **operant conditioning**, as we see in Chapter 4, describes how connections form between reward and behavior – how behavior comes to be controlled by its consequences. This position is fundamentally different from that described by Pavlov and Watson, which maintains that an association forms between two stimuli because of repeated pairings and not because of their consequences. Recall that Pavlov and Watson are contiguity theorists; Thorndike's position (and Skinner's) is based on the consequences of behavior. As is made clear later in this chapter, Hull also accepted Thorndike's view and made it one of the central features of his system.

The Law of Readiness

A third major law formed an important part of Thorndike's pre-1930 system: the **law of readiness**. This law recognizes that certain kinds of learning are difficult or even impossible unless the learner is ready. Readiness to learn has to do with motivation (forces that lead to behavior) as well as with maturation, previous learning, and other characteristics of the learner. When a conduction unit is ready to conduct, says Thorndike, to do so is satisfying and not to do so is annoying. Similarly, when a conduction unit is not ready to conduct, being forced to do so is annoying.

Although Thorndike's use of such vague expressions as "conduction unit" and "ready to conduct" detract from the objectivity of his system, the law of readiness has been made more concrete and more useful in educational practice. Readiness, Thorndike explains, is closely related not only to the learner's maturation and to previous learning, but also has much to do

---

[2] At this point, Old Lady Gribbin got up from the stump and motioned that I should turn off the recorder, and I thought maybe she just wanted to stretch. But no, it seemed a spider had dropped upon her arm from an overhanging branch and now she bent so it might walk down the length of her arm and across the back of her hand onto a smooth boulder by the fire pit. While she did this, she explained that this business of Thorndike's describing how connections form between responses and stimuli might seem like a small point but that it's a fundamentally important one. She said I should repeat it when I transcribe her words into this seventh edition. She said I shouldn't simply assume that you're bright enough to understand everything the first time you're told, that all important things should be repeated at least once or maybe twice or even three times. I defended you, praised your intelligence, said you would be bored rather than enlightened if I were to repeat her words more than once. She took her hat off and looked at me over her spectacles, but I couldn't read her expression. Then, she put the hat back on, sat down, nodded that I should record once more, and continued reading this report. For a moment, I was distracted from her words, watching the spider as it ambled up the smooth side of the white stone and began to cross what must have seemed to it like a vast barren expanse. Did it wonder why its world had changed? Did it understand where it was? Did the heat of the sun-warmed stone reassure it? Did this spider have any of the animal intelligence of which Thorndike wrote?

And then Schrödinger reached out with his paw and smacked the spider hard against the rock.

The Effects of Behavior

with whether an activity is satisfying or annoying. Specifically, a pleasant state of affairs results when a learner is ready to learn and is allowed to do so; conversely, being forced to learn when not ready, or being prevented from learning when ready, lead to an annoying state of affairs.

Subsidiary Laws

As a result of his many experiments with human and nonhuman animals, Thorndike arrived at several additional laws of learning. Five of these are an especially important part of his explanation for learning.

1. The Law of Multiple Responses

The **law of multiple responses** states that in any given situation, the organism will respond in a variety of ways if its first response does not immediately lead to a more satisfying state of affairs. In other words, an individual will attempt to solve problems through *trial and error*, an observation well illustrated in the most famous of Thorndike's hundreds of experiments: the cat-in-the-puzzle-box study described earlier.

2. Set or Attitude

The second law recognizes that learning is partly a function of **attitude**, or **set** (defined as a predisposition to react in a given way). The **law of set** applies to satisfiers and annoyers and to the nature of the responses that will be emitted by a person. There are culturally determined ways of dealing with a wide variety of problems. For example, many cultures find it generally acceptable to react to aggression with aggression. Individuals in these cultures are *set* to respond aggressively. Presumably, doing so has the potential of leading to a satisfying state of affairs for the aggressor (and perhaps an annoying state of affairs for those aggressed upon).

3. The Law of Prepotency of Elements

Thorndike suggests, in his **law of prepotency of elements**, that it is possible for a learner to react only to the significant (*prepotent*) elements in a problem situation and be undistracted by irrelevant aspects of the situation. For example, recognizing that a figure is a square rather than a rectangle requires only that the subject respond to the relationship among the sides of the figure and not to its color, placement, and so on. For this problem, stimuli associated with shape are prepotent; others are irrelevant.

4. Response by Analogy

The fourth principle, the **law of response by analogy**, recognizes that a person placed in a novel situation may react with responses that might be used in other similar situations –

situations that, in Thorndike's words, share *identical elements*. When Cindy uses a subtraction rule she learned at school to determine that if she buys a $1.50 worth of black jellybeans, she will still have $3.50 left from her $5 bill, she is responding by analogy. The reason she does so, explains Thorndike, is that she recognizes important similarities (*identical elements*) between her current situation and a school problem-solving situation. This allows her to *transfer* what she has learned. This principle, Thorndike's theory of transfer, is sometimes referred to as the **theory of identical elements**.

Thorndike's theory of identical elements was his explanation for how people respond in novel situations – that is, how they transfer or generalize responses. When faced with a new situation, "[people's] habits do not retire to some convenient distance," he explains (1913a, p. 28). Instead, people recognize aspects of the novel situation as being similar to some more familiar situation, and they respond accordingly. And if the first response does not lead to a satisfying state of affairs, a second is emitted and then perhaps a third, a fourth, and so on.

Van der Locht, van Dam, and Chiaburu (2013) illustrate how Thorndike's theory of identical elements still plays an important role in contemporary explanations of transfer of training. In their research, they showed that increasing the number of training program elements that are identical to an actual work situation contributes significantly to transfer.

5. Associative Shifting

The last of the five subsidiary principles describes what might also be called *stimulus substitution*. **Associative shifting** recognizes that it is possible to shift a response from one stimulus to another. Thorndike illustrated this process by describing how a cat can be trained to stand. Initially, the cat stands because the experimenter holds up a piece of fish. Gradually, the amount of fish is decreased until the cat stands when the experimenter raises her empty hand.

Associative shifting may explain the effectiveness of countless advertising campaigns that pair a stimulus associated with positive emotions (or with greed or lust) with what might otherwise be a relatively neutral stimulus – for example, liquor brands with deliriously happy juveniles; macho hombres with cigarettes dangling from their lips; ecstatic couples with fists full of lottery tickets; attractive models lounging on vehicle hoods.

Thorndike's Later Theory: Repealed Laws and New Emphases

Although many of Thorndike's beliefs about human learning remained unchanged throughout his long career, he is nevertheless one of several theorists who remained active long enough, and sufficiently open to change, that the system underwent some major modifications. Beginning around 1930, Thorndike admitted he had been wrong about some things.

Repeal of the Law of Exercise

For one thing, I was wrong about the law of exercise, he confessed. Why? Because he had determined through experimentation with humans (rather than simply with cats or chickens)

The Effects of Behavior

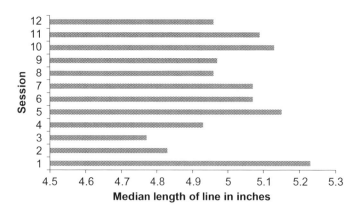

Figure 3.3 Median lengths of 3,000 separate lines drawn by a single subject with eyes closed, over 12 sessions, when instructed to draw a line four inches long. Data from *Human learning* by E. L. Thorndike, p. 9 (table 1). Cambridge, MA: MIT Press, 1931.

that mere repetition does not cause learning. For example, in one experiment, subjects were each given a large pad of paper and a pencil and were asked to draw with their eyes closed, using one quick movement, a line intended to be about four inches long (Thorndike, 1931). They were to do this over a number of sessions on successive days, until they had drawn a total of 3,000 lines, always with their eyes closed.

Results for one subject are shown in Figure 3.3. The results illustrate two general truths, claims Thorndike: "(1) that of multiple response or variable reaction and (2) that of the failure of repetition of the situation to cause learning" (1931, p. 10). In other words, exercise – or repetition – does not affect learning. "The repetition of a situation may change a man as little as the repetition of a message over a wire changes the wire," writes Thorndike. "In and of itself, it may teach him as little as the message teaches the switchboard.... . [T]he more frequent connections are not selected by their greater frequency" (1931, p. 14).

Half a Law of Effect

What does lead to learning is not repetition, Thorndike insists, but the *effects* of the action. Specifically, as he had always maintained, actions that lead to satisfying states of affairs tend to be stamped in and maintained. But recall that he had also thought that responses leading to annoying states of affairs tend to be stamped out. I was wrong, Thorndike admitted again, now claiming that annoying outcomes do relatively little to the strength of a connection.

To investigate the law of effect, Thorndike (1931) devised several experiments. In one of these, nine non-Spanish-speaking participants were asked to select one from among five possible meanings for 200 different Spanish words whose meanings they could not easily have guessed correctly. After each correct selection, the experimenter said "Right"; for each incorrect selection, the experimenter said "Wrong." The procedure was then repeated a second time, then a third, and a fourth. The object was to see whether there would be an increased tendency to select meanings that were initially followed by the response "Right." And, not surprisingly, there was. Subjects were between 50 percent and 90 percent more likely to select a meaning that had twice been followed by the response "Right." Was there a corresponding reduction in the probability of selecting a response followed by a "Wrong"? The answer is no. In fact, subjects were only 7–23 percent less likely to select an incorrect response already selected twice (see

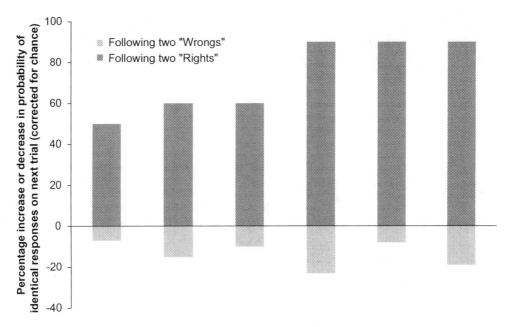

Figure 3.4 The influence of two consecutive "Rights" or "Wrongs" on the next choice of possible word meanings for an unknown word for nine subjects in six experiments. Data from *Human learning* by E. L. Thorndike, p. 44. Cambridge, MA: MIT Press, 1931.

Figure 3.4). "Other things being equal," says Thorndike, "an announcement of 'Right' strengthens the connection which it follows and belongs to much more than the announcement of 'Wrong' weakens the one which it follows and belongs to" (1931, p. 45).

Learning by Ideas

Thorndike revised his theory in several other important ways after 1930. The changes were typically prompted by a need to take into account observations about human learning that didn't readily fit the original theory. Because these observations tended to reveal that thoughts, or ideas, are important in human learning, the theory began to hint at cognitive concerns. For example, Thorndike (1931) now spoke of "ideational learning," described as a "higher" form of learning that involves analysis, abstraction, and meaningfulness. As an illustration of these notions, he refers to the apparently simple task of taming a monkey. To accomplish this task, he says, you cannot simply reach over, grab the monkey, and feed it. Chances are, it just won't get the idea. But if you let it approach on its own and then feed it, the behaviors associated with tame behavior will eventually be *stamped in*.[3] In contrast, humans in the same situation may well form associations among ideas relating to being grabbed by a keeper and subsequently being fed. In Thorndike's words:

---

[3] But Schrödinger still doesn't like you, said the old lady, as a rather unkind aside, sounding almost as though this might please her. I know you've been trying to feed him, but he just doesn't like you, she said again. Maybe he doesn't like me, but you can't please everybody. (Besides, I think she's wrong: He *is* starting to like me.)

> Learning by ideas is, as the name implies, characterized by the frequent presence of ideas as situations or as responses or as both. Whereas the bulk of the learning which dogs and cats and chicks and rats display consists of connections leading from external or perceptual situations straight to bodily acts or to impulsive tendencies closely attached to such acts, the insight learning of man operates with the aid of ideas which are free from narrow confinements. (1931, p. 138)

Although terms such as *ideas*, *analysis*, and *insight* are not defined very clearly in Thorndike's system, they are reflected in two additional concepts that he investigated and incorporated into the system. The first is the **principle of belongingness**, evident in the finding that if two or more elements are seen as belonging together, they are more easily learned. One of Thorndike's (1931) studies illustrating this principle asked subjects to pay attention while the experimenter read out 1,304 pairs of words and numbers. Among these were four words that each recurred 24 times, each time being preceded by exactly the same number. Afterward, subjects were asked to write which numbers came after specific words (including the four frequently repeated words) as well as which words came after specific numbers (including the four numbers each repeated 24 times).

Their performance was no better than would be expected solely by chance. Why? Because, explains Thorndike, they thought each word belonged to the number that followed it rather than to the number that preceded it.

The principle of belongingness is evident in a common memory aid useful for remembering people's names. When you are introduced to Fred and notice that his complexion is red, you might later remember his name. In a sense, his ruddy complexion and his name *belong* together.

The second important post-1930 Thorndikean concept is labeled **spread of effect**. It describes Thorndike's discovery that when a response is followed by a satisfying state of affairs, other related responses also seem to be affected. As an illustration, Thorndike (1931) had subjects choose any number between 1 and 10 to go with each word in a series. In the series were a number of frequently repeated words. Whenever the subject chose the number the experimenter had previously selected for each often-repeated word, he was told he was right. Not surprisingly, "right" numbers increased in frequency. More surprisingly, numbers immediately preceding and following these "right" numbers also increased, although not as dramatically.

Basically, what the principle of spread of effect says is that reinforcement strengthens not only the response that precedes it but also other responses that occur at about the same time. Thus, the effect of reinforcing a student for giving correct answers in class may lead that student to try to continue to give correct answers. It may also *spread* to other accompanying behaviors, such as paying attention in class, focusing on the text, completing assignments, listening when other students respond, and so on.

An Appraisal of Thorndike's Connectionism

Thorndike's laws and principles present a relatively clear picture of his view of learning. According to this view, learning consists of the formation of physiological bonds or connections between stimuli and responses. The bonds are stamped in because of the satisfying nature of their consequences, also influenced by the individual's sense of what goes with what – what belongs.

Basically, says Thorndike, humans arrive at appropriate responses largely through trial and error. They may also respond in given ways because of a predetermined set, or attitude, perhaps determined by culture or by more immediate aspects of the situation. For example, a hungry person will respond to food in a different way than will someone who is not hungry. Some responses will be based on behavior learned in other, somewhat similar situations (response by analogy), whereas others may have resulted from a conditioning procedure (associative shifting). In many cases, the person will engage in behavior only in response to the most important aspects of a situation (the most prepotent elements).

Critics point out that much of Thorndike's theorizing was based on informal observation. Nevertheless, one of Thorndike's very important contributions to the advancement of psychology is that he was largely responsible for the introduction of controlled investigations of animals and people as a means of verifying predictions made from theory.

Critics also point out that Thorndike often appealed to vague internal states as a basis for explaining learning. Satisfying and annoying states of affairs are ill-defined and difficult concepts. As we see in Chapter 4, later theorists – especially Skinner – devoted considerable efforts to finding more objective ways to describe the effects of behavior.

Despite the difficulties associated with Thorndike's use of concepts such as "satisfiers" and "annoyers," one of his most important contributions to the development of learning theory is the emphasis he placed on the consequences of behavior as determiners of what is learned and what is not. The significance of the law of effect in the development of learning theory is apparent in its long-lasting influence. The notion that the effects of reinforcement are central in learning has largely dominated psychology since Thorndike.

Thorndike also made significant contributions in the practical application of psychological principles, particularly in teaching. A large number of his writings are devoted specifically to pedagogical problems in specific areas such as arithmetic (Thorndike, 1922), Latin (Thorndike, 1923), and the psychology of interest (Thorndike, 1935).

Thorndike serves as an example of a theorist strongly committed to a clear and definite viewpoint, yet willing to examine other views, to make dramatic changes in his own thinking, and also to admit that there was still much that his theory could not explain. "The connectionist theory of life and learning," he writes, "is doubtless neither adequate nor accurate. Its explanations of purposive behavior, abstraction, general notions, and reasoning are only a first and provisional attack on these problems. It has many gaps and defects" (1931, p. 131).

Since Thorndike, many others have tried to fill the gaps and fix the defects.

CLARK L. HULL'S HYPOTHETICO-DEDUCTIVE SYSTEM

Among these was Clark L. Hull, probably the most ambitious of the behavior theorists. Hull's dream was to use the rules of logic and of experimentation to discover and to deduce (to infer logically) the laws that govern human behavior – hence, the label **hypothetico-deductive**

system. The result is a system of such complexity and scope that only a brief glimpse of it can be given here. In its entirety, the system is based on 17 laws (called *postulates*) from which he derived more than 100 theorems and many corollaries (Hull, 1943, 1951, 1952).

OVERVIEW OF HULL'S SYSTEM

Science has two essential aspects, Hull tells us (1952). One is concerned with the actual observations (facts) of the discipline; the other tries to make sense of the observations by organizing them into a coherent, logical system or theory. The theory then serves as an explanation for the observations and as a basis for understanding and for making predictions. Hull intended to develop that theory. This energetic, mathematically oriented, and very scientific young man proposed to develop a logical, scientific, and mathematical system that would fully explain human learning and behavior.

Hull called the 17 laws that compose the system *postulates* rather than laws because, science being a young discipline, "a certain amount of uncertainty surrounds these basic laws" (1952, p. 1). These 17 postulates, together with the 133 specific theorems and numerous corollaries he derived from them, describe relationships among the many variables thought to be involved in human behavior.

Although the 17 postulates that are the foundation of Hull's system cannot easily be tested, the theorems and their corollaries can. Each is precise and mathematical; each gives rise to specific predictions that can be tested experimentally. Results can then be interpreted as providing support for, or refuting, not only the theorems or their corollaries but also the postulates on which the theorems are based.

Hull's system is elaborated in two major books. He had also planned a third book describing the application of the system to behavior in social interactions. Unfortunately, he died at about the time he was finishing the second book; the third was never begun.

BOX 3.2 Clark Leonard Hull (1884–1952)

Hull was born in a log house on a farm near Akron, New York, on May 24, 1884. Later, his family moved to Michigan. His was a poor pioneer family; his father had no formal education. He and his only sibling, a brother, began school in a one-room schoolhouse. However, Hull apparently missed a lot of school in his early years because he had to work on the family farm. Much of this work was physically difficult, involving feeding animals, clearing land, chopping wood, and other farm tasks. Sadly, his health was bad throughout much of his childhood, and he had extremely poor eyesight. Still, at the age of 17, he spent a year teaching in a one-room school in Michigan before continuing his education at Alma Academy, also in Michigan. However, early in his college years, he was laid low by poliomyelitis for a lengthy period. The disease left him with a brace on his left leg and dependent on crutches for walking.

BOX 3.2 (cont.)

Hull had considerable talent for mathematics (as well as philosophy), and his initial aspiration was to become a mining engineer. But after reading William James's *Principles of Psychology*, he switched to psychology and went to the University of Wisconsin, where he obtained a Ph.D. in 1918.

Hull's early interests included systematic investigations of human and animal aptitudes, of thinking machines (robots), of hypnosis (to which he devoted a full 10 years of study and research), and of the effect of tobacco on intellectual functioning. In 1929 he went to Yale, where he became a research professor and generated (with a number of ardent disciples) the monumental system that, in extremely simplified form, composes the rest of this chapter. Following his first major descriptions of this system in *Principles of Behavior* (1943), he rapidly became the most frequently cited psychologist in the United States. A final revision of this book was published just after his death in 1952. He, too, served a term as president of the American Psychological Association, as did William James, Edward Thorndike, John Watson, and Edwin Guthrie. (Based in part on Beach, 1959; Kincheloe and Horn, 2007; Leahey, 2000; New World Encyclopedia 2018b)

Main Components of Hull's System

Hull's explicitly behavioristic system is marked by all the behaviorist's concerns for objectivity, precision, and rigor. Thus, although he began by inventing postulates, which sounds like a pretty mentalistic undertaking, his main concern was to derive specific, testable hypotheses from them. Then, he attempted to verify them in laboratory situations. As is clear from an examination of the system, this was a monumental task.

True to the behavioristic approach, Hull began by looking at stimuli and responses. Like Pavlov, Watson, Guthrie, and Thorndike, he was convinced that environmentally conditioned responses underlie behavior. However, he dealt with stimuli and responses in considerably more detail than did most of his contemporaries. Stimuli, he explained, consist of all the conditions that affect the organism but that might or might not lead to behavior. He referred to these conditions as **input variables**; responses are called **output variables**. The main purpose of his theory was to explain the nature of input and output variables as well as to discover the relationships that exist between the two. That relationship is explained largely in terms of a third set of variables referred to as **intervening variables**. These form a central part of Hull's system.

Important aspects of input and output variables can be observed and measured. In contrast, intervening variables are purely hypothetical: They are inferred from input and output. They are the scientist's most educated guesses about what might be happening (*intervening*) between the presentation of a stimulus and the occurrence of a response.

Hull's interest in intervening variables is a significant departure from the preoccupations of early behaviorists such as Watson and Guthrie, who actively shunned speculation, trying to

The Effects of Behavior

keep the study of behavior as objective as possible. For this reason, Hull described himself as a **neobehaviorist** rather than simply a behaviorist. Put another way, he saw himself as an S–O–R theorist rather than an S–R theorist. The "O" stands for organism and indicates that instead of dealing only with stimuli and responses (as Watson did, for example), he also took into account events that occur within the organism.

Hull was greatly impressed by Pavlov's work on reflexive behavior and classical conditioning. This Pavlovian influence is reflected in the fact that the cornerstone of Hull's system is his belief that all behavior consists of S–R connections. Hull thought that conditioning provides a good explanation for the mechanics of learning. But his system goes beyond these mechanics and attempts to explain the motivation that seems to be clearly involved in behavior. Here, the influence of Thorndike, and especially of his law of effect, is most apparent. The influence of reward on learning is the essence of Hull's motivational system and became the main explanatory notion in the final theory.

Graphic Summary of Hull's System

It might seem backward to begin this discussion with a summary. However, in this case, the summary presented in Figure 3.5 serves as a useful outline of the pages that follow.

The complete system is jammed with symbols and mathematical terms and values, all of which seem highly complex and only the most important of which are included in Figure 3.5. In fact, the symbols simplify the theory (although they might impose some strain on memory). Although the theory is very complex in scope and detail, its most basic ideas are very straightforward.

First, to simplify, think of the model in Figure 3.5 not as a general description of human behavior but as representing only one specific behavior for one person at a given time. Applying the system to one behavior makes it much easier to understand.

Next, keep in mind that Hull, the precise and logical mathematician, truly believed that human behavior could be predicted if psychologists had the right information and the right equations. Hence, his main goal was to develop a system that would allow him to do just that – to predict a person's behavior, given knowledge about the stimulus and about the person's history with this stimulus.

Input Variables: Stimuli

In Hull's system, summarized in Figure 3.5, input variables are predictors: They represent the information the psychologist needs to predict correctly how a person will respond (the output variables represent the response, or what is predicted). In different terms, the stimulus variables are *independent variables*, and the response variables are *dependent variables*.

In brief, input variables represent a stimulus. But a stimulus is not just a simple sensation (like the sound of a bell), but is the complex result of a large number of preceding events. As Figure 3.5 indicates, complete knowledge of input requires knowing the following: how many times in the past the S–R bond in question has been reinforced (N); something about the

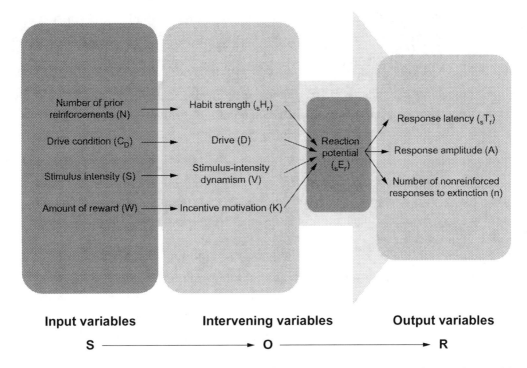

Figure 3.5 A simplified representation of Hull's system. His main goal was to arrive at values and formulas so that it would be possible to predict the output variables given sufficient knowledge about important input variables. While input and output variables are objective and can be measured, intervening variables are hypothetical and can only be inferred.

physical intensity of the stimulus (S); the drive conditions of the organism (CD); and the reward attached to responding (W). Theoretically, all these variables in combination should allow prediction of the output variables. Hence, one of the major difficulties in applying this system to predict behavior is that the psychologist needs a tremendous amount of knowledge about the person's past experiences.

Intervening Variables: Connectors

Although input and output variables are the only directly observable and measurable events described in Hull's system, intervening variables are probably more important for understanding what his theory is really about. These variables have important links with the external variables; they intervene between stimulus events and response events to determine whether a response will occur for a stimulus. They are the "O" in Hull's description of his theory as an S–O–R system rather than simply an S–R system (recall that the "O" stands for organism).

Intervening variables determine responses or the lack thereof. But note that the power of intervening variables in determining responses is completely based on input variables. In a sense, the intervening variables are a mathematical description of S–R relationships. That is, each stimulus (input) variable has a specific intervening variable related to it by some mathematical function. Thus, characteristics of input variables (such as number of prior

The Effects of Behavior

reinforcements) are reflected in the value of intervening variables that, in turn, determine whether a specific response will occur.

Keep in mind that Hull's objective was to develop a mathematical system that would make it possible to calculate human behavior given sufficient knowledge about prior conditions – a sort of human behavior calculator. Viewed in this way, the intervening variables are much easier to understand. The most important of Hull's intervening variables are described below.

1. $_sH_R$

The most important intervening variable, **habit strength** (SHR), is defined as the strength of the bond between a stimulus and a response. Habit strength, explained Hull, is determined largely by the number of previous pairings of a stimulus with a response, provided that reinforcement occurred on every trial. Here, Thorndike's influence on Hull is most evident. Unlike contiguity theorists, Thorndike and Hull maintained that the strength of a habit (of an S–R bond) is a function of reinforcement rather than of simple repetition. Hull introduced specific numerical functions to illustrate the precise relationship between the number of reinforced S–R pairings and habit strength. These are now of historical interest but of little practical value.

2. D

Habit strength is crucially important in determining behavior, but it is not the most important intervening variable: **drive (D)** is. Basically, drive is a tendency to act that is brought about by an unsatisfied need or desire. For example, the need to drink, when unsatisfied, leads to a thirst drive; an unsatisfied need for food leads to a hunger drive.

Drive is a motivational concept that is closely tied with reinforcement. Within Hull's system, drive is the cause of behavior. Accordingly, the system is referred to as a *drive-reduction theory*. Responses become connected with stimuli (that is, become learned), says Hull, when they lead to a reduction in drive. Thus, if the response of eating a strange new thing leads to a reduction in a ravenous hunger drive, stimuli associated with this new thing will tend to become connected with the response of eating it.

Drives are linked with needs, where needs are defined as a lack or deficit in the organism, such as the *need* for food or the need for prestige and money. As a result, drives can be primary or secondary depending on the needs with which they are connected. Primary drives are those associated with physiological needs such as the need for food or water; secondary drives are conditioned to primary drives through contiguity – for example, the need for high grades or money.

As an intervening variable in Hull's system, drive corresponds to the input variable *drive condition*, which is defined by number of hours of deprivation. Hull identified two components of drive: the drive proper increases as a direct function of the length of deprivation, and the *inanition component* is recognition that drive decreases if deprivation (starvation) lasts too long.

Drive has three central functions in Hull's theory: (1) It provides for reinforcement, without which learning would not occur; (2) it activates habit strength – meaning that without drive, behavior will not take place even if there is a strong previously established habit ($_sH_R$); and (3) drive stimuli become attached to specific behaviors through learning. Otherwise, people might engage in completely inappropriate behavior. They might drink when hungry, eat when cold, or cover up when thirsty. Essentially, this distinctiveness of drive stimuli determines whether a response will be reinforcing.

We see later that research has established that even in animals, learning can occur in the absence of drive (when drive is defined in terms of deprivation). This observation does not necessarily invalidate Hull's system, although it does point to some of its inadequacies.

3. V

As Pavlov had demonstrated, the physical intensity of a stimulus increases the probability that a response will occur. This effect is manifested in the intervening variable **stimulus-intensity dynamism (V)**. In general, the more intense a stimulus, (meaning that V is higher), the more probable the response. Stimulus-intensity dynamism interacts with habit strength and drive to determine the likelihood of a response.

4. K

The symbol K in Hull's system stands for **incentive motivation**.[4] In motivational research, incentive motivation is defined in terms of the value the organism associates with different goals. Incentive motivation is determined by the amount of reward associated with a goal (W as an input variable). Hull added incentive motivation to his system as a result of some important experiments reported by Crespi (1942). These experiments made it apparent that drive (D) alone could not account for motivation. In Crespi's experiment, three groups of rats received different amounts of reward (food pellets) for running to a goal box. The fact that the rats that received the greatest reward ran faster than those that received less supports Hull's original notion that drive is reduced more by greater reward, hence leading to a stronger habit. But Crespi also found that when these three groups of rats were subsequently given an identical amount of reward, those that had previously had the least amount now ran fastest, whereas those who had received the greatest amount reduced their speed the most. As a result, Hull now had to modify his system to account for the fact that previous reinforcements can change the *incentive value* of subsequent rewards. *Incentive motivation* interacts with other intervening variables (including drive) to determine the probability that a response will occur.

---

[4] The old lady paused here. She said that some of you – actually, she said the brighter ones among you – might be interested in knowing why Hull chose the letter K for incentive motivation. She said I might want to tell you that he did so to honor his prize pupil, Kenneth Spence. Spence worked so closely with Hull in developing his theory that the system is often referred to not as Hull's theory but as the Hull–Spence system. She said those less bright wouldn't be interested in this little historical footnote. I defended you, said there weren't likely any of you noticeably less bright. The old lady yawned and said nothing for a long time. I thought she might be going to sleep. Then she continued.

5. $_sE_R$

The four intervening variables described thus far ($_sH_R$, D, V, and K) compose the most important term in the equation Hull used to determine the probability that a stimulus would lead to a response. That probability is called **reaction potential** ($_sE_R$) and leads to the formula: $_sE_R = {_sH_R} \times D \times V \times K$. Reaction potential, sometimes called *excitatory potential*, is essentially a measure of the potential that a stimulus has for eliciting a specific response. As the formula indicates, this potential will depend on how many times the stimulus has been paired with the response and with reinforcement, how intense it is, how great the reward, and how strong the drive (in other words, $_sE_R = {_sH_R} \times D \times V \times K$).

Decreased drive after too many hours of deprivation (or satiation)

Because reaction potential is a multiplicative function of these variables, if the value for any of them is zero, reaction potential will also be zero. In practical terms, what this means is that in the absence of drive, it makes no difference how intense the stimulation, how great the reward, or how strong the habit, the response (R) will not occur. Similarly, in the absence of the appropriate stimulus at sufficient intensity, a reaction won't occur; if there is no reward, there will be no response; without an appropriate previously learned habit, the organism will not respond.

To illustrate, consider the case of Emanuel, who finds himself at a table on which is set a variety of appetizing dishes. If he has just eaten, drive (D) might be at or near zero and he might not touch a single dish despite the fact that the stimulus (V), the reward (K), and the habit ($_sH_R$) are all very strong. By way of further illustration, consider the other possibilities: The food is an especially rank presentation of some nameless dead thing (K = 0); Emanuel is blindfolded and his nose is plugged (V = 0); or he has never learned to eat by himself, having always had servants to feed him ($_sH_R = 0$). In none of these cases will the eating response occur.

Note that the probability of responding ($_sE_R$) is a multiplicative function of drive, habit strength, and so on. What this means is that identical changes in one of these variables will have different absolute effects depending on the values of the other variables. For example, doubling drive will make a greater difference if habit strength ($_sH_R$) is already large than if it is small. Put another way, increasing the motivation of a professional golfer should have more effect on her score than increasing that of a rank amateur.

The significance of the magnitude of reaction potential in this system is that a minimum amount of potential is required before behavior will take place. Increasing reaction potential will be reflected in shorter response latency ($_st_R$) (less of a time lapse between the stimulus and the response), more response amplitude (A) (a stronger response), and longer extinction time

(n) (longer time lapse before the organism no longer responds to the stimulus). All of these are characteristics of the output end of Hull's equation.[5]

Output Variables: Responses

The response variables of interest to Hull are the three just mentioned. They include the time lapse between the presentation of the stimulus and the appearance of the response (**response latency**, $_st_R$), the physical amplitude of the response (**response amplitude, A**), and the number of nonreinforced responses that would occur before extinction (**extinction rate, n**). Hull believed that response latency would decrease with increasing reaction potential. That is, the response would occur more rapidly. At the same time, both resistance to extinction and amplitude of response would increase with higher reaction potential.

Put simply, Hull's basic formula for predicting output specified that if reaction potential – which is the product of habit strength, drive, stimulus-intensity dynamism, and incentive motivation – is higher than a threshold (called a **reaction threshold [SLR]**), then a response will occur.

Symbol shock

Hull's Summary Equation Illustrated

To clarify Hull's basic summarizing equation (if $_sE_R [= (_sH_R \times D \times V \times K)] > _sL_R$, then R), consider the following:

Under a given set of circumstances, Willy might go to the movie now playing down the street. Or he might not. In the formula, going to the movie is the response (R). Willy will go to

---

[5] At this point in earlier editions, there appeared in bold print, page center, the expression: ~~BULLSHIT~~. An accompanying footnote explained: "The indelicate expression (delicately crossed out) is not a description of content but simply an antidote to the symbol shock that might by now have overcome the careful reader." When she got to this point, Old Lady Gribbin said, "I've taken it out, you know, your indelicate expression, the one you got away with for several decades now. You should pay more attention to your reviewers." Then, she quoted from the reviewer of the second edition, who said, "This is probably not as exciting now as it might have been in the first edition," and from a third edition reviewer who said, "This strikes me as out of place in a textbook." And she began to quote from another reviewer who said she was deeply offended, but I said, hey, wait, the expression wasn't meant to excite students or to offend them so much as to startle them out of their symbol shock – a sort of shock therapy. And she said, well, it's gone, and besides, that wasn't a very intelligent cure for symbol shock and then she started to read the seventh edition out loud once more without explaining what a good cure for symbol shock might be.

the movie if *reaction potential* ($_sE_R$) is large enough – that is, if it is greater than some threshold (the reaction threshold, represented by $_sL_R$ in the equation). If it isn't large enough, well, he won't go to the movie.

So, what determines if the reaction potential is large enough? Four main factors: First, is Willy in the habit of going to movies? Because if he has gone very often in the past and enjoyed himself when he went (that is, he has been *reinforced* for going to the movies), then the strength of his going-to-the-movies habit is probably much higher than that of, say, Roberto, who seldom goes because he unintentionally wet his pants during *Satan's Slaves*. The strength of the going-to-the-movies habit is represented by the symbol $_sH_R$.

But, of course, the habit of going to the movies is not the only factor that will determine whether Willy or Roberto go to the movies. If Willy has often been reinforced for going to movies, he may be more highly motivated to go again. Put another way, he will be more *driven* in that direction. In Hull's equation, the relevant *drive*, represented by the symbol D, will be high. Roberto's drive may be a lot lower, given his past experiences. But if Roberto's mother, anxious to get him out of the house, offers him a crisp hundred dollar bill to abandon his video games and go to the movies, his drive might suddenly increase dramatically.

Another factor that might come into play is the extent to which the movie has been advertised, the compelling features of the marquee, the word-of-mouth reports about the movie, what Rotten Tomatoes reviewers have said, or the presentation format of the movie. These might all contribute to the intensity of the "movie" stimulus, which is what Hull refers to as *stimulus-intensity dynamism* (V). That the movie is in 3D might well increase Willy's desire to see the movie.

Drive alone, explained Hull, cannot account for motivation. That is, immediate reward, which determines drive, interacts with previous reward to determine *incentive motivation* (K). Given his previous movie-going experiences, if Roberto expects to get a lot of pleasure out of watching the movie now playing, he will be highly *motivated* to go. But if Roberto anticipates little enjoyment from watching the movie, his *incentive* to go will be much lower.

So, given his strong going-to-the-movies habit, high drive, a compelling movie, and a history of enjoying movies, Willy is far more likely to go to this movie than is Roberto. But going to the movies requires effort and money. And maybe Willy has been going so often lately that he is almost tired of movies. Also, there might be other attractions, like Ramona, competing for Willy's time and attention. All these reduce Willy's desire to go to the movie; they are among the *inhibitory* influences that, according to Hull, subtract from reaction potential. If what is left of reaction potential (Hull called this the **net reaction potential**) is larger than the *threshold* value ($_sL_R$), then Willy will go to the movies. And so will Roberto – that is, if his *net reaction potential* is larger than his *threshold*.

Note how this is very much the kind of mathematical formula that a logic machine charged with predicting human behavior might produce. In fact, Hull was very interested in robotics and actually designed a type of computer to sort and score some of his tests.

Not surprisingly, Hull's main problem turned out to be the near impossibility of arriving at precise mathematical functions for each of the variables in the equation. So, even though we can more or less understand how Willy's and Roberto's decision to go or not to go to the movies is affected by each of Hull's variables, we still are not in a position to plug values into the formula and generate a hard prediction.

Still, the system has stimulated an enormous amount of research and led Hull to develop several additional concepts, two of the most important of which are *fractional antedating goal reactions* and *habit-family hierarchies*. These concepts represent significant departures from theories that had preceded Hull.

Fractional Antedating Goal Reactions

Recall that Hull's major explanation for learning is reinforcement. Specifically, he maintains that reinforcement consists of drive reduction, where a drive is a powerful urge or tendency. Hunger and thirst are clear examples of drive. The ordinary way of reducing a drive is to attain a goal or, in Hull's words, to make a *goal reaction*. Goal reactions, as described by Hull, are often responses of consuming (for example, eating or drinking; termed *consummatory responses*). A **fractional antedating goal response (rG)** (called *little r g*) is a conditioned response made by an organism before the actual goal reaction. One of Hull's examples is that of a rat that has learned that there is food at the end of a maze. Through conditioning, the rat's goal reaction (eating) has become linked with the food box as well as with various other stimuli that are also present, such as other sights and smells. Hull suggested that because many of these smells and sights are also found in other parts of the maze, the rat's antedating goal responses might eventually occur when it is first put into the maze. Although overt behaviors might be associated with these reactions, such as the rat licking its chops, fractional antedating goal responses are conditioned *internal* responses.

These antedating (Hull sometimes called them *anticipatory*) responses are important because they serve as stimuli that maintain behavior toward a goal. It is as though there are strings of associated stimuli (little sG) and responses (little rG) (labeled rG–sG) that precede goal reactions. In this sense, they serve the same purpose as Guthrie's MPS. But, unlike MPS, rG–sG are linked with reinforcement and therefore become rewarding.

Foresight and Expectancy

Perhaps most significant, Hull's notions of antedating goal response foreshadowed some fundamental cognitive notions. In effect, what Hull attempted to do with rG–sG was explain in a precise, measurable way behaviors that most people might explain using more vague mentalistic terms such as "knowing" or "anticipating." It was a clever and distinctive contribution to the development of learning theory.

Even though he was determinedly behavioristic, Hull could hardly avoid the use of nonbehavioristic ideas. In a section of his 1952 book entitled *Terminal Notes: Foresight, Foreknowledge, Expectancy and Purpose*, he admits that "since time out of mind, the ordinary man has used the words expect, expectation, expectancy, and expectative in a practically intelligent and intelligible manner" (Hull, 1952, p. 151). Hull goes on to explain that although the fractional antedating goal response is a conditioned mechanism, because it occurs before a response, it "constitutes on the part of the organism a molar foresight or foreknowledge of the not-here and the not-now. It's probably roughly equivalent to what Tolman has called 'cognition'" (p. 151).

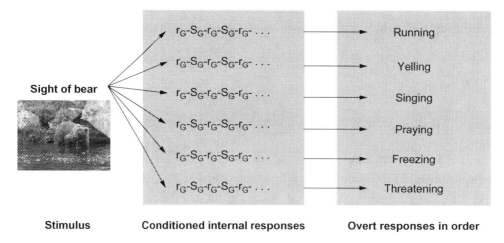

Figure 3.6 A hypothetical habit-family hierarchy. The stimulus input "bear" can lead to a number of different responses associated with the goal of not being molested by this animal. Each is linked to the stimulus "bear" by a chain of conditioned internal responses (called fractional antedating goal responses) arranged hierarchically in terms of the individual's previous learning history. The preferred response – that which is highest in the hierarchy – is the one that has become associated with a higher probability of being reinforced (that is, of leading to the desired goal). So, the individual is most likely to run. If that is impossible (his "friends" have tied him to a tree), he'll yell. If they've also gagged him, he may resort to praying silently.

What Hull was trying to do was to show that it is possible to predict behaviors without resorting to subjective definitions and interpretations. Thus, in a sense, his fractional antedating goal responses are objective, behavioristic ways of accounting for intention and expectancy and even purpose. Although the term *purpose* "has a bad metaphysical history," he wrote, "it represents an undoubted aspect of mammalian behavior" (Hull, 1952, p. 151).

Habit-Family Hierarchies

In the course of learning, or acquiring habits (S–R bonds), an individual will learn a number of different responses for the same stimulus. And in many cases, each response will lead to the same goal. These alternative responses constitute a **habit-family hierarchy** (see Figure 3.6). They are referred to as a *family* because they are related to the same goal and therefore share common fractional antedating goal reactions ($_rG$); they are a *hierarchy* because one alternative will usually be preferred over another, presumably because it has been rewarded more often in the past, and as a result, the reaction potential ($_sE_R$) associated with it is higher. Thus, in the hypothetical habit-family hierarchy shown in Figure 3.6, all responses are related to escaping the danger associated with the stimulus "bear." The most probable response for this individual, running, has presumably been most reinforced in the past.[6]

---

[6] Here, Mrs. Gribbin stopped reading from her notes. Listen, she said to me, I didn't want to explain this any further because we'd be getting ahead of ourselves. But for sure some of your big-brained students will be asking themselves what the devil happens if this is the first time you come across a bear and therefore you've never been reinforced one way or another in that

Summary and Appraisal of Hull's System

At first glance, Hull's behavioristic system might seem overly abstract and difficult. However, its most important ideas can be explained clearly and simply. Basically, the theory says that behavior is lawful and predictable.

Hull believed, as did Thorndike and Guthrie, that an organism placed in the same situation on different occasions will generally respond in the same way each time. If the response is different but the situation is identical, it simply means that the organism has changed. The main purpose of the theory is to discover the relationships that exist between stimuli (input variables) and responses (output) so as to be able to predict output given knowledge about input. This aspect of the system is clear and simple; more complex are the mathematical formulas Hull invented to describe links between input and output variables.

One of the important criteria we have been employing to evaluate psychological theories concerns the extent to which the theory reflects the facts. In one sense, the "facts" of psychological theories are the observations on which the theories are based. To the extent that Hull's system reflects valid observations about input and output, it does reflect the facts well. But at another level, the system deals with hypothetical entities – entities that cannot be observed. That is, much of Hull's system consists of what are termed **logical constructs**. Logical constructs are entities that are inferred: They follow logically from what is observed but cannot themselves be observed or measured. Thus, *reaction potential*, *reaction threshold*, *incentive motivation*, *habit strength*, and the raft of other related "intervening" variables cannot be shown to be facts. This does not mean that they are invalid or that inferred entities have no place in psychological theorizing – quite the contrary. Logical constructs, like other theoretical "truths," should be judged by their usefulness.

So, are Hull's intervening variables useful? Clearly, within the system itself, they are immensely useful in providing a compelling logic that is the hallmark of the system. That they contribute new explanations of human behavior, that they lead to more accurate predictions than would otherwise be the case, that they are clear and understandable, and that they are based on few unverifiable assumptions is not nearly so apparent.

Ironically, then, despite the impressive logic and mathematics that are fundamental to the Hull system, the theory does not fare particularly well with respect to some of our criteria. But Hull's system contributed in many tangible ways to the advancement of psychological theory. First, introducing concepts such as *fractional antedating goal reactions* foreshadowed more cognitive concerns. The concept smacks of intention or purpose, and intention is an important variable in many cognitive theories of learning and motivation.

Second, Hull's insistence on precision, rigor, and quantification, as well as his emphasis on logical consistency, have profoundly influenced how psychological investigations are conducted. These emphases are well illustrated in a large variety of experiments in which Hull systematically compared abilities of hypnotized and awake patients in an attempt to refute

---

situation, either for running or singing or praying or what-have-you. I said yes, that's a good point. Then the old lady said, "Well, tell them, if they haven't already figured it out, that reinforcement doesn't always have to be direct. Tell them ..." Old Lady Gribbin interrupted herself. "On second thought," she said, "they can wait until Chapter 10 to find out about vicarious reinforcement and learning through observation." And then she continued reading.

current misconceptions. These experiments resulted in a major book on hypnosis (Hull, 1933). Decades later, researchers still consider Hull "one of the giants in the world of hypnosis" (Willmarth, 2015, p. 373). Mohl (2012) also notes that many of Hull's typically thorough and highly controlled investigations in hypnosis have led to experimental methods and to conclusions that are still valid, and that many of those experiments should now be replicated. It is perhaps Hull's insistence on systematic experimentation and the application of logic that most sets his system apart from that of other learning theorists, and these are among his greatest contributions.

Third, Hull, along with Thorndike and Skinner, is often credited with popularizing and systematizing the notion that reinforcement is one of the most important forces in shaping behavior. In this sense, these theories involve a Darwinian sort of natural selection: Responses that are accompanied by favorable consequences tend to become more frequent; other responses eventually disappear. It is a principle of natural selection whereby the "fittest" behaviors are those that are reinforced and therefore survive. As McDowell, Caron, Kulubekova, and Berg (2008) explain, it is as though a population of potential behaviors is selected and evolves as a result of environmental pressures related to the consequences of the behavior.

In summary, Hull significantly influenced the development of psychology. In fact, for many years, he was seen as the leading proponent of systematic theories of behavior. As Mills (1998) notes, Hull was very ambitious and very interested in his own personal success as the main spokesman and developer of a complete theory of behavior. At the same time, he was apprehensive, and perhaps a little upset, at the apparent popularity and success of the Gestalt psychologists (which we discuss in Chapter 6). "These gestalt people are so terrifyingly articulate," he wrote in a letter to his student and collaborator, Kenneth W. Spence. "Practically every one of them writes several books. The result is that whereas they constitute a rather small portion of the psychological population of this country, they have written ten times as much in the field of theory as Americans have" (reported by Mills, 1998, p. 112).

Webster and Coleman (1992) note that for about a dozen years following the publication of *Principles of Behavior*, Hull was one of the most influential of all American psychologists. But Hull provided very little research to validate his theories and support his corollaries. By the late 1950s, his influence had diminished dramatically, perhaps because no one had yet succeeded in plugging values into the basic Hullian formulas and predicting with anything approaching machine-like accuracy what the organism would do in various situations. Perhaps it should not be surprising that subsequent theories of learning have typically been much smaller in scope and ambition.

EDUCATIONAL IMPLICATIONS OF THORNDIKE AND HULL

As we noted, Thorndike almost single-handedly defined and established educational psychology. Also, he popularized the use of tests and statistical methods in education as well as in psychology. Moreover, he changed child psychology into an objective discipline. Thorndike and Hull conducted many experiments on learning. It is hardly surprising that their theories should have important educational implications.

Perhaps more than anything else, their recognition of the importance of the consequences of behavior profoundly affected practices in schools. For example, Thorndike's theory stresses that rewards and punishments need to follow correct trials and that they also have to be tailored to the situation. Among other things, the child's readiness needs to be considered.

Thorndike's subsidiary laws also stress the importance of taking students' attitudes into consideration, the value of drawing attention to the most important aspects of a situation, and the worth of teaching for transfer (for generalization). Thorndike suggested that teachers can facilitate transfer by pointing out how different situations are similar.

Although Hull's theory is not so clearly directed at improving educational practice, he is largely credited with popularizing the notion that reinforcement is centrally involved in learning. As we see in Chapter 4, Skinner expanded this notion into an enormously influential system.

Main Point Chapter Summary

1. Thorndike's theory is based partly on his attempts to determine whether animals think – whether they are intelligent in human terms. That they seem to solve problems through *trial and error* rather than through sudden *mental insights* led him to his theory of trial-and-error connectionism.

2. The two main behavioristic explanations for the formation of relationships between stimuli (S–S), between responses (R–R), or between stimuli and responses (S–R) are contiguity and reinforcement. The contiguity explanation maintains that the co-occurrence of the events in question is sufficient; the reinforcement position takes into consideration the consequences of behavior. Watson, Pavlov, and Guthrie were contiguity theorists; reinforcement is central in Thorndike's and Hull's theories, as well as in that of B. F. Skinner.

3. Thorndike described learning as involving the "stamping in" of bonds (connections) between neural events corresponding to stimuli and responses. Forgetting involves "stamping out" of bonds.

4. Thorndike's major contribution to learning theory is the law of effect. It specifies that the effect of a response is instrumental in determining whether it will be learned. After 1930, he stressed that satisfiers (defined objectively as that which the organism does nothing to avoid instead doing things to maintain or renew the situation) are much more effective in stamping in responses than annoyers (that which the organism tries to avoid or not repeat) are in stamping them out. Before 1930, he also believed that repetition (the law of exercise) was important, but he rejected this notion after 1930.

5. Readiness was an important part of Thorndike's pre-1930 system (when an organism is ready to learn, to do so is satisfying; not to do so is annoying); belongingness (things that are seen as belonging together are learned more readily) became more important after 1930.

6. The most important of Thorndike's subsidiary laws is the *law of multiple responses* (learning occurs through trial and error). Other laws state that culture and attitude affect

behavior, that people are selective in responding (prepotency of elements), that behavior is generalizable (response by analogy), and that stimulus substitution or transfer occurs (associative shifting).

7. Among Thorndike's most important contributions is his emphasis on the importance of the consequences of behavior, the popularization of the use of animals in psychological research, and a determined attempt to apply psychological principles to real problems, particularly in the area of education.

8. Hull's analysis of behavior is a highly formalized attempt to account for behavior by attempting to describe the precise relationships thought to exist between input, intervening, and output variables. This hypothetico-deductive system is based on 17 laws (called *postulates*) from which more than 100 theorems and many corollaries are derived.

9. The major Hullian variables and the relationships that exist between them is given by the equation $_sE_R = {}_sH_R \times D \times V \times K$. It reads: Reaction potential (the probability that a response will occur) is the product of habit strength (the number of times a stimulus–response link has been reinforced), drive (the individual's motivation evident in the strength of the urge to respond based on unsatisfied needs), stimulus-intensity dynamism (the physical intensity of the stimulus), and incentive motivation (the value to the organism of the goal). If reaction potential (the tendency to respond) is greater than a threshold value, a response occurs.

10. Two Hullian concepts of special significance in the development of learning theories are fractional antedating goal responses (little rG) and habit-family hierarchies. Fractional antedating goal responses are sequences of internal responses that precede reaching a goal and thus become conditioned. In Hull's system, they're seen as strings of internal stimuli and responses (labeled sG–rG sequences). Habit families are hierarchical arrangements of habits that are related because they have common goals.

11. The concept of fractional antedating goal responses illustrates Hull's belief that it is possible to predict and explain behaviors by using precise, quantifiable notions without resorting to mentalistic and unquantifiable terms. In a sense, these are behavioristic definitions of cognitive concepts such as expectancy or purpose.

12. Despite the impressive mathematics and logic of Hull's system, it has not resulted in useful predictions of behavior. Nevertheless, its contribution to the further development of learning theories is vast. In addition, Hull's work profoundly influenced how psychological investigations are conducted (emphasis on objectivity and experimentation), and he is credited with popularizing the notion that reinforcement is important in learning.

4 Operant Conditioning

Skinner's Radical Behaviorism

CHAPTER OUTLINE

This Chapter	112
Objectives	113
Radical Behaviorism: An Antitheory?	113
An Overview of Radical Behaviorism	114
Reinforcement and Punishment	120
Positive and Negative Reinforcement	122
Punishment	122
Illustrations of Reinforcement and Punishment	123
Primary and Secondary Reinforcers	125
Schedules of Reinforcement	125
Continuous or Intermittent Reinforcement	126
Effects of Different Reinforcement Schedules	128
Concurrent Schedules of Reinforcement	133
Schedules of Reinforcement in Everyday Life	135
Shaping	136
Chaining	137
Shaping and Verbal Instructions in Human Learning	138
Fading, Generalization, and Discrimination	139
Relevance to Human Learning	139
Practical Applications of Operant Conditioning	141
Applications of Positive Contingencies	142
Applications of Aversive Contingencies	144
Other Applications: Behavior Management	147
Skinner's Position: An Appraisal	149
Contributions and Applications of Skinner's Theory	149
Evaluation as a Theory	150
Some Philosophical Objections	150
Main Point Chapter Summary	151

112 Operant Conditioning

It is dangerous and foolish to deny the existence of a science of behavior in order to avoid its implications.

B. F. Skinner (1973)

If people are good only because they fear punishment and hope for reward, then we are a sorry lot indeed.

Albert Einstein

I had agreed to meet Mrs. Gribbin after dark in the back room at the Social House, which Willy is willing to let us use if I'm discreet. There's a back door, which is handy.

Anxious to hear the fourth chapter, and especially curious about this thing called radical behaviorism, I scurried out from behind the hedgerow that borders the park behind Willy's. It was dark back there; somebody, I won't say who, has again shot out the light.

I reached for the door, grabbed the handle, started to turn it . . .

"Don't! They're here." The old lady had been waiting in the dark.

"Who?" I asked, but I already knew.

"We have to go right now," she hissed.

I followed her back beyond the hedgerow and we snaked, hunched over, through the long grass down to the river, where she had tied a boat. We clambered in and pushed out into the current and drifted soundlessly downstream and suddenly Old Lady Gribbin held in her hand a strange tiny light that cast a bluish glow on the stack of pages already spread on her lap and I saw that Schrödinger was there next to her in the boat, but where had he come from?

"We have to hurry," said the old lady, "Get all the chapters done. They're getting closer." How did she know? What did she know?

"What. . ." I started to ask, but she didn't let me finish.

"You won't be able to hide among your radical friends much longer," she said, motioning that I should turn on the recorder. And then she started reading Chapter 4.

THIS CHAPTER

Skinner was one of those, *said Mrs. Gribbin*, motioning that I should now turn on the recorder, that she wanted to record the next chapter. Skinner was a radical. Not like your friends, *she said*, explaining that this chapter deals with radical *behaviorism*, not with radical *misbehavior*, saying how Burrhus F. Skinner's radical behaviorism is undoubtedly the most influential and the best known of all the behaviorist positions. She predicted that some of you, when you finish this chapter, will have been converted to radical behaviorism, saying it almost as though it might be some form of religion.[1]

---

[1] "Don't look so confused," said Old Lady Gribbin, turning from her notes. "I don't mean radical like Skinner was a wild revolutionary bent on vandalizing and looting other people's theories and maybe burning them." She said Skinner used the description in a 1945 article where he was insisting that to be a science, psychology must deal only with public events. In

Objectives

The old lady said to tell you that you would know this has happened when the dreams – perhaps even the nightmares – that awaken you in the night are no longer about the lotteries you fantasize winning or the dramas of which you are the perpetual hero. They will deal instead with the following:

- respondents and operants;
- the basics of operant learning;
- effects of different schedules of reinforcement;
- the nature and uses of non-corporal punishment;
- why opiates make good reinforcers;
- possible origins of superstitious behaviors;
- what's meant by terms such as *fading*, *generalization*, *discrimination*, *aversive control*, and *rat*.

RADICAL BEHAVIORISM: AN ANTITHEORY?

That Skinner even has a theory may seem strange and inaccurate to some, given that he is widely considered to have been deliberately antitheoretical. In 1950, he wrote an article entitled "Are Theories of Learning Necessary?" (Skinner, 1950). His answer, in one word, was "no." In a later article, he declared that theories, although they could be amusing to their creators, were of little practical value (Skinner, 1961).

Hordes of Skinner's critics – and supporters too – concluded that Skinner was against all theories, that he had, as Westby (1966) put it, developed the "Grand Anti-Theory." Skinner disagreed. "Fortunately I had defined my terms," he said of his original article (Skinner, 1969, p. vii). The type of theory he objected to is expressed very clearly in that article: "Any explanation of an observed fact which appeals to events taking place somewhere else."

As an example of the kind of theorizing to which he most strongly objected, Skinner (1969) described an educational film he had recently seen. To illustrate a reflex, this film showed electrical impulses (which looked like flashes of lightning) running up neural pathways and finally appearing on a television screen in the brain. A little man in the brain would then burst into action, pulling a lever that sent return flashes of lightning scurrying down the neural pathways to muscles, which then responded to complete the reflex.

This is similar to a very old explanation for human behavior that dates back to the ancient Greeks, who attributed behavior to a little **homunculus** – a little man inside the big man (or woman, presumably). In Skinner's view, psychological theorizing often takes the form of inventing "little men" in the brain: for example, Freud's notions of the subconscious or cognitive psychology's descriptions of mental maps or other unobserved "fictions" (Skinner's term).

---

this sense, radical means *root*. What Skinner was saying was that public events rather than mental states are the root of psychology. But, *said the old lady*, this doesn't mean denying the private event. Thus, a toothache may be private, but it's also an actual physiological stimulus. The label *radical behaviorism* is commonly used to distinguish between Skinner's behaviorism and that of other theorists who weren't nearly as insistent as Skinner on not making inferences about mental states. Most specifically, the old lady explained, it draws an unmistakable distinction between Skinner's theory and Tolman's *purposive* behaviorism – which is discussed in Chapter 6.

These are misleading and wasteful, Skinner claims; they suggest mysterious intellectual activities and do little to advance science. Behavior, he claims, should be studied and explained in the most direct way possible. "Behavior is one of those subject matters," says Skinner, "which do not call for hypothetico-deductive methods. Both behavior itself and most of the variables of which it is a function are usually conspicuous" (1969, p. xi).

Accordingly, Skinner was not antitheoretical. Rather, what he was opposed to were theories based on speculation about unobservable events and processes. In fact, his acceptance of the central function of theories could scarcely be more explicit: "A theory," he insisted, "is essential to the scientific understanding of behavior as a subject matter" (Skinner, 1969, p. viii). His point is simply that theory should be limited to an effort to understand and organize relationships and events that can be observed. The emphasis of radical behaviorism, as Burgos (2016) points out, is on the practical usefulness of the science of human behavior rather than on testing formal theories. Skinner's approach, in Burgos' words, is "antidualistic and antimentalistic" (2016, p. 1). It is antidualistic in that it rejects the notion that it is useful to separate matter or existence into that which is physical and the nonphysical. And, by the same token, since it rejects the nonphysical, it also rejects the notion that it might be useful to consider events that are purely mental; hence the antidualism and antimentalism of radical behaviorism.

An Overview of Radical Behaviorism

While Skinner's radical behaviorism objected to theories that appeal to unobservable states of affairs or events, it clearly did not deny the existence and importance of unobserved behavior such as thinking, feeling, and other private events (Skinner, 1953). What it rejected was the usefulness of attempting to explain behavior by reference to these unobservable events. For example, he thought Hull's use of intervening variables wasteful and fruitless. Accordingly, there are two overridingly important characteristics of his radical behaviorism: (1) Explanations of behavior rely exclusively on directly observable phenomena, and (2) psychology is considered an objective science whose methods involve the analysis of behavior without appeal to subjective mental events or speculative physiological events.

Basic Assumptions

Skinner's theory is based on two fundamental assumptions. First, he believed that human behavior follows certain laws. Second, although psychology has typically looked for the causes of behavior *within* the person, Skinner started (and ended) with the absolute conviction that its causes are *outside* the person and that these can be observed and studied. What he was looking for was an understanding of the relations between the environment and the organism's behavior. Accordingly, Skinner's theory is the result of an objective search for the laws that govern behavior.

Interestingly, however, Skinner did speculate that his science of behavior could, and should, be widely applied to solve society's ills. As a result, his main critics are those who object to the *control* that applying Skinner's principles implies. As Skinner puts it, "It is true that we can gain control over behavior only insofar as we can control the factors responsible for it" (1953, p. 21). Some critics fear that if science can explain and control all human behavior, the science can then

Radical Behaviorism: An Antitheory? | 115

be misapplied. Others feel that the Skinnerian view of behavior as lawful and therefore explainable through laws makes humans less than they are, that at the very least, the belief that the laws of behavior apply equally to everyone ignores our differences: It robs us of our individuality and of our uniqueness. We look at these criticisms again toward the end of this chapter.[2]

BOX 4.1 Burrhus Frederic Skinner (1904–1990)

Credit: Bettmann / Getty Images. Getty Images 515355234

B. F. Skinner – he was called Fred; Burrhus was his mother's maiden name – is one of the giants of psychology. Only Freud is more readily recognized as an important psychological figure of the twentieth century (O'Donohue & Ferguson, 2001).

Skinner was born in Susquehanna, Pennsylvania, on March 20, 1904, to a staunchly Presbyterian family. His father was a successful, although largely self-taught, lawyer. His mother was an attractive woman who, Skinner claimed, always stood for 20 minutes after

Continued

---

[2] The old lady paused here. She said the biography would come next, explaining there was one for every major theorist in the book. She said biographies might not seem that important to some of you, but sometimes they are, that they're not just there to be interesting or inspiring. She explained that many psychologists think that people's personal lives often profoundly influence their professional lives. For example, Demorest and Siegel (1996; Siegel, 1996) made a detailed study of Skinner's life and of his autobiographical writings. Among other things, they suggest that Skinner's radical behaviorism is a sort of defense reaction that allowed him to cope with his failures – specifically, his apparent failure as a novelist following college.

BOX 4.1 (cont.)

every meal to maintain her figure and her posture. Skinner also confessed that he thought she was frigid.[3]

Skinner attended the same one-room school that both his parents had attended. As a child, he read a great deal, which may have contributed to his desire to become a novelist. He also displayed remarkable mechanical skills, building wagons, roller skates, scooters, gliders, rafts, and even musical instruments. He later put these skills to good use in devising and constructing the devices he later used in his experiments.

Like many of psychology's pioneers, when Skinner went to college, he did not intend to become a psychologist, majoring instead in English (Hamilton College in New York). At the end of his undergraduate career, he met Robert Frost, who read some of the things Skinner had written. Frost's suggestion that he might have some talent convinced Skinner he should be a novelist, so he asked his father to support him for a year while he wrote his first novel. His father reluctantly agreed, and Skinner spent what he was later to describe as "my dark year at Scranton" discovering that he had nothing to say. Subsequently, he undertook graduate studies at Harvard.

Skinner found psychology fascinating. From the very beginning, he was an avowed behaviorist who already dreamed of "making over the entire field to suit myself" (Skinner, 1979, p. 38). In 1931, he obtained his Ph.D. in psychology and spent the next five years doing research before beginning a career as lecturer, researcher, and writer (at the University of Minnesota, Indiana University, and Harvard University, in that order). Chief among his early works was *The Behavior of Organisms* (1938), which laid the groundwork for operant conditioning principles. A novel, *Walden Two* (1948), did much to popularize his conception of an ideal society based on scientific principles of human behavior and engineered in such a way that positive rather than aversive techniques of control would predominate. By the late 1950s, Skinner had become recognized as the leading proponent of the behaviorist position, a position that he continued to develop and defend throughout his life.

In addition to some 200 clearly written scholarly books and articles, Skinner wrote three autobiographical books totaling more than 1,000 pages (Skinner, 1976, 1979, 1983). (Based in part on Ewen, 2010; Goodwin, 2010; Hunt, 2007; Kincheloe & Horn, 2007).

The Experimental Analysis of Behavior

The causes of behavior, Skinner insisted, are outside the organism. The whole point of a science of human behavior, then, is to discover and describe the laws that govern interactions between the organism and the environment. To do so, the psychologist must specify three things:

---

[3] "Do we really care if Skinner thought his mother frigid?" asks Reviewer G, implying that this passage should be deleted. "Leave it in just the same," said Old Lady Gribbin, explaining that maybe that notion is somehow reflected in Skinner's operant conditioning.

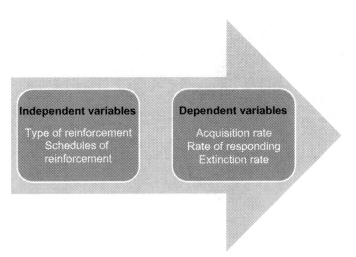

Figure 4.1 Skinner's investigations of operant conditioning looked at the relationships between variables under the control of the experimenter (independent variables) and the organism's behavior (dependent variables).

"(1) the occasion upon which a response occurs, (2) the response itself, and (3) the reinforcing consequences" (Skinner, 1969, p. 7).

Skinner describes his system as involving the **experimental analysis of behavior**. As an experimental analysis, it deals with two kinds of variables: independent variables (factors that can be directly manipulated experimentally, such as reinforcement) and dependent variables (the characteristics of actual behaviors, such as rate of responding). Dependent variables are not manipulated by the experimenter but are affected by the independent variables. The goal is to describe the laws that govern relationships between dependent and independent variables. Achieving this goal would make it possible to increase and refine control over dependent variables – in other words, to control behavior. The essential elements of the system, viewed as dependent and independent variables, are summarized in Figure 4.1.

Operant and Respondent Learning

In his attempts to explain behavior, Skinner had available the classical conditioning explanation that had already been proposed by Pavlov and elaborated by Watson and Guthrie. Although Skinner (1996) expressed considerable admiration for Pavlov, he believed that classical conditioning explained only a very limited variety of human and animal behaviors where the initial response can be elicited by a known stimulus. The learning that then occurs results from pairing this stimulus with another over a number of trials.

Although Skinner accepted this model as accurate for explaining some behavior, he insisted that many human responses do not result from obvious stimuli. Furthermore, the stimuli, whether observable or not, are often not important for an accurate and useful explanation of learning. "Reflexes, conditioned or otherwise," he explained, "are mainly concerned with the internal physiology of the organism. We are most often interested, however, in behavior which has some effect upon the surrounding world" (1953, p. 59).

Responses elicited by a stimulus are **respondents**. They are so labeled because the organism is responding (*reacting*) to the environment. Responses simply emitted by an organism are labeled **operants** because they are actions, or *operations*, performed on the environment. In a

Table 4.1 **Classical and operant conditioning**

Classical (Pavlov)	Operant (Skinner)
Deals with respondents that are elicited as responses to stimuli and appear involuntary	Deals with operants that are emitted as instrumental acts and appear voluntary
Type S (stimuli)	Type R (reinforcement)

sense, respondents correspond to involuntary behavior, whereas operants are more voluntary. However, Skinner probably would not have said this because the terms imply what he would have considered unnecessary speculation. We do not need to ask or wonder whether the organism wants or does not want to do something, Skinner insists; we need only note what it does, the circumstances under which it acts, and the consequences of its actions. The experimental analysis of behavior requires nothing more – or less – than the analysis of these three factors.

Skinner suggested that classical conditioning works only on respondent behavior. He called this type of learning *Type S* (for stimulus) conditioning. He advanced a different model to explain learning based on operant behavior: the model of **operant conditioning**. In a simplified sense, operant conditioning describes behavior change as a result of its consequences. Operant conditioning is also referred to as *Type R* (for response) conditioning or as *instrumental conditioning* because it is based directly on Thorndike's *law of effect* and its role in *instrumental* learning. As Skinner notes, "One of the first serious attempts to study the changes brought about by the consequences of behavior was made by E. L. Thorndike" (1953, p. 59). The distinctions between classical and operant conditioning are shown in Table 4.1.

Prevalence of Operant Behavior

Skinner (1938) believed that most of the important behaviors in which people engage are operant. Walking to school, texting or tweeting, answering a question, smiling at a stranger, scratching a cat's ears, fishing, driving a car, singing, and reading are all examples of operant behaviors. Even thinking is an operant, a covert (internal) form of verbal behavior. Although there might be some known and observable stimuli that reliably lead to some of these behaviors, the point is that stimuli are not central in any learning that takes place. What *is* central are the consequences of the behaviors.

The Influence of Charles Darwin and Edward Thorndike

Skinner's most important ideas owe much to Charles Darwin as well as to Edward Thorndike. In many ways, explained Skinner, learning seems to involve the selection of responses in much the same way as evolution involves the selection of characteristics. Darwin believed that in nature, all sorts of different traits appear over generations; forces of nature act to select those that contribute to survival, precisely because they do contribute to survival. Similarly, in behavior, all sorts of responses appear. Some have consequences that seem to benefit the organism; others do not. The effect of these consequences is that some responses are selected and others are eliminated (Leao, Laurenti, & Haydu, 2016).

That the consequences of behavior lead to the "stamping in" or "stamping out" of responses is the cornerstone of Thorndike's theory of trial-and-error learning. Skinner based his theory of operant learning on much the same idea. Briefly, operant learning is the survival (and death) of responses. "Both in natural selection and in operant conditioning," Skinner wrote, "consequences take over a role previously assigned to an antecedent creative mind" (1973, p. 264).

Pavlov's Harness and Skinner's Box

When Pavlov placed a dog in a harness and injected food powder into its mouth, the dog salivated. That is a clear and unambiguous example of a respondent: a stimulus reliably eliciting a predictable response.

In his investigations, Skinner used a dramatically different, highly innovative piece of equipment now known as a **Skinner box** (he called it an *operant conditioning chamber*).[4] The most typical of these conditioning chambers is a cage-like structure that can be equipped with a lever, a light, a food tray, a food-releasing mechanism, and perhaps an electric grid through the floor.

When a naïve rat is placed in a Skinner box, it does not respond as predictably and automatically as does the dog in the Pavlov harness. In fact, Gallo, Duchatelle, Elkhessaimi, Le Pape, and Desportes (1995) identified 14 distinct behaviors that a rat might display in this experimental chamber. For example, the rat might cower for a while and then it might sniff around the cage, occasionally rearing up on its hind legs to smell the bars and spending a little more time near the food tray as it senses the faint odors of some other rat's long-eaten reward. Eventually, the rat might happen to depress the lever, causing a food pellet to drop into the tray. The rat will eat this pellet and will again eventually depress the lever. And again and again until, finally, the rat runs straight to the lever whenever it is put into the cage. Its behavior has changed as a result of the behavior's consequences: The rat has been operantly conditioned.[5]

---

[4] Skinner was apparently not fond of being an eponym, Old Lady Gribbin said as an aside. But I'm still going to call it a Skinner box, she added, because that's what it's commonly called and that's what students understand. But *experimental conditioning chamber* would be preferable. Then she added, I know this might offend some of your more brilliant readers but maybe you should explain what the word *eponym* means. I expect you are all quite brilliant but to humor the old lady, I have included *eponym* in the glossary.

[5] Do you know about Skinner's baby crib? Old Lady Gribbin asked as an aside as we continued to drift down the river. I think I was going to say "Yes, I do," but she continued before I could answer. Well, it's wrong, she said, what they said about that baby crib. People misinterpreted an article that had appeared in *Ladies Home Journal* titled "Baby in a Box," and thought that Skinner had made a *Skinner box* for his daughter so he could control her environment and study her. That was all hogwash, said the old lady angrily. The truth is that his wife had asked him to make something safer than a crib for their daughter and he had invented this little heated enclosure with plexiglass windows – a wonderfully comfortable place for the baby to play and sleep. But rumormongers claimed that Skinner was experimenting with his daughter and that she grew up confused and melancholy and ended up taking her own life. Slater (2004) later described this misunderstanding and someone reviewing Slater's book misinterpreted the passage and reported it as though it were true – a rumor that was passionately rebutted by Skinner's very-much-alive daughter, Deborah.

Operant Learning

Stated very simply, the operant conditioning explanation says that when a reinforcer follows a response, the result will be an increase in the probability that this response will occur again under similar circumstances. Furthermore, the explanation states that the circumstances surrounding reinforcement may serve as a **discriminative stimulus (S^D)** that can come to have control over the response. Discriminative stimuli include those aspects of the environment that the organism can notice (can *discriminate*). As Skinner explains, "Most operant behavior acquires important connections with the surrounding world" (1953, p. 107). Thus, although operant learning depends on the consequences of a behavior, stimuli that accompany the behavior may become associated with it.

Unlike Thorndike's connectionism, Skinner's theory of reinforcement does not involve the formation of associations between stimuli and responses. In fact, Skinner took pains to point out that he was not an S–R theorist. By definition, an operant is never elicited. Thus, although the rat in the Skinner box might eventually learn to press the lever only when a light is turned on, this particular discriminative stimulus does not elicit bar-pressing, claims Skinner. It simply allows the rat to discriminate reinforcing situations from those that are not reinforcing.

Any behavior that is acquired because of reinforcement can be interpreted as an illustration of operant conditioning. Figure 4.2 shows one example.[6]

REINFORCEMENT AND PUNISHMENT

Skinner's explanation of learning through operant conditioning is based squarely on the notion that the consequences of behavior determine the probability that the behavior will occur again. This is very similar to Thorndike's belief that responses that lead to "satisfying states of affairs" are more likely to be learned. But determined as he was to be objective, Skinner had no place in his theory for subjective terms such as *satisfying* and *annoying*. Thus, Skinner defines a **reinforcer** as an event that follows a response and that changes the probability of a response occurring again. **Reinforcement** is simply the effect of a reinforcer.

This is a clear example of what is meant by an *operational* definition: Reinforcers are defined in terms of observable and measurable behaviors (or *operations*). One important advantage of defining terms operationally is that doing so makes it unnecessary to wonder about subjective states and to speculate about what is pleasant or unpleasant. Whether an event is reinforcing or not depends solely on its effects; the nature of the event and of the organism's emotional reaction to it are irrelevant. Thus, the same event might be reinforcing on one occasion but not on another – or for one individual, but not for another. In Skinner's words, "the only defining characteristic of a reinforcing stimulus is that it reinforces" (1953, p. 72).

---

[6] You can put in your own example, Old Lady Gribbin said. So, I did. When we were at Pigeon Lake, the old lady wouldn't let me fish (she said I had to take notes) and I saw how she stopped using the Wetaskiwin lure after she pricked herself a few times. And I also saw how her rod movements became progressively more agitated as she began to catch more fish. "Isn't your hand getting tired?" I asked. "I can fish for a while." "Why should it be tired?" she snarled. She wasn't even aware that the fish had shaped her behavior (see Figure 4.2.)

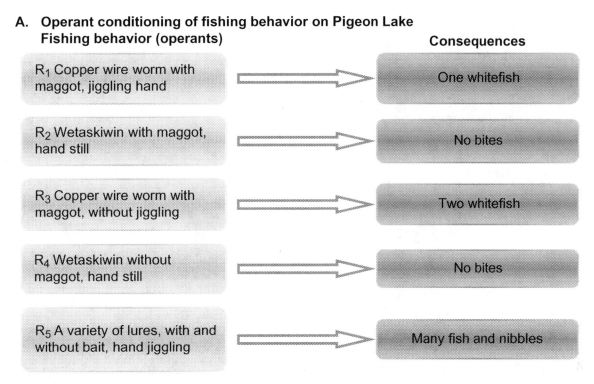

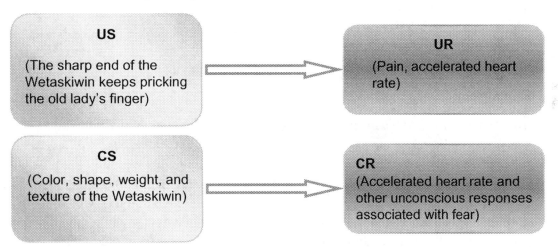

Figure 4.2 A classical (B) and an operant conditioning (A) explanation for changes in Mrs. Gribbin's fishing behaviors.

To illustrate, consider Henry, a freckle-faced, lovable little school child of 10. Henry takes a spelling test for which he has studied very hard by developing a number of mnemonic devices. For example, to remember how to spell *separate*, he talked himself into remembering that there is "a rat" in the word. He receives a score of 95 percent on his spelling test. This event serves as a reinforcer: It increases the probability that Henry will again use mnemonics.

Now consider Agnes, a bright little girl who always gets 100 percent in spelling without using mnemonic tricks. But this time she uses the same mnemonic device as Henry. Unlike Henry, though, she becomes confused, thinks there isn't "a rat" in separate and blows the word. Although she also receives a grade of 95 percent, this outcome is not a reinforcer for Agnes and may well have the opposite effect on her behavior.

Positive and Negative Reinforcement

Skinner distinguishes between two types of reinforcement: *positive* and *negative*. **Positive reinforcement** involves what Thorndike had labeled a "satisfying" consequence of a behavior. In behavioristic psychology, a consequence is more properly referred to as a **contingency** (a contingency is an outcome; that which follows behavior). Defined in objective Skinnerian terms, positive reinforcement occurs when the consequences of the behavior, when added to a situation after a response, increase the probability of the response occurring again in similar circumstances. In common speech, this type of reinforcement is similar to *reward*. It involves a positive contingency.

Negative reinforcement involves consequences that result in the elimination or prevention of what Thorndike would have labeled an "annoying" outcome. It occurs when the probability of a response occurring increases as a function of something being taken away or prevented. In everyday speech, negative reinforcement is similar to *relief*. It involves the removal of a negative contingency.

The effect of both positive and negative reinforcement is to increase the probability of a response's occurring. It is the effect of the outcome (of the contingency), not the nature of the stimulus itself, that determines whether it is reinforcing. Negative reinforcement should not be confused with punishment: Their effects are quite opposite.

Punishment

Like reinforcement, **punishment** is also defined by its effects. However, in this case, the effect is not a strengthening of the behavior, as it is for both negative and positive reinforcement, but its suppression or weakening.

In the same way as there are two types of reinforcers, positive (reward) and negative (relief), there are two types of punishment, each the converse of a type of reinforcer. One is the kind of punishment that occurs when a positive contingency is removed (what might be termed a *penalty* – sometimes referred to as *positive punishment*); the other, where a negative contingency follows a behavior, is what is more commonly thought of as punishment (sometimes referred to as *negative punishment*).

Punishment versus Negative Reinforcement

Because both often involve aversive consequences (negative contingencies), punishment and negative reinforcement are often confused, but they are really quite different. Negative reinforcement is a procedure that increases the probability of a behavior; punishment does

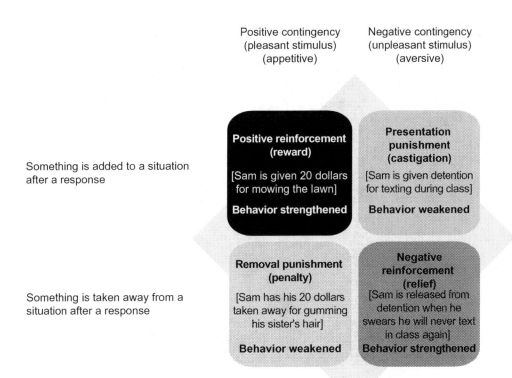

Figure 4.3 In the same way as there are two kinds of reinforcement (positive and negative), so too are there two kinds of punishment (presentation or castigation, and removal or penalty). Both positive and negative reinforcement have the effect of increasing the probability of a behavior; punishment is intended to have the opposite effect. Adapted from Lefrançois, G. R. (2018). *Psychology for Teaching* (2nd ed.). San Diego, CA: Bridgepoint Education, Fig. 5.7. Used by permission.

not. Consequently, negative reinforcement typically involves the termination of an event that might be considered aversive (the termination of a negative contingency); punishment involves introducing a negative contingency or terminating a positive (appetitive) one.

Any lingering confusion can easily be clarified by referring to Figure 4.3, which shows the four possibilities that result when either positive or negative contingencies (appetitive or aversive events) follow behavior or terminate following behavior. In everyday speech, these four possibilities represent reward (positive reinforcement), relief (negative reinforcement), castigation (one kind of punishment, sometimes called *presentation punishment*), or penalty (another kind of punishment, sometimes referred to as *removal punishment*). Each of these four possibilities is illustrated with a rat and then with a person in the following section.

Illustrations of Reinforcement and Punishment

The rat illustrations relate to the behavior of Arnold, a sophisticated white Norway rat in his Skinner box; the people illustrations refer to the behavior of Bill, a rambunctious toddler in his parents' house.

Positive Reinforcement (Reward)

If the consequences of Arnold pressing a lever in his Skinner box is that the food mechanism releases a pellet of food into the tray (positive contingency), the effect may be an increase in the probability that bar-pressing behavior will occur again. In this case, the food is a **positive reinforcer**; its effect is positive reinforcement. It leads to an increase in bar-pressing behavior.

If toddler Bill offers to kiss his mother one morning, and she praises him for this touching filial gesture, there may be an increase in the probability of this kind of behavior in the future. Mama's praise is a positive reinforcer.

Negative Reinforcement (Relief)

If the current is on continuously in the grid on the floor of the Skinner box but is turned off every time Arnold presses the lever (removal of negative contingency), there will again be an increase in the probability of bar-pressing behavior. Termination of the electric current is a **negative reinforcer**; its effect is negative reinforcement. Like positive reinforcement, it leads to an increase in the behavior that precedes it.

If Bill is isolated in his room while having a total meltdown (because his mother insists that no, he cannot sit on the cat like on a horse), allowing him to come out when he stops crying (melting) illustrates negative reinforcement. This event may increase the probability that he will stop crying when again in this situation.

Presentation Punishment (Castigation)

If Arnold, who must stand on the electric grid when he depresses the bar, is given a mild shock every time he does so, he will probably attempt to avoid the bar in the future (negative contingency). The shock in this case is one type of punishment (termed presentation punishment – commonly referred to as castigation). It may lead to what is termed **avoidance learning** (where the organism tries to avoid the situation associated with this negative contingency) or **escape learning** (where the organism, when placed in a situation previously associated with negative contingencies, tries to escape). It does not lead to an increase in the rat's bar-pressing behavior.

However, note that although the electric shock in this case serves as punishment for bar-pressing, it is also an example of negative reinforcement with respect to avoidance learning. That is, if the removal of the shock leads to an increase in avoidance behavior, it serves as negative reinforcement for that behavior. At the same time, if it leads to a decrease in bar-pressing, it serves as punishment for that behavior.

If toddler Bill kicks his sister in the posterior and she then turns around and whacks him on the side of the head, he may be less likely to kick her again in similar circumstances or places. The sister's whack is a castigation kind of punishment.

Removal Punishment (Penalty)

Once the rat has been trained, if the experimenter removes the food pellet (removal of a positive contingency) unless the rat gets to it within a specified time after pressing the lever, the rat may soon stop dawdling and licking its chops on the way to the food tray. In this illustration, removal of the food pellet is an example of punishment involving a penalty (sometimes called *removal penalty*). The responses being punished are those that delay the rat.[7]

If toddler Bill has his jelly beans taken away at lunchtime because he licked them, rubbed them on the wall, ground them into the floor, and then hurled them at his sister, this is an example of a penalty punishment. It might decrease the future probability of some of his jelly bean behaviors.

Primary and Secondary Reinforcers

In addition to distinguishing between positive and negative reinforcement, Skinner classifies reinforcers as being either primary or secondary. **Primary reinforcers** include events that are reinforcing without any learning having taken place. Examples of primary reinforcers are stimuli such as food, water, and sex, each of which satisfies basic, unlearned needs (primary needs).

Secondary reinforcers include events that are not reinforcing to begin with but become reinforcing as a result of being paired with other reinforcers. The light in the Skinner box is sometimes used as a secondary reinforcer. Suppose that over a succession of trials, the light is turned on every time the animal is fed (given a primary reinforcer). Eventually, the animal will respond simply to see the light go on. At this point, the light has acquired secondary reinforcing properties.

The expression **generalized reinforcer** is sometimes used to describe a learned (secondary) reinforcer that appears to reinforce any of a wide variety of seemingly unrelated behaviors. For humans, generalized reinforcers include money, prestige, power, fame, strength, intelligence, and a host of other culturally prized contingencies. These are extremely powerful in determining human behavior.

SCHEDULES OF REINFORCEMENT

To develop a science of behavior, Skinner insisted, the psychologist needs to observe what the organism does, under what circumstances, and to what effect. These are the basic units in the **experimental analysis of behavior**, the phrase often used to describe Skinner's emphasis on analyzing the objective variables involved in operant behavior. Specifically, these variables are what the organism does and what the consequences of that behavior are.

---

[7] This, Old Lady Gribbin admitted, is a hypothetical illustration. She said she could find no evidence in the literature that anyone had actually conducted this experiment. And she claimed she had no time to do it herself, that she was too busy with other far more important research. When I tried to ask what research, she quickly changed the subject.

126 **Operant Conditioning**

In the studies that proved most useful for developing Skinner's views of operant conditioning, rats depressed levers or pigeons pecked at disks. These are easily observed behaviors that Skinner could quantify by how rapidly they were acquired (acquisition rate), how many responses were emitted over a given period (rate of responding), and how long it would take for the responses to stop if reinforcement were discontinued (extinction rate). Recall that these represent *dependent* variables; they are not under the investigator's direct control.

Probably the most easily manipulated and most effective *independent* variable in operant conditioning is the way rewards are administered. In a carefully controlled laboratory situation, experimenters can determine precisely the *what*, *when*, and *how* of reinforcements. In other words, experimenters are in complete control of **schedules of reinforcement**.

Continuous or Intermittent Reinforcement

Basically, the experimenter has two choices: **continuous reinforcement**, in which case every desired response is reinforced; or **intermittent** reinforcement (or *partial reinforcement*), where reinforcement occurs only some of the time (see Figure 4.4). If reinforcement is continuous, there are no further choices to make; every correct response is rewarded in the same way. However, it is entirely possible to use a combination of continuous and intermittent reinforcement schedules. This type of arrangement is sometimes referred to as a **combined schedule**.

Interval or Ratio Schedules

If experimenters use an intermittent schedule of reinforcement, they can make one of two further choices. An intermittent schedule can be based on a proportion of responses (termed a **ratio schedule**) or on the passage of time (called an **interval schedule**). For example, a ratio schedule might reinforce one out of five desired responses; an interval schedule might provide reinforcement once every five minutes.

Fixed or Random Schedules

An experimenter using either of these intermittent schedules (ratio or interval) would further have to decide whether the reinforcement would be administered in a fixed or in a random (variable) way. A **fixed schedule** is one in which the exact time of reinforcement or the precise response that will be reinforced is predetermined and unchanging. For example, in a *fixed-ratio schedule*, reinforcement might occur after every fifth correct response. In *fixed-interval reinforcement*, the reinforcement will be available immediately after the next correct response as soon as the chosen time interval has elapsed.

Random schedules provide reinforcing events at unpredictable times. A random ratio schedule of reinforcement based on a proportion of one reinforcement for five correct responses might involve reinforcing the first four trials, not reinforcing the next 16, reinforcing numbers 21 and 22, not reinforcing the next eight trials, and so on. After 1,000 trials, 200 reinforcers would have been administered.

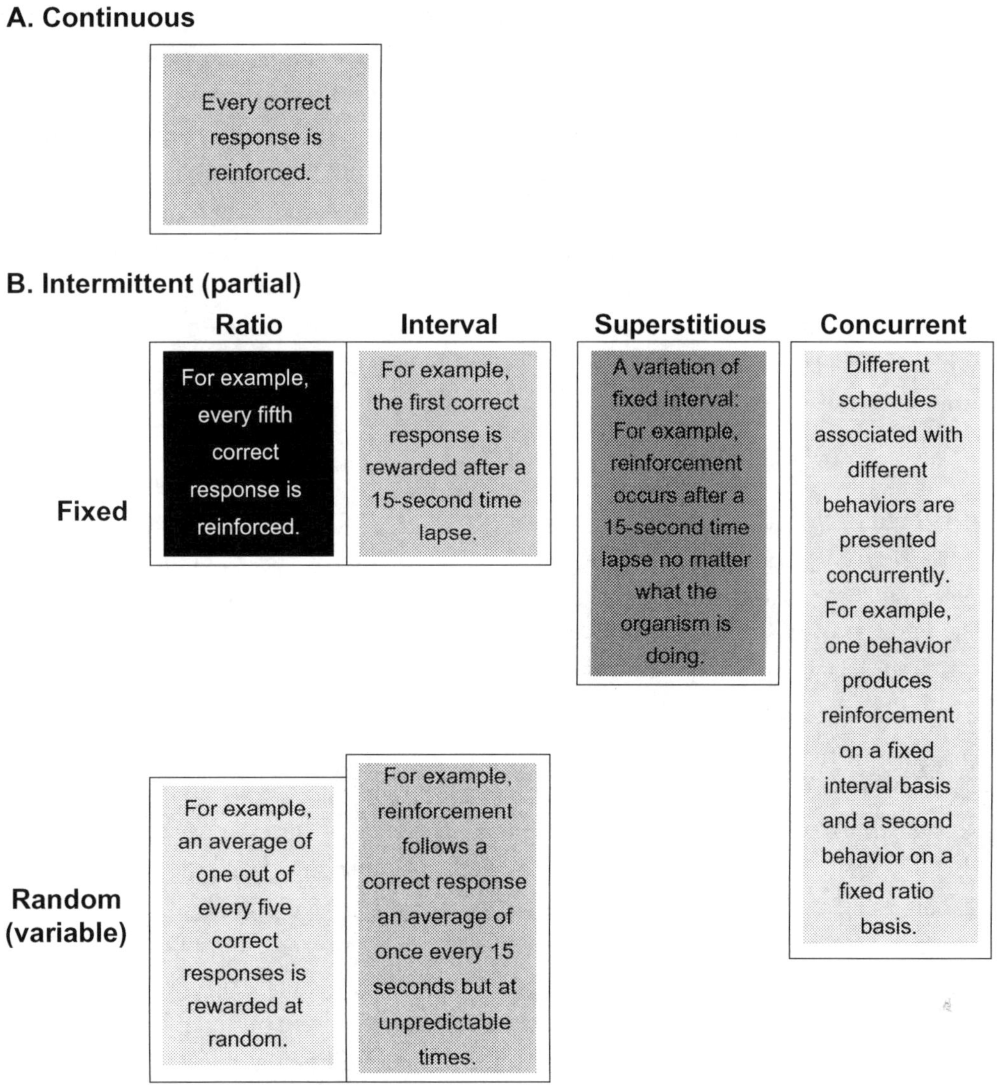

A. Continuous

> Every correct response is reinforced.

B. Intermittent (partial)

	Ratio	**Interval**	**Superstitious**	**Concurrent**
Fixed	For example, every fifth correct response is reinforced.	For example, the first correct response is rewarded after a 15-second time lapse.	A variation of fixed interval: For example, reinforcement occurs after a 15-second time lapse no matter what the organism is doing.	Different schedules associated with different behaviors are presented concurrently. For example, one behavior produces reinforcement on a fixed interval basis and a second behavior on a fixed ratio basis.
Random (variable)	For example, an average of one out of every five correct responses is rewarded at random.	For example, reinforcement follows a correct response an average of once every 15 seconds but at unpredictable times.		

Figure 4.4 In operant conditioning, each type of schedule tends to generate a predictable pattern of responding.

Superstitious Schedules

As noted earlier, the consequences of behavior can involve positive or negative contingencies. By definition, contingencies are consequences. Clearly, however, not all of the positive and negative events that follow behavior are actual consequences of that behavior. Put another way, in many cases, outcomes are *noncontingent*; their occurrence or their failure to occur has nothing to do with the organism's behavior.

A **superstitious schedule** of reinforcement is a special kind of noncontingent fixed interval schedule in which reinforcement occurs at fixed time intervals without the requirement that a correct response precede it. It follows from the law of operant conditioning that any behavior just before reinforcement is strengthened. "We must assume," Skinner explains, "that the presentation of a reinforcer always reinforces something, since it necessarily coincides with

Operant Conditioning

some behavior" (1953, p. 85). Whether the reinforcement is a consequence of the behavior is not always important. It seems that for humans and other animals, temporal contiguity alone is enough to establish a relationship between reinforcement and behavior.

There are many examples of superstitious behavior in experimental animals. In fact, it appears that in most conditioning sequences, there are behaviors that accidentally precede reinforcement and temporarily become part of the animal's repertoire. For example, a rat that has just learned to depress a lever may do so with its head always to the right or with its left leg always dangling. Both actions may be examples of superstitious behavior.

Skinner (1951) left six pigeons on a superstitious schedule overnight; they received reinforcement at fixed intervals no matter what they were doing. By morning, one bird regularly turned clockwise just before each reinforcement, another always pointed its head toward one corner, and several had developed unnatural swaying motions.

Skinner suggests that people often develop superstitious behaviors unconsciously. If you were holding your head just so when you were lucky enough to find a $50 bill, there may be a greater tendency for you to hold your head just so in other similar circumstances, no matter how inelegant the posture might be. For example, during a final exam, you might find students scratching their heads; others frown; some move their lips, hands, legs, or feet; some chew their hair; and others engage in a variety of bizarre behaviors not directly related to clear thinking.

Effects of Different Reinforcement Schedules

Responses like pressing a bar or pecking at a key are easily observed and measured. Displaying his boyhood mechanical skills, Skinner devised a simple and ingenious way of recording such responses by having a pen trace a line on a continually moving drum of paper. Every response (bar-press or key-peck) causes the pen to jump up one step, thus providing a **cumulative recording** of the number of responses on the y-axis (vertical axis). The rate of responding, which is the number of responses emitted during a fixed period of time, is indicated by the slope of the line; the faster the animal responds, the steeper will be the line. A line that stays parallel to the x-axis (horizontal axis) indicates that no response occurred during the period marked.

For example, Figure 4.5 shows a cumulative recording produced by Skinner (1938) of the bar-pressing responses of an initially untrained rat. In the training session, all lever-pressing responses were reinforced. Note how the first three reinforcements (responses – and hence reinforcements – are indicated by the first three upward steps in the recording) seemed to have little effect; the rat took almost two hours to press the lever three times. But immediately after the fourth reinforcement, the rate of responding zoomed upward so almost 100 responses were emitted within the next 30 minutes. When conditioning bar-pressing in rats, a maximum rate of responding is often reached in 30 minutes or less.

Magazine Training

The first step in teaching a naïve rat to depress a lever is to teach it where to go to get its reward. This procedure is called **magazine training**. For example, a typical magazine training session might involve the experimenter depressing a button that delivers a food pellet in the food tray.

Schedules of Reinforcements

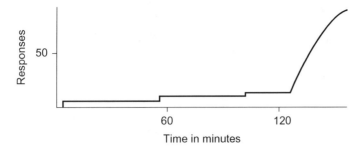

Figure 4.5 A cumulative recording showing the responses of an untrained (naïve) rat on a continuous schedule of reinforcement. Passage of time is shown on the *x*-axis; total number of responses on the *y*-axis. After four reinforcements, this rat's rate of responding, represented by the slope of the graph, increased dramatically. From *The Behavior of Organisms: An Experimental Analysis*, p. 67, by B. F. Skinner. Copyright © 1938 by Appleton-Century-Crofts. Reprinted courtesy of the B.F. Skinner Foundation.

Food delivery is usually accompanied by an audible click. The naïve rat is eventually drawn to the food tray, perhaps by the smell of the pellet. Now the experimenter presses the button again, the mechanism clicks, the pellet drops, and the rat goes for the reward. Within only a few trials, the rat normally goes directly to the food tray upon hearing the click. In Skinner's terminology, the click has become a *discriminative stimulus* that directs the animal toward the food tray. And now the animal is ready to be trained.

When training rats to press levers or pigeons to peck disks, Skinner typically deprived the animal of food for 24 or more hours (sometimes reducing its weight to 80 percent of normal) to increase the effectiveness of the reinforcer. And as we saw, initial training usually begins with "magazine training." After magazine training, all correct responses – and sometimes even responses that merely approximate the desired behavior – are reinforced.

In more recent studies using rats and other animals, opiates and other similar drugs are often used as reinforcers. Not only does this eliminate the need for magazine training, but it provides a very powerful and easily controlled source of reinforcement (for example, Chesworth, Brown, Kim, Ledent, & Lawrence, 2016; Hipolito et al., 2015).

Effects of Schedules on Response Acquisition

Initial learning is usually more rapid if every correct response is reinforced (a continuous schedule). In contrast, changes in responding appear to be haphazard and slow if any of the intermittent schedules of reinforcement are used.

Rate of responding – that is, the number of responses emitted in a given period – is one measure of operant learning. Another important measure is **extinction rate**, defined as the amount of time that passes before the organism stops responding after the withdrawal of reinforcement.

Effects of Schedules on Extinction

Interestingly, although a continuous schedule of reinforcement results in a faster **rate of learning** than does an intermittent schedule, it also leads to more rapid extinction after withdrawal. Furthermore, the fixed schedules of reinforcement, although they have shorter

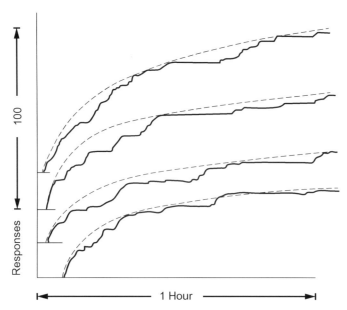

Figure 4.6 A cumulative recording showing four typical extinction curves. Note how rate of responding is high immediately after reinforcement stops (indicated by the steepness of the curve) and then occurs in sporadic outbursts until, less than an hour later, few responses still occur (curve is almost flat). From *The Behavior of Organisms: An Experimental Analysis*, p. 67, by B. F. Skinner. Copyright © 1938 by Appleton-Century-Crofts. Reprinted courtesy of the B.F. Skinner Foundation.

acquisition times associated with them than variable schedules, also lead to more rapid extinction than the variable schedules do. Hence, the best training combination for an animal is usually a continuous schedule initially, followed by a variable-ratio schedule

The ratio may also be varied over training sessions, with a decreasing ratio of reinforced to nonreinforced trials usually leading to even longer extinction periods. This situation defines what is termed a **progressive ratio (PR) schedule** of reinforcement. In PR reinforcement, the response requirements increase systematically during a session. That is, the organism needs to make an increasing number of correct responses to receive reinforcement

A large number of recent studies have investigated the rather complex effects of progressive ratio schedules. These often use touch screens rather than disks or levers and reinforcement is often in the form of self-injection of drugs following the animal's touch on the screen. Commonly used substances in these studies include amphetamines, Oxycontin, heroin, cocaine, methadone, nicotine, and other addictive or at least reinforcing preparations (for example, Hailwood, Heath, Robbins, Saksida, & Bussey, 2018; Powell et al., 2018). Many of these studies are directed toward increasing understanding of addiction; others are explorations of motivation; some are concerned with the role of different brain structures.

Figure 4.6 shows four typical extinction curves following conditioning using variable reinforcement schedules. In each case, reinforcement has been discontinued at the beginning of the one-hour period (indicated on the *x*-axis). Note how rate of responding (indicated by the steepness of the curve) remains unchanged for the first few minutes after reinforcement stops but then rapidly flattens out, showing that few or no responses are occurring.

Spontaneous Recovery

Recall that a classically conditioned response (such as salivation in response to a tone) can be extinguished by presenting the conditioned stimulus (CS; the tone) repeatedly without the

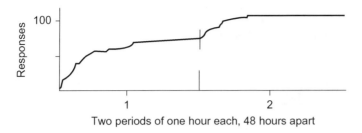

Figure 4.7 A cumulative recording showing initial extinction over a one-hour period (left half of the graph) and spontaneous recovery of the rat's bar-pressing responses over a second one-hour period when placed back into the Skinner box 48 hours later. Note how much more rapidly extinction occurs during the second period (flatter slope). From *The Behavior of Organisms: An Experimental Analysis*, p. 67, by B. F. Skinner. Copyright © 1938 by Appleton-Century-Crofts. Reprinted courtesy of the B.F. Skinner Foundation.

unconditioned stimulus (US; the food). Also, if the CS is presented again a while later, the conditioned response (CR; salivation) might occur again, a phenomenon Pavlov labeled **spontaneous recovery**.

Spontaneous recovery also occurs in operant learning, as is illustrated in Figure 4.7. "If the rat is replaced in the apparatus at a later time," wrote Skinner, referring to a time after a behavior has been extinguished, "a small extinction curve will be obtained" (1938, p. 78). In the case shown in Figure 4.7, the steep slope of the graph during the first half-hour followed by its leveling shows initial extinction of bar-pressing in a rat over a one-hour period during which there was no reinforcement. The next one-hour period shows recovery of the same rat's bar-pressing response when placed back in the cage 48 hours later.

Extinction and Forgetting

In operant conditioning, the terms *extinction* and *forgetting* describe different events. **Extinction** occurs when an animal or person who has been reinforced for engaging in a behavior ceases to be reinforced; the outcome is often a relatively rapid cessation of the behavior. In contrast, **forgetting** is a much slower process that occurs with the passage of time during which there is no repetition of the behavior.[8]

Extinction can be illustrated by reference to a pigeon that has been conditioned to peck at a colored disk. If the food reinforcer for this response is suddenly withdrawn completely, the pigeon will in all likelihood continue to peck at the disk sporadically for some time. However, in a relatively short time, it will stop pecking entirely, at which point extinction will have occurred.

As noted earlier, a behavior that has been extinguished through withdrawal of reinforcement often reappears (that is, recovers spontaneously) without any further conditioning when the

---

[8] Tell your readers, said Mrs. Gribbin, that there's a more detailed discussion of remembering and forgetting in Chapter 8. I said I would.

animal is again placed in the same situation. The extinction period following spontaneous recovery is almost invariably much shorter than the first.

To illustrate *forgetting*, assume that the conditioned pigeon is removed from the experimental situation and is not allowed to return to it for many months. If it does not peck at the disk when it is reintroduced into the chamber, we can conclude that forgetting (not extinction) has occurred.

Skinner reported the case of at least one pigeon that had still not forgotten the disk-pecking response after six years. He also reported one instance of a pigeon that emitted 10,000 unreinforced pecks before extinction.

Effects of Schedules on Rate of Responding

Rate of responding is a dependent variable that is remarkably sensitive to schedules of reinforcement. In general, an animal behaves as might be predicted if it is valid to assume that the animal develops expectations and has some sense of time. For example, under variable schedules of reinforcement, when the animal is less likely to develop an expectation of receiving a reward at a given time, the rate of responding will be uniformly high and relatively unvarying. If the variable schedule is a ratio schedule rather than an interval one, the rate of responding will be uniformly higher. Under a fixed interval schedule of reinforcement, the rate of responding drops dramatically immediately after reinforcement and often ceases altogether. However, just before the next reinforcement, the animal again responds at a high rate (see Figure 4.8).

Under progressive ratio schedules, however, the animal's behavior is not always entirely predictable. That, explain Kileen, Posadas-Sanchez, Johansen, and Thraikill, (2009), may be partly because as the number of required responses increases, the animal may become less motivated. It may also become fatigued, or it may eventually become satiated so that the

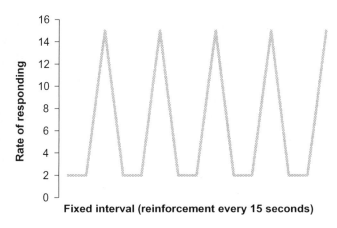

Figure 4.8 Idealized graphs showing the effects of fixed interval and random ratio schedules of reinforcement on rate of responding. With fixed interval schedules, rate of responding increases dramatically just prior to each reinforcement. With the less predictable random ratio schedules, rate of responding remains uniformly high. From Lefrançois, G. R. (2016). *Psychology: The Human Puzzle* (2nd ed.). San Diego, CA: Bridgepoint Education. Fig. 5.8. Used by permission.

reinforcer loses much of its value. This situation is not uncommon when reinforcing the animal with drugs where the effects of one or two administrations may be sufficient for an extended period of time.

Skinner, of course, would not normally use such mentalistic concepts as *motivation, expectation, goal,* or *purpose* to explain why people or animals do things. When he does use such terms, which he does freely when discussing the implications of his science of behavior, he defines them in terms of the organism's reinforcement history. "What gives an action its purpose?" he asks. "The answers to such questions," he then responds, "are eventually to be found in past instances in which similar behavior has been effective" (1969, p. 105).

Concurrent Schedules of Reinforcement

Unfortunately for those who like things to be black and white and uncomplicated, human behavior is seldom as simple as might be the key-pecking of a pigeon or the bar-pressing of a rat. Neither the pigeon nor the rat has a lot of choices in its highly controlled environment: to peck or not to peck; to press or not to press. We, on the other hand, might have a nearly overwhelming array of choices: to go to a movie or not to go; to study or not to study; to call

Operant Conditioning

this friend or that friend or the other friend; to go to the gym; to text a parent; to update our social networking sites; to twitter our current thoughts and activities for the amazement or amusement of friends and strangers, and on and on. To each of these choices is linked the possibility of reinforcement. And each might be associated with very different schedules of reinforcement, a situation that defines a **concurrent schedule of reinforcement**.

In studies of concurrent schedules, the organism can choose among two or more different behaviors, each of which is linked either to a different reinforcer or to a different schedule of reinforcement. For example, a pigeon might be placed in a situation where it can peck one of two different disks, where pecking disk A is linked to a variable ratio schedule and pecking disk B is linked to a variable interval schedule. Studies of pigeons under these circumstances indicate that they typically select which disk to peck and adjust their rate of pecking in clearly predictable ways that tend to maximize reward. A pigeon is not totally stupid!

Most often when dealing with concurrent choices in real life, outcomes are not linked with different schedules of the same reinforcement, but are instead associated with entirely different reinforcers. When you choose between studying and going to a movie, your choices are likely to be determined largely by the very different anticipated positive contingencies associated with each activity and not by the schedules of reinforcement at play.

Concurrent choice investigations with animals present some interesting possibilities. In one study, for example, rats had a choice between a behavior that would lead to a self-administered intravenous dose of cocaine and a behavior that would lead to a food reward (Thomsen et al., 2008), This study, designed to investigate the effectiveness of a drug therapy for psychostimulant addiction, looked at rats' choices following administration of a therapeutic drug under a variety of conditions. The researchers found that under certain conditions, administration of this drug therapy led to a decline in rats' self-administration of cocaine and a corresponding increase in behaviors associated with a natural food reinforcer. This finding might have important implications for treatment of addictions among humans.

That pigeons and other animals *match* their responses to the likelihood and attractiveness of reward has been corroborated in a variety of studies, a fact that led Herrnstein (1974, 1997) to propose that this **matching law** is a generally accurate description of how organisms react when faced with choices.

Not surprisingly, studies with human subjects lead to much the same conclusion: Behaviors in experiments where responses are tied to different schedules of reinforcement tend to be directed toward maximizing reinforcement, as studies of gambling behavior have indicated (for example, Bull, Tippett, and Addis, 2015). Even in highly complex situations where choices must be made extremely rapidly, the matching law seems to apply. For example, studies of shot selection (two- versus three-point field goals) among elite basketball players suggests that choices made tend to match the probability of success (Alferink, Critchfield, Hitt, & Higgins, 2009). Similarly, in a study where six pigeons could make one of four choices, each linked with a different reinforcement schedule, the choice most often made tended to be the one most likely to lead to the next reinforcer (rather than, say, the most recent response made) (Bensemann, Lobb, Podlesnik, & Elliffe, 2015).

Schedules of Reinforcement in Everyday Life

There are many day-to-day examples of the effects of schedules on people's behaviors. The fisherwoman who goes to the same stream time after time although she rarely (but occasionally) catches fish is demonstrating the persistence that results from an intermittent schedule of reinforcement. The small-town student who was at the top of her classes for eight years but now finds herself being outdone in the fierce competition of a new school ceases to study; she is demonstrating the rapid extinction that follows continuous reinforcement. Addicted gamblers, clearly reinforced on variable schedules, persist in their gambling behavior even after disastrously long periods without reinforcement.

Among the most powerful reinforcing events for humans are money, praise, satisfaction, food, and sex. Two of these stimuli, money and food, are often on fixed interval schedules. For a large number of people, money arrives regularly in the form of a paycheck, and food is taken routinely in the form of meals. However, for both of these rather important reinforcers, there are often no immediate, simple operants that predictably result in their presentation. The operants involved in acquiring money have become so complex and so remote from the actual source of reinforcement that it is often difficult to see the relationship between the two. The confusion is further compounded by the fact that the reinforcers themselves are inextricably bound together. That is, money allows one to buy food and, in some cases, praise, satisfaction, sex, and other reinforcers.

The relationship between behavior and reinforcement is not always simple or obvious. But this does not invalidate the conclusion that reinforcers and their scheduling affect many human behaviors. Indeed, in many cases, the person whose behavior is affected remains completely unaware of the relationship between behavior and its consequences. There are countless examples of how behavior is controlled and modified by reinforcements.

Illustration 1

For example, Iris has panned for gold in the same stream for 22 years, gleaning at least a few flecks every outing as well as finding the occasional heart-stopping nugget (continuous reinforcement). Now, after devastating spring floods, she suddenly stops finding any gold whatsoever (withdrawal of reinforcement). After four fruitless trips to the stream, she stops going altogether (rapid extinction following continuous reinforcement).

Illustration 2

Esmeralda has also spent 22 years panning for gold. Sometimes, she finds a little something; sometimes not. On occasion, she finds barely a fleck during an entire season, but she has found as many as five kick-in-the-rump nuggets on a single day (intermittent reinforcement). Now she also stops finding gold (withdrawal of reinforcement). Still, even many years later, she continues to pan the same stream (slow extinction following intermittent reinforcement).

Shaping

Why is it so easy to train a rat to press a bar or a pigeon to peck a disk? Simply because these are among the things that rats and pigeons do. They are operants that almost invariably appear within just a short period in the experimental chambers that Skinner and his followers have provided for these animals. But as Guthrie assures us, "It would be a waste of time to try to teach a cow to sit up" (Guthrie & Powers, 1950, p. 128). This is one of the things that cows do not do. The same is thought to be true of horses. Yet at the National Finals Rodeo a short time back, there was a guy with a horse that not only fetched things the man would throw, much like a dog might, but that also sat down when he was invited to do so. This horse's behavior had been shaped using operant conditioning techniques.

Shaping is the technique used to train animals to perform acts that are not ordinarily in their repertoire. It is not required for behaviors such as pressing a bar in a Skinner box because bar-pressing is one of the behaviors the rat emits in the course of exploring the environment. But if the experimenter wanted to train a rat to go to corner A of the cage, pick up a marble in that corner, carry it to corner B, drop it there, return to the center of the cage, curtsey, lie down, roll over, get up, return to corner B, pick up the marble again, and carry it back to corner A, the rat would probably die of old age before it got around to emitting the desired behavior spontaneously.

Nevertheless, it is possible through shaping to teach a rat to engage in behaviors that are very impressive, if not quite as complex as the behavior just described. Instead of waiting for the final desired response, an experimenter using the technique of shaping reinforces every behavior that takes the animal closer to the final response. For this reason, shaping is sometimes referred to as the *method of successive approximations* or as a method involving the **differential reinforcement of successive approximations** (Skinner, 1951).

Shaping

Most animal trainers employ techniques that amount to shaping procedures. That is how parrots are trained to walk on tightropes, parachute, play tunes, and ride bicycles; porpoises to jump incredible heights with military precision in predetermined order; bears to play guitars; and pigs to poke their noses where experimenters instruct them to (Ueno & Taniuchi, 2016).

One important requirement for the successful use of shaping procedures is that the environment be controlled. For example, the Skinner box is constructed so the rat cannot perform very many responses other than those the experimenter wants to reinforce. Similarly, a professional animal trainer would not attempt to condition a dog when the dog is chasing a rabbit but would first confine the dog and get its attention. In addition, a clever dog trainer might, as Chiandetti, Avella, Fongaro, and Cerri (2016) illustrate, save a lot of time and trouble by first pairing an easy-to-carry-and-administer stimulus such as a clicker with food reinforcement so that the clicker eventually becomes a highly reinforcing sound. These investigators showed that dogs learned as well and as rapidly with this *secondary reinforcer* as did other dogs that were trained with the *primary reinforcer*: food.[9]

Chaining

Recall how Guthrie described conditioning in terms of sequences of what he called *movement-produced stimuli* (MPS). These consist of sequences of responses, imperceptible movements of muscles, tendons, or joints, that give rise to stimuli that in turn lead to other responses, all of which are linked together. Similarly, Hull describes sequences of responses and stimuli, labeled *fractional antedating goal responses* and linked with *little sG* and *little rG*, that also serve to connect behavior with reward.

Skinner describes a similar concept in operant learning, labeled **chaining**. It involves the linking of sequences of responses. Even a behavior as apparently simple as pressing a bar in a Skinner box involves sequences of different responses. "Most of the reflexes of the intact organism are parts of chains," said Skinner (1938, p. 52), going on to describe how chains integrate all behavior.[10] For example, he explained, a rat in a Skinner box makes all sorts of responses. Some of those made in the vicinity of the food tray become learned as a result of being associated with *discriminative stimuli (S^D)*, such as the sound of the food mechanism, that have become secondary reinforcers. Initially, the discriminative stimuli that become secondary reinforcers are those directly associated with reinforcement (such as the sound of the food mechanism). But over time, discriminative stimuli that are further removed (such as the smell of the lever) can also become secondary reinforcers. Thus, a chain of responses can be woven together by a sequence of discriminative stimuli, each of which is a secondary reinforcer associated with, in this case, food as a primary reinforcer.

---

[9] That clicker method is pretty smart, said Mrs. Gribbin, but it isn't the only way to train dogs. Maybe it's not even the best way. I saw a dog on a Facebook post the other day, she said, that sat on its butt and bobbed and swayed and waved its front paws while its master played the guitar. It looked like it was actually dancing to the music. Well, the guy said his dog learned that behavior not through shaping or clicker training but using the "Do as I do" training method. Your brainy students might want to research this, especially if they have dogs. Some researchers, like Fugazza and Miklosi (2015) report that the *Do-as-I-do* method is more effective than shaping and clickers. Works on cats too, she added, looking at Schrödinger. And that miserable creature walked over and jumped on her lap. I didn't know the old lady was on Facebook.

[10] You might point out to your readers, said Mrs. Gribbin, that Pavlov, the then-current giant in psychology, profoundly influenced Skinner. That's why Skinner used the term *reflex* throughout his first major work, as he does in this sentence. But Skinner wasn't speaking about simple reflexes of the type investigated by Pavlov. In his later writing, he largely abandoned the term in favor of *operant* or, simply, *response* or *behavior*.

"Such movements become fully conditioned," Skinner wrote, "and are made with considerable frequency by a hungry rat" (1938, p. 53). Each movement in sequence changes the situation and hence the discriminative stimuli, giving rise to the next response. Vastly simplified, the chain involved in bar-pressing might be something like this: The sight of the inside of the cage serves as an S^D associated with the response of turning toward the bar; the sight of the bar is an S^D for approaching the bar; proximity to the bar is an S^D for pressing it; the sounds and muscular sensations associated with pressing it are S^D for turning toward the food tray; the sight of the food pellet is a stimulus for responses associated with eating.

Skinner argued that most human behaviors, even if they appear simple, consist of chains. For example, combing your hair, should you have any, may require a range of sequential acts: walking to the bathroom, opening a drawer, retrieving a comb, looking at yourself in a mirror, and going through your usual combing motions. If reinforcement (such as your mother saying "Good girl, Sally") is contingent upon you combing your hair, the entire chain of related behaviors is, in effect, reinforced.

Chains in Shaping

When a behavior is shaped, chains are established. What the professional animal trainer tries to do is link a series of discriminative stimuli and responses that are sufficiently long and complicated to astound you and perhaps even your grandmother (although she has seen a lot more than you have). In the final performance, the trainer does not have to hold a steak above the dog's head, yell "Somersault," and move his or her hand quickly backward when the dog leaps for the steak, forcing the animal to describe a crude semicircle in the air. (Your grandmother would not be impressed.)

Holding the steak over the dog's head and "forcing" the somersault is the first step in establishing the chain because chaining typically works backward from a primary reinforcer. During training sessions, a clever trainer arranges for the conditioning of chains by selectively reinforcing certain responses leading to the final and complete sequence of responses. In the end, the dog will bound onto the stage, race through an obstacle course, rescue a drowning baby, spell its name with wooden letters, and finally do a most amazing double somersault. And neither you nor your grandmother will ever see the steak.

Shaping and Verbal Instructions in Human Learning

Human learning often involves shaping. For example, when learning complex motor tasks involving muscular coordination (such as golfing or figure skating), a large number of inappropriate or ineffective responses need to be modified or abandoned. At the same time, more appropriate responses are reinforced and become more firmly established and linked in chains.

The behaviors of both nonhuman animals and humans are shaped through their outcomes (their contingencies), Skinner insists. But, he adds, the behavior of humans is also shaped by *rules* – that is, by *verbal instructions* – that often come from other people. Skinner argued that we first learn to follow rules through reinforcement and shaping when, as children, we experience the consequences of following or not following them. The general tendency to follow rules will eventually be the natural outcome of these consequences.

Many examples of shaping can be found in the classroom. For example, primary-grade teachers reinforce their charges' first fumbling attempts at reading words and making letters, often with praise and little privileges. But as the children age and progress, the same behaviors receive little reinforcement. Now behaviors that are progressively closer approximations to more advanced reading and writing are reinforced. And gradually, children's reading and writing improve.

FADING, GENERALIZATION, AND DISCRIMINATION

Shaping is one technique employed in training animals to perform complex behaviors. Another is **fading** – a conditioning procedure in which certain aspects of a stimulus are gradually changed (faded) until they disappear completely. It is a process that involves both **generalization** (making similar responses in different situations) and **discrimination** (making different responses in similar but discriminably different situations).

As an illustration of fading, Reese (1966) describes a procedure whereby a pigeon is taught to "read" the words *peck* and *turn*. If the pigeon pecks when it sees *peck* and turns when it sees *turn*, says Reese, we can say that it has learned to read.

This type of training presents some special problems. Although it is relatively simple to train a pigeon to peck when shown the word "peck," the bird will then immediately generalize the learned response and peck in response to the word *turn*. But if the two stimuli are made highly different so the pigeon can easily discriminate between the two, it can be taught to respond appropriately to each stimulus through shaping. For example, the word *turn* might be printed in large black letters and the word *peck* in small red letters (pigeons have excellent color vision). After the pigeon has learned to peck and to turn as instructed, the differences between the stimuli are slowly faded out over a number of sessions: The large black letters become smaller, and the small red letters become both darker and larger until finally each word is black and the letters are of uniform size. Through fading, the pigeon has learned to discriminate between two words; in one sense, it has learned to read.

Relevance to Human Learning

Generalization and discrimination are very important in human learning. One example of generalization is that of the pigeon turning in response to the word *peck* before it has learned to discriminate between the words. Another is the perhaps even more impressive finding that pigeons can learn with relative ease to discriminate between spherical and nonspherical stimuli and will, after fewer than 150 trials of training, generalize the "concept" spherical to hundreds of other stimulus objects (Delius, 1992).

Generalization

Examples of generalization in human behavior are numerous. Any five-minute segment of behavior in the life of a normal person is likely to be filled with instances of old behaviors being generalized to new situations. New cars are driven in ways similar to those used in driving old ones; someone who hits a stranger accidentally may apologize although she has never hit this particular stranger before; when faced with the problem of adding 27 kangaroos and 28 zebras, a farmer reasons that the sum is the same as that of adding 27 pigs and 28 horses; people assume that objects fall from mountaintops as they do from treetops; strangers shake hands when introduced; and on and on. All these behaviors are examples of previously learned responses being transferred to new situations because these new situations are similar to situations in which the responses were learned. Generalization is important precisely because not all or even most situations to which a person must react in a lifetime can be covered in schools or in other learning situations. Teaching for generalization (teaching for *transfer*) is one of the main functions of schools.

Discrimination

Discrimination is complementary to generalization. The pigeon's learning to respond differently to the two highly similar situations involved in the presentation of the words *peck* and *turn* requires that the pigeon learn to discriminate between the two similar stimuli.

The importance of discrimination learning is especially apparent in learning socially appropriate behavior. Children must learn to discriminate at relatively early ages between similar situations where different responses are appropriate. For example, they learn that it is permissible to kiss one's parents but not strangers; that sisters should not be punched but perhaps neighborhood bullies can be under certain discriminable circumstances; that it is bad to make noises in quiet churches but permissible to make the same noises in quiet houses; and so on. Thus, socially appropriate behavior is very much a function of having learned to discriminate among situations calling for different types of behavior.

The processes of discrimination and generalization are illustrated in Figure 4.9. In the first case, the appropriate response is to eat any of the five things; in other words, a generalization of the eating response is appropriate. In the second case, it is necessary to discriminate between two stimuli: generalization would not be appropriate.

Individual Differences

It should be noted that, unlike most behaviorists, Skinner recognized the existence of some basic differences among individuals. Early behaviorists, such as Watson, had a tendency to assume that the laws that govern behavior apply equally to all individuals and to all behaviors, and that we are all pretty equal in the beginning. Hence Watson's insistence that he could make whatever he wanted of a dozen healthy infants (see Chapter 2).

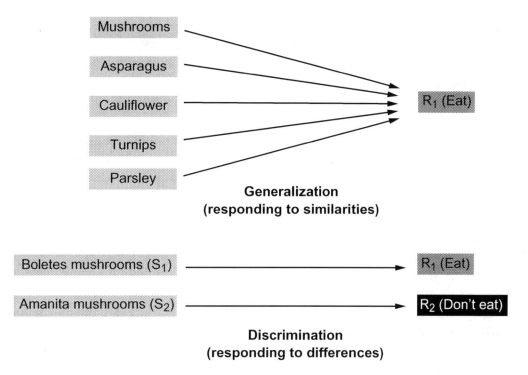

Figure 4.9 Generalization involves responding to similarities and therefore making similar responses for different stimuli. To discriminate is to respond to differences, making different responses to similar stimuli.

On the other hand, Skinner admitted the importance of individual differences. The countless **trait** names that we use are useful and revealing, he says (traits are personality characteristics apparent in words such as *happy-go-lucky*, *cautious*, *brave*, and *impulsive*). "Under certain circumstances," he writes, "everything else about the behavior may be irrelevant, and a description in terms of traits is then highly economical" (1953, p. 195). Knowledge of traits can allow us to predict what a response will be even if we do not know the individual's precise reinforcement history. But, ever the behaviorist, Skinner explains that "some differences are due to the differences in the independent variables to which people are exposed" (p. 195). In other words, some aspects of personality differences are learned through conditioning. However, he also claims that other traits result from basic differences in the rate at which conditioning occurs in different individuals. "The 'intelligent' individual," he writes, "is commonly supposed to show more rapid conditioning and extinction, to form discriminations more rapidly, and so on" (1953, p. 196).

PRACTICAL APPLICATIONS OF OPERANT CONDITIONING

Although it was initially developed largely through the study of rat and pigeon behavior in highly controlled environments, operant conditioning is as much a science of humans as of other organisms. Skinner saw no important discontinuity between how humans and nonhumans respond to the contingencies of their behaviors. And he considered criticisms that accused the system of neglecting higher mental processes such as thinking to be unfair and inaccurate. "A science of behavior does not, as is so often asserted, ignore awareness," he declared. "On the contrary, it goes far beyond mentalistic psychologies in analyzing self-descriptive behavior" (Skinner, 1969, p. 245).

In an article appropriately entitled "Why I am not a Cognitive Psychologist," Skinner (1986) makes it clear that he by no means denies the existence and importance of cognitive phenomena such as thinking, problem solving, and imagining. These are interesting topics, says Skinner; but it is a mistake to try to explain them by reference to inferred "cognitive" processes.

Skinner's behavioristic system did not neglect language and thought. As Lana (2002) explains, acquiring and emitting verbal behaviors is subject to the same rules of operant conditioning as any other behavior. For Skinner, concepts such as *awareness* and *purpose* depend on verbal rules that result from analyzing the relationship between behavior and its contingencies: "An advanced verbal community generates a high level of such awareness" (1969, p. 245).

Initially, argues Skinner (1989), words were used not to describe awareness, purpose, and feelings but, rather, to describe the specific behaviors or situations in which these occurred. Thus, for example, a word such as "love" might be used to describe the action of holding a baby. In time, however, the word would come to be associated with the bodily states – the physiological changes – that accompany the action. Hence, the word eventually describes an emotion and can then be generalized to other situations and behaviors that bring about the same physiological reactions, such as kissing someone or petting a friendly cat.

That humans are responsive to the consequences of behavior seems clear. As we saw, many studies indicate that people are sensitive to variable interval schedules of reinforcement in much the same way as are experimental animals. As we see later, people's responsiveness to the consequences of their behavior is the basis for behavioral therapies – therapies that systematically manipulate rewards and punishments in an effort to change behavior and emotions.

That people are responsive to the effects of reinforcement does not mean that they are always aware of the relationships between their behavior and its consequences. In fact, it is possible to control people through the clever manipulation of rewards and punishments without the awareness of those being controlled – and societies do just that, claimed Skinner.

Applications of Positive Contingencies

As Skinner (1971) notes repeatedly, societies make extensive use of **aversive control** – the use of noxious or unpleasant contingencies – when **positive control** – the use of pleasant and desirable contingencies – would be far more humane and also probably more effective. For example, he writes that the methods of control of the world's major social institutions are based largely on aversive contingencies. These methods are sorely evident in schools, where reprimands, detention, low grades, and threats of punishment are often a more prominent fact of a student's daily life than are praise, the granting of favors, the promise of high marks, or the possibility of other important reinforcement.

A classroom is a little like a giant operant conditioning chamber (*Skinner box*). Teachers play the role of experimenters; they schedule and administer rewards and punishments. Students play the role of Skinnerian rats (or monkeys, if that seems less offensive); their responses are shaped by various teacher-controlled contingencies (and by many other contingencies, such as peer approval or ridicule, that are not under the teacher's control). As experimenters, teachers can profit from knowing that reinforcement is effective in bringing about changes in behavior, schedules of reinforcement can be varied to good advantage, punishment is not very effective for learning, some reinforcers are more powerful than others, and that there should be as short a delay as possible between behavior and its consequences. For example, if teacher comments on student work or grades are used as reinforcement, they should be given to students as soon as possible.

Teacher reinforcement

Teachers can also profit from greater knowledge about sources of reinforcement. We tend to think of reinforcers as easily identifiable stimuli such as the five categories described by Bijou and Sturges (1959): consumables (such as candy bars); manipulatables (like toys); visual and auditory stimuli (for example, a bell or tone that means "good work"); social stimuli (like praise); and tokens (items that can be exchanged for other reinforcers). These stimuli are reinforcing because, as defined by Skinner, they increase the probability of a behavior. Unfortunately, there are a number of problems with this definition. One is that it is rather circular: What is a reinforcer? A stimulus that increases the probability of a response occurring. How do we know it is a reinforcer? Because it increased the probability of a response. Why did it increase the probability of a response? Because it is a reinforcer. What is a reinforcer? And on and on.

A second problem with the Skinnerian definition is that it does not take into consideration the fact that reinforcement is relative; it can vary from one organism to another, and even from one situation to another for the same organism. For example, food is reinforcing at the beginning of a meal, but by mid-meal, it might well have become neutral, and at the end of the meal, it might be punishing.

Operant Conditioning

The Premack Principle

Premack (1965) presents a somewhat different approach to identifying reinforcing events. His approach takes into account the observation that reinforcement is relative; it also takes into consideration the fact that reinforcers can be activities, or responses, rather than only stimuli. Premack's approach, known as the **Premack principle**, holds that behavior that occurs frequently and naturally can be used to reinforce less frequent behavior. For example, being allowed to run in an exercise wheel can be reinforcing for some rats; others find it more reinforcing to be allowed to chew wood. Similarly, some children find it highly rewarding to watch television; others prefer playing with friends; some would rather play video games; still others might prefer reading quietly. Note that each of these is a response. Moreover, each is a response in which the organism will engage freely if given the opportunity to do so, in much the same way as the organism will also drink and eat. To find out what the best class of reinforcers might be for a given organism, suggests Premack, it is often sufficient to observe what the organism does freely. For example, a "with-it" teacher may notice that when students have free time in class, Tara reads, Amy and Juanita talk to each other, Aboud asks to clean the whiteboard, and Ivan draws cartoon characters. Application of the Premack principle suggests that allowing Tara to read might be reinforcing for her but not necessarily for other students; allowing Ivan to draw cartoons might be highly reinforcing for him.

Behavior analysis, based on conditioning principles, is applied extensively in schools. It is also widely used by therapists in a variety of settings. The deliberate and systematic application of operant conditioning principles in an attempt to change behavior is labeled **behavior modification**. Behavior modification is described and illustrated later in this chapter.

Applications of Aversive Contingencies

Skinner describes two types of aversive (or negative) control: punishment and negative reinforcement. Recall that these are fundamentally different from each other: Whereas negative reinforcement increases the probability that a response will occur again, punishment usually has the opposite effect.[11]

The Case Against Punishment

Few topics in child rearing and education have received more attention than punishment. Much of this attention results from the prevalence of punishment rather than from its effectiveness. **Corporal punishment**, also termed *physical punishment*, the use of physical force to bring about pain, is especially controversial.

---

[11] By the way, said Old Lady Gribbin as an aside, you might have noticed that the environment constantly provides people with a huge number of aversive stimuli that appear to be extremely effective in shaping behavior. Stoves that are hot, insects that bite, mushrooms that poison – all these quickly lead to important learning. If they didn't, the human species probably wouldn't have survived this many generations. So, although you need to recognize the importance of emphasizing positive rather than aversive control, aversive control shouldn't be dismissed too glibly.

Most surveys indicate that a variety of physical punishments such as spanking are an extremely common childrearing technique in North America (Chiocca, 2017). In a wide-scale survey, some 76 percent of American men and 66 percent of women "agreed" or "strongly agreed" that children sometimes need to be given a "good hard spanking" (Child Trends, 2018). An increasing number of countries, including India (Cheruvalath & Tripathi, 2015), Bangladesh (Malak, Sharma, and Deppeler, 2015), and Spain (Sirera Miralles, 2015) have banned the use of corporal punishment by parents and by schools. In the United States, the US Supreme Court has affirmed the rights of schools and parents to use corporal punishment (providing it is not grossly excessive). However, many states and some local jurisdictions ban corporal punishment in their schools, although it is still legal in 19 states (Gershoff and Font, 2016).

From a learning theory viewpoint, a number of practical and theoretical objections to the use of punishment can be raised. First, the likelihood that punishment will lead to appropriate behavior is often remote. Essentially, punishment draws attention to undesirable behavior but does little to indicate what the desirable behavior should be.

Second, instead of eliminating behavior, punishment usually only suppresses it; what is affected is the rate of responding. The advantage that nonreinforcement has over punishment is that, theoretically, it leads to the extinction of the unreinforced behavior.

Third, punishment can lead to emotional states that will probably not be associated with love, happiness, or any other positive feeling. Through contiguity, negative emotional states may become associated with the punisher rather than with the undesirable behavior. As a result, corporal punishment is sometimes predictive of later behavior problems. Various studies have linked physical punishment with higher instances of mental illness, aggression, criminal behavior, and substance abuse (for example, King et al., 2018).

Fourth, physical punishment puts children at risk for physical abuse, and parents at risk for becoming abusers (Taylor, Fleckman, & Lee, 2017). A number of studies indicate that parents who were subject to corporal punishment as children are significantly more likely to use corporal punishment on their children and are also more likely to become child abusers (for example, Ellonen, Peltonen, Poso, & Janson, 2017). Hellmann, Stiller, Glaubitz, and Kliem (2018) refer to this phenomenon as the *intergenerational transmission of parental violence*. After corporal punishment was banned by law in Sweden in 1979, instances of both corporal punishment and of physical child abuse have decreased (Annerback, Svedin & Gustafsson, 2010; Ellonen, Lucas, Tinberg, & Janson, 2017).

A fifth, more general objection to punishment is that it often does not work. Considerable research indicates that corporal punishment may have effects opposite to those intended. Numerous studies that have looked at young children's adjustment and behavior over time have found that corporal punishment by parents actually *increases* instances of maladjustment and antisocial behavior (Rebellon & Straus, 2017).

Less Objectionable Forms of Punishment

Psychology's most passionate objections to the use of punishment apply mainly to corporal (*physical*) punishment, such as spanking or strapping. The same objections are not nearly as

Operant Conditioning

relevant for several other forms of punishment, some of which are quite common in schools and homes. These include time-out procedures, response cost, and reprimands.

A **time-out** is a procedure in which children are excluded from ongoing activities. For example, a misbehaving school child might be required to sit at the back of the room, perhaps facing in the opposite direction. Or, at home, the child might be removed from a play area and not allowed to participate in ongoing activities. The key to a time-out procedure is that children are removed from a situation where they might expect reinforcement and placed in another situation where they are less likely to be reinforced. Time-out procedures have been found to be highly effective, report Drayton et al. (2017). And they are even more effective when combined with what are labeled **time-in** procedures. Time-in occurs when children are reinforced by being systematically included, physically touched and praised, and so on. Children who are removed from a classroom in response to misbehavior are being punished not by the administration of an unpleasant stimulus (unless, of course, they are sent to the principal's office or given detention) but, rather, by being removed from what is assumed to be a reinforcing environment.

Among the least objectionable forms of punishment are **reprimands**, most of which are verbal but a number of which might be nonverbal (a negative shake of the head or a frown, for example). A series of studies in classroom situations found that the most effective verbal reprimands are those described as "soft" (O'Leary, Kaufman, Kass & Drabman, 1970). Soft reprimands are those given in such a way that only the child involved can hear them. In classes in which teachers employed loud reprimands, there was a significantly higher incidence of disruptive behavior. In this connection, it is also worth noting that praise, a highly effective reinforcer in the classroom, is far more effective if it is "loud." Not surprisingly, as Spilt, Leflot, Onghena & Colpin (2016) found, the most positive effects in schools are associated with the use of fewer reprimands and more praise

The Case for Punishment

That physical punishment continues to be common in industrialized societies serves as a poor justification for it. Still, a number of arguments can be made for the use of punishment. First, although reinforcement, imitation, and reasoning might all be effective in bringing about and maintaining desirable behavior, in many instances, they do not appear to be sufficient. Nor, of course, is gentle persuasion always going to convince the child immediately that certain behaviors are undesirable. If Johnny persists in throwing his sister into the bathtub even after being told that the poor thing cannot swim, punishment might be in order. And although psychologists have long noted that punishment does not appear to be very effective in eliminating undesirable behaviors, it might be very effective in at least suppressing these behaviors. In fact, the argument that punishment does not lead to the extinction of the behavior in question may be irrelevant. If Johnny now stops tossing the unfortunate sister into the tub, his grandmother will surely not believe that the behavior has been extinguished or forgotten, but she might justifiably hope that he would refrain from doing so in the future.

Despite ethical or moral objections that many feel toward the use of punishment, there are situations in which its use seems the least cruel and the most effective of alternatives. Like reinforcement, punishment appears to be most effective when it immediately follows behavior. However, this observation is far more valid for other animals than it is for humans, presumably because of the human ability to symbolize. This allows for associations between behavior and its consequences even when the consequences occur a long time after the misbehavior.

Negative Reinforcement

Both positive and negative reinforcement, by definition, lead to an increase in the probability of a response occurring – one by being added to a situation (reward) and the other by being removed (relief). However, each of these is likely to have very different effects. You might train a rat to jump onto a stool by feeding it every time it does so (positive reinforcement). Or you might train it to jump onto the same stool by giving it an electric shock when it does not do so. In the end, it may jump onto the stool with equal haste no matter how it has been trained, but it is likely that the positively reinforced rat will display considerably more enthusiasm for jumping than will its aversively trained colleague. There is a fundamental difference between learning an approach response (as is generally the case with positive reinforcement) and escape or avoidance learning (which often results from negative reinforcement).

Much like the rat that has learned to jump onto a stool to escape an electric shock, students who are attentive and studious because of aversive contingencies (negative reinforcement or punishment) cannot be expected to like school as much as those who are attentive and studious because of positive reinforcement.

Perhaps the same is true of those who go to church to avoid hellfire and damnation.[12]

Other Applications: Behavior Management

One goal of the fashion and taste industry is to mold and change people's tastes and, ultimately, their behavior. Similarly, one goal of the business of teaching is to bring about learning which, by definition, involves a change in behavior, and one goal of psychotherapy is to change people's emotional and behavioral responses.

All these involve what is termed **behavior management** – the deliberate and systematic application of learning principles in an attempt to modify behavior. These applications of

---

[12] At about this time, we left the river and worked our way up the bank toward the bush cabin, Schrödinger leading the way. "About hellfire and damnation and rats," Old Lady Gribbin was saying, and she seemed to be speaking to the cat and not to me, "those are old examples left over from some earlier edition." She said she didn't know much about hellfire and damnation. She said, too, that she found the use of such remarkably nonbehavioristic images as that of rats jumping on stools "enthusiastically" at least amusing, if not entirely meaningful or appropriate. When we arrived at the cabin, the old lady went to the cupboard mumbling something about being hungry, which I certainly was. She carved out a thick slab of ham from what was left and I hoped she was making us a sandwich. Schrödinger rubbed hard against the old lady's legs. Yes, the old lady said, and she went over and laid the meat in the cat's dish. He looked up at her as if to say thanks, then bent to gnawing and chewing, making all sorts of disgusting noises. After a while, he looked at me pointedly and belched. Then he went and curled up on the upper bunk. Old Lady Gribbin turned back to her notes. My stomach rumbled.

Operant Conditioning

learning principles are also labeled **behavior therapy** (a term used mainly for the application of Pavlovian principles) or **behavior modification** (used more for the application of operant conditioning principles).

Many different conditioning-based behavior management techniques have been developed. Four of the most common are described briefly here.

Positive Reinforcement and Punishment

As we have just seen, positive reinforcement and punishment – including things such as praise, work bonuses, social approval or time-out procedures, reprimands, penalties, and so on – can be highly effective for modifying behavior and are widespread in everyday life.

Research indicates that specific, well-planned behavior management strategies are typically more effective than are more informal, less-organized approaches. The most effective of these programs are often those based on positive rather than aversive contingencies. When these programs are based on positive reinforcement, they often use tokens as reinforcers. Typically, these can later be exchanged for more meaningful reinforcement (Eby & Greer, 2017). Money is an especially effective token.

Counterconditioning

As we saw in Chapter 2, Guthrie describes how some undesirable habits that have been conditioned to certain stimuli can sometimes be replaced with different, incompatible responses to the same stimuli through a process called **counterconditioning** – a procedure whereby an undesirable response is replaced with one that is more acceptable.

Counterconditioning is sometimes used in **psychotherapy** – the treatment of mental disorders and emotional problems. As we saw in Chapter 2, counterconditioning is well illustrated in *systematic desensitization*, which is used mainly for treating anxieties and phobias (fears). Counterconditioning procedures have also been successfully used in the medical field. For example, Paasch, Leibowitz, Accardo, and Slifer (2016) report that pairing pleasant activities with a simulated medical routine – in this case, an overnight sleep study for children with autism disorders – can be effective for lessening children's anxiety.

Extinction

Just as Skinner's rats can be made to stop pressing a lever by disconnecting the food mechanism or disabling the self-administering drug paraphernalia, so can humans often be made to stop engaging in some unwanted behavior by removing their source of reinforcement. This technique can be used whenever a behavior is maintained by positive reinforcement that is under the control of the experimenter, teacher, parent, or therapist. For example, certain attention-seeking behaviors in young children can be extinguished simply by not paying attention to them.

However, many attention-seeking behaviors are reinforced by peers rather than by authority figures: These are more resistant to parental or teacher attempts to manipulate reinforcers.

SKINNER'S POSITION: AN APPRAISAL

There are some, explain Gentile and Miller (2009), who are convinced that Skinner had all the answers; and there are others who think he was not even asking the right questions.

"Behavioral science," writes Mills, "reached its highest and most complete development in Skinner's writings" (1998, p. 123). More than half a century after the theory was first proposed, it continues to be the most comprehensive and the most researched analysis of human behavior currently available. Skinner's theory has been used as a basis for understanding an enormous range of human behaviors, and has been applied in a huge variety of practical areas, including therapy, education, and business. Not surprisingly, Skinner is widely regarded as one of the "master builders" of psychology; he stands out in the history of psychological thinking as one of its great spokesmen and popularizers. Although Watson defined behaviorism, and many other theorists have contributed significantly to its development, Skinner's name is the one most often associated with behavioristic psychology.

Contributions and Applications of Skinner's Theory

When 186 psychologists were asked to rate psychology's top authors and to list the books that undergraduate psychology majors should read, Skinner's *Beyond Freedom and Dignity* (1971) was among the five books most often listed. These same psychologists also rated Skinner as one of psychology's top five authors (Norcross & Tomcho, 1994).

Probably Skinner's greatest contribution to the understanding of human behavior is his description of the effects of reinforcement on responding. In addition, he extrapolated these findings to individuals and to social groups, and even to entire cultures (for example, see Skinner, 1948, 1953, 1971). As O'Donohue and Ferguson (2001) note, many of today's problems – overpopulation, pollution, conflict, and war – are problems of human behavior. Skinner's dream was that a science that seeks to predict and control behavior would help solve some of these problems.

Through his numerous books and presentations and because of his remarkable leadership skills, Skinner has had a tremendous influence on many theorists, many of whom have incorporated large portions of his system into their own positions. Also, Skinner's emphasis on operational definitions has had a profound and long-lasting influence on psychological theory.

His theory continues to be applied in research in many areas, including the study of drug addictions and behavior, investigations of choice behavior, studies of gambling, and research on memory and reasoning.

Skinner's theory has also had a huge impact on the development of psychotherapies (Thompson, 2014). Behavior modification, for example, is based on the notion that people

Operant Conditioning

are strongly influenced by the actual or anticipated consequences of their behavior. As a result, there are a variety of therapies that are based squarely on the principles of operant conditioning (Johnston, 2013).

Perhaps nowhere is the influence of Skinner's work more apparent than in the development of instructional programs. It was Skinner, for example, who developed **programmed instruction** – an approach to teaching and learning that presents material in very small steps and provides immediate feedback about the correctness of responses (reinforcement). The principles of Skinnerian programmed instruction are now reflected in many computer-based instructional systems. They are also evident in a closely related instructional system developed by one of Skinner's students, Keller: the **Personalized System of Instruction (PSI)** (Keller, 1968, 1969). PSI requires that course material be broken into small units through which learners progress at their own rate. Frequent tests are given to gauge learner progress. The objective is to have each learner master course content. The PSI has been widely studied and used at both the post-secondary and earlier levels (for example, Akera, 2017; Paiva, Ferreira, & Frade, 2017).

Evaluation as a Theory

With respect to the criteria for good theories described in Chapter 1, Skinner's system fares relatively well. It is a well-defined, highly researched system that reflects the facts, especially as they relate to the relationships between reinforcing events and behavior. It is a clear and understandable system that explains some aspects of behavior remarkably well and allows predictions that can be verified. It is not based on many unverified assumptions, and it has led to a tremendous amount of research and advancement in the understanding of behavior.

Some Philosophical Objections

Some critics insist that Skinner's operant conditioning does not explain symbolic processes and says little about other topics of interest to contemporary cognitive theorists, such as decision making, problem solving, perception, and so on. Others are dissatisfied with his attempts to explain language through reinforcement theory. Still others think he neglected the role of biology in learning.

On the other side of the argument are those who argue that Skinner's system does deal with cognitive topics and that many have simply confused radical behaviorism's rejection of the usefulness of invoking mental events as explanations with a rejection of the existence of these mental events.

Skinner's work has been widely misunderstood, claim Malone and Cruchon (2001). For example, summaries of the theory have tended to overlook his contribution to the understanding of verbal behavior. Similarly, psychology tends to ignore Skinner's explanation for "mentalistic" concepts such as self-awareness, which he believed arose from those environmental contingencies that reinforce humans for discriminating (being aware of) their own behavior (O'Donohue & Ferguson, 2001). As Dittrich, Strapasson, da Silveira, and Abreu (2009) explain, Skinner did not ignore "private" events, such as self-awareness. In fact, he recognized the existence of *unobservable* "private" events and the importance of inferences that people make about mental states and behaviors.

If most important human behaviors are operant, the importance of Skinner's explanations can hardly be overestimated. However, there is controversy about the extent to which behavior is controlled by reinforcement contingencies. Many, most notably humanistic psychologists, consider Skinner's view an assault on human freedom and dignity. If we are controlled by the reinforcements and punishments of the environment, the argument goes, then we cannot be free. Thus, on the surface, a Skinnerian position seems incompatible with a concern for human worth and individuality.

"When I question the supposed freedom of autonomous man," Skinner retorts, "I am not debating the issue of free will. I am simply describing the slow demise of a prescientific explanatory device" (1973, p. 261). "Autonomous man," Skinner explains elsewhere, "is a device used to explain what we cannot explain in any other way. He has been constructed of our ignorance, and as our understanding increases, the very stuff of which he is composed vanishes" (1971, p. 200). In brief, Skinner was not trying to provide proof that free will does not exist; rather, he was arguing against what he considered unscientific and futile explanations for human behavior. He was trying to get at the *roots* of behavior.

That, in a nutshell, is radical behaviorism.

Humans are controlled by their environments, Skinner insists, but humans have built these environments, which they continue to control to some extent. A science of human behavior, the development of which was always Skinner's goal, brings the possibility of applying science for the benefit of all humanity. As Clarke (2010) puts it, "The early behaviorists dreamed big dreams." And nowhere is the magnitude of Skinner's dreams more apparent than in his controversial and sometimes violently attacked novel, *Walden Two* (Skinner, 1948). In this novel, Skinner describes his "little utopia," a society where his science of behavior is applied in a community of about 1,000 people. These people lead what Skinner terms "the good life": They work only a few hours a day; enjoy the highest standards of education, health, and recreation; and are intelligent and happy. "Some readers may take the book as written tongue in cheek," he wrote, "but it was actually a quite serious proposal" (Skinner, 1969, p. 29).

One defense against Skinner's critics, proposed by Amsel (1992), is that most don't attack the system as described by Skinner but instead attack a caricature of the system – an exaggeration of its most obvious features. Skinner's ultimate defense against his critics is that many were objecting not to the theory but to their interpretation of its implications. In short, they don't like what humanity seems to be. But as Skinner noted, "No theory changes what it is a theory about; man remains what he has always been" (1971, p. 215).

Main Point Chapter Summary

1. Although sometimes interpreted as antitheoretical, Skinner objects not to theories (he considers them essential) but to the kinds of theories that appeal to speculative, mentalistic

inventions to explain observed events. As a result, it is *antimentalistic* and *antidualistic*. Skinner's radical behaviorism (*radical* meaning *root* – so-called because he was looking for the root causes of behavior) describes human behavior as lawful and insists that psychology should look at external rather than internal factors to explain it.

2. Skinner's experimental analysis of behavior looks for laws that govern interactions between organism and environment. It examines the relationship between independent variables (reinforcement types and schedules) and dependent variables (rate of acquisition, rate of responding, and extinction rate). Influenced by Pavlov, Thorndike, and Darwin, Skinner identifies two major types of learning: that involving stimulus-elicited responses – explainable by using a Pavlovian model (respondents; Type S, or classical conditioning) – and that dealing with emitted instrumental acts – explainable because of their consequences (operants; Type R, or operant conditioning).

3. Piaget used an *operant conditioning chamber* (Skinner box) to investigate the laws of operant conditioning. Operant learning occurs when there is a change in the probability of a response as a function of events that immediately follow it (response contingencies). Events that increase the probability of a response are termed *reinforcers*. Aspects of the situation accompanying reinforcement become discriminative stimuli (S^D) that serve as secondary reinforcers.

4. Reinforcers can be positive (effective through their presentation; reward) or negative (effective through their removal; relief). Removal punishment involves removing a pleasant consequence (penalty); presentation punishment involves presenting an aversive consequence (castigation) following behavior.

5. Primary reinforcers satisfy basic needs (such as food satisfying hunger); secondary reinforcers become reinforcing through association with a primary reinforcer (for example, a light in a Skinner box – associated with food – becomes reinforcing in its own right). Generalized reinforcers (like prestige, praise, and money) are stimuli that have been paired with a variety of other reinforcers and have become reinforcing for many behaviors.

6. Reinforcement schedules can be continuous (every correct response is reinforced) or intermittent (partial). Intermittent schedules can be based on proportion of responses (ratio) or on time lapse (interval). Both ratio and interval schedules can be either fixed (unvarying) or random (variable). Superstitious schedules are fixed interval schedules where reinforcement occurs at fixed times no matter what the organism is doing. Ratio schedules can also be *progressive*, meaning that the number of responses required before reinforcement increases systematically.

7. Continuous schedules lead to rapid acquisition and rapid extinction. Intermittent schedules lead to longer extinction times but are less efficient for early training. Rate of responding typically corresponds to the expectations of reward an animal or person is likely to develop during training. When food is used as a reward, the initial step in operant conditioning in the operant conditioning chamber involves *magazine training*. When self-administered drugs are used with animals, there is no need for magazine training.

8. Extinction (a rapid process, sometimes followed by spontaneous recovery) is the elimination of a behavior through the withdrawal of reinforcement. Forgetting (a slower process) is the elimination of behavior through the passage of time.

9. Concurrent schedules are present when the organism is faced with a choice among various behaviors, each of which is associated with a different schedule of reinforcement or with entirely different reinforcers.

10. Shaping, a technique used to bring about novel behavior in animals, involves reinforcing responses that move in the desired direction until the final response has been conditioned. Chaining is the linking of sequences of responses by virtue of discriminative stimuli that are all linked to the same reinforcer.

11. Fading brings about discrimination learning by exaggerating differences in early training and then phasing them out. Generalization involves transferring one response to other stimuli; discrimination involves making different responses for highly similar stimuli.

12. Social control through the use of positive reinforcement is common and effective. Control through more aversive means (such as negative reinforcement and punishment) is also effective and prevalent. Objections to punishment are based on the observations that (a) it does not tell the offender what to do but merely what not to do; (b) it often results in suppressing behavior but not eliminating it; (c) it may have some undesirable emotional side-effects; (d) it may put the child at risk for physical abuse; and (e) it often does not work, sometimes having effects opposite to those intended. Some forms of punishment (such as reprimands, time-outs, and response-cost methods) are not subject to the same criticisms.

13. Some techniques for modifying behavior include positive reinforcement, extinction, and counterconditioning.

14. Skinner's system explains and predicts certain behaviors remarkably well, is internally consistent and clear, and reflects some facts well. However, it has passionate critics, many of whom object to its search for explanations outside the person and its apparent denial of freedom and autonomy.

5 Evolutionary Psychology

Learning, Biology, and the Brain

CHAPTER OUTLINE

This Chapter	155
Objectives	156
Taste Aversion Learning	156
Conditioning Explanations for Taste Aversions	156
Latent Inhibition and Taste Aversion Learning	159
Blocking	160
Higher-Order Conditioning and Biological Adaptation	163
Darwin's Natural Selection and Psychology	164
Evolutionary Psychology	164
Autoshaping	165
Instinctive Drift	167
Biological Constraints	169
Evolution of the Brain	170
Evolutionary Psychology and Learning	171
Some Reactions to Evolutionary Psychology	172
Sociobiology: A Precursor of Evolutionary Psychology	173
Some Reactions to Sociobiology	175
Evolutionary Psychology: An Appraisal	175
A Transition	176
Learning and the Brain	178
Studying Brain Functions	178
Hindbrain	182
Midbrain	182
Forebrain	182
The Brain and Experience	186
Brain-Based Education	187
Biofeedback and Neurofeedback	189
Conditioning of Autonomic Responses: Early Research	189
How Biofeedback Works	189
Recent Biofeedback Applications	190
Main Point Chapter Summary	191

Think of all the nonsense you had to learn in psychology courses. None of which was testable. None of which was measurable. We had behaviorism, Freudian psychology, all of these theories that you learn in psychology. Totally untestable. Now, we can test it, because physics allows us to calculate energy flows in the brain.

Michio Kaku

Look, said Old Lady Gribbin, and I bent to see what she held toward me. For a moment, I saw nothing and then, as she slowly opened her hand, an orange-colored butterfly perched on her thumb. It stayed there only for an instant and then fluttered away.

She said that this was a monarch butterfly and that most adult butterflies live only about 10 days, which is a great sadness for poets, but that the monarch butterfly can survive for months, and migrates enormous distances over many generations, like from here all the way to Mexico or maybe California. She said I might have noticed that butterflies, especially those that are brightly colored, flit about unpredictably when they fly and their erratic flight makes it difficult for predators to catch them. But the monarch doesn't bounce around unpredictably but instead flies a slow, deliberate pattern. Yet these butterflies fly among butterfly-eating birds at will, without danger. (I really hadn't noticed all that, but I said nothing.)

"Why can they fly so temptingly among ravenous birds and still survive?" The Old Lady asked rhetorically. "Simply because they're so poisonous to birds as to be highly distasteful to them," she answered her own question. "You see," said the Old Lady, when the monarch is still a larva, it chomps away at milkweed plants that contain a compound that is poisonous to vertebrates and it eventually accumulates enough of this compound to become highly distasteful to the birds that would otherwise eat it. So birds avoid these brilliant, slow-flying butterflies.

"Do they avoid these butterflies?" asked the old lady, "because of a built-in, genetically based aversion?" Again she answered her own question, saying that the answer is no. In fact, she explained, naïve birds attack (and generally consume) just about anything that looks like a butterfly or a moth. But once they've eaten one poisonous monarch, they don't eat a second.

They learn this taste aversion after a single unhappy experience. Not only does this prevent them from getting sick or even dying, but it also saves the lives of countless slow-flying monarch butterflies.

The old lady motioned that I should now record her words as she lay back on the grass by the willow, using her boots as a pillow. She had holes in both her socks. I couldn't decide where to sit or whether I, too, should lie down. I stood. It looked like it might rain.

THIS CHAPTER

The importance of taste-aversion learning will become apparent in this chapter, *said Mrs. Gribbin.* And it will also become apparent, *she continued,* that the two basic types of conditioning, classical and operant, described in the first four chapters are not always applicable in all situations. Nor, in spite of what Pavlov, Watson, Guthrie, Thorndike, Hull, and Skinner typically assumed, are the basic explanatory principles of contiguity and reinforcement always appropriate.

Objectives

Tell your readers, *said Mrs. Gribbin*, that Chapter 5 explains how these views are not always entirely correct. Make them understand that after they finish this chapter they will, with startling ease and elegance, be able to write long dissertations explaining the following:

- the meaning of evolutionary psychology;
- the Rescorla–Wagner view of Pavlovian conditioning;
- the significance of phenomena such as blocking, instinctive drift, and autoshaping;
- why surprise and prediction are important in conditioned learning;
- the meaning of biological constraints and preparedness;
- misconceptions and facts about the structures and functions of the human brain;
- the nature and applications of biofeedback.

TASTE AVERSION LEARNING

In psychological terms, *Old Lady Gribbin explained*, what the bird that eats a poisonous butterfly acquires is a **taste aversion**: a marked dislike for a particular food. As the story of the butterfly shows, taste aversions are sometimes very important in biological terms. If poisons have distinctive tastes and if they don't immediately kill the organism that eats them but simply make it sick, then developing a strong aversion to those tastes might prevent a later poisoning. What is important biologically is that the taste aversion be powerful and that it develop immediately, preferably after a single exposure to the poison.

Conditioning Explanations for Taste Aversions

The conditioning theories described in the early part of this book are of two general kinds: those that deal with behaviors resulting directly from stimulation (respondents) and those that deal with behaviors that are simply emitted by the organism (operants). Behavioristic theories offer two different sets of explanations for respondent and operant learning: classical conditioning and the law of effect.

In their simplest and most basic form, the laws of classical conditioning state that when a neutral stimulus is frequently accompanied or slightly preceded by an effective stimulus (for example, a stimulus that elicits a reflex), the neutral stimulus will eventually acquire some of the properties of the effective stimulus. Thus, a dog eventually comes to salivate (CR) in response to a tone (previously neutral stimulus – CS) after the tone has been repeatedly paired with food (effective stimulus – US).

The law of effect, also in its simplest form, maintains that a behavior that is followed by reinforcement will tend to be repeated; one that is not followed by reinforcement will tend not to be repeated. Furthermore, aspects of the situations in which behaviors have been reinforced (or not reinforced) come to exercise a degree of control over the occurrence or nonoccurrence of the behavior. Thus, a dog that is reinforced for rolling over whenever its master says

"Roll over" may eventually discriminate between the commands "Roll over" and "Fetch my slippers." At this point, these verbal commands will have acquired stimulus control over the behaviors in question.

Problems with Classical Conditioning Explanations of Taste Aversions

At first glance, classical conditioning might appear to be a good explanation for taste aversion learning. Neutral stimuli (CS), such as the sight and taste of a butterfly, are paired with a powerful unconditioned stimulus (US), such as the poisons in the butterfly, and become associated with the same illness related responses (CR) (see Figure 5.1).

But several characteristics of acquired taste aversions make a Pavlovian classical conditioning explanation less than perfect. First, a Pavlovian view of classical conditioning maintains that conditioning results from the *repeated* pairing of stimulus and response events; but taste aversion learning often occurs in a single trial.

Second, learning in Pavlovian classical conditioning is thought to depend on contiguity, the near simultaneity of events. In taste aversion learning, though, the unconditioned response (the violent illness) sometimes occurs many minutes or even hours after the CS (Kwok & Boakes, 2015).

Third, classical conditioning principles maintain that any neutral stimulus can be associated with any US if paired with it often enough, but in taste aversion learning organisms often display a marked selectivity in their learning. As a result, certain associations are never learned or are learned only under specific conditions. For example, rats normally acquire taste aversion to a solution they taste shortly before being made to swim. However, as Nakajima (2018) showed, learning the taste aversion is strongly influenced by the temperature of the water in which the rat swims. In his studies, rats who were made to swim in 22 degree (Celsius) water developed the taste aversion; those made to swim in much warmer water (30 or 38 degrees) did not.

These three characteristics of taste aversion learning are well illustrated in controlled experiments with various animals.

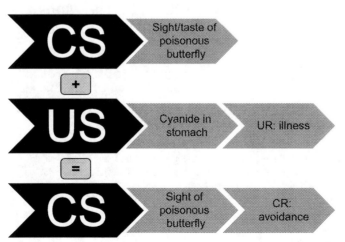

Figure 5.1 A classical conditioning explanation of taste aversion learning. That taste aversions are often learned after a single experience and that there are sometimes long delays between the UR (illness) and the US–UR pairing (eating of the moth and illness) present problems for this explanation.

One-Trial Acquisition of Taste Aversions

Birds don't need to eat bushels of monarch butterflies before learning to avoid them; a single experience is sufficient. Similarly, rats exposed to a single dose of lithium chloride or radiation so they become ill after eating will subsequently avoid the food they ate before getting sick. Thus, a profound aversion to alcohol and other substances can be conditioned in some rats following a single dose of lithium chloride (Nakajima, Ogai, & Sasaki, 2018).

Delayed Conditioning of Taste Aversions

Recall that in Pavlovian conditioning, the normal sequence is to present the conditioning stimulus (bell or tone, for example) just before or overlapping with the unconditioned stimulus (food powder, for example). *Trace pairing* in classical conditioning refers to a situation in which the unconditioned stimulus (US) is presented after the conditioned stimulus. As noted in Chapter 2, trace conditioning is ordinarily very difficult unless the time lapse between CS and US is extremely short (usually only half a second). But taste aversion learning in rats can be extremely powerful even when there is a delay of many hours between the conditioning stimulus (the taste of food, for example) and the effects of the unconditioned stimulus (illness) (Kwok, Sun, & Boakes, 2016).

In humans, too, taste aversions are powerful and quickly learned both by children and by adults. Lin, Arthurs, and Reilly (2017) describe how foods eaten just prior to powerful unconditioned stimuli such as chemotherapy or radiotherapy can, after a single exposure, become linked with strong taste aversions. This happens even though patients know very clearly that the cause of their nausea and illness is the therapy and not the food.[1] "In the most extreme cases," write Lin et al., "the quality of life is so compromised that patients will postpone or abandon chemotherapy or radiotherapy, despite the obvious life-threatening consequences" (2017, p. 340).

Like other forms of classical conditioning, taste aversion learning can also involve stimulus generalization. Thus, aversions are often generalized to other foods that taste or smell similar. For example, among rats, a conditioned taste aversion to *lithium* chloride easily generalizes to *sodium* chloride (ordinary salt) (Rebecca Glatt, St. John, Lu, & Boughter, 2016). Among mice, taste aversions to something like **umami** (one of five tastes humans can detect, described as *meaty*) readily generalize to a variety of substances including sweet substances (sucrose), sour tastes (citric acid), and bitter flavors (quinine) (Delay & Kondoh, 2015).

The fact that taste aversions are easily learned by humans as well as nonhuman animals has led to what are sometimes highly effective therapies for addictions. For example, a therapy that

---

[1] The old lady interrupted her reading. She said she wanted to say something here about the human propensity to think that behavior is mostly a function of conscious awareness. She said that taste aversions are just one of many types of behavior that depend not on conscious awareness but on principles of conditioning as well as on evolutionary factors. She explained that other behaviors, such as phobias, also illustrate the occasional impotence of reason and conscious awareness – such as how people continue to be afraid of things like spiders or snakes or birds even when they know them to be absolutely harmless. Then, she turned to her pages once more. It started to rain a little. She continued reading as if the sudden dampness didn't bother her. I was cold.

is sometimes quite effective, labeled *rapid smoking*, attempts to eliminate nicotine addiction by having participants smoke continually and rapidly, causing nausea and other feelings of ill health and consequent aversion to nicotine (Harris & Reynolds, 2015).

Alcoholism has also been successfully treated using **aversion therapy**. Revusky (2009) reports that chemical aversion treatment of alcoholism was highly prevalent some decades ago. In studies of aversion treatment, patients were typically exposed to the tastes and odors of various alcoholic beverages and subsequently made ill, usually via injections of nausea-producing substances. Although the procedure yielded very positive results, says Revusky, it now appears to be used very infrequently. None of the chemicals most commonly used for alcohol aversion therapy (emetine, apomorphine, and lithium) have been approved by the Federal Drug Administration (FDA) for that purpose (Aetna, 2018).

Selectivity in Taste Aversion Learning

If a rat is injected with a solution of lithium chloride while it is drinking saccharin-flavored water, it will later avoid foods that taste of saccharin (although it doesn't become ill until about an hour after the injection). This observation appears reasonable, given what is known about contiguity and classical conditioning. But if a rat is made ill and exposed to flashing lights or a distinct noise while drinking saccharin-flavored water, it will develop no aversion to the lights or the sound but only to the taste (Garcia & Koelling, 1966).

The same point is made even more dramatically in studies of cross-species aversion learning. Wilcoxon, Dragoin, and Kral (1971) produced aversions in rats and in quail by feeding them blue-colored, flavored water and later injecting them with an illness-inducing drug. The rats and the quail developed marked aversions, but the nature of these aversions was very different. The rats developed an aversion to any liquid with the flavor in question, regardless of its color; the quail developed an aversion to all blue-colored liquids regardless of their flavor.

The best explanation for these findings is that quail have excellent color vision and probably rely to a considerable extent on visual cues to sort what is edible from what is not. In contrast, rats, like most other mammals, depend mostly on olfactory (smell) rather than visual cues. It therefore makes biological sense that rats should make use of smell cues in learning about foods that should be avoided. And it makes biological sense for quail to use visual cues in the same kind of learning.

Latent Inhibition and Taste Aversion Learning

Taste aversions often occur a long time after exposure to an illness-inducing food. For example, if you eat something new that later makes you violently ill, the chances are you will develop a marked aversion to eating whatever made you ill. Interestingly, however, the taste aversion you develop will not be associated with the utensils with which you ate, the television program you were watching at the time, or any of the other familiar things you ate and drank. Instead, it will be associated only with the new taste. And this happens even when the illness occurs hours later.

"But," you say, "we can figure it out. We know that the new food is what made us ill." But no: Taste aversions are not conscious, cognitive decisions, as is evident in the taste aversions that often develop following chemotherapy and radiation therapy (Lin et al., 2017). When you try to poison a rat and you succeed in getting it to take a small bite of your poison, if that bite later makes the rat ill but does not kill it, it may well develop a powerful aversion to anything that smells and tastes like your poison, but not to any of the other foods it may have eaten at about the same time. That is why it is very hard to poison rats. The rat, like most other nonhuman animals, is likely to taste strange foods but not to eat very much of them if there are other, familiar foods around. If the strange new food does not make the rat ill, it may eat a lot more next time. But if the rat later becomes ill, the taste aversion will be associated with the new rather than with the familiar. It is as though the connection between the offending food and its ill effects remain possible until the occurrence, or nonoccurrence, of the unconditioned response (illness). If there is no unconditioned response, no aversion learning occurs. Similarly, when treating human patients with chemotherapy or radiotherapy, if no serious physical symptoms occur, there is no taste aversion learning relative to previously eaten foods.

Research demonstrates that pre-exposure to an inconsequential stimulus (such as the color of food or the physical setting of a clinic), when that exposure is neither reinforced nor punished, makes it less likely that the stimulus will later become associated with a response (Weiner & Arad, 2009). This phenomenon is called **latent inhibition**. For example, in one study, Wang, Chai, and Holahan (2010) pre-exposed a group of rats to a given environment, and another to a different environment. These rats were later trained on avoidance tasks in the first environment. As has been found in many other similar studies, rats pre-exposed to the environment were less reluctant to enter it – a clear demonstration of latent inhibition.

Blocking

It appears that not just any stimulus can be classically conditioned. For example, *latent inhibition* describes how prior exposure to certain stimuli (such as the sights and smells associated with food) can serve to prevent (inhibit) the development of taste aversions associated with those stimuli. And the fact that quail readily acquire powerful aversions associated with color, but rats do not, also indicates that there is more to taste aversion learning than the simple co-occurrence (contiguity) of events. These observations pose problems for a simple, classical conditioning explanation of taste aversion learning.

Kamin (1969) describes another phenomenon that presents problems for classical conditioning. In one demonstration, Kamin used rats who had previously been conditioned to depress a lever to receive occasional rewards. Now, while a group of these rats were busily bar-pressing, he paired two stimuli (a noise and a light) with an electric shock administered to their feet (we'll call these rats the A group). The procedure was to turn both the light and the noise on for three minutes and then follow this immediately with the electric shock. Classical conditioning theory would predict that after enough pairings with the electrical shock, either the light or the noise would bring about reactions similar to those associated with the electric shock. The prediction is

	Pretraining	Conditioning	Testing	Response
• A group (control)	• None	• Noise + light shock	• Light	• Freezing (high fear)
• B group (blocking)	• Noise shock	• Noise + light shock	• Light	• Bar-pressing (no fear)

Figure 5.2 A representation of Kamin's study of blocking in classical conditioning. For rats in the A group exposed to both noise and light followed by a shock, exposure to the light alone leads to a marked suppression of ongoing bar-pressing behavior. But rats in the B group, who had previously learned that noise means shock, failed to learn that light might also mean shock.

correct: Rats in the A group responded with fear to either the noise alone or the light alone by, among other things, immediately stopping their bar-pressing behavior.

Now Kamin threw a twist into the proceedings. First, he conditioned a second group of rats by using only the noise (we'll call them the B group). As before, he followed three minutes of noise with an electric foot shock. Then, after the rats in the B group had been conditioned to the noise alone, he conditioned them in exactly the same way as he had the A group, pairing both the noise and the light again for three-minute periods and then following each pairing with an electric shock.

Now rats in the B group were exposed to the light alone. Recall that when the rats in the A group were exposed to the light alone, they stopped bar-pressing. Classical conditioning theory would predict exactly the same outcome for the rats in the B group because the light had been paired with the noise equally often for both groups. Amazingly, however, the rats in the B group continued to press the bar at about the same rate, seemingly unaffected by the light. It is as though the initial conditioning that linked noise with pain prevented the rat from learning that a light might also mean pain. This defines what is termed **blocking** – the classical conditioning phenomenon where prior learning prevents the formation of a new association. (The procedure is shown in Figure 5.2.)

The Rescorla–Wagner Explanation

Kamin's pioneering experiments in blocking suggest the need for different explanations of what happens, and why, in certain examples of classical conditioning. Among the most widely accepted of the resulting explanations is the one known as the **Rescorla–Wagner model**. What the model says, in effect, is that classical conditioning is not an automatic process solely dependent on the frequency of CS–US pairings; rather, it is dependent on the information the CS provides about the likelihood of the US occurring. In other words, what the organism learns are *expectations* about the probability of the US occurring.

The strength of the link between the CS and the US, explains Rescorla (1988), can be expressed as a number representing *associative strength*. The model assumes that there is a

Evolutionary Psychology

fixed amount of associative strength available for any US–CS pairing and that the various individual stimuli that compose the CS compete for this associative strength. If the CS is composed of two or more stimuli, the strength of the association that forms between any one of these component CSs and the US subtracts from the association strength remaining for other component stimuli. Thus, in Kamin's blocking study, the rats in the B group first learn an association between noise (CS) and shock (US). That is, they develop a very strong expectation that the noise will lead to shock. That they later fail to learn an association between light and shock is explained by the fact that all the associative strength between the US (shock) and the CS has been used up by the noise–shock pairing.

A Biological Explanation

There are other more biologically based explanations of phenomena such as blocking. For example, why might a rat conditioned to associate a noise with shock subsequently be unable to learn that a light might also mean shock?

Well, said Kamin (1968), the most likely explanation is this: Whenever something important happens to an animal, it immediately searches its memory to see what events could have been used to predict the occurrence. When a red-tailed hawk swoops down on a chicken but narrowly misses, scaring the living begorrah out of it, the chicken searches its memory banks for immediately preceding events. And maybe it remembers a swift shadow darkening its path or the whistling of wing feathers braking. And forever after, the chicken flees from shadows and whistling noises.

So, when the rat receives a mild foot shock, it stops and scans its memory to see what was different and unexpected immediately before this event. Because the rat in the A group notes that light and noise always precede the shock, it freezes when it later sees the light or hears the noise.

But the rat in the B group has had different experiences. First, it learned that a noise always precedes a foot shock, so when it again hears this noise, it cowers and stops pressing the bar. Later, it is exposed to both the light and the noise, followed by the shock. But because the shock is already predicted by the noise, the light provides no new information about the occurrence of the CS. There is no discrepancy between what the rats expect (the shock) and what occurs (the shock). So, when the rat in the B group is later exposed only to the light, it keeps right on pressing the bar. In a sense, having learned that noise means a shock is coming blocks the rat from learning that light might mean the same thing.

What this explanation says, in effect, is that classical conditioning means learning *what goes with what*. Contiguity is not as important as the information a stimulus provides about the probability of other events. Thus, what is learned is a connection or an expectation. Pavlov's dog learns that a buzzer or the sight of a handler means it can expect to be fed; a rat learns that a light or a sound means expect a shock. In Rescorla and Holland's words, "Pavlovian conditioning should be viewed as the learning about relations among events" (1976, p. 184).

To summarize, the biological explanation for conditioning and blocking can be simplified in terms of *surprise* and *prediction* (*expectation*). When a rat hears a noise (US), which is initially a neutral stimulus, there is no expectation that a shock (CS) will follow. That there is a shock is initially a surprise; but after the shock and noise have been paired a number of times, the CS–US pairing is no longer surprising: The animal now expects (predicts) that the noise will always be followed by the shock. Learning in classical conditioning, explains Rescorla, occurs when there is new information linked with the CS (in other words, when the organism is *surprised*). When the CS provides no new information, as occurs when the light is added to the noise *after* the rat has already learned that noise means shock, there is no new learning.

Higher-Order Conditioning and Biological Adaptation

In classical conditioning, the organism typically learns about an association between a normally significant event (such as the presentation of food – the US) and one that has less or different importance (such as a tone – the CS). As Pavlov pointed out, though, the relations learned in classical conditioning are not limited to those that might exist between the CS and US, but include what is termed **higher-order conditioning**. In higher-order conditioning, another stimulus becomes a significant event in place of the US. For example, Rescorla (1980) describes how a Pavlovian dog learns a connection between a metronome and food. Later, the metronome is paired with a second stimulus: a black square. And although the black square is itself never paired with food, in time, it too elicits salivation.

As Pavlov (and Watson) interpreted it, higher-order conditioning expands the applicability of classical conditioning tremendously, explaining how associations build on each other to construct a repertoire of responses. For Rescorla, higher-order conditioning is even more important as a way of understanding how associations are formed. In general, says Rescorla, "conditioning [is] the learning that results from exposure to relations among events in the environment. Such learning is a primary means by which the organism represents the structure of its world" (1988, p. 152).

As we saw, one useful way of looking at classical conditioning is in terms of surprise and expectations. As Rescorla (1988) put it, organisms "adjust their Pavlovian associations only when they are 'surprised'" (p. 153). That is because organisms experience surprise only when expectations are not met (in other words, when there is new information). The rat in the B group that has learned an association between noise and shock does not modify that association when noise and light are paired with shock. Thanks to the noise signal, the shock is not a surprise; it doesn't violate expectations. Hence, there is no new information in the light, and no new associations result. Thus, says Rescorla, it is nonsense "that a signal simply acquires the ability to evoke the response to the US" (1988, p. 157), as is suggested by simple interpretations of Pavlovian conditioning.

Learning is essentially an adaptive process. The changes in behavior that define learning are what allow organisms to survive and thrive. At a very basic level, animals need to learn and remember where food sources might be, as does the rat that learns to depress a lever for food; they need to recognize potential enemies, as did the chicken following its near-death experience; they need to avoid potentially harmful substances, as does the bird that has eaten a single toxic monarch butterfly; and they need to stay away from potentially painful or even injurious situations such as electric shocks.

Darwin's Natural Selection and Psychology

That biological and evolutionary pressures toward survival should be evident in the principles that govern human and animal learning is hardly surprising. As Robertson, Garcia, and Garcia (1988) note, Darwin was himself a learning theorist. He was well acquainted with associationistic explanations of learning, and he invoked these principles in his own theory of natural selection. After publishing his classic *On the Origin of Species*, he then published *The Descent of Man* and *The Expression of the Emotions in Man and Animals* (Darwin, 1859, 1871, 1872).

Barrett, Dunbar, and Lycett (2002) summarize Darwin's theory of natural selection in three clear premises and the consequences that logically follow:

- All individuals of a species vary behaviorally and physiologically.
- Some of this variation is genetic (heritable), so offspring will tend to resemble their parents more than they resemble other unrelated individuals.
- Among individuals of any given species, there is typically competition for important resources such as food, mates, and shelter.

The logical consequences of these three premises are clear: Behavioral and physiological variations that allow more success in the competition for resources give certain individuals an edge in the struggle to survive and to procreate. As a result, they produce more offspring who inherit the same advantageous variations. Similarly, individuals whose behavioral and physiological variations place them at a disadvantage produce fewer offspring. This evolutionary process of natural selection leads to the survival of certain variations and the elimination of those that have less desirable consequences.

This theory profoundly influenced conditioning theorists. Theorists such as Skinner and Thorndike noted that all sorts of responses appear when an organism behaves. In biological terms, these different responses are like variations of a characteristic. In the same way as the fitness of an inherited variation is evident in the likelihood of its becoming more frequent in succeeding generations, the fitness of a response, evident in its consequences, is reflected in the probability that it will be retained or eliminated. In brief, conditioning may be described as the survival (and death) of responses. Behaviors whose consequences are most adaptive are most likely to survive.

EVOLUTIONARY PSYCHOLOGY

Thorndike's and Skinner's theories can be interpreted as being influenced by and reflecting Darwinian ideas. A profound Darwinian influence is also found in the works of many other psychologists and sociologists, who are sometimes labeled *sociobiologists* or *evolutionary psychologists*. Among the first of these was George John Romanes (1848–1894). His classical work on animal intelligence (1883) was based on careful observation of the behaviors of dozens of different animals and insects, always with a view to uncovering the causes and the purposes of their actions. His overall objective was, quite simply, to describe the course of mental evolution, much as Darwin had described the evolution of species. Unfortunately, however,

Evolutionary psychologists, notes Hagen (2016), continue to fight the doctrine that has dominated psychology for most of the twentieth century. Briefly, this doctrine asserts that biology does not really matter, that what is most important is the malleability of the mind and the potency of the environment in molding and shaping the mind. This doctrine holds that there is really no such thing as a genetically determined human nature common to all humans. It is the doctrine of the passive mind, of the tabula rasa, the blank slate on which experience writes its messages.

But there *is* a human nature, evolutionary psychologists insist. Evidence that it exists is found in the overwhelming similarities that one sees among all the world's cultures. These similarities reflect common adaptations that have evolved over time, such as color vision that allowed earlier humans to identify ripe fruit. Similarly, all people have a tendency to be concerned about social status and social relations; all feel love and fear and guilt; all gossip about similar things; all have a sense of justice, of envy, of greed, of retribution, of purpose, of love. These feelings are taken for granted and understood everywhere. They are part of human nature.

What is also part of human nature, and this is fundamentally important for biologically oriented learning theory, is a built-in malleability. Malleability is what allows the individual to adapt and survive. But unlike the malleability described by Watson or Skinner, this malleability has limits: It is subject to biological constraints.

The defining characteristic of **evolutionary psychology**, then, is its attention to biology and genetics as sources of explanation for human learning and behavior, for the development of the human mind, and even for the development of cultures (Jonason, 2017; Richardson, 2017). Support for the notions of evolutionary psychologists is sometimes based on situations in which reinforcement and contiguity are inadequate as explanations for learning and behavior. Among these situations are phenomena such as autoshaping and instinctive drift.

Autoshaping

If a pigeon receives reinforcement at intervals regardless of what it is doing at the time, the result might be what Skinner called superstitious behavior. That is, the pigeon may learn some "accidental" behavior such as twisting or swaying.

However, if a response key or disk is illuminated for a few seconds just before the appearance of food, the pigeon will quickly learn to peck at the key or disk. That this behavior occurs and is learned despite the fact that the pigeon's pecking is not related to the appearance of food has led to the use of the term **autoshaping** to describe the learning involved. As is shown in Figure 5.3, this type of learning is easily explained using a Pavlovian model of classical conditioning. The pecking response is initially an unconditioned response elicited by the food (the food is an unconditioned stimulus). However, following the pairing of light and food, the pecking response very quickly becomes associated with the light. Subsequently, experimenters can "shape" the pecking response by making food contingent on its occurrence. In this case, key-pecking could be viewed as an operant rather than simply a conditioned response.

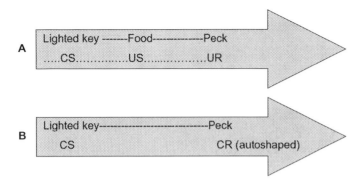

Figure 5.3 In A, a lighted key is paired with food. The pigeon's response to food is to peck. In B, the pigeon pecks the lighted key even though doing so has nothing to do with obtaining food. The pecking behavior has been autoshaped.

Autoshaping can also be demonstrated with rats (for example, Nasser, Lafferty, Lesser, Bacharach, & Calu, 2018). If you place a rat in a cage in which there are two tubes – one an empty feeder tube and the second a spout from which the rat is periodically fed – the rat will lick the empty tube as well as the one through which the food is presented. Eventually, licking the empty tube will become a strong autoshaped behavior, even though it has nothing to do with the rat obtaining food.

Autoshaped responses are remarkably persistent and remarkably resistant to extinction. This is dramatically illustrated in an experiment by Killeen (2003), in which pigeons were taught to peck at a light in the manner described. Then, conditions were changed so the pigeons' pecking would prevent reinforcement from occurring. Despite this, even very hungry pigeons continued to peck at the light for thousands of trials. Nor is autoshaping of key-pecking restricted to pigeons. In other studies, blue jays, robins, and starlings have each demonstrated a propensity for learning to peck lighted keys even when there is no tangible reward contingent on so doing (see Kamil & Mauldin, 1988).

Autoshaping poses a problem for a traditional conditioning explanation of learning. First, it provides an example of behaviors that appear to be learned even though they are not associated with reinforcement. Even more telling, these behaviors often persist even when they are clearly associated with withdrawal of reinforcement.

However, the most important point that studies of autoshaping make is not that reinforcement exercises little control over operant responses. Rather, the point is that pecking among pigeons is not a very good operant behavior for experimental purposes. Nor is bar-pressing for rats. A better experimental operant would be one of several equally probable responses emitted by the organism for no particular reason; the response could then be brought under the control of its consequences. In contrast, pecking is a highly probable food-related response in pigeons, as is bar-pressing among rats. That a pigeon should continue to peck at a lighted disk even when doing so means it will not be reinforced says more about the pigeon's evolutionary history than about the inadequacies of operant conditioning. In the same way, that a rat approaches a lever and explores and pushes at it may reflect the rat's biology as much as its experiences. Levers and lighted disks are, in a sense, *signs* that food (or some other reward) may be imminent. And organisms that have survived the life-and-death struggles of evolutionary history have at least learned to recognize and react to *signs* related to eating, mating, and escaping danger. Not surprisingly, *autoshaping* is often referred to as **sign-tracking** – so-called because the organism is responding to *signs* associated with important, genetically programmed tendencies such as eating and drinking (Smedley & Smith, 2018; Versaggi, King, & Meyer, 2016).

Instinctive Drift

In the early 1950s, two of Skinner's students, encouraged by the remarkable success that experimenters had enjoyed in shaping the behavior of animals, decided to commercialize this process. These students, a husband and wife team, the Brelands, proposed to train a number of animals to perform stunts sufficiently amusing that audiences might pay to see them. Through the "differential reinforcement of successive approximations" (that is, through shaping), they taught a "miser" raccoon to pick up a coin and deposit it in a tin box; a "baseball playing" chicken to pull a rubber loop, thereby releasing a capsule that slid down a chute to where it could be pecked out of the cage; a "hoarding" pig to pick up large wooden "nickels" and deposit them in a piggy bank; and on and on. Operant conditioning procedures worked exquisitely; all the animals learned their required behaviors. The Brelands successfully trained more than 6,000 animals (Breland & Breland, 1961, 1966).

But not all these 6,000 animals continued to behave as they had been trained to behave. As Breland and Breland (1951, 1961) put it, many of them eventually began to "misbehave." For example, the pig took longer and longer to bring its wooden nickel to the bank and deposit it, although it clearly knew that reinforcement depended on doing so.[2] Instead, it spent increasingly longer periods flipping the coins to the ground, rooting around in the dirt with them, and otherwise behaving as might any other uneducated pig on the trail of the elusive truffle. The Brelands tried to remedy the situation by increasing the pig's food deprivation. But that only made matters worse; in the end, the pig was taking so long to deposit the wooden nickels that it was in imminent danger of starvation.

The raccoon fared no better. It too began to take longer and longer in bringing the coins to the metal box. It often refused to let go of the coins, instead dipping them in the box, bringing them out again, and rubbing them between its paws. And not to be left out, the chicken became so engrossed in pecking at the capsule that it seemed to quite forget everything else it had learned.

Researchers have now uncovered a large number of situations in which animals initially learn a behavior quickly and well but eventually begin to resort to other behaviors, the nature of which is highly revealing. It is surely no accident that the pig rooted, the raccoon "washed" its coin, or the chicken pecked. These are, after all, what pigs, raccoons, and chickens do with food. "It seems obvious," claimed Breland and Breland, "that these animals are trapped by strongly instinctive behaviors, and clearly we have here a demonstration of the prepotency of such behavior patterns over those which have been conditioned" (1961, p. 683).

In general terms, this phenomenon, called **instinctive drift**, is the instinctual behavior that takes precedence when there is competition between a biologically based behavior and a learned response. It appears that with repeated exposure to a situation characterized by this kind of competition, organisms tend to revert to the behavior that has a biological,

---

[2] Old Lady Gribbin said this wasn't very scientifically or accurately worded, that we probably shouldn't say that the pig "clearly knew" anything of the sort. She explained that, after all, this was a behavioristic pig, not a humanistic or a cognitive one. She said that all we can say for certain, as behaviorists, is that the pig's shaped responses had been reinforced often enough that the experimenters could justifiably expect it would continue to deposit wooden nickels in piggy banks. She said flatly that what the pig actually thought of the entire process is a matter for speculation, not science.

Evolutionary Psychology

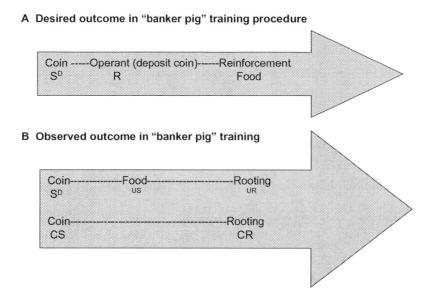

Figure 5.4 The desired outcome of this training procedure, shown in A, is explained by the principles of operant conditioning: Depositing the coin in the bank is an operant whose probability should increase as a result of the reinforcing contingency: food. What actually happens, shown in B, is better explained by a model of classical conditioning: The food serves as an unconditioned stimulus that elicits the unconditioned response: rooting. Repeatedly pairing the coin with the food leads to an association between the two, so the coin eventually serves as a conditioned stimulus for rooting.

evolutionary basis. This, the Brelands are careful to point out, does not invalidate general learning principles. In fact, as is shown in Figure 5.4, instinctive drift presents a good example of classical conditioning. But it is an example that emphasizes the importance of biology. Not all behaviors can be conditioned and maintained through the careful arrangement of response consequences. For example, as Whishaw et al. (2018) explain, there is a spontaneous, presumably biologically based sequence of behaviors that many rodents engage in prior to eating: They pick up food with the mouth, sit back and raise their paws, transfer the food to their paws, and use them to assist in eating. Not surprisingly, elements of these behaviors are frequently observed as autoshaped behaviors learned during conditioning tasks.

Biological Constraints

The main characteristic of evolutionary psychology is its attention to biological influences on learning and behavior. Autoshaping, instinctive drift, and the learning of taste aversions are striking examples of biological influences. They illustrate what evolutionary psychologists refer to as **biological constraints** – inborn predispositions that make certain kinds of learning highly probable and easy and other kinds improbable and very difficult (Overmier & Meyers-Manor, 2015; Seligman, 1975).

As Breland and Breland (1966) note, it is very easy to condition a cat or a dog to sit still or stand motionless. For these animals, which evolved as predators, standing still is an extremely useful, survival-related behavior. But in Breland and Breland's words, "it is almost impossible for a chicken to do nothing" (1966, p. 103). When Breland and Breland tried to teach chickens to stand still, they found these birds absolutely insisted on scurrying around and scratching instead. And, of course, chickens do not have to be trained to scratch. Scratching is how chickens make their living; it has clear survival-related benefits.

The most obvious general principle of a biological constraint is that it will favor behaviors that have survival value and discourage those detrimental to survival. As Kenrick and his associates illustrate, it is possible to predict what will be easy or difficult to learn by reasoning from important social and survival goals (Kenrick, Maner, Butner, Li, & Becker, 2002). For example, that rats (or humans) should learn an aversion to a poisonous taste clearly has survival value. But that they should learn an aversion to a sound or a light when they have been physically poisoned has no such value.

In Seligman and Hager's (1972) terms, organisms are prepared for certain kinds of learning and contraprepared for others, meaning that they are prepared *not to learn* certain things. A rat faced with danger is prepared to flee, fight, freeze, or perhaps become frantic; teaching it to do any of these through the use of aversive stimulation (an electric shock, for example) is a simple matter. But teaching it to engage in a behavior that is opposed to any of these is very difficult. Thus, teaching a rat to depress a lever to escape an electric shock is very difficult (Bolles, 1970). Similarly, a pigeon can easily be taught to peck at a key to obtain food but not to escape an electric shock. In contrast, the pigeon easily learns to flap its wings to avoid a shock but not to obtain food.

Biological constraints are clearly involved in the reversion of pigs to rooting and chickens to pecking in the instinctive drift experiments. Similarly, biological constraints affect autoshaped behaviors. For example, pigeons show a marked preference for pecking at keys that are on the floor rather than on a wall, probably because they feed primarily on the ground (Burns & Malone, 1992). Also, biological influences on learning are dramatically evident in single-trial taste aversion learning.

It is perhaps less obvious that human learning is strongly influenced by biological factors. Still, we know that people are "prepared" to acquire strong taste aversions very easily, which is highly useful if you do not want to poison yourself. Similarly, research indicates that children can acquire fear of snakes exceptionally easily. And that, too, may have survival benefits. Some also argue that humans are biologically prepared to acquire language, perhaps in much the same way as goslings are programmed to acquire a "following" response if given

Evolutionary Psychology

appropriate stimulation at the right time in their development (Chomsky, 1972). Others insist that many human social behaviors are a direct function of inherited predispositions and that these predispositions and biological constraints shape the nature of human culture. Even human marriage and other mating systems reflect biological underpinnings, as do personality characteristics and individual differences (Losos & Lenski, 2017).

Evolution of the Brain

The same evolutionary forces that molded other organs also shaped brains. These evolutionary forces tend to favor behaviors that maximize chances of surviving and reproducing. But they are forces whose effects take shape very slowly over vast stretches of time. On the other hand, the environments in which humans live now change with startling rapidity. As a result, some behaviors that were once highly adaptive persist even though they are now counter-adaptive; witness humanity's peculiar and frightening penchant to destroy its environment and to shorten its lives through resting too much and eating too much of the wrong things. Most of human evolutionary history was spent in Pleistocene environments. These were violent times, explain Mead, Beauchaine, and Shannon (2010), when fierce and hungry predators, and perhaps other evolving humans, posed real and immediate threats. Unfortunately, however, a brain evolved to adapt to violence and to survive becomes maladaptive in less threatening environments. They suggest that such brains bring with them a higher risk of psychopathology. And perhaps they also bring a higher risk of events such as terrorism and wars that have incalculable potential for disaster. Such brains are still adaptive among many reptiles and even other nonhuman mammals, but for today's humans, they are socially maladaptive. As Burgos (2015) explains, they may lead to *misbehaviors* reminiscent of the rooting of the Brelands' pig that stubbornly persisted in spite of the imminent danger of starvation.

There are other ways in which the evolution of our brains is maladaptive. Our brains, suggests Cowley (1989), evolved at a time when snakes and other wild creatures posed far greater threats than water and air pollution; a time when ingesting too much fat, salt, or sugar was laughably unlikely. Also, a well-rested and well-fed animal can more easily survive a cold spell or escape from a predator. It is as though our primitive brains whisper in our ears as we stand before our refrigerators: "Eat while you can. There may be none tomorrow – if there is a tomorrow." And so we eat too much and too often of the wrong things.

Still, if you are human, you know there will be food tomorrow, and you know the saber-toothed tiger is not likely to invade your bedroom this night. You can anticipate with startling clarity; you can plan for times that have not yet come but whose coming can be measured to the very second. Not only can you anticipate the future, but you can also remember the past. And more than all this, you are conscious of your awareness; you can reflect on your own reflections and *communicate* them to others of your species. Language and grammar and the remarkable plasticity of our brains are also products of cultural evolution (Sherwood & Gomez-Robles, 2017).

Put simply, you have a mind that is made possible by your nervous system and your brain.

Evolutionary Psychology and Learning

What is important from a learning theory point of view is that one of the basic ideas of evolutionary psychology is that humans across all cultures have evolved brain structures that prepare them to learn certain things and to behave in certain ways. For example, Geary (2007) suggests that our highly developed frontal lobes are adaptations that facilitate a wide variety of information-processing functions. These processes are related to what he describes as "evolutionary significant content areas" – that is, areas that have important survival implications. They lead to the formation of what he labels *primary* forms of cognition. These include **folk knowledge** – commonly accepted beliefs about people and about natural phenomena. For example, recognition of the meanings of facial expressions and gestures and commonly held beliefs about natural phenomena illustrate folk knowledge. Primary forms of cognition also include the propensity to acquire language and the ability to navigate in physical space. The argument is that this sort of knowledge would have been highly useful to our evolutionary ancestors and that the brain structures that support primary knowledge would therefore have been selected by evolutionary pressures. In his view, humans are motivated to acquire folk knowledge because of an inherited, evolution-based urge to control their environments. Speculation is that in the distant evolutionary past, survival demanded no less.

However, our evolutionary histories did not require that we learn advanced calculus or physics. As a result, our brains do not so easily absorb the complexities of these subjects. As Hunt puts it, "*String theory for dummies* will never make the bestseller lists" (2007, p. 147). Formal education, suggests Geary, leads to a type of *secondary* knowledge. School learning, such as the study of mathematics or physics, represents secondary knowledge. Acquiring knowledge in these domains builds on primary knowledge and abilities and therefore depends on the brain structures that have evolved to support primary knowledge. As Geary puts it, "I assume that primary knowledge and abilities provide the foundation for academic learning" (2007, p. 6). For this reason, he suggests that it is important to understand how brain structures support primary learning, how these structures are organized, and how plastic they are.

Language, explains Klein (2017), has a fundamental evolutionary history tied with our social relations and supported by structures in our evolving brains. He speculates that some very early forms of communication through language, essential for transmitting knowledge about making primitive stone tools, may have existed as far back as two million years ago. In contrast, mathematics is a much more recent invention. As a result, a first language forms part of our *primary* knowledge and is acquired relatively effortlessly. But mathematics is part of *secondary* knowledge and requires considerably more directed effort.

In summary, Geary's view of evolutionary psychology suggests that while primary learning is, in a sense, *natural* and therefore relatively easily acquired, secondary knowledge is not. Thus, self-directed, discovery-oriented approaches to learning may be best for acquiring primary knowledge. For example, early language learning is largely a self-initiated process, as is the discovery of the meanings of facial expressions and gestures. So too is the discovery of many of the important characteristics of the physical world and the acquisition of the knowledge required to find our way in this world – and also our way back. In a sense, our brains have evolved to acquire primary knowledge through our own exploration. But because they have not evolved to acquire secondary knowledge, exploration or discovery learning may not be the best approach for academic subjects. Learning through discovery imposes too great a cognitive strain on many, although not all, learners. Often, suggests Geary, academic learning will require **direct instruction** (*explicit instruction* where the emphasis is on the teacher's role in imparting information) rather than what is currently referred to as **constructivism** (an approach to teaching and learning that focuses on the learner's role in discovering and organizing information).

Some Reactions to Evolutionary Psychology

Many psychologists agree with the principal beliefs and implications of evolutionary psychology. However, there are others who question the scientific basis for many of evolutionary psychology's conclusions. The fact is that we lack the data required to compare our behaviors or our brain structures with those of our evolutionary ancestors. As a result, we really cannot trace the evolution of folk knowledge or even of language and relate these to the evolution of brain structures. Nor, as Templeton (2017) points out, do we have the basis for determining what the future of human evolution will be. What we have instead is speculation. And while the speculation might seem reasonable and useful, it is hardly science.

Buller (2008) describes how evolutionary psychology has captured the popular imagination and led to what he labels a form of *pop evolutionary psychology*. This form of evolutionary psychology is premised on the assumption that if we look at the adaptive problems faced by our distant ancestors, we will find clues about why we are the way we are. For example, we suspect that in prehistoric days, a shortage of food would have driven us to spend considerable effort looking for and consuming nutrients. Now we have only to open our fridge doors to find what our primitive brains crave. And the sugars that might have been laughably scarce at one time now abound. Thus, we eat too much and of the wrong things. As Cosmides and Tooby (1997) put it, "Our modern skulls house a stone age mind."

Perhaps, agrees Buller (2008). Sadly, however, there is little evidence to support many of the claims of evolutionary psychology. Pop evolutionary psychology in particular is characterized by a number of mistaken and misleading conclusions. Among these *fallacies* are the following:

1. **Analysis of Pleistocene adaptive problems yields clues to the mind's design.** Unfortunately, we know very little about the adaptive problems faced by primitive humans, says Buller. The descriptions we have are based solely on speculation.
2. **We know or can discover why distinctively human traits evolved.** But we really don't know why human traits evolved. We assume they resulted from some adaptive function they served. But we cannot know what that adaptive function was. We have no way of comparing the traits humans have evolved with those of other humanoid groups who did not develop the same traits. As Buller puts it, "[A]ll other hominins are extinct. And dead hominins tell (virtually) no tales about their evolutionary histories" (2008, p. 78).

3. **Our modern skulls house a Stone Age mind.** In fact, our evolutionary history stretches back before the Stone Age. So, some of our brain structures and the behaviors they make possible or likely are shared with other primates. Furthermore, argues Buller, significant evolutionary change can occur in as few as 18 generations. Again, we can only speculate about how similar our brains are to those of our Stone Age relatives.
4. **The psychological data provide clear evidence for pop evolutionary psychology.** While the data may sometimes appear convincing, there are often alternative explanations that are just as reasonable but that go unexamined once the basic tenets of evolutionary psychology have been accepted.

These four fallacies simply serve to underline the scarcity of hard evidence to support the claims of evolutionary psychology. They do not disprove the theory or undermine its importance. In Buller's words, "Among Darwin's lasting legacies is our knowledge that the human mind evolved by some adaptive process . . .. We would not have such an organ if it had not performed some important adaptive function in our evolutionary past" (2008, p. 81).

Still, evolutionary psychology does not fare well in terms of its scientific underpinnings. And, as Dennis (2018) points out, its predecessor, *sociobiology*, fared no better and its scientific stature as an explanation for social behaviors is precarious.

Sociobiology: A Precursor of Evolutionary Psychology

In the same way as evolutionary psychologists believe that human behaviors and abilities reflect our evolutionary history, many anthropologists and sociologists argue that human cultures develop and change as a result of evolutionary and biological pressures. This is the belief that underpins the discipline labeled **sociobiology** (the discipline that looks for biological explanations for human behavior).

The single most important assumption of sociobiology is that humans are biologically predisposed to engage in certain social behaviors rather than others. One of sociobiology's principal spokesmen, Edward O. Wilson, defines it as "the systematic study of the biological basis of all social behavior" (1975, p. 4). Put another way, sociobiology is the study of the biological determination of social behavior among all species. Simply defined, social behavior is any form of behavior that requires the interaction of two or more individuals. Thus, mating, aggression, and altruism (helping behavior) are all examples of important social behaviors; each requires interaction between at least two individuals.

Sociobiology is based directly on evolutionary theory and draws many of its illustrations from **ethology** (the study of animal behavior in natural habitats). Sociobiologists believe that certain powerful social tendencies have survived evolutionary processes and are therefore biologically based. Underlying these tendencies is the single most important law of evolution: namely, that processes of natural selection favor the survival of the fittest. Hence, the "fittest" social behaviors (those that have contributed to survival) should be evident as powerful biological predispositions in human behavior.

Inclusive Fitness and Altruism

Note that fitness as defined by sociobiology refers not to the likelihood that a specific individual of a species will survive but, rather, to the likelihood that genetic material itself will survive. Trivers (1974, 2002), Wilson (1976), and other sociobiologists emphasize that the quest for survival is far more meaningful at the group level than at the level of the individual: hence, their use of the concept of **inclusive fitness**, which refers to the fitness of genetically related groups relative to their likelihood of procreation and survival. What is important, says Wilson, is "the maximum average survival and fertility of the group as a whole" (1975, p. 107).

The concept of inclusive fitness is fundamentally different from the Darwinian notion of the survival of the fittest individual. Inclusive fitness emphasizes that the life of a single individual is important in an evolutionary sense only to the extent that it increases the probability that the genetic material characteristic of the group to which the individual belongs will survive and reproduce. Thus, a honeybee will sting intruders to protect its hive even though doing so means that the bee itself will die. Similarly, some species of termites explode themselves when danger threatens, thereby warning other termites, which can now save themselves (Wilson, 1975). These instances of selflessness (or **altruism**) had long puzzled those who interpreted the law of survival of the fittest in the Darwinian sense, as meaning that every single individual does its utmost to survive, come hell or high water. The notion of inclusive fitness presents sociobiology with an explanation for altruism.[3]

Altruism among humans, sociobiologists argue, is a biologically based characteristic ordained by years of successful evolution (for example, see Hamilton, 1970, 1971, 1972; Marsh, 2016). In its purest form, an altruistic act is one that presents some sacrifice to the doer but results in a net genetic advantage to the species. A blackbird that noisily signals the approach of a hawk may well be detected and eaten, but in the grand scheme of things, that is a small price to pay for the eventual survival of many other blackbirds.

Carrying the argument to its extreme, sociobiology predicts that the extent to which an individual will be willing to undergo personal sacrifice will be a function of the net genetic advantage that results for the species; it will also be directly related to the degree of genetic relatedness between the doer of the good deed and those who benefit most directly. Thus, you might hesitate to save a stranger if the probability of losing your life in the process were high; the net genetic advantage in such a situation would be virtually zero. For the same reason, you should scarcely hesitate to sacrifice your life to save many others because the net genetic advantage then is high. It also follows that a father will undergo considerably more risk and sacrifice to save his son than to save a stranger, because he has a great deal more in common genetically with his son. But even saving the life of a complete stranger may present some distinct survival advantages for the entire species. Thus evolutionary pressures may well explain altruism even when it is not directed toward immediately related individuals.

---

[3] Some of your more inquisitive students might also be interested in the possibilities that sociobiological theory offers for explaining suicide, said the old lady. They might think about how honey bees who, when they sting, are not only unable to pull their stinger back out, but also end up leaving behind part of their abdomen and digestive tract, and a mess of muscles and nerves. Which doesn't sound much better than termites that produce a toxic chemical in their abdomens which, when they explode, not only showers the enemy with potentially lethal chemicals, but also quite effectively terminates the

Some Reactions to Sociobiology

In February 1978, reports Alcock (2001), E. O. Wilson gave a talk at the annual meeting of the American Association for the Advancement of Science. While he sat on stage waiting to give this talk, a young woman came over and poured a pitcher of cold water on his head. A small group of accomplices then joined her to wave placards and chant, "Wilson, you're all wet."

Sociobiology has often given rise to this kind of highly emotional negative reaction. Some of this reaction is based on theological arguments that reject the basic notions of evolution (see Cole, 2002). Some is based on a misunderstanding of what sociobiology is and on the fear that it belittles human characteristics by reducing them to mechanistic or animalistic events over which humans exercise little control. And some is based on the lack of data to support the far-reaching claims of many sociobiologists.

In essence, sociobiology suggests that a range of human social behaviors including aggression and sociopathy, sexual mores, gregariousness, scarification rites, and so on, may have biological bases (Ellsworth & Walker, 2015). There are some who even argue that spirituality has sociobiological underpinnings (for example, Galanter, 2009). Advocates of sociobiology argue that this approach provides a scientific basis for understanding social behavior and for guiding social policy. They insist that the contributions of biology to human behavior have long been underestimated. Genes and evolution, claim the sociobiologists, have shaped not only our bodies but also our behaviors.

As noted, these views have met with a great deal of resistance. Many sociologists in particular have reacted very negatively to the notion that much of human social behavior is genetically ordained (for example, see Gould, 2002a, 2002b). A number have objected to what they think is excessive generalization from a handful of evidence, a great deal of which relates more directly to nonhuman animals than to humans (Ruck, 2016).

While sociobiology was being assailed by a number of critics, the field of evolutionary psychology appears to have been steadily progressing, although there are some who wonder whether it will continue to thrive, or even survive, as a distinct discipline (for example, Jonason, 2017; Simon, 2018). Actually, what was once referred to as sociobiology is now often termed *evolutionary psychology*. Thus, in the last few years, the phrase *evolutionary psychology* appears about 13 times more frequently than does *sociobiology* in the PsycINFO database, a database that summarizes psychological research. *Evolutionary psychology* is a phrase with a much lighter burden of negative connotations than that carried by *sociobiology*.

Evolutionary Psychology: An Appraisal

Early behaviorists were optimistic that their theories would be widely applicable. They had little doubt that if they could take a response as arbitrary as bar-pressing in a rat and bring it under the precise control of specific environmental conditions, it would also be possible to take

---

termite. If they want, they should look up the Joiner, Buchman-Schmidt, Chu, and Hom (2017) article that looks at sociobiology and suicide. Then Old Lady Gribbin paused for a long time before she finally added, No, never mind. Maybe it's better if they just go on with the important stuff. And she started to read again.

virtually any operant of which an organism is capable and control it. Similarly, in the same way as it was clearly possible to condition salivation in dogs, eye blinking in adults, and sucking in infants, it should be possible to condition virtually any other reflexive behavior to any distinctive stimulus.

Not so. As we saw, there are situations where classical conditioning does not require repeated pairings of CS and US (for example, in the case of one-shot taste aversion learning). Also, classical conditioning does not occur in some situations even after many pairings (as in the blocking studies).

We also saw that certain behaviors are easily learned when reinforced (for example, a pigeon learning to peck; a pig rooting; a dog fetching: biological preparedness) and others are learned with extreme difficulty (a pigeon flapping its wings for food; a chicken standing still; a cow barking: contrapreparedness). Also, even after certain behaviors have apparently been well learned through operant conditioning, organisms sometimes revert to other more instinctual behaviors that interfere with the learned behavior (instinctive drift).

In brief, there are numerous examples of behaviors that are very difficult or impossible to condition, and of others that are so remarkably easy that they almost appear to be learned automatically. These behaviors, claim evolutionary psychologists, emphasize that learning theorists need to consider biological factors. Although they do not invalidate conditioning explanations, they lead to two important qualifications:

- Classical conditioning is not just a low-level mechanical process whereby one stimulus (the US) passes its control to another (the CS) as a result of repeated pairings. Rather, as Rescorla (1988), Bolles (1979), and others note, through this process, organisms learn what goes with what (they learn what to expect).
- Evolutionary factors are important in explaining and understanding behavior. Recognition of the importance of biological factors in learning is reflected in evolutionary psychology's attempts to understand what knowledge of the evolution of brain structures can do for our understanding of learning. It is also reflected in the search for the biological basis of social behaviors such as altruism, mate selection, sexual jealousy, and even personality differences.

In summary, evolutionary psychology recognizes the importance of genetically determined characteristics – of, if you will, human or animal nature. It admits that one of the most important characteristics of human nature is its malleability, but cautions that this malleability has limits. The first step to understanding the contributions of genetics to our learning and development, says Wright, is to understand "[w]e're all puppets, and our best hope for even partial liberation is to try to decipher the logic of the puppeteer" (1994, p. 37).

But as we saw, we have little data to go on. Much of what passes for science in evolutionary psychology is based on little more than speculation.

A TRANSITION

The rain had gotten a lot heavier, although the old lady seemed not to have noticed. Still, as though responding to some nearly forgotten evolutionary impulse, when she rose, she shook herself like a wet dog might. She said we should go back to the cabin, that the cat would be hungry and besides we should stop here in any case because we were in the middle of a transition that would take us to another chapter. But first, she said she would say more about the transition; she was afraid you might miss its importance. It's more a conceptual than a chronological transition, she explained.

She said one way to simplify the transition would be to say that Pavlovian and Thorndikean and even Skinnerian conditioning deal with the somewhat mechanistic (I mean machine-like, she explained) rules and laws governing relationships among objective, observable events. But now we have suddenly been confronted with phenomena that suggest different explanations – things like one-shot learning and blocking and biological constraints and taste aversions and sign-tracking and.

(A part is missing here – perhaps a paragraph; perhaps as much as a page. As usual, Old Lady Gribbin insisted on leading the way. It was raining very hard. I held the digital recorder inside my jacket, clamping it to my chest, trying to keep it dry, struggling to stay close to the old lady as she plunged through the underbrush. Even in the rain, she refused to follow any of the trails that I have so painstakingly cut and maintained through the years, preferring instead to forge through swamps and thickets that even wild animals avoid. Between where I got tangled up in the branches of a diamond willow near the east slough and where I again caught up to Old Lady Gribbin by the chokecherry bushes on Snake Hill, there's nothing on the recording but the sound of the wind and rain and the swishing and cracking of branches.)

To understand the transition, the old lady was saying as I caught up to her halfway up the hill, you have to realize that learning is essentially adaptive. That's the whole point of the stuff on evolutionary psychology, she said, explaining that changes in behavior – in other words, learning – are what allow organisms to survive and thrive, and we shouldn't be surprised that animals and people learn to avoid potentially harmful foods in a single trial or that they are prepared to learn certain things and not others.

She also said that conditioning should be viewed as learning about what goes with what. She said that in a Skinner box, it's as though the rat develops expectations that one event will lead to the other. But, said the old lady, the behaviorist would not speculate that the rat "figures out" why this is so. To do so would presuppose that it knows something about the mechanical functioning of levers and food-dispensing mechanisms – or something about the minds of psychological investigators. In the behaviorists' view, the rat's "figuring" is limited to a tendency to make associations among things that co-occur or follow one another. As today's psychologists put it, the rat is "sign-tracking"; it is learning about signs associated with reinforcement. Basically, it is learning to eliminate surprises and predict events in its environment.

The old lady stopped and turned so abruptly that I almost ran into her. Despite the rain, her words are very clear on this part of the recording. She said that the words expectations *and* predictions *are too big, too mentalistic, for where we are in this book. She said we should leave words like this for the next chapter, which is more clearly a transition between chiefly behavioristic theories and those that are more cognitive.*

When she said the next chapter, *I thought we were done, and I reached to turn off the recorder, anxious to go back and get out of the rain. But Old Lady Gribbin stopped me.*

She said I shouldn't turn off the recorder yet, that there were some very important things about the brain that you should know before we reach the next chapter. She leaned against a spruce tree and began to speak about the brain, her voice unexpectedly soft, almost reverential. When I listen to the recording now, I have to strain to make out all her words.

LEARNING AND THE BRAIN

The brain is often described as the most complex structure in the entire known universe, with more possible interconnections among its most basic units, **neurons**, than there are particles in that universe. Estimates vary widely, with many researchers claiming that there are around 100 billion neurons in the human brain and perhaps 10 times that number of supporting cells, called *glial cells*. However, recent estimates that take into account the fact that neurons are packed far more densely in some areas of the brain than in others suggest that 100 billion is an overestimate, and that 86 billion may be a closer approximation (Cherry, 2018a; Herculano-Houzel, 2009). In Chapter 6, we look at how these billions of neurons function – how they establish connections and communicate with one another.

We have long known that this lump of tissue that we call the brain is at the very center of our ability to learn, to think, and to feel, and that it somehow determines and defines our very essence. We know that learning depends on the formation of connections among neurons in the brain and that thinking and feeling must involve brain activity. But until recently, much about how the brain works has remained a mystery, although psychologists have long known, or at least suspected, that different parts of the brain might have different functions.

Studying Brain Functions

On September, 13, 1848, Phineas Gage, foreman of a construction crew building a new rail line in Vermont, had a smooth, cylindrical iron rod that measured three feet and seven inches (slightly more than a meter) and weighed a full 13 pounds (about 6 kg) shoot out of a blasting hole and penetrate upward through the left side of his face and out the top of his head! The blow threw Phineas to the ground, but he quickly picked himself up and, with the help of his men, made his way to a cart that carried him to the house where he was staying.

Phineas's physical recovery was rapid and apparently complete. But some reports claim that he was never quite the same person again. He had previously been a kind, gentle, quiet, and hardworking man, but now he seemed moody, fitful, impulsive, selfish, and stubborn; his coworkers and friends no longer recognized him as the person he had been. Unfortunately, however, there is considerable contradiction and perhaps exaggeration in reports of the case of Phineas Gage. Macmillan (2008) points out that no examination of Phineas's brain was ever done, that there is no certainty as to what brain structures were involved, and that there is a strong likelihood that he did not change as dramatically as reported following his accident. That he subsequently began to suffer seizures, eventually dying as a result, also indicates that his recovery might have been far from complete.

Brain Injuries

Brain injuries such as that of Phineas Gage provide one of the earliest clues that different parts of the brain might have different functions. Thus, from Phineas's accident, we might conclude that the part of his brain that was injured had little to do with physiological functions such as breathing (otherwise, he would not have survived), but that it might have been involved with personality characteristics. Unfortunately, however, we have little reliable information about Phineas Gage's brain injury or even about the nature and severity of any personality changes that might have resulted.

Brain Ablations

The problem with using brain injuries to study brain functions is that the main causes of such injuries – accidents, illness, and tumors – usually have nonspecific effects because large parts of the brain are often affected. In addition, researchers cannot control who will suffer from one of these conditions, which can make for poor research.

One way around these problems is to cut out (*excise* or *ablate*) tiny, very specific portions of the brain to see what the effect might be. Karl Lashley (1924) did this to a number of rats that had been trained to run quickly and correctly through a maze. Lashley was convinced that memories must leave a trace in a tiny part of the brain and that if you succeeded in cutting out just the right part, the animal would no longer remember the correct path through the maze. Lashley never did find this memory trace (called an *engram*). It seemed that no matter what part or how much of the brain he cut out, the rats could still find their way through the maze, although they often moved more slowly. The conclusion, later corroborated by more recent studies, is that most memories are scattered in various parts of the brain.

Electrical Brain Stimulation

Another way of mapping brain functions is to stimulate specific areas of the brain, either with chemicals or electrically, and see what the effects of doing so might be. For example, in a very early study, Olds (1956) implanted electrodes in the brains of rats and accidentally discovered that stimulation of a part of the *hypothalamus* seemed highly rewarding for rats. The hypothalamus is located deep inside the brain, near the top of the **brain stem** (the brain stem is the collection of brain structures that links the spinal cord with the brain; see Figure 5.5). When the electrodes were connected so that rats could stimulate their own brains by depressing a lever, they would do so repeatedly. Many rats would even pass up food to stimulate their brains. Olds reports that one rat stimulated himself more than 2,000 times per hour for 24 consecutive hours.

During the same set of experiments, Olds also discovered that if the electrode were implanted somewhat lower in the hypothalamus, the effect of brain stimulation was not rewarding to the rat but was instead punishing. Now rats would go to great lengths to avoid having their brains stimulated. But if the electrode was moved slightly in the direction of what Olds labeled the brain's **pleasure center**, the lure of brain stimulation becomes almost irresistible: One rat

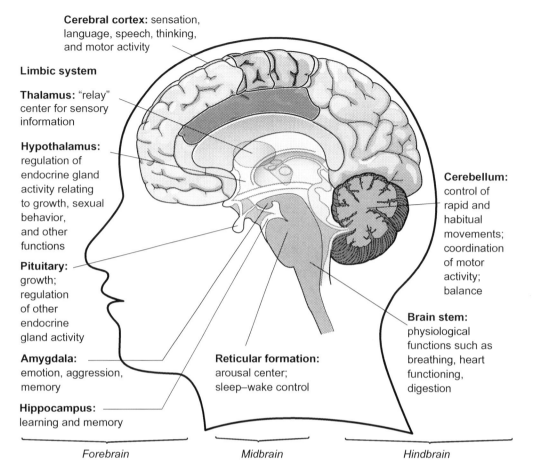

Figure 5.5 A sagittal (bisected front to back) view of the human brain showing some of the major structures that compose the forebrain, the midbrain, and the hindbrain, together with their principal functions.

stimulated himself nearly 7,000 times in a single hour (Olds & Milner, 1954). Mother rats would even leave their newborn pups to stimulate their own brains (Sonderegger, 1970).

Subsequent research has corroborated that there is a reinforcement center in the brains of a large number of animals, including primates such as humans, located in the brain's **limbic system**. This system, which is concerned generally with emotion, memory, and motivation, includes the hypothalamus, the thalamus, and several other structures. Specifically, a group of nerve fibers that runs through the hypothalamus, termed the **medial forebrain bundle**, is linked with reinforcement; another group of fibers, the **periventricular tract**, is associated with punishment (Mihailoff, Haines, & May, 2018).

Chemical Brain Stimulation and Addiction

Implanting electrodes in an animal or a human brain is a difficult and exacting process. A simpler way of stimulating brains is to use chemicals, such as mood-altering drugs. For example, evidence indicates that the neurotransmitter **dopamine** is involved in the activity of some of the neurons associated with pleasure and motivation (Willis & Haines, 2018).

Normally, neurotransmitters such as dopamine are released upon neural stimulation and then quickly recaptured (Kalat, 2016). But certain drugs, such as amphetamines and cocaine, prevent the immediate recapture of the dopamine molecules and are therefore associated with higher levels of dopamine. These drugs are termed **agonists**. An agonist is a chemical that boosts the activity of some naturally occurring chemical. The intensely pleasurable effect of cocaine is thought to be related to the fact that cocaine prevents or delays the recapture of dopamine molecules, so dopaminergic neurons (that is, those that use dopamine for neural transmission) remain active for longer periods. Because dopamine is one of the transmitters associated with neural activity in one of the brain's "pleasure" centers, the ultimate effect of cocaine is to stimulate activity in these centers (National Institute on Drug Abuse, 2018). However, the prolonged use of cocaine leads to the brain adapting to the drug, so the brain synthesizes less dopamine naturally. As a result, in between administrations of the drug, the chronic cocaine user often experiences the opposite of pleasure: depression, sadness, and negative moods. At the same time, there are profound changes in the individual's desire to take the drug, evident in a dramatic change in motivation resulting in addiction (Castine et al., 2018; Nestler, 2016). Also, there is evidence that repeated drug use reduces dopamine receptors, so ever-increasing amounts of the drug are required to satisfy the craving (Kaneda, 2018).

Interestingly, electrical stimulation of the brain also leads to the release of dopamine, as do natural reinforcers such as food, water, and sex, and addictive substances such as nicotine and alcohol (Oscar-Berman & Blum, 2016).

Brain Imaging Techniques

Researchers now have access to a number of powerful, non-invasive imaging techniques for looking at the intact brains of living people. Some of these imaging techniques, such as the **electroencephalogram (EEG)**, are sensitive to actual electrical discharges in the brain. **Positron emission tomography (PET)** records changes in blood flow by detecting the distribution of radioactive particles injected in the bloodstream. **Functional magnetic resonance imaging (fMRI)** detects extremely subtle changes in magnetic fields that accompany changes in blood oxygen level. **Magnetoencephalography (MEG)** allows researchers to detect at the scalp incredibly subtle changes in magnetic fields that occur with neural activity, and **functional magnetic resonance spectrography (fMRS)** uses highly specialized computer software to detect levels of specific chemicals in the fully active brain.

These imaging techniques, together with information derived from brain stimulation studies and from examination of patients with brain injuries, have led to a rapidly increasing amount of information about different brain structures and their functions. Much research on memory now uses EEG and MEG recordings to provide measures of what are termed **event-related potentials (ERPs)** and **event-related fields (ERFs)**. These are changes in electrical potential and magnetic fields, respectively, that accompany neural activity in the brain and that are directly related to external stimulation. As a result, ERPs and ERFs can provide researchers with important information about what happens in the brain when, for example, you look at a picture, hear a word, or are asked to solve a problem in algebra. To understand this information, it is useful to have some knowledge about the brain's anatomy.

Hindbrain

To simplify, the human brain can be divided into three basic parts: the hindbrain, the midbrain, and the forebrain. These are thought to have evolved in that order, with the hindbrain being the oldest and the most primitive structure and the forebrain being the most recent and the most advanced. Not surprisingly, the structures of the hindbrain are present and well developed in nonhuman animals; the structures of the forebrain are more highly developed in humans and other primates.

The hindbrain, physically the lowest part of the brain in an upright human being, includes the lower part of the brain stem, which is concerned with basic physiological functions such as respiration and heart rate, and what is termed the **cerebellum**. The cerebellum (which means "little brain") is a cauliflower-like structure located at the back and lower part of the brain, behind the brain stem. It is centrally involved in movement, locomotion, and balance. Damage to this part of the brain can dramatically impair motor skills such as walking, playing the piano, or catching a baseball. There is also evidence that the cerebellum may sometimes be linked to reading problems and that therapy involving exercises in balance and locomotion might, in some cases, improve performance in reading tasks (Alvarez & Fiez, 2018).

Midbrain

The midbrain includes the upper part of the brain stem, sometimes called the **reticular formation**. As we see in Chapter 9, this structure is largely responsible for regulating waking and sleeping and for controlling general arousal. Also, nerve fibers associated with movement are found in the midbrain. Recall that these nerve fibers are *dopaminergic*, which means that their neural transmission is based on the presence of dopamine. This is why Parkinson's disease, which involves a failure to produce sufficient dopamine, is marked by tremors and other physical motor problems.

Forebrain

The forebrain is the most recent, the largest, and the most complex brain structure; it is also the most important for understanding topics of interest to students of human learning. Its most important parts include the hypothalamus, the thalamus, and other structures of the limbic system, as well as the cerebrum and cerebral cortex.

The Hypothalamus

The **hypothalamus** is a bean-sized structure deep within the brain, near the top of the brain stem. Its major functions relate to regulating physiological functions of the autonomic nervous system and of various glands in the body. Nerve fibers relating to reward and punishment pass through the hypothalamus. The hypothalamus is actually one of the regions of the thalamus (Haines & Terrell, 2018).

The Thalamus

The **thalamus**, another tiny structure at the top of the brain stem, includes a number of structures such as the hypothalamus. It acts as a sort of relay station for sensory information. All incoming neural signals that relate to the senses, except those that have to do with smell, are routed through the thalamus. It is centrally involved in regulating consciousness, sleep, and general alertness.

The Limbic System

The limbic system is usually considered to include parts of the hypothalamus and the thalamus, as well as a network of other structures that are found between the cerebral cortex and lower brain structures. Generally speaking, the structures of the limbic system are involved in emotions. Some are also implicated in memories and in conditioning. Among the important structures of the limbic system are the **amygdala** and the **hippocampus**. The amygdala processes emotional information, especially emotions having to do with fear (Rozeske & Herry, 2018). It is also associated with aggression (Siep et al., 2018). The hippocampus plays an important role in long-term memory and learning (Piskorowski & Chevaleyre, 2018).

The Cerebrum and the Cerebral Cortex

The **cerebrum**, which divides naturally into two parallel halves (the *cerebral hemispheres*), is the largest, most complex, most highly developed, and most obvious brain structure in vertebrates (Haines & Terrell, 2018). Of special importance is its thin outer covering, the cerebral cortex, which is about one-eighth of an inch thick. As Grow (2018) puts it, "The cerebral cortex is the organ of thought. More than any other part of the nervous system, the cerebral cortex is the site of the intellectual functions that make us human and that make each of us a unique individual" (p. 468). The cerebral cortex is responsible for our most advanced forms of mental activity: learning, thinking, and remembering. It underlies our use of language and logic, our imagination, our dreams, our judgment. These are activities responsible for our very sense of consciousness. Interestingly, the cerebral cortex, evolution's most recent legacy, is one of the few parts of the brain that continues to develop and grow through childhood and into early adulthood.

The cerebral cortex is highly convoluted, which increases its surface area enormously. It also has a number of fissures (crevasses) running through it. These fissures result in four natural divisions, termed *lobes*, in each of the two cerebral hemispheres (Figure 5.6). Thus, there is both a left and a right one of each lobe.

Toward the front of the cerebral cortex are the **frontal lobes** – structures involved in motor activity as well as in higher thought processes. Damage to certain parts of the frontal lobes can result in **aphasia** (difficulties in understanding language or producing speech).

To either side of the cerebral cortex are the **temporal lobes**, which are involved in hearing, language, and speech. Just behind the frontal lobes and above the temporal lobes are the **parietal**

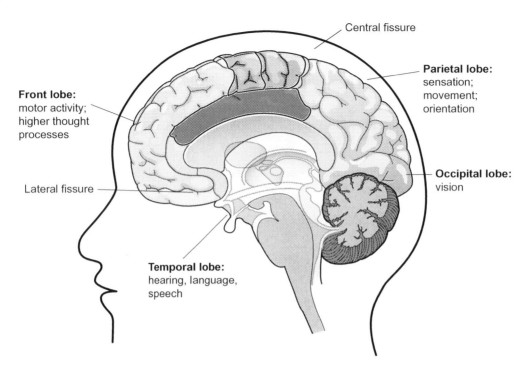

Figure 5.6 The four lobes of the cerebral cortex. The functions of these lobes are highly integrated, so they cannot easily be separated. Still, each lobe is closely associated with the main functions listed.

lobes. These lobes are strongly implicated in physical sensation, movement, recognition, and orientation. At the very back of the brain are the **occipital lobes**, which are involved in vision.

This quick description of the tasks and responsibilities of the different lobes presents a misleading oversimplification: Matters are far from as simple, clear, and definite as this implies. For example, although the temporal lobes are involved in language and speech, other parts of the brain are also centrally implicated. Similarly, as we see in Chapter 9, various kinds of memories may be found in many different parts of the brain. As Sousa (2017) explains, one of the most remarkable characteristics of the human brain is how it is able to integrate all the activities that occur simultaneously in its different specialized areas.

The Hemispheres

As we saw, the brain consists of two highly similar halves separated down the middle, front to back, forming the two cerebral hemispheres and resulting in two of each of the four principal lobes. And although the functions of corresponding right and left lobes are similar in many ways, various studies have shown that the hemispheres do not exactly duplicate each other's functions, a fact referred to as **lateralization**. For example, in general, the right hemisphere controls perceptions of visual and spatial relationships; the left hemisphere is highly specialized for language skills. The cerebral hemisphere that controls language is called the **dominant hemisphere** (Grow, 2018). The left hemisphere is dominant in about 95 percent of right-handed people and in about 70 percent of left-handed people (Holland et al., 2007). At the same time, some evidence indicates that the right hemisphere might be more concerned with emotions and with spatial and temporal things – hence, more with music and art (Workman, Chilvers, Yeomans, & Taylor, 2006).

Findings such as these have led some to speculate that there are "right-brained" and "left-brained" individuals. Those who are left-brained would be expected to perform better on tasks that require logic, math, science, and verbal skills. In contrast, the right-brained would be expected to be more artistic, more musical, and more emotionally intelligent. Some educators argue that schools emphasize the left brain by concentrating on logic, math, science, and language and tend to ignore the right brain (for example, see Dos Santos Fringe, 2018; Sonnier, 1995). These educators advocate what is sometimes termed **holistic education** – education deliberately designed to teach both sides of the brain. Holistic education emphasizes the often-neglected artistic and musical interests and talents of children, and is more person-centered, more ecologically oriented, perhaps more spiritual.

Unfortunately, it has proven difficult to investigate the separate functions of the cerebral hemispheres. Much of what passes for information, suggests Corballis (2007), is speculation rather than fact. The information we have indicates that there is a tremendous amount of overlap between the functions of the cerebral hemispheres. For example, although certain regions of the left temporal lobe are importantly involved in speech and language, when damage occurs to that lobe, speech and language functions are often taken over by other parts of the brain (Nordvik et al., 2014; Uswatte & Taub, 2010). This is especially true if the damage occurs early in life; if it occurs later, there may be less recovery of lost functions. Nor is it clear that the right hemisphere is always more involved in artistic, musical, or spatial functions. For example, an extensive review of studies that have looked at the relationship between the right hemisphere and spatial tasks found that the overall results were highly complex. In general, males seemed to have some slight right-hemisphere preference for spatial tasks, but females did not (Vogel, Bowers & Vogel, 2003).

It's misleading and simplistic to insist that the left hemisphere is logical, scientific, and mathematical, whereas the right hemisphere is artistic, musical, and emotional, and that this brain specialization affects how different individuals learn. As Sousa notes, "there is little scientific evidence to date to support this notion" (2017, p. 192). Although one hemisphere is somewhat better than the other at certain things, there is considerable overlap in their functions.

Still, this may not lessen the importance of holistic education's fear that our curricula may neglect important areas of human interest and ability and its insistence that we should pay more attention to those areas.

Sex Differences in the Brain

Even as males and females are physically (biologically) different, so too are their brains. In fact, says Johnson, "men's and women's brains are nearly as distinct from each other as their bodies are" (2004, p. 14). Sousa (2017) summarizes research that indicates that men's brains are, on average, larger than those of women; those parts of the brain that are linked with sex and aggression are more developed among men; women tend to have a larger volume of gray matter than do men; and men tend to have more white matter. Also, the part of the parietal lobe associated with spatial relationships and mathematics is more developed in males. On the other

Evolutionary Psychology

hand, areas of the frontal and temporal lobes associated with language are larger in women (Sabbatini, 2010).

Not surprisingly, given these differences in the brain, there are differences in the ways men and women process language, spatial information, and emotion. On average, measures of verbal ability often favor girls (Reilly, Neumann, & Andrews, 2016); males perform better in mathematics, physics, and spatial reasoning tasks; girls do better on verbal tasks; even boys as young as five do better on tasks of mental rotation (Hahn, Jansen & Heil, 2010); and males commit about 90 percent of all murders (Fox & Fridel, 2017).

It is important to note that while research has established that there are some real differences between the brains of average men and women, these are not staggering differences. In fact, they tend to be small differences between *average* male and female brain structure and functioning. Our generalizations are never sufficiently sensitive to individual differences. For example, they fail to recognize that some women are far better than most men at navigating in strange places; that some women, given appropriate experiences, become outstanding mathematicians or physicists; that some women are as aggressive as the most bellicose and belligerent of men; and that some men are as sensitive and emotional as any woman.

That differences in brain structures and function underlie some of these sex differences seems clear. In addition, the brains of male and female children are exposed to very different levels of male (testosterone) and female (estrogen) hormones. These hormones have a profound effect on the developing brain (Wierenga, Oranje, & Durston, 2017). Changes in the relative size of brain structures following puberty, when production of these hormones peaks, suggests that they may be partly responsible for some of the male–female differences in brain functioning. In addition, the influence of culture and socialization is also clear: The brain responds to experience.

The Brain and Experience

Riesen, Chow, Semmes, Nissen (1951) raised four baby chimpanzees in a darkened room where they had only about 90 minutes a day of access to diffuse light. After seven months, when these chimpanzees were exposed to a more normal world, none of them had normal vision. The chimpanzees required months before they learned to recognize familiar objects such as their feeding bottles, or learned how to guide their own movements without bumping into things. None ever achieved normal vision.

Many other studies with cats, chimpanzees, and other animals raised in darkness or made to wear goggles that distort the world in different ways dramatically illustrate that most do not learn to see normally when the lights are turned on or the goggles removed. Later examinations of the brains of these animals indicate that they have not developed the same number and kinds of neural connections as animals raised normally (Iliescu & Dannemiller, 2008).

In an early study, Krech, Rosenzweig, and Bennett (1966) raised some rats in a "normal" rat environment and others in a highly enriched environment with large, well-lit cages, wheels to run on, toys to play with, other rats with which to socialize, and friendly human experimenters. The eventual differences between these initially identical groups of rats, explain Krech and associates, were remarkable. Not only did the enriched group learn to run through mazes more easily, but their brains were heavier and appeared to have more interconnections among neurons. These findings have since been corroborated using more advanced and precise methods for examining animal brains (for example, Tropea et al., 2001). As Kolb, Harker, and Gibb (2017) note, developing brains are especially sensitive to a wide range of experiences. By the same token, lack of early experiences can have a significantly deleterious effect on brain development (Stamoulis, Vanderwert, Zeanah, Fox, & Nelson, 2017).

It is clearly impossible to carry out the same sorts of controlled studies with young children as with animals. Investigators cannot simply select a group of children and assign them to enriched environments while subjecting a second matched group to an impoverished environment. However, it is possible to find certain naturally occurring situations that approximate enrichment and impoverishment and to compare developmental outcomes for children from these environments. For example, a large number of studies report a positive relationship between cognitive stimulation and positive outcomes evident in measurable differences in the complexity and extent of neuronal connections or better school achievement (Ghiglieri & Calabresi, 2017). Similarly, Johnson, Riis, and Noble (2016) looked at recent research dealing with the relationship between poverty and the developing brain. They conclude that during periods of highest plasticity, the developing brain is especially prone to adverse effects related to such things as *maternal deprivation* (evident in lack of cognitive and social stimulation as well as nutritional deficiencies), stress (often associated with negative approaches to parenting), and various other environmental factors often linked with poverty.

In the same way as poverty is sometimes connected with environments that are less conducive to optimal development of the highly plastic young brain, so too can higher **socioeconomic status (SES)**, which is typically related to higher income and education, be linked with more optimal brain development (see Sale, 2016).

The general conclusion from these and numerous similar studies is that the brain's development is highly dependent on experience, and especially on early experience. The implications of this conclusion for child rearing and education are tremendous.

Brain-Based Education

There are many different ways of looking at human learning. One collection of important approaches, described in the first part of this text, concentrates on behavior and on the events that underlie changes in behavior. Other approaches are more brain-based; they look at how the brain is involved in learning, giving rise to what is called **brain-based education**: education based directly on scientific knowledge about how the brain functions. As Blakemore and Frith put it, "Only by understanding how the brain acquires and lays down information and skills will we be able to reach the limits of its capacity to learn" (2005, p. 1).

For our purposes, the role of the brain in human learning can be summarized as follows, keeping in mind that this oversimplifies:

1. All information enters the brain by means of our senses. The senses are ultimately our only sources of information about the world. All that brains can know results from the hypotheses they make based on the information they receive through the sensory systems.

Evolutionary Psychology

2. All this sensory information (except for that having to do with smell) is sorted and relayed to appropriate parts of the cerebral cortex via the thalamus. Thus, visual information is sent to what is termed the *visual cortex* in the occipital lobe and auditory information goes to the *auditory cortex* in the temporal lobe. (Sensations having to do with smell have direct links to the *olfactory bulb* which is a structure at the base of the frontal lobe.)

3. Important information having to do with nonemotional facts and events is routed through the hippocampus for long-term storage; important emotional information is routed through the thalamus for processing into long-term memory.

4. Actual processing, involving examining information for meanings and associations, occurs in the cerebral cortex.

This is basically how learning occurs. Certain findings relating to brain development appear to be important for brain-based education. Among these are the following:

- Through a process called *neurogenesis*, the human brain continues to grow new neurons, especially early in life. Neurogenesis can be enhanced by exercise, reducing stress, and nutrition (Tokuhama-Espinosa, 2014).
- Social interactions can improve brain development.
- The high plasticity of the human brain is evident in its ability to rewire itself, a process that can be aided through education.

The main instructional recommendations that flow from these observations include the advisability of teaching cognitive skills as well as a variety of other subjects; of providing time for recreation, stress reduction, and physical activity; and of providing stimulating educational experiences. Interestingly, none of these recommendations is particularly novel.

Farmer-Dougan and Alferink (2013) caution that we must guard against the premature application of brain research to education. They note that brain-based approaches to curricula and to teaching are often based on oversimplifications and misinterpretations of actual findings. For example, there are some who argue that we use only 10 percent of our brains. Furthermore, they argue, our current educational practices emphasize left-brain functions (preoccupation with verbal learning, mathematics, science, and logic) and neglect right-brain functions (art, music, drama, and other creative endeavors). Hence, we should change our educational fare and philosophy to educate both halves of our students' brains and at least some of the 90 percent of their brains currently idling. But as we saw earlier, it is a myth that we use only 10 percent of our brains (Cherry, 2018b). And it is misleading to insist that there are left-brained people (logical, scientific, rational, good at mathematics) and right-brained people (artistic, musical, and emotional), as well as "whole-brained" people (blessed with a *holistic* balance of talents and abilities). "This," write Blakemore and Frith, "is pop psychology but not scientific psychology" (2005, p. 60).[4]

---

[4] Mrs. Gribbin motioned for me to turn off the recorder as she pulled her ever-present pack of gum from one of her many pockets, retrieved a piece, unwrapped it, and slipped it into her mouth. For a while, she said nothing as she slowly chewed the gum. She seemed to savor it immensely. I thought she might offer me a piece, but she didn't. Let me give you one example of a brain-related educational fad, she said, chewing excessively loudly. Chewing gum, she continued. They're actually doing it in some schools! It's apparently based on "scientific" research that shows that chewing gum makes students smarter. Do a quick internet search, she said, and you'll find references to studies and conference presentations that insist that students should be encouraged to chew gum. Interestingly, she added, much of this research is supported by at

BIOFEEDBACK AND NEUROFEEDBACK

Another brain-based innovation in education and therapy is labeled biofeedback. **Biofeedback** is a procedure by which individuals are given information about their biological functioning, such as heart rate or brain activity, with a view to helping them acquire control over that function. Biofeedback that involves information about neurological functioning is sometimes referred to as **neurofeedback**.

There have recently been a huge number of studies looking at the application of biofeedback as a therapeutic approach in the treatment of a wide range of medical and psychological problems, including anxiety, insomnia, asthma, breathing disorders, chronic pain, depression, posttraumatic stress disorder (PTSD), and many others (for example, Caldwell & Steffen, 2018; Lehrer & Gevirtz, 2014; Schuman & Killian, 2018). The results of many of these investigations have been highly promising (Austad & Gendron, 2018).

Conditioning of Autonomic Responses: Early Research

Early investigations of classical and operant conditioning led quickly to the conviction that the types of behavior being explained by each were fundamentally different. Most theorists assumed that autonomic (involuntary) behaviors such as salivation or eye blinking could not be brought under stimulus control through operant conditioning, although they responded very well to classical conditioning procedures. Also, it seemed that operants became more or less probable solely as a function of reinforcement contingencies and not as a function of contiguity.

These assumptions were incorrect. Salivation can be conditioned using operant procedures and so can heart rate, blood pressure, bladder functioning, and a host of other involuntary autonomic functions. Miller (1969) was among the first to demonstrate some of these phenomena when he conditioned increases or decreases of heart rate in rats in response to a combination of a light and a tone. And in a related study, Miller and Carmona (1967) conditioned dogs to salivate or not to salivate simply by rewarding a group of thirsty dogs with water when they salivated spontaneously and rewarding another group with water when they refrained from salivating. What these studies show is that operant conditioning procedures can be used to bring about control over behaviors that are normally *autonomic* (involuntary).

How Biofeedback Works

Although people are ordinarily unaware of most aspects of their physiological functions (heart and respiration rates, blood pressure, electrical activity in the brain), monitoring devices used in

---

least one chewing gum company. She chewed without talking for a while longer. Then, she continued reading her manuscript.

I did a quick search and found many studies, references, and recommendations, as Old Lady Gribbin had said I would. There's even a chewing gum company website that claims wonderful benefits for chewing their gum (Wrigley, 2017). It strikes me that this might be a good research topic for a clever student anxious to impress.

biofeedback can easily and accurately provide information about these functions. For example, in some early biofeedback experiments, participants were connected to a device that records brain waves (called an *alpha recorder*) and that emits a distinctive stimulus such as a tone whenever the subject produces the right type or frequency of waves. Participants were simply instructed to try to activate the tone as often as possible. Using this equipment, many participants could quickly learn to control aspects of brain wave functioning. Using an operant conditioning explanation, investigators argued that the tone (or light or other distinctive stimulus) serves as a reinforcer and the behaviors involved in controlling the autonomic response are operants.

Recent Biofeedback Applications

Using more sensitive and sophisticated instruments to monitor brain activity, many researchers have since confirmed that at least some participants are able to learn to control specific kinds of brain waves. For example, Shtark et al. (2018) report a study in which 18 of 35 participants were successful in learning to increase *alpha* brain waves when given biofeedback indicating the nature of their brain activity. Increased alpha activity is associated with reduced levels of anxiety.

Other research has looked at the use of biofeedback in the preparation of athletes. For example, Blumenstein and Orbach (2014, 2018) describe how biofeedback that provides the athlete with information about physiological functions such as heart and respiration rate, blood pressure, muscle tension, brain activity, and electrical activity of the skin (a measure of stress or anxiety) can be directed toward increasing the athlete's control over these functions and, as a result, enhance athletic performance.

Among the many other practical applications of biofeedback are attempts to treat attention-deficit disorders, autism and Asperger's syndrome, learning disabilities, and misbehaviors in schools (Barth, Mayer, Strehl, Fallgatter, & Ehlis, 2017; Keith, Rapgay, Theodore, Schwartz, & Ross, 2015).

In a typical neurofeedback training session for attention-deficit disorder, autism, or Asperger's syndrome, children are connected to brain wave recorders capable of sensing brain wave patterns that indicate attention or lack thereof. The children are subsequently rewarded for attention-related brain wave activity (specifically, *beta* activity) or for suppressing other activity (for example, *theta* waves), often while engaged in computer-based activities. Over successive training sessions, the activities require progressively longer periods of attentiveness. Many researchers report relatively high levels of success using such procedures (for example, Bakhtadze, Beridze, Geladze, Khachapuridze, & Bornstein, 2016).

Early replications of biofeedback research did not always duplicate earlier results (for example, see Ramsay, 2010). However, there has been an enormous surge in biofeedback research in recent years (more than 800 studies reported in psycINFO in the last five years). Much of this research uses far more sophisticated equipment than was available for earlier studies, and, building on earlier research, procedures appear to have become more standardized and more effective. Still, as with any new and complex approach to therapy, there is always a need to guard against the misapplication of "science" and to be wary of applications based on misconceptions, oversimplifications, and exaggerations of potential benefits. Perhaps we need to think twice and wait for more research (or do it ourselves!) before we run out and buy a year's supply of chewing gum and our own personal brain wave recorders and biological functioning monitors.

Main Point Chapter Summary

1. Taste aversion learning is not well explained by a Pavlovian view of classical conditioning because (a) it may occur in a single trial, (b) it often involves an effect that occurs long after the conditioning stimulus, and (c) it occurs more readily under certain conditions and for certain stimuli than others. These observations suggest that biological and evolutionary pressures might be involved.
2. Latent inhibition describes the phenomenon where pre-exposure to a stimulus reduces the likelihood that the stimulus will later become conditioned to a subsequent unpleasant outcome. In blocking, establishing a simple conditioned reaction is prevented by previous learning.
3. Rescorla and Wagner suggest that what is learned in classical conditioning is an association between component stimuli and a conditioned response. Because a limited amount of associative strength is available, when all of it has been used up for one component of the compound stimulus, further learning is blocked.
4. A biological explanation for conditioning and blocking has to do with surprise and expectation. When the outcome of a behavior is expected and there is no surprise, no new learning occurs. But when the outcome is unexpected, there is surprise, new information is being provided, and learning may occur. One way of looking at conditioning is to say that it involves learning what goes with what.
5. Higher-order conditioning refers to the process by which various neutral stimuli assume some of the functions of an unconditioned stimulus as a result of being paired with it.
6. Evolutionary psychology uses biology and genetics as explanations for human learning and behavior. Evolution-based predispositions are seen as explanations for autoshaping (learning a highly probable but nonreinforced response, such as key-pecking in pigeons), *instinctive drift* (where the organisms reverts to a more *instinctual* behavior), and *biological constraints* (predispositions that make certain kinds of learning highly probable and others less likely).
7. Geary relates evolutionary psychology to learning by suggesting that the human's highly developed frontal lobes have evolved to support acquisition of *biologically primary knowledge* (*folk knowledge* about people and natural phenomena, language, and spatial navigation skills). *Biologically secondary knowledge*, represented by academic learning, is less well supported and consequently more difficult to learn. Given the lack of historical records about the evolution of the brain, of language, of social behaviors, and so on, the

scientific basis of evolutionary psychology has been questioned and the term *pop evolutionary psychology* is often used to describe it.

8. Sociobiology, a precursor to evolutionary psychology, assumes that there are genetic and evolutionary explanations for much animal and human social behavior (altruism, for example). With its approximately 86 billion neurons, the brain is centrally implicated in everything we think and do. It is the basis of our consciousness.

9. Information about the brain and its functioning derives from studies of brain injury and disease, surgical procedures and physical examination of the brain, electrical and chemical stimulation of the brain, and imaging and scanning procedures such as fMRIs, MEGs, fMRSs, and PET scans.

10. Among other things, studies of brain functioning have identified "pleasure" and "punishment" centers in parts of the hypothalamus and have shown how some neurotransmitters such as dopamine may explain the rewarding and addictive effects of electrical stimulation of the brain and of certain drugs like alcohol, cocaine, and heroin.

11. The most recent brain structures in an evolutionary sense, those that compose the forebrain and especially the cerebrum, are most highly developed in humans and are centrally involved in higher mental functioning. Hindbrain structures, more involved in physiological functioning and in movement, are older and often highly developed in nonhuman animals.

12. The cerebral cortex, the thin, convoluted outer covering of the cerebrum, seems to divide naturally into four lobes on each hemisphere. Each lobe is primarily associated with one or more functions, although there is considerable overlap and integration of functions (frontal lobes: higher mental processes; parietal lobes: sensation, movement, recognition, and orientation; occipital lobes: vision; and temporal lobes: hearing, speech, and language).

13. Some evidence suggests that the two halves of the cerebral cortex differ in their involvement with various functions. Specifically, the left hemisphere is said to be more logical, mathematical, and verbal; the right hemisphere is thought to be more emotional, artistic, spatial, and musical. These beliefs are an oversimplification. In fact, cerebral functions overlap considerably.

14. There are consistent differences between *average* male and female brains. The development of the brain seems to be highly dependent on experience, especially in the early years. Brain-based approaches to learning look at how the brain responds to stimulation and processes information, but are often founded on misconceptions and oversimplifications. Few brain-based educational recommendations are novel.

15. Biofeedback is information that organisms receive about their biological functioning. Neurofeedback refers specifically to information about neural – and especially brain – functioning. Biofeedback research attempts to increase people's control over physiological functioning by providing them with information about it. Biofeedback and neurofeedback techniques are sometimes used in therapy (for relieving stress and headaches, as a treatment for learning problems, as a therapy for autism and related disorders, and so on).

Part III

The Beginnings of Modern Cognitivism

6 Transition to Modern Cognitivism

Hebb, Tolman, and the Gestaltists

CHAPTER OUTLINE

This Chapter	196
Objectives	197
Hebb's Theory	197
Higher Mental Processes	197
The Physiology of Learning	200
The Central Nervous System	200
Hebb's Main Assumptions	203
Neurological Basis for Learning	205
Reactivity and Plasticity	206
Mediating Processes	207
Thinking and Learning in Hebb's Theory	209
Set and Attention	210
Educational Applications of Hebb's Theory	210
Appraisal of Hebb's Theory	211
From Behaviorism to Cognitivism	213
Mechanistic Behaviorism	214
Tolman's Purposive Behaviorism	214
Do Rats have Purpose?	216
What Is Purposive Behaviorism?	218
Educational Implications and Summary Principles of Tolman's System	219
Appraisal of Tolman's Purposive Behaviorism	220
Gestalt Psychology	221
Insight or Trial and Error	223
Gestalt Means "Whole"	224
Principles of Perception	224
Gestalt Views of Learning and Memory	226
Beyond Perception: The Behavioral Field	228
Gestalt Psychology and Modern Cognitivism	229
Educational Implications of Gestalt Psychology	230
Appraisal of Gestalt Psychology	231

Metaphors in Psychology	232
Metaphors in Behaviorism	232
Metaphors in Cognitivism	233
Main Point Chapter Summary	234

Behaviorism proposes to study human behavior according to the methods developed by animal and infant psychology. It seeks to investigate reflexes and instincts, automatisms and unconscious reactions. But it has told us nothing about the reflexes that have built cathedrals, railroads, and fortresses, the instincts that have produced philosophies, poems, and legal systems, the automatisms that have resulted in the growth and decline of empires, the unconscious reactions that are splitting atoms.

Ludwig von Mises

Schrödinger was waiting when we arrived, looking drenched and pathetic, rubbing hard against the closed door. Even in the rain, I could smell the roast Old Lady Gribbin had put to bake in the ancient wood-burning stove, and I was suddenly ravenous. "Are you hungry?" I asked hopefully as she filled the cat's dish with juicy slivers of meat. "Not yet," she said, spreading scraps of scribbled notes and soggy pages of manuscript on the table where I had thought to eat. "I want to get into Chapter 6 before dinner." But instead of beginning to read and lecture from her notes, she said she wanted to say something about ideas and theories first. She explained that new ideas seldom appear completely out of the blue. She said that if we look carefully at the history of human ideas, we see that long before the appearance of an apparently new idea, there are almost invariably hints that it is coming. Sometimes we find that the idea has appeared fully formed decades or even centuries earlier. Such precocious ideas, and their perpetrators, are often ridiculed loudly and doomed to a premature death: an idea before its time, the philosophers say. But they're wrong, explained the old lady, because ideas are never truly before their time; it's people who are behind their own time and therefore can't recognize the ideas' importance.

The old lady was silent for a long time, as though thinking important thoughts. "Are you hungry now?" I asked again. "Turn on the recorder," she said as if she had not heard my question.

THIS CHAPTER

This sixth chapter, *she said*, looks at ideas that in many important ways were ideas "before their time" – hints of ideas yet to come. At the same time, many of these ideas were reflections of thoughts already spoken and written. Thus, Donald Hebb's behaviorism reflects the ideas of conditioning theory, but in it are many hints of the connectionism and neural networks that underlie computer models of human thought processes developed decades later (Chapter 11). His theory foreshadows current attempts to understand learning and behavior by looking at what happens in the brain. Similarly, the ideas of Tolman and the Gestaltists express growing concern with contemporary cognitive topics, such as perception, problem solving, and decision making.

Objectives

The old lady said that after you've read this chapter eight times, you'll be able (and willing), she promised, to mumble your way through spectacularly long discourses on the following:

- Hebbian cell assemblies and phase sequences;
- neural transmission;
- arousal theory;
- purposeful rat behavior;
- Tolman's purposive behaviorism;
- the basic laws of Gestalt psychology.

She said you would also know something, but not a whole heck of a lot, about saber-toothed tigers. And then she bent to her notes once more.

HEBB'S THEORY

The relevance of saber-toothed tigers, *she read*, has to do with the fact that when people come face-to-face with their first saber-toothed tiger, they immediately turn and run like stink. But when they come to a stream and find that the stones they had laid in it to step across are gone, they are forced to stop. Perhaps they now sit for a while on the bank, grunting and gesticulating at each other. Later, they may decide to get other stones to replace those that are missing.

In addition to the obvious lack of similarity between running from a saber-toothed tiger and sitting on a riverbank, there is an important distinction between these two behaviors. The first behavior can be interpreted in terms of the now familiar stimulus–response (S–R) model: The tiger serves as the stimulus; running is the immediate response.

The second behavior presents a different situation. Although in a sense the missing stones serve as a stimulus and the act of leaving to get replacements is a response, the problem with this S–R interpretation is that there might be a delay of minutes or even hours between the presentation of the stimulus and the response. This delay strains the S–R model and leads to a fundamentally important question: What occurs during the lapse of time between a stimulus and a response?[1]

Higher Mental Processes

It is likely, says Hebb, that something related to the stimulus and response must be occurring at least part of the time because the eventual behavior (response) reflects the

---

[1] Here, Mrs. Gribbin interrupted herself. We could have used the roast as an example, she said, pointing out that although I seemed very hungry, my hunger stimulus didn't automatically lead to my eating. She said I was able to delay my response for various reasons, including the fact that I could imagine the consequences both of waiting and of not waiting. She said that the ability to delay our responding and the ability to imagine the consequences of so doing are fundamentally important to understanding human behavior. Schrödinger had now finished licking his empty dish and sat grinning at me. I thought I delayed my eating only because I was offered no food.

Transition to Modern Cognitivism

situation (stimulus). One phrase that labels what goes on between the stimulus and response is **higher mental processes**. In laypersons' terms, higher mental processes are thinking or thought processes. However, a label is just a name: It is not an explanation or even a description.

Hebb describes higher mental processes as "processes which, themselves independent of immediate sensory input, collaborate with that input to determine which of the various possible responses will be made, and when" (1958, p. 101). In other words, higher mental processes are activities that mediate responses; they are *mediating* processes. What this means is that they are processes that link stimuli and responses, sometimes over long periods of time. From the actor's point of view, these processes are experienced as "thinking."

Although Hebb wanted to explain higher mental processes, he is clearly a behaviorist. "The evidence which psychology can be sure of consists of what man or animal does," he claims. "The evidence does not include sensations, thoughts, and feelings" (1966, p. 4). But, he hastens to point out, psychology "is essentially concerned with such processes; they're known by inference, not directly" (p. 4). He adds: "Everything you know about another person's thoughts or feelings is inferred from behavior. Knowledge of behavior is factual. Knowledge of mental processes is theoretical, or inferential" (p. 4).

Here is a profoundly important departure from early behaviorism. With its insistence that the science of behavior be based solely on observations of objective events such as stimuli and responses, early behaviorism seemed to deny the existence of mental processes. But behaviorism never really denied that these processes occur, Hebb informs us. What John B. Watson, Skinner, and others emphatically rejected was the scientific value of concepts such as consciousness, imagination, and thinking, as well as the scientific value of an approach, such as introspection.[2] Hebb is now suggesting that inferences about such processes might be useful if they are based on actual observations and if the psychologist keeps clearly in mind the distinction between fact (observation) and inference (theory). "Theory is always open to argument," claims Hebb, "but useful argument is possible only when there is some agreement concerning the facts" (1966, p. 4).

Recall that Clark L. Hull had also suggested that human behavior can be understood through hypothetical (that is, inferred) variables that mediate between stimulus and response. But one important difference between Hebb's and Hull's mediational constructs is that Hull's inferences are unrelated to the structure or functioning of the nervous system: They are largely hypothetical. In contrast, Hebb's variables are physiological: They are based on the neurological facts then available and on speculation.

---

[2] Old Lady Gribbin shook her head – almost sadly it seemed – when she read this line. You know, she said to me, I find it astounding how your psychologists have treated consciousness. She said she thought we would recognize that consciousness is absolutely central to the experience of being human but that despite this, it has occupied such an uncertain and controversial role in the development of human psychology. In the beginning, she explained, consciousness was the very center of the science; later, it was sometimes ignored or even denied. Psychologists are still not at all certain what they should make of it. I wondered why she said *your* psychologists. Why not just *psychologists*?

BOX 6.1 Donald Olding Hebb (1904–1985)

Credit: Chris F. Payne/McGill University Archives, PR000387

Hebb was born in the small Canadian town of Chester, Nova Scotia, on July 22, 1904. He spent his childhood in this region, eventually going to Dalhousie University in Nova Scotia. Interestingly, like Skinner, his early ambition was to become a novelist (Hebb, 1980).

Both of Hebb's parents were physicians, and his mother homeschooled him until the age of eight. Two years later, he had been promoted to the seventh grade. He later failed 11th grade – but so did most of his classmates.

When he later went to university, Hebb was reportedly not an outstanding student, perhaps because of a somewhat rebellious nature; his grade point average was just barely enough for him to be granted a B.A. in 1925. After Dalhousie, he was admitted as a part-time graduate student partly because the psychology department chair was a friend of his mother's. He later went to the University of Chicago to study with Karl Lashley, whose investigations of memory storage in rats' brain profoundly influenced Hebb's theory (Dewsbury, 2002). Hebb obtained an M.A. in Chicago and later went to Harvard University where, at age 32, he was granted a Ph.D.

Hebb then went on to academic appointments at Harvard, at the Montreal Neurological Institute, and at Queen's University in Kingston, Ontario. Other positions included a stint as editor of *The Bulletin* of the Canadian Psychological Association, a research position

Continued

BOX 6.1 (cont.)

with the Yerkes Primate Laboratory, the presidencies of both the Canadian and the American Psychological Associations, and a professorship in psychology at McGill University in Montreal.

Among Hebb's many honors were the Warren Medal (presented by the Society of Experimental Psychologists), which was also won by Hull; a distinguished scientific contribution award, also won by Jean Piaget; and a large number of honorary degrees. Hebb's publications include many important papers and two major books: *The Organization of Behavior*, published in 1949, and *A Textbook of Psychology*, the third edition of which was published in 1972. (Based in part on Gentile and Miller, 2009; Seung, 2000.)

The Physiology of Learning

Hebb points out that psychology deals with the behavior of biological organisms; accordingly, it has to be concerned with humans as products of evolution as well as with the functioning of glands, muscles, and other organs. Perhaps most important, argues Hebb, psychology needs to take into account the functioning of the nervous system, and especially the brain.

Although other behaviorists, such as B. F. Skinner, accepted the existence and the importance of human physiological and neural systems, they deliberately avoided speculation about what these systems do. Such speculations, claimed Skinner (1938), are fictions; they deal with a *conceptual* rather than a *central* nervous system.

Hebb, in contrast, deliberately chose to speculate about what he labeled, perhaps to mock Skinner, "the *conceptual nervous system*." What he proposed was that the mental processes that intervene between stimulus and response can be understood and described as neurological events. This belief is a cornerstone of his theory, which he described as *pseudo-behavioristic* because it is concerned mainly with explaining thought processes and perception, topics not often considered within behavioristic positions (Hebb, 1960).

To understand Hebb's system, it is useful to look at some of the main features of the human nervous system.

The Central Nervous System

The human **nervous system** consists of some 86 billion cells called *neurons*. Most of these are located in the brain and in the spinal cord, which together compose the **central nervous system (CNS)**. The rest are found throughout the body in the form of complex neural pathways and branches.

A **neuron** is a specialized cell whose function is to transmit impulses in the form of electrical and chemical changes. Neurons are the link between receptors (for example, sense organs) and effectors (muscle systems, glands) and thereby ensure that the responses made by an organism will be related to the stimulation it receives. Bundles of neurons form **nerves** that compose the nervous system.

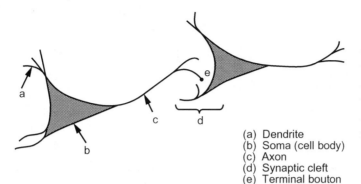

Figure 6.1 Idealized representation of two neurons. Neural transmission ordinarily involves electrical impulses traveling from the cell body, down the axon, and crossing the synaptic cleft to the dendrites of adjoining cells. These adjoining cells can then transmit impulses to other neighboring cells.

(a) Dendrite
(b) Soma (cell body)
(c) Axon
(d) Synaptic cleft
(e) Terminal bouton

Like all cells, neurons consist of a cell body, labeled **soma**, and several arms that extend from this cell body. One of these is the **axon**; the others are **dendrites** (see Figure 6.1). The axon is a conductor of neural impulses. In most cases, transmission occurs in only one direction: from the cell body outward along the axon. Axons may be microscopically short, but some extend all the way from the brain through the spinal cord, a distance of about a meter (about 40 inches) in an adult. Near their ends, axons branch out and terminate in a number of little bulbs called **terminal boutons** (sometimes called **synaptic knobs**). These are not connected directly to other neurons but end close to them. The gap between the terminal bouton and an adjacent neuron is a **synaptic cleft**.

Dendrites are hair-like extensions on a neuron's cell body. Whereas neurons have only one axon, they may have a few or many dendrites. The function of dendrites is to receive impulses and transmit them to the cell body.

Neural Transmission

Neural transmission involves electrical and chemical activity. Each neuron is like a little battery. If you were to use a sensitive voltmeter to measure a currently inactive neuron, you would find that it has a charge of some 70 millivolts (a negative charge of some 70/1000th of a volt). That is the **resting potential** of a neuron; it describes an inactive neuron (a neuron that has more negative ions inside its cell walls than there are positive ions immediately outside the cell).

When the cell is stimulated, certain chemical substances, of which more than 100 have now been identified, are released by the neuron, effectively serving to "open the switch" and cause a flow of charged particles to shoot down the axon to the dendrites of adjacent neurons. This flow of charged particles is called an **action potential.** Within approximately two milliseconds of the initial stimulation, the neuron regains its resting potential. But for a brief period, termed a **refractory period**, it is essentially discharged and thus no longer has the potential to fire.

The chemicals involved in changing the electrical potential of cells, thus leading to neural transmission, are called **neurotransmitters**. Of the 100 or so neurotransmitters that have now been identified, some of the most important are dopamine, norepinephrine, acetylcholine, and serotonin.

Dopamine

Dopamine is centrally involved in the functioning of neurons associated with pleasure and reinforcement. Hence, dopamine is an important neurotransmitter for motivation. But it also has many other functions, some of which have to do with movement, cognition, sleep, memory, and learning.

As we saw in Chapter 5, almost all abused drugs are effective precisely because they increase the availability of dopamine in certain areas of the brain. Research with mice indicates that a single dose of cocaine or of amphetamine is sufficient to cause a marked increase in dopamine and to increase the probability of addiction (Runegaard, Jensen, Wortwein, & Gether, 2018). Alcohol, too, activates the dopamine system, and various studies indicate that individuals most likely to become addicted to drugs are those who have low levels of dopamine available for neural transmission in the first place, sometimes for identifiable genetic reasons (for example, Jerlhag, 2018; Kaneda, 2018).

Norepinephrine

Norepinephrine, sometimes called *noradrenaline*, is a neurotransmitter linked with arousal as well as with memory and learning. At times of crisis, parts of the brain, including the hypothalamus and the amygdala, are suddenly flooded with norepinephrine. This signal of alarm tells the brain that it must now prepare the body to respond to the crisis, perhaps by fleeing or perhaps by fighting.

As a drug, norepinephrine increases blood pressure, which typically causes a reduction in heart rate. As a neurotransmitter, it functions as a result of being released by nerve cells at the synaptic junction. Evidence indicates that it may be implicated in some instances of **attention-deficit hyperactivity disorder (ADHD)** (for example, Navarra & Waterhouse, 2018). One of the effects of drugs such as Ritalin, commonly used to tread ADHD, is to increase levels of norepinephrine and dopamine (King et al., 2018).

There is also indication that some manifestations of depression are linked with the norepinephrine system. Many common antidepressant drugs (for example, those labeled *tricyclic antidepressants*) serve to increase norepinephrine levels (Mayo Clinic, 2018).

Acetylcholine

Acetylcholine is a neurotransmitter found in the central nervous system (the brain and spinal cord) as well as in the *peripheral nervous system* (receptors such as the senses, as well as effector systems, such as muscles and glands). As such, it is importantly involved in conscious activity such as muscle movement. It is also involved in the largely unconscious functioning of the *autonomic* nervous system (the part of the nervous system concerned with physiological functions such as heart and respiration rate, digestion, salivation, perspiration, and so on).

As a neurotransmitter in the central nervous system, acetylcholine is involved in arousal and reinforcement as well as in learning and memory (Solari & Hangya, 2018). Its role in learning and memory is thought to be partly related to increases in *plasticity* resulting from its presence during neurotransmission. It can also serve to increase the reactivity of neurons or to inhibit their responsiveness.

Serotonin

The bulk of the **serotonin** in the human body is found in the gut, where its main role seems to be to regulate intestinal functions. In the central nervous system, serotonin is implicated in neural transmission in much of the brain, especially in areas having to do with emotion. Its other functions also include regulating sleep, appetite, and cognitive activity related to learning and memory (Kim et al., 2018).

Serotonin is present not only in humans but in most other animals as well as in some plants and seeds, many of which are toxic or at least cause pain. In fact, pain is one of the side-effects of large amounts of serotonin in the blood. Interestingly, wasp venom contains serotonin, which serves to increase the painfulness of wasp stings (Moreno & Giralt, 2015).

Too low levels of serotonin have been linked with depression, aggression, and even violence. Accordingly, many antidepressants and antianxiety drugs are substances that affect serotonin levels (Shapiro, 2018).

Hebb's Main Assumptions

When Hebb proposed his pioneering ideas on the neurological basis of learning and behavior, relatively little was known about how the human nervous system functions or about the role of neurotransmitters. From his point of view as a learning theorist, what was important was the knowledge that the effect of stimulation is to activate neural cells, which can then stimulate one another in sequence as impulses cross the gaps (called **synapses**) between neurons. This transmission of impulses is what underlies thought and emotion and causes glands to secrete or muscles to contract. The basic question for the learning theorist is this: What changes occur in neurons or in neural transmission when the organism learns?

Although Hebb didn't know the answer to this question, he made a number of assumptions that suggested an answer highly compatible with what we now know to be correct. The most basic of these assumptions, known as the **Hebb rule**, is this: Repeated transmission of impulses between two cells (that is, between two neurons) leads to permanent facilitation of transmission between these cells.

Permanent facilitation means, in effect, learning. What Hebb was saying is that if a neurological event such as the firing of a sequence of neurons occurs repeatedly, it will become progressively easier for the first neurons in the sequence to activate subsequent neurons.

A second assumption central to Hebb's theory is that neural cells may be reactivated repeatedly because of their own activity. Stimulation of cell A might cause cell B to fire. This in turn might fire cell C, and cell C might then reactivate the first cell in the sequence, cell A, which again activates B, then C, then A again ... and again ... and again (see Figure 6.2). The resulting circular pattern of firing is called a **cell assembly**.

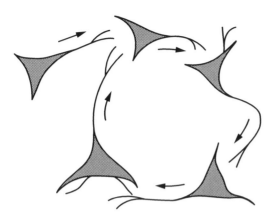

Figure 6.2 Cell assemblies consist of activity in a large number of related neurons. They correspond to relatively simple input.

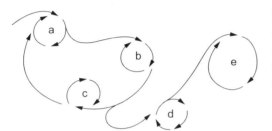

Figure 6.3 Schematic representation of a phase sequence: a, b, c, d, and e can be thought of as cell assemblies. A phase sequence is equivalent to a concept and may consist of activity in a large number of related neurons (see Figure 6.2)

A third important assumption is that if a number of related cell assemblies are simultaneously active, they will become linked in what Hebb labels a **phase sequence** (see Figure 6.3). These hypothetical structures (they are hypothetical because they are imagined rather than demonstrably real) play central roles in Hebb's proposal for a theory of learning.

Each cell assembly, explains Hebb, corresponds to "relatively simple sensory input" – for example, a color or a sensation. Hence, the recognition of even very simple objects will involve the activation of a large number of such cell assemblies or phase sequences.

To summarize, the three basic assumptions that underpin Hebb's learning theory are:

1. The Hebb rule: The repeated firing of two neurons strengthens the link between them.
2. Separate neurons can fire in a circular pattern, so the original neuron is eventually reactivated by another neuron in the pattern (a cell assembly).
3. Simultaneously active cell assemblies become associated so they can activate each other mutually (a phase sequence).

An Illustration of Hebb's Theory of Perception

Another way of describing a cell assembly is to say that it is a network of neurons that is activated repeatedly during a mental process. Say, for example, that the mental process is that of looking at your new car. A car is a very complex stimulus, but Hebb might simplify the illustration by suggesting that the shape of the car, perceived through the sense of vision and perhaps touch, gives rise to activity in a group of related neurons thus forming a *cell assembly* corresponding to shape. At about the same time, another cell assembly (or many such assemblies) relating to color will be activated. And perhaps many other assemblies, such as those having to do with the smell of the new leather seats, activated by the olfactory receptors, will also fire. Now, explains Hebb, there is a tendency for these many related cell assemblies to become associated and to, in a sense, facilitate activity in each other. These interconnected cell assemblies form a *phase sequence* corresponding to this car and, at a more abstract level, perhaps to the entire class of things that can be called *cars*. And maybe when, many decades later, you smell this particular leathery smell while lounging in your deck chair on your luxury yacht off Homer, Alaska, you will suddenly remember the car you once knew so very far away in time and space. Why? Because this precise smell activates a cell assembly that in turn activates a group of related cell assemblies that were linked because of their simultaneous activation in the distant past.

Neurological Basis for Learning

It is important to keep in mind that cell assemblies and phase sequences are hypothetical constructs: They are Hebb's inventions designed to organize what was then known and to lead to new insights. Reassuringly, however, recent evidence of neurological functioning suggests that brain cells tend to fire in groups (assemblies) and to reactivate each other much as Hebb had speculated they might (for example, see Higgins, Stringer, & Schnupp, 2017). Actually, Hebb's notion of cell assemblies plays an increasingly important role in current psychological research and theory, not only in relation to computer-based neural networks (discussed in Chapter 11) but also in a variety of studies that look at topics such as language learning, amnesia, and memory (for example, Magro, Attout, Majerus, & Szmalec, 2018).

The *Aplysia*: Habituation and Sensitization

We know that the transmission of neural impulses underlies sensation, behavior, and higher mental processes (thinking). But what, exactly, happens when an organism learns something? In other words, what neurological changes underlie learning?

Studying changes in human neurons is very difficult and complex, especially given how many there are in the human nervous system. But a number of invertebrates have only a few neurons. And some of these have very large neurons, whose functioning can be studied. Among these invertebrates is the *Aplysia*, a slug-like snail that can be almost as big as a small cat. The *Aplysia* is an especially valuable organism for neurological research: Its nervous system is relatively simple and well mapped, and the electrical and chemical details of neural transmission in the *Aplysia* are very similar to those of neural transmission in vertebrates. As a result, it continues to be extensively studied (for example, Briskin-Luchinsky, Levy, Halfon, & Susswein, 2018; Perez, Patel, Rivota, Calin-Jageman, & Calin-Jageman, 2018).

Not only does the *Aplysia* respond predictably by retracting its gills when its siphon (spout) is touched, but it quickly *habituates* to repeated light touches. After a short while, it stops responding. **Habituation** (becoming less responsive to stimulation so that reactions to it diminish or stop altogether) is clear evidence that something has been learned. It is a highly common phenomenon among most organisms. People quickly stop paying attention to repeated mild stimulation such as the sensation of their clothing, the monotonous humming of an air-conditioning unit, the incessant chirping of sparrows. In the same way, a city dog quickly habituates to traffic noises and pays them little attention. In contrast, a rural dog may pay considerable attention to the much less frequent traffic noises it hears.

There are instances in which repeated stimulation leads not to habituation but to its opposite: **sensitization** (an increase in responses to a given stimulus complex). This is most likely to occur for highly intense stimulation. Thus, if instead of gently touching the *Aplysia*'s siphon, you administer one or two electric shocks just about anywhere on its body, it may become highly *sensitized* as a result of the shocks. Now a very gentle touch of the *Aplysia*'s siphon causes instant and very decided retraction.

Examination of the *Aplysia*'s neurons before and after habituation and sensitization does not indicate that new synapses are formed (or lost) but, rather, that the axons of the sensory neurons become more or less responsive to stimulation (Lodish et al., 2016). With increasing habituation, the amount of transmitter chemicals released by the stimulated neuron declines measurably. But in the event of sensitization, a second neuron, termed an *interneuron*, becomes active. The net effect is that subsequent stimulation will now lead to measurable increases in the amount of transmitter chemicals released. Thus, at least in the *Aplysia*, a chemical change in the cell itself accounts for learning evident in changes in behavior.

Reactivity and Plasticity

In Hebb's theory, as in most other accounts of learning, two properties of the human organism play a central role: reactivity and plasticity. *Reactivity* refers to the capacity of the organism to react to external stimuli; *plasticity* is the property of the organism that allows it to change as a function of repeated stimulation. A simple demonstration can be used to illustrate these two properties. The procedure involves placing a subject two or three feet in front of the experimenter. Without warning, the experimenter then kicks the subject squarely and soundly where he sits. The subject's immediate behavior is an example of reactivity; subsequent refusal to repeat the experiment is an example of plasticity.[3]

Plasticity, the capacity to change as a function of experience, is what accounts for learning. Brain plasticity refers to the fact that activities such as thinking and learning result in actual changes in the brain's physical structure (in its anatomy) as well as in its organization. For example, we know that neural connections that go unused often disappear, a process termed *synaptic pruning*. Thus, in the first four months of **gestation** (prenatal development), more than 200 billion neurons are formed. But in the fifth month, as many as half of these atrophy and die, apparently because they fail to connect with other parts of the brain. This, explains Sousa (2017), prevents the brain from becoming overcrowded with useless neurons. In much the same

---

[3] Mrs. Gribbin said she didn't like this example. She explained that she was leaving it in because someone had thought of it and must have decided it illustrated the point. She said she found it demeaning to think of being hoofed in the unmentionables, or even of doing it to someone else. Schrödinger watched the old lady intently while she spoke. The kerosene lamp's flame danced in its single pupil.

way, neural connections that are thought to be unnecessary or overly simple tend to be pruned and perhaps replaced by more complex and more useful structures.

Plasticity is evident in the *Aplysia*'s habituation as well as in its sensitization to stimulation. It is also apparent in the neurological changes that occur following habituation and sensitization. Neurologically, sensitization leads to **long-term potentiation (LTP)** – that is, to a lasting increase in the responsiveness of neurons. In contrast, habituation leads to **long-term depression (LTD)** – a lasting decline in the responsiveness of relevant neurons. Research involving the electrical stimulation of neurons illustrates that the facilitation (potentiation) and inhibition (depression) of neural activity involve lasting changes in the release of chemical transmitter substances (Greenwald & Shafritz, 2018).

The biochemistry of neurological events involved in learning is now increasingly well understood. It is interesting and impressive that Hebbian theory explains behavior in terms of neurological events at a time when he could do little more than speculate about these events. The *Hebb rule*, his belief that the probability that neuron A will lead to activity in neuron B increases with co-activation of A and B, is basic to current neurological research.

Mediating Processes

Hebb's primary concern was to explain higher mental processes, or thought, which he referred to as *mediating processes*. Thinking (or *mediation*), says Hebb, consists of "activity in a group of neurons, arranged as a set of closed pathways that will be referred to as a cell assembly, or of a series of such activities, which will be referred to as a phase sequence" (1958, p. 103).

How are cell assemblies formed?

The Hebb Rule

A cell assembly (or mediating process) is established as the result of the repeated firing of cells. It is the outcome of the repetition of a particular kind of sensory event. That is because the repeated presentation of a specific stimulus will tend to reactivate the same assemblies each time, leading to changes that facilitate transmission of impulses across the synaptic spaces between the neurons involved. Hence, repetition has a facilitating effect on further neural activity (the Hebb rule). Evidence of this effect is clear in the fact that it is considerably easier to multiply two numbers if they have been multiplied many times previously. Similarly, it is easier to recognize an object if it has often been seen than if it has been seen only once. This property of neural transmission illustrates what plasticity of the nervous system means. And as we saw, there is evidence of changes in neurons that account for increases and decreases in synaptic strength.

Co-activation of Cell Assemblies

Hebb assumes that if two cell assemblies are repeatedly active at the same time, an association between the two will tend to form. In other words, if cell assembly A is always (or often) active when B is active, the two will tend to become associated neurologically. As a result, the firing of cell assembly A may lead to firing in B and vice versa. The result will be the formation of phase sequences – arrangements of neurons that tend to fire in sequence and that can reactivate each other.

This assumption explains conditioning through contiguity. If cell assembly A corresponds to one specific sensory event and B to another, then after repeated simultaneous activation, the activation of one may lead to the activation of the other. For example, if A corresponds to the buzzer in the classical Pavlovian demonstration and B corresponds to food, after sufficient pairings, activation of A alone may lead to responses previously associated only with B. Similarly, if A and B represent the components of thought (mediation), then establishing a relationship between A and B means that presentation of the event associated with A may *remind* a person of the event associated with B. Intuitively, this makes sense. If you always see Jorge with a cigar in his mouth, then it is likely that anything that reminds you of Jorge will also bring the cigar to mind. In much the same way, the smell of wood smoke evokes thoughts of fire; lilacs go with spring; the letter *q* in a word (usually) means *u* is next; and motherhood and apple pie are good things.

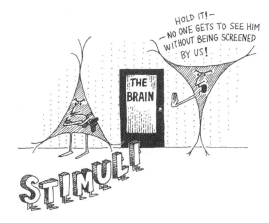

This assumption also explains the perception of objects even with incomplete sensory data. For example, the lines in Figure 6.4 are almost always perceived as a triangle, although they really are not. (This phenomenon is discussed later in this chapter.) For the sake of simplicity, the cell assemblies associated with triangularity can be said to include units representing each of the corners A, B, and C of the triangle as well as each of the sides. Because these features of triangles have been experienced in contiguity many times, associations have formed among the cell assemblies that represent them. It is now sufficient to present limited sensory input (the three sides of a triangle but no corners) to evoke activity in the entire sequence of assemblies corresponding to "triangle."

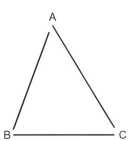

Figure 6.4 Perception with incomplete data. It looks like a triangle, and most people will perceive it as such. But it is really just three lines that do not quite meet.

Learning: The Forming of Associations

Hebb suggests that an assembly that is active at the same time as an *efferent* pathway (a neural pathway leading *outward* from the CNS) will tend to form an association with it. This allows Hebb to explain the formation of associations between events that are in temporal contiguity. Activity in an efferent pathway may result in some sort of motor activity. Hence, the associations explained by this assumption involve behavioral events and thoughts or sensations. For example, particular sights, sounds, or smells might become associated with a specific motor activity so that engaging in the activity then recalls the sensory impression.

The reverse is also true; activity in assemblies that have often been active during some motor response would tend to elicit the same response. For example, in Pavlovian conditioning, assemblies relating to the sounding of a buzzer are always present at the time of salivation and are eventually sufficient to elicit salivation. Thus Hebb's theory offers a simple, neurologically based explanation for Pavlovian conditioning.

Thinking and Learning in Hebb's Theory

For Hebb, the term *mediation* is a word for *thinking*. Mediation, explains Hebb, consists of activity in assemblies of neurons, and the nature of the mediation (or of the thought) is determined by the specific assemblies involved. He believed that the activated area of the cortex, rather than the nature of the neural activity itself, determines the subjective experience of the organism. For example, it is possible to stimulate the optic nerve electrically or by using pressure. In either case, the effect is the same: The subject sees light (Hebb, 1966, p. 267). In contrast, the activation of specific receptors will always affect the same area of the cortex (and presumably the same cell assemblies). Hence, it is possible to "feel" the same reaction for the same stimulation on different occasions. If this were not true, of course, human awareness as it is now known would not exist.[4]

In Hebb's theory, the repetition of the same sensory event leads to the same pattern of neural firing and, eventually, to the formation of associated assemblies of cells. Conduction among these cells becomes easier with repetition. Put very simply, learning is the "permanent facilitation" of conduction among neural units. What Hebb labels a phase sequence is a neurological

---

[4] Old Lady Gribbin interrupted herself and motioned that I should turn the recorder off. "Do you think," she asked, "this means that scientists will one day be able to tell exactly what you're thinking simply by hooking you up to a machine that will detect precisely which neurons are active in your brain?" She got up and put more wood on the fire. Then, she said that no, she didn't think scientists would ever be able to tell exactly what you're thinking just by knowing which of your brain cells are active. She said Goldblum (2001) put her finger on it when she said this would never happen because the neurons that are active in your brain when you're thinking that, say, "$2 + 2 = 4$" are different from the ones active in her brain when she's thinking the same thing. In the end, she says, science might be able to figure out what she's thinking when they detect exactly the same pattern of activity in her brain on different occasions. But if they then detect exactly the same pattern of activity in someone else's brain, all they'll be able to do is guess the general area to which the thought relates. Because the same pattern of neural activity might be used to encode entirely different thoughts in different people, they won't know what that other person is thinking. Do you know what I mean? she asked. I wanted to say I wasn't sure, but she said to never mind and to turn on the recorder again because she had more to say.

unit where the transmission of impulses has become so easy that the activation of one part of the sequence is sufficient to activate the entire organization.

Hebb's neurologically based explanation for learning explains the formation of stimulus and response associations. These, says Hebb, are connections that are formed between their corresponding neurological counterparts (active cell assemblies or phase sequences). Higher processes involved in learning (insightful problem solving, for example) are assumed to involve the combination of phase sequences (sometimes through chance) in higher order organizational units that he labels *supraordinate* phase sequences.

Hebb's notion of cell assemblies and phase sequences provides an explanation for conditioning and suggests the beginning of an explanation for higher mental processes. It also offers explanations for two other interesting phenomena: set and attention.

Set and Attention

When a starter at a race tells the contestants that she'll fire her pistol a few seconds after saying "On your mark," she is attempting to establish **set** (a predisposition to respond in a certain way). If she succeeds, the contestants will sprint forward when the pistol sounds.

A simple behavioristic interpretation of this situation might be that the sound of the pistol is the stimulus that elicits the response of running. But consider what might have happened if the starter had said, "I'm going to fire this pistol to test whether it's working. Just relax." If she then fires the pistol and no one runs, it becomes obvious that the pistol alone is not the stimulus that leads to the running response. Clearly, the initial instructions are also important. In other words, both the *set* given to the contestants and the stimulus influence the behavior.

Consider further what would happen if a celebrity strolled along the track just before the sounding of the gun. Would the contestants' perspiration change? Would their blood pressure and heart rate go up? Would their temperature jump? Probably not. But if these same contestants had already finished the race and were lounging around recuperating when the celebrity walked by, the phase sequences activated might be quite different. This illustrates the effect of **attention**, a narrowing and focusing of perception. *Set* refers to selectivity among responses; *attention* refers to selectivity among input.

According to Hebb, both set and attention are functions of the preactivation of specific cell assemblies. When racers are told to get ready to run, they are *set* to respond by running when they hear a bang. When they are paying attention to the impending sound, they are less likely to attend to other distracting stimuli.

Educational Applications of Hebb's Theory

Set and attention are especially important for teachers. Attention is essential if learning is to occur, and set is involved in choosing appropriate responses. In addition, attention and set are closely related to **arousal** (the person's alertness or vigilance, evident in certain physiological changes). Arousal is central to Hebb's theory of motivation. (That theory is summarized and discussed in Chapter 9.) According to this theory, arousal is an essential condition of learning.

Humans behave as though they need to maintain an optimal level of arousal, explains Hebb (1966). When arousal is too high, the individual feels anxiety or perhaps even panic. Too low a level of arousal results in boredom, lethargy, perhaps even sleep.

Arousal level is, in large part, a function of the amount and variety of stimulation to which the organism is exposed. As we see in Chapter 9, teachers control much of the most significant stimulus input for students in the classroom. The intensity, meaningfulness, novelty, and complexity of what teachers say and do affect students' attentiveness and arousal level. The aim, suggests Hebb, is to maintain student arousal level at an optimal level, where they are attentive and interested rather than bored or anxious.

In addition to its important implications for student motivation, Hebb's theory provides an explanation for why repetition is important in learning (that repetition is important is a finding that has been corroborated in more recent research, discussed in Chapter 8). According to Hebb, repetition of stimulation leads to repeated activation of the same sets of neurons and to the eventual formation of cell assemblies and phase sequences. The establishment of these neurological patterns defines learning.

Appraisal of Hebb's Theory

Hebb's theorizing represents a significant departure from the more traditional S–R theories we considered earlier. Most notably, it is mainly concerned with internal neurological events, few of which are nearly as objective as the stimuli and responses that interested Watson and Skinner. Hebb's goal was less to explain the formation of relationships between stimuli and responses than to account for higher mental processes. In this sense, Hebb's ideas serve as a transition between behaviorist and more cognitive theories.

Much of Hebb's theorizing is based on speculation about the nature of neurological events that mediate between stimuli and responses. Largely because of this, he claimed that his descriptions and assumptions were not really a theory but instead a proposal for one. Nevertheless, his ideas represent a coherent and systematic attempt to explain important observations and can be evaluated as a theory.

Hebb made at least three important contributions to the development of learning theory. First, he brought a consideration of physiological mechanisms back into the study of learning and behavior (much as Pavlov had many decades earlier). Some of the implications of his ideas are now apparent in the neural network models described in Chapter 11.

Second, Hebb's work on arousal theory gives him an important position as a motivational theorist. His work set the stage for a considerable amount of research on the relationship between motivation and performance.

Third, his work on sensory deprivation, discussed in Chapter 9, has had an important influence on research in learning. Among other things, it called attention to a completely new class of motivational systems relating to curiosity, novelty, and exploration.

Hebb's theory has significantly influenced research in neuroscience and on brain-based learning as well as the study of emotions, memory, perception, human development, and the development of theories of intelligence (for example, Brown, 2016; Brown and Milner, 2004). In particular, Hebb's suggestions regarding the neurological underpinnings of perception and thinking and his introduction of the Hebb rule, often now called *the repetition effect* (the notion that the repeated simultaneous activation of neurons leads to permanent changes facilitating subsequent firing of the same neurons) are central to behavioral neuroscience (see Chapter 11).

Viewed in light of the criteria we have been employing, Hebb's theory can be described as reflecting some facts rather well. Thus, it is highly compatible with what is known about neurological functioning, despite the fact that instrumentation to detect and measure brain activity was not sufficiently developed in Hebb's time to permit him to verify his neurological speculation. Now there is increasing evidence that neurological functioning in the brain is organized in ways similar to Hebb's description of cell assemblies and phase sequences.

It is also clear, as Hebb speculated, that a large range of neural changes are linked with experience, and underlie learning and remembering. These include changes in brain size and weight, in neuron size, in the number of dendrite branches, in the number and complexity of synaptic connections between neurons, and even in the number of neural cells. Furthermore, research with the *Aplysia* and related findings about neural transmission supports Hebb's neurological assumptions and his belief that repeated co-activation of related neurons facilitates neural transmission among them.

In support of Hebb's theorizing, it is interesting to note that half a century later, a summary of findings from neuroscience reflects some of the key assumptions of Hebb's theory: "Learning," write Bransford, Brown, and Cocking, "changes the physical structure of the brain. These structural changes alter the functional organization of the brain; in other words, learning organizes and reorganizes the brain" (2000, p. 115). In a nutshell, that is what Hebb said.

It bears repeating that the concepts represented by inventions such as cell assemblies have an important explanatory function. Like all theories, Hebb's hypotheses should not be judged by their "truthfulness" but by the extent that predictions based on these hypotheses agree with actual observations and the extent to which they provide clear and useful explanations of observations. Indeed, no psychological theory need be blessed with "truthfulness." Science would not recognize it in any case. Science insists on objectivity, replicability, consistency, and usefulness; usefulness is sometimes better judged by history than by science.[5]

FROM BEHAVIORISM TO COGNITIVISM

Isms seem to have been a little like religions among many psychologists. Even when dealing with what are meant to be scientific systems of ideas, faith and emotion often seem to have as much to do with people's responses as does science or good sense. That's the way it has been with behaviorism and cognitivism.

Amsel uses a parliamentary metaphor to describe historical confrontations between behaviorism and cognitivism. "I like to point out," says Amsel, "that the S–R psychologists, who at one time formed the government, are now in the loyal opposition, the cognitivists being the new government" (1989, p. 1). But the change in government from the first behaviorists (who shunned all mentalistic concepts) to current cognitive psychologists (who have largely abandoned the stimuli and responses of the first behaviorists) did not happen overnight. It happened slowly. And it happened partly as a result of the influence of Hebb, Tolman, and others like them.[6]

Talking about what he describes as "the war between mentalism and behaviorism," Uttal (2002) describes the two principal points of view in the early development of psychology. On the one hand, he says, there is the belief that the subject matter of psychology is mental activity itself and that it can be studied directly. The opposing viewpoint is represented by a collection of behaviorisms that maintain that it is not the mind but observable behaviors that should be the target of a science of psychology. The main difference between these two points of view, says Uttal, has to do with disagreement over whether external behaviors can be used to make valid inferences about underlying mental states.

For his part, Hebb was a **neobehaviorist** – a *behaviorist* who did not limit theory to observable events but also considered the mental or neurological events that intervene between stimuli and response. While he retained a commitment to the need to preserve the objective, scientific nature of psychological investigation, he also sensed the need to include inferences about profoundly important mental processes such as thinking and imagining.

---

[5] The old lady reshuffled her pages almost haphazardly, it seemed. For a long while, she said nothing, just sat there on the straight-backed chair staring at the window, although it seemed her eyes were focused not on the pane but on the darkness beyond. Schrödinger sat on the table on his haunches, looking out into the darkness, his one eye wide and unflinching, his ears turned like a horse's toward what had drawn his attention, no doubt even in that black night sensing things of which I couldn't be aware. I reached to touch him. He grunted and stepped away.

And then, as if she hadn't paused, Old Lady Gribbin began to speak once more, although she didn't immediately reach for her notes. I went to turn on the recorder, but it had never been off. During this time, the only noise on the machine is the cat's strange guttural cry.

[6] Nor, to extend the metaphor, said Old Lady Gribbin, has psychology's parliamentary system been strictly a two-party system. In the government, there have always been other -isms (such as humanism), -ologies (such as sociobiology), and -yses (such as psychoanalysis) – some with very loud voices; others very quiet. And sometimes, she continued, there have been revolutions that have perhaps had little noticeable effect on the established system of government – grassroots revolts by peasants with machine guns and new theories. As if bored, Schrödinger curled up on the old lady's notes and closed his good eye. She continued as though she had never needed notes.

MECHANISTIC BEHAVIORISM

The behaviorism associated with theorists such as John B. Watson, Edwin Guthrie, Ivan Pavlov, and even B. F. Skinner and Edward Thorndike is sometimes referred to as a **mechanistic behaviorism** because they emphasize and try to understand the predictable, *machine-like* aspects of human behavior. Skinner used the phrase *radical behaviorism* to denote a behaviorism that does not make inferences about mental states.

Mechanistic theories share several characteristics: First, they arose largely as a reaction to the more mentalistic approaches that had previously dominated psychology. In contrast to these mentalistic approaches, behaviorism tries to be completely objective. Accordingly, its most devoted theorists concentrated almost entirely on aspects of behavior that could be observed and measured. The science of behavior thus became a question of discovering reliable relationships between stimuli and responses. And when theorists such as Hebb and Hull began to break away from this orientation by including intervening (mediating) variables in their systems, they were always careful to link them as directly as possible to observable events.

A second characteristic of mechanistic behavioristic theories such as those of Watson, Guthrie, and Skinner is that they make few assumptions about the objectives or purposes of behavior except insofar as these can be related directly to specific needs or drives. Typically, a behavioristic interpretation of a behavior does not ask any questions about the intentions or the wishes of the actor. It simply looks for relationships between response consequences and behavior or it searches for an understanding of how contiguity of stimuli, responses, and response consequences are important in determining behavior.

Behavioristic theories such as those described by Watson and Guthrie are labeled **reductionist** or *molecular* because they try to explain behavior by analyzing it at a molecular level – that is, by reducing it to its smallest elements or components. For example, Watson and Guthrie based their theories on the physiology of the reflex and believed that the most useful approach to understanding and explaining behavior was to look at the most basic (molecular) response. For these theorists, behavior consists of chains of reflexes and reactions.

In contrast to the reductionist or molecular approach, behaviorists such as Hull, Hebb, and Skinner (as well as Tolman) looked at the organism's behaviors from a more *molar* (as opposed to *molecular*) perspective. They assumed that behavior could be understood "as a whole" without being reduced to its individual components. For his part, Tolman who, like Hebb, was a neobehaviorist, deliberately gave behaviorism a different twist: He gave it a purpose.

TOLMAN'S PURPOSIVE BEHAVIORISM

Even in the heyday of behaviorism, not all psychologists enthusiastically embraced mechanistic behaviorism's emphasis on the predictable, machine-like characteristics of human functioning. In fact, there were some strong negative reactions to behaviorism, evident in the beginnings of **cognitivism**. Cognitivism is an approach in psychology that is concerned more with decision making, thinking, problem solving, imagining, and related topics than with observable behavior.

One of the early roots of cognitivism is German Gestalt psychology, which is discussed later in this chapter. Another is Tolman's theory, which challenged behaviorism's removal of purpose and consciousness from psychology. All behavior has a purpose, insisted Tolman (1967): All actions, whether that of rat or woman or man, are directed toward a goal by **cognitions** (things that are known, imagined, anticipated, etc.). Behavior is seldom simply the result of mindless S–R connections. But ever a behaviorist, Tolman insisted, "Mental processes are to be identified in terms of the behaviors to which they lead" (1932, p. 2). In other words, his intervening variables, like those described by Hull, are tied to observable behaviors. But he insisted that observable behavior, including even that of animals such as rats, has a purpose.

BOX 6.2 Edward Chace Tolman (1886–1959)

Edward Chace Tolman was born into a Quaker family in Newton, Massachusetts, on April 14, 1886 (also the year of Guthrie's birth). His was a hardworking family that valued social responsibility and education. His father was on the board of trustees of the Massachusetts Institute of Technology, which he later attended at least partly because of family pressure (Tolman, 1952). In 1911, he received a B.S. in electrochemistry from MIT and then went to Harvard where he obtained an M.A. in 1912 and a Ph.D. in 1915, both in psychology. Heavily influenced by the writings of John B. Watson, Tolman became a behaviorist while at Harvard. But at the same time, he was also exposed to the new ideas of the Gestalt psychologists. As a result, he became a behaviorist with very different ideas.

Tolman began his university teaching career at Northwestern University. However, he was let go three years later, apparently because of incompetence as a teacher but perhaps more likely because of his Quaker-based pacifist convictions in a time of war. From Northwestern, he went to the University of California at Berkeley, where he spent most of the remainder of his academic career. For a number of years, though, Tolman was also compelled to leave Berkeley, this time after refusing to take a controversial loyalty oath spawned by the McCarthy purges. As a result, in 1950 he accepted teaching positions at the University of Chicago and at Harvard. As a member of the American Civil Liberties Union, Tolman was instrumental in bringing about guarantees of certain academic freedoms. As a result of his involvement in this effort, he was able to return to Berkeley in 1953, apparently with back pay.

Tolman, like Watson, Thorndike, Guthrie, Hebb, Hull, Bruner, and Bandura, also served as president of the American Psychological Association. Still, he was often accused of not being as serious and single-minded as he might have been regarding the development of his theories. His writings are filled with whimsy and anecdotes, and he wrote somewhat disparagingly about his own theorizing and research. "The system may not stand up to any final rules of scientific procedure," he says. "But I do not much care .... In the end, the only sure criterion is to have fun. And I have had fun" (Tolman, 1959, p. 140). And perhaps his tongue was at least partly in his cheek when he dedicated one of his most important books to *Mus norvegicus albinus*, the white Norway mouse, although he probably meant the white Norway rat. (Based in part on Encyclopædia Britannica 2010a; Sahakian, 1981; Tolman, 1952; Woodworth & Sheehan, 1964.)

Do Rats have Purpose?

What evidence is there that a rat directs its behavior as if it had certain definite purposes? Why should the psychologist believe that cognitions, rather than simply a series of mindless S–R connections, are what drive the rat's behavior?

The Blocked-Path Study

The evidence, claimed Tolman, is convincing. For example, take the blocked-path study (Tolman & Honzik, 1930). In this study, a rat is released into a maze with several different routes to a goal and is allowed to run freely until it has learned the maze. The next step is to place barriers in some of the paths and then observe the rat's reaction. Figure 6.5 shows an approximate representation of the Tolman and Honzik maze. The paths vary in length from the shortest, most direct route (path 1) to the longest (path 3).

As expected, once they have learned the maze, hungry rats almost invariably select path 1 when given a choice. And, as might also be expected, when path 1 is blocked at point A, rats usually select path 2 (about 93 percent of the time).

The situation becomes more interesting when path 1 is blocked at point B. S–R theory might still predict that the rat would select path 2 because the entrance to it isn't blocked and it should be second in overall preference given how much shorter it is than path 3. How can a rat be expected to figure out that the block on path 1 at B also serves as a barrier for path 2 and that there is now only one path to the goal?

But the rat does figure it out, consistently selecting path 3 rather than path 2 (14 out of the 15 rats involved in the original experiment selected path 3). Should psychology assume that these rats "know" the same thing you and I do – that they have, in fact, developed some sort of cognitive grasp of the maze?

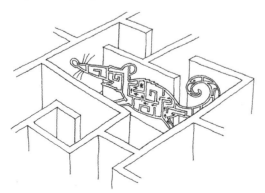

Tolman: Learning involves the development of cognitive maps

Yes, said Tolman, psychology should assume just that. Experiments such as these illustrate that learning involves the development of **cognitive maps**. A cognitive map is an internal representation of relationships between goals and behaviors as well as knowledge of the environment where the goals are to be found. What happens is that the organism develops a series of expectations with respect to behavior. These expectations are part of what Tolman

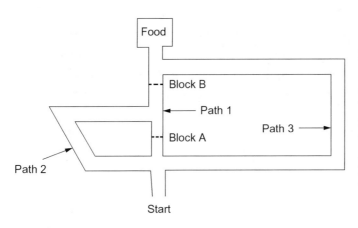

Figure 6.5 In the Tolman and Honzik (1930) blocked-path study, rats that had learned this maze almost invariably selected path 3 when path 1 was blocked at B. It seemed they somehow knew that the barrier at B also blocked the much shorter path 2. From Lefrançois, G. R. (2016). *Psychology: The Human Puzzle* (2nd ed.). San Diego, CA: Bridgepoint Education, Fig. 5.11. Used by permission.

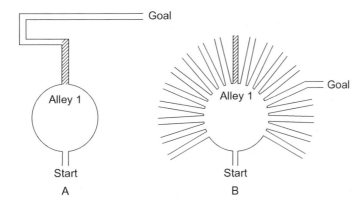

Figure 6.6 In the Tolman, Ritchie, and Kalish (1946) study, rats learned a simple maze with an indirect path to the goal. In the second part of the experiment, the position of the goal and of the starting area remained the same, but the original path was blocked, and 18 new paths were available.

labels *sign–significate relationships*. A sign is simply a stimulus; a significate is the expectation of reward that results from learning.

An Expectations Study

Even nonhuman animals behave as though they have expectations. Tinklepaugh (1928), one of Tolman's many students, placed a banana under a cup in full view of a monkey. Then, when the monkey wasn't watching, he substituted a piece of lettuce for the banana. The monkey was allowed to turn the cup over, which it did very eagerly, immediately becoming extremely agitated, searching here and there and snarling at Tinklepaugh. The monkey's behavior seemed to indicate clearly that it had expected to find the banana under the cup. Its agitation and continued search would be difficult to explain using simple conditioning theory.

A Place Learning Study

In a classic experiment, Tolman, Ritchie, and Kalish (1946) trained rats to run across an open, circular area and into an alley that, after three right-angle turns (left, right, and right), led to a goal box with a food tray (maze A in Figure 6.6). In the next part of the experiment, the alley leading to the goal box was blocked, and 18 new alleys were made available to the rats (maze B). Which alley are the rats most likely to choose?

Behavioristic theory would predict that the rat would most likely choose one of the alleys closest to the previously rewarded alley. Not so. In fact, most rats chose alleys that go in the general direction of the original goal box. It appears that what these rats learned was not a series of connected responses, duly reinforced and stamped in, but a *place*. In Tolman's terms, they developed a cognitive map of the area, together with related expectancies, both of which directed the rats' behavior.

A second experiment, reported by Macfarlane (1930), makes much the same point in a dramatic way. It also involved rats that were taught to find a goal box in a maze, but these animals had to swim through the maze rather than run. A plausible behavioristic interpretation of this phenomenon would maintain that the specific responses involved in swimming are chained together, reinforced, and eventually learned as a complete sequence. This same interpretation would also predict that if the maze were drained, making the learned S–R chains involved in swimming completely useless, the rats would have to learn the maze all over again. In fact, however, when the maze was drained, the rats ran to the goal box without hesitation and with no more errors than they had been making while swimming.

A Latent Learning Experiment

These studies strongly suggest that there is more to learning mazes than the simple acquisition of stimulus–response or response–reward connections – a point that is dramatically underlined by the latent-learning experiment described in Chapter 1. In this study, Buxton (1940) allowed rats to spend several nights in large mazes without reward. Some behavioristic pioneers would surely predict that these rats would learn very little from their exposure to the mazes. They might be more than a little amazed to find that when Buxton fed the rats briefly in the goal box and then placed them in the start box, half of them ran to the goal box without a single error. It appears that rats are capable of developing cognitive maps even in the absence of a food reward. Because it is delayed, this learning is sometimes called *latent*.

What Is Purposive Behaviorism?

These and many related studies carried out by Tolman and his students tended to support the conclusion that the notion of *cognitive maps* is the best explanation for how rats learn mazes. Thus, without being reinforced for so doing, they learn how to take shortcuts, how to make detours, or how to navigate a complex maze in which they have never previously had any reinforcement. That the rat's learning and its behavior appear to be purposeful explains Tolman's use of the label **purposive behaviorism**, a label that emphasizes that behavior is goal-directed.

Although, as Rescorla (2009) points out, Tolman's ideas were controversial, many psychologists accepted the notion that animals and humans develop cognitive maps – representations of what the world is like. But, explains Rescorla, the rat's mental maps are not quite like a human mental map: They do not have the same logical qualities; they don't permit logical deduction and inference. But they do serve remarkably well as guides for navigating and reaching goals.

Educational Implications and Summary Principles of Tolman's System

Four major themes summarize Tolman's theory of purposive behaviorism. Each has clear implications for educational practice.

Behavior Is Purposive

First and most important, Tolman believed that all behavior is purposive. By this, he meant that all behavior is guided by goals and expectancies. In its simplest sense, the purpose that guides the organism's behavior is the expectation of a reinforcing outcome.

It follows from this principle that if teachers are to influence and guide students' behavior, they need to find ways to influence and guide their goals and expectations. The best ways of doing this are implicit in the next summarizing theme.

Behavior Is Cognitive

The expectations that underlie and guide behavior are cognitions. They consist of the organism's awareness of possible (or probable) connections between certain actions and certain outcomes. These cognitions develop after experiences with stimuli and rewards. In effect, what is learned, says Tolman, isn't a specific behavior in response to a stimulus or reward but a cognition, an item of knowledge concerning a link between stimuli and expectancies of acquiring a goal (also referred to as a *sign–significate* relationship).

Note that a cognition is an abstraction – a theoretical invention. Tolman, a behaviorist, believed that cognitions should only be inferred from behavior, not through introspection.

One of the means by which teachers can influence students' expectations and goals is by arranging for their most desirable behaviors to be followed by positive outcomes. What students learn, Tolman explains, is an expectation that certain behaviors will lead to certain outcomes. Clearly, teachers have considerable control over the outcomes of school-based behaviors.

Reinforcement Establishes and Confirms Expectancies

A third underlying theme in this system relates to the role of reinforcement in learning. Tolman's system deals with connections between stimuli and expectancies. Because expectancies develop in situations in which reinforcement is possible or probable, the role of reinforcement is primarily one of confirming expectancies. The more often expectations are confirmed, the more likely it is that the stimuli (signs) associated with them will become linked with the relevant significates (expectancies). For example, if Sabrina expects high grades as a result of studying hard and long, that expectation will be confirmed to the extent that she receives high grades on a Monday test after studying all weekend. If she does not, her expectations will be shattered and her study habits may well change. If she and her classmates typically receive high grades when they do not study, their expectations and their behaviors are likely to change accordingly.

A Theory of Purposive Behaviorism Is Molar, Not Reductionist

A final important principle of Tolman's system is his emphasis on the molar rather than the molecular aspects of behavior. Unlike Watson and Guthrie, Tolman did not reduce behavior to its smallest units but dealt instead with large units of behavior that are unified in the sense that they are governed by *purpose*. Purpose (a search for rewarding goals), rather than the reward itself, directs behavior. Put another way, the connections that explain behavior in Tolman's system involve links between stimuli and expectancies rather than between reinforcement and responses or between stimuli and responses. And the expectancies themselves develop as a function of exposure to situations in which reinforcement is possible. If you do not expect reinforcement in a given situation, you are not likely to be disappointed; but if you do expect reinforcement, whether you obtain it may well affect your subsequent behavior.

From an educational perspective, this final theme leads to a less mechanistic, less rigid view of the learner than might be implied by the behavioristic theories discussed in earlier chapters. Tolman's learner is not so much moved blindly this way and that by the rewards and punishments that the world provides; rather, this learner is a more thoughtful being, a learner more likely to develop expectancies and to weigh the possible outcomes of various behaviors.

Appraisal of Tolman's Purposive Behaviorism

One of Tolman's important and often overlooked contributions to the development of psychology relates to his use of mazes in studies of rat behavior. He and his students designed dozens of ingenious mazes and conducted countless clever experiments with them. The study of behavior in mazes continues to be a useful and important way of studying the cognitive mechanisms used to represent space and to direct movement. In addition, maze learning provides an important way of studying memory.

Tolman's principal contribution to the development of psychological theory lies not so much in the advances in knowledge and prediction made possible by his work as in the transition from behavioristic to more cognitive interpretations. Tolman's emphasis on the importance of cognitive variables such as expectancies is a significant departure from behavioristic theories such as those of Skinner, Watson, and Guthrie which rejected speculation about events that might intervene between stimuli and responses. But, notes O'Neil (1991), it is never entirely clear whether Tolman was actually making claims about what he considered to be "real" internal states or processes or whether he was just speaking "as if." Hence, relative to the criteria described in Chapter 1, Tolman's position might be faulted for a certain inconsistency or lack of clarity. In fact, his writings and research do not point to a very clear theoretical orientation. Nevertheless, his notion of *cognitive maps* as internal representations that guide movement in space continues to be explored in psychological research (for example, Epstein, Patai, Julian, & Spiers, 2017; Sato, Fujishita, & Yamagishi, 2018).

It would be far from accurate to convey the impression that psychology went directly from the mentalistic concepts of the early introspectionists to the interpretations of behaviorists, such as Watson and Guthrie, and then finally to a more enlightened cognitivism. Actually, cognitivism is approximately as old as behaviorism because Gestalt psychology (one of the earliest forms of cognitive theory) developed at about the same time as early behaviorism. It is nevertheless true that North American psychology went from a period when Watsonian and Thorndikean behaviorism were supreme, both in theory and in practice, to a later period when interest turned increasingly to cognitive topics (although behaviorism continued to flourish). Thus, it is relatively common in psychological literature to speak of the period during which behaviorism dominated in American psychology (from the 1920s to around the middle of the century) followed by a "cognitive revolution," which began around the middle of the twentieth century.

In some important ways, Tolman's thinking reflects something of both schools. This should not be surprising given that, although one of his first courses in psychology used Watson's brand-new and thoroughly behavioristic book, Tolman had traveled to Germany and met with leading Gestaltists, including Köhler and his associates, before finishing his graduate work at Harvard (Tolman, 1952). Some 10 years later (around 1923), he returned to Germany to study with the Gestalt psychologists.

GESTALT PSYCHOLOGY

At the time World War I broke out, Wolfgang Köhler, a young German psychologist, found himself marooned on the island of Tenerife, unable to return to his home because of the war. On Tenerife, there was a research station for studying apes; Köhler studied them during the four years he spent on the island, summarizing his studies in the book *The Mentality of Apes* (1925).

There are bright apes and stupid apes, Köhler concluded. Stupid apes seem to learn by association and repetition, practicing the same behaviors repeatedly. In their attempts to solve problems, said Köhler, they make "bad errors," errors based on old and inappropriate solutions. In contrast, bright apes learn very much like people do, repeatedly displaying an astounding capacity for *higher mental processes*. Even when they fail to solve a problem, they nevertheless make "good errors," attempting solutions that, upon reflection, should have worked but didn't.

Köhler arrived at his notions about the minds of apes by designing studies to observe their problem-solving behavior. These studies often required that the ape invent or discover a solution for the problem of obtaining a bunch of bananas hanging outside the ape's cage. In some studies, the ape had to use a long stick to reach the bananas. In others, it would have to join several sticks together so they would be long enough. In one study, the ape had to use a short stick to drag another longer stick within reach before joining the sticks. In Köhler's "box" problems, the ape had to move a box underneath the bananas or pile boxes one on top of the other to reach them.

BOX 6.3 Kurt Koffka (1886–1941), Wolfgang Köhler (1887–1967), and Max Wertheimer (1880–1943)

Max Wertheimer. Credit: Bettmann / Getty Images. Getty Images 514896776

The ideas and theories of Koffka, Köhler, and Wertheimer are almost inseparable, as are their lives. All graduated from the University of Berlin (they became known as the "Berlin group"), all had training in philosophy and psychology, and all eventually emigrated to the United States courtesy of Hitler's persecution of Jews (Koffka and Wertheimer were Jewish). They worked together, sharing their convictions and united in their attacks against introspectionism and behaviorism. And they were close friends: Köhler's 1929 book *Gestalt Psychology* is dedicated to Max Wertheimer, and Koffka's 1935 book *Principles of Gestalt Psychology* bears the inscription, "To Wolfgang Köhler and Max Wertheimer in gratitude for their friendship and inspiration."

Wertheimer, half a dozen years older than Köhler and Koffka, was born in Prague on April 15, 1880. Before going to Berlin, he studied law in Prague. He obtained his Ph.D. in 1904. His many interests included writing poetry and composing symphonies.

Although acknowledged as the intellectual leader of Gestalt psychology, Wertheimer wrote little and did far less to popularize the movement than did Köhler and Koffka. But he designed a number of important experiments, elaborated Gestalt principles in his lectures, and recruited Koffka and Köhler to work with him. In 1933, Wertheimer emigrated to the United States, where he remained until his death in 1943.

BOX 6.3 (cont.)

Köhler was born in Reval, Estonia, on January 21, 1887. He obtained his Ph.D. from the University of Berlin in 1909 and subsequently, along with Koffka, worked with Wertheimer in Frankfurt. During World War I, he spent four years on Tenerife as director of the anthropoid station there, studying the behavior of apes (and of chickens). The results of his investigations were published in *The Mentality of Apes* (1925). About the mentality of chickens, he wrote little.

After Köhler returned to Berlin, he published extensively, becoming one of the most important spokesmen for the Gestalt movement. Conflict with the Nazi regime forced him to emigrate to the United States in 1935, where he was to stay until his death in 1967. Köhler continued to write important books in the United States, engaging in fierce battles with behaviorists such as Hull and even publicly debating against Watson. He was awarded the distinguished scientific contribution award by the American Psychological Association and, like Tolman, Watson, Thorndike, Guthrie, Hebb, Hull, Bruner, and Bandura, served as president of that association.

Koffka was born in Berlin on March 18, 1886, went to the university there, and obtained his Ph.D. in psychology in 1909. He had earlier studied science and philosophy in Edinburgh. From Berlin, he went to Frankfurt, where he and Köhler worked with Wertheimer. There, he began the extensive writings that later became influential in popularizing Gestalt psychology. He was the most prolific writer of the trio, publishing a large number of important and sometimes difficult books.

Like Köhler and Wertheimer, Koffka spent some time lecturing in the United States before moving there permanently in 1927. There, he lectured at Smith College and continued to write until his death in 1941. (Based in part on Boring, 1950; Encyclopædia Britannica, 2010b, 2010c, 2010d, 2010e; Sahakian, 1981; Woodworth & Sheehan, 1964.)

Insight or Trial and Error

Thorndike was wrong, claimed Köhler: Intelligent apes don't learn simply by trial and error. They don't just go about their cages lunging repeatedly at unreachable bunches of bananas, climbing the bars, and doing other well-practiced ape things. Instead, some apes appear to solve complex problems very suddenly, as if they had just now grasped the solution. For example, when Sultan, perhaps the most famous of Köhler's apes, found he could not reach the bananas with his short stick, he stopped and, in Köhler's words, "gazed about him." Then, as if galvanized into action by his vision of the correct solution, "[he] suddenly carried out the correct reactions in one consecutive whole" (Köhler, 1927, p. 150). The Gestalt term for the process involved in this kind of solution is **insight**: the perception of relationships among elements of a problem leading to an apparently sudden realization of a solution. In Köhler's (1927) words, insightful thinking is a type of *relational thinking*. It requires a mental reorganization of problem elements and recognition of the correctness of the new organization. Insight is the cornerstone of Gestalt psychology.

But, cautions Köhler, just because the term *insight* or *relational thinking* is used to describe what might be considered an extraordinary accomplishment in an ape, we should not misinterpret it to mean "some special and supranatural faculty producing admirable and otherwise inexplicable results. As I used and intended the term, nothing of that sort should be implied in it" (1929, p. 371). As Köhler uses it, the term applies to understanding common facts and solving general, everyday problems.

Among the most important of Köhler's convictions is the belief that trial and error plays a minor role in problem-solving behavior, especially among humans, but even among apes and chickens. "I am not sure that even after years of trial and error," Köhler writes, "a child would learn to organize [a sensory field]" (1929, p. 177). Organizing perceptions, he claims, is far more important than the specific properties of what is perceived. Why? Because it is only through an understanding of their organization and their structure that people know things.

Take something as simple as a melody. You know that a melody is composed of individual notes. But you would not understand the melody were you to hear the notes in a completely random arrangement. Similarly, the meaning of a geometric figure derives not from each of its elements (number of sides, dimensions of its parts, angles of corners) but from their relationships to each other.

Gestalt Means "Whole"

That the whole is greater than the sum of its parts is the saying most closely associated with Gestalt psychology. Thus, the melody, not its individual notes and rests, is the whole, the organization, the *Gestalt* – as is the trapezoid, the triangle, and the square. Their meaning comes not from summing their parts willy-nilly but from the ability of humans (and apes) to perceive their organization. To perceive organization or structure is to achieve insight. *Gestalt* is German for *whole*; hence, the name for this approach to psychology.

Not surprisingly, one way of summarizing Gestalt psychology is to describe its laws of perception, laws that were developed and elaborated largely by the three founders of the Gestalt movement: Wertheimer (1959), Koffka (1922, 1925, 1935), and Köhler (1927, 1969).

Principles of Perception

The first and most basic argument advanced by Gestaltists against procedures that emphasize the analysis of behavior is that behavior cannot be understood through its parts: It cannot be reduced to isolated sensations (as the German psychology of introspection tended to do) or to distinct stimuli and responses (as American behaviorism did). This is not to deny that the whole is composed of parts or that the parts can be discovered through analysis.

The thrust of the argument is that the whole (the Gestalt) is different from the parts, as is evident in countless daily events. In the same way as the overall perception when listening to music is not of isolated notes but, rather, of bars or passages, so too do physical objects derive their identity from the way their parts are combined. An object as simple as an apple is no longer simply an apple after it has been put through a blender; nor is a house a house when all its timbers, nails, and other parts have yet to be assembled.

Prägnanz: Good Form

The first concern of the Gestaltists was to discover the laws governing the perception of wholes, where perception refers to the process by which physical stimuli are interpreted and become meaningful. These laws, first described by Koffka (1935), are summarized briefly here. The laws are primarily perceptual and are most easily described and illustrated as such. However, Gestalt psychologists see no discontinuity between perception and thinking: They consider these laws applicable to both.

A single overriding principle governs perception and thinking: **prägnanz** (meaning "good form"). As Köhler noted, insightful solutions often seem to involve an "abrupt reorganization of given materials, a revolution, that suddenly appears ready-made on the mental scene" (1969, p. 163). How does the person (or the animal) recognize that this reorganization is right? At least part of the answer, argues Köhler, is that the brain appears to be directed by a tendency for whatever is perceived to take the best form possible.

The exact nature of that form for all perceptual (and cognitive) experiences is governed by four additional principles.

Principle of Closure

Closure is the act of completing a pattern or Gestalt. It is clearly illustrated in the fact that when you look at an incomplete figure (such as in Figure 6.7), you tend to perceive a completed design. The same phenomenon is readily apparent in perception of a melody with missing notes or of incomplete words, such as p–ych–l–gy.

Although the term *closure* was originally employed only with perceptual problems, psychologists now use it in a variety of situations, retaining much of its original meaning but also adding some broader significance. For example, the phrase *achieving closure* is often used to refer to solving a problem, understanding a concept, completing a task, or achieving resolution of a personal crisis.

Principle of Continuity

Perceptual phenomena tend to be perceived as continuous. For example, a line that starts as a curved line (see Figure 6.8) tends to be perceived as having continuity (as continuing in a curving fashion). Similarly, if you see the front end of a truck poking around a corner, you are

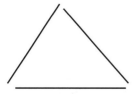

Figure 6.7 Closure is the tendency to perceive incomplete objects (or thoughts) as being complete. Here the figures tend to be perceived as a triangle and a square rather than as individual lines that do not meet.

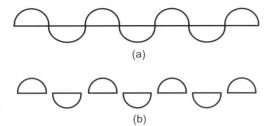

Figure 6.8 An illustration of the Gestalt concept of continuity. The lines in (a) tend to be perceived as a straight line running through a curved one rather than as a set of semicircles as in (b).

Figure 6.9 People have a tendency to perceive similar input as belonging together. The figure is seen as four rows of identical letters rather than as 10 columns of different letters.

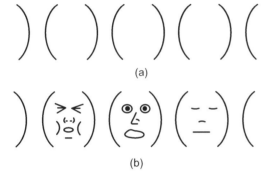

Figure 6.10 There is a tendency to perceive things that are close together as belonging together. Part a is seen as four sets of curved lines; b is seen as three faces.

also likely to *see* (or at least imagine) the unseen rest of the truck continuing, uninterrupted. The principle of continuity, also referred to as the principle of "good continuation," tends to ensure that we don't perceive whole objects as isolated and broken parts.

Principle of Similarity

The principle of similarity holds that objects that are similar tend to be perceived as related. For example, a person who hears two melodies at the same time recognizes each as a separate melody rather than hearing both as one. In Figure 6.9, there appear to be four rows of identical letters rather than 10 columns of different letters.

Principle of Proximity

Objects or perceptual elements tend to be grouped by their proximity. For example, (a) in Figure 6.10 shows four sets of curved lines, whereas (b) is perceived as three faces.

Gestalt Views of Learning and Memory

These principles, along with several others, were developed by Wertheimer and later applied by Koffka to thinking as well as to perception. But because the Gestaltists were not concerned with molecular aspects of learning and behavior, such as stimuli and responses, their explanations of learning and memory are considerably more global and nonspecific than those of the behaviorists.

In general, the Gestaltist view is that learning results in the formation of memory traces. The exact nature of these traces is left unspecified, but a number of their characteristics are detailed. The most important characteristic is that learned material, like any perceptual information, tends to achieve the best structure possible (prägnanz) relative to the laws of perceptual organization just discussed. Hence, what is remembered is not always what was learned or perceived, but is often a better Gestalt than the original. Wulf (1938) described three organizational tendencies of memory.

Leveling

Leveling is a tendency toward symmetry or toward toning down the peculiarities of a perceptual pattern. Figure 6.11 presents a hypothetical illustration of leveling. Koffka assumed that the process of leveling is also applicable to cognitive material. For example, when recalling the feeling of traveling in a train, a person may remember a generalized impression of forward motion and of countryside sweeping by without also remembering the sensation of swaying from side to side.

Sharpening

Sharpening is the act of emphasizing the distinctiveness of a pattern. One characteristic of human memory is that the qualities that most clearly give an object identity tend to be exaggerated in reproducing that object. For example, Figure 6.12 shows how successive recollections of a face with distinctive eyebrows tend to exaggerate the eyebrows.

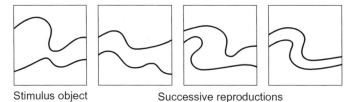

Figure 6.11 Leveling describes a tendency toward symmetry and toward reducing abnormalities and peculiarities.

Stimulus object   Successive reproductions

Figure 6.12 Sharpening is evident in a tendency to emphasize the distinctiveness of a pattern.

Stimulus object   Successive reproductions

Stimulus object　　　　Successive reproductions

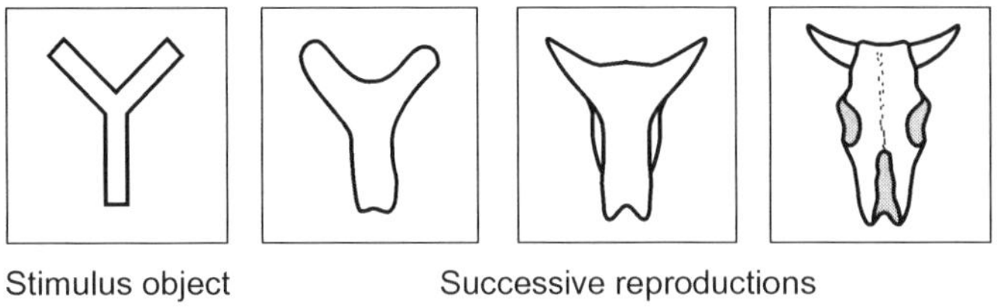

Figure 6.13 Normalizing is the tendency to perceive (and remember) what is expected.

Normalizing

Normalizing occurs when the reproduced object is modified to conform to previous memories. This modification usually tends toward making the remembered object more like what it appears to be. A hypothetical illustration of normalizing is presented in Figure 6.13, in which successive reproductions of the same stimulus object over a period of time become progressively more like something familiar (and, hence, something "normal").

Beyond Perception: The Behavioral Field

The world as it might be seen and described by physics is one thing, Koffka points out; the world as the individual perceives it is quite another matter. And this, the world of "direct experience," is far more important for understanding the individual's behavior.[7]

The Lake of Constance

To illustrate, Koffka (1935, p. 28) tells the story of a man on horseback who struggles through a fierce blizzard across an open plain, finally arriving at an inn. "Gawd, which way did you come?" asks the innkeeper. The man, half frozen, points out the direction. "Do you know," asks the innkeeper in amazement, "that you have ridden across the Lake of Constance?" And the man, stunned, drops dead at the innkeeper's feet.

There's only one behavior here: that of riding across a frozen lake through a winter blizzard. But, Koffka points out, the psychologist knows that the man's behavior would have been very different had he known he was crossing the lake and not a barren plain. If this after-the-fact thought frightened him so much that it killed him, he surely would not have crossed the lake had he been aware of it beforehand.

---

[7] "There's an interesting philosophical issue here," said Old Lady Gribbin. "Let me read to you from this book by Lehar," and she motioned that I should turn off the recorder but said nothing when I continued to take notes. Then, she read different lines from here and there, which seemed to say, according to my hurried notes, that we can't personally know the reality with which physics deals, but that neither can physics know our personal realities. Consciousness is a "deeply mysterious" thing according to Lehar (2003). He explains that if you think about it, you'll eventually realize that the reality you know, your consciousness, is all inside your head. It can't really be anywhere else. What you're observing when you think you're looking at reality is in fact your personal consciousness of reality. Consciousness, says Lehar, is directly observable; the external reality of physics isn't. Plato was right: The world is all inside your head. "Did you know that?" asked the old lady, and I swear she was talking to Schrödinger. He purred. Then, she turned back to her pages.

The Behavioral Field

From the man's viewpoint, his behavior took place in a very different environment – in what Koffka calls the **behavioral field** (or the *psychological field*). The behavioral field is the actor's personal view of what is real. In this man's behavioral field, there was a windswept plain. As he later discovered, though, in the real physical world, there was a deadly dangerous frozen lake.

The behavioral field and the physical environment always affect a person's behavior, claims Koffka. And although the physical environment clearly affects the behavioral field, the two are not the same. Koffka describes as another example the behavior of two apes in separate cages, each of which can reach a bunch of bananas only by stacking boxes one on top of the other. One, the bright ape, eventually does so, climbs up, and retrieves the bananas. The stupid one ends up sitting on one of the boxes, staring sadly at the unreachable bananas. These two apes are in exactly the same physical field. But in the behavioral field of the bright ape, there are stacking boxes that reach way up; in the behavioral field of the other, there is only a box on which to sit and cry for a bunch of unreachable bananas.

Appearance versus Reality

The Gestalt laws of perception point out that what people see is not necessarily what is really out there. Your reality, as Lehar (2003) puts it, is all within your head. When you look at the book you are now reading, you are looking at your personal, entirely internal consciousness of this book. There may well be an objective, physical reality beyond the confines of your skull, but you can only "know" it within your consciousness. And your knowledge of it may not be accurate. Thus, when you saw a complete triangle in Figure 6.7, you did not perceive the physical field accurately. But that there is a triangle in Figure 6.7 becomes an actual part of your psychological reality. Gestalt psychology emphasizes the difference between physical reality and what *seems* to be real.

The Gestaltists believed that to understand behavior, it is necessary to know something of the individual's perception of reality (that is, of the person's behavioral, or psychological, field). This is because people respond to appearance (what they think is real) rather than to reality. The task of psychology, claimed Koffka, is "the study of behavior in its causal connection with the psychophysical field" (1935, p. 67). In many ways, this is a far more complex task than the behaviorists had set themselves – namely, that of understanding responses to real stimuli in the actual physical environment. At the same time, because the psychological field includes people's individual perceptions of other people (as well as of things, animals, and all else that might be relevant), this approach lends itself more easily to understanding social behavior.

Gestalt Psychology and Modern Cognitivism

Gestalt psychology is considered the beginning of contemporary cognitive psychology for two main reasons: (1) because of its concern with perception, awareness, problem solving, and insight and (2) because it rejected behaviorism for being overly mechanistic, incomplete, and unsuitable for explaining higher mental processes. Köhler, in particular, felt that approaches such as Hull's were impractical because they were too insistent on objectivity and too determined to reject the usefulness of trying to understand individual perceptions and private awareness.

However, in several important ways, Gestalt psychology and contemporary cognitivism represent different interests and different approaches. Contemporary cognitive psychology deals with subjects such as problem solving, decision making, information processing, and understanding (the theories of Jerome Seymour Bruner and Jean Piaget, discussed in Chapter 7, are examples). Cognitive theorists conduct research on a wide range of topics, primarily using human subjects. Topics include understanding prose, memory for words, paraphrasing, language learning, and reading. In contrast, Gestalt psychology made extensive use of animal (as well as human) experimentation and dealt mainly with problems of human perception.

Educational Implications of Gestalt Psychology

Gestalt psychology presents a dramatic contrast to some of the more behavioristic approaches that we have considered in earlier chapters in at least two ways: First, it rejects the trial and error explanations favored by psychologists such as Thorndike. People learn through insight, not through trial and error, explain the Gestaltists.

Second, Gestalt psychology rejects the "reductionist" approach of early behaviorism. Psychologists who want to understand learning and behavior, insist the Gestaltists, should not try to reduce it to simple elements such as stimuli and responses. Instead, they should look at the more *molar* aspects of behavior; that is, they should look at the whole rather than its parts.

These – the belief that learning occurs through insight and the belief that psychology should concentrate on the molar rather than the molecular aspects of learning – are two of the important themes that summarize Gestalt psychology. Because Gestalt psychology does not present learning principles that are as simple and clear as, say, those of Skinnerian behaviorism, it is not as easily applied to the nitty-gritty of classroom practice. But these two underlying themes do have very clear and very powerful implications for teachers.

The rejection of trial and error as a useful way of learning means, very clearly, that teachers and parents should not present learners with problems that require them to attempt a wide variety of different solutions until they finally "get it right." Instead, learning situations should be structured in such a way that learners can eventually achieve insight. But how is this to be done?

First, suggests Wertheimer (1959), the problems selected for presentation to a learner should not be problems that can be solved by memorizing a series of steps. People who learn in this way, he explains, are prone to the learning difficulty referred to as *response set*. Response set is a strong tendency to respond or to perceive in a predetermined way even when there are more appropriate responses. Such learners are likely to *reproduce* answers. They are what Wertheimer labels *reproductive thinkers*. The aim of schools should, using Wertheimer's expression, be to foster more **productive thinking** (thinking that is creative) (Wertheimer, 1959).

Second, Wertheimer argues that problems should be presented in meaningful, real-life situations so learners can see their importance and their relationship to real, day-to-day problems. Learners need to be encouraged to understand the problem rather than to attempt to copy a set of prescribed procedures. Accordingly, the guidance that teachers provide students should be geared toward helping them discover solutions for themselves. Ideally, they should achieve insight on their own rather than be directed toward ready-made solutions by the teacher.

In the jargon of current educational psychology, the Gestalt perspective supports what is termed **constructivism** rather than **direct teaching** (Lefrançois, 2018). Constructivist approaches are methods that are highly learner-centered and that reflect the belief that meaningful information is constructed by learners rather than given to them. In contrast, direct teaching implies more teacher-directed approaches. The methods of constructivism encourage discovery learning, cooperative approaches in the classroom, and active learner participation in the teaching/learning process. As we see in Chapter 7, these methods are most compatible with cognitive theories such as those of Bruner and Piaget.

Appraisal of Gestalt Psychology

Gestalt psychology was an important reaction against the introspectionism that had preceded it as well as against the behaviorism that came to dominate much of American psychology in the first half of the twentieth century. For example, Köhler felt that a behaviorism such as Hull's theory was wrong in rejecting the scientific value of concepts like consciousness or thinking. "I find myself therefore with a profound aversion and guard against the behaviorist, or any other one-sided and impractical purism in science," wrote Köhler (1929, p. 34). He argued that the behaviorists' insistence on dealing only with objective reality forced them to reject the validity and importance of what he called "direct experience": "There cannot be the slightest doubt for me that, as a child, I had 'direct experience.' . . . There were experiences which belonged to me personally and privately" (p. 20).

In some ways, Gestalt theories don't fare especially well with respect to the criteria listed in Chapter 1. "The theoretical ideas of the Gestaltists were notoriously vague," write Holyoak and Spellman (1993, p. 268). As a result, they are not especially useful for predicting or explaining behavior. "In the view of most contemporary observers," says Gardner, the theoretical program of Gestalt psychology was not well founded . . .. [T]here are too many exceptions or indeterminate cases" (1987, p. 114).

One example of vagueness in Gestalt theory relates to their use of the words *whole* and *part*, both of which are fundamental to the theory. At times, the word *parts* seems to mean specific units of perceptual analysis, such as notes for music or angles and lines for geometric shapes; at other times, it seems to refer to physiological or neural activity in the brain. In this connection, the Gestalt theorists often spoke of what they called *phenomenal units*, which seem to be subjective units of perception, but the precise nature of phenomenal units remains unclear.

Gestalt theories have also been criticized for simply describing rather than explaining. As Jäkel, Singh, Wichmann, and Herzog (2016) put it, this apparent weakness of Gestalt theory is related to the general lack of quantitative concepts and precise terminology in early Gestalt theorizing. Accordingly, the theory provides a set of descriptive principles for perception but no real explanations to account for it. "What happened to the Gestalt school that always aspired to provide a unified vision of psychology?" ask Jäkel et al. (2016, p. 7).

Transition to Modern Cognitivism

However, relative to some of the other criteria, Gestalt theory fares very well. For example, Gestalt psychology continues to be widely applied in counseling and therapy (Bandin, 2017; Houston, 2018). Gestalt-like notions of the behavioral field and of the self play an important role in humanistic theories of counseling, such as those of Carl Rogers. Rogerian therapy is premised on the notion that to understand a person's behavior, it is essential to look at it from that person's personal view; change in behavior results when the person's views of reality change.

Perhaps even more important, Gestalt theory has proven highly thought-provoking. Among other things, it provided psychology with the beginnings of a new metaphor.

METAPHORS IN PSYCHOLOGY

A metaphor is a comparison. Metaphors abound in literature and especially in poetry, where their purpose is to evoke images (sometimes impossible ones) that are more startling, clearer, and more moving than the reality they represent. For example, in Pablo Neruda's poem "Little America," the woman the poet loves isn't just a woman. She's a country, with "boughs and lands, fruits and water, the springtime that I love . . . the waters of the sea or the rivers and the red thickness of the bush where thirst and hunger lie in wait" (1972, p. 110).[8]

In psychology, as in poetry, metaphors abound. But their purpose in psychology is less to move or startle than to inform and clarify. In the psychology of cognition, claims Bruner, "it is apparent that there have been nothing but metaphors" (1990a, p. 230). Perhaps the most common of all current metaphors for human cognition is the computer, from which psychology draws notions of humans as information-processing organisms and psychologists create cognitive models that speak of processing, storing, retrieving, input, output, and on and on.

But the metaphor was not always entirely welcome in psychology or in science. For years, physical scientists were convinced that the result of their many investigations would be a complete, accurate, and absolutely literal description of the physical world and how it functions. In 1910, there seemed to be little reason to suspect that science might someday discover something about the world that could only be described in terms of black holes, quarks, antimatter, quantum reality where Schrödinger's cat can be in two places at the same time, string theory, and other metaphorical concepts. Indeed, even in the twenty-first century, many scientists still do not suspect that there might be something not quite literal about their knowledge.

Metaphors in Behaviorism

And so it was in psychology. During the first half of the twentieth century, a period dominated largely by behaviorism, psychologists searched valiantly for reliable facts, laws, and principles that might provide a literal description of human learning and behavior. The emphasis,

---

[8] The original is as follows: "ramas y tierras, frutas y agua, / la primavera que amo, / la luna del desierto, el pecho / de la paloma salvaje, / la suavidad de las piedras gastadas / por las aguas del mar o de los rios / y la espesura roja / del matorral en donde / la sed y el hambre acechan." (GRL)

especially for behaviorists such as Skinner and Watson, was on keeping theorizing as close to the data as possible. And even neobehaviorists like Hull and Hebb, who allowed themselves to invent new metaphors in the form of hypothetical somethings that mediate between stimuli and responses, nevertheless tried to define things operationally (that is, in terms of actual behaviors). This was the legacy of "logical positivism," a philosophy of science based on the assumption that things are real and exact and that they can therefore be described literally and measured accurately.

But as Smith (1990) points out, the behaviorists also found themselves using metaphors to explain and clarify. For example, Hull used machine models of human functioning, describing his theory as the "robot approach." "So far as the thinking processes go," wrote Hull in one of his unpublished diaries, "a machine could be built which would do every essential thing that the body does" (quoted in Hays, 1962, p. 820). That is an impressive foreshadowing of the dreams that drive many of those who now work in the field of *artificial intelligence* (see Chapter 11).

Tolman, too, began to glimpse new metaphors in the imagination of the white Norway rat, for it seemed to Tolman that even the rat learns more than just S–R connections. Rather, it builds representations of the world in the form of cognitive maps of what is out there. And it develops notions that somehow allow it to connect what is out there with behavioral choices. Tolman called these notions "expectancies," and his view of human learning explored the metaphor of cognitive maps and hypotheses. Thus, Tolman's expectancies are representations of the world. But they're not the literal representations that a logical positivist might seek; they are metaphors.

Even Skinner used metaphors, claims Smith, although he was probably the most determinedly positivistic of the behaviorists and consequently held the "aim of eliminating metaphorical discourse from science" (1990, p. 255). His principal metaphor is a Darwinian, evolutionary one. In the same way as species survive or die out as a function of natural pressures interacting with "fitness," so too are responses selected by their consequences. Behaviors survive or are eliminated as a function of how they are reinforced, ignored, or punished.

Metaphors in Cognitivism

As noted earlier, cognitive psychology is a psychology of metaphors. To explain human functioning, cognitive psychology uses metaphors of mental structures, describing things that don't actually exist to represent things that cannot be described literally. All theoretical cognitive concepts, such as *operations*, *short-term* and *long-term memory*, and *neural networks*, are metaphors. And most descriptions of how humans function (that is, of how cognitive structures are developed and used) rely on metaphors.

But metaphors in psychology are not simply comparisons meant to evoke images and feelings, as might metaphors in poetry. Rather, they are meant to explain, to illustrate, and to predict. The behaviorist metaphor that compares human functioning to that of a machine says much about how the theorist expects to explain and predict behavior. And as we see in the next few chapters, the computer metaphor, often favored by cognitive psychology, also says much about what the cognitive theorist expects in the way of explanation and prediction.

Main Point Chapter Summary

1. Hebb's model is based largely on knowledge and speculation about neurological and physiological processes. Its aim is to explain the higher mental processes that mediate between stimuli and responses.

2. The human nervous system is composed of cells called *neurons*, which consist of a cell body (*soma*), receiving extensions called *dendrites*, and an elongated part called an *axon*. Transmission among neurons involves electrical and chemical activity. It proceeds from the cell body down the axon and across the synaptic cleft to the dendrites of an adjacent cell. Important neurotransmitters include dopamine, serotonin, acetylcholine, and norepinephrine.

3. For Hebb, higher mental processes (thinking) involve activity in neural assemblies. He reasons that this activity must take the form of neurons arranged in such a way that they can keep reactivating one another in patterns he calls *cell assemblies*; arrangements of related cell assemblies are called *phase sequences*.

4. Important assumptions underlying Hebb's theory are that repeated firing of neurons facilitates subsequent firing of these neurons (the Hebb rule), which eventually become linked in cell assemblies, which can then become associated in phase sequences (thus explaining conditioning).

5. Research with the *Aplysia* snail illustrates that habituation (long-term depression [LTD]) and sensitization (long-term potentiation [LTP]) involve chemical changes at the level of the neuron. This research provides support for Hebb's assumptions about neural transmission.

6. *Set* refers to selectivity among responses; *attention* refers to selectivity among input. Set and attention are central processes in learning and perception.

7. Hebb's theory has important educational applications relating to motivation. Much of his speculation about neurological events has been confirmed by subsequent research. His theory continues to have a profound influence on contemporary research in motivation, neurology, and other areas of psychology.

8. The mechanistic behaviorism of theorists such as Guthrie and Watson (and even Skinner and Thorndike) seeks to be impeccably objective, analyzes behavior at a molecular level, and makes no assumptions about any intentions the actor might have. In contrast, Tolman believed that all behavior is purposive; that behavior involves cognitive elements such as expectancies that can also be described as cognitions or cognitive maps; that behavior should be analyzed at the molar rather than the molecular level; and that expectancies develop as a function of exposure to situations in which reinforcement is possible (sign–significate relationships).

9. Gestalt psychology is a forerunner of contemporary cognitive psychology. Cognitive approaches to learning are characterized by a preoccupation with topics such as under-standing, information processing, decision making, and problem solving. Two of the main

beliefs of the Gestaltists are: (a) The whole is greater than the sum of its parts; and (b) people solve problems through insight rather than through trial and error.

10. The founders and popularizers of the Gestalt school were Wertheimer, Köhler, and Koffka. As a system, Gestalt psychology is closely linked with studies of perception and the formulation of laws of perceptual organization, such as prägnanz, closure, continuity, similarity, and proximity. These laws are assumed to apply to thinking as well as perception.

11. Gestalt studies of memory have led to the observation that structural changes in information over time involve the processes of leveling (making symmetrical), sharpening (heightening distinctiveness), and normalizing (rendering more like the object should appear).

12. Gestalt theorists make an important distinction between external reality (the physical field) and the individual's perceptions (the behavioral or psychological field). Both need to be considered to understand behavior, a notion that is basic to Gestalt approaches to psychotherapy.

13. Psychology makes extensive use of metaphors. Various machine metaphors have long been popular and are evident in Hull's "robotic approach" and, more recently, in the human-as-computing-machine metaphor.

Part IV

Mostly Cognitive Theories

7 Three Cognitive Theories

Bruner, Piaget, and Vygotsky

CHAPTER OUTLINE

This Chapter	240
Objectives	241
Cognitive Psychology	241
Cognitivism Compared with Behaviorism	242
The Main Metaphor in Cognitive Psychology	243
Principal Beliefs of Cognitive Theories	243
Bruner's Theory: Going Beyond the Information Given	244
Evolution of the Brain	245
Evolution of Mind	246
Symbolic Representation and Cognitive Theory	248
Bruner's Theory of Representation: Categorization	248
Categories as Rules	249
Coding Systems	250
Research on Concept Formation	252
Meaning and the Construction of Reality	254
Educational Implications of Bruner's Theory	257
Jean Piaget: A Developmental-Cognitive Position	258
The Méthode Clinique	259
Theoretical Orientation	260
Adaptation Through Assimilation and Accommodation	260
Play	261
Imitation	262
Piaget's View of Intelligence	263
The Sensorimotor Period: Birth to Two Years	264
Preoperational Thinking: 2–7 Years	265
Operations	268
Concrete Operations: 7–11/12 Years	269
Formal Operations: After 11 or 12 Years	271
Piaget's Theory as a Theory of Learning	272
Educational Implications of Piaget's Theory	273
Appraisal of Piaget's Position	274

Lev Vygotsky: Social/Cognitive Theory	276
Main Ideas in Vygotsky's Theory	278
The Role of Culture	278
Language and Thought	279
Educational Applications: The Zone of Proximal Development and Scaffolding	281
Appraisal of Vygotsky's Theory	284
Main Point Chapter Summary	285

The essence of creativity is figuring out how to use what you already know in order to go beyond what you already think.

Jerome Bruner

Curled up like a dog in the grass beneath the wild raspberry canes, Old Lady Gribbin seemed to be sleeping. She had said I should meet her here below the rock face, that she would deliver Chapter 7 this afternoon. Anxious to continue, I wanted to awaken her but didn't dare. Thick yellow bees swarmed over the raspberry bushes and ants crawled through the heavy berries the old lady had gathered in a bowl. She held the bowl safe in the crook of her arm while she slept, and a smile played at the corners of her mouth.

Suddenly, a bird swooped across the cliff, swirled around the raspberry bushes, and in a swoosh of braking wing feathers, landed gently by the old lady and she was instantly awake, sitting, as though she had never slept, smiling at the blue-gray rock dove, stroking its iridescent cheeks and smoothing the purplish feathers on its back. Schrödinger appeared suddenly, as he so often does, crouched in his lion pose, his one good eye fixed unblinking on the bird, his tail swishing hypnotically, and I knew that here was his dinner; I have seen him hunt birds. But no. Gently, he rose, ambled past the dove, lay down by the old lady, stretched way out in that luxurious pose. The old lady set the dove down by the cat. Startled, I watched as he licked the bird's shining neck.

And didn't bite it.

What, I asked Old Lady Gribbin, is going on here? But she ignored my question, just motioned that I should turn on the recorder and started to talk again.

THIS CHAPTER

What's a cat to a pigeon? Or a pigeon to a cat? *Mrs. Gribbin mused.* And what's a person to a pigeon? What does a pigeon think of people when it swoops above their houses or flies above their fields and forests? Of what does it dream, hunched in a city tree or huddled on the edge of a roof as people scurry about beneath its perch? In the pigeon's thoughts, is a person just another big, earthbound thing, indistinguishable from horses, cows, goats, cats, and trucks? Does the pigeon have a concept of "peopleness"? Is the pigeon capable of any thoughts of this kind?

Objectives

Tell your readers, *said Old Lady Gribbin*, that this is one of the questions this chapter answers as it looks at the topics of cognitive psychology and at what Bruner (1985) describes as the human taste for knowledge and the human hunger for information. More than that, claims Bruner, humans are forever going beyond the information given.

Explain to them, *said the old lady*, that even if they don't go beyond the information given in this chapter, they'll be astounded to discover that once they have finished digesting its contents, they'll be able, while standing or sitting, to answer remarkably complex questions relating to what Bruner meant by:

- concept formation;
- categories and coding systems;
- going beyond the information given;
- personal narratives.

They'll also know what Piaget intended when he wrote of

- adaptation, assimilation, and accommodation;
- play, imitation, and intelligence;
- sensorimotor, preoperational, concrete, and formal developmental stages.

And they'll have insights into the meanings and educational implications of Vygotsky's notions of

- the zone of proximal development;
- scaffolding.

Even better, *said the old lady*, they'll also have stunning new insights into what pigeons know about people.

COGNITIVE PSYCHOLOGY

It's no easy matter for people to ask pigeons what they know and think. But Herrnstein, Loveland, and Cable (1976) gathered some pigeons and, in a fashion, asked them what they thought of people. Even more astounding, the pigeons answered.

What these investigators did was present pigeons with series of slides, some of which contained one or more people doing various things, dressed differently (or even nude), and sometimes partly hidden behind objects like trees. The pigeons were reinforced whenever they pecked in the presence of a slide containing a person.

Sure enough, the pigeons learned to do this. They seemed to have what Herrnstein and his associates call "natural concepts" that include complex notions such as what a person is. And they were able to identify slides representing this concept even when the "peopleness" of people was disguised in different activities, contexts, or clothing.

In a similar study, Watanabe (2010) had human judges sort children's art into "good" and "bad" art. He then reinforced pigeons for pecking at "good" paintings until they learned to discriminate between the good and the bad. He then showed the pigeons children's paintings they had never seen before. The pigeons proved astonishingly good at discriminating between novel "good" and "bad" paintings. As Watanabe explains, the results suggest that pigeons may be able to learn complex human concepts such as those that define abstract qualities, like "beauty."

Pigeons, of course, are not the only nonhuman animals to form concepts. For example, recall Tinklepaugh's (1928) research in which monkeys were shown either a lettuce leaf or a banana, which was then hidden. If the monkey remembered the hiding place and found the object, it was allowed to eat it. Monkeys seemed quite delighted to eat whatever they found no matter whether lettuce or a banana was used. But when Tinklepaugh showed the monkey a banana, surreptitiously switched it, and the monkey later found a lettuce leaf hidden where the banana should have been, it became very upset. Not only did it ignore the lettuce (which it presumably would have eaten had it been expecting to find it), but it continued to search for the missing banana. This is strong evidence, claimed Tinklepaugh, that the monkey learned not only where the object was hidden but also had a clear and stable concept of what should have been in that location.

Studies such as these present serious challenges to behavioristic explanations. If the simpler behaviors of animals cannot be adequately explained using behaviorist positions, then the presumably more complex behaviors of humans might be even less well explained. And if even animals can think and form concepts, psychology should perhaps concern itself with these as well as with more easily observed and described behaviors. Enter **cognitivism**, an approach to theories of learning concerned primarily with intellectual events such as problem solving, information processing, thinking, and imagining.

COGNITIVISM COMPARED WITH BEHAVIORISM

Tolman's behaviorism, with its description of expectancies, goals, and purpose, and Gestalt psychology, given its concern with perception, awareness, problem solving, and insight, both foreshadowed cognitivism. Their emphases underline some of the important differences between cognitive psychology and behaviorism.

First, cognitive psychology is mainly interested in higher mental functions rather than observable behavior. The most important of these higher mental functions have to do with perception (how physical energies are translated into meaningful experiences), concept formation, memory, language, thinking, problem solving, and decision making. These topics are reflected in the information-processing or computer metaphors that characterize cognitive psychology.

Second, the shift to cognitivism also saw a shift from animal research to a renewed emphasis on human research. Topics such as language learning, reading, strategies in concept attainment, and the growth of logic cannot easily be investigated with rats and pigeons.

Third, the principal aim of behaviorist theories has typically been to determine the relationships that exist between behavior and its antecedents and consequences. In contrast, the principal goal of cognitive theories is to make plausible and useful inferences about the mental processes that intervene between input and output.

Table 7.1 **Principal differences between behaviorism and cognitivism**

	Behaviorism	Cognitivism
Principal concepts	Stimuli, responses, contiguity, reinforcement	Higher mental processes (thinking, imagining, problem solving)
Main metaphors	Machine-like qualities of human functioning	Information-processing and computer-based metaphors
Most common research subjects	Animals; some human research subjects	Humans; some nonhuman animal research
Main goals	To discover predictable relationships between stimuli, responses, response consequences	To make useful inferences about mental processes that influence and determine behavior
Scope of theories	Often intended to explain all significant aspects of behavior	Generally more limited in scope; intended to explain more specific behaviors and processes
Representative theorists	Watson, Pavlov, Guthrie, Thorndike, Skinner, Hull	Gestalt psychologists, Bruner, Piaget, Vygotsky, connectionist theorists

Fourth, cognitive theories tend to be less ambitious in scope than were the behaviorist theories of people like Skinner or Hull. Most cognitive theorists are not trying to build theories to explain *all* human learning and behavior. The emphasis in the last several decades has been on intensive research in specific areas rather than on the construction of general systems (see Table 7.1).

The Main Metaphor in Cognitive Psychology

The dominant metaphor in cognitive psychology is essentially a computer-based, **information-processing (IP)** metaphor. Information processing refers to how information (input) is modified or changed. The emphasis is on the perceptual and conceptual processes that allow perception, that determine how the actor acts, and that underlie thinking, remembering, solving problems, and so on.

The single most important common characteristic of the topics of cognitive psychology is that they presuppose mental representation and information processing. Accordingly, cognitive theory building has taken the form of metaphors relating to the nature of mental representation and to the processes involved in constructing and using these representations.

Principal Beliefs of Cognitive Theories

Cognitive theories are grounded in a number of common assumptions and beliefs.

Three of the most important of these are as follows.

1. Current Learning Builds on Previous Learning

Cognitive approaches stress the importance of the learner's previously acquired knowledge and skills. This is in contrast to behaviorist approaches that tend to view all learners as equally susceptible to the effects of rewards and punishments. Cognitive psychology's view emphasizes that learners come with different motives, different background information, different interests, different genetic characteristics, and so on. As a result, even in identical situations, they often learn and behave differently.

2. Learning Involves Information Processing

The dominant metaphor in cognitive psychology does not view the learner as a *passive* receiver of information reacting mindlessly to the prodding of stimuli and their consequences. Rather, the learner is an *active* participant in the learning process, striving to discover and organize, and capable of using strategies to arrive at concepts and arrange them in memory.

3. Meaning Depends on Relationships among Concepts

Take a sentence as apparently simple as "It won't work without a hook." What does this straightforward sentence mean?

It depends on the context. If the reference is to fishing, then perhaps the meaning has to do with a fly by means of which you might land a trout. If we are talking about rolling logs into a sawmill, then the meaning might relate to a cant hook, a useful tool if you need to roll a heavy log up a ramp. If we are discussing a new song, then the hook may be a riff or a phrase that will "catch" listeners and have them thinking the song all day. If we're commenting on the coat rack you are trying to invent or on the computer program you are currently writing or the butcher shop in which you work, then we are talking about a range of other "hooks."

Meaning, cognitive psychologists explain, results from actively processing *input*, builds on previous learning, and depends on relationships among concepts (sometimes labeled *schemas*) that are currently active. Among important theoretical contributions to the development of contemporary cognitive psychology are those made by Jerome Bruner, Jean Piaget, and Lev Vygotsky, whose theories are discussed in this chapter. Subsequent chapters deal with specific areas where current research is primarily cognitive: memory, motivation, social learning, and artificial intelligence.

BRUNER'S THEORY: GOING BEYOND THE INFORMATION GIVEN

In a classic article, Bruner (1964) compares the development of a child to the evolution of the human race.

Evolution of the Brain

In the beginning, says Bruner, humans were far from the fastest, the fiercest, or the strongest of predators on the planet. A number of fearsome beasts would probably have decimated the human population had it not been for one simple fact: In the end, humans proved to be more intelligent than all who preyed on them. So intelligent was this creature that it eventually took the course of evolution into its own hands: It used its brains.

"Brains are wonderful things," Johanson and Shreeve tell us. "There is no better solution to one's environment – no claw so sharp, no wing so light that it can begin to bestow the same adaptive benefits as a heavy ball of gray matter" (1989, p. 262).

BOX 7.1 Jerome Seymour Bruner (1915–2016)

Courtesy of Harvard University, Department of Psychology

Jerome Bruner, whose father was a watchmaker, was the youngest of four children in a Jewish family living in an affluent New York suburb. He describes his parents as "remote grownups." His father died when he was 12, after which his mother moved the family every year (to Florida, to California, to "the country"). Bruner found these many moves "too sudden a transformation" (Bruner, 1983, p. 5). He writes of changing schools constantly but never quite shifting his allegiances before moving again. "My formal secondary schooling was appalling," he writes (1983, p. 17), lamenting that he never stayed in one school long enough to develop any good relationships with teachers, although his marks were acceptable.

Bruner describes himself as shy and ill at ease as an adolescent, and thought himself ugly. At age 16, he and some friends acquired a motorized racing hull that they smoothed and

Continued

BOX 7.1 (cont.)

polished and with whose engine they tinkered until they had become experts. In 1932, they won the Round Manhattan race ("heady stuff," says Bruner). Much later, at age 57, Bruner and his wife, with a few friends helping as crew, sailed across the Atlantic in his sailboat.

At 17, Bruner entered Duke University in Durham, North Carolina, where he obtained a B.A. in 1937. Four years later, he received his Ph.D. from Harvard. Subsequently, he taught at Harvard as well as at Princeton, Cambridge, Oxford, and at the New York University School of Law. He was one of the founders and a director of the Center for Cognitive Research at Harvard.

Bruner's research has been highly eclectic and highly influential in education as well as in psychology. He is widely recognized as one of the leaders of the "cognitive revolution" of the 1950s and 1960s (Haste & Gardner, 2017) and also served as president of the American Psychological Association. He has been a prolific writer, with more than a dozen books and many articles to his name. Even in his eighties, Bruner continued to write about topics such as the development of the self (Bruner, 1997c), the development and meaning of *meaning* (Bruner, 1996a), and the history and the future of the cognitive revolution (Bruner, 1997d). In 1983, he concluded an autobiographical essay with the note, "I suppose my life has been a good one . . . . [P]sychology has certainly helped it to be so, psychology as a way of inquiry rather than as a basis of wisdom" (1983, p. 293). (Based in part on Gale Group, 2001; Kincheloe & Horn, 2007.)

Advantages of Brains

At the dawn of civilization, human brains allowed access to food sources that would be overlooked by humankind's finned, feathered, or clawed competitors, many of whom had better noses, keener eyesight, swifter movement, and stronger beaks and jaws. Brains are what permitted people to make the connection between sharp sticks and digging into the ground for roots and tubers or between heavy rocks and stunned prey (or predators). Eventually, brains led to stone and wooden tools, agricultural and hunting implements, the wheel, the rocket, the computer, and artificial intelligence. And perhaps even more important, brains led to the development of language and **culture**, and consequently to the possibility of sharing information and of transmitting it among individuals and across generations. Thus, although the raw matter of our nervous systems may be a product of genetic transmission, the products of our brains are transmitted in other ways, most of which depend on language or other symbol systems.

Evolution of Mind

In the same way as language is one of the products of cultural evolution made possible by the brain, so too is that ill-defined entity we call the **mind**. The term refers primarily to human consciousness – the awareness we have of being, of thinking, of feeling (our *self-consciousness*). Clearly, *mind* is closely associated with cognitive activities such as thinking, perceiving, and imagining.

The evolution of the mind, Bruner (1964, 1966) notes, is evident through three waves of remarkable inventions, each serving different functions. First, humans succeeded in developing devices that could amplify their motor capacities: simple machines (levers, pulleys, inclined planes, perhaps even the legendary wheel) and combinations of machines to make weapons (knives, arrows, spears, and hatchets). By amplifying their motor capacities, humans became stronger and faster, better able to build shelters, and far less vulnerable to predators and to natural catastrophes.

Centuries later – quite recently in human history – a second group of inventions dramatically altered the pattern of human evolution: inventions that amplified sensory rather than motor capacities. They include the telescope, radio, television, and all the other instruments that expand humans' ability to see, hear, feel, and sense things they could not otherwise sense.

The final group of very recent human inventions includes those that amplify what Bruner terms *ratiocinative* (intellectual) capacities. These are human symbol systems and theories; they include computer languages and systems. Almost all human mental work, claims Bruner (1997b), is now done with the aid of the technology that cultures provide their members. These technologies enrich human competencies enormously.

Representation in Children

Bruner suggests that the representational systems children use as they develop closely parallel the history of human inventions. Thus, at the earliest ages, children represent objects through their own immediate sensations and actions. Bruner labels this **enactive representation**. Enactive representation, says Bruner, corresponds to the period in human evolution when the emphasis was on the amplification of motor capacities.

Early in development, children progress from a strictly *motoric* (or enactive) representation to representation that involves the use of mental images. Bruner calls this **iconic representation** because an icon is an image. Iconic representation corresponds to the period during which human inventions were directed at amplifying sensory capacities.

The most advanced form of representation uses symbols such as words and numbers, and is therefore called **symbolic representation**. The fundamental difference between a symbol and an icon is that the icon bears a literal resemblance to its referent whereas the symbol does not. A symbol is completely arbitrary: The numeral "2" does not look like a collection of two objects any more than the word *turkey* looks like that bird. But humans have absolutely no difficulty understanding what is meant by either of these or, indeed, by most of the thousands of other symbols in this text. Symbolic representation parallels the development of inventions that amplify intellectual capacities.

Although enactive, iconic, and symbolic representation develop sequentially, they don't replace one another. Adults continue to represent both enactively and iconically as well as symbolically. Thus, people "know" how to ride a bicycle, stroke a cue ball, or execute a golf shot not in symbols or in images but in the body – which is why it is so difficult to explain in

Three Cognitive Theories

words how these things are done. In contrast, we recognize faces not in activity or even in symbols but in images (icons).[1]

Symbolic Representation and Cognitive Theory

In summary, adults have at least three distinct modes for representing not only the effects of sensory experiences but also thoughts. The importance of representation in cognitive theory – and especially of symbolic representation – can hardly be overestimated.

A symbolic representational system, most importantly, language, is essential to systematic reasoning and is necessary for sharing knowledge among people. Ultimately, representation is fundamental in determining human culture and in shaping the experience of living a human life. Representational systems, claims Bruner, are "a very special kind of communal tool kit whose tools, once used, make the user a reflection of the community" (1990c, p. 11). The mind, he insists, can reach its full potential only through participation in a culture (Bruner, 1996b).

Bruner's Theory of Representation: Categorization

Learning and perception, argues Bruner (1957a), are information-processing activities that reflect our need to simplify and make sense of the world. Essentially, we simplify by putting things into **categories** – abstract representations based on common elements among events and experiences. **Categorization** is Bruner's term for the formation of **concepts** where concepts are defined as abstractions that reflect the common properties of related objects or ideas. All human cognitive activity involves categories (concepts), Bruner informs us. All interaction with the world involves classifying input in relation to categories that already exist. Completely novel experiences are "doomed to be a gem serene, locked in the silence of private experience," writes Bruner (1957b, p. 125). In short, people probably cannot perceive completely new stimulus input; if they can, they cannot communicate it. Hence, to understand Bruner's theory, it is important to know what a category is, how it is formed, and of what value it is.

What Is a Category?

If you see a pinkish apple sitting in a bowl on a table, is that all you see? In a literal sense, yes. But in another sense, you see much more. You *see* at once that this apple belongs to the *pink lady* category. And you see, too, that it has a core in which there are seeds, that it has whitish flesh under its skin. Perhaps, in your *mind's eye*, you also see that it is tangy, sweet, crisp, and juicy.

But you cannot actually perceive these things, so what you do, in Bruner's words, is "go beyond the information given" (1957a). First, you note that this object is an *apple*; second,

---

[1] That's true, said Old Lady Gribbin as an aside: You can't describe a face, not even your own, so some stranger could easily recognize it in a crowd of other faces. Unless, of course, there's something especially odd about your face. And then she added, rather unkindly, "Perhaps your face isn't that good an example."

Bruner's Theory: Going Beyond the Information Given | 249

you make inferences about the object based on what you know about similar objects. According to Bruner, these inferences are made possible because of your category *apple*. A category is a *concept*: It is a representation of related things. It is also a **percept** in the sense that it is *perceived* through the senses. Percepts and concepts are roughly equivalent in Bruner's system.

Because categories are classifications of objects relative to properties that are redundant for that type of object, they are based on associations developed largely through frequency or redundancy.[2] For example, if the first aliens to arrive from Mars all have warts, then warts will eventually become an essential feature of the category *Martian*. In Hebbian terms, the cell assemblies activated by warts will become associated with others activated by Martians.

Categorization, as Iordan, Greene, Beck, and Fei-Fei (2016) point out, is closely tied to similarity and typicality. That is, objects tend to be placed in the same categories based on the similarities that are typical among them. Thus, apples are categorized as apples because of their typical shared characteristics.

Categories as Rules

"To categorize," writes Bruner, "is to render discriminably different things equivalent, to group the objects and events and people around us into classes, and to respond to them in terms of their class membership rather than in terms of their uniqueness" (Bruner, Goodnow & Austin, 1956, p. 1). Hence, one way of looking at the term *category* is to define it as though it were a rule (or a collection of rules) for classifying things as being equal. For example, the concept (or category) *book* can be thought of as an implicit rule that allows an individual to recognize an object as a book. In fact, this category is a collection of rules that specify that to be a book, an object must have pages, a cover, writing, and a title (among other things).

Attributes

Categories say something about the characteristics that objects must possess before they can be classified in a given way. Hampton and Passanisi (2016) explain that concepts are represented mentally in terms of the class (category is Bruner's equivalent term) to which objects belong (this notion is referred to as class **extension**). Concepts are also represented in terms of what researchers call class **intension**: their identifying features. Bruner's equivalent term for the characteristics of objects is **attribute**. In short, a concept such as *apple* is defined as the collection (or class or category) that includes all objects recognized as apples (*extension*); objects are identified as belonging to the same category because they share common, identifying attributes (*intension*).

---

[2] You will have noticed, said Mrs. Gribbin, that Bruner's categorization is similar to Hebb's cell assemblies and phase sequences. Both are established as a result of repeated, redundant experiences. You know what I mean? But she didn't really expect me to answer. I don't think she wanted me to. She just jumped right into her little Martian example. You see how she is?

Bruner defines attributes as "some discriminable feature of an object or event which is susceptible of distinguishable variation from event to event" (1966, p. 26). Attributes are therefore properties of objects that are not possessed by all objects. They are further distinguished by whether they play a role in the act of categorizing. Attributes that define an object are called **criterial attributes**; they are features that determine category intension (Djalal, Storms, Ameel, & Heyman, 2017). Attributes that don't define an object are irrelevant for categorizing.

Rules for Categorizing

As rules, categories specify the nature of the similarities (and differences) required for membership in a category. Specifically, categories as rules spell out four things about objects being categorized.

First, the rule states that for membership in a given category, it is essential that the object possess one or more of a combination of attributes. For example, the rule for the category *car* might specify that the object must have a motor, a place to sit, and certain control devices. The attribute *color* is irrelevant for membership in this class.

Second, a category specifies the manner in which attributes are to be combined. For example, if a car were disassembled and the parts placed in wooden bins, it is unlikely that anyone would look at the bins and say, "nice car." The rule for the category *car* says that the parts must be assembled in a certain way. As the Gestalt psychologists insist, the whole is greater than the sum of its parts.

Third, a category assigns weights to various properties. A car might continue to be classified as a car even if it had no bumpers and no windows. But if it had no motor and no body, it might be categorized as something else because these properties are more criterial (more essential) for membership in the category.

Fourth, a category sets acceptance limits on attributes. A car typically has four wheels. If it has eight wheels – or only two – the implicit *car* rule might specify that it is no longer a car.

Decision Making

In Bruner's system, decision making is simply another aspect of information processing involving categorization.

First, to identify an object is to decide whether it belongs in a given category. Second, once an object is categorized (identified), there is inherent in the category a decision about how the object should be reacted to. For example, the act of categorizing stimulus input as an example of the category *red light* implies the decision not to walk across the street.

Coding Systems

Categories allow the classification and recognition of sensory input. But going beyond the immediate sense data involves more than simply making inferences based on the category into

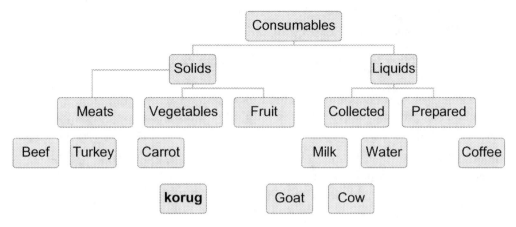

Figure 7.1 Schematic representation of a coding system. Coding systems are hypothetical groupings of related categories. From Lefrançois, G. R. (2018). *Psychology for Teaching* (2nd ed.). San Diego, CA: Bridgepoint Education, Fig. 6.2. Used by permission.

which the input has been classified. More importantly, it involves making inferences based on related categories. For example, the inference that a new object (let's call it a "korug") is edible might be made not simply because the korug is pear-like and pears are edible but also because the korug is orange-like and oranges are also edible. In fact, the korug is identified and predictions are made about it based on a variety of related categories. Bruner calls these related categories a **coding system** (see Figure 7.1).

Coding systems can be thought of as hierarchical arrangements of related categories, such that the topmost category in the system is more general (*generic* is Bruner's term) than are all the categories below it. As one moves up from the specific instances that define related categories, each subsequent concept (or category) is more abstract – freer of specifics, as Bruner puts it. To remember a specific, it is usually sufficient to recall the coding system of which it is a member. The details of the specific instance can then be recreated. And placing an event or experience in a coding system allows the individual to make generalizations based on what is known about other events that compose the coding system. Thus, categorizing and placing concepts (categories) into coding systems is basic to generalizing (transfer). For example, there is a significant amount of transfer involved in the decision that an appropriate behavior toward a korug might be to eat it.

Research on Concept Formation

Bruner's description of categories and of the processes involved in categorizing continues to play an important role in cognitive research. "A category," write Mervis and Rosch, "exists whenever two or more distinguishable objects or events are treated equivalently" (1981, p. 89) – a definition essentially identical to that first advanced by Bruner a quarter of a century earlier. "Once categories are established," note Markman and Gentner (2001), "people can use them to infer features of a new situation" – a notion highly reminiscent of Bruner's claim that categorizing allows people to "go beyond the information given."

There is currently a great deal of research on concept formation. What does this research tell us about categorization and concepts?

Developmental Trends in Concept Learning

Nouns and verbs are a simple way of defining concepts. Nouns, such as dog, ditch, door, and Dilbert, represent categories of related characteristics that are actually perceived when we interact with one of these: Each defines a category of perceptual experience. Verbs express relations among nouns, generally indicating things such as states, causes, movements, and other changes.

Linguists tell us that virtually all languages in the world make the noun–verb distinction and that nouns are in many ways simpler than are verbs. As a result, it is far easier to translate nouns from one language to another than it is to translate verbs. As Medin, Lynch, and Solomon (2000) note, there is far more interlanguage variability for verbs than for nouns.

In many, but not all, of the world's languages, children tend to learn nouns and therefore the concepts associated with nouns before they learn verbs (Ferguson & Waxman, 2017; Waxman & Lidz, 2006). But, strangely, they don't begin by learning the most specific concept and progressing from there to the most general. Instead, they typically start by learning concepts of intermediate generality and then learn those that are more specific. Later, they develop more all-encompassing categories ("coding systems," in Bruner's terms). For example, a child doesn't begin by learning the concept *German shepherd*, a highly specific category, but instead learns the far more general concept *dog*. Eventually, concepts such as *poodle*, *German shepherd*, and others at a similar level of specificity will be learned. Later, the child will be ready to understand the even more generic concept *mammal*.

Category Boundaries

Items or events that are included in the same category are not all equivalent, even though they may be reacted to as though they were. For example, although a large range of stimulus input will be interpreted as being blue, some of that input will clearly be more blue and some far less blue.

In the same way, individuals who fit into the categories *thin* and *fat* are not all equally thin or fat. Category boundaries are not always well defined, and the definitions that exist may be arbitrary and individualistic. Not only might two different people disagree with respect to the attributes that are *criterial* for membership in fat and thin categories, but when pressed, they would also be forced to recognize that their personal categories for these qualities have somewhat fuzzy boundaries.

The Neurobiology of Categories

Earlier, we discussed Herrnstein, et al.'s (1976) pioneering work in which they demonstrated that pigeons could develop abstract concepts such as "human" and "nonhuman." Since those studies, other researchers have demonstrated that pigeons can form concepts that allow them to identify various concepts such as cubist paintings, good and bad art, and English and non-English writing. Using modern brain activity imaging instrumentation, these researchers have been able to look at the neurology of categorization and concept formation. For example, Gunturkun, Koenen, Iovine, Garland, and Pusch (2018) found that among pigeons, categorization of perceptual input first occurs rapidly in the visual forebrain areas of the pigeon brain. Following this, the dopaminergic areas of the pigeon's brain are involved.

Evidence suggests that a similar two-part process is also involved in primate perceptual categorization, with perceptual input first being processed in the temporal lobes before dopaminergic areas of the brain are involved. Recall that dopamine-based neural activity is centrally related to reinforcement.

Learning and the formation of categories involve changes in the brain. What is learned has to be represented in some way in one or more brain areas. As we saw in Chapter 5, our exquisitely sensitive imaging and measuring devices have allowed us to detect at least some of the areas of the brain that are involved when, for example, we perceive a dot of light or hear a single note. These instruments indicate that perceptual representation of sensory categories occurs in the part of the cerebral cortex labeled the *parietal lobe*. They also suggest that the more abstract aspects of categories are represented in the *frontal lobes* (Keri, 2003). After all, that part of the brain deals with higher thought processes. Abstraction is among the highest of thought processes.

Abstraction

At a superficial level, it might seem that perceiving objects simply involves matching sensations with appropriate categories. Thus, to recognize someone as belonging to the category *thin* or *fat*, it should suffice to do no more than sense thinness or fatness (probably through vision or maybe also by touch). In fact, however, fatness and thinness cannot be sensed directly; they are *abstractions*. Thus, even at the most elementary level of perceptual recognition, abstraction is often involved.

Two Models of Abstraction

Actually, abstraction is involved in virtually all models of categorization. The main question these models try to answer is this: How do people abstract the central characteristics of a class of objects or events as a result of exposure to examples of that class?

One answer is that people develop a generalized notion of the most typical or representative features of a concept. This abstraction is a **prototype model**, or *generalized model* (Rosch, 1977). Thus, after seeing thousands of different trees, Jane has developed a highly abstract notion of "treeness." If she could represent this abstract notion accurately, she might find that it doesn't resemble any specific tree or kind of tree but instead embodies all that is essential in trees. Whenever she sees some new tree-like thing, she simply compares it to her prototypical tree.

Another possibility is that while learning about trees, Jane has stored in memory a number of good examples of trees. The **exemplar model** approach argues that concepts are represented by memories of specific examples that have actually been experienced rather than an abstraction of some ideal prototype (Bowman & Zeithamova, 2018). According to this model, a person determines whether a thing is a tree by comparing it to examples that illustrate *treeness*.

One important difference between these two models is that the prototype model assumes a higher level of abstraction. For example, a prototypical category for "birdness" is an abstraction of the characteristics of many examples of birds. In contrast, an exemplar category for *bird* is defined by examples of real birds.

Rosch (1973) argues that the prototype model is better than the exemplar model because for many concepts, it is difficult to find good examples that resemble each other closely. For instance, an automobile is a good example of a vehicle and so is a passenger truck or a van. But a bus is less so, a train even less, and a child's wagon far less. In classifying each of these as vehicles, argues Rosch, it is likely that the person relies on an abstract, or prototypical, notion of what vehicles are.

Considerable research has been conducted to evaluate these two approaches and to determine which approach should be emphasized in teaching and learning (for example, Nosofsky, Sanders & McDaniel, 2018). Thus far, the research seems to indicate that both highly abstract prototypes and more specific examples are involved in concept learning. However, there is some preliminary suggestion from neurobiological research looking at brain activity that the prototypical model may be somewhat dominant. Much of the brain activity relating to developing prototypes seems to occur in the hippocampal regions of the brain (Hutter & Wilson, 2018).

Meaning and the Construction of Reality

Bruner's cognitive theory deals with mental representation and the formation of concepts – a process he describes as *categorization*, with a *category* being roughly equivalent to a concept. The development of that part of the theory dates back to 1956 with the publication of *A Study of Thinking* (Bruner et al., 1956).

His later writings deal less with the details of concept learning than with larger issues relating to how we understand reality. The goal of cognitive psychology, Bruner insists, has been to understand the mind and how it achieves *meaning* (Harre, 2015). However, he believes that much of cognitive psychology's early efforts were sidetracked by its focus on the computer metaphor and a consequent emphasis on information processing. One of the results of this emphasis was the notion that if we could devise programs that realistically simulate cognitive

Bruner's Theory: Going Beyond the Information Given | 255

processes, we would by that very act understand those processes. "In the place of the concept of meaning," writes Bruner, "there emerged the concept of computability" (1990a, p. 6).

In a sense, Bruner is saying that the scientific **paradigm** (model or pattern that guides science) that is the basis of cognitive psychology has reached its limits and cannot easily look at the central question that cognitive psychology started out to address: How does the mind create meaning? To answer that question, says Bruner, we need to discard the computational model of mind.

Constructivism and Narration

Bruner believes that we construct our own notions of reality – that we make our own meanings. This belief is fundamental to what is labeled **constructivism** in education. Essentially, constructivism describes a student-centered instructional approach that emphasizes the learner's role in discovering relationships and *constructing* meaning. Constructivist approaches are often contrasted with the methods of **direct instruction** that grant the teacher a more important role.

In a series of more recent articles and books, the latest published when he was 89, Bruner advances yet another view of how we go about making meaning (Bruner, 1991, 2004). Logical thought, he suggests, isn't the most common form of thinking. Instead, we engage in another form of thinking to try to make sense of who we are and of the lives that we are leading and have led. It is a form of thinking that is profoundly influenced by culture and especially by language and other symbol systems. This form of thinking is what allows us to tell ourselves (and others) stories about our lives. Put another way, we construct the reality of our lives through **narratives**.

The notion of the construction of reality though narratives isn't an entirely new one. Researchers in the field of human life span development had begun to look at personal narratives a handful of decades earlier. "We tell ourselves stories in order to live," Didion informs us (1979, p. 11). These stories, called *personal narratives*, are stories about our own lives. They result from our attempts to weave the different events of our lives into a meaningful, coherent story that integrates past and present happenings and that often includes a vision of the future. Its principal character is the self, explains McAdams (1984), and its main themes are love and power.

Our narratives tend to describe not only what we have done (Bruner refers to this as the "landscape of action") but also what our thoughts and feelings were at the time and often what we assume the thoughts and feelings of others to have been (Bruner's "landscape of consciousness") (Bruner, 1986). They are a fundamental part of ourselves beginning in childhood and continuing through life and are importantly involved in our ability to choose, to act, to imagine, and to understand (Stapleton & Wilson, 2017). They can reveal much about our lives and our cultural commonalities and differences.

One of the functions of these narratives is to provide us with a sense of stability and consistency, a feeling of continuity, of orderliness and predictability. As Bruner notes, narratives give us a means for describing and making sense of the time we have lived and the time we yet hope to live. In the end, says Bruner, "the culturally shaped cognitive and linguistic processes that guide the self-telling of life narratives achieve the power to structure perceptual experience, to organize memory, to segment and purpose-build the very events of a life" (2004, p. 694). In a real sense, we *become* the narratives we tell about our lives.

Appraisal of Bruner's Position

Evaluating a cognitive position such as Bruner's presents an interesting difficulty. Whereas some behaviorist positions attempt to describe matters in a relatively exact and literal manner and can therefore sometimes be judged by how accurate the description appears to be, cognitive theories are more abstract and therefore more difficult to evaluate.

An additional problem with evaluating Bruner's theory is that its emphases changed over the decades, so what can be said about his notions of categorizing and the formation of coding systems might be quite different from what can be said about his notions of meaning-making, constructivism, and personal narratives.

Still, Bruner's notions do not do great violence to what people intuitively suspect about human functioning. More than that, they appear to be relatively clear and understandable as well as consistent. Both of these attributes are important criteria of a scientific theory.

Perhaps the most important question that needs to be asked of any psychological theory concerns its usefulness in predicting and explaining. And although cognitive theories such as Bruner's aren't very useful for explaining specific behaviors of the kind more easily explained by behavioristic positions, they can be useful in beginning to explain higher mental processes such as decision making and the formulation of personal narratives. Unfortunately, however, they present only the beginnings of explanations. That the narrator and the principal character are one and the same leads inevitably to distortion in the narration. As critics are quick to point out, narratives are highly subjective, difficult to analyze, and not always highly revealing.

One of the major contributions of Bruner's writing and theorizing has to do with his role in the so-called *cognitive revolution* – the revolution by which the cognitive party replaced the behaviorist party in what Amsel (1989) describes as psychology's parliamentary system.[3] "We were not out to 'reform' behaviorism," says Bruner, "but to replace it" (1990c, p. 3).

What was this revolution? "It was," claims Bruner, "an all-out effort to establish meaning as the central concept of psychology – not stimuli and responses, not overtly observable behavior, not biological drives and their transformation, but meaning" (1990b, p. 2). But the revolution was only partly successful, Bruner laments, because the emphasis changed from "constructing meaning" to "processing information." And the dominant metaphor became that of the computer, which unfortunately led to the requirement that new models and theories be "computable."

Bruner argues that there has not been just one cognitive revolution but that cognitive revolutions are ongoing. And he suggests that the most fruitful direction for the next cognitive revolution is that it should focus on discovering how people construct meaning, how they make sense of the jumble of physical sensations that the senses provide (Bruner, 1997d). There is perhaps a third revolution in the offing, claims Shotter (2001). This next revolution may deal more specifically with the uniqueness of the person and with the meaning of the self in the context of culture.

The proper study of man, says Bruner in his book of that title, is man (and, presumably, women and children too). "There is no one explanation of man," he explains, adding that no

---

[3] Perhaps he was wrong, Old Lady Gribbin chuckled. Maybe it wasn't a parliamentary system after all but a dictatorship – a benevolent dictatorship. Otherwise, why the need for a revolution? She chuckled again and then looked at me strangely as though seeing something she hadn't seen before. Maybe I shouldn't laugh about such important matters, she said, turning once more to her notes.

explanation of the human condition can make sense "without being interpreted in the light of the symbolic world that constitutes human culture" (1990c, p. 138).

Bruner's more recent work, some of which is described in Chapter 12, deals increasingly with humans in the context of culture. This work places increasing emphasis on the importance of language, on the significance of the stories we tell ourselves about our lives (our personal narratives), and on the analysis of language and of grammar as a way of discovering things about the self (Bruner, 2002, 2004; Marsico, 2015).

Bruner's work continues to be enormously influential in culturally based approaches to psychological and anthropological research and theory (Marsico, 2015, 2017). Among other things, it has encouraged the development of what is often labeled the "narrative" approach to research and analysis and a study of "narrative" as opposed to "logical" thinking.

Educational Implications of Bruner's Theory

Bruner's theory fares especially well with respect to its **heuristic** value (the extent to which it continues to engender research and debate, leading to new discoveries); it also fares well in terms of its practical implications. He has been especially concerned with pointing out some of the instructional implications of his work (Bruner, 1966, 1983, 1990a, 1996b).

Bruner's emphasis on the formation of coding systems, together with his belief that abstract coding systems facilitate transfer, improve retention, and increase problem-solving ability and motivation, has led him to advocate a discovery-oriented approach in schools. This emphasis on **discovery learning** is premised partly on his belief that the formation of generic coding systems requires the discovery of relationships. Accordingly, Bruner advocates the use of techniques by which children are encouraged to discover facts and relationships for themselves. A major theme in his approach to instruction is that learning is an *active* rather than a *passive* process. As we saw, these notions are basic to a *constructivist* approach to instruction.

Bruner suggests that some form of spiral curriculum is often the best for learner-centered education. A spiral curriculum is one that redevelops the same topics at succeeding age or grade levels as well as at different levels of difficulty. For example, in early grades, learners are exposed to the simplest concepts in a particular area; at succeeding grade levels, they are re-exposed to the same area but at progressively more advanced conceptual levels.

Renewed interest in discovery approaches to education is evident in the constructivist approach to teaching advocated by various educators. The whole point of constructivism, say Gabler and Schroeder, is to shift students from "the familiar role of listener to that of active learner" (2003, p. xvii). Constructivism is in close agreement with Bruner's argument that learners need to build knowledge for themselves – that, in his words, they need to "make meaning." Not all educators or theorists are as enthusiastic as Bruner about the use of discovery methods in schools (for example, see Ausubel, 1977; Ausubel & Robinson, 1969). A relatively mild controversy pitting discovery teaching against more didactic approaches (sometimes called **reception learning**) has been going on in educational circles for several decades. Research that has attempted to examine the relative merits of these two approaches doesn't clearly favor one over the other (see Lefrançois, 2018). This need not be of any great concern though. Teachers do not need to use only one of these methods; they can use both.

JEAN PIAGET: A DEVELOPMENTAL-COGNITIVE POSITION

Another cognitive theorist whose research and theories have enormously influenced psychology and education is Jean Piaget. Piaget's system is unmistakably cognitive; its overriding concern is mental representation. It is also a developmental theory; it looks at the processes by which children develop progressively more advanced ways of knowing and thinking. In brief, Piagetian theory is an account of human cognitive development. His work covers an enormous range of topics – for example, language (1926); reality (1929); morality (1932); causality (1930); time (1946); intelligence (1950); play, dreams, and imitation (1951); consciousness (1976);

BOX 7.2 Jean Piaget (1896–1980)

Credit: Ben Martin / Archive Photos / Getty Images. Getty Images 1034835480

Jean Piaget was born in Neuchâtel, Switzerland, in 1896, the first child of Arthur Piaget, a professor of medieval literature. There are indications that he was a precocious child. At age 11, he published his first "scholarly" paper: a one-page note on a partly albino sparrow, and throughout his teen years, he produced a series of papers on mollusks that were widely published and read. Apparently his readers, not realizing he was still a teenager, considered him an expert.

Jean Piaget: A Developmental-Cognitive Position | 259

> **BOX 7.2 (cont.)**
>
> Piaget's interest in biology led him to the University of Neuchâtel, where he obtained his Ph.D. at age 22. By age 30, he had already published more than two dozen papers, most relating to mollusks.
>
> After receiving his doctorate, Piaget spent a year wandering through Europe, uncertain about what to do next. During this year, he worked in a psychoanalytic clinic (Eugen Bleuler's), studied psychology under Carl Jung for one semester, and worked in a psychological laboratory (that of Wreschner and Lipps). He eventually ended up in Alfred Binet's laboratory, then under the direction of Théodore Simon, where the famous Stanford–Binet intelligence test originated.
>
> One of Piaget's duties while in the Binet laboratory was to administer an early intelligence test, Burt's Reasoning Tests, to young children to standardize the items. This period marks the beginning of his lifelong interest in the thought processes of children. It was also at about this time that Piaget's first child was born. He and his wife, Valentine Châtenay, had three children, each of whose development he studied in detail. These studies are incorporated in the origins of his theory. The bulk of Piaget's work is found in *Archives de Psychologie* (of which he was coeditor); much of it remains untranslated.
>
> In 1980, Piaget was still publishing and doing research at an amazing pace. In fact, a book he finished shortly before his death introduces important changes and advances in his thinking (Piaget, 1980). And even 20 years after his death, previously unpublished essays and new translations of his work continue to appear (for example, Piaget, 2001). In Piaget's own words, "At the end of one's career, it is better to be prepared to change one's perspective than to be condemned to repeat oneself indefinitely" (quoted in Inhelder, 1982, p. 411).
>
> One indication of his stature in psychology and education is the website www.piaget .org, the official site of the Jean Piaget Society, a group of academics and educators devoted to studying and applying Piaget. The society's official journal is entitled *Cognitive Development* (Nucci & Turiel, 2001). (Based in part on Jean Piaget Society, 2018; Kincheloe & Horn, 2007; Smith, 1997.)

and much more. The theory is scattered in more than 60 books and several hundred articles, many of which were coauthored by Piaget's long-time assistant, Bärbel Inhelder (1913–1997).

The Méthode Clinique

Much of the data on which Piaget based his theories was derived from a special technique he developed for studying children: the **méthode clinique,** a semistructured approach to research in which participants are often asked to explain their answers and in which their responses determine what the next question will be. This is quite unlike the more conventional approach, in which predetermined questions are presented sequentially.

The méthode clinique is borrowed from clinical psychology and especially from psychoanalysis. Santiago-Delefosse and Delefosse (2002) speculate that Piaget's psychoanalyst, Sabina Spielrein (1885–1942), may have strongly influenced the development of this

Three Cognitive Theories

research method.[4] Likewise, the psychoanalyst Pierre Janet (1859–1947), also a contemporary of Piaget's, used this method extensively in his practice. As Piaget describes the method, it requires that the interviewer listen while letting the child talk. And it also requires that the interviewer go where the child's explanations and questions lead (Piaget, 1926).

One of the advantages of the méthode clinique lies in the considerable flexibility it permits. Piaget argues that when investigators do not know what all the answers might be, they are hardly in a position to decide beforehand how the questions should be phrased or even what questions should be asked. The "father/experimenter" role of the méthode clinique has sometimes led to surprising observations.

Theoretical Orientation

Perhaps the most basic of all of Piaget's ideas is this: Human development is a process of adaptation. And the highest form of human adaptation is cognition (or knowing).

This view stems directly from Piaget's early training in biology. Consistent with that training, Piaget began by borrowing two of zoology's biggest questions: (1) What properties of organisms allow them to survive? And (2) how can species be classified? These he rephrased and directed at the development of children: (1) What characteristics of children enable them to adapt to their environment? And (2) what is the most accurate and most useful way of classifying child development? Hence, Piaget's theoretical orientation is clearly biological and evolutionary as well as cognitive: He studies the development of mind (a cognitive pursuit) in the context of biological adaptation.

Adaptation Through Assimilation and Accommodation

The newborn infant, Piaget notes, is in many ways a stunningly helpless organism, unaware that the world is real, ignorant of causes and effects, with no storehouse of ideas with which to reason or any capacity for intentional behaviors. All the newborn has are a few simple reflexes – and an amazing capacity to adapt.

In the language of the computer metaphor, newborns are remarkable little sensing machines that seem naturally predisposed to acquire and process a tremendous amount of information. They continually seek out and respond to stimulation, notes Flavell (1985). As a result, the infant's simple reflexes – the sucking, reaching, and grasping – become more complex, more coordinated, and more purposeful. This occurs through **adaptation**, a process of gradual change by which organisms, or behaviors, become better suited to environmental demands.

---

[4] The old lady stopped and motioned that I should turn off the recorder. Your students, she said, might want to know how Sabina Spielrein came to be Piaget's psychoanalyst. You could tell them she was born in Russia but her parents, who were Jewish, sent her to Switzerland when she was 19 so Carl Jung could treat her for some nervous malady she had. Jung had just begun to use Freud's new methods of psychoanalysis. Psychoanalysis fascinated Sabina, so she stayed in Switzerland to study medicine and become a psychoanalyst and eventually ended up working at the Jean-Jacques Rousseau Institute in Geneva, where Piaget worked. Later, at age 38, she returned to Russia with her two little girls. Mrs. Gribbin paused for a long time, and I thought she had finished. Then, she said that no, even very studious students probably wouldn't be interested in this aside and that I shouldn't put it in. It's too sad, she said, because, in 1942, Sabina Spielrein, along with her two daughters and a host of other Jewish people, were executed by German soldiers.

The short answer for the first of Piaget's questions – what characteristics of children enable them to adapt to their environment? – is simply **assimilation** and **accommodation**. Assimilation involves responding to situations using activities or knowledge that have already been learned or that are present at birth. Accommodation involves change in existing activities or knowledge.

To use Piaget's example, an infant is born with the ability to suck – with a sucking **schema**, in Piaget's terms (pluralized as *schemata* or as *schemas*, sometimes used interchangeably with *scheme*). Schemas are important concepts in Piaget's system. Essentially, a schema is a behavior, together with neurological structures related to that behavior. In Piaget's theory, any distinct activity can be labeled a schema. Thus, there are looking schemas, talking schemas, schemas evident in the child's ability to add 2 + 3, and so on. Objects or situations are said to be assimilated to a schema when they can be responded to using previous knowledge. Thus, the sucking schema allows the infant to assimilate a nipple to the behavior of sucking. Similarly, children who have learned the rules of addition can assimilate a problem such as 1 + 1; that is, they can respond appropriately because of previous learning.

Often, however, the child's understanding of the world is inadequate. The newborn's sucking schema works for ordinary nipples but is not very effective for fingers or pacifiers. Similarly, preschoolers' understanding of number allows them to keep track of toes and fingers, but it does not impress kindergarten teachers. If there is to be any developmental progress, changes are required in information and behavior. These changes define *accommodation*.

In summary, assimilation involves reacting based on previous learning and understanding; accommodation involves a change in understanding. And the interplay of assimilation and accommodation leads to adaptation.

Equilibration

All activity, claims Piaget, involves both assimilation and accommodation. The child cannot react to an entirely new situation without using previous learning and behaviors (hence, assimilating). At the same time, reacting to the same situation even for the thousandth time implies change, however subtle (hence, accommodation). Flavell (1985) notes that these activities are simply two sides of the same cognitive coin.

It is important, explains Piaget, that there be a balance between assimilation and accommodation – an equilibrium. He uses the term **equilibration** to signify the processes or tendencies that lead to this balance. If there is too much assimilation, there is no new learning; if there is too much accommodation (that is, change), behavior becomes chaotic.

Assimilation and accommodation are clearly illustrated in two important activities of early childhood: play, which involves mainly assimilation, and imitation, which is mostly accommodation.

Play

When children play, Piaget explains, they continually assimilate objects to predetermined activities, ignoring attributes that don't really fit the activity. For example, when children sit astride a chair and say "Giddyup," they are not paying attention to those attributes of the chair that don't resemble a horse.

This type of play behavior involves little change and thus little accommodation, which isn't to deny its importance. Indeed, Piaget does quite the opposite, emphasizing that although young children engage in activities (such as playing "horse") simply for the sake of the activity, the effect is to stabilize the schema (the activity), to make it more readily available, and, consequently, to set the stage for further learning.

Imitation

Play involves a preponderance of assimilation because, during play, objects and situations are continually assimilated to ongoing activities. Thus, when the "horse riding" schema is active, a chair becomes a horse as easily as does a stuffed teddy bear or the family dog. These objects are *assimilated* to the "horse riding" schema; the child need not *accommodate* to the different characteristics of the chair, the dog, or the teddy bear.

In contrast, imitation is primarily accommodation (Williamson & Gonsiorowski, 2017). When they are imitating, children constantly modify their behavior in accordance with the demands imposed on them by their desire to be something or someone they are not. Piaget argues that through the imitation of activity, children's repertoires of behaviors expand and gradually begin to be internalized. In Piaget's terminology, **internalization** is equivalent to the formation of concepts. Internalization is the process by which activities and events in the real world become represented mentally: It is the basis of cognitive learning. First comes the activity and then comes a mental representation of it.

Many of the young infant's imitative behaviors occur only in the presence of the model being imitated. For example, even very young infants can imitate simple behaviors such as blinking, winking, and opening the mouth (Meltzoff & Moore, 1989), but the imitation doesn't continue when the model is no longer present. That, says Piaget, is because the infant fails to realize that objects continue to exist independently even when the child is not actually looking at them, touching them, or otherwise sensing them. The world of the infant is a world of the here and now; it does not include an understanding of the permanence of objects.

At about age one, an important change occurs when Juanita puts on her mother's jacket, takes her little backpack, and climbs into the box that has suddenly become her car. She is now pretending that she is going to work after her mother has already left for work. Piaget explains that this kind of **deferred imitation** – the ability to imitate things and people not immediately present – is evidence that the infant has internalized a representation of that which is being imitated. It is also evidence that the infant has begun to realize that things continue to exist on their own even when out of sensory range – evidence, in other words, of the object concept.

Piaget's View of Intelligence

Piaget was very familiar with Gestalt theory. In his book *The Psychology of Intelligence* (Piaget, 1950), he devotes most of a chapter to examining the Gestalt notion that perceptual activity underlies intelligence. In the end, although he greatly admired Gestalt theory and shared its emphasis on perception, he concludes that intelligence is a more active process than portrayed by the Gestalt theorists. Also, his concept of intelligence differs markedly from the traditional measurement approach. Instead of describing intelligence as a relatively fixed quality or quantity, Piaget describes it as *mobile* – as something that moves (that changes). Intelligence, he argues, exists in action. As Muller, Ten Eycke, and Baker (2015) explain, mental and physical action are the basis of Piaget's theory. In this theory, intelligence is the property of activity that is reflected in maximally adaptive behavior, and it can therefore be understood as the entire process of adapting.

To review briefly, adaptation is the process of interacting with the environment by assimilating aspects of it to **cognitive structure** (defined by Piaget as mental representations and actions) and by modifying (or accommodating) cognitive structure. Both activities occur in response to environmental demands. Also, both are guided by cognitive structure and result in changes in cognitive structure. However, this entire process can be inferred only from actual behavior. The substance of Piaget's view of intelligence is summarized in Figure 7.2.

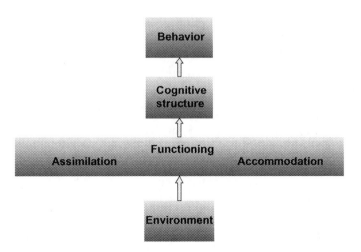

Figure 7.2 Piaget defines intelligence in terms of the individual's interactions with the environment. Intelligent interaction involves a balance of assimilation (incorporating aspects of the environment to previous learning) and accommodation (changing behavior in the face of environmental demands). The result of this interaction (of this functioning) is the development of cognitive structures (schemas and operations), which are then reflected in behavior.

Piaget's View of Cognitive Structure

Although this view of intelligence may be useful for understanding some of the processes involved in intelligent behavior, it is not immediately useful for measuring it. But one aspect of the model has implications for developing tests of intelligence: the part defined by the expression *cognitive structure*.

Piaget's description of cognitive structure (of what he describes as mental representation) is essentially a description of the characteristics of children at different ages. This description is his answer for the second of the questions he borrowed from biology: What is the most accurate and most useful way of classifying or ordering child development? Hence, Piaget's description of changes in cognitive structure is a description of the stages of human cognitive development. This part of his system has received the most attention.

Piaget's Stage Theory: A Summary

Piaget believed that development progresses through a series of stages, each characterized by the appearance of new abilities or, more precisely, each consisting of a more advanced level of adaptation. He describes four major stages and several substages through which children progress in their development:

- *Sensorimotor (birth to 2 years)*
- *Preoperational (2–7 years)*
  - *Preconceptual (2–4 years)*
  - *Intuitive (4–7 years)*
- *Concrete operations (7–11/12 years)*
- *Formal operations (11/12–14/15 years)*

Each stage can be described by the major identifying characteristics of children at that stage and by the learning that occurs before transition to the next stage.

The Sensorimotor Period: Birth to Two Years

The most striking characteristics of child behavior in the first two years of life relate to the absence of language and of internal representation. Because it cannot be represented mentally, the child's world is a *world of the here and now*. In a very literal sense, it is a world where objects exist only when the child actually senses them and does things with them – hence, the label **sensorimotor intelligence**. At this stage, when objects are not being sensed, they cease to exist; infants have not yet acquired the **object concept** (a realization of the permanence of objects).

The Object Concept

Piaget investigated the development of the object concept by presenting young children with an attractive object and then removing it after they had become interested in it. In the earliest stages of development, they show no signs of missing the object – proof, claims Piaget, that out of sight is literally out of mind. However, in later stages, children will look for objects they have seen being hidden; at around age one, they will search for objects they remember from some previous time.

Achievements by Age Two

Piaget's labels for his developmental stages typically reflect the characteristics that are most common throughout the stage rather than the newly developing characteristics that lead to transition into the next stage. Thus, the sensorimotor stage is so labeled because for most of their first two years, children react to the world in a sensorimotor fashion: They understand the environment largely through their sensations of it (hence, *sensori*) and their actions toward it (hence, *motor*). However, each stage is a preparation for the next, and the achievements of each are important in explaining the transition to the next stage.

Among the most striking and important achievements of the sensorimotor period is the development of the ability to symbolize and to communicate. The use of symbols and especially of language emerges from sensorimotor experience (Meadows, 2018). Language accelerates thinking and makes possible the transition to a more cognitive interpretation of the world. A second achievement, already noted, is the development of the object concept – the discovery that the world continues to exist even when it is not being seen, felt, heard, smelled, or tasted.

The culmination of sensorimotor learning is marked by a third accomplishment: the child's increasing ability to coordinate separate activities. Adults take the ability to coordinate complex activities very much for granted, but it is no small or unimportant achievement for the child. In the absence of cooperation between simple activities such as looking and reaching, the child could never obtain the object looked at and desired. Even for so uncomplicated a behavior as picking up a pen, vision must direct the fingers and the hand, the arm, the shoulder, the torso, and perhaps even the head must be pressed into service.

A final sensorimotor achievement is that of recognizing cause-and-effect relationships. At birth, infants do not know that if they reach toward an object, they can grasp it and bring it closer. This kind of learning is precisely what allows them to develop intentionality, for until children know what the effects of their activities will be, they cannot clearly intend these effects.

Preoperational Thinking: 2–7 Years

The next stage in the cognitive evolution of the child is **preoperational thinking** – so-called because the child's thinking exhibits serious shortcomings in terms of the ability to understand and use logical *operations*. The preoperational stage is divided into two substages: the preconceptual and the intuitive.

Preconceptual Thinking: 2–4 Years

The stage of **preconceptual thinking** is characterized by the child's inability to understand many of the properties of classes. Piaget, whose early work was often based on observations of his own children, illustrates this by reference to his son's reaction to a snail they saw as they were walking one morning. "Papa," said the boy, "regarde l'escargot." Which they did. But later, when they came across a second snail, the boy said again, "Poup, regarde l'escargot. C'est encore l'escargot!"[5]

The preconceptual child has acquired the ability to represent objects internally (that is, mentally) and to identify them based on their membership in classes, but now reacts to all similar objects as though they were identical. For a while, all men are "Daddy," all women are "Mommy," animals are all "doggie," and the world is simple. If Samuel sees a teddy bear like his at a friend's place, he knows that it's his teddy bear, and the tricycle at the store is clearly his. Children understand enough about classes to identify objects, but their understanding is incomplete: They cannot yet distinguish between apparently identical members of the same class (hence, the term *preconceptual*). Santa Claus continues to be the one and only individual of his type, even though he may be seen in 10 places the same day.

Another feature of the child's thinking during this stage is that it is **transductive** rather than **inductive** or **deductive**. Deductive reasoning proceeds from the general to the specific. For example, if you accept the generalization that all birds have wings, when you are told that the water ouzel is a bird, you can deduce that it has wings. Inductive reasoning goes from specifics to a generalization. For example, after you have observed a hundred species of birds and have noted that they all have wings, you might induce that all birds have wings.

Inductive and deductive reasoning are valid methods of thinking logically. In contrast, transductive reasoning is a faulty type of logic that involves making inferences from one specific to another. For example, the child who reasons "My dog has hair, and that thing there has hair; therefore, that thing is a dog" is engaging in transductive reasoning. Transductive reasoning can lead to correct conclusions but is not guaranteed to do so. The hairy thing might well be a dog, in which case transductive reasoning results in an accurate inference. But if the furry thing is a skunk, the same reasoning process has a less happy outcome.

---

[5] Old Lady Gribbin said I should translate this for you. I said okay. The first conversation means, "Father, look at the snail." The second one, in response to a different snail, means, "Pops, look at the snail. It's the snail again."

Intuitive Thinking: 4–7 Years

By the time children reach age four, they have achieved a more complete understanding of concepts and have largely stopped reasoning transductively. Their thinking has become somewhat more logical, although it is governed more by perception than by logic: hence the label **intuitive thinking**.

The role of perception is evident in children's lack of **conservation** – that is, in their failure to realize that quantitative attributes of objects do not change unless something is added or taken away. A typical conservation problem goes like this: Children are shown two identical beakers filled to the same level with water (as in part (a) of Figure 7.3). The experimenter then pours the contents of one of the beakers into a tall, thin tube (as in part (b) of Figure 7.3). Children who had previously said the amounts in each beaker were equal are now asked whether there is as much, more, or less water in the new container. At the intuitive stage, they will almost invariably say that there is more because the water level is much higher in the tube. They are misled by appearance (perception) as well as by a lack of some specific logical abilities.

The thinking of intuitive-stage children shows not only lack of conservation but also a marked **egocentrism** – an inability to easily accept the viewpoint of others. To illustrate this, an experimenter holds in each hand one end of a wire on which a boy doll and a girl doll are strung side by side. The child is shown the dolls, which are then hidden behind a screen, but the hands remain in plain view. The child is asked which doll will come out first if they are moved out on the left. The child's answer is noted, the dolls are returned to their original position, and the question is repeated. Again, the dolls come out on the left; thus, the same doll comes out first. The procedure is repeated a number of times.

Reasonably intelligent children generally answer correctly at first. However, after a while, they change their minds and predict that the other doll will come out first. If asked why they think so, they are unlikely to claim they distrust psychological investigators. Instead, they may say something like, "It's not fair. It's her turn to come out next." Responding in terms of how things should be from the child's own point of view illustrates the role of egocentrism in intuitive thinking.

Although children at this stage can identify objects based on class membership, they do not yet completely understand how classes can be nested within larger classes. A four-year-old who is shown a handful of seven candies, two of which are chocolates and five of which are

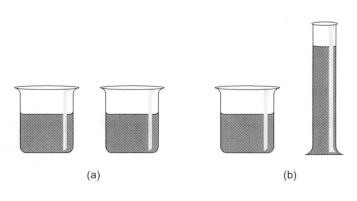

Figure 7.3 Material for a simple conservation of liquid experiment. One of the containers from (a) has been poured into a taller, thinner container in (b). The nonconserving child will assume there is more liquid in this new container because it is "taller" – or less because it is "thinner."

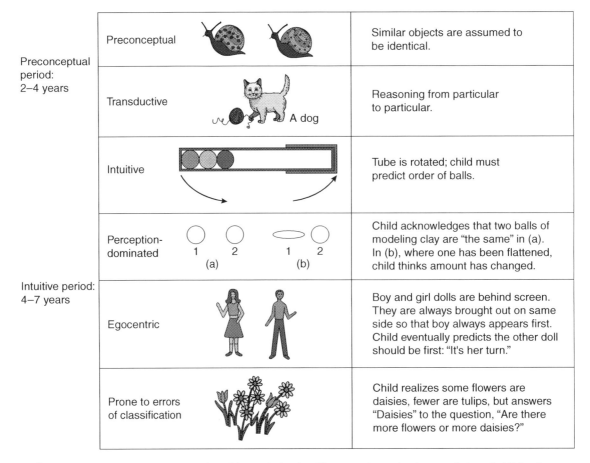

Figure 7.4 Some of the demonstrations Piaget devised to illustrate the main characteristics of children's thinking between the ages of 2 and 7. Relative to older children, the reasoning of pre-operational children tends to be egocentric, dominated by perception, and prone to errors of logic. Adapted from Lefrançois, G. R. (2018). *Psychology for Teaching* (2nd ed.). San Diego, CA: Bridgepoint Education, Fig. 2.5. Used by permission.

jelly beans, immediately recognizes that they are all candies. However, if the experimenter asks, "Tell me, are there more jelly beans than candies or fewer or the same number?" the child may well say that there are more jelly beans than candies! When a class is broken down into subclasses and children are asked to reason about the subclass (jelly beans) and the larger class (candy), they find it very difficult to do so. For them, the original division destroyed the parent class. (See Figure 7.4 for a summary of some of the characteristics of preoperational thinking.)

Operations

The preconceptual and intuitive stages are substages of the lengthy preoperational period. The stage is labeled *preoperational* because before age seven, the child doesn't reason with **operations**. An operation can be defined as an internalized activity (in other words, a thought) that is subject to certain rules of logic.

Concrete Operations: 7–11/12 Years

At about age seven or so, children make an important transition from preoperations (prelogical, egocentric, perception-dominated thinking) to **concrete operations** – more rule-regulated thinking, but where the rules of logic are applied to real, *concrete* objects and situations and not to hypothetical situations. Concrete operations are well illustrated in the acquisition of the concept of conservation.

The Conservations

Conservation is the realization that certain quantitative attributes of objects do not change unless something is added or taken away. In the demonstration illustrated in Figure 7.3, children have acquired conservation when they realize that pouring water from one container to another doesn't change its amount, regardless of the shape of the container.

There are many types of conservation, each relating to a specific quantitative attribute of an object and each acquired in highly similar order by most children. These, with approximate ages of attainment, are shown in Figure 7.5. Research suggests that children's ability to conserve is closely tied to their performance in related school subjects, such as mathematics (for example, Bond & Parkinson, 2010).

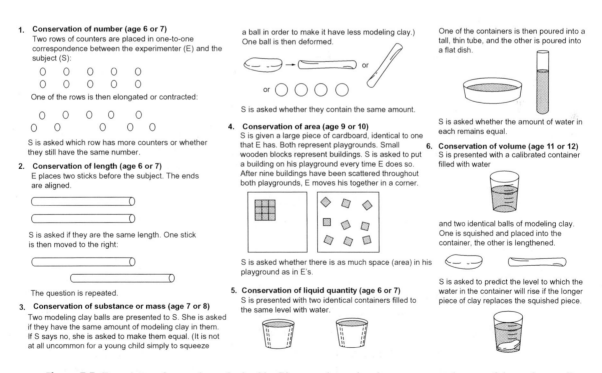

Figure 7.5 Experimental procedures devised by Piaget to determine the presence or absence of the understanding of conservation in each of a variety of different areas such as volume, number, length, and liquid quantity.
Adapted from Lefrançois, G. R. (2016). *Psychology: The Human Puzzle* (2nd ed.). San Diego, CA: Bridgepoint Education, Fig. 4.8. Used by permission.

The importance of conservation in Piaget's theory is that it illustrates the use of one or more of the rules of logic that now govern thinking. What has happened is that while interacting with things and events and learning about self and world – "constructing knowledge" is Piaget's (1972) phrase; "meaning making" is Bruner's (1996a) – the child discovers that logic governs actions and relationships.

The first of three rules of logic that become apparent at this stage is **reversibility** – the realization that actions (and thoughts) can be reversed and certain logical consequences follow from doing so. For example, with respect to the problem of conservation of liquids described earlier, a child might reason, "If the water were poured out of the tall tube and back into its original container, it would still have as much water as before, so it mustn't have changed." That, in a nutshell, is reversibility.

Alternatively, the child might reason that nothing has been added to or taken away from either container and that there must then still be the same amount in each. This is an example of the rule of **identity**, which states that for every operation (action), there is another operation that leaves it unchanged. Adding or taking away nothing produces no change.

A third way of reasoning might be this: "The tube is taller, but it is also thinner, so it balances out." Piaget and Inhelder (1941) refer to this reasoning as **compensation** (or *combinativity*), a property defined by the logical consequences of combining more than one operation or, in this case, more than one dimension.

Classifying

With the appearance of the logical properties of thinking that define operations, children also acquire new skills in dealing with classes, numbers, and series. Piaget assumed that these abilities depend on interacting with and manipulating real objects. For example, by combining objects, separating them, or arranging them into groups, children learn about class membership and develop the ability to reason about nested classes. The candy problem cited earlier (whether there are more jelly beans or more candies) would present so slight a problem for concrete-operations children that they might snort in derision if the question were put to them.

Seriating

As a result of experiences with real objects, children learn not only about classes, but also acquire the ability to order objects in series and to set up correspondences between more than one series. Piaget investigated the understanding of seriation by presenting children with jumbled collections of objects that can easily be ranked, as shown in Figure 7.6. Before concrete operations, children rank objects by comparing two of them at once, but they seldom make the necessary inference that if A is greater than B and B is greater than C, then A must also be greater than C. It does not embarrass preoperational children to put C before B if they have just been comparing A and C. The concrete-operations child seldom makes an error of this kind (Figure 7.6).

Figure 7.6 A test of a child's understanding of seriation. The elements of the series are presented in random order, and the child is asked to arrange them in sequence by height. The top row was arranged by a 3½-year-old and the bottom by an eight-year-old. Adapted from Lefrançois. G. R. (2018). *Psychology: The Human Puzzle* (2nd ed.). San Diego, CA: Bridgepoint Education, Fig. 4.9. Used by permission.

Dealing with Numbers

Understanding numbers flows directly from the child's developing ability to classify and deal with series. Understanding the cardinal properties of numbers (the fact that numbers represent classes of different magnitude: one thing, two things, three things, etc.) depends on classification. Understanding the ordinal properties of numbers (their ordered sequence: first, second, third, etc.) depends on understanding the rules of seriation.

Formal Operations: After 11 or 12 Years

Formal operations, the ability to apply rules of logic in a wide variety of abstract as well as concrete situations, present some important advances over concrete operations. First, concrete-operations children apply their logic directly to real objects or to objects that are easily imagined (hence, the label *concrete*). They do not yet deal with what is merely hypothetical unless it can be tied directly to concrete reality. Their ready answer for the question "What if Doris Adler had small ears?" is "Doris Adler does not have small ears!" In contrast, adolescents are potentially capable of dealing with the hypothetical (the nonconcrete). That Doris Adler has large ears does not prevent them from imagining the consequences of her having small ones.

Abstract Relations

An item from Binet's *reasoning test* illustrates dramatically an important difference between formal operations and concrete operations thinking. The item deals with abstract relations: Edith is fairer than Susan; Edith is darker than Lilly. Who is the darkest of the three? This problem is difficult not because it involves seriation, which has already been mastered in the stage of concrete operations, but because of its abstract nature. If Edith, Susan, and Lilly were all standing in front of 10-year-old Sean, he could easily say, "Oh! Edith is fairer than Susan, and she's darker than Lilly – and Susan is the darkest." But when the problem is not concrete but verbal, it requires thinking that is more formal (abstract).

Three Cognitive Theories

Table 7.2 **Piaget's stages of cognitive development**

Stage	Approximate age	Major characteristics
Sensorimotor	0–2 years	World of the here and now No language, no thought in early stages Motoric intelligence No notion of objective reality
Preoperational **Preconceptual** **Intuitive**	2–7 years 2–4 years 4–7 years	Egocentric thought Reason dominated by perception Intuitive rather than logical solutions Inability to conserve
Concrete operations	7–11/12 years	Ability to conserve Logic of classes and relations Understanding of numbers Thinking bound to concrete Development of reversibility in thought
Formal operations	11/12–14/15 years	Complete generality of thought Propositional thinking Ability to deal with the hypothetical Development of strong idealism

Adapted from Lefrançois, G. R. (2018). *Psychology for Teaching* (2nd ed.). San Diego, CA: Bridgepoint Education, table 2.4. Used by permission.

Hypothetical Nature of Thought

The last stage in the evolution of thought is marked by the appearance of what Piaget labels **propositional thinking** – thinking that isn't restricted to the concrete or the potentially real but instead deals in the realm of the hypothetical. (A proposition is any statement that can be true or false.) Children can now reason from the real to the merely possible or from the possible to the actual. They can compare hypothetical states of affairs with actual states or vice versa. As a result, they can become profoundly upset at the seeming irresponsibility of a generation of adults that has brought itself to the edge of untold disasters. (See Table 7.2 for a summary of Piaget's stages.)

Piaget's Theory as a Theory of Learning

Piaget's position is primarily a theory of human development. However, largely because of its emphasis on the development of knowledge, it is also a theory of learning. As a theory of learning, it can be simplified and reduced to the following set of statements:

- The acquisition of knowledge is a gradual developmental process made possible through the interaction of the child with the environment.
- The sophistication of children's representation of the world is a function of their stage of development. That stage is defined by the thought structures they then possess.

- Maturation, active experience, equilibration, and social interaction are the forces that shape learning (Piaget, 1961). **Maturation** is a biologically based process related to the gradual unfolding of potential. *Active experience* refers to actual activities that enable the child to know and to internalize things. *Social interaction* (interaction with other people) permits the child to elaborate ideas about the world and about others. And equilibration is the tendency toward finding an optimal balance between assimilation and accommodation.

Educational Implications of Piaget's Theory

The impact of Piaget's theory on school curricula, on instructional procedures, and on measurement practices is profound and significant. For example, as shown in Table 7.3, each of the forces that shape development has important educational implications.

Theories such as Piaget's and Bruner's emphasize that learning is far more than simply moving items of information from out there into the child. These theories support *constructivism*, an approach to teaching and learning that gives the child an active role in the construction of knowledge. Constructivist methods, explain Gabler and Schroeder, are those that encourage "students to be critical thinkers and independent learners, with the teacher acting as a mentor and a facilitator" (2003, p. xvii).

Table 7.3 **Four forces that shape human development**

Force	Explanation	Educational Implication
Equilibration	A tendency to maintain a balance between assimilation (responding using previous learning) and accommodation (changing behavior in response to the environment).	Children need to be provided with tasks at an optimal level of difficulty – not so difficult that they're too challenging but not so easy that they require no accommodation.
Maturation	Genetic forces that, although they don't determine behavior, are related to its unfolding.	Teachers need to know something about how children think and learn – about their level of maturation and understanding – to optimize their educational experiences.
Active experience	Interaction with real objects and events allows individuals to discover things and to invent (construct) mental representations of the world.	This supports a *constructivist* curriculum where the learner is actively involved in the process of discovering and learning.
Social interaction	Interaction with people leads to the elaboration of ideas about things, people, and self.	Schools need to provide ample opportunity for learner–learner and teacher–learner interaction in academic (classroom) and nonacademic (playground, library, etc.) areas.

Piaget's work suggests a number of very specific instructional approaches and principles. For example, it follows directly from the theory that in early stages, interaction with real objects is crucial to the growth of knowledge and to the development of the understandings and abilities that underlie thinking. Hence providing opportunities for both mental and physical activity is a basic educational implication of Piaget's theory (Lefrançois, 2018).

Piaget's theory also suggests that schools should take pains to provide students with tasks and challenges of optimal difficulty. Material presented to learners should not be so difficult that it cannot be understood (assimilated) nor so easy that it leads to no new learning (no accommodation). Hence, it is very important for teachers to know how children develop, how they learn and think, and what the limitations and the potential of their thinking are.

In describing the forces that shape the child's development, Piaget gave a very important role to social interaction. Through social interaction, children become aware of the feelings and thoughts of others, they develop moral and games rules, and they develop and practice their own logical thought processes. Instructional methods that reflect Piaget's theory need to provide many opportunities for social interaction.

Appraisal of Piaget's Position

Piaget's critics, of which there are a significant number, have advanced a few standard complaints. One of the earliest centered on the small number of subjects in his research: The méthode clinique doesn't lend itself easily to large samples. This criticism is not particularly relevant, except where more careful studies with larger groups have contradicted Piaget's findings.

Criticisms and Research

Thousands of studies have investigated and sometimes elaborated on Piaget's work. As Fuson (2009) notes, "[T]here has been a huge explosion of research in children's mathematical thinking stimulated by Piaget" (p. 343). Many of these studies support Piaget's general description of the sequence of intellectual development, especially at the earliest stages (for example, Giles et al., 2018; Hebe, 2017). In contrast, research provides less sweeping support for Piaget's description of the ages at which major intellectual changes occur.

Piaget Underestimated Young Children

Critics point out that Piaget seems to have drastically underestimated the ages at which young children are capable of certain important behaviors. Indications are that verbal difficulties might often have been implicated in Piaget's failure to find certain abilities and understanding during the earlier developmental periods. When the tasks are made simpler and less dependent on advanced language development, children sometimes respond quite differently.

For example, Baillargeon (1987, 1993) reports studies that seem to indicate young infants have some notion of the permanence of objects much before Piaget thought they did.

When three- and four-month-old infants saw an object apparently passing through a space that should have been occupied by another solid object, they seemed surprised. Similarly, Charles and Rivera (2009) found that five- and six-month-old infants will often actively *look* for an object before they actually reach for it. Looking for an object is a strong indicator of a developing notion of object permanence. However, when Piaget's object permanence tasks are replicated as he described them, results corroborate his findings with respect to age of attainment (Paolini & Oiberman, 2017).

Gelman, Meck, and Merkin (1986) and Aubrey (1993) also point out that preschoolers typically have a well-developed understanding of number that Piaget thought more characteristic of older, concrete-operations children.

Formal Operations Are Not Highly General

In his earlier writings, Piaget left little doubt that he considered formal operations to be generally characteristic of older adolescents as well as of most adults (Inhelder & Piaget, 1958). However, several studies provide convincing evidence that this is probably not the case (for example, Modgil & Modgil, 1982). Many of these studies have failed to find much evidence of formal operations among adults – let alone adolescents (Oesterdiekhoff, 2016). Ironically, it seems that although Piaget underestimated the abilities of young children, he may have overestimated those of older children and adolescents.

Given these findings, Piaget (1972) modified his earlier position by conceding that the formal-operations stage is probably not nearly as general as he had first thought. Available evidence suggests that formal operations are best viewed as cognitive processes that are potential rather than probable. In short, formal operations are probably impossible in middle childhood or earlier; they are possible but far from completely general in adolescence or adulthood.

The System Is Too Complex

Another criticism has to do with the difficulty of understanding the system and with the use of complex and sometimes nebulous terminology. For example, Morgado (2003) points out that Piaget's use of important terms, such as *representation*, is sometimes ambiguous. In addition, in trying to describe logical thinking, Piaget used a difficult logic whose contribution was not always readily apparent. Lourenco and Machado (1996) suggest that many of these criticisms are based on misinterpretations of Piaget's theory, sometimes resulting from difficulties in translating from the original French.

How Damaging Are These Criticisms?

Although more numerous and detailed than indicated here, these criticisms are probably not very damaging to the basic theory. At most, the various well-substantiated contradictions of Piagetian theory suggest that the ages of attainment are approximate – a point that Piaget always maintained. They further suggest that children may develop more rapidly in certain areas than

Piaget suspected (particularly at the sensorimotor level) and that the final stage in Piaget's description isn't generally descriptive. This is not unduly disturbing for Piagetian theorists, providing that the preceding stage, concrete operations, remains descriptive of those who have not achieved formal operations.

What the criticisms point out most clearly is that a child's cognitive development is far more complex than Piaget had thought – perhaps more complicated than psychologists still think.

An examination of Piaget's system with respect to the criteria described in Chapter 1 reveals, among other things, that the theory is remarkably consistent, coherent, and comprehensive. However, some research indicates that Piaget's system may not reflect all the facts accurately. On occasion, it underestimates children's abilities, but at other times, it may be guilty of overestimating abilities.

Is the theory clear and understandable? Yes and no. At the level of describing stages, it can be presented simply and clearly. But at the level of abstract logical systems, it is less clear and perhaps not very useful in any case.

Does the theory explain and predict well? Again, yes and no. It explains some behaviors that were largely undiscovered previously (conservation and the object concept, for example), and in a general way, it predicts the type of cognitive functioning that might be expected of children at various stages of development. The predictions are not always entirely appropriate, however, especially when tied to Piaget's approximate ages.

Finally, how useful and influential is the theory? Very. Piaget's impact in psychology and education has been enormous, even if it has also been controversial. The theory has generated thousands of studies and countless applications in schools. Piaget is largely responsible for converting a generation of teachers, parents, and child care workers into fascinated observers of children and their development. And although some theorists now argue that the influence of the theory is waning, many continue to praise his contributions and to extend his work (for example, see the Jean Piaget Society, 2018; Martí & Rodríguez, 2012).

LEV VYGOTSKY: SOCIAL/COGNITIVE THEORY

Not all psychologists have always praised Piaget's work or sought to extend it. In fact, one of Piaget's contemporaries, Soviet psychologist Lev Vygotsky, apparently spent a considerable amount of effort attacking and criticizing Piaget's work and trying to get Piaget to engage in debate and dialogue with him (Obukhova, 2016; Van der Veer, 1996). As was his custom, Piaget never responded, although it is not clear whether this was because he chose not to respond or whether it was because he might not have been very familiar with Vygotsky's work. After all, much of Vygotsky's writing wasn't translated into English until many years after his untimely death (at age 38, in 1934).

But, argues Pass (2007), there is evidence that Piaget and Vygotsky did communicate with each other. And each seems to have modified his theories as a result of the other's work. After reading Vygotsky, says Pass, Piaget began to acknowledge that social influences are one of the important forces shaping development. And after reading Piaget and writing prefaces for two of his books, Vygotsky modified his notion of developmental stages. Unfortunately, says Pass,

Stalin's blockade of East–West communications effectively terminated their exchanges after a short period. Apparently, Vygotsky made repeated attempts to smuggle his work out of Russia to Piaget. In the case of his 1926 book *Psychological Pedagogy*, he wasn't successful until 1932. In fact, for several decades after he died, Vygotsky's work was banned in the Soviet Union (see Vygotsky biography). Ironically, as Mironenko (2009) notes, history now suggests that Vygotsky single-handedly introduced one of the two biggest ideas that Russian psychology has contributed to the world: the notion of the zone of proximal development. (The other great idea was Pavlov's notion of the conditioned reflex.)

BOX 7.3 Lev Semenovich Vygotsky (1896–1934)

Credit: Heritage Images / Hulton Archive / Getty Images. Getty Images 520714133

Vygotsky was born to middle-class Jewish parents in the town of Orscha (sometimes spelled differently) in what is now Belarus. He was raised in Gomel, some 400 miles west of Moscow. His Jewish ancestry placed significant limitations on his educational and career possibilities. As a result, a private tutor educated him during his earliest years before he entered a Jewish high school. That he was later admitted to Moscow University was a matter of sheer luck, there then being in place a lottery system by which only a very small number of Jewish youth were admitted each year.

Because his parents insisted, Vygotsky enrolled in the medical school at Moscow University. He quickly decided he did not want to become a doctor, so he switched to

Continued

BOX 7.3 (cont.)

law and simultaneously studied history and philosophy at a second university (Shaniavsky University). After graduating from these two universities in 1917, he went back to Gomel and began teaching in a state school. Sometime later, he contracted tuberculosis, apparently while caring for members of his family who had become ill with the disease. Fortunately, he survived this first bout.

Strikingly, although he was to become an outstandingly influential psychologist during his lifetime, and remain so for decades after his death, Vygotsky did not become interested in psychology until 1924, when he was already 28 years old. A mere 10 years later, on the morning of June 11, 1934, he died of tuberculosis. Nevertheless, in the intervening 10 years he had pioneered research and ideas that still seem fresh. Despite the fact that his most famous work, *Thought and Language*, was not published until after his death, during his extremely short career he became one of the most important intellectual forces in the Soviet Union. Sadly, however, his work was suppressed two years after his death and was not well known in the West until at least two decades later. Soviet authorities had determined that the child science he had pioneered, known as **pedology**, was a decadent "bourgeois pseudoscience" (partly because it used Western tests for assessing and diagnosing learning difficulties).

Toulmin (1978) has described Vygotsky as the Mozart of psychology – its child genius. By age 28, says Toulmin, Vygotsky had assimilated all of psychology's major theories and findings and had begun to map out new ideas that are still highly influential. What might his career and his contribution have been had he lived as long as Piaget? (Based in part on Kincheloe & Horn, 2007; Kozulin, 1990; New World Encyclopedia, 2018.)

Main Ideas in Vygotsky's Theory

The central emphasis in Piaget's theory, says Bruner (1997a), has to do with understanding the logical systems involved in the child's construction of meaning. Vygotsky's theory is also concerned with the making of meaning; as a result, his theory is often referred to as an example of *constructivism*. But in contrast to Piaget, Vygotsky emphasizes how culture and social interaction are involved in the development of human consciousness. Thus, whereas Piaget's theory gives a primary role to forces that are *within* the child (the tendency toward equilibration, for example), Vygotsky's system emphasizes forces that are *outside* the child – in other words, the forces of culture (Ardila, 2016).

Three overriding themes unify Vygotsky's far-reaching theory: These deal with the importance of culture, the role of language, and the relationship between learner and teacher.

The Role of Culture

The single most important theme in Vygotsky's theory can be summarized in one sentence: Social interaction is fundamentally involved in the development of cognition. By social interaction, Vygotsky meant the child's interaction with what we label **culture** (the customs, beliefs, shared language, etc. of a group). We are very different from other animals, Vygotsky explains. Why? Because we use tools and symbols, and as a result, we create this thing called *culture*. Cultures are very powerful, dynamic, changing things that exert a tremendous influence on each of us. Culture specifies what the successful outcome of development is; it determines what it is we have to learn and what sorts of competencies are required for successful adaptation to our worlds. Cultures, as Vygotsky explained, necessarily shape human mental functioning. "Every function in the child's cultural development appears twice," he writes. "First, on the social level, and later, on the individual level; first, between people (interpsychological) and then inside the child (intrapsychological). This applies equally to voluntary attention, to logical memory, and to the formation of concepts" (Vygotsky, 1978, p. 57).

Perhaps even psychological theories are shaped by culture, says Perinat (2007), who argues that Vygotsky's theory was profoundly shaped by the politics of his culture. That Vygotsky's theory reflects his Marxist-socialist beliefs, particularly in the role he gives culture and social interaction in determining development, is a common thesis (for example, Ratner & Silva, 2017). In addition, his writing and theorizing make it clear that he was very familiar with the research and theorizing of his contemporaries.

We are not only *culture-producing*, notes Bronfenbrenner (1989), but also *culture-produced*, giving voice to one of the most fundamental contemporary themes underlying the study and understanding of human development. Amazingly, more than six decades ago, Vygotsky had already adopted this theme as the very basis of his theory.

The importance of culture in Vygotsky's theory is highlighted in the distinction he makes between *elementary mental functions* and *higher mental functions*. Elementary functions are our natural, unlearned tendencies and behaviors, evident in the newborn's ability to suckle and gurgle and cry. During development, these elementary mental functions are transformed into higher mental functions, such as thinking, problem solving, and imagining, largely through the social interactions that cultures make possible. After all, culture makes language possible. And social interaction brings about the learning of language.

Language and Thought

Without language, Vygotsky explains, the child's intelligence would remain a purely practical, purely natural capacity similar to that of animals, such as apes – a capacity limited to elementary mental functions and animalistic activities like sensing and perceiving. But with language, we can interact socially. And with social interaction comes what Vygotsky describes as "upbringing and teaching," which are essential for development (Davydov, 1995). Thus, cognitive development is mainly a function of the largely verbal interaction that occurs between the child and adults. Through these interactions, the child develops language and, as a result, logical thinking.

To understand intellectual development, says Vygotsky, it is necessary to understand the relationship between thought and language. Traditionally, psychology has suggested two possibilities: One is that thought might be identical to language, a view sometimes attributed

Three Cognitive Theories

to behaviorists such as Watson, who claimed that thinking is simply internalized speech. In fact, the relationship between thinking and language seems so profound that some linguists, such as Sapir and Whorf, believed that thinking is completely determined by language (Carroll, 1997; Sapir, 1921). Another possibility is that thought and language are basically independent but influence each other.

Vygotsky proposed to examine these possibilities by looking at the vast body of literature in this area and by devising a series of investigations of children's development of language. He quickly reached the conclusion that the so-called *strong* form of the **Sapir–Whorf hypothesis** – the belief that language is essential for thought and *determines* it – is not tenable. Contrary evidence includes manifestations of thinking among nonverbal infants as well as among certain nonhuman animals. In addition, even adults highly skilled in the use of one or more languages sometimes think in terms of images or other symbols. Also, as we see in Chapter 8, we all have *implicit* memories – memories that cannot easily be verbalized, such as how to ride a bicycle or hit a golf ball, or even our "thoughtless" responses to situations that frighten or excite us. That thoughts cannot be verbalized does not deny their existence.

The other possibility – that language and thought are basically independent of each other but extremely closely intertwined – is closer to Vygotsky's conclusion. While language is an extraordinarily powerful tool for organizing and manipulating thoughts, thinking is not entirely dependent on language.

The Vygotsky Blocks Study

To study how language and thought develop in young children, Vygotsky devised a number of ingenious studies. Using what are now known as the **Vygotsky blocks**, one of these studies presents children with a set of 22 blocks, no two of which are identical. These blocks vary in shape, color, height, and size. Underneath each block is one of four labels: lag, bik, mur, and cev. None of these labels are real words; none could have been "learned" beforehand. But the labels are used systematically, so regardless of the block's color or shape, all tall, large blocks are labeled *lag*; all short, large blocks are *bik*; all short, small blocks are *cev*; and all tall, small blocks are *mur*. Children are shown the label underneath a sample block and asked to pick out all other blocks they think are the same kind. When the child has finished turning up blocks, the examiner selects one that is of a different kind and shows the child the label underneath. The child tries again and again. Typically, the experiment continues until the child solves the problem and realizes that the words are labels for blocks that are identical on two of the four dimensions: height and size.

By observing problem-solving sequences among several hundred children of different ages and by observing their use of speech in this and other investigations, Vygotsky arrived at the conclusion that speech and thought are initially independent, but that culture and language complexity are instrumental in determining the level of conceptual sophistication the child reaches. Thus, during the earliest months, there is little relationship between speech and thought; the two develop independently. But with increasing language sophistication, thought and language become progressively more closely related.

Stages of Language and Conceptual Development

In many ways, Vygotsky's description of language development anticipated important aspects of Piaget's description of stages in the development of knowledge. For example, Vygotsky describes how, as a result of social interaction, the child progresses through three stages in the development of language as well as in the development of thought (Vygotsky, 1962).

The first stage in language development is that of **social speech** (also termed *external speech*) – speech that is used mainly to influence the behavior of others. It spans the first two or so years of life. The beginning of this stage, essentially a *prespeech* period, is characterized by non-word sounds such as cries, gurgles, wails, and grunts. These sounds express simple emotions and physiological states such as hunger, anger, and contentment. Later, the child makes more repetitive and more meaningful sounds like babbles, coos, and gurgles. Still later, the first words appear. With words comes *social speech* that can be used to control the behavior of others (as in "Give me milk!") or to express simple concepts.

With the discovery of words and eventually of primitive sentences, thought becomes progressively more verbal, says Vygotsky. Words become powerful abstractions that can be used to organize and to communicate simple concepts.

The next stage, **egocentric speech**, appears between ages three and seven. During this stage, children often speak to themselves, as though in an effort to guide their own behavior rather than simply that of others. For example, in the Vygotsky block problems, young children can often be heard verbalizing the reasons for their choices, urging themselves on, or praising or chiding themselves. Egocentric speech serves as a bridge between the highly public (external) speech of the first stage and the more private (inner) speech of the third stage.

The final stage, **inner speech**, is the stage of self-talk – the stage of what William James called the "stream of consciousness" (1890). Our self-talk (our inner speech) is what tells us that we are alive and conscious. It allows us to observe and direct our thinking and, by the same token, our behavior. Inner speech is what makes all higher mental functioning possible. The block problem reveals that during this stage, the child's thinking has reached a higher level of conceptual sophistication. When children solve the problem correctly, it is because they have successfully identified and abstracted the relevant dimensions.

In summary, language starts out as a sort of tool that is highly useful in social interaction as well as in guiding personal behavior, as happens with self-talk. In time, self-talk becomes inner speech. Whereas self-talk guides the child's early actions, inner speech serves more to guide thinking. In Vygotsky's words, "Speech is initially a means of socializing with those around the child and only later, in the form of internal speech, does it become a means of thinking" (1960/1997, p. 4) (see Table 7.4).

Educational Applications: The Zone of Proximal Development and Scaffolding

Vygotsky's theory says a great deal about the forces that shape children's learning. It emphasizes the role of culture and of language in cognitive development. And it says much about the special relationship that exists between teachers and learners. Not surprisingly, it has been of profound

Table 7.4 **Vygotsky's stages of language and conceptual development**

Stage of language development	Approximate age	Characteristics and functions of speech	Conceptual development
Social	To age 3	Prespeech sounds (express emotional states like hunger or anger) Meaningful sounds; first words Simple sentences (control the behavior of others; express simple thoughts and emotions)	Thought is independent of language; speech is independent of thought.
Egocentric	Ages 3–7	Characterized by self-talk; often spoken out loud (serves to guide and control child's own behavior)	Speech is more conceptual; thought more verbal. Disorganized attempts at solving Vygotsky blocks Haphazard groupings
Inner	Age 7 onward	Silent self-talk; defines "stream-of-consciousness" (makes it possible to direct thinking and behavior; involved in all higher mental functioning)	Thinking is highly verbal. More complex groupings based on characteristics of blocks Ability to analyze and synthesize abstract dimensions

interest to educators, even leading to the development of a program, the Tools of the Mind curriculum, based squarely on the theory. This curriculum, designed for early childhood education, focuses on both cognitive skills such as self-regulation (awareness and control of cognitive processes), and academic skills relating to subjects like language and mathematics. Its instructional approach emphasizes social and verbal interaction with peers and teachers, often in a context of play (Farran, Wilson, Meador, Norvell, & Nesbitt, 2015). Thus, it uses cultural forces to bring about and shape cognitive growth, culture and social interaction being the main drivers of cognitive development in Vygotsky's system. It has proven effective in various early-education contexts (for example, Campbell, Chen, Shenoy, & Cunningham, 2018; Solomon et al., 2018).

The Tools of the Mind curriculum reflects two aspects of Vygotsky's theory that have especially clear and important educational implications: his notions of the *zone of proximal development* and of *scaffolding*.

The Zone of Proximal Development

Much of the current popularity of Vygotsky's theoretical framework has to do with his description of the relationship between learner and teacher, or between parent and child.

In Vygotsky's theoretical framework, this relationship involves teaching and learning for both parties – that is, the teacher learns from and about the child even as the child learns because of the teacher's actions. This relationship is best summarized by Vygotsky's notion of the **zone of proximal development**.

The simplest way of explaining the concept of zone of proximal development is to say that it is a sort of potential for developing. To clarify: Take Raoul and Alisha, two seven-year-olds who can both answer roughly the same questions as can average seven-year-olds and who can accomplish the same tasks in about the same amount of time. The measured intelligence of these children is about average. But suppose that when prompted and helped by a competent adult or older child, Alisha can successfully accomplish tasks and answer questions normally more characteristic of nine-year-olds, but Raoul cannot. It would be accurate to say that Alisha's *zone of proximal development* is greater than Raoul's: It spans a greater range of mental functions.

Davydov explains the zone of proximal development as follows: "What the child is initially able to do only together with adults and peers, and then can do independently lies exactly in the zone of proximal psychological development" (1995, p. 18).

Vygotsky's notion of the zone of proximal development has been extensively researched and applied in educational practice (for example, Griffin, 2017; Nguyen, 2017). It is one of two enormously important contributions to instructional theory and practice; the other is his closely related concept of *scaffolding*

Scaffolding

The task of the teacher and the parent, explained Vygotsky, is to arrange for children to engage in activities that lie within their zone of proximal development – activities that are not so easy that the child can accomplish them immediately, nor so difficult that even with help, they cannot be accomplished. How the learner can be helped is described by the concept of **scaffolding**. In education, scaffolding refers to instructional approaches designed to assist learners in their gradual progress toward greater understanding and competence.

To illustrate: If you were to build an especially tall outhouse, it might be very useful to have a scaffold upon which to stand. Initially, the scaffold would be a sturdy affair, solid and low to the ground. And as the structure rose, your scaffold would also rise, making use of its original base to remain strong and in the right location. But the scaffolding might no longer need to be so extensive and so strong. In fact, you might now be able to climb on the wall plates and rafters of your own construction, and eventually right onto the roof, with little need of the scaffolding that was so essential in the beginning.

Scaffolding for teaching/learning works in much the same way, claims Vygotsky. In the early stages of learning, scaffolding (that is, guidance and support) are often essential. A preschooler can hardly be expected to discover rapidly and easily the sounds that each letter of the alphabet represents. But in later stages, the bright and successful learner will quickly be able to pronounce brand-new words. Older learners who have learned how to learn need far less support, instead building on previous learning and well-rehearsed strategies.

By telling, demonstrating, showing, correcting, pointing, urging, providing models, explaining, procedures, asking questions, identifying objects, and so on, teachers and parents build scaffolds for children. As Moll (2014) points out, scaffolding allows children to perform tasks that would be beyond their abilities if they were working alone. Research supports Vygotsky's notion that scaffolding can increase the complexity of children's thinking and affect both learning and development positively (for example, Hebe, 2017; Veraksa, Shiyan, Shiyan, Pramling, & Pramling-Samuelsson, 2016).

Scaffolding leads to a model of learning through gradual increments, and it emphasizes the importance of interaction between educator and learner. Moreover, it highlights the importance of understanding the principles of child development and learning because the scaffolds that the educator builds need to lie within the zone of proximal development. That is, they must present the learner with challenges that lie within the range of what the child can accomplish with the help of a competent adult or older child.

Appraisal of Vygotsky's Theory

Like many other cognitive theories, Vygotsky's cultural/cognitive theory can easily be criticized on the grounds that it does not provide precise measurements or lead to many verifiable assumptions – that it is not a highly scientific theory. Interestingly, these are some of the same criticisms that Vygotsky himself directed at the Marxist psychology of his day in one of his early works (Vygotsky, 1927/1987). In particular, he was aghast at the notion that "scientific" theories were often supported mainly by references to quotations from Marx and Engels or Lenin. Vygotsky argued that psychology needed to use objective methods of investigation and that it should abandon the more intuitive, introspective approaches that were still widely popular. In addition, he rejected the reductionist approaches of the more behavioristic theories, preferring to analyze behavior in more holistic terms (Lantolf, 2003).

Some critics argue that Vygotsky's description of stages in language development is not particularly useful or accurate, and that it really is not a theory of language use (for example, Kellogg, 2017). Others point out that translations of his work have often been inaccurate and misleading (Gillen, 2000). However, many consider him to be one of the most influential and important psychologists of the twentieth century. Ironically, however, the Soviet state censored and banned his work for a 20-year period (Fraser & Yasnitsky, 2016).

Vygotsky's theory fares well relative to many of the major criteria of good theories: It is clear and understandable; it attempts to simplify complex observations relating to human learning and development; it is consistent; and it has very important practical implications, especially in child rearing and education. Also, it continues to stimulate and guide a considerable amount of research in the social sciences. But, caution Lambert and Clyde (2003), the application of Vygotsky's theoretical framework to research and education may have been marked by an excess of enthusiasm that might have blinded researchers and practitioners to the possibility that there are better ways of understanding children and of teaching. In addition, Lambert and Clyde suggest, the desire to make his theory fit current practices has sometimes led to taking his writing out of context and to making it conform to current beliefs. But that, to the extent that it is true, is the fault of those who interpret and apply the theory rather than of the theory or of the theorist.

Main Point Chapter Summary

1. Cognitive theories are mainly concerned with explaining higher mental processes (perception, information processing, decision making, and knowing), are based more on human than on animal research, and often reflect an information-processing model.

2. Bruner compares the development of the child to the evolution of the human race: from enactive (motoric) representation (corresponding to inventions that amplify motor capacities), to iconic (in the form of images) representation (corresponding to inventions that amplify the senses), and finally to symbolic representation (corresponding to inventions that amplify intellectual capacities).

3. In Bruner's system, forming concepts involves *categorization*. Concepts represent classes (categories) to which objects or ideas belong (class *extension*). A category can be thought of as a rule that specifies the attributes (qualities) that objects must possess to belong to a category (class *intension*). Information processing and decision making involve categorization. Categorizing implies the possibility of "going beyond the information given" (of making predictions about events or objects based on their category membership).

4. Coding systems are hierarchical arrangements of related categories. Higher-level categories are more generic in that they subsume more examples and are freer of specifics (that is, are less defined by small details).

5. The *prototype model* of abstraction says that people abstract highly general notions of concepts from exposure to various examples of the concept; the *exemplar model* (which is less abstract) says people remember specific, representative examples of concepts.

6. Bruner's recent writings deal with how we understand reality (*make meaning*) and how we use personal narratives to make sense of our lives. He is a strong advocate of discovery-oriented, constructivist teaching methods.

7. Piaget's theory can be viewed as an attempt to answer two biology-related questions: What are the characteristics of children that enable them to adapt to their environments? What is the most accurate and most useful way of classifying or ordering child development?

8. Assimilation and accommodation are the twin processes that underlie adaptation. To assimilate is to respond using previous learning; to accommodate is to change behavior in response to environmental demands. Play involves a preponderance of assimilation; imitation, a predominance of accommodation; and intelligent adaptation, equilibrium between the two.

9. A here-and-now understanding of the world, lack of the object concept, and absence of language characterize the beginning of the sensorimotor stage (to age two). Through interaction with the world, the infant builds a representation of reality that includes the development of language, the ability to coordinate activities, the appearance of intentionality, and the recognition of cause-and-effect relationships.

10. Errors of logic, transductive reasoning (from particular to particular), intuitive problem solving, egocentrism, reliance on perception, and absence of conservation characterize

preoperational thinking (ages 2–7). The stage nevertheless encompasses remarkable advances in language, mathematical understanding, and reasoning.

11. The appearance of the ability to conserve (reflecting logical rules of reversibility, compensation, and identity) marks the transition from preoperational to operational thought. In addition, children can now deal more adequately with classes, series, and numbers. However, their thinking is tied to what is concrete.

12. Formal operations (beginning at age 11 or 12) are defined by the appearance of propositional thinking. The child's thought processes are freed from the immediate and real and are potentially as logical as they will ever be.

13. Among the instructional implications of Piaget's theory are suggestions relating to providing for concrete activity, optimizing the difficulty of tasks, trying to understand how children think, and providing opportunities for social interaction.

14. Research suggests that sensorimotor children may be more advanced than Piaget suspected, that the sequence he described for cognitive development is relatively accurate, and that formal operations may not be generally characteristic of adolescence or adulthood. It is nevertheless a highly influential theory that has stimulated a tremendous amount of research and writing.

15. Vygotsky's cultural/cognitive theory stresses the importance of culture and of its principal invention: language. Culture, and especially language, removes us from a lower animal-like realm of reflex and reaction and makes higher mental processes (thinking) possible. Children progress through three stages in their learning of language: social (external) speech (before age three) used mainly to control the behavior of others; egocentric speech (ages three to seven), which is often spoken out loud but is geared toward directing one's own behavior; and inner speech (after age seven), which is "stream of consciousness" self-talk.

16. Thought and language are initially independent. The infant is characterized by nonverbal thought and nonconceptual speech. Thought becomes progressively more verbal as the child develops.

17. Vygotsky's zone of proximal development is the child's potential for development, defined by what the child cannot initially accomplish alone but is capable of with the help of competent others. Scaffolding describes an interactive teaching or learning technique in which educators or parents provide learners with various forms of support designed to help them progress gradually.

8 Learning and Memory

CHAPTER OUTLINE

This Chapter	288
Objectives	289
Memory Metaphors	289
What Is Memory?	290
Exceptional Memories	290
Implicit Memories	291
Storage and Retrieval	292
Early Memory Research	292
Modal Model of Memory	294
Sensory Memory	295
Working (Short-Term) Memory	296
Levels of Processing	301
Long-Term Memory (LTM)	302
Working and Long-Term Memory Compared	305
Categories of Long-Term Memory	306
Explicit (Declarative) and Implicit (Nondeclarative) Memory	306
Declarative Memories	307
Models of Declarative Long-Term Memory	308
Physiology of Memory	311
The Engram	311
Brain Imaging: ERPs and ERFs	312
Summary of Modal Models of Memory	315
Why We Forget	315
Brain Injury	315
Fading Theory	316
Distortion Theory	317
Repression Theory and False Memories	317
Interference Theory	318
Retrieval-Cue Failure	319
Learning and Remembering: Educational Applications	319
What Works in Education	320
How Important are Teachers?	321
Main Point Chapter Summary	323

The Right Honorable gentleman is indebted to his memory for his jests and to his imagination for his facts.

Richard Brinsley Sheridan (in *Sheridaniana*; a speech in reply to Mr. Dundas)

It is a poor sort of memory that only works backwards.

Lewis Carroll (in *Through the Looking-Glass, and What Alice Found There*)

Mrs. Gribbin said that we would climb the rock face today, that my fear of heights wasn't an issue, that she would show me where to put each foot and each hand, that she would guide me as might a mother her child. She refused my protests, insisting that Chapter 8 would only be told from above the land.

We left at dawn before the sun had warmed the air. Schrödinger lay curled on the sunny side of the largest of the birch trees, watching as we inched our way up the smooth face. Within minutes, my hands were slick with sweat, my muscles strained with fear. The old lady said I should pay attention, do exactly what she did, put my hands and my feet in the holds she found, trust in the rope that joined us like an umbilical cord. She explained that trust is a thought, a conclusion. She said that I need only believe it, and it would be mine.

But I couldn't stifle my dread, and when I had not yet reached as high as the youngest of the birch, I could climb no more, and Old Lady Gribbin lowered me to the ground, dropping the rope, useless, like a dead snake at my feet. When I turned to sit weakly against the birch, the cat rose and left, and when I looked up again at the old lady climbing, I saw that the cat waited for her at the very top, although it was not possible that he would have arrived so soon.

The old lady climbed swiftly like some hairless simian, never resting, until she stood next to Schrödinger, and she motioned to my astonishment that I should now record her words and she began to shout very loudly, as though enjoying that she needed to do so, the words of Chapter 8. Most of them are very clear on the recording.

Here's what she bellowed from that great height while I listened through the early morning, too far away to ask questions.

THIS CHAPTER

My body knows how to climb, *she yelled.* It knows this in its muscles and tendons and maybe elsewhere, but it is knowledge that cannot easily be put into words. That is why I cannot tell you how to climb or how to ride a unicycle. Memories for complex learned actions like these are implicit; they cannot easily be made explicit. In contrast, I can easily describe what I remember of what I did last night.

This chapter looks at the differences between memories that are implicit and those that are explicit. It explores the astonishing power of human memory, and it also recognizes its imperfections and limitations. As Johnson declared, "When put on the witness stand, we can swear before God that we will tell the truth, the whole truth, and nothing but the truth. But the best we can really do is read out what is left of our memories, recollections that have been inevitably altered by time" (1992, p. 233).

OBJECTIVES

Let your readers know, *said Mrs. Gribbin*, that they will understand what this means after they have read and studied this chapter – that is, if they remember it. And if their memory serves them well, they will then be able to weave fascinating tales dealing with:

- sensory, working, and long-term memory;
- flashbulb memories;
- two kinds of long-term memory;
- the Jennifer Aniston neuron;
- event-related activity in the brain;
- theories of forgetting;
- the most effective techniques for learning and remembering.

They will also have a clearer idea of what works in education.

MEMORY METAPHORS

As I have noted on a number of occasions, *Old Lady Gribbin's voice rang out from her lofty perch*, cognitive psychology is a psychology of metaphors. It seeks to understand the grand complexities of human cognitive functioning not so much by uncovering its precise mechanics and exposing its structures and functions but by inventing the most compelling and the most useful metaphors to describe it. In the end, however, the value of the metaphor will be judged not only by how well it reflects the facts but also by how well it explains and how useful it is for making predictions. Thus, the search for metaphors is premised on the results of scientific investigation. If psychology cannot trust its facts, how can it trust its metaphors?

It bears repeating that the metaphors of cognitive topics such as memory are not the moving images of literature. They are nothing more than models – often simple models. What they say is not "Attention is a damsel with flowers up her pointy nose" or "Memory is the proboscis of an ancient, wrinkled elephant." Rather, the metaphors of cognitive psychology are prosaic metaphors. They say only that humans behave "as though" or "as if," and they describe what it is that humans behave "as if." These, explain Oswick, Keenoy, and Grant (2002), are the comfortable metaphors of similarity. They elaborate and explain by emphasizing likenesses.

Over the years, an enormous number of different metaphors have been used to describe memory – perhaps testimony to how difficult a concept it is and how uncertain psychologists have been of their models. For example, the index to Draaisma's *Metaphors of Memory* (2000) lists some 43 different memory metaphors. Memory, different thinkers have assured us, is like an abbey with many rooms. Or maybe it is more like a book with many pages of information, table of contents, and index. Or perhaps it resembles a library or a mirror, a loom, a palace, a camera, a purse, a treasure chest, a vault, a wine cellar . . . and on and on (p. 240). Recently, of course, computer metaphors have become increasingly popular. After all, computers allow storage and retrieval, and these are two of the essential features of memory. But as we see in this

Learning and Memory

chapter, the computer metaphor, and indeed all our common metaphors, does little justice to something as rich and as complex as is human memory.

What Is Memory?

It is very difficult to separate attention, memory, and learning, so closely linked are they. Learning is a change in behavior that results from experience, memory is the effect of experience, and both are facilitated by attention. Clearly, there will be no evidence of learning without something having happened in memory; by the same token, something happening in memory implies learning. Studying memory is, in effect, another way of studying learning.

Still, there is far from unanimous agreement among psychologists about what memory is and how it should be studied. One simple definition of **memory** is this: Memory is the ability to retain and retrieve recollections of past events or experiences or acquired information. From cognitive psychology's point of view, memory is the information-processing system involved in encoding, storing, and retrieving information.

But, as Quiroga points out, these definitions are too narrow. In his words, "Not only does [memory] underlie our ability to think at all, it defines the content of our experiences and how we preserve them for years to come. Memory makes us who we are" (2017, p. 3). When our memories are gone, either because we have died or had some system catastrophe (like dementia or severe brain injury), will we still be us, the "me" of our consciousness?

Exceptional Memories

Leonard Euler, reports Draaisma (2000), was both a child prodigy and a mathematical genius. He had apparently memorized *The Iliad* (more than 15,000 lines) and could recite it flawlessly until the day he died. They say that one night when he could not sleep, he worked out the first six powers for numbers 0 through 99, generating a mental table of 600 numbers that he could read off at will weeks later. He seemed to remember everything that he heard or read, so even though he was completely blind for the last 15 years of his life, this hardly affected his work. He had a huge slate-covered table installed in the middle of his workroom, and he walked around this table, writing down formulas and ideas that his students, including his sons and grandsons, organized, wrote, and read to him. The result was that during the 15 years of his blindness, he published an astonishing 355 scientific papers, mostly in mathematics and applied science.

But not all people with remarkable memories are so well adjusted and so productive. Some extraordinary memories may be quite trivial and useless. For example, there is the so-called **idiot savant** – the mentally limited person who possesses a remarkable but highly specific talent, such as the guy who could watch a freight train pass by and memorize all the serial numbers on the boxcars.

There is also the well-documented case of a man known to us only as S, described by Luria (1968). S was in most ways an ordinary man who had not been very successful as a musician or as a journalist but who had an astounding memory. On one occasion, Luria presented S with an

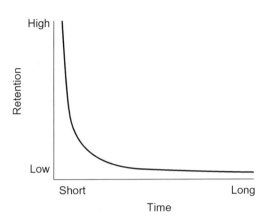

Figure 8.1 An idealized memory curve, similar to some generated by Ebbinghaus. The curve indicates that most of what is forgotten is lost very quickly after learning. Longer-term retention tends to be relatively stable.

array of 50 numbers arranged in four columns (with only two numbers in the last row). After examining the table for three minutes, S reproduced the numbers flawlessly in 40 seconds, reciting rows and columns in any order when so instructed. And one of the absolutely remarkable things about his memory was not so much that he could memorize numbers so quickly but that he could remember them without error as much as 16 years later without having been asked to remember them once in the interim. The only difference was that when asked to recall complex arrays months or years after learning them, he needed a few minutes to "revive" the memory. He would usually sit with his eyes closed, Luria tells us, and he might comment, "Yes, yes . . .. This was a series you gave me once when we were in your apartment . . .. You were sitting at the table and I in the rocking chair . . .. You were wearing a gray suit and you looked at me like this . . .. Now, then, I can see you saying . . ." (1968, p. 12).

Most memories are not so phenomenal, as is well illustrated by "memory curves" that represent the results of some of the first experiments on memory, many of which were carried out by pioneering memory researcher Ebbinghaus (1885). Figure 8.1 shows an idealized summary of these curves. The most striking thing these early memory curves indicate is that people tend to forget most of what they learn almost immediately after learning it. In Ebbinghaus's original investigations, subjects were typically asked to learn a list of nonsense syllables – meaningless combinations of letters, such as *kiv*, *gur*, or *lev*. Even though these subjects could successfully recall the syllables immediately after learning them, within about 20 minutes they had usually forgotten more than 40 percent of them; within an hour, more than half had been forgotten. However, most of the nonsense syllables that were remembered for half a day could still be recalled a month later. Hence, although the bulk of what people learn (at least with respect to meaningless items) tends to be forgotten very quickly, some information is retained over long periods.

Implicit Memories

In everyday speech, the term *memory* refers to the availability of information and implies being able to retrieve previously acquired skills or information. It clearly presupposes learning. The computer metaphor leads naturally to the notion that to remember is to be able to retrieve from storage and that if a memory is to influence behavior, it has to be retrievable. But this is not so. There are numerous examples of what is sometimes termed *implicit memory* (or *unconscious memory*) – past learning that cannot be remembered consciously but that can nevertheless affect later behavior. This happens, for example, when someone rapidly relearns a long-unused and apparently forgotten poem. Similarly, some people with amnesia know all sorts of things that they cannot remember having learned. Current models of memory take into consideration different kinds of memory as well as different ways of storing memories and of working with them.

Storage and Retrieval

Studies of amnesiacs, and experiences in our own daily lives, make it clear that some stored experiences may not be retrievable. Put another way, there are often things you *know* that you cannot quite *remember*. Remembering, in the sense of *recollecting*, says Tulving (1989), is not quite the same thing as knowing. He explains that trees with their growth rings, just like musical recordings and memory sticks, have memory; that is, they have a *record* of the past. But they remember nothing.

To clarify these concepts, Tulving (2002) suggests that psychologists need to pay attention to the two distinct aspects of memory: *storage* and *retrieval*. What trees and electronic memory devices have is storage of certain effects; what humans have is storage and retrieval. Being able to retrieve presupposes storage because things that have not been stored (learned) cannot be recalled. However, not all that has been stored can be retrieved. And evidence from studies that use **functional magnetic resonance imaging (fMRI)** to pinpoint brain activity during storage and retrieval tasks suggests that different parts of the brain may be involved in storage and retrieval. We look more closely at the role of the brain in memory later in this chapter.

Forgetting

If the coin of learning has two sides, memory is one side, and forgetting is the other. Like memory, forgetting relates to both storage and retrieval. Thus, forgetting, which implies a loss of memory, might involve either an inability to retrieve or an actual change in or loss of the physiological effects of experience. Or perhaps it can involve both.

Early Memory Research

It can be said that a person remembers if behavior or responses reflect previous learning, whether or not the person remembers the learning consciously. If Ralph stays away from snakes because he had a frightening experience with one when he was three, it is accurate to say that this early snake experience changed his behavior and that he learned something about snakes because of that experience. That he no longer consciously recalls anything about the experience does not contradict that fact. However, most early studies of memory dealt only with conscious retrieval: They simply looked at people's ability or inability to reproduce items of information that were presented to them.

Studies of this kind can sometimes lead to unclear results if participants have learned related things previously. One way of getting around this problem is to use material that is entirely new

Table 8.1 Testing retroactive interference

Experimental group (A)		Control group (B)
Time sequence	1. Learn X	1. Learn X
	2. Learn Y	2. Do unrelated things
	3. Recall X	3. Recall X

Note: Lower scores of group A relative to group B indicate the extent to which learning Y has interfered with the recall of X.

Table 8.2 Testing proactive interference

Experimental group (A)		Control group (B)
Time sequence	1. Learn X	1. Do unrelated things
	2. Learn Y	2. Learn Y
	3. Recall Y	3. Recall Y

Note: Lower scores of group A compared with group B indicate the extent to which X has interfered with Y.

for all learners. Ebbinghaus (1885) solved the problem by inventing more than 600 **nonsense syllables** – arrangements of letters that have a clear phonetic sound but no meaning, like *gev*, *kor*, *rel*, and so on. For a number of years, he sat faithfully at his desk at periodic intervals, memorizing lists of nonsense syllables and testing his retention of them. The plotted results of these experiments, with Ebbinghaus as the sole subject, provided the first *memory curves* – graphical portrayals of how people learn and forget. As illustrated in Figure 8.1, these curves show that the bulk of what is forgotten is lost very rapidly. At the same time, what is retained for a longer period (say, 10 days) is less likely to be forgotten even after a much longer passage of time (for example, 40 days or sometimes even 40 years).

Subsequent early research on memory continued to make extensive use of nonsense syllables in a variety of experimental situations. Sometimes, these syllables were paired with other syllables, or meaningful words were paired with other words, and subjects were required to learn what went with what. This is called *paired-associate learning*. At other times, subjects were asked to learn sequences of stimuli (*serial learning*).

In numerous studies, subjects learned two different sets of material and were then asked to recall one or the other in an attempt to determine whether recall would be interfered with. It often was. When earlier learning interferes with the recollection of subsequently learned material, **proactive interference** is said to have occurred (*proactive* meaning moving ahead in time). When subsequent learning reduces recall of material that has been learned earlier, **retroactive interference** is said to take place (see Tables 8.1 and 8.2). If you half-learn a

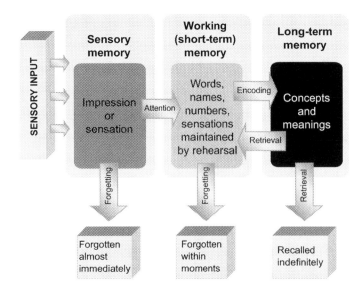

Figure 8.2 A widely used model of human memory. Note that these three components of memory do not refer to three different locations in the brain or other parts of the nervous system but, rather, refer to how we classify memory storage. The goal of teaching is to bring about changes in long-term memory. From Lefrançois, G. R. (2016). *Psychology: The Human Puzzle* (2nd ed.). San Diego, CA: Bridgepoint Education, Fig. 6.1. Used by permission.

language, such as French, and later on try to learn a related language, such as Spanish, you might well find yourself recalling French words when searching for newly learned Spanish words (proactive interference). Later, when you have mastered Spanish, you might find it very difficult to remember some of the French words you previously knew (retroactive interference).

MODAL MODEL OF MEMORY

One important contribution of early studies of memory, in addition to their many isolated findings, takes the form of several closely related models of human remembering. The best known of these, first proposed by Atkinson and Shiffrin (1968), is the **modal model of memory** (in this context, *modal* means the most widely accepted). This model distinguishes between *working* (or *short-term*) and *long-term* memory as well as between a third component relating to sensation, called *sensory* memory (also called the *sensory register*). The main differences between these three stages of memory has to do with (a) the amount of information each can hold, (b) how long they can hold material in storage, and (c) their most important functions. The modal model is summarized in Figure 8.2.

Keep in mind that this model, like most psychological models, is a metaphor. As such, it probably says as much about the ways psychologists choose to investigate and talk about memory as it does about memory itself. In brief, there is not a particular "box" or structure in human brains that corresponds to working (short term) memory and another that corresponds to long-term memory. These are not physical structures but abstractions.[1] These abstractions allow researchers to make inferences about actual structures and functions in the brain.

---

[1] Do you see what I mean about metaphors? Old Lady Gribbin shouted from the top of the rock face, throwing her arms out wide almost as if she were about to break into a sermon – or about to leap into space and plunge or glide down to where I stood. But she had neither of those acts in mind. Do you see, she asked rhetorically, how this model of memory is one more example of how selective humans have been in their attempts to explain what's inside the "black box" and how

Sensory Memory

When we are awake and conscious, our sensory systems (vision, hearing, taste, touch, smell) are constantly bombarded by an overwhelmingly wide range of stimulation. If you *consciously* think about it, at this very moment, you can sense the clothing on your body. You can also hear all kinds of ambient noises; perhaps you can smell some of the aromatic molecules that surround you; you might even taste the remnants of your last meal. And if you look around, you will see that there are an enormous number and variety of shapes and colors around you. If you were constantly conscious of all these sensations, you might be completely overwhelmed. But the fact is that you are aware of only a very limited number of these potential sensations, and most of them are fleeting. They *flit* from your memory before you become aware of them.

Sensory memory is a term for the immediate, *unconscious* effects of stimuli. One of the interesting and useful features of sensory memory is that although it refers to fleeting and unconscious effects of sensory input, there is convincing evidence that sensory impressions have an effect even when we are not aware of them. This phenomenon is easily demonstrated in crowded social situations where groups of individuals carry on conversations while they apparently remain oblivious to other nearby conversations. But if someone in one conversation mentions a topic of vital interest to someone in another conversation, such as their name, for example, their attention might switch immediately. Because this characteristic of sensory memory is a common occurrence in social gatherings, it is labeled the **cocktail party phenomenon**.

The cocktail party phenomenon seems a clear indication that even sensory impressions to which the individual is not paying attention do have at least a momentary effect. Early investigations of the cocktail party phenomenon corroborated this. In a typical study, stereo headphones are used to feed different messages to each of a subject's ears. Under these conditions, most subjects are easily able to listen to either ear simply by intending to do so. In a variation of this study, Broadbent (1952) had subjects repeat everything they heard in one ear as they heard it – a process called *shadowing*. Using this approach, Broadbent discovered that subjects do not remember what goes on in their other ear. When the language was changed from English to German in the unattended ear, the subject remained completely unaware of it. Moray (1959) found that even if the same word were repeated as many as 35 times, the subject was not able to remember having heard it. Strikingly, however, if the subject's name was said a single time, that was usually enough to cause a shift in attention. It seems clear that sensory events have some momentary effect even when they are not being attended to. These effects define what is meant by sensory memory.

---

they've been guided by the metaphor of the day. For example, in the case of memory, for a long time, their explanations were shaped by a metaphor that saw the human mind as some sort of filing cabinet that slipped items of information into logically ordered files, many of which were later lost. Another metaphor viewed the human mind as a kind of motion picture camera that makes a continuous record of everything it experiences. And this more current computing metaphor pictures human memory as an information-processing system whose storage is determined by the nature of the processing it does.

The "cocktail party" phenomenon

More recent research on the cocktail party phenomenon has typically used recordings of brain activity in response to visual and auditory stimulation, often using noninvasive techniques such as *magnetoencephalography* (for example, Bradley, Joyce, & Garcia-Larria, 2016; Ding & Simon, 2012).

Because the effects of sensory stimulation remain available for a very brief period of time, almost like an echo, Neisser (1976) called it *echoic* (for auditory stimuli) or *iconic* (for visual stimuli). Echoic memory is easily illustrated: If someone were to read you a long list of numbers in an unusually dry monotone and then ask you to repeat the numbers 10 seconds later, you would probably not remember very many, if any. But if the reading were suddenly interrupted and you were asked, "What was the last number?" you might well respond correctly. It is as though the number is still there as a sort of echo that will disappear within a fraction of a second if it is not attended to.

Research that monitors brain activity, reviewed later in this chapter, indicates that, except for olfaction (which is connected directly to the amygdala and other parts of the brain), signals relating to incoming sensory stimulation involve neural relays that first go to the thalamus. It appears that it is the thalamus (a tiny structure at the base of the brain) that then monitors these incoming signals and in just a few milliseconds, determines, on the basis of past experience, whether this signal is important enough to be attended to. The vast majority of sensory signals, explains Sousa (2017) are of little consequence and we are never consciously aware of them.

Working (Short-Term) Memory

The main function of sensory memory is to keep sensory impressions momentarily available for further processing. Note that the emphasis is on *momentarily*. In order for impressions to be available for longer periods of time, the individual has to pay attention.

So, another way of looking at sensory memory is to say that it precedes **attention** (conscious awareness) – that, in other words, it is something that occurs without the individual being aware of it occurring. But when the thalamus has determined that a particular stimulus is important, it slips into a sort of *temporary* memory called **working memory** (or **short-term memory**).

Sensory memory refers to a phenomenon that lasts milliseconds; working memory is a phenomenon that lasts seconds, not hours or even minutes. Specifically, working (or short-term) memory refers to the awareness and recall of items that will no longer be available as soon as the individual stops rehearsing them.

Working memory is what makes it possible for Harvey to look at a phone number and then key it in without having to look at the second digit after keying the first, at the third after inputting the second, and so on. That he forgets the number as soon as he has finished inputting it and that he has to look it up once more if he needs to call again are also characteristics of working memory. Long-term memory (LTM) is what would be involved if Harvey decided he might need to use the number again and "memorized" it. It would also be involved if the symmetry and poetry of the number so moved him that he found himself remembering it the next day.

A Classical Study of Working Memory

Among the most common early techniques for studying working memory was one developed by Peterson and Peterson (1959) in which participants are presented with a single nonsense syllable and then asked to recall it. Immediate recall is typically close to 100 percent. But greater delay between the presentation of the word and its recall results in lower retention, the extent of which depends on the participant's intervening activities. Those who are not required to do anything and who know they will be asked to recall the syllable usually rehearse it to make sure they can remember it. But those who are asked to engage in some unrelated activity beginning immediately after presentation of the nonsense syllable (such as counting backward in time to a metronome), recall far less well. For example, in the Peterson and Peterson (1959) study, subjects recalled 80 percent of the syllables correctly when given three seconds to rehearse them but only 60 percent of them when given no opportunity to rehearse them. Eighteen seconds after the stimuli had been presented, subjects still remembered 33 percent of them if they had been given an opportunity to rehearse for three seconds, but only 14 percent of the syllables when given no opportunity to rehearse (see Figure 8.3).

Limited Capacity

Working memory refers to the brief availability of a small number of items. This availability begins to deteriorate within seconds and is usually completely gone within 20 seconds in the absence of rehearsal. Short-term memory is what makes it possible for readers to "keep in mind" the words that they are currently reading (or writing) long enough to make sense of the sentence. Put another way, short-term memory is what is conscious at any given time. As Baddeley (2002) explains, it is a sort of "scratch pad" for thinking.

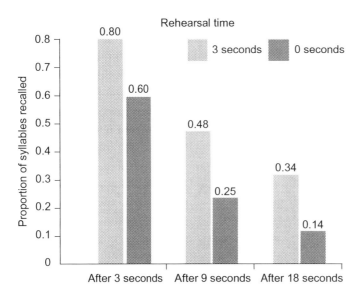

Figure 8.3 Proportion of nonsense syllables recalled correctly when subjects were given no time for rehearsal, compared with those allowed to rehearse for 3 seconds. From Peterson, L. R. & Peterson, M. J. (1959) "Short-term retention of individual verbal items," In the *Journal of Experimental Psychology*, vol. 58, p. 197. Copyright © 1959 by the American Psychological Association. Reprinted by permission of the American Psychological Association.

Following his investigations of short-term memory, Miller (1956) concluded that the average adult's working memory capacity is seven plus or minus two items. According to Miller, it is as though there are about seven slots in working memory (plus or minus two). When these are filled, there is no room for more until one or more of the slots are again emptied; this happens within seconds.

Working memory capacity for younger children is less than seven. Indications are that for most children, adult-like capacity is reached at around age seven (Plebanek & Sloutsky, 2018). Not surprisingly, with advancing age, there is often a reduction in working memory capacity (Teng et al., 2018).

Chunking

The limited capacity of short-term memory is not a great problem for most people, says Miller (1956), because the items that fill each of these slots do not have to be unitary (a digit or a letter, for example). Instead, they might be composed of a **chunking** of items. Thus, the short-term memory slots might be filled with seven letters or with seven words. The seven words represent chunks of information that are far more economical (and probably more meaningful) than seven unrelated letters. Miller explains chunking by making an analogy to a change purse that can hold only seven pieces of money (here is the "change purse" memory metaphor). If there are seven pennies in the purse, it will be full; however, it could have held seven quarters or seven dollars – or even seven gold coins.

Baddeley's Model of Working Memory

Working memory is the stage of memory that describes immediate awareness or attention. During this stage, information is kept in mind long enough to make sense of sequences of words, to solve problems, to make decisions, or to do mundane things such as dial telephone numbers.

This is why Baddeley and Hitch (1974; Baddeley, 2000) label short-term memory, *working memory*. The label describes the *function* of this level of memory rather than simply its duration.

Baddeley's model of working memory is designed to describe what happens in short-term memory. Put another way, it describes our immediate *consciousness* – what we are aware of (what we are thinking). In a sense, it attempts to clarify the processes involved in paying attention, in learning, and in remembering.

Just how does working memory work? Baddeley proposes an intriguing model (Baddeley, 2007; Baddeley & Hitch, 1974). First, he explains, there must be a **central executive system** – a sort of controlling system to supervise and direct the workings of memory. Its most important functions are (1) to regulate the flow of information from sensory storage (that is, to bring information into conscious attention); (2) to process information for longer-term storage; and (3) to retrieve information from long-term storage (Baddeley, 1997, 2007). In a sense, it supervises and controls our ongoing, conscious cognitive processing.

Second, what we know about the workings of short-term memory suggests that there must also be at least two systems to maintain verbal and visual/spatial information in immediate consciousness. These are referred to as *slave systems* because of their relationship to the central executive system. The two slave systems are the **phonological loop** and the **visual-spatial sketch pad**. The phonological loop maintains verbal information, such as words or numbers, and is important in learning things such as new words. The visual-spatial sketch pad is concerned with processing material that is primarily visual or spatial. The main function of the slave systems is to maintain information so it remains available to working memory.

Finally, Baddeley supposes that there must be some sort of *buffer* between short- and long-term memory as well as between the two slave systems. This buffer would be capable of integrating information from the two slave systems and perhaps other information not covered by these systems (for example, musical information) to create a coherent *episode*. It would also be capable of remembering information temporarily. This system is labeled the **episodic buffer** (see Figure 8.4).

What the Baddeley model says, in effect, is that the slave systems maintain (as a sort of loop) the effects of sensory stimulation so the central executive might have access to them. In the meantime, the episodic buffer organizes this information into a form that makes sense and that can be processed for long-term memory and retrieval. Note that in this model, one important function of the central processor is to transfer material into long-term storage as well as to retrieve from storage.

Research on Working Memory

An enormous amount of research on working memory has been published in very recent years. For example, a search of the main psychology database, psycINFO, using the phrase *working memory* as a key word, lists an astonishing 11,234 different articles published in just the past five years.[2]

---

[2] You might suggest to your more agile-brained readers who dream of graduate degrees, shouted Old Lady Gribbin from the cliff top, that there are thousands of ideas for their theses and dissertations lurking in these publications. I said I would.

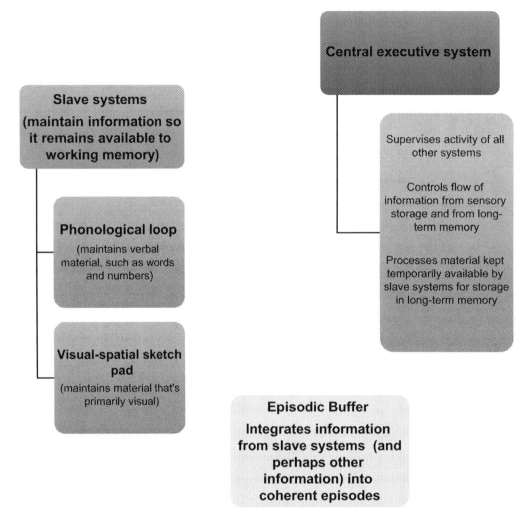

Figure 8.4 A representation of Baddeley's model of working memory. Information that we remember must first be sensed and then must somehow be held on to and processed if it is to be transferred to long-term memory. Baddeley's model describes how memory functions. The central executive system supervises activity in working memory, controls the flow of information from sensory storage and from long-term memory, and processes it for long-term storage. The slave systems maintain information so it is available for processing. The episodic buffer integrates information from the slave systems into coherent episodes. Adapted from Lefrançois, G. R. (2016). *Psychology: The Human Puzzle* (2nd ed.). San Diego, CA: Bridgepoint Education, Fig. 6.3. Used by permission.

What Baddeley's model of working memory suggests is that there are at least two different and independent types of processing available in working memory. Experimental evidence that this might be so comes from studies using a dual-task paradigm devised by Baddeley and his associates. For example, subjects might be asked to learn a list of words that are being presented visually (a *visual-spatial sketch pad* task) while retaining a sequence of six or fewer numbers presented aurally (a *phonological loop* task). One might expect that there would be tremendous interference between these tasks. But that there is typically only minor interference is strong evidence, suggests Baddeley (2007), that the slave systems are independent.

Additional evidence that the slave systems represent distinct processes comes from studies that look at brain activity while subjects are engaged in memory tasks. These studies indicate that distinctly different regions of the brain are involved in the different aspects of working memory (Sousa, 2017; Swanson, Kudo, & Van Horn, 2018).

The importance of working memory is highlighted by a large number of studies that indicate that problems in visual or verbal attention – that is, problems related to maintaining visual and verbal material in consciousness – may underlie problems in mathematics (Charest-Girard & Parent, 2018) and in speech (Schulze, Vargha-Khadem, & Mishkin, 2018). They might also be manifested in memory disorders such as Alzheimer's disease and other forms of dementia (Poos, Jiskoot, Papma, van Swieten, & van den Berg, 2018; Yin, Fang, & Zhang, 2016), as well as in attention disorders such as ADHD (Maehler & Schuchardt, 2016).

Levels of Processing

Craik and Lockhart (1972) suggest that the short-term duration of working memory is often a matter of how and to what extent information is processed or, in their words, **level of processing**. For example, a simple stimulus such as a word might be processed relative to its physical appearance. This is a relatively low level of processing referred to as *orthographic* or simply *visual*. Alternatively, a word might be processed by its sound (*phonological processing*), which is a somewhat deeper level of processing. Or it might be processed for its meaning (*semantic processing*), the deepest level of processing.

Craik (2002) devised experiments in which subjects were given word analysis tasks that required them to process words at different levels, but they didn't know they would be required to remember the words later. For example, subjects might be asked whether a word was in capital letters (shallowest processing: orthographic); whether it rhymed with another word (intermediate processing: phonological); or whether it meant the same thing as another word (deepest level of processing: semantic). Not surprisingly, the proportion of words later recognized by participants increased with depth of processing. These findings were later confirmed by Rose, Myerson, Roediger, and Hale (2010), who found that level of processing had little effect on tests of working memory but that semantic processing significantly improves long-term memory.

In the sensory register, notes Craik, no processing occurs. With deeper processing (involving activities such as analysis, organization, and recognition of meaning), material is transferred to long-term memory and hence is not lost immediately. Forgetting in working memory is thus presumed to result from lower levels of processing (Cermak & Craik, 1979). However, loss of immediate awareness of items in working memory is often not a problem. After all, the function of short-term memory is simply to retain information for only as long as it is useful and then to discard it. If people did not function this way, it is likely that their memories would be cluttered with all sorts of useless information, and retrieval might be far more difficult than it now is.

Loss of material from working memory becomes a significant problem in those cases when disease, injury, or aging shortens short-term memory to the point that ongoing functioning suffers. That is essentially what happens when people forget what they were going to say after they have started to say it. Or what they were going to write next . . .

Long-Term Memory (LTM)

Before the 1950s, most research on memory dealt not with the transitory and unstable recollections of working memory but with the more stable and, by definition, longer-lasting remembrances of **long-term memory (LTM)**. Psychologists did not begin to recognize the usefulness of distinguishing between working (*short-term*) and long-term memory until the mid-1950s.

Two other changes in memory research have been (a) a shift from the use of nonsense syllables and paired associates to the use of meaningful material and (b) a change in emphasis from measuring memory span and the effects of interference to examining models for long-term storage and retrieval.

All that a person can remember that has not just now occurred composes long-term memory. Thus, all that is retained of educational experiences, a complete working knowledge of language, and all stable information about the world are in long-term memory. Among the characteristics of long-term memory, four are especially important.

1. Long-Term Memory Is Highly Stable

Much of what you remember today and tomorrow you will also remember next week and perhaps even next year. The faces and other perceptual patterns you recognize today you will also recognize tomorrow. (Interestingly, however, research suggests that you are more likely to remember angry faces than happy ones [Tay & Yang, 2017]). And the general information you have retained to date from your schooling will also in all likelihood be retained next month.

Some recollections, such as those having to do with smells, are astonishingly resistant to the passage of time and provide powerful cues for a large variety of recollections (Hacklander & Bermeitinger, 2017). In fact, research reveals that olfactory cues are more effective than visual cues in activating autobiographical memories (de Bruijn & Bender, 2018). Thus, the sight of a stove identical to your grandmother's is less likely to evoke memories of her kitchen than is the smell of her baked beans.

Memory for odors is unique in that it is independent from memory for verbal or visual information and is highly resistant to interference. For example, in an intriguing study, Goldman and Seamon (1992) bottled 14 odors, half of them associated with childhood (for example, crayon shavings, Play-Doh, finger paints, bubble soap) and the other half partially or entirely associated with adulthood (chocolate, popcorn, soap shavings, cigarette tobacco). Adults correctly identified about 90 percent of recent odors and more than three-quarters of sometimes very distant odors (see Figure 8.5). "Significant memory for odor–name associations remains even over very long recall intervals," Goldman and Seamon conclude, "much longer than any tested to date" (1992, p. 562).

2. Long-Term Memory Is Generative

Memory, explain Mahr and Csibra (2018), "should not be equated with beliefs about the past. Instead, empirical findings suggest that the contents of human episodic memory are often

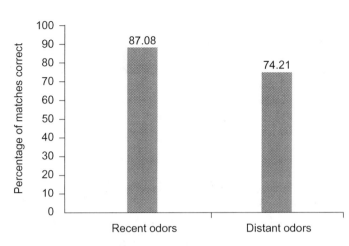

Figure 8.5 Accuracy of memory for recent and distant odors. In this study, thirty 17–22-year-old students correctly matched odors with names at least two out of three times. Based on "Very Long-Term Memory for Odors: Retention of Odor–Name Associations," by W. P. Goldman and J. G. Seamon, 1992. In the *American Journal of Psychology*, 105, pp. 549–563 (Table 1, p. 553). © 1992 by the Board of Trustees of the University of Illinois. Used with permission of the University of Illinois Press.

constructed in the service of the explicit justification of such beliefs" (p. 1). Preconceived notions and beliefs about what goes with what, sometimes termed *schemata* or *scripts*, profoundly influence memories. These schemata may lead people to remember things that have never happened and to generate rather than reproduce. For example, Johnson, Bransford, and Solomon showed subjects this passage (1973, p. 203):

> John was trying to fix the birdhouse. He was pounding the nail when his father came out to watch him and to help him do the work.

Later, subjects were shown the previous two sentences along with several others, one of which was the following:

> John was using the hammer to fix the birdhouse when his father came out to watch and to help him do the work.

Most subjects were more convinced that they had seen this sentence rather than either of the sentences they had actually seen. Why? Because, say Johnson and associates, although the word *hammer* was not mentioned in either of the first two sentences, subjects recalled the idea of the sentences clearly, and based on their knowledge that hammers are what is used to pound nails, they generated the word into their recollections.

That memory tends to be highly generative (or constructive) has especially important implications in judicial systems that tend to rely heavily on human testimony. For example, as we see later, investigations show that under a variety of circumstances, witnesses can be expected to remember incorrectly or to remember events that have not occurred (Laney & Loftus, 2010; Loftus, Feldman & Dashiell, 1995).

3. Understanding Influences Long-Term Memory

Long-term memory is also influenced by what we understand and by our intentions. As Linderholm (2006) points out, we read and remember very differently depending on the purposes for which we read. Reading a novel for enjoyment is quite different from reading

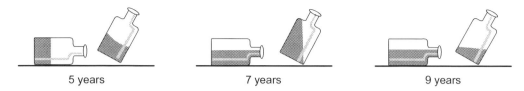

Figure 8.6 Children's drawings of water lines. Note how the children do not draw what they have seen and remember. They draw the water line correctly only when they understand the principle that water tends to remain level.

the same novel for an English class. In the second case, we modify our strategies. We analyze, we review, we think about; in short, we process what we read at a very different level. But, says Linderholm, if we have learned to read in order to *memorize* the content rather than to understand it, we might struggle mightily when asked to generalize what we have learned.

What people remember is often a meaning – a central idea. We don't recall the detail so much as the *gist*, explain Koriat, Goldsmith, and Pansky (2000). For example, when Isaac hears a story and then repeats it, typically what he remembers of it is its general "drift" – its setting and plot. When he repeats the story, he does not remember each of the sentences, pauses, and gestures of the original storyteller. Instead, he generates his own based on his understanding of the story.

The relationship between understanding and long-term memory is illustrated in a study by Piaget and Inhelder (1956) in which young children are asked to draw lines representing the level of water in tilted jars. Although all children have seen fluids in tilted glasses or bottles, it is clear from their reproductions that they do not actually remember what this looks like (shown in Figure 8.6). Only after children understand that water remains horizontal do they remember correctly.

4. Some Things Are More Easily Remembered

Meaningful material, as we just saw, is remembered far more easily and for longer periods than is material that is less meaningful. Memory for odors also appears to be very persistent. And personal recollections of real-life, day-to-day events are often remarkably accurate, although their reliability and accuracy decline with advancing age (Robin & Moscovitch, 2017).

Particularly striking, important, or emotional events are often remembered for longer periods than are more mundane happenings. Such events sometimes give rise to what are called **flashbulb memories** (Hirst & Phelps, 2016). Flashbulb memories are extremely vivid recollections associated with first becoming aware of some especially emotionally charged event (Lanciano, Curci, Matera, & Sartori, 2018). Flashbulb memories sometimes occur in response to events that are highly personal. They occur more often in response to highly negative rather than positive emotional events (Xie & Zhang, 2017). Often, they are associated with mass phenomena, such as occurred with the assassination of President Kennedy in the United States. Over 95 percent of individuals later surveyed remembered vividly where they were, how they became informed, and what they were doing at the time they heard of the attacks (Dumas & Luminet, 2016).

Although flashbulb memories typically include the subjective impression of extraordinarily clear and precise recall, much of the research suggests that these recollections are not especially accurate. When Hirst et al. (2015) looked at flashbulb memories of the September 11, 2001 attacks over a 10-year period following the event, they found that there had been very rapid forgetting in the first year, with a leveling off in subsequent years. They also found that although much had been forgotten in the first year, confidence in the accuracy of recall had not declined. Furthermore, inconsistencies and errors in recollection were more likely to be repeated than corrected over the years. Similarly, when Talarico and Rubin (2003, 2007) tested university students' recollections of the September 11 attacks, they found that their memories had become progressively more confused over time. However, students' belief in the accuracy of their recollections scarcely diminished. As the title of the Talarico and Rubin (2003) article puts it, "Confidence, not consistency, characterizes flashbulb memories."

Working and Long-Term Memory Compared

Working memory is active memory. As such, it is basically equivalent to span of attention. Hence one of the obvious distinctions between working memory and LTM is that working memory is in fact *short-term* memory (it is often called *short-term memory* rather than *working memory*).

Other differences between working memory and LTM (summarized in Table 8.3) include the fact that as an active, ongoing process, working memory is easily disrupted by external or internal events. In contrast, LTM is far more passive and far more resistant to disruption.

Table 8.3 **Three levels of memory**

	Sensory	Working (or short-term) memory	Long-term memory
Alternate labels	Echoic or iconic	Primary	Secondary
Duration	Less than 1 second	Temporary; less than 20 seconds	Permanent; indefinite
Stability	Fleeting	Easily disrupted	Not easily disrupted
Capacity	Limited	Limited (7 ± 2 items)	Unlimited
General characteristics	Momentary, unconscious impression; a passing sensation or association	What we are paying attention to; immediate consciousness; active; maintained by rehearsal	All our knowledge; passive; the result of encoding, storage, and retrieval of information

Adapted from Lefrançois, G. R. (2018). *Psychology for Teaching* (2nd ed.). San Diego, CA: Bridgepoint Education, table 7.1. Used by permission.

Also, as we have seen, working memory is far more limited in capacity, being essentially synonymous with active attention or immediate consciousness.

Finally, retrieval from working memory is immediate and automatic, a fact that is hardly surprising because what is being retrieved is either immediately conscious or not available. Retrieval from LTM may be far more hesitant, may require a search, and may result in a distortion of what was originally learned.

CATEGORIES OF LONG-TERM MEMORY

One of the most important insights to emerge from memory research is the gradual realization that long-term memory is not just one thing: It consists of different components. Different researchers and theorists have proposed various labels as metaphors for these components. Among the most useful and widely investigated are what are labeled *implicit* and *explicit memory*.

Explicit (Declarative) and Implicit (Nondeclarative) Memory

When a meddling philosopher asked a centipede how it managed to walk with its many legs, the poor thing was totally bewildered. You see, it had never really thought about the problem; it just darn well knew how to walk. Sadly, after it had been asked the question, it began to try to understand the process, tried to figure out which leg went where, when, which next, and on and on, until, finally, completely perplexed and befuddled, it had wrapped its hundred legs into the world's biggest headache of a knot.

Much of our knowledge is a lot like the centipede's knowing how to walk. Our memories relating to how to keep upright on a bicycle, how to hit a home run, or how to do a triple Lutz in ice skating are **implicit memories** – also termed **nondeclarative memories** because they cannot readily be recalled and put into words (in other words, they cannot be *declared*). The sorts of memories that led Watson's subject, Little Albert, to whimper when he saw a rat are implicit.

But we also have many memories that we *can* put into words, such as memories relating to people's names and addresses, their telephone numbers, the name of our dog, the capital of France. These are **explicit memories** – also termed **declarative memory** because they can be put into words (they can be *declared*). Other examples of explicit memory include our recollections of our last birthday or what we did last Christmas or our first day at school.

"The main distinction," claim Squire, Knowlton, and Musen, "is between conscious memory for facts and events and various forms of nonconscious memory" (1993, p. 457). One way to remember the difference between explicit and implicit memories relates to the difference between knowing and remembering. Explicit memories can be remembered and verbalized; that is, they can be brought to mind (made explicit). In contrast, implicit memories, although they involve things that one knows (such as riding a bicycle, for example), cannot be verbalized: They cannot be made explicit.

Physiological Evidence

The distinction between implicit and explicit memories is sometimes well illustrated in amnesiacs, some of whom have been extensively studied by psychologists. Some amnesiacs have lost huge chunks of declarative (explicit) memory, often forgetting who they are, where they went to school, what they did for a living, who their spouse, children, parents, and friends are, and so on. But they often retain many implicit memories relating to motor skills and other items. Not surprisingly, in simple memory experiments, amnesiacs often do quite well on tasks of implicit memory while manifesting impaired recall for explicit learning (Addis, Barense, & Duarte, 2015). Similarly, patients with Alzheimer's disease (which is associated with memory loss) also do relatively well on tests of implicit memory despite severe impairment for explicit memory tasks (Broster et al., 2018; Deason, Strong, Tat, Simmons-Stern, & Budson, 2018).

As we see later in this chapter, there is also evidence from studies of brain activity in normal subjects as well as from studies of people with brain injuries that different parts of the brain are involved in implicit and explicit memory.

Declarative Memories

Studies of amnesiacs also provide evidence of an important distinction between two kinds of declarative memory. For example, there is the case of K.C., a man who, when he was 30, missed a curve with his motorcycle and suffered severe brain damage, becoming permanently amnesiac (Tulving, Schacter, McLachlan & Moscovitch, 1988). K.C. is incapable of bringing to conscious memory anything that he has ever done, seen, or felt in the past. He cannot remember himself ever experiencing or doing anything. "K.C.," writes Tulving, "knows that his family owns a summer cottage, knows where it is located, and can point out the location on a map of Ontario, and he knows that he has spent summers and weekends there. But he does not remember a single occasion when he was at the cottage or a single event that happened there" (1989, p. 363). K.C. remembers all sorts of things that are political, geographical, and musical. In fact, he remembers well enough that his measured intelligence is quite normal, and those talking with him might not notice anything wrong. But he remembers nothing of the personal episodes of his life.

Semantic and Episodic Memory Declarative Memories

There are at least two distinct types of declarative long-term memory, claims Tulving (1989, 2002). On the one hand, there is stable knowledge about the world, such as abstract knowledge, knowledge that is necessary for understanding and using language, knowledge of principles, laws, and facts, and knowledge of strategies and heuristics. These illustrate **semantic memory**. It appears that K.C. has retained his semantic memory.

On the other hand, there is a body of knowledge consisting of personal memories of events that have happened to the individual. These are not abstract memories (as are rules and principles, for example) but are specific memories tied to a time and place. They are *autobiographical memories*. These memories, which K.C.'s amnesia obliterated, are labeled **episodic memory** (sometimes also called *autobiographical memory*).

Tulving argues that these two types of memories are sufficiently distinct that it is useful to consider them separately. He suggests that there might be some important differences in the way material is stored in each as well as in how it is remembered and forgotten. For example, episodic memory seems to be far more susceptible to distortion and forgetting than is semantic memory: We have considerably more difficulty remembering what we ate for breakfast three days ago than in remembering a poem or a name we learned in elementary school.

Episodic memory, according to Tulving (1989), depends on semantic memory. When Georgina remembers the experience of eating breakfast this morning, she might also remember a variety of abstract things about eating, about breakfasts, or about kitchens or restaurants. In contrast, semantic memory seems to be able to operate independently from or even in the absence of episodic memory. Thus, K. C. can know how to play chess, and know that he knows how to play chess, without any memory of ever playing a single game of chess. As Tulving put it, "It is possible for an individual to know facts without remembering learning them, but not possible to remember without knowing what it is that is being remembered" (1989, p. 365).

Episodic memory, explains Tulving (2002), is closely tied to a subjective sense of time.[3] When people recall specific episodes in their lives, they are also recalling a specific time and place. K. C., whose episodic memory had disappeared with his accident, had also lost all sense of personal time. Although he understood the concept of time and could discuss it as well as any normal person, he had no sense of subjective time. In Tulving's words, "The impairment does not encompass only the past; it also extends to the future. Thus when asked, he [K. C.] cannot tell the questioner what he is going to do later on that day, or the day after, or at any time in the rest of his life. He cannot imagine his future any more than he can remember his past" (2002, p. 14).

Distinctions among the various kinds of long-term memory are shown in Figure 8.7.

Models of Declarative Long-Term Memory

An early metaphor for long-term memory portrays the mind as a sort of motion picture camera (complete with audio, video, smell, touch, taste, and so on; Koffka, 1935). This model views memory as a complete, sequential record of experiences from which people retrieve the isolated bits of information that remain accessible after the passage of time. This is a *nonassociationistic* model of memory.

Almost without exception, contemporary models of LTM are *associationistic*. This means they are premised on the fundamental notion that all items of information in memory are associated in various ways. Thus, when you "search" your memory for some item of information,

---

[3] Your more astute students might want to digress a little here, Mrs. Gribbin yelled down at me. They might want to take a time to think about time. Maybe they should read Manrique and Walker's (2017) *Early Evolution of Human Memory: Great Apes, Tool-Making, and Cognition*. It might lead them to reflect on the possibility, suggested by Tulving (2002), that no nonhuman animal is able to ever think about subjective time. Because episodic remembering takes the form of "mental travel through subjective time," it is accompanied by a special kind of self-awareness (labeled *autonoetic*) that animals aren't thought to have. In reference to the suggestion that animals might have some version of autobiographical memory, Harpaz writes, "That is dead stupid. Until an animal has enough intelligence to have self-awareness, it cannot have episodic memory by definition. Even if it does, it has to be intelligent enough to discuss it with us for us to know it" (2003). Colombo and Hayne agree with Tulving. "No single study," they declare, "yields conclusive evidence for episodic memory in animals, infants, or very young children" (2010, p. 617).

Categories of Long-Term Memory | 309

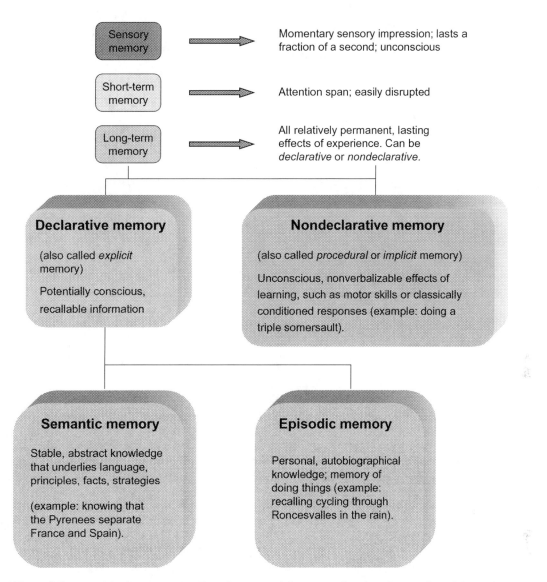

Figure 8.7 A model of memory. Studies of memory failure as well as imaging studies of the brain suggest that different parts of the brain are involved in each type of memory. From Lefrançois, G. R. (2016). *Psychology: The Human Puzzle* (2nd ed.). San Diego, CA: Bridgepoint Education, Fig. 6.5. Used by permission.

you don't haphazardly produce a long sequence of unrelated responses; instead, you narrow in on the missing item through a network of related information.[4]

---

[4] Abruptly, Old Lady Gribbin stopped. She was still on top of the rock face, but she no longer stood as she had earlier, like a preacher trumpeting out psychology's messages of memory. Instead, she sat on the edge of the cliff, legs dangling into space, apparently unconcerned about the danger of falling. She yelled did I need a break, but I wasn't doing anything, just worrying whether my recorder might need to be recharged, only half listening in the early morning sunshine, so I shook my head no, and the old lady said maybe here I should point out, as an aside for all you quick-witted readers, that the concept of associations is fundamental to most of the earlier, behaviorist theories described in the first chapters of this report. She explained that many of these theories deal with how associations between stimuli and responses are affected by repetition or reward. She said associations are also very important in the area of cognitive psychology. But cognitive

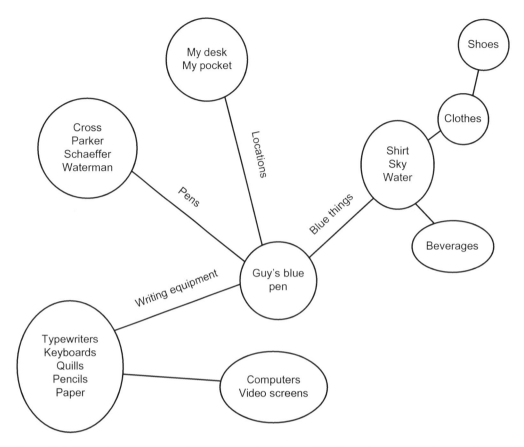

Figure 8.8 Node theory suggests that we remember abstractions (meanings, associations, and gists rather than specifics). Thus, "Guy's blue pen" is depicted as a "node" embedded in a complex web of abstractions (for example, "blue things"), each of which relates to many other nodes that are not shown here.

Associationistic models of long-term memory are essentially cognitive models. Not surprisingly, they often use a variety of abstract concepts, such as Bruner's *categories* and *coding systems*, Piaget's *schemata*, Hebb's *cell assemblies* or *phase sequences*, or other abstractions, such as *nodes*. But *node, category, schema, cell assembly*, and related terms are simply metaphors, not actual structures. They are metaphors for what can be represented in the "mind." Their single identifying attribute is that they represent. Nevertheless, there is ample reason to believe that there *are* actual structures and patterns of activation in the brain that correspond to the concepts represented by these metaphors.

For example, a node model of mental representation is a model that says people store knowledge through representations (called *nodes*, although they could as easily have been called anything else) that are related in countless little-understood ways. Figure 8.8 presents one version of how a tiny part of a node model might be depicted.

theorists are concerned more with associations among ideas (concepts) and how they're affected by meaning. Then, she continued to read from her notes.

The usefulness of a node model for human memory is that it emphasizes memory's associationistic features. Models of LTM are basically information-processing models. As such, they have much to say about the processes involved in memory (such as attending, rehearsing, and organizing). Not surprisingly, most cognitive theorists no longer study learning and memory as separate subjects.

PHYSIOLOGY OF MEMORY

Learning and remembering result in some sort of change in the brain. Understanding the precise nature and location of this change should be very useful for understanding what learning and memory are all about.

The Engram

It makes sense, thought the first memory researchers, that a specific and permanent trace should be left in the brain for every experience that is remembered. The trick is to find this trace, labeled an **engram**. The search for this trace includes some fascinating studies.

Lashley's Rats

Karl Lashley (1924) was convinced that experiences leave specific *engrams* in the brain, and he was determined to find them. As we saw in Chapter 5, Lashley trained rats to run through a maze, and once a rat knew the maze well, he systematically lobbed off tiny little chunks of its brain, keeping a careful record of exactly what it was he had removed. Then, he would release the rat back into the maze. He knew that he would eventually cut out just exactly the right piece, and the rat would have no idea how to get through the maze.

But it didn't work that way at all. It seemed that no matter what part of the brain Lashley excised, as long as he did not kill the rats or incapacitate them physically, they continued to run through the maze (although they did so more and more slowly). He was eventually forced to conclude that memories are scattered throughout the brain rather than located in just one place.

Penfield's Patients

Wilder Penfield (1969), a brain surgeon, thought he had begun to discover and map human memories when he stimulated the brains of some of his fully conscious patients as they were undergoing brain surgery. Tiny amounts of stimulation applied with minute electrodes seemed to stimulate very vivid and detailed recollections of past experiences. However, more careful examination later revealed that these memories were not very reliable: One subject who

Learning and Memory

described in detail a visit to a lumberyard had never been there. It is likely, claims Squire (1987), that Penfield's subjects were fantasizing, constructing memories, or perhaps even hallucinating.

Rat Brain and *Planaria* Studies

A series of studies of rat brains (Krech, Rosenzweig & Bennett, 1960, 1962, 1966) seemed to show that learning causes specific, measurable chemical changes in the brains of rats. But the changes that were found turned out to be highly global and not very informative. In addition, these studies have seldom been replicated and are generally considered invalid (Johnson, 1992).

Similarly, McConnell (1962, 1976) reports studies that seemed to show that conditioning *Planaria* (flatworms) to curl up in response to a light causes permanent chemical changes that can then be transmitted to other *Planaria* simply by mincing the trained worms and feeding them to untrained worms. However, other researchers were unable to duplicate these results, and McConnell was later accused of "overselling" his *Planaria* research and of being a "popularizer" (for example, see McKeachie, 1997; Rilling, 1996).[5]

Brain Imaging: ERPs and ERFs

Although the precise physiology of memory remains undiscovered, early studies of amnesiacs and of those suffering from brain injuries suggested that different brain systems are involved in different types of memory. More recent studies have been greatly aided by the use of new imaging techniques that allow researchers to study neurological functioning in normal patients rather than only in those suffering from brain injuries or amnesia. These imaging techniques, described in Chapter 5, include EEG (electroencephalogram) recordings, positron emission tomography (PET), functional magnetic resonance imaging (fMRI), magnetoencephalography (MEG), and functional magnetic resonance spectrography (fMRS).

---

[5] So, do you know anything about the Heisenberg uncertainty principle? Old Lady Gribbin shouted down at me, literally out of the blue. But before I could even think to answer, she had already begun to explain how the Heisenberg uncertainty principle is drawn from quantum mechanics and how it implies that for no state of any system can all dynamic variables be simultaneously and exactly known. Then, for a long time, she said nothing, just sat up there watching the golden eagle mounted on a wide-swirling mass of rising air, and I thought I'd missed the point, but then she started talking again, explaining how studies such as the *Planaria* research are good examples of the urgent need for replication in human sciences. She said there are simply too many variables human scientists still haven't learned to control in their experiments. She said scientists haven't yet learned how to counter all the confounding effects of their own investigatory procedures, although they now recognize that these effects do exist. And that, she said, that phenomenon, that's the Heisenberg uncertainty principle, which, in a nutshell, means that investigators almost always have a *considerable* but not always *considered* effect on their own investigations. I wanted to protest, tell her it wasn't all that clear, ask her to explain again, but she turned once more to her notes.

Event-Related Potentials and Fields

When brain activity recordings are taken while a person (or an animal) is exposed to a specific stimulus, it is possible to detect electrical activity in the brain that is directly related to that stimulus. That activity is called an **event-related potential (ERP)**. Related to ERPs are **event-related fields (ERFs)**, which are measures of changes in the magnetic field that result from the flow of electrical currents among nerve cells. These changes can be detected by means of a **magnetoencephalogram (MEG)**, which involves a recording of the magnetic field at the scalp, even though that field is less than one-billionth as strong as Earth's magnetic field (Yamagishi, 2008).

Jennifer Aniston Neurons

Event-related potentials and event-related fields are now among the most often studied variables in investigations of memory and learning, as well as in studies of learning disabilities and mental disorders. In one of these studies, neuroscientists were looking at ERFs in an effort to locate areas of the brain associated with epileptic seizures when they found that one of their patients had a neuron that fired reliably whenever she looked at a photo of Jennifer Aniston, but this specific neuron did not fire for other celebrities (Quiroga, Reddy, Kreiman, Koch, & Fried, 2005). Other patients, and later, other normal people, were also shown to have a single cell that fired in response to a specific stimulus or concept. These neurons, capable of being reliably elicited by a given stimulus, are sometimes called **Jennifer Aniston neurons** (or simply *concept cells*). Jennifer Aniston neurons are reminiscent of what are called **grandmother cells**, which are *hypothetical* neurons that fire in response to complex but highly specific concepts (Gross, 2002; Jagadeesh, 2009). These cells might be activated when, for example, you recognize your grandmother or even just think about her. However, the Jennifer Aniston neuron is a specific neuron rather than a hypothetical grouping of related neurons. And, as Quiroga and Kreiman (2010a) point out, discovery of the Jennifer Aniston neuron is probably the best experimental evidence there is to corroborate the existence of something like grandmother cells.

What both the Jennifer Aniston neurons and grandmother cells suggest is that very specific and localized brain activity may be associated with facial recognition and with specific concepts. But neither the Jennifer Aniston Neuron nor the grandmother cell is the engram for which Lashley was searching. That is, they do not represent a single, unitary memory trace, the loss of which would result in the complete disappearance of the associated recognition or recollection. There is considerable redundancy among *grandmother cells*: If one is lost, the person still recognizes grandmothers and knows much about what they represent. Similarly, Quiroga (2017) has been at pains to point out that people do not have single Jennifer Aniston-like cells whose sole function is to recognize a specific person. It is likely, Quiroga explains, that many other cells are involved in recognizing Jennifer Aniston. And it is also likely that this single Jennifer Aniston cell would also respond to other concepts.

Memory and the Brain

Studies that have looked at ERPs and at ERFs have been a rich source of information about how the brain is involved in learning and remembering. Many of these studies use auditory stimuli, such as words or tones; others use visual stimuli, such as photos of Jennifer Aniston and Tom Cruise. These studies typically show that ERPs related to verbal material occur in both hemispheres but tend to be stronger and more localized in the left temporal lobe (for example, Lombardi et al., 2016; Manuel & Schnider, 2016).

Studies of ERPs and ERFs have repeatedly found abnormalities in various mental disorders, such as schizophrenia (for example, Lavigne et al., 2015). The most common finding is that of reduced ERP amplitude among schizophrenics. Reduced ERP amplitude has also been associated with poorer personality development as well as with learning disabilities (Lorusso, Burigo, Borsa, & Molteni, 2015).

Research using this new technology indicates that the medial temporal lobe is highly involved in long-term memory (for example, Zhang, van Vugt, Borst, & Anderson, 2018). Injury to these parts of the temporal lobe, or neurological problems in the temporal lobe such as would be found in temporal lobe epilepsy, are also associated with long-term memory deficits (Tramoni-Negre, Lambert, Bartolomei, & Felician, 2017). Similarly, pathological temporal lobe changes such as those found with diseases like Alzheimer's are typically linked with impairments in long-term memory (Mendonca et al., 2018).

In particular, the hippocampus, which is located in the medial temporal lobe of the brain, appears to be essential for consolidating declarative memory and for spatial navigation (Rubin & Cohen, 2017). Research conducted by Laczo et al. (2009) suggests that impairment of hippocampal functioning, which is often manifested in problems with spatial navigation, might be an early indicator of Alzheimer's disease.

On the other hand, nondeclarative (implicit) memory seems to be associated with other brain structures, such as the amygdala, which is located in the frontal portion of the temporal lobe (Gotzsche & Woldbye, 2016). In particular, the emotional aspects of memory seem to be closely related to the amygdala (Dolcos et al., 2017).

In spite of the fact that certain memories are often linked with specific brain structures, the bulk of the evidence indicates that human learning and memory are seldom associated with a single site in the brain. Even a learning task as simple as the classical conditioning of the eye-blink reflex involves activity and change in different brain structures.

Many details of the physiology and neuroanatomy of learning remain unknown. For example, the precise nature of the changes that must occur during learning, and that therefore account for memory, remains speculative. Still, research has now led to the widely held view that memories are stored in changes of synaptic strength – that is, in changes in the probability that one neuron will activate another, much as the Hebb metaphor had speculated more than half a century ago. It is likely that as more is learned, metaphors will become even more appropriate. In time, psychology might even move from the metaphor to a literal description.

Summary of Modal Models of Memory

The most widely accepted current models of memory describe a three-component memory storage system: sensory memory (the momentary effect of sensory stimulation); working memory (*short-term memory*: fleeting, immediately conscious memory); and long-term memory (relatively permanent storage).

Also widely accepted and the basis of a great deal of current memory research is Baddeley's model of working memory, which is an attempt to describe how information is processed and manipulated in conscious awareness. The Baddeley model describes an executive controller that interacts with two systems that keep visual/spatial (the *visual-spatial sketch pad*) and auditory (the *phonological loop*) information available for processing, and a third system (the *episodic buffer*) that serves to integrate and make sense of information currently being processed. Working memory refers to a way of processing information as well as to a type of storage that is highly limited in duration and in capacity.

Baddeley's model has proven especially useful in directing, organizing, and summarizing much of the research on memory that has been undertaken since it was first proposed. The later addition of the *episodic buffer* made it possible to explain how information from the two slave systems, along with information from long-term memory, could be integrated to arrive at coherent, meaningful awareness.

Models of long-term memory are primarily associationistic. Research indicates that our LTM tends to be relatively stable, although not always exceptionally reliable. For one thing, it tends to be highly *generative*: We remember the gist of certain things and generate the rest. And we often misremember. Sometimes, we remember things that never happened; other times, we don't remember things that actually did happen. What we remember and what we forget can have important implications in our lives – and in courts of law.

WHY WE FORGET

To forget, as the term is ordinarily used, is to be unable to bring into immediate consciousness. Clearly, forgetting does not prove, or even imply, complete loss from memory. There are many things people learn implicitly (like how to skip a stone) whose underlying memories they cannot easily translate into symbols or examine consciously. Also, there is a possibility that when someone cannot recall something, it has not been lost but simply cannot be retrieved. Like a stubborn name lurking on the tip of the tongue, perhaps it will be retrievable later – and perhaps not.

Many answers have been proposed for why people are unable to remember.

Brain Injury

Brain injuries might impair memory because they affect normal brain functioning. They might also affect memory as a sort of protective mechanism. For example, a relatively common outcome of traumatic war experiences with mild brain injury is **amnesia**, a total or partial impairment of memory. Bryant et al. (2009, 2015), who studied survivors of traumatic injury, suggest that posttraumatic amnesia appears to protect the individual from re-experiencing the trauma.

Because different parts of the brain are more involved than others in certain kinds of memory, brain injury might result in different kinds of memory impairments. Recall the case of K. C., who had suffered a brain injury in a motorcycle accident and who had lost all *episodic* (*autobiographical*) memory. Although K. C. was unable to remember personal experiences, he remembered all sorts of more general information. That is, his *semantic* memory remained intact.

The case of K. C. is not totally isolated. Knight and O'Hagan (2009) asked 19 people who had sustained severe traumatic brain injury at least six years earlier whether they recognized the names of 115 famous persons who had become prominent between 1960 and 2005. They typically had little difficulty recognizing many of these famous persons and explaining why they were famous. However, most were unable to recall specific episodic memories connected with the names. For example, they could not recall when they become familiar with the famous person, nor did they remember ever listening to the person sing, watching the person act, seeing the person dance, and so on. In other words, their episodic (autobiographical) memories were significantly impaired, much as was Tulving's patient, K. C.

Fading Theory

Brain injury is an uncommon cause of forgetting; there are other far more common causes. For example, one possibility is that people forget some things simply as a function of the passage of time – that whatever traces or changes learning leaves behind become less distinct as time passes. Evidence for this **fading theory** rests on the observation that people often remember recent events more clearly than very distant ones. Clara might at this moment be able to remember most of the items of clothing hanging in her closet, but she would not fare so well at describing what she had in her closet six years ago (unless she was in prison then). But if she has periodically reviewed mentally what was in her closet at that time, she will probably do much better. Items that are occasionally remembered are far more resistant to the presumed ravages of time than are items that have never been recalled. Every recollection is a sort of rehearsal and an opportunity for relearning.

It is worth noting that many psychologists do not consider fading (or decay) theory very useful or accurate. These psychologists point out that time, by itself, does not cause forgetting any more than it causes the erosion of mountains or the disappearance of the passenger pigeon. These are caused by other things that happen during the passage of time. These other things, ERP and ERF research suggest, might have to do with less effective functioning of the brain, often associated with loss of gray matter as well as with various diseases of aging (Ramanoel et al., 2018).

Distortion Theory

Memories that are forgotten do not always disappear completely. Instead, some are distorted or confused with other memories. As Loftus (2007) explains, it is as though various features of a single past experience were not adequately bound together. As a result, when the person tries to recall the experience, only fragments are available. These are combined with other memories in a recollection that makes sense even if it is a distortion of the original experience.

Distortion theory recognizes that when people search their memories, what they remember are main ideas and abstractions, the gist of the story but not the details. Later, they generate the details, often distorting the original. Recall that in the Johnson, Bransford, and Solomon (1973) study, subjects were convinced they had seen a never-before presented sentence simply because it made sense.

Eyewitnesses, Loftus (1979) notes, are notably unreliable and easily misled. In one study, she had subjects view a film in which a sports car was involved in an accident. While later interviewing the participants as witnesses, some were asked "How fast was the sports car going when it passed the barn while traveling along the country road?" Others were asked "How fast was the sports car going while traveling on the country road?" And although there was no barn along the road, about one-fifth of those who had been asked the first question swore they had seen one; fewer than 3 percent of the second group thought they had seen a barn.

Repression Theory and False Memories

The notion of memory repression dates back to Freud, who speculated that individuals sometimes unconsciously repress experiences that are traumatic (highly disturbing; anxiety provoking). For example, this might be the case when an adult experiences difficulty remembering childhood traumas, such as sex abuse (Woodiwiss, 2010). Freud's notion of **repression theory** was that experiences that are overwhelmingly traumatic are pushed back into the subconscious. But although the individual is no longer consciously aware of the experiences, they can nevertheless have a profound effect on psychological well-being. Freud believed that recovering these memories was often critical to resolving any resulting psychopathology.

How common are repressed memories? And how reliable are recovered memories? These are difficult questions. Loftus's research reports numerous instances of memories of traumatic occurrences that are so highly distorted that the memories are, in fact, largely false (Loftus & Cahill, 2007). **False memory syndrome**, the label sometimes given to this phenomenon, may be of considerable importance in courts of law where people are asked to recollect traumatic experiences that occurred in the distant past. There are instances where alleged victims of sexual abuse have provided testimony confirming the abuse but have later retracted their testimony. Among the most notorious of these cases is that of Beth Rutherford who, after a number of sessions with a counselor, recalled a long-suppressed memory of having been raped repeatedly by her father when still a child, and having twice been pregnant and undergone forced abortions as a result. Armed with these recollections, she sued her clergyman father who, humiliated and disgraced, was forced to resign. But a subsequent examination revealed that Beth Rutherford was still a virgin who had never been pregnant (Loftus, 1997). It appeared that Beth was the victim of what Shaw (2016) describes as a *memory illusion.*

Following this and a number of similar cases, a group of individuals, many of whom felt they had been victims of accusations stemming from false memories, formed the False Memory Syndrome Foundation (2018). The foundation offers support to those who claim to be falsely accused.

To date, questions relating to the validity of repressed memories remain highly controversial (Follette & Davis, 2009; Greenhoot & Tsethlikai, 2009). Because unconscious repression applies only to rare, highly emotional, and highly negative experiences, repression theory is of limited value as a general explanation of forgetting.

Interference Theory

Many researchers suggest that forgetting has little to do with the passage of time but that it is more often due to interference (Domjan, 2018). **Interference theory** holds that new learning can interfere with the recall of old learning (*retroactive interference*) or that old learning can interfere with the recall of new learning (*proactive interference*). These two kinds of interference have been a consistent phenomenon in studies of long-term memory, often employing nonsense syllables. In these studies, learning one list of words and then learning a second related list leads to (a) more difficulty in remembering the first list (retroactive interference) and (b) more difficulty in learning the second list (proactive interference) (see Tables 8.1 and 8.2).

Interference has also been extensively studied in language learning (for example, Bartolotti, Bradley, Hernandez, & Marian, 2017). Not surprisingly, interference appears to be higher for words that are most similar, and interference decreases with increasing exposure to the second language. Retroactive and proactive interference have also been implicated in certain cases of amnesia as well as in gradual memory impairment related to aging (Plancher, Boyer, Lemaire & Portrat, 2017; Postma et al., 2018).

What happens in forgetting via interference, suggests Domjan (2018), is that recent experiences are simply not "consolidated"; that is, the neurological changes that underlie memory do not occur. Until a memory is consolidated, it is especially vulnerable to the interfering effects of ongoing mental activity and to the formation of other memories (Cherdieu et al., 2018). This explains why sleep and even certain drugs often improve memory for recent learning. In effect, sleep and drugs (such as alcohol) have the effect of diminishing competing mental activity.

Fortunately, interference is often more descriptive of what happens in the laboratory than of what actually happens in people's daily lives. Although people might occasionally become confused because of competition among items they are trying to remember, indications are that they can continue to learn all sorts of things without running the risk of becoming progressively more subject to the effects of interference.

Retrieval-Cue Failure

Ed Landry, an English teacher, would often realize just as he was about to go into class that he had forgotten something. And even if he stood there for long minutes, scratching and sniffing around in his memory, he was often unable to remember what it was that he had forgotten. So he would go back to his office because he knew that is where it had occurred to him to bring whatever it was that he had now forgotten. And as soon as he entered his office, it would come to him. "Shoot. It's the green book I wanted to bring!"

Ed Landry's office served as a powerful **retrieval cue**, a stimulus that facilitates recall. As Homa (2008) explains, learning always occurs in a specific context, which includes the individual's current mood, thoughts, and preoccupations, as well as the external environment. Aspects of these can serve as important memory cues. That is one of the reasons why witnesses are sometimes brought back to the scene of the crime, or why victims themselves sometimes go back. The hope is that some aspect of the scene may jog memory, serving as a retrieval cue.

Retrieval-cue failure is yet another explanation for why we forget. As noted at the outset, perhaps people do not actually forget but simply cannot remember. That something cannot be remembered is not very good evidence that it is completely gone from memory. The problem might be one of retrieval rather than of storage.

Tulving (1974) recognized this possibility in his description of two kinds of forgetting. There is a kind of forgetting, he explains, that simply involves an inability to recall – a *retrieval-cue* failure. This very common type of forgetting is called **cue-dependent forgetting** (forgetting related to the unavailability of appropriate cues for recall). In cue-dependent forgetting, not remembering has to do with being unable to discriminate the item from other possibilities at the time of remembering rather than at the time of learning.

A second type of forgetting involves actual changes in the memory trace itself and is therefore labeled **trace-dependent forgetting**. The five possibilities described earlier (brain injury, fading, interference, distortion, and repression) relate primarily to trace-dependent forgetting.

For declarative (conscious, explicit) material, recall seems to be better with certain types of cues. For example, Tulving (1989) reports that the most effective memory cues are those that match the type of recall required. In studies in which subjects are required to remember the meanings of words, cues that emphasize meaning are best. But when subjects are asked questions relating to the spellings or sounds of words, retrieval cues that emphasize the sounds (phonemes) or the letters in the words work best. Also, as Wheeler and Gabbert (2017) explain, self-generated cues, and especially highly distinctive cues, can improve recall.

LEARNING AND REMEMBERING: EDUCATIONAL APPLICATIONS

One of the principal aims of education is long-term remembering. And fortunately, the common belief that students begin to forget much of what they have learned very soon after their examinations may not be especially valid. That is because schools do not usually provide

What Works in Education

A great deal of research has looked at which instructional approaches are most effective for learning and remembering. Brown, Roediger, and McDaniel (2014) have synthesized much of this research in their book *Making it Stick: The Science of Successful Learning*. Another summary is that of Dunlosky, Rawson, Marsh, Nathan, and Willingham (2013), who looked at the wealth of research that has examined the effectiveness of 10 different techniques for learning.

One general conclusion based on all these summaries is, in the words of Brown et al., that "People generally are going about learning in the wrong ways" (2014, p. ix). The most effective learning strategies, they explain, are not intuitive: Rather, they are based on good cognitive science and research. Intuitive methods such as rereading material over and over are not only time-consuming, but don't really improve memory. What they do, say these authors, is give learners the *illusion of knowing*.

So, what are the most effective and the most generally useful strategies for learning and remembering? To answer the question briefly, of the 10 distinct approaches evaluated by Dunlosky et al. (2013), five were considered highly, or at least moderately, useful; five were considered of relatively low value. Unfortunately, some of the five approaches that were found to be the least effective are among the most commonly used by students, at least at the post-secondary level. Among these are study approaches such as summarizing, highlighting, using keyword mnemonics, using imagery for learning textual material, and rereading.

Note, however, that the last of these low-efficiency techniques, *rereading*, can also be highly effective under certain circumstances. In fact, one of the most effective techniques identified by both Dunlosky et al. (2013) and by Brown et al. (2014) is **spaced repetition** (or *spaced rereading*). Spaced repetition occurs when the learner practices a skill, rereads material, or rehearses information during brief, separate periods of time. Spaced repetition is contrasted with the more common **blocked repetition** approach, a technique in which the learner attempts to learn the skill or the information in a single, uninterrupted block of time. Blocked repetition is one of the five techniques identified by Dunlosky et al. (2013) as not very effective.

In most surveys and reviews of effective learning techniques, there is one that is even more effective than spaced repetition: **interleaving**. Interleaving describes an approach where learners intentionally practice several unrelated skills or rehearse and review distinctly different groupings of information in sequence. For example, the learner practices one skill for a while, leaves it to practice a second, unrelated skill (or to rehearse different material), turns perhaps to a third area of study, then back to the first, then the second, and so on. As Pan (2015) put it, "research in schools finds that interleaving produces dramatic and long-lasting benefits."

Interestingly, in spite of the demonstrable advantages of spaced and interleaved repetition, learners seem to prefer blocked repetition, a technique that Brown et al. (2014) identify as a common, intuitive approach. When Zulkiply and Burt (2013) asked research participants which

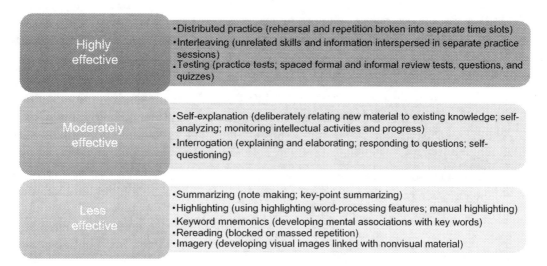

Figure 8.9 Summaries and interpretations of vast amounts of educational research have identified 10 distinct learning strategies. They are shown here in their apparent order of effectiveness. Keep in mind that the effectiveness of any given strategy is often dependent on the purposes for which the individual tries to remember as well as on the material being learned. Based in part on Dunlosky, J., Rawson, K. A., Marsh, E. J., Nathan, M. J., & Willingham, D. T. (2013). Improving students' learning with effective learning techniques: Promising directions from cognitive and educational psychology. *Psychological Science in the Public Interest*, 14(1), 4–58; and on Brown, P. C., Roediger, H. L. III, & McDaniel, M. A. (2014). *Making it stick: The science of successful learning*. Cambridge, Mass.: The Belknap Press of Harvard University Press.

they thought to be more effective, they chose massed (blocked) repetition over interleaving even when results of the research in which they had participated showed exactly the opposite!

Third in effectiveness in the Brown et al. (2014) summary is *memorizing*. The reason why memorizing is important is because of its role in bringing about some of the most important outcomes in education: namely those having to do with higher cognitive activities such as evaluating, analyzing, synthesizing, and creating. If learners are to succeed in these tasks, they claim, they need to be able to retrieve from memory a variety of facts, procedures, formulas, relationships, and so on.

Also important as a learning technique is what Brown et al. (2014) label the **testing effect**. The phrase recognizes the fact that testing, which includes the variety of informal as well as formal testing situations to which learners are exposed (for example, quizzes, impromptu questions, brief assignments), has been shown to have a highly positive and long-lasting effect on learning and retention.

Figure 8.9 summarizes the effectiveness of different approaches to learning and remembering.

How Important Are Teachers?

Hattie (2009) synthesized more than 800 separate **meta-analyses** concerned with identifying the most powerful influences in school achievement. Later, he summarized another

1,200 meta-analyses that examined influences in post-secondary education (Hattie, 2015a, 2015b). A meta-analysis is an approach to research where investigators combine and analyze the results of a large number of related studies to arrive at an overall, generally valid conclusion.

In the first of these analyses, more than 50,000 separate studies were combined; total samples exceeded 200 million students (Hattie, 2009). These 50,000 studies looked at how six different factors contribute to learning and achievement: the home, the school, the child, the teacher, the curricula, and approaches to teaching.

The results seem clear, says Hattie: The single most important factor in determining children's school achievement is what they, themselves, bring to the learning situation. Most significant among child characteristics is prior cognitive ability; also important are factors such as motivation and personality characteristics, such as persistence.

Second in importance in terms of their contribution to educational outcomes are teachers. This finding is true both in schools and at the post-secondary level. And among the most important aspects of teacher–learner interaction, says Hattie, is **feedback** – information teachers and students receive about their performance and use to adjust their actions. In Hattie's (2009) words, speaking about *excellence in education*, "It is about how teachers and students strategize, think about, play with, and build conceptions about worthwhile knowledge and understanding. Monitoring, assessing, and evaluating the progress in this task is what then leads to the power of feedback" (p. 238).

Feedback, says Hattie (2012), is one of the most powerful influences on learning. One form of feedback is simply information about the correctness and appropriateness of responses (or other behaviors). In effect, this kind of feedback is a response consequence that illustrates reinforcement, or the lack thereof, in a Skinnerian sense. The teacher's simple comment, "Good work," can be a powerful positive reinforcer. "You'll have to do that over" is not as clearly a positive reinforcer, but can also be highly useful feedback.

Hattie (2009) lists six signposts that indicate progress toward excellence in education. Implicit in these are suggestions for worthwhile teacher behaviors, attitudes, and beliefs (based on Hattie, 2009, pp. 238–239):

1. Teachers are among the most powerful influences on learning.
2. Teachers need to be directive, influential, caring, and actively engaged in the passion of teaching and learning.
3. Teachers need to be acutely aware of what each student is doing to provide appropriate feedback.
4. Teachers need to know the criteria of success in their lessons: "Where are you going?" "How are you going?" "How will you know you are there?" "Where to next?"
5. Teachers need to go from single ideas to multiple ideas, relating and extending ideas, helping learners *construct* knowledge.
6. Teachers need to create environments where error is welcomed as a learning opportunity and where participants can feel safe to learn, relearn, and explore.

Teachers, the very best research tells us, are important.

Main Point Chapter Summary

1. Memory makes us who we are. It is ordinarily defined as the availability of information (recall or retrievability); however, some aspects of memory are not conscious (they are implicit rather than explicit). Not all that is stored can be retrieved. Ebbinghaus pioneered the early scientific investigation of memory using nonsense syllables, discovering that much of what is forgotten is lost very soon after learning.

2. The modal model of memory describes three memory storage stages: sensory register, working (short-term) memory, and long-term memory. The sensory register describes the momentary effect of stimulation (includes echoic or iconic memory). Studies of the cocktail party phenomenon demonstrate that even material not attended to remains available for a fraction of a second.

3. Working memory refers to the ongoing availability in immediate attention or consciousness of a small number of items (seven plus or minus two). It lasts only seconds (seldom more than 20), unless there is continued rehearsal (in which case the information may be coded into long-term memory). Its capacity may be increased through chunking – the grouping of related items.

4. Baddeley's model of working memory describes an executive control system concerned with controlling the flow of information in and out of working memory; two slave systems (the phonological loop and the visual-spatial sketch pad) concerned with maintaining auditory or visual material ready for access by the executive system; and an episodic buffer that integrates information from the slave systems and from long-term memory and makes coherent sense of it.

5. Forgetting in working (short-term) memory may be related to decay (loss of memory traces), displacement (replacement of old with new material because of space limitations), interference (where previous learning interferes with new learning), or level of processing (Craik and Lockhart's model).

6. Long-term memory is highly stable (notably so for images and odors), is generative rather than simply reproductive, is influenced by understanding, and is better for some items (those that are more striking, more meaningful, or more emotional, sometimes leading to flashbulb memories) than for others. Flashbulb memories are more often linked with negative than with positive emotions. They are often distorted over time, but are characterized by very high confidence in their accuracy.

7. A comparison of working (short-term) memory and long-term memory (LTM) reveals that working memory is an active, continuing process; that it is easily disrupted by ongoing activities; and that it is highly limited in capacity. In contrast, LTM refers to a more passive process, not easily disrupted by ongoing activities, and essentially unlimited in capacity. Retrieval from working memory is immediate and automatic or does not occur; retrieval from LTM may be considerably slower and more groping.

8. Long-term memory systems include explicit (declarative) memory – consisting of potentially conscious, recallable information – or implicit (nondeclarative or procedural)

memory – consisting of unconscious, nonverbalizable effects of learning (for example, as in skill learning or classical conditioning).

9. Declarative (recallable) memory is composed of semantic memory and episodic memory. Semantic memory includes general, stable, abstract facts and principles (for example, knowledge of language or of the world). Episodic memory refers to private knowledge tied to specific personal events and to a time and place (hence, autobiographical memory).

10. Some early models of memory were nonassociationistic (Koffka's notion of a continuous record, such as a videotape); current models emphasize associations among items in memory and frequently make use of schema or node models – a node or schema being simply whatever it is that represents an idea.

11. Historical events in the search for the physiology of memory include Lashley's ablations of rat brains (he didn't find the engram); Penfield's stimulation of his patients' brains (their memories may have been fantasies and hallucinations rather than specific memories); dissections of the brains of enriched rats (changes were global and imprecise); the feeding and injection of trained *Planaria* into untrained *Planaria* (the studies don't easily replicate and, 30 years later, seem to have led nowhere); the study of amnesiacs' memories (these support distinctions among different long-term memory systems and indicate that different brain systems may be involved in each); and the development of connectionist models (which argue that memories reside in patterns of neurons rather than in specific changes within single neurons).

12. A great deal of current memory research uses electroencephalograph (EEG) and magnetoencephalograph (MEG) recordings. These provide real-time recordings of event-related potentials (ERPs) (changes in the electrical potential of nerve cells as they fire) and of event-related fields (ERFs) (changes in magnetic fields during neural activity). Although individual neurons have been identified that are readily activated by a specific stimulus (Jennifer Aniston and grandmother neurons), it is likely that many cells are involved in all mental processes.

13. Research on ERPs and ERFs suggests that long-term memory (LTM) involves permanent structural or chemical changes in the brain, with the left temporal lobe being more involved than the right in relation to long-term memory of verbal material. The hippocampus appears to be essential for declarative memory and spatial navigation. Nondeclarative memory and emotional memory appear to be associated more with the amygdala.

14. Forgetting may result from brain injury; some might result from an ill-explained "fading" or decay process. In addition, some forgetting probably results from distortion. Other explanations for forgetting include repression theory (uncommon, most appropriate for experiences laden with negative emotion, and sometimes linked with erroneous recollections as in *false memory syndrome*), interference theory (proactive and retroactive interference), and retrieval-cue failure (absence of appropriate cues to retrieve learned material).

15. The most effective techniques for improving learning and remembering are distributed (spaced) practice as opposed to blocked (continuous) practice; interleaving (different skills interspersed in separate practice sessions); and testing (use of practice tests and a variety of formal and informal testing). Moderately effective strategies include self-explanation (deliberate personal analysis, appraisal and direction of learner's cognitive activities), and interrogation (explaining and elaborating material to be learned). Less effective are activities such as summarizing, highlighting, keyword mnemonics, rereading (blocked repetition), and the use of mental imagery.

9 Motivation and Emotions

CHAPTER OUTLINE

This Chapter	326
Objectives	327
Motivation and Emotions	327
Reflexes, Instincts, and Imprinting	328
Reflexes	328
The Orienting Reflex	328
Instincts	329
Imprinting	330
Psychological Hedonism	332
Drive Reduction and Incentives	332
Needs and Drives	333
Psychological Needs	333
Need/Drive Positions: An Appraisal	334
Incentives	335
Maslow's Hierarchy	336
Arousal Theory	338
Emotion and Motivation: Level of Arousal	338
The Yerkes–Dodson Law	338
Hebb's Arousal Theory	340
Sources of Arousal	342
Social Cognitive Views of Motivation	342
A Theory of Cognitive Dissonance	342
Intrinsic and Extrinsic Motives	346
Attribution Theory	349
Dweck's Theory: Performance versus Mastery Goals	350
Self-Efficacy	353
Intentions, Goals, and Expectancy–Value Theory	356
Self-Determined and Self-Regulated Learners	358
Applications and Implications of Motivation Theory	359
Predicting Behavior	359
Controlling and Changing Behavior	359

Motivation in the Classroom	360
The ARCS Model of Motivation	363
Main Point Chapter Summary	364

No one asks how to motivate a baby. A baby naturally explores everything it can get at, unless restraining forces have already been at work. And this tendency doesn't die out, it's wiped out.

B. F. Skinner

Mrs. Gribbin seasoned the fish and wrapped them in what looked like thick pastry. Then she scratched the glowing embers apart and laid them directly in the ashes, covering them with more ashes and embers. The cat appeared suddenly from the black night. He made a wide circle around me to reach and sniff disapprovingly at his empty dish. Thinking I would befriend him, I hurried over and filled it generously with that very expensive Blue Buffalo "succulent and nourishing" cat food I had bought. Schrödinger glared at me, and walked back into the darkness. You just can't please some people.

Later, the old lady cracked open and discarded the blackened shells and laid the steaming fish on our plates and we ate them, one each. And when we had done the light was gone, and the wolf howled from the deep darkness, and I would have added wood to the fire to warm the night and ease my fears, but Old Lady Gribbin said not to, that tonight she wanted that nothing should dim the stars and for a long time, she lay on her back gazing at the sky and it seemed that her eyes didn't move, almost as though she might be looking at something she had recognized, something familiar. But when I peered hard where I thought she might be looking, I saw nothing, just a maze of tiny stars lost in the confusion of the Milky Way. Then, the wolf howled again, so close this time that between his howls, I could hear the rasping in his throat, and I would have asked the old lady once more if I might build the fire up just a little, but I saw that she had turned her face to the northern sky where the aurora had just now begun to shimmer and dance in the cold night, brushing the sky with greens and pinks, and for a time, the wolf was silent.

Suddenly, Old Lady Gribbin rose and heaved great lengths of wood on the fire until the flames leaped and flailed about, throwing sparks like diamonds into the night, and the cat appeared once more, strutting like he had just laid waste to a thousand mice, and the old lady nodded that I should turn on the recorder once more.

THIS CHAPTER

We have done and felt much tonight, *said Old Lady Gribbin*, about which Chapter 9 speaks. We've eaten and drunk and burned our fears and gazed at splendor – which is to say that we have been moved by thirst and hunger, perhaps by fear and cold, maybe even by love and kindness and beauty. These are precisely the things with which this chapter is concerned, *she said*: What moves human beings? Or to put it another way, what are the reasons and causes for what people do?

Objectives

Tell your readers, *said Mrs. Gribbin as she fed still more birch to the fire*, that they'll know the difference between causes and reasons once they are completely done with this chapter – that is, after they have read it and carefully translated it into every other language they know. At that point, they will be in the enviable position of being able to write tiny but brilliant truths, of the kind that might be baked into fortune cookies, explaining, among other things:

- the meaning of motivation;
- what imprinting is and whether it applies to human behavior;
- what needs, drives, and incentives are;
- the meaning and importance of arousal;
- the intricacies of attribution theory;
- how the mental calculus people use to compute costs, values, and expectations directs actions;
- Dweck's notions of *mindsets* and how they affect behavior.

In addition, *she said*, they'll have new insights into the causes and reasons for their own uninspiring but nevertheless inspired actions. She sat close to the fire now, once more taking up her sheaf of notes. Number One Head: Motivation and Emotions, *she began*.

MOTIVATION AND EMOTIONS

Are you motivated to learn? Motivated to succeed? Motivated to eat parsnips and cabbage? Or do you lack motivation?

A big and important word, motivation, inextricably linked with learning and very closely tied to performance in school and in life (Linnenbrink-Garcia et al., 2018). Its importance in all endeavors can hardly be overstated.

The Latin origin for the word **motivation** means *to move*. Hence, motivation deals with action. A motive is a conscious or unconscious force that incites a person to act or, sometimes, not to act. In this sense, motives are **causes** because, says the dictionary, causes are agents or forces that produce an effect or an action. Thus, the study of human motivation is the study of agents and forces that cause behavior. And the study of learning, as we saw, is the study of changes in behavior; hence, the link between learning and motivation.

But the study of human motivation is not just the study of causes; it includes a study of **reasons** for behavior. Reasons are rational explanations. They typically involve deliberation, purpose, anticipation of the results of behavior – in other words, reasoning. When Sherlock Holmes enquires about the killer's motives, he is asking for the killer's purposes – her reasons.

To illustrate the distinction between reasons and causes: If Joe naïvely places his hand on a hot stove, the heat (or, more precisely, Joe's sensation of heat) causes him to withdraw his hand at once. The reason why Joe later avoids going near the stove is his realization that doing so might be painful. The study of human motivation is a study of both reasons and causes.

Motivation and Emotions

It is important to note that motives are very closely tied to emotions. Emotions may be centrally involved as causes and reasons for a very large number of human actions. Just as powerful negative emotions accompany painful sensations of heat, so too might powerful positive emotions accompany compelling attractions or great ambitions.

Emotions are complex states tied not only to motives but reflected as well in activity of our nervous systems. Emotions can be very general states experienced as "feeling good," "feeling bad," "feeling energized," and so on. When these states are linked directly to some cause such as an activity or an object, they can become very powerful sources of motivation.

REFLEXES, INSTINCTS, AND IMPRINTING

Motivation theory recognizes that there are biological causes for behaviors such as Joe's sudden withdrawal from heat. These have to do with his nervous system and its wired-in tendency to react to certain situations reflexively.

Reflexes

Hence, a **reflex** is one kind of motive – one sort of explanation for behavior. As we saw in Chapter 2, a reflex is a simple unlearned act that occurs in response to a specific stimulus. Children are born with a limited number of reflexes, such as the blinking reflex in response to air blown on the eye, the knee-jerk reflex, withdrawal from pain, and startle reactions. All these reflexes are also normally present in adults. In addition, several human reflexes are present at birth but soon disappear. These include the Babinsky reflex (curling of the toes when the sole is tickled), the grasping reflex, the sucking reflex, and the Moro reflex (flinging out the arms and legs when suddenly startled or dropped). (See Table 2.1 for a summary of infant reflexes.)

Most reflexes, such as sucking, swallowing, and withdrawing from pain, have clear survival value. Some hypothesize that even the **Moro reflex** might have been useful in some distant past when a tree-dwelling infant accidentally slipped from a perch or was dropped by a careless mother and the sudden flinging out of its arms helped it find another branch to grasp.

The Orienting Reflex

Another type of reflexive behavior, the **orienting reflex (OR)**, is a general tendency to respond to new stimulation by becoming more alert. In most mammals, it typically consists of a shift in gaze often accompanied by head and eye movements. Thus, when dogs hear a new sound, their heads turn, their ears perk up, and their entire posture says "What the @#$*! was that?" Not surprisingly, the orienting response is often called the "What is it?" response. It appears to be present even in very young infants who tend to orient toward new stimuli, an inclination that might well have survival value given that sudden change in stimulation is often related to feeding and caring for the infant or perhaps to danger. The orienting response is an evolutionary development that enables organisms to assess the environment quickly to uncover potential threats and opportunities. Hence, it has important implications for survival.

In humans, the orienting response is not as obvious as in cats or dogs, but it serves the same alerting function. Thus, when exposed to a novel stimulus, heart and respiration rates may decelerate momentarily (this explains the expression "to hold one's breath"), conductivity of the skin increases, and electrical activity in the brain changes (Barry, De Blasio, Bernat, & Steiner, 2015).

One very important function of the orienting reflex in humans relates directly to learning and development. Orienting occurs in response to novelty; as the novel becomes familiar (becomes *habituated to*), the orienting response ceases (Barry, MacDonald, De Blasio, & Steiner, 2013). Thus, in studies with preverbal infants, the disappearance of an orienting response is often used as an indication that learning has occurred. In current research, cessation of the orienting response is usually determined by looking at changes in *event-related potentials (ERPs)* (measures of electrical activity in the brain).

Reflexes as Explanations

Pavlov and Watson made extensive use of reflexes in their theories, and they were at least partly successful in explaining some simple types of learning such as emotional responses or taste aversions. Note that these classes of learning can be important for the organism's survival. For example, the classically conditioned fear of a snarling noise might lead an animal – even a human one – to avoid a tiger when it hears one clear its throat. And a learned taste aversion might prevent the animal from eating a poisonous toadstool.

Because of their link with survival, reflexes are valid, biologically based explanations for some behaviors. However, they have limited generality and usefulness as explanations for most human behaviors, the bulk of which are not reflexive.

Instincts

Reflexes are simple unlearned (inherited) behaviors; **instincts** are more complex inherited patterns of behavior that are common to an entire species and are generally associated with survival and procreation (for example, nest building in birds or the avoidance of predators). Some early theorists, including James, thought that humans had an enormous number of instincts – more than any other animal. In addition to instincts for jealousy, cleanliness, sucking, pointing at, clasping, and biting (among hundreds of others), James listed a tendency toward kleptomania as a human instinct (James, 1890)! McDougall (1908) and others went so far as to argue that all human behavior results from unlearned tendencies to react in given ways – in other words, from instincts. These theorists thought up long lists of supposed instincts, such as gregariousness, pugnacity, flight, self-assertion, self-abasement, and hunger. At one point, Bernard counted more than 6,000 "instincts," including inclinations as unexpected as "the tendency to avoid eating apples that grow in one's own garden" (1924, p. 212).

Motivation and Emotions

But most of these tendencies are not really instincts at all. After all, instincts are complex behaviors (such as migration or hibernation), they are general to all members of a species (the "following" behavior of young ducks or geese, for example), and they are relatively unmodifiable (birds' nesting behaviors, for example). Given these observations, many psychologists argue that there is no convincing evidence that there are any instincts among humans, although instincts are clearly evident in other animals.

Still, not all psychologists believe that instincts play no role in human behavior. For example, Freudian theory is premised on the notion that powerful, instinctual tendencies, mainly associated with survival and procreation (collectively labeled **id** and often manifested in sexual urges termed **libido**), underlie much of behavior (for example, see Thurschwell, 2009). According to Freud, these instincts are sometimes apparent in dreams as well as in actual behavior.[1] Also, as we saw in Chapter 5, evolutionary psychologists look to biology and genetics as important sources of explanation for human learning and behavior. For example, sociobiology argues that human behavior is profoundly influenced by unlearned instinct-like tendencies.

Imprinting

Similarly, theorists such as Bowlby (1982) believe that early attachment between human mother and child has important parallels with **imprinting** among animals. Imprinting describes an instinctual, unlearned behavior that is specific to a species and does not appear until an animal has been exposed to the appropriate stimulus (called a *releaser*), providing that exposure occurs at the right period in the animal's life (the **critical period**). The classical example of imprinting is the "following" behavior of ducks, chickens, or geese, which typically imprint on the first moving object they see. Fortunately, that object is usually their mother, but it need not be. Lorenz (1952) reports the case of a gosling that imprinted on him and followed him around much as it might have followed its mother. As the time for mating approached, much to Lorenz's embarrassment, this goose insisted on foisting its affections on him. The story is that this goose, in a gesture of devotion and love, insisted on depositing beakfuls of minced worms in Lorenz's ear. Its love, as far as science knows, remained unrequited (see Figure 9.1).

Imprinting among animals is not limited to acquiring "following" behavior in *precocial* (fast-maturing) birds; it also appears to play an important role in their later sexual behavior. For example, various studies have shown that the sexual behavior of adult birds is strongly influenced by their exposure to appropriate stimuli during critical periods early in their development. This is perhaps why adult birds typically seek to mate with members of their own species. When Plenge, Curio, and Witte (2000) raised female birds with parents that had

---

[1] There's not much about Freud in this book, said Old Lady Gribbin as an aside. But some of your students might be interested in the Crews (2017) biography of Freud. Crews went through piles of old archives and he concluded that Freud was a charlatan, that he had invented his persona as a great mental detective, that he never succeeded in actually curing anyone, often simply recommending to his patients that they should use this miracle drug, cocaine, that he himself quite loved. But, added the old lady, Freudian theory still exerts enormous influence in psychotherapy.

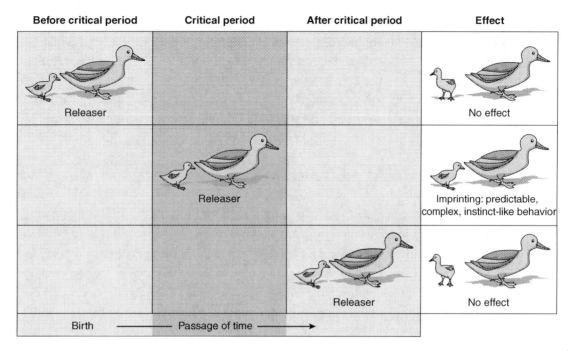

Figure 9.1 Under appropriate conditions, exposure to a releaser (a mother duck, for example) during the critical period (within a few hours of hatching) leads to imprinting, which is evident in the "following" behavior of the hatchling. Imprinting does not occur in the absence of a releaser or if the releaser is presented too early or too late.

been adorned with a bright red feather on their heads, these female birds later chose to mate with similarly adorned adults.

Although humans do not imprint as do many other animals, a number of researchers have looked at the possibility that sexual attraction and preference might be subject to something like imprinting. For example, there is some suggestion that human sexual responses to attributes such as the size and shape of buttocks and breasts in women, or muscular development and facial and body hair in men, might reflect imprinting-like influences. These might serve as signals of virility in men, fecundity in women, and general good health in both (Valentova, Bartova, Sterbova, & Varella, 2017a; Valentova, Varella, Bartova, Sterbova, & Dixson, 2017b). That human responses to these attributes are relatively general suggests the possibility of genetic influences that, in the words of these researchers, are *imprinting-like*.

Other researchers have sometimes suggested that many children tend to *sexually imprint* on their parents or even siblings. For example, based on an analysis of anonymous responses to a computerized questionnaire, Griffee et al. (2017) report that 19 percent of women and 16 percent of men recognize that they are attracted to people similar to their opposite-sexed parent (or, in some cases, sibling).

Similarly, Bowlby (1982) and others (for example, Hazen et al., 2015) argue that there is a "sensitive period" during which bonds between mother and infant form most easily and that this provides a biological explanation for early attachment. Interestingly, research indicates that the development of those parts of the brain most responsive to emotion, specifically, the amygdala and the hippocampus, are measurably affected by the nature of caregiver–infant interaction

Motivation and Emotions

during a sensitive period early in life. For example, Lyons-Ruth and associates (2016) found significantly smaller amygdala volumes among adults who had been subject to disrupted and inadequate maternal interaction as infants. Similarly, Perry, Blair, and Sullivan (2017) report that research on optimal development of the amygdala and the hippocampus appears to depend on infant–caregiver attachment during a sensitive period early in life. Quality of infant care, they explain, shapes emotional development in later adulthood.

PSYCHOLOGICAL HEDONISM

Considerable evidence, and intuitive good sense, indicates that we are drawn to that which is pleasant and try to avoid the unpleasant. At first glance, this notion, labeled **psychological hedonism**, would seem to be a good general explanation for many human behaviors. Unfortunately, it is not a very useful idea. The main problem with the notion is that it cannot be used to predict or even to explain behavior unless pain and pleasure can be defined clearly beforehand, which is not often possible. For example, it might appear wise to say that Samantha braves the Arctic cold in an uninsulated cabin because doing so is pleasant, but it is quite another matter to predict beforehand that Samantha will retire to that frosty cabin. The difficulty is that pain and pleasure are subjective emotional reactions. Although it might be true that many people are hedonistic, motivational theory can profit from this bit of knowledge only if pain and pleasure can be described more objectively. For this, we would need to know something about the subjective "hedonic" calculus that each person uses to evaluate different payoffs. As Milkman and Sunderwirth (2010) point out, some people's *hedonistic* drives push them toward obsession and addiction and "counterfeit" pleasures such as cigarettes, alcohol, drugs, sex, food, gambling, and so on. Others are driven more quietly in other directions. And some, as we see shortly when we look at Maslow's theory, are driven not by *hedonistic* motives but by a *eudemonic* approach to life (also spelled *eudaimonic*). This is an approach where well-being is defined not in terms of pain avoidance and pleasure attainment, but in more existential terms relating to self-fulfillment and to becoming the best, most highly developed, fully functioning individual possible (see, for example, Vitterso, 2016).

DRIVE REDUCTION AND INCENTIVES

One approach to defining pain and pleasure more objectively is implicit in operant conditioning theory's definitions of reinforcement and punishment. At a simple level, positive reinforcers might be considered pleasant, whereas punishment and negative reinforcers generally would not be.

Another approach to clarifying the hedonistic notions of pain and pleasure is to look at basic human needs and drives, assuming that satisfying needs is pleasant and leaving them unsatisfied is unpleasant. Historically, there have been two ways of looking at motivation, says Covington (2000). One view, for a long time the most popular, sees motives as drives that urge the individual to action. Recall that a **drive** is a tendency to behave brought about by an unsatisfied

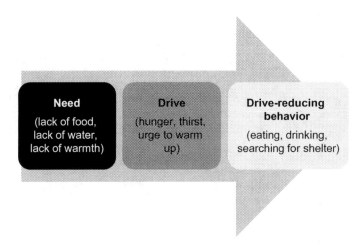

Figure 9.2 The drive-reduction model of motivation: A need (lack) gives rise to a drive (urge), which in turn leads to a behavior whose goal is to remedy the lack. This model is useful for explaining many physiologically based behaviors but does not effectively explain why some students work hard to learn their subjects and others play computer games instead. From Lefrançois, G. R. (2018). *Psychology for Teaching* (2nd ed.). San Diego, CA: Bridgepoint Education, Figure 8.4. Used by permission.

need. Thus, the need for food, when unsatisfied, gives rise to the hunger drive, which then motivates behavior.

The other view sees motives less as drives that impel the individual to act but rather as goals toward which the individual strives. The difference between these two views is mainly one of emphasis. Drives, such as the sex drive, clearly have goals associated with them. Similarly, a goal, such as the desire to achieve great fame, may lead to powerful drives to act in certain ways. As we see later, the emphasis in most current approaches to motivation, which tend to be more cognitive than behaviorist, is toward viewing motives as goals rather than as drives.

Three physiological motives are central to the lives of all humans: hunger, thirst, and sex. These have been studied mainly as drives rather than as goals.

Needs and Drives

Each of the three physiological motives is linked with a need – a lack that gives rise to a desire for satisfaction. The tendency to act to satisfy a need is what defines a drive. For example, to be thirsty is to be in a state of need for liquids; this need leads to the thirst drive. Thirst leads to drinking, and the need disappears. Thus, needs bear the seeds of their own destruction (see Figure 9.2).

This explanation of behavior, termed *drive reduction*, is well illustrated in Hull's theory. Hull believed that drive reduction is what accounts for the effects of reinforcers and leads to learning.

Psychological Needs

What the basic **physiological needs** (or *physical needs*) are seems clear: They include the need for food, drink, and sex and the need to maintain body temperature. Most psychologists also believe that people have **psychological needs**, although there is considerably less agreement about what these might be. Likely candidates include the needs for affection, belonging, achievement, independence, social recognition, and self-esteem. Research clearly supports the notion that satisfying psychological needs is important for psychological well-being and

334　Motivation and Emotions

is closely related to school achievement. That nonhuman animals also have psychological needs is less clear and somewhat controversial.[2]

One main difference between physical and psychological needs is that physical needs and their satisfaction result in tissue changes. Psychological needs, in contrast, are not necessarily manifested in bodily changes but have more to do with the intellectual or emotional aspects of human functioning. In addition, physiological needs can be completely satisfied whereas psychological needs are relatively insatiable. People can eat until they are not at all hungry, but they seldom receive affection until they desire absolutely no more from anyone.

Need/Drive Positions: An Appraisal

Need/drive models are important explanations in behavioristic learning theories. Skinner's and Thorndike's conditioning theories are founded largely on the effectiveness of basic drives as human motives. Similarly, Hull relied on drive reduction to explain why habits are acquired and how fractional antedating goal responses become connected. Not surprisingly, common reinforcers in animal research are things that satisfy basic unlearned needs like food and drink. And among the most common reinforcers in studies of human operant conditioning are those that satisfy learned or psychological needs (praise, money, tokens, high grades, and so on).

Some Problems with Need/Drive Theory

Even though need/drive theory appears to have considerable relevance for explaining human behavior, it has a number of problems. First, need/drive theories typically suggest that behavior results from a need or deficiency in the organism. It would seem logical to assume, then, that the satisfaction of needs should lead to rest. However, often this is not the case. Even rats that presumably are not in a state of need, having just been fed, given drink, and loved, often do not simply curl up and go to sleep. Instead, they may even show increases in activity.

A second problem with need/drive theory is that there are many instances of behaviors that human beings and even lower animals engage in with no possibility of immediate or delayed satisfaction of a need – as when a rat learns to run a maze in the absence of any reward (Tolman, 1951) or a person gets bored and looks for sensory stimulation (Hebb, 1966). Evidence of exploratory behavior has led some theorists to suggest that a curiosity or exploratory drive motivates many human behaviors (for example, Berlyne, 1960, 1966).

A third major shortcoming of need/drive or drive-reduction theories is that they try to account for behavior through inner states and urges (for example, need for food is an inner state, and the hunger drive is an urge). As a result, they are hard-pressed to explain why behaviors also seem to be affected by external stimulation. If hunger were solely an internal

---

[2] At this point, Old Lady Gribbin muttered something I couldn't quite make out. I don't really think she said what I thought I heard. Maybe she did. When she spoke again, she sounded very angry. Do you really believe the cat doesn't have psychological needs? She asked. I said nothing. It was surely another of her rhetorical questions. Schrödinger lay snuggled up against her scrawny neck. His single good eye seemed to be glaring at me.

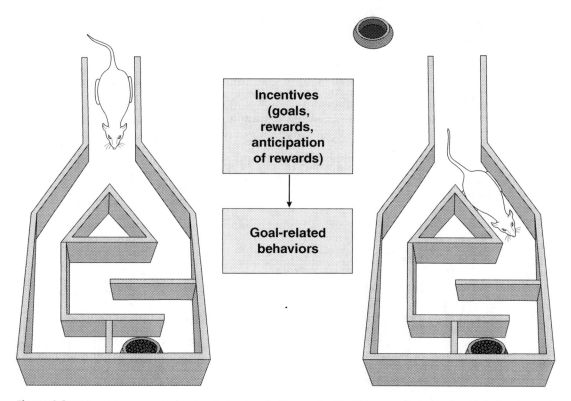

Figure 9.3 Drives alone cannot explain behavior. In Zeaman's (1949) experiment, rats that had already been given some food (right maze) performed better on a maze that they knew led to food than did hungry rats (left maze).

state, people would always eat only enough to activate the physiological mechanisms that relate to stopping eating. But many people eat far more if the foods appear more appetizing; others seem to become far hungrier if they are allowed to anticipate beforehand what they will be eating. Even rats that are given a small taste of food before being placed in the start box of a maze run faster toward the goal box than do rats that have not been "primed" (Zeaman, 1949). If an inner state of hunger is the motive, it follows that the taste of food, however small, should reduce the hunger drive somewhat and make the rats run more slowly (see Figure 9.3).

Incentives

What need/drive positions need to account for is the *incentive value* of motivation (termed **incentive motivation**). Even for rats, a taste of food seems to serve as an incentive, urging them to run faster. For us, gifted as we are with the ability to imagine and to anticipate, there is no need for a taste beforehand. All we need to know is that the world's most exquisite Crêpe Suzette is to be found yonder under the purple sign that reads "Suzie's," and we walk a little faster.

Basically, the term *incentive* relates to the value of a goal or reward. Thus, a goal is said to have high incentive value when it is particularly powerful in motivating behavior, and to have low incentive value if it is not very motivating. Hull was among the first to use the concept of

336   Motivation and Emotions

incentives in his theory (for which he used the symbol K; see Chapter 3). He recognized that drive alone could not account for motivation. Among other things, the amount of reward a rat receives affects its behavior, as does its history of past rewards.

The introduction of the concept of incentives into a discussion of need/drive theory makes it possible to account for the fact that monkeys will work harder to obtain a banana than a piece of lettuce and that a person might pay more to eat a steak than a hamburger. It also brings what is essentially a behavioristic theory of motivation somewhat closer to the cognitive positions because anticipating goals and estimating their values involve what are essentially cognitive processes. Later in this chapter, we deal in more detail with goals and rewards and how they relate to motivation.

Maslow's Hierarchy

There are two major systems of needs, says Maslow (1970): basic needs and **metaneeds**. The basic needs are called *deficiency needs* because they lead to behavior if the conditions that satisfy them are lacking. Basic needs include the physiological needs (need for food, drink, and sex, for example), safety needs (such as the need for security), love and belongingness needs, and self-esteem needs.

In contrast with the basic *deficiency* needs, the metaneeds are *growth* needs. They are marked by a human desire to grow, to achieve, to become. They include the need to know and achieve abstract values such as goodness and truth, to acquire knowledge, and to achieve *self-actualization* (discussed in more detail next).

Maslow assumes these need systems are hierarchical in that higher-level needs will not be attended to until lower-level needs have been satisfied. Thus, starving people do not hunger for knowledge. And the elderly whose basic needs are met but whose higher-level needs are ignored might remain unhappy (see Figure 9.4).

Self-Actualization

The most important of Maslow's metaneeds is **self-actualization**, a difficult-to-define concept. It is best described as the process of becoming oneself, of actualizing (making actual) one's potential. Self-actualization is the basic goal of the **eudemonic** (as opposed to *hedonistic*) orientation. It is an orientation that aspires to a sense of well-being determined by the extent to which the individual strives to become the best, most fully functioning person possible. But, as Maslow admitted, "The exploration of the highest reaches of human nature and its ultimate possibilities and aspirations is a difficult and tortuous task" (1970, p. 67). Even decades later, say Leclerc, Lefrançois, Dube, Hebert, and Gaulin (1998), the concept of self-actualization remains unclear. That is partly because there has been a tendency to view self-actualization as a state that the individual reaches when all of that person's potential has finally unfolded. In Maslow's words, self-actualized people "may be loosely described as [making] full use and exploitation of talents, capacities, potentialities, etc." (1970, p. 150). But when Maslow searched among 3,000 college students, he found only one person that he considered truly self-actualized, using this definition.

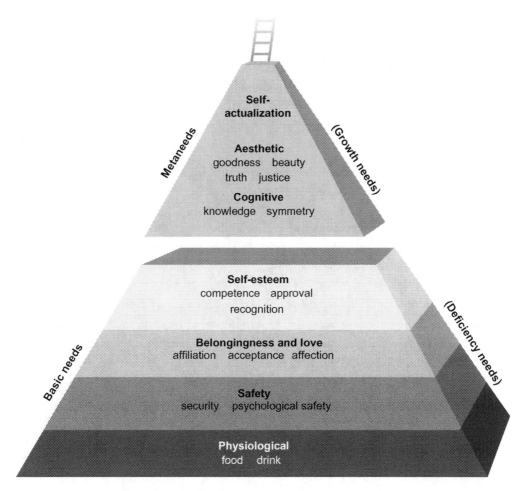

Figure 9.4 The hierarchy is shown in the form of a pyramid depicting lowest-level needs, such as the need for food and drink, at the bottom. When lower level needs are satisfied, the individual attempts to look after higher level needs. The open pyramid, suggested by Rowan (1998), indicates that self-actualization is a never-ending process rather than an ultimate, achievable goal. From Maslow, Abraham H.; Frager, Robert D.; Fadiman, James. MOTIVATION AND PERSONALITY, 3rd EDITION©1987. Printed and electronically reproduced by permission of Pearson Education, Inc., New York: New York.

The problem, says Rowan (1998), is that self-actualization is not a state but a process, an ongoing search to develop and to grow. As a result, the triangle that has typically been used to represent Maslow's hierarchy of needs is misleading because it is closed at the top. "What is wrong with the triangle," explains Rowan, "is that it suggests that there is an end point to personal growth" (1998, p. 88). But we never reach that end point (see Figure 9.4).[3]

---

[3] There are those, said Old Lady Gribbin, who believe it's possible to go beyond this end point, beyond the hedonistic and the eudemonic – that is, beyond the meager sense of well-being afforded by a succulent meal or the feelings of a job well done, or the self-congratulatory notion that one has become all that one can be. Inspiration makes it possible to transcend all this, as might a truly holy person.... But I would lose many of your readers if I tried to explain that, the old lady said sadly. Those on the brink of eudemonic self-fulfillment might want to do a little research to clarify their paths. Tell them they could start with the chapter by Belzak, Yoon, Thrash, and Wadsworth (2017) listed in the references.

AROUSAL THEORY

Three things affect how much effort a person is willing to make (that is, how motivated a person is), according to Brehm and Self (1989): internal states (such as needs); potential outcomes; and the individual's estimate of the probability that a behavior will lead to a desired outcome. This recognizes both the physiological and the cognitive aspects of behavior, much as Hull's system tried to do.

Emotion and Motivation: Level of Arousal

Most of our important behaviors are intentional, and are directed by a desire to attain goals or to avoid certain outcomes. When we succeed in reaching a goal or avoiding a negative outcome, we feel positive **emotions**; failure leads to negative emotions (emotions are feelings or subjective reactions describable in terms such as angry, anxious, ambivalent, annoyed, agitated, and hundreds more). Hence, emotions are strongly linked with the reasons why we do or do not do things.

Emotion is both physiological and psychological. Some of the physiological aspects of emotion can be detected and measured. We know that the physiological changes that accompany increasing motivation and emotion are changes in the **sympathetic nervous system** – the part of the nervous system involved in changing heart rate, constricting blood vessels, and raising blood pressure. These are all changes that accompany strong emotions. These changes define what is meant by *arousal*.

The term **arousal** has both psychological and physiological meaning. As a psychological concept, it seems to have at least two dimensions, explains Dickman (2002). One dimension relates to tension and ranges from high anxiety or even panic at one extreme to great calmness at the other. The other dimension has to do with energy and refers to the degree of alertness, wakefulness, or attentiveness of a person or animal. The energy dimension of arousal may also be evident in the organism's vigor, notes Dickman, which appears to be somewhat different from wakefulness.

As a physiological concept, arousal refers to the degree of activation of the organism through activation of the sympathetic nervous system. Physiological arousal is often measured through changes in heart rate and blood pressure, changes in conductivity of the skin to electricity (called **electrodermal response**), and alterations in electrical activity of the brain. Specifically, with increasing arousal, the electrical activity of the cortex (as measured by an electroencephalograph [EEG]) takes the form of increasingly rapid and shallow waves (called **beta waves**). At lower levels of arousal (such as calm meditation), the waves are slower and deeper (called **alpha waves**).

Increasing arousal defines increasing intensity of motivation (and of emotion). But the relationship between arousal and intensity of motivation is not perfectly linear; that is, a person does not continue to become increasingly motivated as arousal increases.

The Yerkes–Dodson Law

At the very lowest levels of arousal, motivation tends to be low and behavior ineffective. This can easily be demonstrated by asking someone at the lowest normal level of arousal

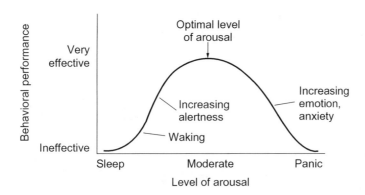

Figure 9.5 The Yerkes–Dodson law describes the relationship between behavioral performance and arousal level. In general, the most effective performance occurs at an intermediate level of arousal. Note that this is more a general observation than an actual law.

(namely, sleep) a simple question, such as "How many are five?" As arousal increases, behavior becomes more highly motivated and more interested; the person can now tell you with stunning clarity how many five are and all sorts of other things.

But if arousal continues to increase, as might happen if what woke the person up were an earthquake, performance might deteriorate badly. Often evident in high anxiety or even fear, high arousal explains why students in tense oral examinations are sometimes unable to remember anything and sometimes cannot even speak. Anxiety in test situations clearly lowers test performance (von der Embse, Schultz, & Draughn, 2015). And, not surprisingly, decreasing anxiety can contribute to increased test performance. Khng (2017) trained 122 fifth-grade students to perform a series of deep-breathing relaxation exercises and had them perform these exercises just prior to a timed mathematics test. Subsequent measures revealed two important findings: First, the exercises produced measurable reductions in students' feelings of anxiety; and second, test performance was significantly enhanced, especially for the more anxious learners.

Studies indicate that negative emotions associated with tests, such as anxiety over the personal consequences of failing or doing poorly on a test, increases general levels of anxiety and may have a detrimental effect on test performance. In contrast, more positive emotions such as anticipation without high levels of personal concern or worry can increase general arousal to the point that there is a positive influence on test performance (Chin, Williams, Taylor, & Harvey, 2017).

In summary, the relationship between performance and arousal, depicted in Figure 9.5, takes the form of an inverted U-shaped function. This observation, first described by Yerkes and Dodson (1908), is known as the **Yerkes–Dodson law**. Basically, this law says that there is an optimal level of arousal for the most effective behavior; arousal levels above and below this optimal level are associated with less effective behavior. This law has been widely accepted in psychology. It has also been corroborated in various studies with animals. For example, Bray, MacLean, and Hare (2015) compared the performance of *assistance* dogs, trained for low arousal, with that of pet dogs, whose normal levels of arousal were measurably higher than those of the assistance dogs. In their study, dogs were exposed to a novel task (a detour problem) under conditions of increasing arousal. Investigators increased the dogs' arousal by eagerly encouraging them. Mounting arousal level in dogs is easily measured in tail wagging rate. As would be predicted by the Yerkes–Dodson law, the performance of dogs at an initially low arousal level increased with increasing arousal; in contrast, performance of dogs who were normally highly aroused deteriorated with further increases in arousal.

Hebb's Arousal Theory

Hebb's **arousal theory** of motivation is based directly on the Yerkes–Dodson law. This law, claims Hebb (1972), gives rise to two important assumptions. First, optimal level of arousal differs for different tasks. Thus, intense, concentrated activities, such as studying or competing on a television quiz program, demand higher levels of alertness (arousal) than do more habitual behaviors, such as driving a car. For most routine activities, moderate levels of arousal are probably best. Second, the organism behaves in such a way as to maintain the level of arousal that is most appropriate for ongoing behavior. If arousal is too low, the organism will try to increase it; if it is too high, an attempt will be made to lower it.

The value of arousal as a motivational concept is based largely on the validity of this second assumption. If people try to maintain an optimal level of arousal, then it should be possible to predict at least some behaviors. For example, students who are bored in a classroom (too low an arousal level) would be expected to do things to increase their arousal. Actually, this is what happens when students daydream, throw paper wads, play games on their smartphones, or talk out loud with other bored students.

Two Functions of Stimuli

Stimuli have two important functions, claimed Hebb (1972): the **cue function** and the **arousal function**. The cue function is the message function; it tells the organism how to feel, think, or react. The arousal function is defined by the general activating, or arousing, effect of stimuli. Interestingly, Hull made exactly the same distinction, referring to the cue and the drive components of stimuli.

In Hebb's terms, the cue function involves the activation of the specific cell assemblies corresponding to the stimulation. For example, a red light at a traffic intersection gives rise to a complex of stimuli that activate cell assemblies that permit the individual to recognize the stimulus and react appropriately. This is the *cue function* of this stimulus complex: its meaning. In contrast, the arousal function involves the activation – or, more precisely, preactivation – of a larger number of cell assemblies. This preactivation is brought about through the **reticular formation**, a structure that forms part of the brain stem and through which most neural pathways branch on their way from sensory systems to the brain. Arousal (preactivation of cell assemblies) is essential for the cue to have its effect, claims Hebb. At low levels of arousal, the individual is totally relaxed or even asleep and stimulation might have no discernible effect.

The Need for Stimulation

Unless they are tired and in need of sleep, humans, and, indeed, many other organisms, appear to have a clear and strong need to maintain relatively high levels of arousal. When Hebb and his co-researchers lowered students' arousal levels dramatically and kept them at low levels for long periods, they observed some surprising outcomes (Bexton, Heron & Scott, 1954; Zubek, 1969). In the classic experiments related to this, male college students were asked to volunteer for an experiment. They were told they would be paid $20 a day for doing absolutely nothing (Heron, 1957) – a substantial sum in those days.

During the experiment, participants were forced to lie on cots, getting up only to use the toilet and sitting up only to eat their meals. Each cot was isolated in a soundproof cubicle, and subjects wore translucent visors that did not allow them to see, but permitted diffuse light to enter. Over their ears, they wore U-shaped foam pillows designed to prevent hearing. As a further precaution against the perception of sounds, air-conditioning equipment hummed ceaselessly and monotonously. In addition, participants wore cotton gloves and had cardboard cuffs that extended over their fingertips to discourage tactile sensation. In short, the experimenters tried to make sure that participants would experience a minimum of sensory stimulation as long as they remained in isolation.

Interestingly, none of the subjects lasted more than two days. In some later experiments where conditions of deprivation were more severe (for example, complete darkness, no sound, body immersed in water to simulate weightlessness), subjects often did not last more than a few hours (for example, see Barnard, Wolfe & Graveline, 1962; Lilly, 1972).

Because the chief source of arousal is sensation, perceptual deprivation should result in a lowering of arousal. This assumption has been confirmed through measures of electrical activity in the brain (EEG recordings) before, during, and after isolation (Heron, 1957; Zubek & Wilgosh, 1963). After prolonged isolation, the brain activity of subjects who are awake is often similar to that normally associated with sleep.

Other effects of sensory deprivation include impairment in perceptual and cognitive functioning evident in performance on simple numerical or visual tasks (Heron, 1957). In addition, subjects often become irritable, easily amused or annoyed, and almost childish in their reactions to limited contact with experimenters. For example, they often desperately attempt to engage the experimenter in conversation, acting in much the same way a child does when trying to gain the attention of a preoccupied parent.

Among the most striking findings of sensory-deprivation studies is that subjects sometimes report experiencing illusions of various kinds, and in some cases hallucinations, after prolonged isolation. These are relatively infrequent and are markedly affected by the subject's preisolation attitudes (Zubek, 1969). However, more recent research has found that even short periods of sensory deprivation can lead to perceptual distortions, paranoia, and other disturbances, especially in hallucination-prone individuals (Mason & Brady, 2009).

These studies of sensory deprivation tend to add further support to arousal-based explanations of human behavior. There seems to be little question that behavior is more nearly optimal under conditions of moderate arousal. In addition, it seems that people try to maintain arousal at that level. For example, subjects in isolation often talk to themselves, whistle, recite poetry, or (as noted earlier) attempt to draw the experimenters into conversation. Such behavior led Schultz (1965) to hypothesize that the need for arousal is really a need for stimulation.

Almost all the more recent studies on sensory deprivation have been conducted with animals (often with rodents such as mice) rather than with human participants. In general, many of these studies indicate that sensory deprivation often leads to an increase in neural activity, particularly in the hippocampus (for example Denizet, Cotter, Lledo, & Lazarini, 2017; Milshtein-Parush et al., 2017). Recall that this temporal lobe structure is closely involved in learning and memory. It is as though, in the absence of external stimulation, the brain itself becomes more active, thus, in a sense, increasing its own arousal.

Sources of Arousal

The principal source of arousal is stimulation. But perhaps even more important for theories of motivation, it is the meaningfulness, the novelty, and the surprisingness of stimulation that increases arousal or fails to increase it (Berlyne, 1965, 1966). Much of people's exploratory behavior – that is, behavior designed to discover and learn things – stems from a need for stimulation, says Berlyne.

Arousal is also related to a variety of personal and cognitive factors. As Brehm and Self (1989) note, the more difficult and the more important a behavior is, the higher the arousal associated with it will be. Similarly, motivational arousal may be a function of the extent to which the actor assumes personal responsibility for the outcomes of behavior versus the extent to which these are attributed to luck or other factors over which the person has no control. These are some of the things that social cognitive theories of motivation look at.

SOCIAL COGNITIVE VIEWS OF MOTIVATION

Some early behavioristic theories in learning and in motivation were characterized by what has been described as a mechanistic and passive view of the human organism. For example, in theories such as Hull's, motives for behaving consist largely of the urge to reduce drives related to unsatisfied needs. Behavior is viewed as a question of responding to internal or external prods to which the individual reacts in a relatively helpless way.

In contrast, cognitive positions present a more active view of human behavior. Individuals are seen as actively exploring and manipulating, as predicting and evaluating the consequences of their behavior, and as acting on the environment rather than simply reacting to it.

Note that although some behavioristic positions do tend to see the individual as more reactive than active, many do not. For example, Skinner also sees the organism as acting on the environment, as exploring and manipulating, as emitting responses rather than simply responding blindly. Accordingly, a better contrast between behaviorist and cognitive approaches to motivation is that cognitive theories explain the effectiveness of environmental circumstances such as rewards and punishments in terms of the individual's understanding and interpretation. Behavioristic theorists see no need to resort to these cognitive events.

A Theory of Cognitive Dissonance

That individuals act on the basis of their information and beliefs seems clear, claims Festinger (1957, 1962), author of an intriguing cognitive theory of motivation known as the theory of

cognitive dissonance. Simply stated, the theory holds that when a person simultaneously possesses two contradictory items of information (a situation that defines cognitive dissonance), that person will be motivated to reduce the contradiction. As Morvan and O'Connor (2017) explain it, Festinger's theory describes how people have developed mechanisms to reduce the stress associated with holding two incompatible beliefs at the same time, or with behaving in ways that contradict beliefs. In this sense, cognitive dissonance serves as an explanation for behavior (hence, as a *motive*).

In one study, Festinger (1962) subjected individual college students to an exhausting and boring one-hour session that the students thought had to do with motor performance. After the session, each participant was told that the experiment was over, but each was then asked to help the experimenter with the next subject. The participants were told that it was important for the research that the incoming person believe the experiment would be interesting and pleasant. Each participant agreed to lie to that person. As a result, says Festinger, participants would be expected to experience conflict (or dissonance) between their behavior and their beliefs.

Cognitive dissonance theory predicts that subjects will try to reduce the dissonance. One way of doing this would be to retract the lie, which was impossible under the circumstances. The alternative would be for subjects to change their private opinions by modifying their beliefs.

Festinger used two different treatments in this experiment. Although all subjects were paid to tell the lie, some were given $20, but others received only $1. The effect of this differential treatment was remarkable. The obvious prediction is that those paid the larger amount would be more likely to change their beliefs than would those paid the smaller amount. But the opposite was consistently true! Those who received small sums often became convinced that the session was really enjoyable; those who were paid the larger sum remained truer to their original beliefs.

Brehm and Cohen (1962) later corroborated these findings in a similar study in which they paid participants $10, $5, $1, or 50 cents for lying. As in the Festinger study, those subjects paid the smallest sum changed their opinions the most, whereas those paid $10 didn't change appreciably.

The explanation for these unexpected results is that the magnitude of dissonance brought about by a behavior contrary to one's beliefs will be directly proportional to the justification that exists for the act. Students paid $20 to lie have a better reason for doing so and will therefore feel less dissonance. These studies lead to the interesting observation that if criminals (thieves, for example) initially know that their behavior is immoral and if they are highly successful at their chosen vocation, they will be "better" people than if they are unsuccessful. If they make a lot of money by stealing, they are more likely to continue to believe that stealing is an immoral act, justified by its material rewards. But if they make very little money stealing, they are more likely to change their opinions about their criminal activities and view it as morally acceptable.

In another study, Tanford and Montgomery (2015) looked at college students' spring break travel decisions when they had to make a choice between a green (environmentally friendly) and a non-green resort. Student choices were influenced by reviews describing the resort either positively or negatively and recommending them accordingly. Subsequent measures indicated that participants who initially had strong pro-environmental attitudes experienced considerable dissonance when, as a result of the social pressure of traveler recommendations, they chose the non-green option. And, consistent with earlier findings, they now tended to evaluate the resort they had chosen more favorably than the one not chosen.

Reducing Dissonance

Dissonance can lead to uncomfortably high arousal, as several studies have shown (for example, Martinie, Milland, & Olive, 2013; McGrath, 2017). Dissonance is an important motivational concept because it provides an explanation for behaviors designed to reduce it. There are many different ways in which this can be done (Festinger, 1957; Morvan & O'Connor, 2017).

1. **Attitude change:** One way of reducing dissonance, as the experiments just described illustrate, is to change beliefs (or attitudes). Consider the case of Sam Plotkin, who dislikes schoolteachers intensely but who, at a local dance, falls in love with Mary Rosie. When he discovers that Mary is a teacher, he is subjected to a great deal of dissonance, which will disappear when he decides that he does not like Mary or that teachers really are not that bad.

Cognitive dissonance theory is widely used in social psychology as a way of explaining attitude change and as a basis for suggesting how people might be influenced to change. For example, Cooper, Feldman, and Blackman (2018) had individuals identified as Republicans or Democrats imagine the statements members of the other party would make if forced to defend or attack Obamacare in opposition with their beliefs. As predicted by dissonance theory, Republicans placed in this situation experienced what the authors labeled *vicarious* (second-hand) dissonance, leading to a subsequent change in attitudes and a greater support for Obamacare. Democrats who had now imagined statements that opposed Obamacare showed only marginally reduced support for the act. These results illustrate how deliberately manipulating dissonance can bring about attitude change.

2. **Compartmentalization:** If Sam Plotkin, in love with Mary but negatively predisposed toward teachers, decides that Mary is really not like other teachers – that she is a different type of person, despite the fact that she teaches – what he is doing is placing her in a different "compartment." Compartmentalization, says Festinger (1962), is a fairly common dissonance reducer.

3. **Exposure to or Recall of Information:** Sometimes, when two items of information conflict, gaining more information can reduce dissonance. If a rumor is circulated that wheat flour turns the human liver white, it will probably create some conflict in those who have been in the habit of eating food made with wheat flour. If a person were exposed to the information that white livers are really quite functional, the dissonance might disappear. Similarly, dissonance resulting from doing poorly on a test (a discrepancy between expectations and actual performance) would be greatly reduced if the student learned that all other students had done as poorly.

4. **Behavioral Change:** Situations characterized by dissonance sometimes lead to changes in behavior. Tobacco smokers whose behavior is at odds with the information they have about the effects of smoking might stop smoking, thereby eliminating all dissonance.

5. **Perceptual Distortion:** However, quite frequently, smokers find it simpler to use other techniques for coping with this problem. For example, they might convince themselves that there is yet no conclusive proof that smoking is harmful, thus using a strategy of selective exposure to information or perceptual distortion. To avoid dissonance, these smokers might simply insist that all that has been clearly demonstrated by numerous smoking-related studies on experimental animals is that *Rattus norvegicus* would do well to stay away from the weed.

Reducing dissonance

Not surprisingly, when Gibbons, Eggleston, and Benthin (1997) looked at the attitudes of individuals who had stopped smoking but later started again, they found that these relapsers had significantly distorted their perception of the risks associated with smoking.[4]

---

[4] One of Festinger's most fascinating studies, the one that started the whole theory, said Old Lady Gribbin taking in an unbelievably huge breath, is his *end of the world* study about the cult that absolutely knew the world was about to end but a flying saucer was coming to save them at midnight so they needed to be ready and waiting with no metal objects on them but the saucer didn't show up at midnight like it was supposed to and these people had gone to extraordinary lengths to be prepared for its arrival giving up their jobs and leaving their families and giving away their money and so how would they resolve the dissonance they might now feel and I think your students whose brains are like fat mushrooms should Google that study or get hold of that 2012 book by Joel Cooper called *Cognitive Dissonance: Revisiting the End of the World Study*. She said all this without throwing in a single comma. I don't really know what she meant about your brains.

Summary of Dissonance Theory

Cognitive dissonance is the motivating state that occurs when an individual is in conflict. Ordinary sources of dissonance are incompatibilities between beliefs, between behavior and private opinion, or between two items of information. Dissonance theory holds that these states lead to behavior intended to reduce the conflict and reflects the amount of conflict and stress that exists (see Figure 9.6).

Cognitive dissonance has become a relatively common intervention technique in a variety of therapeutic settings. For example, changes in the eating habits of patients with different eating disorders can sometimes be brought about by creating cognitive dissonance among these patients, often through discussion, exercises, homework, social pressure, and so on (for example, Taylor, Fitzsimmons-Craft, & Goel, 2018). Similarly, Auer and Griffiths (2018) suggest that dissonance-based approaches might be useful for treating gambling addictions.

Intrinsic and Extrinsic Motives

Cognitive theorists insist that the urge to understand and explain to ourselves why we do things is fundamentally human. We need to be able to attribute our behavior to some recognizable cause – to make sense of the things we do.

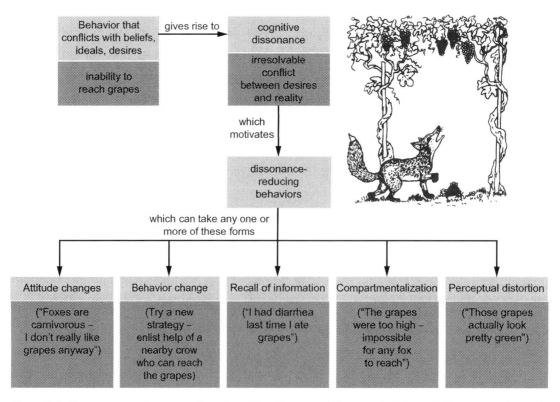

Figure 9.6 Everyone experiences conflicts (cognitive dissonance) between beliefs or desires and reality. This conflict can be arousing and disturbing and can serve as a motive for behavior designed to reduce it. There are many ways of trying to ease cognitive dissonance. From Lefrançois, G. R. (2016). *Psychology: The Human Puzzle* (2nd ed.). San Diego, CA: Bridgepoint Education, Fig. 8.5. Used by permission.

Some causes of behavior seem clear. For example, we do many things for external goals and rewards, such as a steak or a hamburger or a fifty-dollar bill. These external rewards are closely tied to **extrinsic motives** – motives relating to *external* sources of reinforcement. Extrinsic motives are what investigators use when they give rats and pigeons food rewards for their actions, and when they give students high marks and verbal praise for their behaviors. But praise is not something that can be eaten like a candy to satisfy an urge and then it's gone. Praise, and perhaps the candy too, might do more than simply satisfy a passing urge. Each might bring about the realization that one has done well, and each might lead to feelings of pride and satisfaction. These feelings, cognitive psychologists insist, can be extremely powerful **intrinsic motives** – motives tied to *internal* sources of reinforcement. In business and education, where motivating people is tremendously important, appeal to intrinsic motives may be more important than appeal to external motives.

Can External Rewards Decrease Intrinsic Motivation?

"When individuals are intrinsically motivated," explain Eccles and Wigfield, "they engage in an activity because they are interested in and enjoy the activity. When extrinsically motivated, individuals engage in activities for instrumental or other reasons, such as receiving a reward" (2002, p. 112).

External rewards, such as money, are very powerful motives; witness the lengths to which many people will go to get some. But, caution Deci and Flaste, "While money is motivating people, it is also undermining their intrinsic motivation" (1995, p. 27). As counterintuitive as this may seem, some studies seem to indicate just that. For example, Lepper and Greene (1975) gave two groups of children some geometric puzzles to solve. One group was told that they would be rewarded by being allowed to play with some toys; the other group had no reason to expect any reward. Subsequently, both groups were allowed to play with the toys. And both were later observed to see whether they would be sufficiently interested in the puzzles to play with them spontaneously. Surprisingly, as is shown in Figure 9.7, significantly more of those who had not expected a reward were motivated to play with the puzzles.

Lepper and Greene (1975) suggest that perhaps the most plausible explanation for this is a cognitive one. It is important for us to make sense of our behaviors, to understand why we do things. Typically, they explain, we resort to one of two types of explanations for our behaviors: We recognize that we do things for external rewards, such as being paid or being allowed to play with a toy (extrinsic reward); or we believe we do things because we are interested in them, enjoy the activity, and derive personal satisfaction from it (intrinsic reward). Or we do things for both internal and external motives.

When external motives are large, obvious, and expected, we are most likely to use these motives to explain our behaviors, notes Lepper (1981). That is, we are then most likely to be extrinsically motivated. But when we expect no significant external reward, we have to explain and justify our behavior with more intrinsic motives. Thus, those who expect no external reward subsequently display more intrinsic motivation, and consequently more interest, in the activity. However, if you expect no reward but receive one, as was the case for the children in

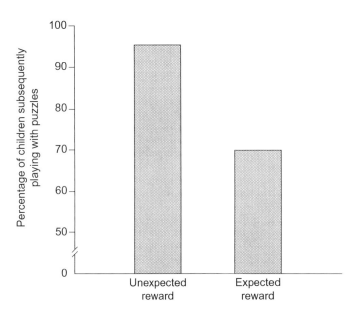

Figure 9.7 The overjustification hypothesis suggests that rewarding certain activities unexpectedly or excessively can undermine intrinsic motivation for those activities. The results of the study summarized here indicate that significantly more children who had not expected a reward showed higher intrinsic interest by subsequently playing spontaneously with the geometric puzzles. Based on data from M. R. Lepper and D. Greene (1975), "Turning play into work: Effects of adult surveillance and extrinsic rewards on children's intrinsic motivation." In the *Journal of Personality and Social Psychology*, 31, 479–486.

the Lepper and Greene (1975) study, the external reward might have the effect of undermining your intrinsic motivation to continue engaging in the activity. This situation is labeled the **overjustification hypothesis**. What it says, in effect, is that because extrinsic rewards provide strong justification for doing something, intrinsic reasons for engaging in that activity are weakened. The implication of this hypothesis is that providing external rewards for various activities might not always be a good thing. For example, when Warneken and Tomasello (2014) gave little toys and gifts to a group of 20-month old children who spontaneously helped others, they found that these children were subsequently less likely to engage in these altruistic behaviors than were other children who had not been rewarded for so doing.

However, not all researchers agree that the *overjustification* effect is important or that it even exists. For example, Pope and Harvey (2015) provided incentives during two semesters to one group of first-year college students for meeting certain health-related fitness-center goals; a second group was given no incentives for meeting these goals; and a third group received incentives during the first semester but not the second. They found that, during this period, intrinsic motives for these activities did not decrease for any of the three groups.

The finding that extrinsic rewards can sometimes undermine intrinsic motivation is not entirely clear. In fact, an analysis of 96 studies that examined the relationship between intrinsic and extrinsic motivation concluded that reinforcement does not lower intrinsic motivation (Cameron & Pierce, 1994). Perhaps, suggest Ryan and Deci (2008), that is because many behaviors that appear to be directed toward external rewards are a result of the individual's basic internal needs. Most important among these are the need to be competent and to be self-determining (autonomous). For example, explain Deci and Ryan (2008), the student who chooses a major because it will earn him a lot of money may seem to be guided entirely by extrinsic motives but, in fact, may be strongly influenced by the basic needs for self-determination and competence. Self-determined individuals – those who select their own activities freely and autonomously – are those who have internalized what might otherwise seem to be external reasons for behaving.

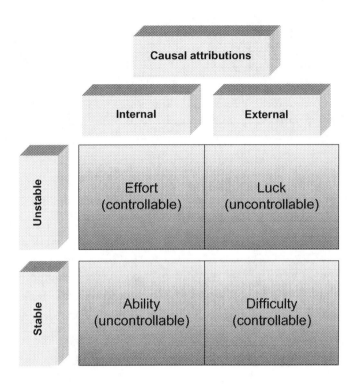

Figure 9.8 Four important possible attributions for success and failure. Our explanations for why we succeed or fail can be internal or external; they can also invoke causes that are either stable or unstable and that are controllable or uncontrollable. From Lefrançois, G. R. (2018). *Psychology for Teaching* (2nd ed.). San Diego, CA: Bridgepoint Education, Fig. 8.6. Used by permission.

Attribution Theory

This belief is directly tied to **attribution theory** – the theory that searches for predictable regularity in the ways people explain things. To *attribute* is to assign responsibility or to impute motives. If Rod attributes his stupidity to his parents, he is assigning them responsibility for that condition.

Rotter (1954) was among the first to suggest that people can be differentiated by their tendencies to attribute their successes and failures to internal or external causes. In his words, there are people whose **locus of control** is external; others are more internally oriented. *Locus* is Latin for a place or a locality. Hence *locus of control* refers to whether an individual attributes the outcomes of behavior to *external* or *internal* sources. Those who are externally oriented, says Weiner (1986, 2008), tend to attribute their successes and failures to task difficulty, bad luck, good luck, or other factors over which they have no control. In contrast, internally oriented individuals are more likely to explain the outcome of their behavior in terms of their own ability and effort (see Figure 9.8).

Attribution and Dissonance

If you want to do well and think you should but do not, you may well experience some *cognitive dissonance*. But if you attribute your failure to do well to external causes, that means you have little personal responsibility for your successes and failures. As a result, you will not be subject to cognitive dissonance in the same way as are individuals who are more internally oriented. By the same token, those who are internally oriented are far more likely to feel pride when they succeed and shame when they fail. Thus, dissonance and internal orientation are likely to be associated with emotion, and the motivating power of emotion is considerable.

Development of Attribution Tendencies

Some people habitually attribute success and failure to either internal or external causes; the tendency to do so seems to be a relatively predictable and stable personality characteristic. However, this is not the case for children younger than nine. Before that age, Folmer et al. (2008) explain, children have not yet differentiated between factors such as ability and effort. They think those who know the most are the most "intelligent." In their view, those who work hard and succeed are the smartest.

At around age 10, children begin to consider ability as a separate factor that contributes to success. But even at this age, "smartness" is still equated with hard work. However, by age 11, children typically share our intuitive notions about the distinctions among ability, luck, effort, and task difficulty (Dweck, 2002a).

Interestingly, research indicates that attributions are often related to the nature of the event being considered. For example, positive events are most likely to be attributed to internal, stable factors over which the individual has control. However, negative outcomes are more likely to be attributed to external, unstable events that are beyond the individual's control (for example, Titova & Sheldon, 2018).

Dweck's Theory: Performance versus Mastery Goals

Some of us, says Dweck (1986, 1999), seem to believe that intelligence is fixed and unchanging: We have an **entity theory** of intelligence (we believe it is an unchanging *entity*). Others behave as though they think intelligence is malleable and can change: These people subscribe to the **incremental theory** of intelligence.

Those who subscribe to the entity theory tend to have what are termed **performance goals**; they try to perform well so others will judge them competent and will think they have an impressive amount of this fixed quality we call *intelligence*. On the other hand, those who subscribe to the incremental theory believe they can increase their competence through effort. As a result, their goals will be **mastery goals** (also termed *learning goals*). Mastery goals are directed toward increasing competence rather than simply trying to perform well.

Attribution research strongly suggests that students whose basic orientation is toward performance goals (those who subscribe to the entity theory and therefore see intelligence as being fixed) need to believe they have very high ability to be willing to accept challenges. Those with lower confidence are more likely to give up and to suffer from feelings of "helplessness" because they see failure as a direct reflection of their lack of ability. In contrast, those who view intelligence as malleable and who are therefore oriented toward mastery are more likely to accept challenges and to be persistent. Because they believe that effort contributes to ability, they are more likely to strive toward high achievement. For them, the cost of failure is not as high as it is for those who see ability as fixed and unchangeable (Blackwell, Trzesniewski, & Dweck, 2007; Dweck & Grant, 2008) (see Table 9.1).

Table 9.1 **Achievement goals and achievement behavior**

Theory of intelligence	Goal orientation	Confidence in present ability	Behavior pattern
Entity theory (intelligence is fixed)	*Performance goal* (goal is to gain positive judgments/avoid negative judgments of competence)	*If high*	*Mastery oriented* (seeks challenge; high persistence)
		If low	*Helpless* (avoids challenge; low persistence)
Incremental theory (intelligence is malleable)	Learning goal (goal is to increase competence)	*If high or low*	Mastery oriented (seeks challenge that fosters learning; high persistence)

Source: Adapted from C. S. Dweck. (1986). "Motivational processes affecting learning." *American Psychologist*, *41*, 1040–1048. Copyright © American Psychological Association. Used by permission.

Implications of Mindsets About Intelligence

Dweck argues strongly that belief in the malleability of intelligence and the performance-oriented goals that come with that belief contribute to successful achievement in important ways (Dweck & Yeager, 2018). Unfortunately, however, many of us naïvely believe that intelligence is fixed: We have this *mindset*, claims Dweck in a book by that title (Dweck, 2006). The sad thing is that our *mindsets* shape our goals, our efforts, our attitudes – even our relationships. Those who are convinced that intelligence is fixed may go to great lengths to convince people that they have a lot of this thing we think of as intelligence. And they will avoid challenges that might expose their shortcomings. That, argues Dweck, is the road to stagnation. But those who know that intelligence is malleable – who have a *growth* rather than a *fixed* mindset – know that with effort, they can develop astonishing skills and talents.[5]

Furthermore, as Dweck and Yeager (2018) explain, the judgments about themselves and about others made by those who hold an entity theory and have fixed mindsets are likely to be relatively permanent judgments. If you believe intelligence is fixed and also believe that you, or Rebo, do not have much of this thing, this can have lasting repercussions for your future undertakings and for your relationships with Rebo. Mindsets, explains Dweck, can determine and explain important outcomes. She urges that interventions are needed to focus people on

---

[5] It might be intelligent, said Old Lady Gribbin, waiting with her finger raised so I would turn off the recorder – it might be intelligent to point out to your students that unless they happen to be one of those narcissistic types who absolutely know that they're more intelligent (among other good things) than just about anyone else, believing that intelligence is fixed seriously limits the possibilities they might envision for themselves and the efforts they're likely to make to achieve those possibilities. That's another long sentence, I ventured. Read it again if you don't understand it, she retorted, gathering up her crumpled pages and reading on.

growth rather than fixed mindsets. Growth mindsets have tremendous potential to increase academic performance and reduce a variety of negative outcomes associated with feelings of hopelessness and inadequacy (Claro, Paunesku, & Dweck, 2016; Haimovitz & Dweck, 2017).

Unfortunately, as Haimovitz and Dweck (2017) explain, even parents who have growth mindsets do not automatically pass these mindsets on to their children through a natural process of socialization. Too often, their children grow up with the notion that they have a fixed amount of ability and that they can do little to change it. However, there is considerable research supporting the notion that a growth mindset can be taught using a variety of approaches, including in-person workshops, tutoring sessions, online programs, and other interventions that emphasize how brains can develop and grow (for example, Yeager et al., 2016).

What do parents and teachers need to do to promote growth mindsets? Studies indicate several possibilities and at least one caution: The caution is simply that when children are repeatedly praised for being intelligent (you are really smart, Ishmael!), or worse (Ishmael, we think college is going to be out of your reach), they are likely to develop fixed mindsets. But if they are praised for their efforts and their strategies they are far more likely to develop growth mindsets. However, praise for effort that has not been effective is, as Haimovitz and Dweck (2017) put it, "like giving them the consolation prize of effort praise" (p. 1854). The most effective praise is that which is aimed at effort and strategies that are successful. One of the tasks of both parents and teachers is to provide children with challenging tasks *at which they can succeed* – tasks that, in Vygotsky's terms, are within the child's *zone of proximal development* (Chapter 7)

Attribution and Achievement Goals

How people explain their successes and failures appears to be closely related to what psychologists call **need for achievement** – the individual's need to reach some standard of excellence. It seems that those with a high need to achieve are far more likely to attribute the outcomes of their behavior to internal causes. Thus, if they are successful, they are likely to attribute their success to effort (and perhaps also to ability); if they are not successful, they continue to invoke internal factors, often blaming a lack of effort. In contrast, individuals characterized by a lower need for achievement may attribute their success to ability, effort, ease of the task, or luck. Put another way, high-need achievers will tend to be internally oriented, whereas low-need achievers will more likely attribute their performance to external factors (Mueller & Dweck, 1998). Not surprisingly, individuals who score high on measures of achievement motivation also tend to be high achievers in school (Capa, Audiffren, & Ragot, 2008).

High-need achievers are typically moderate risk-takers. Tasks that are moderately difficult provide them with a challenge while keeping the probability of success fairly high. Surprisingly, however, individuals with a low need to achieve will often attempt tasks that are either quite difficult or quite easy. Why?

The answer may lie in attribution theory. As a low-need achiever, if I attempt a very difficult task and fail, I can attribute my failure to the difficulty of the task – a factor over which I have no control; hence, I will assume no personal responsibility and experience no negative

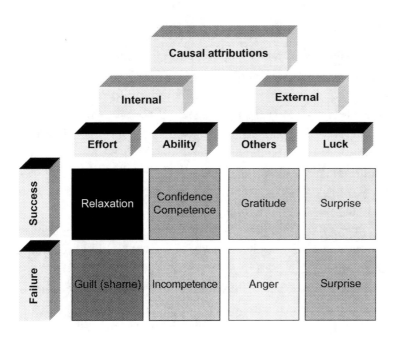

Figure 9.9 Relations between causal attributions and feelings associated with success and failure. Based on Bernard Weiner, "The Role of Affect in Rational (Attributional) Approaches to Human Motivation." In *Educational Researcher*, July/August 1980, pp. 4–11. Copyright © 1980. American Educational Research Association, Washington, D.C. Used by permission.

affect (emotion). If I am successful, there is again little positive affect because my success is due to external factors over which I have no control. However, if I am a high-need achiever and take moderate risks, I can attribute success to my skill or my effort; similarly, I can also attribute failure to personal factors. In either case, there is considerably more emotional involvement in the outcomes of the performance.

This social/cognitive view of motivation is based on the assumption that people continually evaluate their behaviors, look for reasons behind their successes and failures, anticipate the probable outcomes of intended behaviors, and react emotionally to success and failure. And here is the key concept in attribution theory: It is not the attribution of behavior to one cause or the other that motivates behavior, says Weiner (1992); it is the emotions that occur as responses to specific attributions. The outcomes of attribution, he suggests, might be anger, guilt, gratefulness, or a variety of other emotions (see Figure 9.9). It seems logical that if the emotions are positive, subsequent behaviors will attempt to maintain the conditions that made the attribution possible.

Self-Efficacy

Social/cognitive theories of motivation show how our explanations for the outcomes of our behaviors – that is, the *attributions* we make – are fundamental in determining what we do and how we feel about it. And basic to our explanations and our reactions are our estimates of our competence – of what Bandura (1991) labels **self-efficacy**. Put very simply, self-efficacy has to do with our estimates of our personal effectiveness. "Perceived self-efficacy," Bandura writes, "refers to beliefs in one's capabilities to organize and execute the courses of action required to produce given attainments" (1997, p. 3). Those with high self-efficacy see themselves as capable and effective in dealing with the world and with other people. (See Chapter 10 for a biography of Albert Bandura.)

Importance of Self-Efficacy Judgments

Self-efficacy judgments are significant in determining what people do; hence, they are important as motives. Under most circumstances, people don't do things at which they expect to do very badly. "Efficacy beliefs," says Bandura, "influence how people feel, think, motivate themselves, and behave" (1993, p. 118). Not surprisingly, research indicates that level of self-efficacy is one of the variables that differentiates between high- and low risk-takers in sports such as kayaking, skiing, rock climbing, and stunt flying (for example, Babskie, Powell, & Metzger, 2017; Baretta, Greco, & Steca, 2017). Individuals with the highest judgments of self-efficacy – of personal power – are those who are most likely to engage in activities that demonstrate the validity of their judgments.

Judgments of personal efficacy influence not only what people will do but also how much effort and time they will devote to a task, especially when they are faced with difficulties. The more Consuelo believes in herself (the higher her estimates of personal effectiveness), the more likely she will be to persist. In contrast, if she does not see herself as being very capable, she is more likely to become discouraged and to give up. This is why self-efficacy judgments are so important in school. For example, in a study that looked at self-efficacy and performance in mathematics in 33 schools, Williams and Williams (2010) found a significant positive relationship between high self-efficacy and high achievement. There is a **reciprocal determinism** at play, they explain, where high achievement contributes to high self-efficacy, and high self-efficacy contributes to high achievement. In fact, self-efficacy judgments are among the best predictors of future educational achievement among secondary school students (Ocumpaugh et al., 2016).

Notwithstanding the positive role that high self-efficacy plays in relation to goal setting and performance, it nevertheless appears to be true that under some circumstances, high self-efficacy judgments are associated with stubborn commitment to a losing effort. For example, Whyte, Saks, and Hook (1997) demonstrated that many students characterized by a firm conviction that they would succeed (marked by high self-efficacy) escalated their commitment to a failing course of action even beyond the point at which it should have become apparent they would fail. This reveals that although positive evaluations of competence are closely related to setting high goals and investing effort in attaining them, unrealistically high appraisals of one's competence might be associated with improbable goals and inappropriate persistence.

Factors in the Development of Efficacy Judgments

Beliefs about self-efficacy are often measured with simple tests and questions, such as "How good do you think you are at math?" and "How smart do you think you are?" (Bandura, 2006). Responses are often on a **Likert scale** – that is, a scale where the respondent chooses from a range of responses (say, from "very smart" to "not very smart at all") or indicates degree of agreement with a statement such as "I'm very smart" (strongly agree, agree, disagree, strongly disagree).

Children typically begin with very global notions of self-efficacy, particularly with respect to qualities like "smart" or "not smart," with a definite bias toward "smart" (Harter, 2006, 2012).

Early in elementary school, children tend to have overly optimistic notions of their competence. But with increasing experience, notions of self-efficacy change in two ways: First, they become more differentiated. Children no longer see themselves simply as being "smart" or "not smart"; instead, they develop notions of themselves as effective in some endeavors and less effective in others. Second, their general estimates of self-effectiveness tend to decline and become more realistic, as revealed in self-reports surveys (Harter, 2018). Still, we don't always judge our competence very accurately; our assessments of our capabilities are often overestimates or underestimates.

Why do some people typically have high judgments of personal efficacy and others much less favorable judgments? The answer, suggests Bandura (1986), lies in the combined effects of four main sources of influence.

First are the individual's *personal experiences* – that is, the effects of the individual's behavior, especially as they are reflected in success or failure. Other things being equal, people who are generally successful are likely to develop more positive evaluations of their personal effectiveness than are people who typically fail. However, as Weiner (1980) points out, people who attribute their successes and failures to factors over which they have no control (such as luck or task difficulty) are less likely to base judgments of personal efficacy on the outcomes of their behaviors. After all, it is not their fault the test was too hard or they studied the wrong sections.

A second influence is *vicarious* (secondhand); it comes from observing the performance of others. That we do well or not well *compared with* others may contribute a great deal to our judgments of how competent we think we are. The most useful comparisons, Bandura (1981) notes, are those that involve potential equals. Thus, children who do better than their age-mates are likely to develop positive judgments of self-efficacy. That these same children might be blown away by somebody older or more experienced would be less relevant for judgments of self-efficacy.

Verbal persuasion is a third possible influence on self-judgments. Those with lower self-confidence can sometimes be persuaded to do things they would not otherwise do. One of the possible effects of persuasion is that people will interpret it as evidence that others think them competent. As Bandura (1997) notes, "[I]t is easier to sustain a sense of efficacy ... if significant others express faith in one's capabilities than if they convey doubts" (p. 101).

High arousal can also affect self-judgments, says Bandura, leading to either high or low estimates of capability, depending on the situation and the person's previous experiences in situations of high arousal. For example, some athletes who are anxious before a competition view this emotion as helpful to their performance; for others, arousal may be interpreted as negative. These personal experiences in anxiety-producing situations may subsequently influence the extent and direction of the effects of arousal on self-judgments. Thus, an extreme fear of drowning might lead a person to decide she is incapable of an act such as swimming across a river. In contrast, extreme fear might lead the same person to decide that she is capable of swimming across the river to save her son, who is marooned with deranged baboons on the other side.

To summarize, Bandura's four sources of influence on judgments of self-efficacy are *enactive* (reflecting the results of the individual's own actions), *vicarious* (based on

Motivation and Emotions

Table 9.2 **Four sources of information related to judgments of self-efficacy**

Sources of information	Examples of information that might lead Joan to arrive at positive estimates of her personal efficacy
Enactive	She receives an A in mathematics.
Vicarious	She learns that Ronald studied hard but only got a B.
Persuasory	Her teacher tells her she can probably win a scholarship if she tries.
Emotive	She becomes mildly anxious before a test but feels exhilarated afterward.

comparisons between self and others), *persuasory* (the result of persuasion), and *emotive* (reflecting arousal or emotion). Examples of each of these types of influence are shown in Table 9.2.

Intentions, Goals, and Expectancy–Value Theory

Our choices of actions, explain Eccles and Wigfield (2002), as well as our persistence and our performance, are strongly influenced by our expectancies for success (or failure) as well as by the values related to our various options. The interplay of these two variables – expectancy and value – define Eccles's **expectancy–value theory** of motivation (Wigfield, Tonks, & Klauda, 2009).

Expectancy–Value Theory

According to this theory, behavior is determined by two things: the value of the goal(s) toward which the behavior is directed (*value*); and the confidence with which the individual expects to reach the goal (*expectancy*).

Expectancy in expectancy–value theory is defined in much the same way as Bandura defines self-efficacy: "individuals' beliefs about how well they will do on upcoming tasks, either in the immediate or longer-term future" (Eccles & Wigfield, 2002, p. 119). The *value* associated with a choice is described in terms of four distinct components: *attainment value*, *intrinsic value*, *utility value*, and *cost*.

Attainment value is the personal importance of the task to the individual. Among other things, attainment value reflects such things as how well an activity fits into an individual's plans, and how well it reflects the person's self-image. A person who sees herself as "good" and law-abiding is not likely to ascribe much value to the option of accompanying her cousin while he robs the local convenience store.

Intrinsic value refers to the personal satisfaction and enjoyment that the individual derives from an activity. As Deci notes, people tend to seek out challenging activities for which they

Social Cognitive Views of Motivation   357

Table 9.3 **Main concepts in Eccles's expectancy–value theory of motivation**

Summary of theory	Choice, persistence, and achievement are directly linked to the individual's expectancy- and task-related (value-related) beliefs.
Expectancy	Personal beliefs about how well the individual is likely to do now and in the future.
Value	Task-related beliefs that define the value and cost associated with each option.

Components of value judgments	
1. Attainment value	Importance to the person of doing well; does the option fit in with self-image?
2. Intrinsic value	How enjoyable and personally satisfying is the option?
3. Utility value	How well does each option fit in with immediate and future goals?
4. Cost	How much effort is required? How stressful will each option be? What am I giving up?

have an expectation of success – a feeling of competence or of self-efficacy (Deci & Flaste, 1995). Such activities, he claims, tend to have high intrinsic value. That is, they are highly intrinsically motivating.

Utility value has to do with whether an activity fits in with present and future objectives. If Robert, whose goal is to be accepted in a doctoral program, is motivated to take a series of difficult summer courses in physics when he could be lounging about at the lake instead, his choice might well be because of the very high utility value of his chosen option.

Cost of an option, a very critical factor in determining an individual's choices, has to do with the various negative possibilities associated with a task. These include such things as the probability of failure, the actual effort required in undertaking the task; stress and anxiety associated with the task, loss related to other alternatives that might need to be abandoned; and emotional costs linked with the choice. Flake, Barron, Hulleman, McCoach, and Welsh (2015) suggest that research has frequently overlooked the importance and the complexity of *cost* in the individual's mental calculus when trying to select among options.

In summary, expectancy–value theory is a social/cognitive approach to motivation that holds that people make choices based on a sort of mental calculus where the most important factors are expectancy of success and feelings of competence on the one hand (self-efficacy, in other words) and the values associated with the various options (their personal importance; how they fit into plans, goals, and self-image; their intrinsic value; and the cost associated with each option in terms of effort, loss of other opportunities, stress, etc.) (see Table 9.3).

Investigations of Expectancy–Value Theory

Expectancy–value theory provides an important framework for understanding the mental calculus involved when individuals set goals, select options, and translate their intentions into

Motivation and Emotions

action. It is a clearly cognitive position that views the individual as a rational, thoughtful organism – an organism that does not simply react to external forces that push it this way and that, but that imagines consequences, anticipates outcomes, evaluates costs and benefits, and selects the most reasonable and rewarding of alternatives.

Clearly, however, our decisions and our behaviors are not always the most ideal. Our mental calculus is often affected by wishes that are too overwhelming, expectations that are ridiculously unlikely, and estimates of our capabilities that are shockingly inaccurate.

Expectancy–value theory has been extensively researched and applied in recent years. Among other things, it has been found to be highly useful in predicting students' academic choices. For example, research carried out by Ball, Huang, Cotten, and Rikard (2017) indicates that students' expectations relating to the likelihood of their succeeding in STEM careers (**s**cience, **t**echnology, **e**ngineering, and **m**ath), together with their assessments of the costs associated with embarking on these careers, are important determiners of their post-secondary academic choices.

Other research links personal calculations of expectancies and values with alcohol consumption. When Nicolai, Moshagen, and Demmel (2018) compared alcohol-related values and expectancies among a group of 1,053 college students and a second group of 699 alcohol-dependent inpatients in a treatment facility, they found expected relationships between drinking behaviors and individual outcome expectancies. As might be predicted, positive and negative expectations were associated with drinking or abstaining. Among inpatients, expectations of tension-reduction seemed to be an important motivational factor.

Other studies indicate that expectancy–value theory is useful for understanding students' achievement-related behavior as well as their occasional procrastination with respect to academic tasks (Wu & Fan, 2017); that it can explain attitudes toward cow's milk and other milk alternatives (Kempen et al., 2017); that it provides a basis for predicting risk-taking behaviors among adolescents (Dever, 2016); and that it might even be useful in attempts to change personality (Magidson, Roberts, Collado-Rodriguez, & Lejuez, 2014).

Self-Determined and Self-Regulated Learners

The mental calculus implicit in expectancy–value theory paints a picture of learners whose choices are based on their judgments of their personal effectiveness (their *self-efficacy* beliefs), whose intentions are colored by their goals, and whose decisions reflect a consideration of the expected outcomes of their actions, of the values of those outcomes, and of the costs associated with them. Put another way, the cognitive view of today's ideal learner is that of **self-regulated learners** – learners who take responsibility for their learning and control of the behaviors that lead to learning. Self-regulated learners are what Deci and Ryan (2008) label *self-determined* learners. The single most important assumption of Deci and Ryan's **self-determination theory** of motivation is, as the label implies, that people need to be self-determining – to feel that they are in control of their own actions. By definition, to be intrinsically motivated, we need to be able to attribute the causes of our behavior to intrinsic factors over which we have control, such as our personal interest and ambition rather than to external causes, such as expected monetary or social rewards.

Self-regulated learning describes learning where individuals assume responsibility for planning and directing their own learning. It implies three things: (1) learners set their own goals; (2) they select, devise, and apply appropriate strategies to reach these goals; (3) they constantly evaluate and modify strategies in response to feedback telling them how successful the strategies are in leading them toward intended goals.

Zimmerman (2001, 2008) summarizes these characteristics of self-regulated learning in terms of three sequential phases: *forethought* (the process of analyzing a task, setting goals, and selecting or devising appropriate learning strategies); *performance* (application of the strategies); and *reflection* (evaluating the effectiveness of strategies to determine whether they need to be modified).

APPLICATIONS AND IMPLICATIONS OF MOTIVATION THEORY

Knowledge about why people behave the way they do can greatly facilitate the psychologist's task of predicting what a person will do in a given situation and of controlling behavior when it isn't unethical to do so.

Predicting Behavior

Normal social interaction depends largely on being able to predict many of the ordinary activities of others. If these activities were not at least partly predictable, social relations would be chaotic and confusing. When Joshua meets his grandmother and says "Hello," he expects that she will return either the same greeting (or some other appropriate greeting) or that, at worst, she will ignore him. He would be understandably surprised if, instead of responding as expected, she chose to kick him in the shins, run away, faint, or curse in some foreign language.

Controlling and Changing Behavior

Knowledge about motivation has important implications for the control of behavior, a subject that has led to considerable debate among psychologists. Should behavior be controlled? How should it be controlled? Who should control it and to what end? In short, what are the ethics of behavior control (see Rogers & Skinner, 1956)?

Despite the somewhat appealing humanistic arguments against behavior control, deliberate behavior control is not only a reality but in many cases highly desirable – as a parent whose young child has recently been toilet trained would quickly admit. Toilet training is just one of many behaviors that involve systematic and deliberate attempts to modify behavior.

Motivation plays a key role in changing and controlling behavior. For example, toilet training a child might involve manipulating goals (for example, getting little Sammy to view cleanliness as a desirable condition). In addition, rewards and punishments, which also relate to motivation (and to learning), can be employed. Cognitive dissonance also may be implicated in toilet training: Children who think being clean is desirable may feel considerable dissonance when they have what is euphemistically referred to as "an accident."

Motivation in the Classroom

Motivation theory is highly relevant for teachers, whose function is largely one of changing the motivation and the behavior of students, often by helping them develop and implement realistic and worthwhile goals and appropriate expectations. It is important that teachers know something about the individual needs and goals of students, about the effects of cognitive dissonance, about the role of arousal in learning and behavior, and about the factors involved in the cognitive activities at play in the mental calculus that underlies goals, expectations, intentions, and choices.

Needs, Psychological Hedonism, and Eudemonic Motives

Theories based on a recognition of the importance of needs and of the human tendency to seek pleasant outcomes and avoid those less pleasant have obvious instructional implications. For example, it is clear that basic physiological needs, such as for food and drink, should be reasonably well satisfied if learning is to be optimized. It is less obvious but no less true that children's psychological needs – for example, the growth needs described by Maslow – also need to be attended to. Among these growth needs are those that define *eudemonic* goals where well-being has less to do with pain avoidance and pleasure attainment than with becoming a fully functioning, fully developed individual – with, in Maslow's terms, constantly striving toward self-actualization.

Arousal

The role of arousal in behavior can also be crucial for teaching. Recall that it is the combined novelty, intensity, and meaningfulness of stimuli that most affect level of arousal. Teachers are one of the most important sources of arousal-inducing stimulation for students. The impact of what teachers say and do and how they say and do it is important in determining whether students are either bored or sleeping (low arousal) or attentive (higher arousal). This observation leads directly to an argument for meaningfulness, variety, novelty, and intensity in classroom presentations and assignments.

Cognitive Dissonance

Cognitive dissonance is one possible source of arousal. Motivation theory suggests that students who are experiencing cognitive dissonance will attempt to reduce the dissonance and, consequently, to reduce the accompanying arousal. For example, dissonance may occur when students become aware of a discrepancy between their behavior and what a teacher or some other important model (such as a book) considers ideal. Such dissonance may well lead students to try to become more like the teacher's description of the ideal. As we saw, dissonance can be reduced in various ways, including behavior change, attitude change, or exposure to new information. Teachers can clearly play an important role in setting up dissonant situations to motivate students and in helping them find ways to reduce the dissonance.

Intrinsic and Extrinsic Attributions

The tendency to attribute success and failure to internal or external causes may be a relatively stable personality characteristic, says Dweck (2006). Children who are most likely to make internal attributions – that is, to take personal responsibility for their successes and failures – are also the children who are most likely to strive toward increasing their competence. Externally oriented children are less willing to accept challenges and less likely to strive to improve their competence. One of the objectives of schools and teachers is to make children more internally oriented – more intrinsically motivated. In this regard, teachers need to take pains to make sure that students perceive classrooms as being oriented toward mastery (rather than simply toward performance) and to arrange learning experiences so all students can develop a sense of personal competence and self-efficacy. Among other things, it is important that teachers present students with a variety of short-term goals that are challenging but that can be accomplished with reasonable effort – that, in other words, are within what Vygotsky calls the learner's *zone of proximal development*. It is also important that an effort be made to ensure that school work is personally involving, that teachers focus on the processes of learning rather than on its outcomes, that individual progress be emphasized, and that comparisons with other students be minimized.

Goals and Beliefs About Intelligence

Among the big ideas that, in Dweck's words, "make smart people dumb," believing that intelligence is fixed ranks very high (Dweck, 2002b) (see Table 9.4). One of the tasks of schools, says Dweck, is to instill beliefs that deny "dumb" ideas. This isn't to say that all "dumb" ideas are entirely false. For example, we know that measured intelligence does have a substantial hereditary basis, and it is a strong predictor of academic achievement. But Dweck's (2006) focus, as she explains, is less about the true nature of intelligence than about the consequences of what people believe about intelligence. "A fixed view of intelligence," she writes, "discourages students from taking active charge of their learning, whereas a malleable

Motivation and Emotions

Table 9.4 **Dweck's three big ideas that make smart people dumb**

Beliefs that make smart people dumb	Consequences of "dumb" idea	Opposing belief
"Entity theory": Intelligence is fixed and unchanging.	Efforts directed toward "proving" intelligence. Avoidance of challenges that might expose intellectual shortcomings.	Intelligence is malleable; it can be developed through effort.
Performance reflects intelligence and worth.	Fear of failure. Feelings of worthlessness in the face of failure. Avoid challenges. Avoid opportunity to learn because of associated risks.	Your current performance tells you where you are and what efforts you need to make.
Truly intelligent people don't need to make an effort to realize their potential.	Don't make effort necessary to achieve to potential. Less likely to convert high intelligence into very high achievement.	Everyone needs sustained effort to achieve as well as they can.

Source: Based in part on Dweck (2002b, 2006).

view of intelligence encourages students to undertake, regulate, and motivate their own learning processes" (Dweck & Master, 2008, p. 31).

Self-Determination, Self-Regulation, Self-Efficacy, and Expectancy–Value Theory

People need to be self-determining, explain Deci and Ryan (2008). They need to feel a sense of autonomy and of personal competence. Defined in other terms, personal competence translates into personal estimates of self-efficacy. As Shell and Husman (2008) point out, there is a strong relationship among self-regulation, self-efficacy, a tendency to attribute success and failure to effort rather than to innate ability, and a mastery orientation.

It is worth repeating that judgments of self-efficacy are powerful motivators: They profoundly influence a person's thoughts and emotions. Those who have low judgments of self-efficacy are also likely to feel poorly about themselves, to attempt fewer difficult tasks, and, ultimately, to be less successful. Our choices, according to Eccles and associates' expectancy–value theory, are the result of a mental calculation in which we consider our expectancies of success or failure and weigh these expectancies against our personal judgments of the value and costs associated with the options we contemplate.

Teachers play a crucial role in providing children with the sorts of experiences that contribute to positive judgments of self-efficacy. Teachers can also play an important role in determining student goals and self-image – important factors in how students judge the value of different outcomes and the potential cost of the efforts required to reach these outcomes.

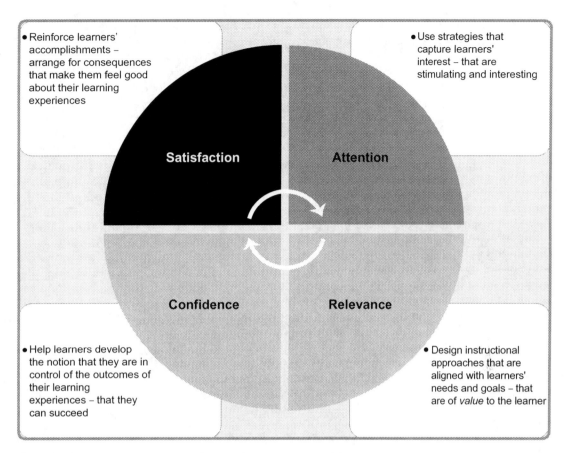

Figure 9.10 Keller's ARCS model of instruction design suggests ways in which teachers can design instruction to foster and maintain high levels of motivation among learners. From Lefrançois G. R. (2020). *Of Learning and Assessment* (2nd ed.). San Diego, CA: Bridgepoint Education, Fig. 3.9. Used by permission.

The ARCS Model of Motivation

Keller's (2010) **ARCS model of motivation** provides an excellent general outline and summary of the sorts of instructional strategies and teacher behaviors that can be used to create and maintain a high level of motivation (Figure 9.10). The Model is defined in terms of four key elements implicit in the acronym, ARCS: **A**ttention; **R**elevance; **C**onfidence; and **S**atisfaction.

Attention, explains Keller, can be gained and maintained by using surprise or novelty to grab interest, and by presenting challenging and intriguing questions and problems. Relevance is brought about by selecting topics and examples that are meaningful for learners and that relate to learners' goals. Confidence is inspired by providing material within learners' zones of proximal development – material that is challenging but that they can understand and master, initially with the help of others but in the end as a result of their own efforts. And satisfaction implies that the learning process needs to be rewarding. For truly self-regulated learners, one of the highest forms of reward is the sense of accomplishment that comes upon reaching goals that are self-defined, challenging, and worthwhile, and that are attained as a result of the learner's own efforts.

364 | **Motivation and Emotions**

Main Point Chapter Summary

1. Motives are the forces that incite a person to act. Psychological theories of motivation deal with both the reasons (explanation for an action) for behavior and the causes (forces that produce an action or an effect) of behavior.

2. Reflexes are simple, unlearned, stimulus-specific responses that explain some elementary human behavior. The orienting reflex (OR), related to arousal, is the general reflexive response an organism makes to novel stimuli. Instincts are more complex unlearned patterns of behavior that are more relevant for animal than for human behavior. Imprinting is a complex, instinct-like pattern of behavior manifested following exposure to an appropriate stimulus (*releaser*) during a critical period. Some researchers speculate that infant–caregiver attachment reflects imprinting-like learning.

3. Psychological hedonism is the notion that people act to avoid pain and to obtain or maintain pleasure. The *eudemonic* approach suggests that well-being is closely related not to hedonistic concerns but to self-fulfillment and full human functioning. Physiological needs are states of deficiency that give rise to drives, which in turn impel the organism toward activities that will reduce the deficiency. Psychological needs are sometimes described as learned needs. Incentive refers to the value of a goal or reward for the individual.

4. Maslow, a humanistic psychologist, describes a hierarchy of basic or deficiency needs (physiological, safety, belongingness, and self-esteem) and meta- or growth needs (cognitive, aesthetic, and self-actualizing). Self-actualization is more a process of developing the highest levels of potential of humanness possible than a state that can be reached. It underlies the *eudemonic* (as opposed to *hedonistic*) orientation.

5. Arousal is the degree of alertness of an organism. Too low or too high arousal is related to less optimal behavior than is a more moderate level of activation (the Yerkes–Dodson law). High anxiety often has a detrimental effect on performance.

6. Hebb's theory of motivation claims that there is an optimum level of arousal for maximally effective behavior and that people will behave to maintain that level. Stimuli have both cue (message) and arousal functions. Studies of sensory deprivation support the belief that humans need a variety of sensory stimulation.

7. Social/cognitive theories present a more active view than do traditional behaviorist theories. Cognitive dissonance assumes that conflict among beliefs, behavior, and expectations leads to behavior designed to reduce the conflict (for example, attitude change, compartmentalization, acquisition or recall of information, behavioral change, or perceptual distortion).

8. Extrinsic motives relate to external rewards; intrinsic motives have to do with personal satisfaction and interest in an activity. Some controversial evidence indicates that excessive reliance on external rewards might undermine intrinsic motivation (the *overjustification hypothesis*).

9. Attribution theory describes how individuals assign responsibility for the outcomes of their behaviors. Internally oriented individuals frequently ascribe success or failure to ability or

effort; externally oriented individuals are more likely to invoke luck or difficulty of the task. Internally oriented individuals are often characterized by higher need for achievement.

10. Some people act as though they believe that intelligence is fixed (entity theory); others as though it is malleable (incremental theory). Entity theory is associated with performance goals (designed to prove high intelligence); incremental theory is linked with mastery goals (designed to learn and become more competent). A common mindset sees intelligence as fixed and limits the possibilities that individuals select. Those high in need for achievement tend to be mastery-oriented (rather than performance-oriented). A growth mindset and mastery orientation present clear advantages for achievement.

11. Self-efficacy judgments have to do with personal estimates of competence and effectiveness. High evaluations of efficacy are associated with persistence, high achievement, and positive self-concepts. Notions of self-efficacy are influenced by the outcomes of behavior, comparisons with others, persuasion, and arousal.

12. Expectancy–value theory is a motivational theory that describes some of the variables that are considered in the mental calculus that leads to choice among options: specifically, expectations of success or failure (self-efficacy) factored in with the value of each of the options (attainment value, intrinsic value, utility value, and cost).

13. Self-determination theory is premised on the assumption that individuals have a need for personal autonomy – that is, a need to be responsible for their own actions (to be intrinsically motivated). Self-determined and self-regulated learners are those who take personal responsibility for their learning, setting their own goals, selecting and implementing strategies to reach them, and monitoring, evaluating, and modifying goals and strategies as appropriate.

14. Knowledge about human motivation is important for predicting behavior, for controlling it, and for changing it. In a practical sense, it is especially important for teachers. The ARCS (**A**ttention, **R**elevance, **C**onfidence, and **S**atisfaction) model presents suggestions for designing instruction so as to foster and maintain a high level of motivation.

10 Social Learning

Bandura's Social Cognitive Theory

CHAPTER OUTLINE

This Chapter	367
Objectives	367
Social Learning	368
Socially Accepted Behaviors: The Product	368
Learning Social Behaviors: The Process	370
Overview of Bandura's Social Cognitive Theory	371
Models	371
Processes in Observational Learning	372
Operant Conditioning in Observational Learning	374
Sources of Reinforcement in Imitation	375
Classical Conditioning in Observational Learning	375
Three Effects of Imitation	376
Cognitive Control in Bandura's Social Cognitive Theory	380
Behavior Control Systems	381
An Illustration of Behavior Control Systems	382
Bandura's Agentic Perspective	383
Reciprocal Determinism	386
Applications of Bandura's Social Cognitive Theory	388
Observational Learning	388
Behavior Control Systems	389
Personal Agency and Self-Efficacy	390
Bandura's Social Cognitive Theory: An Appraisal	391
Main Point Chapter Summary	392

Children are more in need of models than of critics.

Joseph Joubert

Accomplishment is socially judged by ill defined criteria so that one has to rely on others to find out how one is doing.

Albert Bandura

When I arrived at the bush cabin, Old Lady Gribbin said to come in and sit down; she wanted to show me something. She acts very much like the cabin is hers and I'm only a guest, although I'm the one who built it and it's really mine. So, I went in and pulled a chair up close to the table. I could smell the pot of beans the old lady had just taken from the oven, and on the table was a loaf of freshly baked bread. I was suddenly very hungry. But the old lady said no, not to sit at the table, motioning that I should sit on one of the bunks instead. Then, she took a plate and heaped it with beans and cut a thick slab of bread, which she buttered very slowly. I thought she might now give the plate to the cat to spite me, beans being one of Schrödinger's many addictions: He attacks them like he thinks they're wild catnip. But no, she offered neither the cat nor me anything. Instead, she sat at the table and began to devour the beans, scooping them into her mouth as fast as she could using both hands, stopping now and again to stuff a chunk of bread into her cheeks so they bulged grotesquely on either side of her face. The cat pretended he wasn't the least bit interested. I tried to do the same. Still, the old lady stuffed beans and bread into her maw, and when the plate was half empty, she buried her face directly into it, slurping up great mouthfuls of beans, making all sorts of grunting and snorting noises. When the last of the beans was gone, she licked the plate clean. Then, holding one nostril firmly between thumb and forefinger, she blew the other forcefully into the plate, belched, and blew out her other nostril. The cat got up and left, and the old lady motioned that I should turn on the recorder, that she was ready to start the next chapter.

THIS CHAPTER

You're shocked and disgusted aren't you, said Old Lady Gribbin as she stacked the dirty plate in among the clean dishes and wiped her nose with the back of her hand, bean juices dripping from her chin and eyebrows, her glasses smeared a revolting molasses brown. But she said I shouldn't be shocked, that the way she had just eaten would seem perfectly normal and exquisitely polite to the people in an Amazonian tribe she knew well. She said you would understand this more clearly once she had finished with Chapter 10.

Objectives

Tell your readers, *said the old lady*, that once they have finished this chapter, they will be moved by an unresistable urge to create blogs in which they can, for the amazement and enlightenment of the people, expose their stunningly clear understanding of:

- what social learning is;
- the three effects of modeling;
- the agentic perspective and reciprocal determinism;
- the various systems that control human behavior;
- the cumulative and long-term effects of screen violence;
- the importance of a sense of personal power and effectiveness.

In addition, *she said*, tell your students that they will have a keener appreciation of the significance of will and intention in their lives. Also, they will understand why rich corporations gladly pay "stars" obscene sums of money to endorse their products.

SOCIAL LEARNING

Psychologists often use the phrase **social learning** without defining it, *she read from a hopelessly bean-stained sheet of paper*. It's as though everybody already knew what it meant. But, actually, the phrase can be used in at least two distinct senses.

Social learning can mean all learning that occurs as a result of social interaction or that in some way involves social interaction. Or it can mean the sort of learning involved in finding out which behaviors are socially expected and acceptable in social situations – for example, in finding out that sucking up one's food and licking one's plate and belching and other happy creature behaviors are wonderfully appropriate in Korukaka but not so much in Des Moines. Put another way, the phrase *social learning* might refer to the *process* by which we learn (specifically, a process that involves social interaction) or to the *product* of social learning (that is, the learning of socially appropriate behaviors).

Socially Accepted Behaviors: The Product

The product of social learning is knowledge of what is socially acceptable. Through a process of social learning, children learn that it is acceptable to ask a parent or a grandparent to take them to the store and buy them purple gumdrops, and that it is unacceptable to make the same request of a stranger. It is also through a lengthy process of **socialization** – the process of learning what is acceptable and what is not in a given social environment – that people learn how to eat a plateful of beans. They also learn that acceptable behaviors can vary from culture to culture and that they can be very different for different ages and sexes. For example, in some Asian countries, it is quite acceptable, perhaps even expected, for students to bow to their professors and maybe even to offer them small gifts. In contrast, in North America, few students feel inclined to bow to their professors or to offer them gifts. To do so might indicate lack of social intelligence.

In the same way that socially accepted behaviors can vary among cultures, so too might they vary for different ages and sexes. For example, whereas adults freely call each other by their first names, young children are seldom expected to call adults by their first names. For eight-year-old Charles to call his grandmother Rhonda might be taken as a sign of lack of respect (or of exceptional precocity – or of an especially advanced sense of humor).

One of the most important tasks of child rearing is to *socialize* youngsters – that is, to teach them socially appropriate behaviors. A society's chief socializing agencies are its major cultural institutions: family, school, church, playground, communication media, and so on. These institutions transmit to children the **mores** (distinct, established social conventions and customs that identify a group), customs, values, habits, beliefs, and other trappings that define human **cultures**.

BOX 10.1 Albert Bandura (1925–)

Credit: NurPhoto / Getty Images

Albert Bandura was the youngest of six children born to an immigrant family in a small farming community in Canada, about 50 miles from Edmonton, Alberta.[1] Later, he moved to the southern coastal area of British Columbia, where he did his undergraduate work at the University of British Columbia (UBC), graduating in 1949.

"What influenced you to become a psychologist?" Evans asked Bandura. "I have come to the view," Bandura replied, "that some of the most important determinants of career and life paths often occur through the most trivial of circumstances" (Evans, 1989, p. 3). He goes on to explain how, because he commuted to the university with a group of pre-med and engineering students who had to go in very early, he took a psychology course to fill a gap in his early morning schedule. The subject fascinated him and, three years after graduating from UBC, Bandura obtained his Ph.D. in clinical psychology from Iowa State University. A year later, he joined the faculty at Stanford University eventually becoming a professor and department chair.

Bandura's early writings and theorizing stemmed from the predominant theories of the day: Skinnerian and Hullian forms of behaviorism. But even at the dawn of his career, he had already begun to break away from the behaviorists' rejection of the importance of thoughts and intentions. Bandura's approach was more socially oriented; he looked at how people influence each other and at how social behaviors are acquired through imitation. His approach was also more cognitive, assigning an increasingly important role to the human ability to anticipate the consequences of behavior.

In the end, his is a social cognitive theory of human behavior, summarized in his aptly titled *Social Foundations of Thought and Action: A Social Cognitive Theory* (1986).

Continued

---

[1] You know what? said Old Lady Gribbin. Some of your readers might be interested to know that the small town Bandura grew up in is Mundare and that Mundare is almost walking distance from the bush cabin we're in right now. And maybe they'd also want to know that your university gave him an honorary degree a few years ago. Or maybe they wouldn't really care, she added cynically, turning once more to her disorganized and grimy notes.

Social Learning

> **BOX 10.1 (cont.)**
>
> Artino (2007) notes that Bandura has few peers in terms of contributions and awards. He has published more than 200 articles and a large number of books and book chapters. He has held office in more than a dozen scientific organizations and received a large number of state and national awards and honors. Among them are the E. L. Thorndike Award, the APA Award for Outstanding Lifetime Contribution to Psychology, and the University of Louisville Grawemeyer Award (which includes a $200,000 prize). Like Watson, Tolman, Thorndike, Guthrie, Hebb, Hull, and Bruner before him, he served as president of the American Psychological Association. (Based in part on Bandura, 2007; Evans, 1989; Pajares, 2004; Sheehy, 2003; and Zimmerman & Schunk, 2003.)

Learning Social Behaviors: The Process

Given the importance and prevalence of social behavior, a fundamentally important learning-theory question is, "How do children and adults learn socially appropriate behavior?"

One of the most widely accepted answers is based on Bandura's theory of social learning through **imitation**, also referred to as **observational learning** – learning by copying or mimicking aspects of the behavior of others. Bandura's theory was partially derived from Miller and Dollard's (1941) theory. The original Miller and Dollard theory was a highly behavioristic approach that closely followed Hull's notions of drive reduction. Basically, the theory argued that behavior occurs as a response to specific drives (such as hunger). These drives are linked to stimuli (such as internal feelings of hunger). Reducing the drive gets rid of the stimulus; this is reinforcing and leads to learning.

What Miller and Dollard did is argue that people have a natural drive to imitate, and that imitation involves social interaction which is then reinforced and becomes learned as a result. One of the problems with this approach is that the existence of a common, natural drive to imitate cannot readily be demonstrated.

A second problem is that drive-reduction theories, as we saw in Chapter 9, cannot account for the fact that humans and nonhuman organisms engage in many behaviors that do not seem to be directed toward eliminating or reducing drive-related stimulation. For example, recall the Hebb sensory deprivation studies in which participants actively seek stimulation when they became bored.

A third problem with behavioristic, stimulus–response, drive-reduction theories is that they do not explain some of the most important kinds of human learning. For example, as Chomsky (1972) argued, they say very little about language learning. And, as Bandura makes clear, they fail to take into consideration the influence of social variables, especially in the acquisition of novel behaviors. As a result, they cannot easily explain many human behaviors.

What Bandura did is modify Miller and Dollard's theory of imitation by getting rid of the Hullian drive-reduction component. However, Bandura's early theorizing was still initially based squarely on B. F. Skinner's theory of operant conditioning (Bandura & Walters, 1963). Very shortly, though, Bandura revised and expanded his theorizing as he came to recognize the importance of cognitive activities such as imagining and anticipating (Bandura, 1977, 1986,

OVERVIEW OF BANDURA'S SOCIAL COGNITIVE THEORY

1997, 2001). The theory is now commonly referred to as a **social cognitive theory** (meaning that it is a theory that takes into consideration the importance of cognitive activities in explaining social learning).

OVERVIEW OF BANDURA'S SOCIAL COGNITIVE THEORY

We learn a great deal through operant conditioning, explained Bandura early in the development of his theory (Bandura & Walters, 1963). But in many ways, operant learning by itself can be a highly inefficient and often ineffective way of learning. Imagine if all we could do is wait for a socially desirable behavior to be emitted as an operant and then hope that subsequent circumstances might prove reinforcing. For example, take the simple social behavior of learning how to shake hands. How likely is it that young Shia will spontaneously emit the "hand shaking" operant one day, under the appropriate circumstances, to be sure, and that someone will immediately reinforce him? Or consider the problem of learning how to drive a car. How reasonable is it to expect that if Sheila is given a set of keys and a car, she will quickly learn to drive simply as a result of, by chance, emitting the right sequence of operants and being reinforced for these operants before running up against the side of the house?

Actually, it would be difficult to learn how and when to shake hands or how to drive if the completely inexperienced learner were required to emit spontaneously the appropriate series of responses without any sort of guidance. But the point is that there are very few completely inexperienced would-be hand shakers or car drivers. Almost all youngsters have seen their parents and others shaking hands and driving. Many will even have read instruction booklets describing rules of the road, and they will have listened to peers and siblings talk about how you start and drive cars. In Bandura's terms, they have been exposed to many different **models**, where models are simply actual or symbolic examples of ways of thinking, behaving, or being.

Much of our learning, says Bandura, is *observational learning* (*learning through imitation*): It results from imitating models. Learning through imitation, says Bandura in his early explanations of his theorizing, is really a form of operant learning. That is because an imitative behavior is much like an operant; it is not a response to a specific stimulus (as is the case for a respondent) but, rather, an emitted response. And imitative behaviors, as we see shortly, are often reinforced and therefore become learned.

Models

Although there is a tendency to think that models are people whose behavior is copied by others, the term is far more inclusive than this. Models are best defined as any representation of a pattern for behaving. Thus, although a model may be an actual and perhaps very ordinary person whose behavior serves as a guide, a blueprint, or an inspiration for somebody else, many models are symbolic. **Symbolic models** include the great variety of models that are represented by things such as oral, written, printed, or digital instructions, pictures, book characters, mental images, cartoon or film characters, television actors, and so on. Symbolic models also include computer-based software such as might be used for various kinds of training programs like pilot training or

Social Learning

medical instruction, often using computer-controlled **virtual-reality (VR)** simulations (simulations that typically involve one or more senses to heighten the sensation of realism).

While models may sometimes be adults and experts who serve as examples of highly advanced skills and competencies, they need not be. Even two- and three-year-olds imitate and learn from each other, explain Abravanel and Ferguson (1998). And, as we saw in Chapter 3, various studies have shown that monkeys, dogs, and many birds and dolphins can learn various behaviors by observing their trained fellow animals perform these behaviors (for example, Sclafani, Paukner, Suomi, & Ferrari, 2015; Subiaul, Renner, & Krajkowski, 2016). In many of these studies, obvious food rewards are associated with the imitated behavior. For example, capuchin monkeys who observe other monkeys performing a complex task to obtain food tend to learn the task far more easily than they otherwise would (Dindo, Whiten, & de Waal, 2009).

Processes in Observational Learning

Models inform us not only about how to do certain things, but often, they also tell us what the consequences of our behaviors are likely to be. Accordingly, observational learning is very much a *cognitive* process. Bandura (1977) describes four distinct processes that are involved in learning through observation.

Attentional Processes

To begin with, we have to pay attention. We learn very little from observing behaviors that have little value for us and to which we therefore pay little attention. Thus, 30-year-old Cedric may have seen his mother making him crêpes a thousand times. But if he were asked to make his own crêpes, he might well be at a complete loss. Despite the inordinately high value he places on eating crêpes with wild chokecherry syrup, his mother's crêpes-making behavior is of so little value to him that he has learned virtually nothing from observing her these countless times.

Whether we attend to a potential model's behavior, Bandura informs us, depends very much on the value of the model's behavior. (Is it important for the observer to be able to sing a song that well? Make such delicate crêpes? Hit a golf ball so far? Dance the salsa and the tango that way?)

Whether we pay attention also depends on how distinctive, how complex, how prevalent, and how useful a behavior is. We are less likely to attend to behaviors that are highly common and not very distinctive or that occur only rarely or that are complex and difficult to perform. Not surprisingly, the most effective models – those that command the greatest attention – are those that are most attractive, most trustworthy, and most powerful (in terms of social power, which can come from knowledge, money, or prestige). That is one of the reasons why actors and sports stars can be such effective models – sometimes positive and perhaps sometimes negative.[2]

---

[2] Their power as models is why corporations gladly pay them such ridiculous sums of money to wear their logos and pretend to eat their potato chips and drive their cars, said the old lady somewhat testily, adding that nobody was paying her a dang thing to wear her jacket. Actually, it was my jacket that she had taken from behind the door – the jacket with the John Deere™ crest on it. They don't pay me to wear it either.

Retention Processes

To learn from a model, the observer not only needs to pay attention but must also be able to remember what is observed. This, explains Bandura, might involve one of two different types of representation: visual or verbal. For example, to learn a complex motor skill, it is sometimes useful to observe someone carrying out the skill and then try to remember a visual sequence of the behavior. Thus, an aspiring athlete watching an Olympic performer might represent and retain the behavior to be imitated as a series of visual images rather than as a series of words. There is research indicating that mentally rehearsing a complex motor sequence (as in high jumping, diving, gymnastics, or golf, for example) can significantly improve performance (Rymal & Ste-Marie, 2017). Bandura (1977) suggests that the best way to learn from a model is to organize and rehearse the observed behavior mentally and then act it out.

While a motor sequence is sometimes more easily represented visually, much of what an observer sees can be described in words (verbal representation). Thus, a novice driver learning how to operate a standard shift vehicle might well be able to verbalize the required sequence of actions – depress clutch, place gear shift into first gear, slowly release clutch while applying pressure to the accelerator . . .. A visual representation of the driving instructor's behavior might not be especially useful in this case.

Motor Reproduction Processes

Imitating requires transforming imagined (visually or verbally represented) actions into actual behaviors. Doing so may well call for certain motor and physical capabilities or perhaps some verbal and intellectual capacities. In addition, successful imitation implies the ability to monitor and correct performance. For example, a coach might repeatedly demonstrate how to cut in from the wing in ice hockey or how to jump for a slam in basketball, but it will all be to no avail if the observer lacks the combination of well-practiced physical skills required to successfully imitate the coach. Similarly, if the athlete remains unaware of how poorly she skates or of how she cannot jump high enough to reach the basket – in other words, if she cannot monitor and correct her performance – she is unlikely to be able to imitate successfully. Successful reproduction of motor sequences typically requires monitoring, evaluating, and gradually improving component behaviors.

Motivational Processes

Finally, the observer has to be motivated. As we saw in Chapter 9, motives impel and direct our behaviors. When Cedric's mother announced that because he refused to leave the house she

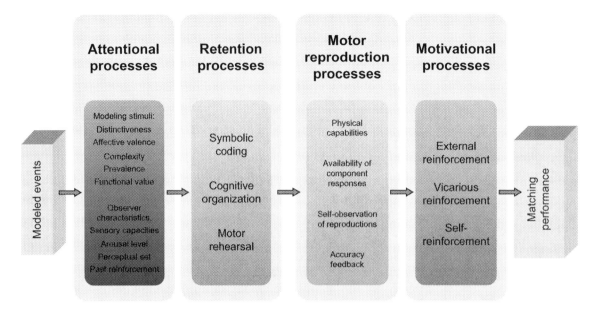

Figure 10.1 The four processes involved in observational learning. If a behavior is to be imitated, it is important that the imitator attend to the behavior, remember its characteristics, be capable of reproducing it, and be motivated to do so. From A. Bandura, *Social Learning Theory*, © 1977, p. 23. Reprinted by permission of Pearson Education, Inc., New York, New York.

would be moving out, he suddenly had an important reason for learning how to make his own crêpes. This newfound motivation became apparent when he now learned to make crêpes after observing his mother making them only once or twice more.

The distinction between acquisition and performance is important in social learning theory because, as we have noted, much of what is observed and presumably acquired is never performed. Whether the modeled behavior will ever be performed is a function of motivation – a concept closely related to reinforcement or, perhaps more precisely, to anticipated reinforcement.

To summarize, observational learning begins with a modeled event (perhaps a real-life model doing something, a symbolic model, or a combination of these) and culminates in some sort of matching performance from the observer. Four processes are at play here: First, the observer must pay attention; second, the observer must represent the observed behavior cognitively, store it, and perhaps rehearse it mentally; third, given the required capabilities, the observer reproduces and refines the observed behavior; and fourth, under appropriate motivational conditions (defined mainly in terms of anticipated reinforcement), the observer performs the learned behavior. (See Figure 10.1 for a summary of these four processes.)

OPERANT CONDITIONING IN OBSERVATIONAL LEARNING

Simply put, Skinner's model of operant conditioning describes learning as an increase in the probability of occurrence of an operant (emitted response) as a function of reinforcement. As we saw, Bandura's theory of social learning assumes that imitation is a type of emitted behavior that results from observing a model and that is reinforced. Hence, imitative behaviors are learned in the same way as any operant.

Imitative behaviors, explains Bandura, are extremely common. Similarities in the ways people dress, eat, walk, and talk, and differences between cultures, are testimony to the prevalence and the power of imitation. Imitation ranks high as an explanation for social learning because it provides a good explanation for complex learning. Skills such as learning to fly a plane cannot easily be acquired solely through contiguity or trial and error; they require the presentation of models (usually other pilots as well as verbal and written instructions). Similarly, children would probably never learn to speak if they had to do so through trial and error, without benefit of the models that are presented by other speaking humans. Also, as we saw earlier, it seems clear that people learn what is acceptable and unacceptable in matters of speech, dress, and behavior largely by observing the models presented by others.

Sources of Reinforcement in Imitation

There are two main potential sources of reinforcement for the observer in observational learning, claim Bandura and Walters (1963). In addition, the model might also be reinforced.

First, imitated behaviors are often subject to **direct reinforcement**, when their immediately apparent consequences are reinforcement. For example, an imitator is often reinforced directly by the model whose behavior is being copied. Proud parents are quick to praise their children for behaviors that resemble those of Daddy or Mommy. That a grandmother says, "Look at little Norbert standing there with his finger in his nose, just like his daddy" might well be *directly reinforcing* for said little Norbert.

A second source of direct reinforcement has to do with the actual consequences of the imitated behavior. If the activity is socially acceptable or leads to a reward, it is often reinforced by its own consequences. A child who learns to say "milk" as a result of hearing her mother say the word 40 times a day for 12 months may actually get milk as a result of saying the word.

Second, in addition to the possibility of direct reinforcement, the observer in a modeling situation often appears to be influenced by what Bandura (1969) calls **vicarious reinforcement**. This is an important type of secondhand reinforcement in which the imitator is not actually reinforced directly. It is as though the observer assumes that if the model does this or that, then this or that must be reinforcing. Therefore, in the imitator's unconscious logic, a similar sort of reinforcement is expected for the imitator.

Another source of reinforcement for imitative behavior, which affects the model rather than the observer, is based on the supposition that simply being imitated may be reinforcing. Thus, entertainers who wear bizarre clothes or hairstyles and are subsequently imitated by their fans may be more likely to persist with their unusual tastes.

Classical Conditioning in Observational Learning

Imitative behavior, as we saw, is typically an operant response whose probability increases or decreases because of the reinforcement contingencies associated with it. Hence, operant conditioning is clearly involved in this kind of learning.

Social Learning

Classical conditioning may also occasionally be implicated in learning through imitation. Specifically, many of the emotional responses associated with models may be acquired through classical conditioning. If you see a group of your cohorts laughing uproariously, clearly having a wonderful time, it is likely that their manifestations of fun and happiness will trigger similar emotions in you. Why? Simply because hearing people laugh and seeing them smile has been repeatedly paired with your own emotional reactions of joy, beginning right in infancy. As a result, other people's joyful behavior now serves as a conditioned stimulus (CS) for your own joyful **conditioned emotional reaction (CER)**. (A CER is a largely unavoidable, classically conditioned emotional reaction brought about by a specific stimulus.)

Not all conditioned emotional reactions are positive. Many social behaviors and gestures, such as cries, tears, frowns, raised eyebrows, head shakes, and finger wags, are conditioned stimuli for powerful negative CERs. These behaviors have been linked with negative emotions often enough that, through classical conditioning, they readily elicit negative emotions in observers. This might happen, for example, when you hear people screaming in panic and see them running madly toward the exits.

Conditioned emotional reactions may have a profound influence on the likelihood that a model will be imitated. If you witness Eduardo being punished for climbing on the roof, the CERs that you experience may discourage you from imitating his roof-climbing behavior. But if, instead, Eduardo clearly has a wonderful time on the roof and, furthermore, Candy smiles at him and praises him for his courage, you might well find yourself trying to imitate him.[3]

Three Effects of Imitation

In advanced technological societies, symbolic models such as those presented by books, verbal directions, and technological media are extremely important. In fact, explains Bandura, one problem with older theories of learning is that "most of them were cast long before this tremendous technological revolution in communications . . . . These theories do not encompass the tremendous power of the symbolic environment" (Evans, 1989, p. 6).

Through observational learning, children (and adults) learn three different classes of responses, which Bandura and Walters (1963) describe as the three effects of imitation. These are described here and summarized in Table 10.1.

The Modeling Effect

When observers learn through imitation something that is new for them, they are said to *model*. Hence, the **modeling effect** involves the acquisition of novel responses. When grandmothers

---

[3] Remember the car, Old Lady Gribbin said, interrupting her reading and pulling out the magazine ad she had shown me many weeks earlier – the one with the model lounging over a car. I was puzzled that she still had it. "If we measured changes in your blood pressure and your heart rate and perspiration and all that," she said, "we'd find that you had a CER when you looked at this ad. And that's exactly what the advertisers were shooting for." And then, although I know she doesn't smoke – at least not much – she pulled out a pack of cigarettes (one of those with the dire warnings printed on the side, along with a picture of a cancerous lung). "Now here," she said, "when you look at this warning, that's a different kind of CER. But it's the same learning principle."

Operant Conditioning in Observational Learning 377

Table 10.1 **Three effects of imitation, Bandura's theory**

Type of effect	Description	Illustration
Modeling effect	Acquiring a new behavior as a result of observing a model.	After watching a martial arts television program, Roberto tries out a few novel moves on his young sister, Juana.
Inhibitory–disinhibitory effect	Stopping or starting some deviant behavior after a model is punished or rewarded for similar behavior.	After watching Roberto, Dick, who already knew all Roberto's moves but hadn't used them in a long time, now tries a few of them on the family cat (disinhibitory effect). Dick abandons his pummeling of the cat when Juana's mother responds to her wailing and soundly punishes Roberto (inhibitory effect).
Eliciting effect	Engaging in behavior related, but not identical, to that of a model.	Reba starts piano lessons after her cousin receives a standing ovation for singing at the family reunion.

describe how their grandchildren acquire undesirable habits from the neighbor's undisciplined ruffians – habits that are clearly novel because the grandchildren never did such things previously – they are describing the modeling effect.

The classical experimental illustrations of the modeling effect with respect to aggression in young children are the "Bobo" clown experiments. In the first and most famous of these experiments, Bandura, Ross, and Ross (1961) exposed 72 children (aged 37–69 months) to adult models and a large, inflated, plastic Bobo clown. One group saw the model being physically aggressive with the doll (punching it, striking it with a mallet, kicking it, sitting on it, and so on). This physical aggression was also accompanied by verbally aggressive comments, such as "Hit him down . . .," "Sock him in the nose . . .," "Throw him in the air. . . ," and "Pow . . ." (Bandura et al., 1961, p. 576).

A second group saw the experimenter completely ignore the doll (nonaggressive model). And children in a third group were not exposed to the Bobo doll until the testing part of the study. In this part of the study, the model leaves the room and participants are exposed to the same doll and observed for 20 minutes through a one-way mirror. Participants are given no instructions. They are free to play with the Bobo or with other toys in the room.

The results of this, and of many subsequent studies, seem clear: When left alone with the doll, children exposed to aggressive models behave significantly more aggressively than children exposed to nonaggressive models or not exposed to any models at all. Furthermore, children's aggressive behaviors are often precisely imitative. If the model kicked the doll, that is what the child is most likely to do (see Figure 10.2).

Studies such as this have been widely used to support the belief that aggression is often learned through imitation and that television, because of its violent content, is highly influential in fostering

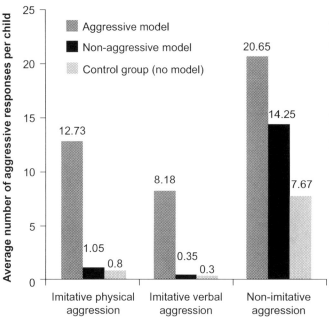

Figure 10.2 Some of the results from Bandura, Ross, and Ross's (1961) study of children's interactions with a Bobo doll following exposure to models interacting aggressively or nonaggressively with the doll. From Lefrançois, G. R. (2018). *Psychology for Teaching* (2nd Ed.). San Diego, CA: Bridgepoint Education, Fig. 5.12. Used by permission.

aggressive behavior. Others point out that these studies involve laboratory situations that are somewhat unrealistic and that aggression directed at an inanimate object is a far cry from aggression against real people in real life. However, ethical considerations prevent the use of babies (or even five-foot grownups) instead of dolls in these experiments. It is therefore difficult to illustrate the acquisition of meaningful aggressive responses experimentally. Still, a comprehensive review of 60 years of research on the effects of what the authors term *screen violence* (entertainment-based violence found in video games, films, the internet, and television) leaves little doubt that there are both short- and long-term negative effects associated with screen violence. As the authors of this review phrase it: "The vast majority of laboratory-based experimental studies have revealed that violent media exposure causes increased aggressive thoughts, angry feelings, physiologic arousal, hostile appraisals, aggressive behavior, and desensitization to violence and decreases prosocial behavior (eg, helping others) and empathy" (Anderson et al., 2017, p. S142).[4]

Inhibitory and Disinhibitory Effects

Imitation sometimes leads not to the learning of novel responses but, rather, to the suppression or disinhibition of previously learned deviant behavior. Inhibition and disinhibition usually

---

[4] I have another example of modeling for your keen-brained students, said Mrs. Gribbin, indicating that this wasn't to be recorded. She said it's an example described by Bandura. It involves the film *The Doomsday Flight*, in which an altitude-sensitive bomb is used in an attempt to extort money from an airline. Bandura wrote to the Federal Aviation Administration to find out about extortion attempts before and after airings of this film. As he expected, these attempts went up dramatically – often on the day following an airing. What's perhaps most striking is that many of these attempted extortions involved very precise modeling, including the use of allegedly altitude-sensitive bombs designed to explode at an altitude below 5,000 feet. One would-be extortionist out of Montreal on a London-bound flight was foiled when the airline decided to land in Denver (altitude 5,300 feet) instead. But in Alaska, an extortionist received $25,000; in Australia, another succeeded in getting $560,000 from Qantas Airlines (Evans, 1989).

occur as a result of seeing a model punished or rewarded for doing something deviant. For example, a group of thieves may stop stealing after a member of the group is apprehended and punished (the **inhibitory effect**: the suppression of a behavior as a consequence of modeling). Conversely, the same group may have begun stealing as a result of seeing a member become wealthy through stealing (the **disinhibitory effect**: engaging in a previously inhibited deviant behavior as a result of observing a model).

A striking illustration of the power of models in disinhibiting deviant behavior is found in some classic punishment studies (Walters & Llewellyn, 1963; Walters, Llewellyn, & Acker, 1962). In these studies, subjects were asked to volunteer for what was described as an experiment in memory. They were then shown one of two short sequences of film: a violent scene from *Rebel Without a Cause* or an excerpt from a film showing adolescents engaged in artwork. Afterward, subjects were asked to help the experimenter with another study designed to investigate the effects of punishment on problem-solving behavior.

Another male student, who posed as a subject but who was in reality a confederate of the experimenter, sat at a panel working out problems and signaling his answers by pressing a switch. Whenever he answered correctly, a green light would flash on a second panel; when he was incorrect, a red light would go on. This second panel also contained 15 toggle switches labeled 15 volts, 30 volts, 45 volts, and so on. The switches appeared to be connected to the electrodes fastened to the impostor subject's wrists. The actual subject was instructed to administer punishment in the form of an electric shock every time the imposter subject made an error (after he himself had been administered a mild shock to ensure he realized what he was doing).

Results of this study indicated that exposure to films with violent content significantly increased the intensity of shocks subjects were willing to give (the confederates weren't actually given shocks because one electrode was always disconnected). As we saw earlier, studies like this have often been cited as evidence of the potentially harmful effects of televised violence.

The Eliciting Effect

A third manifestation of the influence of models on human behavior, the **eliciting effect**, involves eliciting responses that, instead of matching the model's behavior precisely, are simply related to it. In a sense, it is as though the model's behavior encourages similar behavior in the observer. For example, a boy's being praised for winning athletic competitions might encourage his brother to try to excel academically. Similarly, the tastes and the fashions of television and movie heroes might influence the tastes and fashions of their admirers, *eliciting* related but not precisely imitative behavior in them. The eliciting effect, explains Bandura, "is the social facilitation function ... . The whole fashion and taste industry relies on that modeling functioning" (Evans, 1989, p. 5).

COGNITIVE CONTROL IN BANDURA'S SOCIAL COGNITIVE THEORY

As we saw, although Bandura's early formulation of his theory of observational learning (or imitation) was based squarely on a model of operant conditioning, his later writings have taken a decidedly cognitive twist (Bandura, 1986, 2007).

Some of our behaviors, explains Bandura (1977), are instigated by environmental events and bodily conditions such as those relating to hunger, thirst, and pain. But, in his words, "A great deal of human behavior, however, is initiated and sustained over long periods in the absence of compelling immediate external stimulation. In these instances, the inducements to action are rooted in cognitive activities" (Bandura, 1977, p. 161).

In Chapter 9, we saw the cognitive side of Bandura's theorizing in a discussion of the aspect of his social cognitive theory that deals with what is termed **self-referent thought**. Self-referent thought is thought that involves our own mental processes. Recall that a fundamentally important aspect of self-referent thought concerns the individual's personal assessments of competency and effectiveness. What Juan thinks of himself (his sense of **self-efficacy**) is inextricably linked with decisions he makes about what he will do as well as with the amount of effort and time he is willing to devote to different activities. If he firmly believed himself to be stupid and incapable of understanding the concepts in this book, he probably would not read it. Thus, cognitions drive actions.

Even in operant learning, claims Bandura, what is most important is the ability to symbolize and to anticipate the consequences of a person's own behavior (as well as the behavior of others). Moreover, says Bandura, people strive to control events that affect them. "By exerting influence in spheres over which they can command some control," writes Bandura, "they are better able to realize desired futures and to forestall undesired ones" (1995, p. 1). This is the *reciprocal determinism* of which we spoke earlier: The individual controls and influences the environment – sometimes by selecting it; sometimes by changing it – and the punishments and reinforcements that characterize the environment affect the individual. But although punishments and reinforcements affect behavior, they do not exert control as if people were thoughtless puppets. Rather, these effects are largely a function of awareness of relationships

Behavior Control Systems

Bandura (1969) maintains that it is impossible to explain human behavior solely by reference only to internal or external stimulus events; both are inevitably involved in most human behavior. Behaviorism is marked by its preoccupation with external events, whereas cognitivism deals mainly with internal events; Bandura's view tends to integrate the two approaches.

When Bandura refers to external stimulus events, he means simply that the physical environment is at least partly responsible for human behavior. People respond to the environment. Not to do so would be a mark of a completely nonfunctional being. Even such phylogenetically low forms of life as *Planaria* and *Aplysia* are responsive to external stimulation.

Internal stimulation refers to more cognitive events (in the form of images, memories, feelings, instructions, verbalizations, anticipations, and so on) that compose human thought processes. That these events influence behavior is clear: Grandmother would need no convincing whatsoever. Interestingly, though, psychologists sometimes do. To this end, Bandura (1969) cites an experiment performed by Miller (1951) in which a group of subjects were conditioned by means of electric shocks to react negatively to the letter T and positively to the number 4. After conditioning, subjects consistently gave evidence of greater autonomic reaction (arousal) for the stimulus associated with shock (in this case, T). Miller subsequently instructed subjects to think of the stimuli alternately as a sequence of dots was presented to them (T for the first dot, 4 for the second, T for the third, and so on). That there was now greater autonomic reaction to odd-numbered dots demonstrates the effect of internal processes on behavior.

Bandura describes three separate forces, or *control systems*, that interact with one another in determining behavior.

Stimulus Control

One class of human behaviors consists of activities directly under the control of stimuli. Such behaviors include the host of autonomic (reflexive) acts in which people engage when responding to certain specific stimuli. Sneezing, withdrawing from pain, flinching, the startle reaction, and so on, are all examples of behavior controlled by external stimuli.

Behaviors under control of stimuli also include responses learned through classical conditioning and through reinforcement. When a specific stimulus is always present at the time of the

---

[5] And students study night and day, Old Lady Gribbin grumbled, motioning that this was an aside, not to be recorded. They study and study, she said, even with no likelihood of immediate rewards for their efforts. They know that they'll eventually have fascinating and rewarding careers. She paused for a moment and then added, "At least, the clever ones will."

Social Learning

reinforcement, it acquires control over behavior in the sense that it eventually serves as a signal for a response. One illustration of this type of control is found in the contrast between the behaviors of some school children when their teachers are present and when they are not. By granting rewards for good behavior and punishment for less desirable activity, teachers become stimuli capable of eliciting obedience, fear, caution, respect, love, or a combination of these responses.

Outcome Control

Some behaviors, explains Bandura, are under the control of their consequences rather than their antecedents – that is, they don't appear to be under stimulus control. The outcome control system, which has been extensively investigated by Skinner, relates specifically to activities that become more probable as a function of reinforcement or less probable as a function of either nonreinforcement or punishment. In this behavior control system, control is achieved through operant conditioning.

Symbolic Control

The third behavior control system includes the range of human activity that is influenced by "mediation," or internal processes. Thought processes can affect human behavior in several ways. Internal verbalization of rules (self-instructions) can direct behavior, as in the Miller (1951) experiment in which subjects instructed themselves to think T, then 4, and so on.

A second way in which symbolic processes direct behavior has to do with the fact that imagining the consequences of behavior affects ongoing activity. Were it not for the ability to represent long-range outcomes symbolically (in other words, to anticipate outcomes), many tasks that are not associated with either an immediate stimulus or an immediate reward would never be undertaken. Why sow a field of corn if you cannot anticipate a crop in the fall? Why study medicine if you cannot imagine yourself as a doctor?

The importance of symbolization for human behavior seems to be much greater than that of the other two behavior control systems. It also appears that as one goes down the phylogenetic scale, the importance of outcome control and of direct stimulus control increases. Lower animal forms seem to react more to specific external stimulation than to behavioral outcomes. In addition, symbolization does not appear to play an important (if any) role in directing the behavior of many lower animals.

An Illustration of Behavior Control Systems

Although stimulus, outcome, and symbolic control are clearly distinguishable on theoretical grounds, they are not necessarily separate in practice. Much human activity is probably directed by a combination of these three. For example, consider a woman who pursues a bucktoothed, cross-eyed, knock-kneed, pigeon-toed, skinny, pointy-headed man. Because of stimulus

Table 10.2 **Behavior control systems in Bandura's theory***

Control system	Definition	Example
Stimulus control	Behaviors controlled directly by antecedent conditions (by stimuli)	Reflexes and classically conditioned responses (e.g., Watson's Little Albert crying when he sees a white rat)
Outcome control	Behaviors controlled by their consequences	Behaviors learned through operant conditioning (e.g., Sarah, who has occasionally won a small "jackpot," plugs dollar after dollar into the slot machine – until she finally reaches her last dollar)
Symbolic control	Behaviors controlled by thought processes, such as the ability to visualize and anticipate	Behaviors without immediate rewards but associated with anticipation of long-term rewards (e.g., Edward studies like a fiend all week, hoping to ace the exam and win a scholarship)

* Note that many behaviors may be influenced (controlled) by two or more of these systems at the same time. Thus, the behavior of a young lad who races to sit at the front of the gym during a film presentation may be controlled by (1) negative conditioned emotional reactions (CERs) relating to punishment he received for misbehaving in the back of the gym (stimulus control); (2) the fact that when he sat in the front, he was among the first to receive his bag of popcorn (outcome control); (3) his anticipation that sitting in the front will allow him to see the action more clearly (symbolic control).

generalization, the pursuer reacts to this man as she would to any other (the stimulus man has been present at the time of many previous reinforcements).

But human behavior is not this simple. The pursuer does not just respond to the stimulus in the blind manner expected of an unsophisticated rat. If her initial approach encounters strong resistance, she may modify it; if it is rewarded, she may intensify it. If the intensification leads to more reward, it may be reintensified; if it leads to a cessation of reinforcement, it may be diminished. Thus, the human female is capable of changing her behavior in accordance with its immediate outcomes.

The direction of activity is even more complex because symbolic processes also guide actions. For example, the woman can represent in her imagination the consequences of succeeding in capturing this unattractive male with the pointed head. She likely believes that such an ugly man must possess hidden talents to offset his lack of obvious physical qualities. Perhaps she anticipates that he will be an excellent cook (see Table 10.2).

Bandura's Agentic Perspective

People are agents of their own actions, Bandura insists. "They are agents of experiences rather than simply undergoers of experiences. The sensory, motor, and cerebral systems are tools

384   **Social Learning**

people use to accomplish the tasks and goals that give meaning, direction, and satisfaction to their lives" (2001, p. 4).

There are three main features of human agency, explains Bandura – three human characteristics that define this **agentic perspective**, where *agentic perspective* simply means that people are largely in control of their actions.

Intentionality

People can only be agents of their actions if they perform these actions intentionally, explains Bandura (2008a).[6] If Graciela gets pushed into her professor, accidentally causing the professor to spill her coffee, she would not be considered the agent of that action. But if Consuelo, who pushed Graciela, did so deliberately, Consuelo would be the agent.

Forethought

Intentionality implies planning and anticipation. That is, it implies forethought. As we noted earlier, the ability to symbolize allows people to anticipate the consequences of their actions. Were it not for the ability to predict the likely consequences of behavior, we could hardly intend to achieve them. Thus, if Consuelo could not foresee the consequences of pushing the hapless Graciela, she could hardly intend to get her into trouble.

Self-Reflection

As Bandura puts it, "Through the exercise of forethought, people motivate themselves and guide their actions in anticipation of future events" (2001, p. 7). This requires that people be able to examine and react to their own functioning. As an agent of her own actions, Consuelo can not only intend to push Graciela and foresee the consequences of so doing, but she can also reflect on her own actions as well as on their consequences, and she can react to them. That is, she can reflect upon (think about) the likely long-term consequences of her behavior and she can react to these consequences both before and after they occur. Also, she can change her intentions and her actions as she reflects and reacts.

The fundamentally important point, according to Bandura, is that we are in charge: We are the *agents*. As Bandura (2008b) explains, to be an agent is to deliberately attempt to direct our own behavior and influence the course of environmental events. This is not to deny that powerful biological forces shape many of our behaviors. Nor does it deny that much of what we do is under the control of various stimuli and under the control of anticipated outcomes. Likewise, there are accidental outcomes, unintended behaviors, and unexpected eventualities

---

[6] Your most discerning students will have realized, interrupted Old Lady Gribbin, that Bandura's description of the human being as an *agent* presupposes that this being is endowed with volition. It's a difficult issue in psychology but one that Bandura doesn't entirely skirt. The title of his 2008 chapter is "Reconstrual of 'free will' from the agentic perspective of social cognitive theory."

over which we exercise little control, often precisely because we could not have anticipated them. Clearly, had Graciela expected Consuelo to push her, things might have gone quite differently.

Personal Efficacy

If we are to truly be agents of our own actions, claims Bandura (2008b), nothing is more central than our beliefs about our personal efficacy. As we saw earlier, judgments of self-efficacy have a profound influence on what we do or do not do. If Sarah thinks she is especially good at making public speeches – that is, if her judgments of self-efficacy relative to public speaking are highly positive – she may be strongly motivated to seek out and accept opportunities to speak. In contrast, if she has low estimates of self-efficacy in this area, she will probably be far more likely to avoid public speaking occasions.

Of course, judgments of self-efficacy are not always accurate. There are those who continue to see themselves as efficacious (decidedly capable) in activities in which they perform appallingly poorly. Others have just the opposite problem: They see themselves as incapable and try to avoid activities where they would perform astonishingly well.

As we saw in Chapter 9, judgments of self-efficacy reflect four distinct influences: *enactive* (the direct effects of behavior), *vicarious* (the effects of comparisons with the behavior of others), *persuasory* (the effects of persuasion), and *emotive* (the effects of emotions).

The effects of our behaviors on others or their effects in a more objective sense often tell us how effective we are. If Samuel repeatedly fails in school, that would be objective evidence of low effectiveness. And if his parents, his teachers, or his friends make disparaging comments about his performance, the effects of his behavior on others would be an additional, very powerful social influence that would tend to lower his estimates of self-efficacy.

Similarly, comparisons that Samuel makes between his performance and that of his peers should tell him something about how effective he is. And significant others, such as parents, teachers, or peers, might succeed in persuading him that he really is a competent and effective individual, and that he need only apply himself more diligently.

Collective Efficacy

Bandura speaks not only of *self-efficacy*, which is a *personal* sense of competence and probable effectiveness, but also of **collective efficacy**, which is a shared belief about the efficacy of a group. In Bandura's words, "[P]erceived collective efficacy is defined as a group's shared belief in its conjoint capabilities to organize and execute the courses of action required to produce given levels of attainments" (1997, p. 477).

We do not live in social isolation, explains Bandura. As a result, no matter how powerful and effective we are as *agents* of our own lives, there are aspects of our environments and of our lives over which we have little individual control. But as members of various groups, we can sometimes exercise considerable power. For example, important political movements and decisions that can sometimes have profound influences on individual lives are often the result of concerted action by groups. Organized lobby groups, activists, people united by virtue of common religious beliefs – these are examples of just a few of the many *collectives* that can be described in terms of their sense of *collective efficacy*. Groups characterized by a high sense of *political* efficacy are those who hold the conviction that they have the power to effect political change.

Increasing economic and social globalization[7] coupled with technological change, explains Bandura (1997), are rapidly creating a world in which the exercise of collective agency becomes progressively more important if individuals are to retain a sense of control over their lives, and therefore a sense of personal self-efficacy.

Reciprocal Determinism

Bandura's early explanations of social learning, based as they were on a model of operant conditioning, can be summarized as follows:

- Much human learning is a function of observing and imitating the behaviors of others or of symbolic models such as fictional characters in books, television programs, video games, and so on. In Skinner's terms, imitative behaviors can be considered *operants*.
- When imitative behaviors have positive outcomes or result in the removal or prevention of negative consequences, they become more probable.

As we saw, Bandura's theory changed in important ways as he incorporated new ideas over the years, and responded to changing interests and emphases. In the end, besides being based on operant conditioning principles, and perhaps even more important, the theory became more cognitive as well as more social. It is now a theory that recognizes the fundamental importance of the individual's ability to symbolize, to understand cause-and-effect relationships, and to anticipate the outcomes of behaviors.

True to his Skinnerian roots, Bandura points out that the environment clearly affects our behavior: We engage in many behaviors because of the reinforcing consequences of so doing and we avoid other behaviors because of their negative consequences. But reinforcement and punishment do not control us blindly, pushing us mindlessly in this or that direction. Their effects depend largely on what we know of the relationship between our behavior and its outcomes. It is the individual's *anticipation* of future consequences that affects learning and behaving (Grusec, 2006).

Not only do we anticipate the consequences of our behavior and govern ourselves accordingly, but we also often deliberately shape our environments. That is, to the extent that we

---

[7] That's not entirely true, grumbled Old Lady Gribbin, suddenly very angry. This business of increasing globalization is hogwash! Back when I first spent time with Marshall McLuhan, she said, it was truer. "We're fast becoming a global village," he would say to me over drinks and canapés: "We're tearing down borders. We're all becoming citizens of the same world." He thought media, especially television, was seeing to globalization. But now, the old lady harrumphed, the media are fracturing rather than uniting us. The watchword is no longer *globalization*; it's now *tribalization* and by all means keep the other tribes out! She took a deep, shuddering breath and seemed to lose much of her anger. Now she looked profoundly dejected. After a while, she sighed again, and then turned once more to her ragged notes. She had not told me that she and Marshall McLuhan were friends.

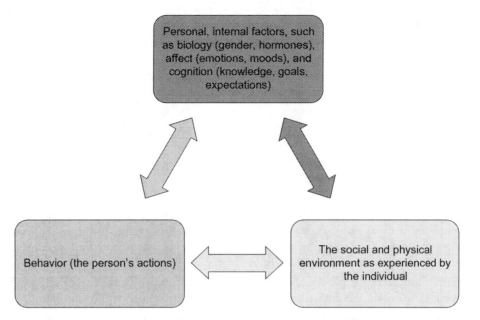

Figure 10.3 Bandura's notion of triadic reciprocal determinism. Behavior, the person, and the environment all mutually influence and change each other. From Lefrançois, G. R. (2016). *Psychology: The Human Puzzle*. San Diego, CA: Bridgepoint Education, Fig. 5.12. Used by permission.

choose what we do, where, and with whom, we create significant aspects of our environments. For example, if we are gifted at riding horses, and we therefore receive a lot of reinforcement from riding them, we might well choose a career on a ranch. Now we find ourselves in an environment that we have selected and perhaps shaped, and the environment in turn affects and shapes us. Those like you, who are wonderful students, *choose* to be in an academic environment. This environment constrains and shapes your behaviors, and it metes out your immediate and long-term rewards.[8]

This, the apparently causal interrelationship between environment, behavior, and person, is the source of Bandura's concept of **reciprocal determinism**. Put simply, this concept refers to the notion that we affect and are affected by our environment. In fact, explains Bandura, the three principal components of our social cognitive realities – personal factors (such as what we know and feel), our actions, and our environments – all influence each other reciprocally to determine our behaviors (Bandura, 1997).

Bandura (1997) refers to this kind of *reciprocal determinism* as **triadic reciprocal causation**. The three points of the triad, shown in Figure 10.3, are the person, the person's

---

[8] There's a lot that could be said here, Mrs. Gribbin interrupted her reading. A lot. And then for a long time, she was silent. About what? I asked, and for a second, I think she looked disappointed when she glanced at me, but in the dim glow of the kerosene lamp, I couldn't be certain. About free will, she answered. That you can choose to be here or there and that you can choose how you eat your beans – well, doesn't that mean that you have volition? Some of your brighter students might want to look at the Miller and Atencio (2008) chapter where they argue that volition is one of the factors that accounts for some of the variance in behavior. But most psychologists aren't certain what to make of free will. So, they make nothing of it. With some exceptions, like Skinner's 1971 book *Beyond Freedom and Dignity*. So, do we have free will? I asked. Do some research; think about it, the old lady replied, and she started to read once more.

actions, and the environment. Personal factors, such as our mood, our knowledge, and perhaps our personality traits, clearly affect our behavior. They can also affect our environments. But just as clearly, aspects of our environments, such as the social systems in which we operate, affect our behaviors even as they can also affect personal factors, such as how we feel. But not all these forces, Bandura explains, are always equally and simultaneously reciprocal. Qualities such as high self-efficacy can lead people to make considerable efforts to master their environments; those with lower estimates of personal efficacy may be more *mastered* than masterful.

APPLICATIONS OF BANDURA'S SOCIAL COGNITIVE THEORY

Bandura's theory has several important facets: One, based partly on Skinner's model of operant learning, deals with observational learning (learning through imitation). This aspect of the theory looks at the extremely powerful and pervasive influence on learning and behavior of both actual and symbolic models. It looks at the different processes that are involved in observational learning (attention, retention, reproduction, and motivation) and at the different effects of observational learning (modeling, inhibition–disinhibition, and eliciting).

A second facet of the theory introduces a more cognitive orientation. It recognizes that even in observational learning, the individual's ability to symbolize and to anticipate is fundamentally important. This aspect of the theory looks at the three different control systems that direct human behavior: stimulus control, outcome control, and symbolic control. The first of these, stimulus control, has to do with classically conditioned behaviors; the second, outcome control, deals with operant learning; and the third, symbolic control, refers to the role of cognitive activities such as thinking and imagining.

A third aspect of the theory, even more cognitive, underlines Bandura's belief that we are not simply pawns pushed hither and yon by our reflexes, our drives, or the contingencies of our behaviors. We are in charge, Bandura insists. Despite there being powerful biological forces and behavioral consequences that shape our behaviors, we are the agents of our own actions. We intend them, we anticipate their consequences, and we reflect on our behaviors, our effectiveness, and ourselves as human beings.

Each facet of this theory has clear applications.

Observational Learning

Observational learning has to do with learning by imitating models. As we saw, imitation might be evident in novel behaviors (modeling effect), in the suppression or appearance of deviant behaviors (inhibitory–disinhibitory effect), or in the appearance of behaviors related to those of the model (eliciting effect). Also, recall that some of the most important models in advanced technological societies are symbolic rather than actual. These include books, fictional characters, verbal instructions, social media, and so on.

Teachers use models extensively in the classroom. The instructions and directions they provide are, in effect, models. So too is the teacher's behavior and that of other students. Research suggests that not all models have the same influence on children. Children are most likely to imitate people who are important to them, such as parents, siblings, close friends, and respected teachers. Also, as we saw, they are most likely to imitate highly valued behaviors. Each of the three effects of imitation described by Bandura can be used systematically to promote desirable behavior and to eliminate deviant behaviors.

For example, children might be taught something new by being shown what to do (modeling effect); they might be discouraged from doing something by witnessing someone else being punished for the behavior (inhibitory effect); or they might be encouraged to engage in a certain class of behaviors after being exposed to a relevant model (eliciting effect).

One example of using models to modify behavior comes from a study Martens and Hiralall (1997) conducted in which a teacher was instructed in a three-step procedure for changing inappropriate play behaviors among nursery school children: (1) identifying sequences of inappropriate behavior; (2) rescripting these behaviors by working out more acceptable inter-actions; (3) acting out the modified scripts for the children. These investigators found that the teacher was quickly able to learn and implement this procedure and that the effect was a measurable increase in acceptable play behavior.

Behavior Control Systems

Some classroom behaviors appear to be under relatively direct control of specific stimuli. Thus, early in the school year, most teachers establish clear rules and routines that ensure the smooth and orderly functioning of their classrooms. A verbal signal, a bell, a buzzer, or a gesture might be a specific stimulus that says, "Yes, you may now go to the bathroom," "It's time to put away your books," "You're dismissed for recess," "Take out your math books," and so on. Such routines, says Doyle (1986), are fundamental to effective classroom management. Bringing them under the control of clear stimuli can greatly facilitate teaching.

Many classroom behaviors are affected by outcomes rather than mainly by preceding stimuli. Among important outcomes that are under teacher control are things such as praise and criticism as well as the enormous range of other reinforcers and punishers that schools can provide for children (see Chapter 4 for a discussion of some of these). For example, **time-out** procedures are based on the behavioral principle that outcomes affect behavior. Thus, when Roberta is excluded from ongoing classroom activities because she has repeatedly activated her phone to text Camilla, the expectation is that because she is being removed from a situation where she might expect positive reinforcement, her subsequent behavior will be affected. As Drayton et al. (2017) explain, time-out is the most common behaviorally based disciplinary technique currently used in North America. Research and theory such as that of Bandura and Skinner illustrate that changes in behavior result from the relationship that exists between what children do, what happened before they do it, and what happens afterward.

Closely related to stimulus or outcome control, explains Bandura, are the effects of the individual's ability to symbolize, imagine, and anticipate the likely consequences of various behaviors. That Vladimir so carefully follows all the rules and routines in his classroom has to do with his ability to imagine what the consequences of not doing so might be. Similarly, that Eugenio studies so hard may well relate to his ability to anticipate how his parents and teachers will react to his performance on various tests. And his studying may also be linked to his anticipation of a brilliant future as a nuclear physicist.

Personal Agency and Self-Efficacy

Eugenio has strong, highly positive notions of self-efficacy. Self-efficacy judgments are a very important aspect of self-knowledge, says Bandura (1997). Among other things, our judgments of self-efficacy are important determiners of what we do and what we do not do. In addition, positive judgments of self-efficacy are associated with higher physical and mental health. Bandura explains that high self-efficacy provides people with the tools they need to cope with the situations life offers. As a result, anxieties and phobias, important manifestations of human distress, are far less common among those whose judgments of self-efficacy are positive. In contrast, those who have low evaluations of their personal competence are more likely to judge themselves negatively and to have poorer self-esteem and life satisfaction (Martinez-Marti & Ruch, 2017).

Not surprisingly, therapeutic interventions based on Bandura's notions of self-efficacy have become increasingly common. For example, Scott and Cervone (2008) describe how interventions designed to strengthen feelings of self-efficacy not only are effective in doing so but often result in reductions in avoidant behavior. Such therapies – sometimes labeled **guided mastery therapy** – have been shown to be especially effective in combating phobias (Hoffart, 2016). Their effectiveness is most often explained in terms of the assumption that phobias often result from individuals' lack of a sense of self-efficacy – that is, lack of a feeling of confidence that they can deal with the object of their phobia.

Developing positive self-concepts (positive evaluations of self-efficacy) in children, together with an accompanying sense of personal power (of personal agency), is an important task for parents and teachers. Bandura describes four main sources of influence that can affect these concepts, each of which is at least partly under the control of parents and teachers. For example, enactive influences are those related to the effects of the child's actions. Hence, the importance of presenting children with tasks that allow them to experience success, but that are not so simple as to be meaningless. Tasks within Vygotsky's zone of *proximal development* are ideal.

Vicarious influences relate to the effect of comparing one's achievements with those of others. In this connection, many educators recommend that teachers avoid highly competitive school situations where learners are placed in a win–lose struggle to see who's best (Johnson & Johnson, 1994). Instead, teachers are encouraged to provide students with their own learning goals so they can work individually as well as cooperatively at their own pace and in a way that ensures that every student achieves success and feels personally responsible for doing so.

Teachers are also important agents of what Bandura calls *persuasory influences* as communicators of confidence or doubt. That Sarah's teacher has suggested she not attempt the extra assignment in mathematics because it will be too difficult for her will do very little that is positive for her self-judgments of personal competence.

Physiological states of arousal, evident in high or low excitement or anxiety, also influence judgments of self-efficacy, explains Bandura. As we saw in Chapter 9, arousal is at least partly under a teacher's or a parent's control. Teachers are among the most important sources of stimulation in the classroom. What they say and do as well as the tasks they present their charges can do a great deal to increase or decrease arousal. Bandura suggests that high arousal can affect self-judgment in different ways. For example, great fear might lead to judgments of low personal competence. If Jessica is deathly afraid of being afraid if she tries to climb the rock wall, she may well judge herself incapable of doing so. On the other hand, if Jessica is deathly afraid of being attacked by a rampaging bear, she might judge herself capable of outrunning or outwitting it, or of climbing the wall to escape.

BANDURA'S SOCIAL COGNITIVE THEORY: AN APPRAISAL

Bandura's social cognitive theory serves as an important bridge between behavioristic and more cognitive theories. Its behavioristic roots are evident in his use of an operant conditioning model to explain learning through imitation. And its cognitive orientation is apparent in its recognition of the power of our ability to imagine the consequences of our actions, in its insistence that we are the agents of our own actions, and in the central role it assigns self-referent thought in motivating and directing behavior.

Bandura's theory also serves as an excellent example of how theories in psychology do not need to be – and probably should not be – static and unchanging things. As the spirit of the times change and as science provides theorists with new information and new possibilities, good theories can also change. After all, our psychological theories are not judged by some absolute criteria of rightness or wrongness. Instead, we judge them by how well they reflect the facts as we know them and, perhaps most important, we look at how useful they are in any of a variety of ways.

Bandura's theorizing does no great violence to the facts as we know them. It tends to reflect research findings well and has successfully incorporated new findings and new ideas over a span of decades. For example, Bandura's notions about self-efficacy and his assertion that we are agents of our own actions are in close agreement with current notions about expectancy–value theory and self-determination in motivation theory (Chapter 9).

That the theory is useful in a practical sense also seems clear. As Artino (2007) puts it, "[T]he work of Albert Bandura and his co-authors has had an immeasurable impact on the field of psychology, in general, and educational psychology, more specifically" (p. 2). For example, observational learning theory has been used extensively in an effort to understand the influence of television on aggression and violence among children and adults. The theory also suggests useful explanations for the effectiveness of incarceration and other forms of punishment.

Many aspects of Bandura's theory have had a profound influence on the development of therapies. For example, his notions of personal agency and the role of self-referent thought, and especially of the individual's sense of self-efficacy, underlie a variety of social cognitive therapies. These have proven especially effective in the treatment of phobias.

Bandura's writings have also exerted a huge influence on the study of motivation, learning, and social psychology. For example, his theory of observational learning has become nearly synonymous with the field of social learning theory; his notions regarding self-efficacy have stimulated an enormous amount of recent research in personality and motivation; and the impact of the Bobo doll studies continues unabated almost half a century after they were first reported. In fact, Bandura reports that whenever he is invited to give a talk somewhere, someone almost invariably brings along a Bobo doll and asks him to sign it (Bandura, 2007).

It is perhaps fitting that in their study of the most eminent psychologists of the twentieth century, Haggbloom et al. (2002) ranked Bandura fourth. First was Skinner, followed by Piaget, and then Freud.

Main Point Chapter Summary

1. Social learning can mean learning that occurs as a result of social interaction (a *process* definition) or the sort of learning that is involved in discovering which behaviors are expected and acceptable in different social situations (a *product* definition). Socially accepted behaviors vary from one culture to another as well as for different ages and sometimes for different sexes.

2. The chief agents of socialization are the culture's main institutions: the family, the school, the church, peer groups, media, and so on.

3. Bandura's theory of social learning is a theory of imitation (observational learning), stemming from Miller and Dollard's drive-reduction theory of imitation and based heavily on Skinner's theory of operant conditioning, with a recognition of the importance of cognitive variables that became clearer and more emphatic as the theory developed.

4. Imitative behaviors are operant responses subject to the laws of operant learning. Models can be people or more symbolic patterns for behavior, such as are provided by books, instructions, religions, television, computers, and so on.

5. Reciprocal determinism refers to the fact that we shape and control our environments even as they shape and control us. It is also evident in that we are culture-produced and culture-producing.

6. Observational learning depends on four related processes: attentional (the need to pay attention), retentional (the need to be able to remember and represent what is observed), motor reproduction (the need to be able to produce the observed behavior), and motivational (the need to be motivated – to have a reason to imitate).

7. Imitation can be reinforced directly (by the model or through its own consequences) or vicariously (as a result of seeing someone else rewarded or punished).

8. Conditioned emotional responses (CERs) – acquired through classical conditioning – are often involved in determining whether a behavior will be imitated.

9. Observational learning may be apparent in the modeling effect (novel, precisely imitative responses), the inhibitory or disinhibitory effects (the suppression or appearance of deviant behavior), and the eliciting effect (social facilitation of related responses). The Bobo doll experiments are classic illustrations of observational learning involving aggression. Its findings have been replicated in numerous studies of the effects on viewers of screen (television, film, video games, the internet) violence.

10. Bandura integrates behavioristic and cognitive models by describing three behavior control systems involving different classes of responses: those that are under direct stimulus control, those that are affected by their consequences, and those that are directed by means of symbolic processes. Symbolic processes are heavily involved in self-referent thought – our ability to think about our *selves* and to evaluate our personal effectiveness (our self-efficacy).

11. We are agents of our own actions, says Bandura, as is evident in our intentionality, our forethought, and our self-reflection.

12. One of the most important aspects of self-knowledge is reflected in personal judgments of competence, termed *self-efficacy*. Positive evaluations are associated with high achievement and good physical and mental health. Self-efficacy is influenced by the outcomes of our behavior (enactive influences), by comparisons with other people's behavior (vicarious influences), and by the effects of persuasion (persuasory influences) and of arousal (emotive influences).

13. Bandura's theory reflects scientific findings well, is highly compatible with current developments in social-learning and motivation theory, and has important practical implications for parenting, teaching, and therapy.

11 Machine Learning and Artificial Intelligence

The Future?

CHAPTER OUTLINE

This Chapter	395
Objectives	396
The Computer and the Brain	396
People and Machines: Computer Metaphors	397
Serial and Parallel Processing	399
Symbolic and Connectionist Models	400
Symbolic Models	400
Appraisal of Symbolic Models	403
Connectionist (Neural Network) Models	403
Artificial Intelligence	410
Historical Approaches to Artificial Intelligence	410
Why Make Computers Smarter	411
Can Machines Think? The Turing Test	412
Recent Developments in Artificial Intelligence	415
Appraisal of Connectionist (Neural Network) Models	417
Educational and Social Implications	419
A Field in Progress	421
Main Point Chapter Summary	421

I visualize a time when we will be to robots what dogs are to humans, and I'm rooting for the machines.

Claude Shannon

Mrs. Gribbin said to meet her that night on the ridge behind the bush cabin where the trail forks, that she would be there to tell me the story of the next chapter. "If you're not there," said she, "the thread of the story will be broken." She said that the breaking of the story might not seem a big thing but that it would be far bigger than itself. "All happenings are connected to other happenings," she said very solemnly. And then, very suddenly, she thrust a small black box into my hands.

"Tell me what's in this box?" she said. I turned the box this way and that, searching in vain for a way to open it. "I don't know what's in the box," I said. "I can't open it."

"Is that the only way you can find out what's inside?" asked the old lady. But before I could answer, she snatched the box from my hand and whirled quickly around so I could see only her back. A moment later, when she turned to face me once more, she held what looked like a fried chicken leg in her hand, which Schrödinger took so delicately from her, and I knew that somehow, the old lady had opened the box. "How did you . . . ?" I began to ask, but she had disappeared into the trees. The cat, too, had vanished.

I found her that night huddled by a fire not where the trail forks on the ridge's flank but farther back on the edge of the crest where no trees screen the stars, and again she didn't greet me but motioned that I should sit and nodded that I should turn on the recorder. As I did so, a wolf howled. Every time I listen to the recording now, the howl somehow seems more desolate, more mournful.

I squatted on the other side of the fire watching the fire shadows dancing on Old Lady Gribbin's face as she spoke Chapter 11, the recorder squeezing her words into invisible electronic paragraphs.

THIS CHAPTER

She said that much of this chapter deals with how things are connected in vast, complex networks. To understand these networks, *she explained*, it's important to clarify a mysterious term often used in psychology: **black box**.

Black box is an expression psychologists have used to describe the contents of the mind. Interestingly, however, psychologists haven't yet decided what a mind actually is – although the term is used constantly, as in, "I've a good mind to . . ." or "I've changed my mind" or "They're always mindful of it" or "She's out of her ever-loving mind" or "Mind the kids now" or "Mind the dog" or "Out of sight is out of mind" or . . . well, never mind.

The expression *black box* implies that the contents of the mind are unknown and perhaps unknowable. So, *black box* is often linked with behaviorists such as Watson and Skinner, who thought it was a waste of time to speculate about what happens between the presentation of a stimulus and the appearance of a response.

But as we saw, some behaviorists thought maybe the black box should be opened – which they couldn't quite do. What they did instead was try to guess as intelligently as possible what sorts of things might be going on up there (or down there) in the mind – or in the brain because most psychologists believe that if the mind is ever discovered, it will be found somewhere in the brain.

Neobehaviorists, such as Clark L. Hull, Edward Chace Tolman, and Donald Hebb, invented their own versions of what they thought might be in the black box, being very careful all the while to tie their inventions to things they could actually see and maybe measure. At the same time, cognitivists also tried to crack the black box's lid. Some of them – Jerome Bruner and Jean Piaget, for example – became so engrossed in the structures and processes they glimpsed inside that, in the end, they ripped the lid right off and filled the box with so much jargon and stuff that the lid probably would not go back on at all anymore. And now, far more recently in

Machine Learning and Artificial Intelligence

the history of the black box, a new army of brain/mind explorers, driven by powerful and sometimes intricate computer metaphors, has begun to map regions of the box few had dreamed of. Many of these explorers are no longer content simply to invent metaphors for the mind and the brain. Instead, they try to actually simulate what it is that the brain/mind does. Their theories are, in Harnish's words, "connectionist computational theories of mind" (2002, p. 15).

Objectives

Tell your readers, *said the old lady*, that the paths on which these mind/brain explorers have set out is the subject of this chapter. Try to convince them that once they have finished learning the chapter, they will probably want to rent television time so they might explain to everybody the significance of:

- artificial intelligence and computer simulation;
- symbolic representation systems;
- parallel processing and connectionism;
- machine learning and deep learning;
- why robots play chess;
- how to test the intelligence of an artificially intelligent machine.

Tell them, too, that they will also know more about how new *connectionist* machines with names like Thinker, Zappa, Deep Blue, and Watson are shedding new light on that lump of tissue inside their skulls that they call a *brain*. But they will not yet know where the paths of this newer connectionism lead because human history, perversely tied to linear notions of time, provides no glimpse into the future. Maybe we really will be like robots' dogs when, and if, robot intelligence ever becomes real rather than artificial.

The old lady fell silent for a moment. The wolf cried again, more moan than howl. Then, she began reading from her notes.

THE COMPUTER AND THE BRAIN

In their characteristically human way, people have assumed all along that a truly smart computer would be quite a lot like a human. It is surely no accident that most of the computers and computerized robots of popular fiction are given personalities. These fictional computer-driven creations are superbly "intelligent" in their memory and computational abilities, and they all have a degree of willfulness and of personal idiosyncrasy. Their creators have tried to make them human.[1]

---

[1] I find this an astonishingly presumptuous intention, Old Lady Gribbin said, explaining that it's obvious to all clear thinkers that human-type life-forms cannot simply be invented and built. She said that real robots are simply machines; they don't have personalities because personalities are properties of *persons*. What they have, she said, is *machinalities*, chuckling at her lame attempt at humor. She said that this is why the human-invented robots of fiction will always be fictions. She seemed angry but ignored me when I tried to ask her if these things disturbed her. Schrödinger appeared suddenly from the shadows and laid what I thought must be a mouse at the old lady's feet. But when she picked it up,

People and Machines: Computer Metaphors

Mechanical metaphors, says Shanks (2002), have been rich sources of inspiration for scientists and philosophers. But these metaphors have not been without controversy. There are those who argue that viewing humans as machines robs them of the most important aspects of their humanity. After all, machines have no emotion and no volition. Metaphors and models based on machines cannot explain or account for affect (emotion).

It is important to keep in mind that metaphors are, as the term implies, just comparisons. Models are simply conceptual or physical representations of something else. We need not believe that computers are in any way human for computer metaphors and analogies to be useful. We need only accept that, at least in some ways, computers and humans are sufficiently similar that some features of one can be used as a sort of pattern for some aspects of the other.

As Milkowski (2018) points out, the information processing capacities of computers are a useful metaphor for nervous systems that are basically computational, and that require information processing for its cognitive activities. As a result, computer metaphors are extremely common in what are sometimes called the *cognitive sciences*. Similarities that have historically been most important for these computer metaphors have to do with both structure and with function. Structurally, computers consist of complex arrangements of electronic components: chips, disks, drives, central processing units, random access memory, connectors, and so on (called **hardware**), as well as input and output devices like keyboards and screens. The human brain consists of complex arrangements of neural material: neurons, various other cells, amino acids, chemical transmitter substances, and so on (termed **wetware**), as well as input and output devices like the senses and the ability to produce sound and movement. The basic computer metaphor, represented in Figure 11.1, compares hardware to wetware. Similarly, it equates input and output with stimuli and responses.

Although the computer's hardware permits it to function (even as wetware permits humans to function), its instructions or programs (termed **software**) determine whether and how it will function. With respect to functioning, the basic computer metaphor compares the computer's programmed operations with human cognitive processes. Hence, these human cognitive processes are labeled **information processing**. After all, information processing is what computers do. And in the same way as a computer can become infected with **malware**, such as computer viruses, Trojan horses, spyware, worms, and so on, so too can the human brain be attacked by viruses that cause diseases, such as encephalitis and meningitis.

The potential of the comparison between human and computer functioning lies in the possibility that a truly smart computer – one that responds like an intelligent human being – might function as does a human. Put another way, the memory and programs of a smart computer might in some important respects resemble the memories and cognitive processes of the human.

I saw that it was a tiny, flaming yellow, wild Lady's Slipper orchid. Holding it to her nose with one hand, she scratched the cat's ruff with the other while murmuring gentle words in a language I did not recognize. The cat seemed to shrug as if to say, "It's nothing really," but for a second, I thought I saw Mrs. Gribbin's eyes water. I wished I had thought of looking for a wild orchid. Then the old lady nodded that I should start the recorder and began to speak once more, using a language I mostly understood.

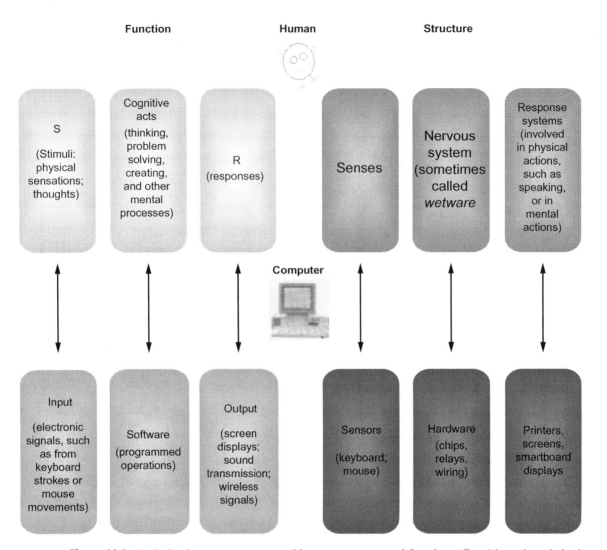

Figure 11.1 Analogies between computer and human structures and functions: Cognitive science's basic computer metaphor compares input to stimuli, output to responses, and the cognitive functioning of the nervous system to the computer's software-driven operations.

However, keep in mind that even a computer that does very human-like things might nevertheless use very different processes to do them. A machine can milk a cow far more rapidly than a grandmother can, but this certainly does not prove that the machine has hands (or that the grandmother has suction tubes!). And it might also be important that although the machine does not sing as it milks, the grandmother sure as the devil does.

Important Differences Between Brains and Computers

Despite their similarities, brains and ordinary computers are different in some important ways. For one thing, brains are very slow; computers are lightning fast. A neuron in the cerebral cortex can respond to input in thousandths of a second; a signal within a computer can be activated in just a few **nanoseconds** (one nanosecond is *one-billionth* of a second).

So transmission of impulses in the brain is maybe 100,000 times slower than transmission in a computer. As Sejnowski and Delbruck (2012) note, the brain is a product of evolution, not engineering design, and nature is not always the most intelligent designer.

But a single human brain can, in an instant, greet by name a man who has just shaved off his beard, dyed his hair, and changed his clothes; understand five languages spoken in dozens of different accents; recognize a drinking container no matter what style of mug, glass, flask, vessel, goblet, tumbler, cup, jug, beaker, carafe, pot, or flagon it is; write a novel; and on and on.

"What makes a bunch of neurons so smart?" asked Allman a few decades ago (1989, p. 6). He answered his own question by saying that it is a collective phenomenon; it has to do with organization. What intelligent living things have in common is organization and complexity. Thus, from a physical point of view, the human nervous system is incredibly more complex than even the largest and most sophisticated of modern computers. As a result, claimed Allman, from a psychological viewpoint, the brain's "tangled web displays cognitive powers far exceeding any of the silicon machines we have built to mimic it" (1989, p. 3). He goes on to explain that the human ability to store information in memory is virtually unlimited; no computer even comes close.[2]

At the time that Allman wrote, no computer could yet match the human ability to perceive and to recognize complex, changing patterns or even to defeat the best human game players. But that was 1989, and computers have come a very long way since then. As we see in a later section, there are now computer systems that easily trounce the best *Go* or chess players in the world. Too, there are machines that reliably beat humans at identifying common objects, at picking out faces from among millions of similar faces, and at transcribing speech – even machines that play Pac-Man better than any human Pac-Man addict (Vincent, 2017). The modern computer's ability to retrieve flawlessly from memory and to perform arithmetical computations rapidly and accurately far exceeds that of humans. Computers do complex calculations in elaborate arrays (such as spreadsheets) in fractions of seconds. Using the brain to do the same sort of thing, claims Allman (1989), is like using a wrench to pound in a nail: It will work, but that is not what it is made for.

Serial and Parallel Processing

One of the problems with earlier brain–computer metaphors was simply that, for many years, all computers were **serial processing** digital machines: They carried out a single operation at a time, albeit extremely rapidly so that it seemed that they were manipulating a host of operations simultaneously. But the brain is a computer that does not do things one after another with lightning rapidity, arriving at its solutions in less time than it takes to say "Bob's your uncle."

---

[2] Are you worried that really smart robots might one day take over the world? asked Old Lady Gribbin. You shouldn't be, she answered her own question. Brooks (2002) says that even when or if robots ever become truly intelligent, you won't have to worry that they'll decide that you're stupid and useless and take over the world. Why? Because, writes Brooks, "there won't be any us (people) for them (pure robots) to take over" (p. ix). You want to know why? asked the old lady. And again she answered her own question. It's because by then, according to Brooks, all humans will have robot parts imbedded in them – parts to make their joints and muscles faster and stronger, their hearing more acute, their vision clearer and, yes, even their brains incredibly more powerful. "Robot-humans," said the old lady, "will always be a couple of jumps ahead of the pure robots." I didn't feel reassured.

The truth is that if the brain actually worked that way, it would take you a staggering amount of time to blurt out "Bob's your uncle." Instead, the brain is more like today's 8- or 16-core computer that does more than one thing at the same time. A computer that does many things at once is also called a **parallel processing** computer. As we see shortly, not only do these newer computing technologies make the brain–computer metaphor more appropriate, but they provide scientists with powerful new tools for mimicking, simulating, and perhaps even duplicating and enhancing human cognitive functions.

SYMBOLIC AND CONNECTIONIST MODELS

Just how useful are computers for studying human information processing? Is it possible to design and program them so they perceive the environment as humans do? Can they be made to learn and use language as do humans? Can they be taught to read?

And if a computer can be made to do some (or all) of these things, will its processes be anything like human cognitive processes? Will it then be a "thinking machine"? Will it reveal things about human cognitive processing that are not now known?

There have historically been two different approaches to the computer-based study of human cognitive processes – each tagged with a sometimes-bewildering array of labels. On the one hand is the **symbolic model** (also associated with the labels *production system* or *declarative knowledge*); on the other is the more recent **connectionist model** (also associated with the labels *procedural*, *automatic*, and *implicit*).

Symbolic Models

Given that all computers were initially digital, serial-processing machines, early models of human thought processes reflect the characteristics of these machines. These models view intellectual functioning largely as a sequence of acts (rather than as a number of acts carried out simultaneously). The tremendous power of the serial computer is that it can carry out a staggering number of operations (calculations) in a very short time, not simultaneously but successively. In the vernacular of computerese, its strength is one of *brute force*.

The basic assumption of symbolic models is that all meaning and therefore all thought processes can be represented by symbols, such as language. According to this model, all processing of information – and, hence, all thinking – can be interpreted through identifiable rules. Simply put, the external world is represented mentally by symbols; thinking involves manipulating these symbols according to certain logical rules. Therefore, for a computer programmer to simulate thinking, it is necessary to program into the system symbols that correspond to items of information as well as rules for dealing with these symbols.

Logic Theorist and the General Problem-Solver

An early example of a symbolic model is the proposal by Newell, Shaw, and Simon (1958; Newell, 1973; Newell & Simon, 1972) for a theory of human problem solving. The proposal took the form of a complex program designed to discover proofs for theorems in symbolic logic. The program, called Logic Theorist (LT) was based on *Principia Mathematica* (Whitehead & Russell, 1925) and consisted of storing the axioms of *Principia Mathematica* in the computer, together with all the processes necessary for discovering proofs. The first 52 theorems of the text were then presented to LT; it succeeded in proving 38 of the theorems, almost half of them in less than one minute. It even proved a theorem not previously proven.

Although it was reasonably adept at solving mathematical theorems, the Logic Theorist program could not be used to solve other kinds of problems. So, Newell and his colleagues developed a more general problem-solving program, aptly titled *General Problem-Solver* (GPS) (Newell & Simon, 1972). Simplified, the program used any of a number of available operations to reduce the difference between the present state of affairs (the problem) and the desired state of affairs (a solution for the problem). That is, the program was designed to allow comparisons between the desired end state and the current state and to make a succession of changes (using the logical and mathematical operations available to it) until a solution was reached.

GPS was used to solve a variety of logical and mathematical problems, and the problem-solving steps used by the computer were then compared with those used by human problem solvers. These comparisons, report Newell and Simon (1972), suggested that the behavior of GPS was like that of a human in several ways. Much like humans, GPS solved some problems, although not all; it did better if the information was presented systematically; it performed better with instructions that provided direction; it used processes suggestive of "insight" rather than blind trial and error; it used concepts in solving problems to the extent that axioms can be considered to be concepts; and it organized itself to do these things by using past discoveries to guide future endeavors.

In the end, GPS did not actually reveal anything new or very important about human problem solving. It did only what it had been programmed to do, so it tended to reflect only what was then known or suspected about cognitive processing. But one thing it did show was that human subjects are far more flexible than GPS (Wagman, 2002). Moreover, humans have a degree of self-awareness and a range of knowledge about the world that cannot easily be programmed into a computer.

Chess Computer Masters

Logic Theorist and the General Problem Solver were among the first modern attempts to develop *thinking* machines. But the technology available for these machines was a far cry from that available for today's machines.

Early machines led to a tendency to think of computers as mechanical wizards endowed with a type of brute cognitive force that humans do not even remotely approach. In the main, this estimate of the computer, although not entirely incorrect, is misleading. For example, take a straightforward game, such as chess. The rules of the game are marvelously explicit; each piece can move only in prescribed ways and only on a conventional, easily defined area. The object of the game is simple and clear: capture the opponent's king. At any given point, there are a limited number of possible moves, a finite number of possible countermoves, and so on.

Surely such a powerful brute as the computer can be programmed to consider and keep in memory all possible moves, countermoves, and responses to countermoves, together with the eventual implications of each of these moves. In other words, a well-programmed computer could at least play to a draw but more likely beat any chess master in the world.

Not quite so easily. The total number of moves possible in a chess game approximates 10^{120} – a figure that may not look like much sitting here on this page, but that is absolutely staggering. "There haven't been that many microseconds since the big bang," writes Waldrop (1992, p. 151). Hence, no conceivable computer could represent all possible alternatives.

The computer, like people, must rely on **heuristics** rather than **algorithms** for situations such as this. An algorithm is a problem-solving procedure in which all alternatives are systematically considered and a correct solution is pretty well guaranteed. An algorithmic solution for chess problems relies on the computer's *brute force*. In contrast, a heuristic approach to problem solving makes use of various strategies that eliminate and select from among alternatives without having to consider every one separately, but with no guarantee of a correct solution. For example, a computer programmed to play chess might make use of heuristics (strategies) designed to protect the king, attack the opposition's queen, control the center of the board, and so on.

When artificial intelligence investigators first began to program computers to play chess, none of their serial processing computers were large enough or fast enough to make very good use of brute force; hence, programmers were compelled to build their programs around the kinds of strategies human chess players might use. Chess masters could lick these early chess-playing computers with one hand.

But now, today's multi-core computers are incredibly faster and infinitely larger, and some of them can look ahead and see the implications of millions of different moves within seconds. Modern chess programs have largely given up trying to imitate human chess-playing strategies. They have reverted instead to using sheer brute force, coupled with a few key strategies. Their strength is not that they "think" better chess than average human players, but that they can mechanically compute millions of moves and countermoves within a few seconds. In fact, the IBM chess computer Deep Blue is described as a "massively parallel processing" machine whose chips can each consider and evaluate 2–2.5 million moves per second. In total, Deep Blue can attain speeds of more than 300 million positions per second.

So, how good are the best chess-playing computers now? Quite good. Chess masters no longer laugh when they watch good computers play and most would not gladly accept a computer challenge. Even if they played with both hands, they would likely lose each time they played. In fact, as far back as 1997, Deep Blue, which had previously lost to world champion Garry Kasparov, won the rematch (although the match was close – 3½ to 2½ in a six-game match, with one point awarded for a win and half a point for a draw). Some years later, grandmaster Vladimir Kramnik played a six-game match against Deep Fritz. And even though Kramnik was allowed to study Deep Fritz's program, he wound up losing two of six matches and drawing the other four (*Chessbase News*, 2006).

Now, chess programs with various names like Junior, Jonny, Thinker, Stockfish, Komodo, Shredder, and Zappa have little interest in playing against human chess grand masters: Human competition has become too laughably easy. Instead, they play each other in intense world tournaments (for example, ICGA Tournaments, 2018). The most recent winner of one of the major machine-chess tournaments in the world was Stockfish; Komodo came in second (Top Chess Engine Championship, 2018).[3]

Appraisal of Symbolic Models

Symbolic models are based on the assumption that meaning and, therefore, thinking can be represented by symbols such as words and that intellectual functioning can be described in terms of a sequence of actions – a *serial-processing* model. These are the assumptions that underlie many computer simulations of human thinking, such as are evident in computers programmed to play chess.

As we saw, one of the problems with these models is that the human mind is extraordinarily slow compared with a computer. The computer responds to input within *nanoseconds*; the human brain neuron typically requires as much as 300 *milliseconds* to begin to respond. As a result, to account for the amount of information it processes, functioning of the human brain is probably better explained by a model of *parallel* rather than *serial* processing. As we see in the next section, *connectionist* models provide that alternative model.

In spite of the fact that symbolic models do not represent all human intellectual functioning very accurately, they can nevertheless be highly useful in modeling and clarifying specific mental activities, such as those involved in solving problems, and perhaps even learning languages or developing strategies in games such as chess.

Connectionist (Neural Network) Models

Chess masters and computers don't play chess the same way. Human chess players do not – in fact, cannot – rely on brute force. Their computational capabilities don't allow them to foresee the consequences of very many moves and countermoves at one time. But what they can do that the machine does not do is recognize patterns on the chessboard based on their previous experiences with similar though probably not identical patterns. And they can select the best move on that basis, synthesizing the effects of previous experience without necessarily following explicit rules. It is as though the human chess player learns from experience, developing implicit, nonverbalized rules. Moreover, the logic that characterizes the chess player's behavior is not a formal logic that always leads to one correct solution. Instead, it is termed **fuzzy logic** – logic that is relativistic, considers a variety of factors, and has a not entirely predictable probability of being correct.

---

[3] Victories over human chess grand masters by Deep Blue and his progeny may not be entirely trivial, said Old Lady Gribbin – not just another chess match won and lost. She explained that it might herald the next major blow to humanity's collective ego. She said that there have already been at least three such blows in relatively recent human history. The first was Copernicus's discovery that humans aren't the center of it all. The second was Darwin's suggestion that the human animal evolved from other animal forms. The third, closely associated with Freudian theory, was the realization that humans aren't in complete rational control of everything. And now computers can beat human chess champions so easily they don't even bother playing with them. Will the next major blow be the reluctant realization that whatever qualities make *Homo sapiens* human can be duplicated – perhaps even improved – in a machine?

If all this is true, it suggests that the symbolic model is inadequate or incomplete. Recall that this model is based squarely on the assumption that all information can be represented in symbols (like language), that learning is explicit, and that information processing (thinking) involves the application of identifiable rules.

Implicit Learning

But not all learning is explicit, representable in symbols, conscious, and subject to definite rules. If Martha throws darts at a dartboard long enough, she might eventually reach a point where she will hit the double- or triple-20 spaces almost at will. But she will remain essentially unaware of precisely what it is that she has learned. Her learning will be **implicit learning**, learning that is not easily represented in symbols. In this case, the learning may be implicit in a complex web of connections between her eye and hand, involving millions of relays among neurons and muscles.

Habitual, well-practiced motor skills are just one example of implicit or unconscious learning. It appears that people also learn all sorts of cognitive things unconsciously. For example, there have been a number of studies of gender-based expectations using what are termed *artificial lexicons* (invented words that do not exist in the participant's language). These studies reflect the observation that even in languages such as English that do not assign gender to common nouns (unlike languages such as French or Spanish), as a result of cultural patterns, stereotypes, and word usage, speakers nevertheless develop certain gender expectations associated with specific words. For example, words such as *nurse*, *caregiver*, and *ballerina* are still likely to elicit female connotations; words such as *lumberjack*, *pipefitter*, and *mechanic* are more likely to trigger a male connotation.

Öttl and Behne (2016, 2017) report several studies where participants are presented with various meaningless words embedded in meaningful, gender-suggestive context, and are later asked what they think the gender association of these artificial words is. In one study, gender cues were provided by pairing nonsense words with novel imaginary figures whose features were stereotypical masculine or feminine (e.g. bright lipstick on one of a pair of identical figures; heavy eyebrows on the corresponding male figure). In this study, 12 *pseudoword* stems such as *bon*, *jel*, and *rin*, were paired with one of two different *pseudosuffixes*: *tef* and *tok*, with *tef* always used with the female figure and *tok* with the male. In studies such as these, participants typically respond correctly far more often than would be expected by chance when they are later asked what gender is associated with a given nonsense word, although they seldom perform very well on complex tasks of this sort. Strikingly, however, they are usually unable to verbalize the rules by which they arrive at their judgments. That they have learned something is clear from their behavior, but what they have learned is implicit rather than explicit.

Much the same thing happens when children learn language. Within an astoundingly short period, they learn to say all sorts of things in ways that are largely correct grammatically. But they cannot make explicit their knowledge of the rules that allow them to generate correct language or to recognize good or bad grammar. Even among adults who are exposed to a second language that they do not know and are not currently learning, there is evidence of implicit learning (Kerz, Weichmann, & Riedel, 2017).

Explicit Learning

Cognitive scientists have typically assumed that the mind uses rules and symbols to think, and that much of what we learn is deliberate, **explicit learning** – that is, learning that we are aware of and that can be put into words. The principal appeal of the computer as a model of cognitive processes rests with the metaphor of information zipping through the brain in the form of electric impulses, much as it does in the serial digital computer. In this metaphor, the end result of cognitive processing is knowledge in the form of concepts and thoughts that we are aware of – that, in other words, is *explicit learning.*

But what we know of the physiology of the brain no longer supports this type of metaphor, no matter how useful and instructive and even inspirational it might once have been. We now know that cognition occurs in the brain not as a series of processes but more as patterns of activation (much as Hebb had suspected). And we also know that these patterns of activation require that many things be happening simultaneously and very rapidly.

Early cognitive scientists had also assumed that the logic governing human cognitive activities would be a precise and predictable, machine-like sort of logic. And the outcome could, at least theoretically, be duplicated by any machine given access to the appropriate symbols and programmed to apply the underlying logic. In other words, a machine can be built to do anything that can be represented by an algorithm. However, the key word is algorithm. Recall that an algorithm is a clear, logical, systematic step-by-step procedure for solving a problem. Although a machine can perhaps be built to solve any problem for which an algorithm can be found, many problems do not easily lend themselves to algorithms. As we saw, some problems are more likely to require heuristics – more general, alternative-eliminating problem-solving strategies that do not promise a correct solution. The logic of heuristics is a fuzzier logic than the logic of algorithms. Activities such as playing chess, learning grammar, recognizing a dog, or mistaking a flying shoveler for a mallard illustrate a more typically human, prone-to-mistakes, fuzzy logic kind of thinking. If computer scientists are to investigate and model this kind of thinking, they clearly need something other than the algorithm-driven, symbol-manipulating calculating machine that is the serial digital computer.

Neural Networks as Connectionist Models

What they need, and have, is a parallel processing computer of the kind that can easily trash the world's best chess player. This parallel processing computer with its solid-state drives and its multiple cores gives rise to the connectionist model of cognitive architecture, whose development was pioneered by McClelland and Rumelhart (1986). It is a model that attempts to duplicate the structure and function of the networks of biological neurons that compose our brains – our actual human neural networks. Current usage of the phrase **neural network** typically refers to artificial rather than biological neural networks.

Neural networks, which are often simply referred to as *connectionist models*, are complex arrangements of computer units that activate each other much as might groupings of neurons in the brain. They typically consist of a set of processing units whose structure (architecture) is designed to mimic that of the brain's neurons. Thus, these separate units can be considered to represent words, letters, sounds, elements of visual perception, variables related to financial markets, global weather data, and so on. They are connected to each other in complex and changing ways, as are actual neurons in the brain. The pattern of connections determines what the system knows and how it will respond. Learning within such a system involves changing the strength of connections among units, in a manner highly reminiscent of Hebb's description of the formation of cell assemblies.

Uses of Neural Network Models

Research and development in the area of neural network technologies has mushroomed in the last 30 years. Neural network software is now used for research in a wide variety of fields in science and in brain-related research. It is also widely used in efforts to understand, predict, or modify environmental change, financial crises, medical conditions, weather patterns, academic performance, even terrorist locations and voting patterns.

The common, parallel processing computer serves as a model of how the brain might work – a model labeled *connectionism* (or *connectionist*). Recall that the term *connectionism* was first used in Chapter 3 in relation to theories such as that of Edward Thorndike. Thorndike was concerned with connections between stimuli and responses. He made inferences about these connections by looking at actual behavior. The new connectionists are concerned with connections among neural units. Much like Hebb, they make inferences about these connections. But unlike Hebb, their inferences are based less on supposition and speculation than on observation of the functioning of computers programmed as artificial neural networks.

What the connectionist model supposes is that the brain's collection of neurons is like the processing units in a computer. In effect, these processing units form a neural network. No central organizer or processor governs their activities. Instead, thousands (or millions) of these units are simultaneously active. They activate each other, establishing new connections, getting rid of old ones, and modifying the strength of connections. In a sense, they learn through experience, ultimately achieving understanding, making decisions, and initiating actions.

It is important to keep in mind that in cognitive research, neural networks are not physical arrangements of actual networks of neurons. Rather, what cognitive research deals with are artificial neural networks represented by the functioning of a computer. In effect, this approach to understanding human thinking and learning uses the physical hardware and software of the computer to model the functioning of actual neural networks in humans. They are useful for mimicking how humans learn. And, as Ninness, Ninness, Rumph, and Lawson (2018) explain, they may also be useful for explaining and predicting human responses.

Whether it be biological or artificial (computer-based), learning may occur in a neural network in three ways: New connections might develop, old connections might be lost, or the probability that one unit will activate another might change. Connectionists have worked extensively on this last possibility.

Biological neural networks as they exist in the brain are not simple to explain and understand; nor are the artificial neural networks that have evolved from what we understand of how the brain functions. One way of simplifying them is by reference to one of the first well-known attempts to develop a functioning neural network: NETtalk.

An Historical Illustration: NETtalk

It is extremely complex to program into a serial-processing computer all the rules it would need to read a letter or a poem, as a bright six-year-old might. How a word is pronounced depends on what words come before or after, what sorts of punctuation marks accompany the sentence in which it is found, when it is being said, by whom, intended meanings and emphases of the reader, and on and on. So many exceptions and qualifications have to be built into such rules that even linguists cannot agree on all of them. Actually, it may well be that the six-year-old does not learn to read by first learning all the appropriate rules and exceptions and then applying them as required (a symbol production model) but, rather, that the "rules" are unconsciously made up in the process of learning how to match spoken words to printed symbols (a connectionist model). This is essentially the reasoning that led Sejnowski and Rosenberg (1987) to develop a connectionist program that might learn to read. The result, NETtalk, is at once a machine and a *neural network model*. Its units serve as an analogy for actual neurons in the brain; in the model, they are also referred to as *neurons*.

As a machine, NETtalk consists of a "window" that can scan seven letters at a time. Each of the seven slots in this window is connected to 29 neurons (input units), corresponding to the 26 letters of the alphabet plus punctuation and space marks. Hence, there are 203 input units. At the output end of the machine are another 26 neurons (output units), each of which is linked with one of the 26 phonemes (simple sounds) that compose the English language. When one of the output neurons selects a phoneme, it is played through a loudspeaker, thus giving NETtalk its "voice" (see Figure 11.2).

The guts – or, better said, the brains – of NETtalk consist of 80 *hidden units* that intervene between the 203 input units and the 26 output units. Each of the 203 input neurons is connected to every one of the 80 hidden units, as is each of the 26 output neurons. Thus, there are 18,320 connections in this neural network. And each of these 18,320 connections is weighted, meaning that some of the connections are strong (the important ones), and some are weak (those that are irrelevant). The highest of weightings (that is, the strongest of connections) might mean that activation of one unit would always lead to activation of the next; conversely, the lowest of weightings would mean that the activation of a unit would never lead to activation of the second.

The essence of the task for NETtalk is stated simply: Learn to read text. Unfortunately, in English, there is no direct, one-to-one link between a letter and a sound or even between combinations of letters and a sound. The *a* in can is quite different from the *a* in cane. Although there is a simple rule to cover this situation, how about the *a* in ah? Or in far? Or the *a*s in

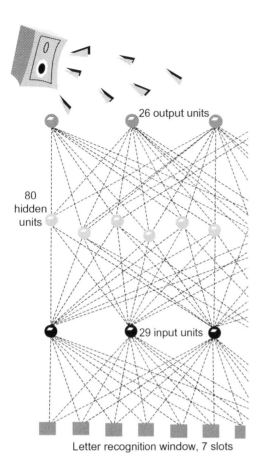

Figure 11.2 A schematic representation of NETtalk, a neural network model. The machine is a computer programmed to learn how to translate written English text into accurately spoken words by adjusting the weights among its interconnected units. Only a few of the units and 18,320 possible connections are shown.

façade? Or in aaaargh? Or how do you explain why the "ough" sounds so different in cough, bough, through, rough, and thorough? So, the solution for the NETtalk task (learn to read) is not so simple. It requires that the weightings among the hidden units be arranged in such a way that patterns activated by letters lead the machine to select correct phonemes. Sejnowski and Rosenberg (1987) did not know, of course, what these weightings would be, so they proposed to let the machine learn them itself by using what is called the **back-propagation rule**. Essentially, a model that uses a back-propagation rule uses information about the correctness or appropriateness of its responses to change itself so the response might be more correct or more appropriate. For example, in learning to read, children already know something about combinations of sounds that are correct (and meaningful). They know that in the sentence "The stink is all through the house" the *ough* sounds like "threw" and not like "dough." The computer does not know this.

The solution, Sejnowski and Rosenberg reasoned, might lie in letting the computer know what spoken text should sound like. So, they presented NETtalk with 1,000 words of text read by a first-grader. And they gave it the *back-propagation rule*, in effect telling the computer to compare its output with the first-grader's reading and work back through its hidden units, readjusting weights to reduce the difference between what it says and what the kid said.

And the computer did so. Because the initial weights had been set at random, its first pass through the text produced pure garbage. But over and over again, the text was fed through

NETtalk's input neurons, and over and over again, the computer spluttered and babbled strings of phonemes, initially garbled and meaningless but eventually clearer and more systematic. It was teaching itself to read.

After a day of practice, NETtalk could read not only most of the 1,000-word text it had been studying so hard but other texts it had never seen. It had learned rules and exceptions, it had learned to generalize, and it had made some of the same sorts of errors that children make when they first learn to read – for example, pronouncing *have* as if it rhymed with *cave* and *rave*. And in much the same way as the human brain, by the end, NETtalk used only a small portion of its potential connections.[4]

Summarizing and Simplifying Neural Networks

NETtalk provides a good illustration of the basic components of a simple artificial neural network. Artificial neural networks such as this are modeled on the architecture and the functioning of the biological neural networks in the brain. Accordingly, they typically consist of input units, corresponding to the sensory systems that transmit signals to the brain. They have units corresponding to the neurons that are found in the brain. These are sometimes termed *hidden units* in artificial systems although, even here, they are often referred to as neurons. And they have units that allow the system to respond. These are called *output units*; they correspond to the systems that allow organisms to act. Human outputs can take a variety of forms, including speech, gestures, facial expressions, bodily movements, cries, and so on. Outputs in artificial neural networks are often simple choices, predictions, or actions limited by the mechanics of the system. However, given appropriate hardware and software, these systems are sometimes complex enough to drive cars, move robots to smile, laugh, and perhaps even generate novel speech. Spontaneous humor remains a challenge.

The hallmark of a neural network application is that the nature of its functioning and its output are basically unknown. They do not function as do systems that have been programmed so that their outputs are completely predictable from their software.

NETtalk was one of the first widely known applications of a neural network. There have since been hundreds of different networks developed, researched, and applied in a huge variety of fields. A more current illustration of a neural network model is one labeled *emergent virtual analytics* (EVA) (Ninness et al., 2018). This is a simpler structure, consisting of only six neurons in the input layer, two hidden neurons, and only two output neurons. In its beta version, it is freely available, and runs on Windows 7–10 operating systems. It is designed for academic and demonstration purposes, and can be downloaded from www.chris-ninness.com. (See Ninness et al. 2018 for more details.)

Neural network systems are the basis for *artificial intelligence*.

---

[4] I'm sure some of your students would be interested in more information here, said Old Lady Gribbin, once more straying from her notes. Some, she explained, might want to know that other researchers have developed programs similar to NETtalk but using feed-forward rather than back-propagation rules. That is, the neural net is so structured that the computer has access to rules designed to eliminate or minimize certain errors. Others have developed similar programs to enable computers to teach themselves how to count. The result can sometimes be quite impressive (for example, see Westermann & Monaghan, 2017).

ARTIFICIAL INTELLIGENCE

Artificial intelligence (AI) has to do with developing computers that can do some of the things that people do that presumably require intelligence – things like perceiving and identifying objects, recognizing and responding to speech, making decisions, and reasoning.

But, says Vincent (2017), we don't have IQ tests for computers, although we could easily program one so that it would breeze through any of our conventional intelligence tests. But a computer armed with this kind of software would not be *artificially* intelligent: It would simply regurgitate responses programmed into it. "Our most advanced computer systems are dumber than a rat," says Yann LeCun (Facebook head of AI, quoted in Vincent, 2017). Although AI systems do a few things better and faster than human brains, they are still highly limited.

There is too much hype about AI and killer robots, says Sejnowski (2018), too many doomsday scenarios. "Imagine how a medical robot, originally programmed to rid the world of cancer, could conclude that the best way to obliterate cancer is to exterminate humans who are genetically prone to the disease" wrote Nick Bilton in the *New York Times* (quoted in MIT Technology Review, 2018). Or, as Stephen Hawking told the BBC, "The development of full artificial intelligence could spell the end of the human race . . .. It would take off on its own, and re-design itself at an ever increasing rate. Humans, who are limited by slow biological evolution, couldn't compete, and would be superseded" (Cellan-Jones, 2014).

Historical Approaches to Artificial Intelligence

We have not quite yet been superseded. But computer applications in fields like psychology, neuroscience, finance, and automation, like the technology of computers themselves, is extremely dynamic, changing at lightning rates. **Moore's law**, a prediction initially made in 1965 by Gordon Moore, cofounder of Intel, holds that the number of transistors that can be placed on a chip will double approximately every two years, essentially doubling computing power. Remarkably, that prediction has proven largely accurate – a fact that accounts for the mind-boggling storage capacity and speed of hand-sized contemporary computing devices. So rapidly does the field of computer technology and application change that almost everything written as recently as even a decade ago is so far out of date that it is now simply history.

Much of the older research in computer applications to psychology, firmly based on a computer metaphor, tried to understand the ways in which brains are like computers and tried to devise computer systems that could accomplish the same things as humans. The field quickly came to be known as artificial intelligence. Those who now work in the field are a varied collection of psychologists, neuroanatomists, physiologists, linguists, computer specialists, entrepreneurs, and others. They are united in their efforts to develop programs, procedures, devices, or mechanisms to simulate, duplicate, and improve upon some of the intelligent functions of human mental activity.

Artificial intelligence is sometimes distinguished from **computer simulation**. Artificial intelligence is concerned with devising systems – primarily computer software – that can accomplish or exceed the same things as humans can (learning language or solving problems, for example). The emphasis in the AI enterprise is on the accomplishments of the system in terms of developing intelligent behavior where intelligent behavior involves reasoning, learning, communicating, perceiving, diagnosing, predicting, and acting in complex environments. In contrast, computer simulation attempts to mimic the functioning of the human (including errors and biases). Hence, in computer simulation, the emphasis is on the processes rather than on the outcome.

In a sense, AI is a branch of computer science that tries to make computers smarter. A smart computer needs to be *rational*. Such a computer is one that is expected to be able to act autonomously, perceive the environment, adapt to change, develop and pursue goals, and strive for the "best" outcome. Developing such a computer is the goal of many in the field of AI.

Many people think computers are stupid, says Raphael (1976); they think that computers are nothing more than "big fast arithmetic machines" and "obedient intellectual slaves" that can do only what they have been programmed to do. These are myths, claims Raphael. And the first myth – namely, that computers are nothing more than computational machines – is easily dispelled. The functioning of many computers involves countless operations that are not computational, including storing in memory, searching memory, making sequences of decisions, activating and turning off equipment, sensing and responding to external conditions, recognizing speech and visual patterns, and perhaps even learning to read.

The second myth, that of the computer as slave, is more complex. It is true that computers do what they are programmed to do, and in that sense, they are slaves to their programs (or, perhaps more precisely, to their programmers). But this does not mean that all computers need be programmed in such a way that their activities will always be completely predictable. As we now know, with the development of sophisticated neural network systems, it is possible to program computers so they can learn new things and perhaps surprise us in unexpected ways.

Why Make Computers Smarter

There are at least two good reasons why people might want to make a smarter computer. One is that such a computer might do some marvelous things for people, freeing them to move on to

Machine Learning and Artificial Intelligence

other even more marvelous things. That, in effect, is the goal of that part of the AI enterprise that is aimed at developing artificially intelligent systems that accomplish clever things for humans. One example of this effort can be found in autonomous vehicles that may soon take over piloting all our transportation devices. Another example is found in the growing use of **intelligent tutor systems** that are responsive to learner strengths and weaknesses and adjust their offerings accordingly.

Perhaps more important for psychology, the other reason for trying to make a smarter computer is that doing so might answer many questions about human cognitive processes. A truly intelligent computer is one that is capable of what scientists now refer to as *deep learning* or *deep thinking* (Chen, 2018). Such a computer is truly intelligent to the extent that it can solve problems without being specifically programmed to do so. And in so doing, it might reveal important things about human cognitive processes.

Many of those involved in the computer simulation enterprise are mainly concerned with the second of these benefits. Their quest is to discover what the study of computers can do for the study of humans. They use computers in two distinct ways: first, to mimic the functioning of the mind; and second, to generate metaphors of human functioning. The hope is that the machines and programs that result will reveal information not previously known. Furthermore, attempts to simulate human processes in machines may serve as a fundamentally important test of what psychologists think they know about these processes, and might have important practical applications in teaching human learners.

Can Machines Think? The Turing Test

What sorts of human activities can computers mimic? For example, can they actually *think*?[5] Human thinkers have long struggled with this old but fundamentally important question. For example, Sternberg and Ben-Zeev (2001) suggest that neither the computer simulation of human thought processes nor the development of problem-solving computers provide examples of machines (or programs) that can actually think. Computers cannot think, they argue, although they can sometimes be programmed to respond *as if* they are thinking.

Another argument goes like this: If it is true that people can think and if it is true that a machine can be developed to do everything that a person can do when the person is thinking, then it follows that the machine can think.

---

[5] At this point in the recording, there is a long period when all you can hear is the muted crackling of the fire and, once, the hooting of a great horned owl. I remember that Mrs. Gribbin's voice had trailed off as though she were lost in thought and then she asked that I pause the recorder for a bit. Then, she repeated the question again: "Can machines think?" as though if she asked it of herself, the answer might be clearer. She said that the great French philosopher Blaise Pascal had tried to answer precisely this same question. She said that some two centuries ago, Pascal – whose IQ was estimated by someone clearly less intelligent to be above 200 – had invented a primitive, computer-like calculating machine that he called an *arithmetic machine*. And in one of his *Pensées*, he had written, "The arithmetic machine does things that are closer to actual thinking than anything that animals do." But, explained the old lady, Pascal then concluded this thought by saying, "But, unlike animals, the machine does nothing to indicate that it has willfulness" (Pascal, 1820, vol. 2, p. 184). When I began to ask her to explain what she meant, the old lady said that I should put more wood on the fire and turn the recorder on, and she started to read once more.

Now consider this situation, described by Turing (1950) and since dubbed the **Turing test**: A computer (A) and a person (B) are placed in a room. An interrogator (C) in another room must discover which of the two is human and which is a machine. At the end of the game, C must say "A is a computer, and B is a person" or "A is a person, and B is a computer." To discover which is which, C is allowed to ask them questions. A and B print out their responses. The object of the game for A is to impede the interrogator. In contrast, B attempts to help the interrogator. Obviously, if B attempts to do so by telling the truth ("I'm a person. Really! Believe me!"), A can do exactly the same thing ("Don't believe him; I'm the person!").

Turing says it will soon be possible to construct a machine that will converse with a human interrogator in such a way that the interrogator will not have more than a 70 percent chance of identifying it as a machine after five minutes of conversation. That, essentially, is the Turing test of machine intelligence.

Reductio ad Absurdum

Consider a second Turing test that does not even involve a machine (described by Searle, 1980). Instead, it involves a human student, Bob. Bob finds himself alone in a room, sitting at a table in front of which is a slot. Through this slot, some Chinese psychologists pass a slip of paper on which is written a string of Chinese characters – which are all Greek to Bob. But he has at his disposal a heavy book, and in this book, he finds a string of Chinese characters identical to those on the paper, together with instructions to copy out a second string of characters. He does this and passes the paper back through the wall.

The Chinese psychologists examine the characters he has written, nod in approbation, and pass him a second piece of paper with a different string of characters on it. Again, he responds as his book instructs. After several repetitions, the Chinese psychologists conclude that the machine – or the room – into which they have been passing these pieces of paper understands Chinese. What they have been doing is asking questions about a story, and Bob has been answering correctly. But he knows, of course, that he understands no Chinese. Thus, the Turing test is meaningless; it has been reduced to the absurd (**reductio ad absurdum**).

It's a strange thing, notes Searle (1980), that so many psychologists behave as though they believed in the validity of the Turing test. They assume that if a machine simulates intelligent behavior, then the machine must itself be intelligent; that if a machine produces correct responses for complex problems, it must understand these problems; and, presumably, that if a slot in a wall returns insightful responses in Chinese script, then something or someone beyond the wall knows not only Chinese but also stories. It is a mistake, notes Searle, that people do not make in other areas where computers are used to simulate complex systems: The meteorologist who tracks the movements and implications of weather systems by simulating them on a computer knows that the computer cannot generate hurricanes or hailstorms. Similarly, a computer that accurately imitates human-like processes or that selects responses identical to those a human might select does not become human because of this.

Back to the Turing Test

So, has it been possible to design a machine that can fool a human even 30 percent of the time? A decade ago, the answer was clearly no; no computer had yet passed a well-designed Turing test. In 2008, Collins wrote that no machine was likely to pass a test that actually requires the machine to *think* like a human. Nor will the machine ever be able to, he claimed, "unless we find some means of embedding it in lived social life" (Collins, 2008, p. 309).

In one challenge reported by Floridi, Taddeo, and Turilli (2009), four judges sat in front of a computer and interacted for five minutes each with two unknown entities by means of instant messages. Judges were to determine whether the entity was a person or a machine. Machine responses to questions such as, "If we shake hands, whose hand am I holding?" "I have a jewellery box in my hand; how many CDs can I store in it?" or "The four capitals of the UK are three, Manchester and Liverpool. What's wrong with this sentence?" were dead giveaways. In the authors' words, "the computer went bananas" (p. 147). The best-performing machines in this annual competition fooled only three out of 12 people.

But newer machines may have higher IQs. Warwick and Shah (2016) report on a series of Turing test studies carried out at the Royal Society London on June 6–7, 2014. Five different machines were involved in these studies, along with 30 different judges. The highest-performing of these machines, named Eugene Goostman, became the first to pass the Turing test using unrestricted conversation. This meant that both the machine and another human (both hidden) carried on individual five-minute conversations with each of the 30 judges without guidance or preplanning. At the end of each conversational session, the judge had to decide whether the machine and the human were human or machine. Eugene Goostman, the best of the five machines, deceived the judges 33 percent of the time.

Now, more than 60 years after the original Turing paper, a large number of studies describe situations where a participant is unable to distinguish between the performance of a machine and that of another human (for example, Hernandez-Orallo, 2017; Turnwald & Wollherr, 2018). So, does this mean that machines like Eugene Goostman can actually think? Or is it simply that their software is so well designed that they *seem* to be thinking?

According to the Turing test, the answer to the original question, can machines think, appears to be yes. Or is it? Is there more than one way to solve a problem? To remember a poem? To recognize a word? Will studies of AI and computer simulations discover a computer way of thinking quite distinct from the human way? And will humans never know whether a machine can think – until, perhaps, it's too late?

Is it even clear what thinking is? Does the fact that human behavior appears purposive, whereas the behavior of a computing machine does not, prove that humans can think and that the machine cannot? Would psychology be more convinced that a machine can think if it could change its "mind"? If it could deliberately lie? Or if it simply became petulant and refused to answer our silly questions?

"But," the skeptic protests, "the machine wouldn't be thinking. It would just stupidly be churning out responses programmed into it."

There are situations in which a machine may consistently fool the "man in the street" and pass the Turing test. But, as Floridi and associates put it, "Why (artificial) intelligent behavior should be tested by the untrained, naïve and often uninformed 'man in the street' remains a mystery to us . . .. Unless that is the sort of dude you wish to fool" (2009, p. 148).

Does the Computer Need to Think?

In the final analysis, that the computer may not be able to think – that it is not a mind and the mind is not a computer – may not be very important. As Gunderson put it, "In the end the steam drill outlasted John Henry as a digger of railway tunnels, but that didn't prove the machine had muscles; it proved that muscles were not needed for digging railway tunnels" (1964, p. 71). And your washing machine does a much better job of washing your clothes than you would by hand. But that does not mean that the washing machine has hands!

Similarly, computers don't need to "think" or to feel joy or anger to do what they do so well. And that they might not be able to think and feel does not imply that computer models are either useless or flatly wrong.

Recent Developments in Artificial Intelligence

Artificial intelligence tries to imitate human intelligence. The AI systems that drive your autonomous vehicle are designed to react to things like traffic flows, signals, road conditions, and the sudden appearance of a cat strolling in a crosswalk in much the same way as might a skillful and prudent human driver. Unlike NETtalk and EVA, these systems are built with multiple layers of hidden units. They illustrate what Sejnowski (2018) describes as **deep learning**, the capability of learning as a result of exposure to unstructured data without being specifically programmed and supervised to do so. Deep learning systems take the form of neural networks that are modeled on the brain, where the architecture includes multiple layers of hidden units (neurons), much like those found in the brain. It is a type of machine learning inspired by the biological neural networks of human brains.

The most successful neural networks, explains Sejnowski, are what are called *convolutional neural networks* which are made up not only of layers of units, but also of units of varying complexity. These mimic the neural architecture of the human visual system which involves both simple and more complex cells. Using complex, deep learning networks, it is possible to develop networks that actually generate output as a result of activity within the network itself rather than simply as a response to input.[6]

Deep learning and other neural network applications also give rise to the possibility of unparalleled, *Big Brother* kinds of control and surveillance. There is currently an arms race in AI, claims Pedro Domingos (Scheuermann & Zand, 2018). Although some of today's leading companies in AI are behemoths like Google, with units like Deep Mind and Google Brain, the

---

[6] And that, said Old Lady Gribbin, opens up the possibility of building machines whose unexpected behaviors might be a staggering shock for their creators. "I don't want to really scare you," said James Barrat, author of *Our Final Invention: Artificial Intelligence and the End of the Human Era*, in a *Washington Post* interview, "but it was alarming how many people I talked to who are highly placed people in AI who have retreats that are sort of 'bug out' houses, to which they could flee if it all hits the fan" (Miller, 2013).

main players in this arms race are China and Russia (Domingos, 2018). Both of these countries are determined to dominate AI, and both are bent on developing the algorithms that will allow them to seek out, mine, and understand data at a rate and in ways never before imagined.

The AI systems that we currently have are stunningly stupid, says Domingos, pointing out that there is little real intelligence in applications like Siri and Alexa. But, we are prone to obeying leaders, and the next generation of Siris and Alexas just might be our leaders.

Perhaps something like that is already happening in some Chinese cities where, as Mozur (2018) describes them, the leadership's dreams are **dystopian**. Dystopian has to do with imaginary places or states where everything is bad, undesirable, even frightening. Dystopia is often associated with totalitarian regimes.

Mozur describes how police wear facial recognition goggles in various Chinese cities. Although these are still primitive and error-prone, they have apparently led to the identification and arrest of a number of criminals. Perhaps even more frightening, especially for law-breakers, is the fact that, in addition to all the systems that track how people use the internet, where they travel, their communication, even their car movements, there are now several hundred million cameras watching the daily (and nightly) movements and activities of hundreds of millions of Chinese citizens. Government agencies are rapidly developing technologies like facial recognition, driven by AI systems, to pick out people from crowds, to monitor their activities, and, ultimately, to control them. The aim is to develop a massive, national, surveillance system. New AI technology provides a wonderful tool for authoritarian nations. Even when these still-primitive systems don't work very well, says Mozur, they still work because if people think they are being watched, they tend to follow the rules. Just in case.

There are many other possibilities implicit in the neural networks that make AI possible. For example, Richardson (2017) describes how private entrepreneur, Bryan Johnson, dreams of controlling evolution by building what are termed *neuroprostheses*, devices that will enhance human brain functioning enormously. He envisions a world where non-invasive interfaces like tiny sensors injected in the brain or genetically engineered, wireless neurons, would be used to serve as a bridge between brain structures and physical neural networks. These might allow people to learn faster, remember with stunning clarity, solve problems in nanoseconds, and perhaps even develop extrasensory capabilities like telepathy.

Richardson also describes how Zuckerberg, of Facebook fame, is working on machine-to-brain interfaces where it might be possible for the machine to read signals from neurons. If, for example, a machine could read human thoughts as they take the form of words, it might be a very simple step for the machine to recast those words into code that could then be sent to a computer for storage or for immediate printing. And the human thinker may then be throwing out dozens of elegant printed pages every minute. Or dozens of pages of garbage. But there is little reason not to believe that this smart machine could not weed out the garbage.

Still, notes Richardson (2017), in spite of all these efforts and all this human brain-power dedicated to the development of AI, aspects of human functioning such as imagination and creativity are so complex that all the neuroscientists in the world may never completely understand, let alone duplicate them.

The next big break, says Knight (2018), may come from looking at how infants learn and building a machine that starts out by trying to learn as do the young of the human species.

Appraisal of Connectionist (Neural Network) Models

The point of all this is that neural networks (connectionist models) are designed to respond very much like humans. Their fuzzy logic takes the imprecision of the real world into account. In fact, the role model for the logic that drives neural networks is the human mind. The possibility of developing truly intelligent machine systems is a tantalizing goal.

A truly intelligent neural network system is one that can make inferences without being given specific rules for so doing. As Allman (1989) notes, if you see the word *bat* along with the words *ball*, *diamond*, and *base*, you know something very different about *bat* than if you see the same word along with *witch*, *Halloween*, and *cave*. As Bruner explains, our inferences are based on experiences that allow us to categorize and relate things and "go beyond the information given" (Bruner, 1957a). Given the right series of experiences, a neural network might well do exactly the same thing. In a sense, its structure and functioning allow it to reach something that looks like insight. It might eventually discover on its own that bat in one context is different from bat in another.

So, connectionist neural network models – and the parallel processing computers that make them possible – may in the end be relatively good models of some human cognitive processes. Among other things, these models suggest that people do not always think all that rationally. They do not systematically consider all the pros and cons, bringing the cold rules of logic to bear and calculating what the correct response is. Connectionist models allow for a fuzzier kind of logic and they emphasize that many aspects of a situation (or of many situations) might be involved in a response or a conclusion. In addition, neural network models have the advantage of more accurately reflecting the actual physiological structure of the human nervous system with its maze of neurons and interconnections. Still, the most complex of neural network machines is ridiculously simple compared with the fully functioning human brain. As Josh Tenenbaum, head of the MIT Quest for Intelligence project, put it, "None of them have the flexible, common sense, general intelligence of a two year old, or even a one year old" (quoted in Knight, 2018).

Neural network models also present a functional analogy for the notion that experience alters the brain's wiring, as Hebb had theorized so long ago. For example, a neural network that adjusts its own connections is highly compatible with Hebb's notion that neurons that repeatedly activate each other become increasingly more likely to do so. In fact, the **Hebb rule** is basic to many neural network programs (Kuriscak, Marsalek, Stroffek, & Toth, 2015). The *Hebb rule* is Hebb's supposition that the repeated simultaneous firing of adjacent neurons increases the strength of the link (synapse) between them.

Connectionist, or neural network, approaches now dominate the study of human cognitive processes. Connectionist models are rapidly leading to new insights in understanding the course of human development, individual differences, and atypical development. They've been applied to the study of autism (Church et al., 2015), generalizing and discriminating (Hilbig & Moshagen, 2014), and reading and writing (Holman & Spivey, 2016). Also, as we saw, connectionist model applications stretch well beyond the cognitive sciences and psychology. Neural networks are rapidly spreading into a huge variety of endeavors, including prediction of the weather and the performance of financial markets, medical diagnosis, engineering, object recognition, petroleum and mineral exploration, detection of explosives, speech recognition, the development of autonomous transportation systems and devices, even the attempted enhancement of human cognitive functioning.

For example, Watson, IBM's deep-thinking computer named after IBM's founder, Thomas Watson, was first developed to compete on the television quiz show *Jeopardy*. As far back as 2011, it ended up trouncing the two long-time Jeopardy champions, winning a $1 million dollar prize in the process. At that time, it was a massive, noisy piece of equipment, occupying roughly the space of a large bedroom and requiring complex systems of fans to stay cool enough to function. Now, it is approximately the size of an average desktop computer and many times faster (Best, 2012). And it has quickly progressed from being a game-playing machine to being developed and commercialized to answer questions and provide direction in a wide range of highly specialized fields, including the treatment of cancer, banking services, education, weather forecasting, tax preparation, and a variety of other fields described as "information intensive" (Best, 2012; IBM, 2018; Leopold, 2017).

Some Cautions and Criticisms

There is a sort of biological realism to connectionist models. Because of their close resemblance to the structure and functioning of the human nervous system, it is easy to mistake connectionist models for the real thing – that is, for real, functioning nervous systems. But they are not real nervous systems; they are just machines and metaphors. As metaphors, they describe and they suggest, but it would be a mistake to confuse a description or suggestion with an explanation.

Connectionist models are not perfect analogies for human thought processes. There are three standard criticisms of computer simulation models of human thought processes, The first is that computers do not simulate human emotions well. As DeLancey puts it, the failure to imbue machines with "passions" makes "a strict version of the computational theory of mind untenable" (2002, p. 187).

A second standard criticism is that computer simulations do not reveal the insight of which human problem solvers are capable. In the Gestalt view, such simulations are woefully inadequate models of human cognitive processes.

The third common criticism is that computer programs tell us very little – if anything at all – about how the human nervous system works. For example, as Li (2002) points out, the successful functioning of connectionist models depends on certain properties of their units that are not properties of the human nervous system. Thus, by changing their weightings, these units can inhibit activity in some units while facilitating it in others; neurons in the human brain do not do this.

There are a number of other reasons why connectionist models are not always very informative or useful and why they should not be taken too literally. A connectionist model with 360 units that successfully duplicates some human cognitive functioning does not reveal that the cognitive function requires 360 neural units in the human brain. The same cognitive activity could conceivably be predicted with a model consisting of only 250 units or perhaps 400.

Another ongoing issue in connectionist modeling of human cognitive activity is the debate and uncertainty concerning whether mental representations are *distributed* in neural connections in various parts of the brain or whether they are *localized* in specific neurons or neural connections. Parallel processing (connectionist) models typically assume that representation is distributed. However, there is evidence of highly selective responding to familiar stimuli – an observation that has given rise to the notion of **Jennifer Aniston** and **grandmother cells**, neurons that are thought to be activated by a specific, complex stimulus (Coltheart, 2017; Quiroga, 2017). They were so named because they were first introduced in reference to a mother and then a grandmother around 1969. The theory is that the "grandmother cell" becomes active when a stimulus such as a grandmother (or Jennifer Aniston) is presented, whether she is seen from the front, the back, upside down, inside the house, out by the barn, upright, or standing on her head. And perhaps her name, her voice, her smell, or the sight of her cane will all elicit activity in the same grandmother cell.

Brain activity recordings do indicate that there are specific visual neurons in human (and monkey) brains that respond selectively to stimuli such as human faces. However, there is no evidence that these cells would not fire for a wide variety of faces – and perhaps for names as well as faces (Quiroga & Kreiman, 2010a). However, it is important to note that there is considerable redundancy among grandmother cells, so if one is lost, the person might not lose the grandmother *percept* (Quiroga & Kreiman, 2010b).

Some researchers suggest that grandmother cells are biologically plausible and that they are incompatible with parallel distributed processing models (for example, Bowers, 2010). Others argue that the biological research supports the notion of distributed representation and that grandmother cells are simpler *sparser* representations involving fewer cells (Quiroga & Kreiman, 2010a).

EDUCATIONAL AND SOCIAL IMPLICATIONS

Computer technologies and successful simulation of human learning and thinking have enormous educational and social implications, not all of which are clearly positive. For example, as we saw in Chapter 10, a review of more than half a century of research on the effects of *screen violence* leads to the clear conclusion that it has lasting negative effects (Anderson et al., 2017). The screens referred to in this research include television, films, video games, and internet-based offerings. The authors of this review point out that exposure to violent media is associated with increased aggressiveness, hostility, desensitization to violence, and a reduction in altruism and prosocial behavior.

Other research has found a link between screen time, especially that involving the use of smart phones, tablets, and computers, and differences between today's learners and yesterday's learners. Today's learners, explains Prensky (2016), are learners who are expert at navigating virtual electronic technology. They are used to receiving information extraordinarily rapidly in all sorts of mind-blowing, attention-compelling forms, but always in short, captivating bursts rather than in longer, more thought-provoking expositions. As a result, they are easily bored, quickly distracted, and soon impatient: Their attention spans are shorter. Also, they have become more visual than text-based learners, accustomed to immediate feedback and instant access to information. In addition, many of them are overwhelmed by the wealth of information that bombards them and by the sometimes-enormous assortment of in- and out-of-school activities that eat up their time.

There is also the possibility, suggest Cavanaugh, Giapponi, and Golden (2016), that although digital technology might improve some cognitive skills (such as the ability to multi-task), it might also detract from others such as those associated with what they call *deep-thinking skills*. Some of these skills might be lost because of negative changes in the developing brain as a result of overexposure to technology. For example, some research suggests that the amount of time spent on smart phones and related devices is negatively related to the ability to remember, think, pay attention, delay gratification, and regulate emotion (Wilmer, Sherman, & Chein, 2017). Bowles (2018) reports that, in his words, "A dark consensus about screens and kids begins to emerge in Silicon Valley." He describes how many of Silicon Valley's most knowledgeable technologists have begun to severely limit their children's screen time. For example, Bill Gates reportedly banned cell phones until his children were teenagers; his wife supposedly said they should have waited longer.

All of this makes the tasks of teachers, and of parents, at least different, if not more difficult. However, we should not overlook the contribution of technology and of connectionist models in areas such as the development and application of **intelligent tutoring systems (ITS)** – systems that are designed to obtain information about each learner so that, like good human tutors, they can make qualitative judgments about the learner and modify their teaching strategies accordingly. Intelligent tutoring systems are used to monitor students' progress and to act like a teacher by guiding students, asking questions, uncovering misconceptions and errors, and so on.

Computer simulations that mimic phenomena other than human thought processes also have increasingly important instructional applications. For example, programs that mimic the in-flight responses of specific aircraft are used to train pilots, and others that model the functioning of the circulatory system are used in medical schools. A simulation of a physics or chemistry laboratory can be used to teach students the likely outcomes of combining, chilling, pressurizing, and heating or even eating various substances without the risk of losing an actual laboratory, a school, or a student in the process.

Interactive, computer-based simulations of various environments, labeled **virtual reality (VR)**, also have instructional applications. In education, virtual reality describes a type of computer–learner interaction whereby the learner experiences certain events and environments and makes choices within that environment. Many virtual reality systems involve more than one sensory system. For example, the computer's display systems may include helmets and goggles so the visual presentation occupies the subject's entire visual field and changes as the learner moves. Similarly, learners might wear headphones that provide authentic "surround" sound as well as "gloves" that give them the sensation of being able to manipulate objects in the virtual world.

Another important use of computers and technology in schools is to teach students programming skills. In the same way that flint knapping and spear-throwing skills might have been essential to survival at the dawn of civilization, so too might programming skills become indispensable survival tools in a world populated by artificially intelligent machines. (See Aoun (2018) for a description of rapidly growing applications of AI.)

A FIELD IN PROGRESS

Much of this book is historical: It deals with theories, the meat and gristle of whose principles and assumptions have been well chewed. That, of course, is not necessarily because they are less current or tougher than younger fields. It is simply because they are of a greater age and have therefore been around to be gnawed at much longer.

In contrast, the subjects of this chapter are of a younger age; they have yet to be digested by generations of scholars and thinkers. Thus, this chapter cannot really be concluded nor can the models and findings presented in it be evaluated. History, as is her habit, will judge.

Main Point Chapter Summary

1. The basic computer-as-cognitive-processor metaphor sees parallels between computer hardware (physical components) and the human nervous system and especially the brain (wetware), as well as between human cognitive functioning and computer programs (software).
2. Brains are much slower than computers and far inferior at doing computations, but they have traditionally had certain rapidly disappearing advantages in recognition tasks and in reasoning where insight and fuzzy logic are required. They are also enormously more complex in organization and size. Parallel processing computers appear to work more like brains, doing many things simultaneously.
3. The symbolic model is based on the serial-processing digital computer; it assumes that knowledge can be represented symbolically and manipulated with rules. Newell, Shaw, and Simon's Logic Theorist (LT), which is capable of finding proofs for theorems in symbolic logic, and their GPS, a more general problem-solver, are symbolic models.
4. Not all human learning is explicit and describable in symbols and rules. Much is implicit or unconscious, including motor skill learning and the learning of abstract relationships through experience. Implicit learning is better modeled on *parallel processing* machines than on serial-processing machines.
5. Software using multi-core, parallel processing computers has produced machines capable of easily defeating world champions in games like chess and Go. These computers lend themselves to *connectionist* (*neural network*) models and applications, and underlie the development of AI. Biological neural networks are complex arrangements of neurons in the brain; computer-based neural networks are complex arrangements of computer units that activate one another and that have the ability to change activation strengths and patterns as a result of feedback.

6. The branch of computer science that tries to develop models, procedures, or devices intended to accomplish some of the intelligent functions of human mental activity is labeled *artificial intelligence. Computer simulation* attempts to mimic actual cognitive functioning.

7. Connectionist models lead to machines whose functioning resembles that of humans in some respects. They allow for thinking that is not completely logical, that sometimes leads to unforeseen results, and that can be shown to mimic learning (for example, NETtalk). They also reflect some aspects of human neurological structure well. But they are descriptions rather than explanations, do not always generate plausible results, and do not always function as a human (for example, they do not simulate emotion well, and cannot easily be programmed to reflect insight, spontaneous humor, and intuition).

8. Two myths characterize human reactions to computers: that they are merely computational machines and that they are nothing more than slaves to their programmers. However, parallel processing computers can "learn," and they sometimes surprise their programmers. The consensus is that despite the exaggeration and hype surrounding AI, in many ways, computers are still as dumb as fence posts and not very likely to take over the world. Yet.

9. The Turing test is like an intelligence test for computers. It says that if A can do X, Y, and Z, and B can do X, Y, and Z exactly, then B must possess whatever attributes A has that allow it to do X, Y, and Z. The test reduces easily to the absurd and does not answer the question of whether machines can think. They probably do not need to: They can do other things – including pass the Turing test.

10. Recent developments in AI research and applications include advances in the development of autonomous vehicles, *deep learning* research that mimics the architecture of parts of the human brain, frightening applications in the field of human surveillance and control, the possibility of enhancing human sensory and cognitive functioning, and the development of machines such as IBM's Watson, capable of answering questions and assisting human decision making in a huge variety of "information-intensive" fields.

11. Connectionist models are not perfect analogies for human cognitive processes, provide poor models of human insight, and are not always very informative. In addition, there is evidence that screen time and screen violence may have lasting negative effects on children. But there is enormous potential in the application of digital technologies to a vast array of different fields.

12. Artificial intelligence applications in education include the use of intelligent tutoring systems, simulations of systems and situations to teach things such as how to drive a car or conduct experiments in chemistry, virtual reality programs to teach aspects of history or medicine, and a variety of programs designed to teach programming and computer literacy skills, problem solving, memory improvement, verbal interaction skills, and so on.

Part V

Summary

12 Summary, Synthesis, and Integration

CHAPTER OUTLINE

This Chapter	426
Objectives	426
Two Major Approaches to Learning Theory	427
Summaries of Key Theories and Approaches	428
Early Approaches: Structuralism and Functionalism	430
Mostly Behavioristic Positions	431
Transitions to Modern Cognitivism	434
Modern Cognitivism	436
Factors Affecting Learning	438
Social Learning	440
Machine Learning and Artificial Intelligence: The Future	441
Synthesis and Appraisal	442
Strengths and Weaknesses	442
An Integration	446
Jerome Bruner: Models of the Learner	446
A Last Word	449
Main Point Chapter Summary	450

The problem of far greater importance remains to be solved. Rather than build a world in which we shall all live well, we must stop building one in which it will be impossible to live at all.

B. F. Skinner

A theorist is an artist, someone with a talent for weeding the essential from the inessential and constructing these marvelous orders.

George Johnson

We spent the morning drifting soundlessly down the Beaver River, far beyond the last of the empty trappers' cabins, Old Lady Gribbin sitting on her lifejacket in the bow, neither of us saying very much, just looking and pointing at the goldeneyes whistling along the banks and at the mergansers in winter colors low in the water under the willow branches. Bald eagles patrolled the shoreline from above, and the old lady said not to start the motor yet, why spoil such a place and such a day?

When the current had taken us beyond the mouth of the creek-with-no-name to the edge of the riffles that mark the beginning of the rapids, the old lady said we could stop, that my enemies wouldn't find me here, and I wondered how did she know, and she took the oar from my hand and pushed hard against the bottom and steered us against the long sandbar at the edge of the island, and I made a fire while Mrs. Gribbin cast into the pool and caught a walleye, which we cooked and ate, a gray jay appearing as they always do to see would we leave something for it to eat, which we did. And Schrödinger also appeared, although I could swear that he had not been in the boat, and he too ate of the walleye, sitting on his haunches, his one good eye fixed firmly on me as if he, too, knew.

Later, Old Lady Gribbin said it was time for the very last chapter, and once more, I turned on the device, and on this recording, you can hear the river and the sounds of ducks and songbirds. And, toward the very end, the whup-whup-whup of the helicopter. The old lady was wrong: They found me.

THIS CHAPTER

This chapter, *said the old lady*, undertakes a very complex task: that of summarizing and evaluating the learning-related theories that make up the chapters of the book. There are two great techniques for taking care of things that are complex, *she continued and I couldn't tell whether she was being serious*: oversimplifying and lying. *She said she used one of these techniques repeatedly in this ambitious chapter, but she didn't say which*. The chapter, *she explained*, presents a summary of the major learning theories discussed earlier, follows that summary with a rapid evaluation, and ends with a synthesis. In short, the chapter is a summary, an analysis, and an integration of the 11 chapters that have come before.[1]

OBJECTIVES

If I were speaking directly to your readers, *Mrs. Gribbin said*, I would say to them (if they cared to listen), "Much of science is a shared hallucination, a network of self-reinforcing beliefs" (Johnson, 1992, p. 53).

And I think they might shake their heads and say, "Does this mean I've wasted my time studying these theories of learning and behavior – these shared hallucinations?" I would answer no, *the old lady explained*, because there is nothing more useful than a theory, even if it is an

---

[1] Mrs. Gribbin said maybe I should tell you that much of this chapter could – and maybe should – have come at the beginning of the book. She explained that this final chapter is like the skeleton of the book, the emperor *sans clothes*; the first 11 chapters are the various imperial garments, and she laughed when she said this, as if she had invented a joke. She said that if you had glimpsed the emperor first, you might have seen better how the vestments would hang on his frame. But she said she thought there was a danger that the naked emperor would prove not too shocking or too outrageous but simply too bewildering for a naïve and sensitive student. She said to tell you that here, finally, is the essence of imperial power: the emperor stripped.

invention or a fantasy. A theory doesn't have to be true, although it does have to be other important things: useful, logical, consistent, clear, and so on.

So, tell your students to keep studying, *said Old Lady Gribbin, absently tossing a pebble into the river.* Tell them to read this last chapter and reflect on it well. And when they have finished, each student should discuss it with his or her grandmother because in it are hidden truths and insights that might impress even someone as wise as she. When grandmother and student have talked it over, students will finally understand:

- why we absolutely need theories;
- how theories actually work;
- the distilled essence of each of the major theories that compose this text;
- why theories of learning and behavior are really models of human learners;
- how this entire text might be synthesized.

There is also a small chance that they will have learned to simplify – without lying.

TWO MAJOR APPROACHES TO LEARNING THEORY

Theories are invented not just because they might be useful, *the old lady read from her notes.* Humans also seem to crave them – or at least seem to crave the order that theories bring. You see, there is much in human behavior that is chaos, but humans want it to be orderly. "There is an ancient human longing," says Johnson, "to impose rational order on a chaotic world. The detective does it, the magician does it. That's why people love Sherlock Holmes. Science came out of magic. Science is the modern expression of what the ancient magician did. The world is a mess, and people want it to be orderly" (1992, p. 114).

But science does not work quite the way it is pictured, Johnson informs us. It isn't simply a question of having a theory, generating hypotheses from it, testing them, and throwing out the theory if the hypotheses do not pan out. Many theorists love their theories so much they are seldom willing to abandon them. Sometimes, they stick with them long after everybody else has left.

A theory, Johnson explains, is a form of architecture, maybe a little like a cathedral. When the theory ages and threatens to become useless, theorists don't just build a brand-new one. What the smart theorists do instead is shore up their old ideas: put in new joists, new rafters, brace the old walls, redo the decaying foundation, patch the roof, paint a little here and there, polish the old gold, and so forth. Those less smart try to make do with what they have (and the rats move in)[2].

That, in a sense, is what has happened repeatedly in the history of learning theories – not the rats so much as the repairing and renovating. From the very beginning, there were at least two different ways of looking at human behavior and learning, two broad orientations that gave rise to different cathedrals. One orientation assumes that human behavior is, at least in some measure, influenced by activities such as thinking, feeling, intending, wanting, expecting, reasoning, remembering, and evaluating. These processes define what is thought of as "mind." They are cognitive (or intellectual) processes; hence, this orientation is that of the cognitive psychologists.

The other orientation does not flatly contradict the first but insists that little scientifically valid knowledge about human behavior can be gained by investigating the nebulous processes of the mind. Instead, advocates of this orientation concentrate on examining actual behavior and the observable conditions that lead to behavior: These are behaviorist psychologists.

SUMMARIES OF KEY THEORIES AND APPROACHES

Few positions are entirely and exclusively behavioristic or cognitive; to say that they are is often a shameful oversimplification (though not an outright lie)! Nevertheless, these labels are very useful for indicating the theorist's general orientation and the sorts of topics with which the theory is most likely to be concerned. By definition, behaviorist theories deal mainly with relationships among stimuli, responses, and the consequences of behavior. In contrast, cognitive psychologists are less interested in stimuli and responses than in more intellectual processes: problem solving, decision making, perception, information processing, concept formation, self-awareness, and memory, among others. Table 12.1 distinguishes among the major divisions in learning theory. Each of these positions is summarized in the following sections.[3]

---

[2] And Schrödinger might move in too, I said to Mrs. Gribbin, thinking it might make her chuckle. She scowled at me; she doesn't like to be interrupted.

[3] Old Lady Gribbin pointed at the recorder, which meant I should turn it off, that she was going to stop for a while and I wondered, did she need to go to the bathroom? She didn't. She said she thought some students might be interested in another of Blaise Pascal's *Pensées*, the one in which Pascal wrote that science has two closely related extremes: One is pure, natural ignorance, the state in which all humans are born; the other is a state reached by those lofty souls who have learned all that it is possible for humans to know and who, finally, arrive at the realization that they know nothing – that

Table 12.1 Major divisions in learning theory

	Variables of interest	Representative theorists
Early approaches		
Structuralism	The mind Feelings Sensations Immediate experience "Elements of thought"	Wundt Titchener
Functionalism	The mind Purpose of behavior Adjustment to the environment Stream of consciousness	James Dewey
Later approaches		
Behaviorism	Stimuli Responses Conditioning Reinforcement Punishment	Thorndike Pavlov Guthrie Watson Skinner Hull
A transition: the beginnings of modern cognitivism	Evolutionary psychology Sociobiology Stimuli Responses Reinforcement Mediation Purpose Goals Expectation Representation	Rescorla–Wagner Wilson Hebb Tolman Koffka Köhler Wertheimer
Cognitivism	Representation Self-awareness Information processing Perceiving Organizing Decision making Problem solving Attention Memory Culture Language	Bruner Piaget Vygotsky Bandura

Table 12.1 (cont.)

	Variables of interest	Representative theorists
	Deep learning Cognitive models of memory and motivation Computer metaphors Neural networks Connectionist models and artificial Intelligence	

Early Approaches: Structuralism and Functionalism

Interest in the human mind [*the recording missed the first words but these five make sense*] is probably as old as, well, the human mind. It's unlikely that it dates back only to the Greek or Roman philosophers who had the foresight to make written records of their thoughts. We have no reason to believe that our cave-dwelling ancestors did not occasionally wonder about things psychological – things such as what ideas or dreams or wishes or feelings are, where they come from, why we are moved to do this or that or the other thing. Perhaps they, like Aristotle and most of the other Greek and Roman philosophers who took quill in hand to hurl their thoughts forward in time, believed that the mind is to be found in the heart.

We no longer believe that; the brain is now our organ of choice.

Nor do we trace the beginnings of modern psychology to our earliest ancestors, nor even to the Greek and Roman philosophers.

Structuralism

We only go back as far as Wundt, who, when he established a psychological laboratory at Leipzig, Germany, in 1879, is considered to have established the very beginnings of "scientific" psychology. Not that Wundt was especially scientific by our standards. His investigative method of choice was *introspection* – a sort of navel-gazing enterprise where the sole subject is the investigator, and there is, of course, only one investigator. The goal of structuralism was to analyze the structure of consciousness, eventually arriving at an understanding of the elements of which it is composed. In their discussions of psychology, structuralists such as

they are once more in a state of ignorance. But it's a far wiser ignorance than the first state, an ignorance that sees and judges things more clearly. The unfortunate ones, says Pascal, are the ones who have only gone halfway between the extremes – those who have learned much of what science knows but who have failed to learn that they know nothing. These are the souls who most trouble the world and who see things most obscurely (Pascal, 1820, p. 121). I wanted to protest and explain that you aren't ignorant or even half ignorant, but the old lady started to read the manuscript once more, and I hurried to turn on the recorder. I had already missed the first few words she said.

Wundt in Germany and Titchener in the United States made extensive use of highly mentalistic concepts like sensation, feeling, and imagining.

Functionalism

James did not argue with the methods of structuralism; he, too, relied heavily on instrospection to discover how the mind works. But he thought the search to understand the *structure* of the mind was misguided, and that it would be far more fruitful to look at its functioning (hence, the label *functionalism*). His focus was on behavior's purposes, and many of the concepts he investigated were less *mentalistic* than those of the structuralists. He was heavily influenced by Darwin and consequently more concerned with objective events that appear to cause behavior (stimuli). Both structuralism and functionalism were soon abandoned in favor of more *behavioristic* positions.

Mostly Behavioristic Positions

Among the major predominantly behaviorist positions are those of Pavlov, Watson, Guthrie, Thorndike, Hull, and Skinner. Each is summarized briefly here.

Pavlov: Classical Conditioning

Largely as a result of a single physiological study of a dog being trained to salivate in response to a tone, Ivan P. Pavlov set the stage for much of the entire world's next 100 years of research and theorizing in human learning and behavior. The model of classical conditioning described by Pavlov, and illustrated by his famous dogs, is part of almost every current course in introductory psychology. More than this, it served as the basis for the development of the first clearly behaviorist positions in psychology. Why? Partly because it provided what seemed like a simple way of explaining both animal and human behavior; perhaps even more, because it pointed toward an approach based on objective, replicable, scientific methods in contrast with the more subjective and introspective approaches that had previously been widely current. Interestingly, many principles of classical conditioning (of generalization and extinction, for example) continue to be applied in clinical psychology, in education, in industry, and elsewhere.

Watson: American Behaviorism

Pavlov's classical conditioning was quickly embraced and championed by John B. Watson, one of the first North American psychologists to define the science of psychology in completely objective terms. He saw psychology as a science that deals with the observable rather than the merely hypothetical – a definition that gave rise to North American behaviorism. Watson assumed that individuals are born with a behavioral repertoire consisting of only a few reflexes

432 **Summary, Synthesis, and Integration**

and that these early responses become conditioned to other stimuli by being repeatedly paired with them.

Watson was also an important spokesman for environmentalism: the belief that the environment (the nurture side in the historical nature–nurture dispute) determines personality, intelligence, and all other human qualities. One of his better-known claims was that he could make whatever he wanted out of a dozen healthy infants if he were given a free hand in their upbringing.

Guthrie: One-Shot Learning

Like Watson, Edwin R. Guthrie was firmly behavioristic. His theory can be summarized in several major laws, the most important of which states that whenever a response follows a stimulus, there will result a tendency for the same response to occur again the next time the stimulus is presented (*one-shot learning*). Thus, Guthrie maintained that learning is complete with the first pairing of a stimulus with a response and that further practice will not strengthen the response, although it will help ensure that the person (or animal) learns it in many different situations.

Although learning occurs and is complete and relatively permanent after a single trial, said Guthrie, it is possible to remove undesirable habits simply by learning new habits that are incompatible with the old ones. Guthrie suggested three ways in which this can be done: the fatigue technique, the threshold approach, and the method of incompatible stimuli.

Note that for Watson and Guthrie, the consequences of the behavior are not important in bringing about learning. According to Guthrie, the effect of punishment or reward is simply to change the stimulus situation, thereby either increasing the likelihood of a response in various circumstances or bringing about its replacement with another response.

Thorndike: Trial and Error and the Law of Effect

But consequences can be extremely important, argued behaviorist Edward L. Thorndike, who is generally credited with introducing the notion of reinforcement in contemporary learning theory through his *law of effect*. This law states that learning is a consequence of the outcome of behavior. Specifically, responses that lead to a satisfying state of affairs will tend to be repeated. At first, Thorndike had also believed that unpleasant or annoying states would have an opposite effect, but he rejected this belief after 1930. Similarly, before 1930, he had believed that stimulus–response events that are practiced tend to be more strongly linked, whereas those that fall into disuse tend to be forgotten (the law of exercise). Thorndike later rejected this belief too. Thus, Thorndike is an example of a theorist whose ideas changed in important ways as a result of new findings and new insights.

For Thorndike, learning consists of the formation of bonds between stimuli and responses largely as a function of the consequences of the responses. He labeled the process of learning a *stamping-in* process; forgetting involves *stamping out*. The system includes a number of subsidiary laws, the most important of which is the *law of multiple responses*. This law holds that when faced with a problem situation, people tend to respond in various ways until one of the responses emitted is reinforced. In other words, learning occurs through a process of trial and error. Additional laws note that behavior is generalizable, that people respond to the most striking features of the environment, that cultural background affects behavior, and that learning through contiguity does occur.

Hull: A Hypothetico-Deductive System

Clark L. Hull carried to an extreme the scientific approach of behaviorists such as Watson, Guthrie, and Thorndike, developing a resolutely objective and highly complex *hypothetico-deductive* system. He dedicated himself to one of the most monumental tasks ever undertaken by a psychologist: formalizing all knowledge about human behavior to make it possible to predict responses on the basis of knowledge about stimuli. Although the system was never completed, Hull's work stands as an overwhelmingly ambitious attempt at formal theory building.

Hull's investigations and consequent formulas and equations deal with three aspects of human behavior: input variables (which include physical stimuli as well as factors such as drive condition, previously learned habits, and amount of reward available), intervening variables (which consist mainly of the assumed effects of input variables on the organism), and output variables (which are the characteristics of actual behavior in terms of response latency, frequency of responding, and time to extinction). The system may be partly summarized by the equation $_sE_R = {_sH_R} \times D \times V \times K$ (meaning reaction potential is equal to habit strength times drive times stimulus intensity times incentive motivation).

One of the central concepts in Hull's theory is that of *habit*, which is an S–R connection. A collection of such connections forms a *habit-family hierarchy*, which is a hypothetical preferential ordering of related alternative behaviors. Habits are related in that they have common goals, represented by Hull's concept of fractional antedating goal responses. An antedating goal reaction is any one of the many reward-related responses that an organism makes as it nears a goal. For example, as it turns the last corner in a maze, a rat may lick its chops.

Fractional antedating goal responses are important because they represent Hull's behavioristic definition of *expectancy* or *purpose*, and they foreshadow important cognitive concerns. In a sense, his use of the concept of intervening variables serves as a link between his system and more cognitive interests. However, note that Hull's intervening variables are tied directly to input and output variables.

Skinner: Operant Conditioning

B. F. Skinner stands out as one of the great system builders in twentieth-century psychology. He developed a model of operant conditioning whose most basic notion is that learning results from the reinforcement of responses emitted by an organism. Much of Skinner's work dealt with the effects of different ways of presenting reinforcement (schedules of reinforcement) on rate of learning, response rate, and extinction rate (extinction refers to the cessation of a response after reinforcement has been discontinued). Among his most important findings is that learning is facilitated in its initial stages by continuous reinforcement, but extinction is slower following intermittent reinforcement. Although Skinner experimented extensively with animals, many of his results are generally applicable to human behavior.

One technique developed by Skinner for teaching complex behaviors to animals is shaping, which involves reinforcing successive approximations to the desired behavior. It is widely employed by professional animal trainers.

Skinner discusses the applications of his work to human behavior in several books, including *Walden Two* (1948), *Science and Human* Behavior (1953), and *Beyond Freedom and Dignity* (1971). In addition, many principles of Skinner's theory have been extensively applied in education, medicine, advertising, psychotherapy, and other human activities. Behavior modification, which includes various systematic programs for changing and controlling behavior and is based primarily on Skinnerian principles, is widely used in education and psychotherapy.

Transitions to Modern Cognitivism

Watson's insistence that behaviorism must be limited to events that can be observed proved a difficult constraint even for those as staunchly behaviorist as Thorndike and Hull. For example, Hull found himself having to invent unobservable *fractional antedating goal responses* to explain observable connections. And Thorndike (1931), who had initially vigorously attacked the Gestalt psychologists for resorting to insight as an explanation for learning, found himself speaking of "ideational learning" to explain insight learning.

Evolutionary Psychology

Thorndike's and Skinner's theories were strongly influenced by Darwinian ideas. In a sense, they are theories of the survival-of-the-fittest responses, a notion reflected in *evolutionary psychology*. The primary identifying characteristic of evolutionary psychology is its attention to biology and genetics as sources of explanation for human learning and behavior. Phenomena such as single-trial, taste aversion learning or *autoshaping* and *instinctive drift*, in which animals revert to instinctual patterns of behavior despite reinforcement contingencies that urge different responses, provide strong support for biological explanations. It is as though inherited biological constraints make certain kinds of learning and behaving highly probable and other responses far more improbable.

Sociobiology, a forerunner of evolutionary psychology, looks at inherited predispositions as the underlying causes of all social behavior. It draws its evidence heavily from ethology, which is the study of the behavior of nonhuman animals in natural settings.

Evolutionary psychologists believe there is an inherited "human nature," which is apparent in the similarities that one finds among the world's many cultures. Among these are the human tendency to worry about social status; a number of basic male–female differences; the tendency of humans everywhere to feel guilt, to seek justice and retribution, and to feel pride, remorse, love, empathy.

But, counter critics of some of evolutionary psychology's claims, our long-ago ancestors left no record of their social behaviors or of their development of culture and of language. As a result, we cannot really trace the evolution of the traits and behaviors that evolutionary psychology now tries to explain. Because of the intuitive appeal of biological explanations for behaviors such as altruism and mating, to mention only two examples, a sort of unquestioned acceptance of these explanations has led to a form of *pop evolutionary psychology.*

But today's evolutionary psychologist does not believe that all explanations lie in a genetically determined human nature. Malleability, notes Wright (1994), is built into human nature. Malleability, evident in responsiveness to environmental and cultural realities, is what makes learning and adaptation possible. And underlying this malleability is the wonderfully complex human brain, whose chemical and electrical mysteries we are beginning to unravel. The brain appears to be highly plastic, and especially sensitive to environmental influences in early development.

Hebb: The Neurophysiology of Learning

Donald O. Hebb's attempt to explain higher mental processes is a much clearer departure from some of the constraints of behaviorism. His is a somewhat speculative, neurophysiological proposal designed to explain thinking and learning by looking at activity in neurons. Thinking, he suggests, involves activity among groups of neurons arranged in closed loops (called *cell assemblies*) or of activity in more complex arrangements of such loops (termed *phase sequences*). Absolutely central to Hebb's theory is the notion that transmission among neurons appears to be facilitated by repeated firing among them. This is a still-popular notion now known as the *Hebb rule*. This phenomenon of neural activity ostensibly accounts for learning. A cell assembly corresponds to some simple sensory input (for example, the color of an object or one part of one of its dimensions), whereas activity in a phase sequence corresponds to the whole object. Through learning, cell assemblies and phase sequences eventually achieve some correspondence to the environment; because different parts of an object are usually sensed in contiguity, cell assemblies related to different aspects of an object will often be simultaneously active and will therefore become related. Interestingly, many of Hebb's notions about neural activity have been supported by more recent research using sophisticated techniques of brain imagery (EEGs and MEGs, for example) and related measures of change in event-related potential (ERPs) and event-related fields (ERFs). The recent development of computer-based neural networks also reflects the Hebb rule and confirms some of Hebb's most important speculations.

Hebb has been largely responsible for the development of an arousal-based theory of motivation. This theory is premised on the assumption that optimal human functioning is made possible by a moderate level of arousal, and an organism therefore behaves in such a way as to maintain that level. Other theorists (for example, Bruner) have subsequently incorporated these same notions into their systems.

Tolman: Behavior Has a Purpose

Edward C. Tolman was among the first North American psychologists to begin with a behaviorist orientation and eventually develop a system far more cognitive than behavioristic – a theory of *purposive behaviorism.*

Summary, Synthesis, and Integration

Tolman's system reflects three basic beliefs. First, all behavior is purposive. By this, Tolman meant that behavior is directed, that it is guided toward goals not by stimuli (as in Hull's system) but, rather, by cognitions (conscious awareness). These cognitions take the form of expectancies that the organism develops with respect to reward.

Second, Tolman emphasized the *molar* rather than *molecular* aspects of behavior. In other words, he was not concerned with discrete S–R events as much as with the more global aspects of behaving.

Third, Tolman insisted that what is learned as a function of reinforcement is not a response–stimulus link or a response–reinforcement link but a cognition in the form of an awareness that reward is likely to follow certain behaviors. This awareness or expectancy guides behavior, thus making it reasonable for Tolman to describe his system as one of purposive behaviorism.

The Gestaltists: German Cognitivism

The first cognitive position in American psychology was associated with the *Gestalt school*, a system advanced by a group of three German psychologists: Wolfgang Köhler, Kurt Koffka, and Max Wertheimer. All eventually emigrated to the United States and did much of their research, lecturing, and writing there.

That Gestalt theory is a cognitive position is evident in its preoccupation with perception and in its rejection of trial-and-error explanations of human learning. The Gestalt explanation is that people learn through insight.

The Gestalt approach is one of synthesis: Even physical objects cannot be completely known or understood through an analysis of their parts. "The whole is greater than the sum of its parts" became the familiar Gestalt slogan.

The chief concern of Gestalt psychology was to discover the laws governing perception. The Gestaltists were responsible for the elaboration of "laws" such as closure, proximity, symmetry, continuity, and prägnanz.

That the Gestaltists used people for their research about half the time represents an important transition in the history of learning theories; behavioristic psychologists had conducted most of their research on animals. In addition, Gestalt theory's interest in the individual's private experience – the *behavioral* or *phenomenological* field – presents a dramatic departure from the main concerns of most behaviorist positions. This interest has led to continuing applications of Gestalt theory in counseling and therapy.

Modern Cognitivism

This text's chronology (from behaviorism to cognitivism) might make it seem as though more recent formulations are more enlightened, more accurate, and more useful and that they must therefore have completely replaced older theories by now. This is not entirely so. Many aspects of earlier positions have survived and continue to appear in current theories and applications, although not always in completely recognizable guises. And behaviorism is still a vigorous and growing orientation in psychology; it is well represented in current professional literature as well as in countless educational and therapeutic programs. But cognitive metaphors are now in the majority.

Bruner: Going Beyond the Information Given

Jerome S. Bruner has developed a loose-knit cognitive theory intended to explain various phenomena in perception, decision making, information processing, conceptualization, and development. His earlier writings deal primarily with concept learning; his more recent interests are largely in the area of development.

Bruner's theory is sometimes referred to as a *theory of categorizing*. To categorize is to treat objects as though they were in some ways equivalent; accordingly, a category can be thought of as a rule for classifying objects by their properties (attributes). Bruner devoted much of his early work to investigating the strategies people use in learning how to categorize stimulus events.

Bruner's approach to learning and problem solving is premised on the assumption that the value of what is learned can be measured by how well it permits the learner to go beyond the information given. He argues that concepts and perceptions are useful when organized into systems of related categories (coding systems) that have wide generality.

One of Bruner's major contributions has to do with his role in the so-called cognitive revolution – his championing of approaches that rejected the constraints of behaviorism. In addition, his theories have found wide application in *constructivist* (learner-centered) approaches to education.

Piaget: Development and Adaptation

Jean Piaget's theory is a system unto itself; it is not easily compared with other positions. Although Piaget's major focus is human development, much of what he says is relevant to learning and behavior because of the close relationship between learning and development.

Piaget describes development as the evolution of a child's ability to interact with the world in an increasingly appropriate, realistic, and logical fashion. Hence, part of his work is a description of children at different stages of development: the sensorimotor stage (birth to two years), the preoperational stage (2–7 years, comprising preconceptual and intuitive thinking), the period of concrete operations (7–11/12 years), and the stage of formal operations (11/12–14/15 years). Each stage is marked by characteristic abilities and errors in problem solving, results from activities and abilities of the preceding period, and is a preparation for the next stage.

Another aspect of Piaget's work discusses the properties of children that enable them to make progress in their development. Thus, he describes intelligence as a biologically oriented process involving a combination of using previously learned capabilities (*assimilation*) and modifying behavior as required (*accommodation*). An optimal balance between these processes (equilibrium) constitutes maximally adaptive behavior. Maturation, active experience, social experience, and a tendency to achieve a balance between accommodation and assimilation shape learning and development. Children construct a view of reality, says Piaget, rather than simply

438 | Summary, Synthesis, and Integration

discovering it or learning it passively. Thus, they build notions of time, space, causality, logic, geometry, and so on.

Piaget's impact on psychology and on education has been enormous.

Vygotsky: Culture and Language

Had the Soviet psychologist Lev Vygotsky lived beyond his short 34 years, his impact might have been even greater than Piaget's. There is little doubt that he would stand very tall among the giants of psychology. When he died, this "Mozart of psychology" had apparently mastered all the leading theories of his day and had already developed a far-reaching theory of human learning and development. This theory grants an especially important role to culture and especially to its most important invention: language. Cultural interaction, together with the language that culture grants us, insists Vygotsky, is what makes all higher mental processes possible.

Vygotsky was especially interested in the intellectual development of children. He worked in the field of pedology, the then-popular Soviet discipline of child development that used tests to determine the developmental level of children. One of Vygotsky's important notions was that children who are capable of X on their own might be capable of X plus, say, Y, with the help of some competent adult or older child. This Y, specifically that which the child is capable of achieving with prompting and other kinds of assistance, is the *zone of proximal development*. Good teaching and learning, explains Vygotsky, requires that the educator or parent present the child with tasks that fall within this zone; tasks that are neither so simple that they can be accomplished easily by the child alone nor so difficult that even with assistance, the child remains incapable of successful performance. *Scaffolding* is a general term for the kind of assistance that skilled educators and parents present children. It can include demonstrating, explaining, providing written or real-life models, systematically developing prerequisite skills, asking leading questions, suggesting, correcting errors, and so on – all within the zone of proximal development.

Factors Affecting Learning

Among the important factors that are inextricably implicated in human learning are memory and motivation. In fact, studying memory is another way of studying learning. And by definition, motivation deals with the causes and the reasons for behavior and for behavior change (and behavior change defines learning). Theories in each of these areas include behaviorist and cognitive orientations, although recent investigations of memory and motivation tend to be based primarily on cognitive models.

Memory

One common memory model is a three-stage storage model that says people process and remember information as though they had three separate memory storage areas or processes: One involves the momentary, unconscious effects of sensation (*sensory memory*); it precedes attention. Another, called *working memory* (or short-term memory), has to do with immediate, conscious awareness. It lasts seconds rather than minutes. The third deals with long-term memory (LTM). Working memory is an active, ongoing process that is easily disrupted and highly limited in capacity; LTM is more passive, relatively stable, and virtually unlimited in capacity.

Baddeley's model of *working memory* attempts to describe not so much how or where memories are stored but how they are processed (that is, how memory *works*). This model describes a *central executive system* that oversees the workings of two *slave* systems that maintain information so that it is available for processing (the *phonological loop* and the *visual-spatial sketch pad*) and an *episodic buffer* that integrates information into a coherent episode.

Current models of long-term memory tend to be associationistic: They assume that all knowledge is related. They often distinguish between explicit, potentially conscious memory (termed *declarative*) and the implicit, unconscious, nonverbalizable effects of learning (termed *nondeclarative* or *procedural*). Explicit or declarative memory includes *semantic memory* (stable, abstract knowledge) and *episodic memory* (personal, *autobiographical memory* tied to a specific time and place). Studies of amnesiacs and neural imaging studies of brain activity, often using *magnetoencephalography*, indicate that different parts of the brain might be involved in each of these types of memory. These newer brain imaging technologies are sensitive to electrical activity in the brain (*event-related potentials* [ERPs]) and to changes in magnetic fields associated with brain activity (*event-related fields* [ERFs]). They can even detect activity in single neurons, leading to the labeling of *Jennifer Aniston* and *grandmother* neurons.

The causes of forgetting are varied and not always obvious. They include brain injury, fading or decay over time, distortion, repression, interference, and lack of retrieval cues. Research indicates that what works best for facilitating recall in education are strategies such as *spaced repetition* (rather than *blocked repetition*), *interleaving*, *memorizing*, the frequent use of *testing*, and the use of *feedback*. Teachers are also very important, second only to what learners bring with them in terms of skills, ability, motivation, and prior learning.

Motivation

Motivation theory addresses the whys of behavior – a question with many answers. Some behaviors are reflexive: simple unlearned responses to specific situations. Others might result from instincts, which are more complex inherited tendencies common to all members of a species but not readily apparent in humans. Still others might result from urges (termed *drives*) associated with basic biological needs (such as the need for food or drink) or perhaps with psychological needs (such as the need for achievement, affection, or self-esteem). Some motives appear to be primarily hedonistic (designed to obtain pleasure and avoid pain), although some theorists suggest that the measure of well-being is not found in hedonistic pursuits but more in *eudemonic* approaches to life (related to self-fulfillment).

Social/cognitive theories of motivation present a more active view of human behavior that is quite distinct from that of a reactive organism pushed and prodded by hungers and drives over which it has little control. Maslow's theory recognizes the importance of both basic (deficiency)

440 | **Summary, Synthesis, and Integration**

needs and metaneeds (growth needs), with the highest human need being that of self-actualization. Arousal theory looks at the motivating consequences of too low and too high arousal and at the need to maintain a relatively high level of arousal, as is evident in behaviors during conditions of sensory deprivation. Cognitive dissonance theory describes how conflicts among beliefs, behaviors, and expectations give rise to behaviors designed to reduce or eliminate the conflicts. Self-determination theory looks at the human need to be autonomous and self-determining. There is some disputed and controversial evidence that external rewards can sometimes decrease intrinsic motivation (the *overjustification hypothesis*).

Attribution theory explores systematic tendencies for people to attribute the outcomes of their behaviors to causes they either can or cannot control. Carol Dweck's theory looks at how our implicit notions (*mindsets*) about intelligence contribute to our goals (*mastery* or *performance*) and to our efforts to reach those goals. *Growth mindsets* (belief that intelligence is malleable) have clear advantages for motivation and performance relative to *fixed mindsets* (belief that intelligence is fixed and unchanging).

Albert Bandura's account of the role of *self-efficacy* judgments shows how personal estimates of competence and effectiveness are associated with persistence, achievement, and positive self-concepts. Expectancy–value theory describes how our motives are determined by a sort of mental calculus that we use to determine the personal benefits and costs associated with our various options. What these newer cognitive approaches to motivation have in common is that they describe behavior as involving a conscious attempt to make sense out of self and environment. In essence, they describe a *self-regulated* learner – one who accepts personal responsibility for setting goals, selecting strategies for attaining these goals, and monitoring and controlling goal-directed behaviors. Keller's *ARCS* model (**A**ttention, **R**elevance, **C**onfidence, and **S**atisfaction) summarizes instructional strategies designed to encourage and maintain high levels of motivation among learners.

Social Learning

Social learning refers to the learning of socially appropriate behavior as well as to the processes by which humans learn through social interaction. The phrase *social learning* has become almost synonymous with learning through imitation or observational learning. Bandura's theory of observational learning describes three possible effects of observing models: (1) We learn new behaviors as a result of seeing others (models) engaging in these behaviors (the *modeling effect*); (2) deviant behaviors can be encouraged or discouraged largely as a function of what we observe to be the consequences of such behaviors (*inhibitory and disinhibitory effect*); and (3) seeing models engage in what seem to be highly rewarded behaviors can elicit similar but not necessarily identical behaviors in observers (the *eliciting effect*).

Bandura's theory of observational learning was initially based largely on a Skinnerian model of operant conditioning: Imitative behaviors are learned because they are reinforced either directly (for example, by the model or because of the imitated behavior's direct consequences) or vicariously (a type of secondhand reinforcement where the consequences of a behavior for the model seem to be reinforcing for the observer). Research indicating that screen violence has lasting negative consequences is often cited as evidence of the power of observational learning (of learning through imitation).

But, explains Bandura, not all human behaviors are under the direct control of their outcomes, as Skinner might have argued. Some behaviors are controlled more directly by stimuli, as in the case of classical conditioning. Others, perhaps far more important for understanding human behavior, are under symbolic control. What is truly important, says Bandura, are perhaps less the direct and immediate consequences of an action or of a stimulus than the peculiarly human ability to imagine the action's consequences, to discover cause-and-effect relationships, to anticipate. As a result of so doing, we enthusiastically engage today in behaviors that have no possibility of being reinforced for weeks, months, and even years.

These three behavior control systems – stimulus control, outcome control, and symbolic control – provide a clear and useful summary of the major learning theories discussed in this text. They illustrate the progression from early emphases on understanding the relationship between stimuli and behavior (evident in theories based on a model of classical conditioning), to an emphasis on the consequences of behavior (apparent in theories such as those of Thorndike and Skinner), and finally to a progressively more cognitive orientation. In the final analysis, says Bandura, humans are agents of their own actions. As agents, they clearly demonstrate intentionality, forethought, and self-reflectiveness. In a kind of reciprocal determinism, people affect their environments (sometimes by selecting and shaping them), and are affected by their environments. And especially important in determining motivation and behavior are the individual's personal estimates of effectiveness – of *self-efficacy*.

Machine Learning and Artificial Intelligence: The Future

With its systems and functions, the computer has become increasingly common as a metaphor for human cognitive activity. This metaphor compares human neurology, and especially the brain (wetware), to computer hardware (physical components) and computer software (programs) to human cognitive functioning. The two most common forms of computer metaphor are the *symbolic* (based on the serial functioning of earlier digital computers) and the *connectionist* (based on the functioning of today's multi-core, parallel processing computer). Symbolic models assume that all knowledge can be represented in symbols and manipulated using rules; connectionist models recognize that some learning is implicit (rather than explicit) and cannot easily be verbalized.

Connectionist models consist of interconnected units rather than central processors and are therefore also called *neural networks*. In neural networks, patterns and strengths of connections represent knowledge. Connectionist models are based on the architecture of the human brain and lead to machines whose functioning is in some ways similar to that of humans in that it is not completely logical or predictable. But these models are descriptions rather than explanations, do not always generate plausible results, and don't always function as a human would. However, they do lead to artificially intelligent machines that can now perform pattern recognition and facial recognition tasks far better and more rapidly than can humans, that can destroy world chess and Go champions so easily that they now have their own

Summary, Synthesis, and Integration

machine-vs-machine tournaments, that can predict financial, meteorological, transportation, and other patterns with uncanny and often surprising accuracy, that can drive our vehicles, fly our planes, and on and on. And this is probably just the beginning.

Some argue that humans are on the verge of making machines that can actually think – taking into account all the variables, the contingencies, the qualifications that a human might consider. These would be machines that do not think in a completely predictable, linear, old-fashioned-logic kind of way but in a fuzzy logic, neural network manner in which the programmer does not really know beforehand what the computer will decide because the problem is too complex to program symbolically.[4]

SYNTHESIS AND APPRAISAL

The preceding sections summarize most of the learning positions described in this text. Table 12.2 and Figure 12.1 synthesize that information. Table 12.2 lists key terms associated with each theoretical position. Figure 12.1 is more visual; it consists of diagrammatic or symbolic representations of the central aspects of each theory. Neither pretends to be a complete representation of the theories in question.

Strengths and Weaknesses

An appraisal section follows each of the major learning theories described in this book. This section does not repeat all those evaluations but simply brings together in one place some of the most important features of earlier evaluations. The following comments are not meant to be an exhaustive catalogue of all the good and bad features of each theory. Besides, criticism and evaluation are often subjective in the first place, often a matter of taste, or upbringing, or religion. So, these evaluations are presented only as suggestions.

Behaviorism

A common criticism of behaviorism is that through its mechanization of humanity, it has dehumanized the human animal. Critics point out that humans possess awareness, that feeling is very much a part of behaving, and that surely human interaction with the environment is more than simply a matter of stimuli and responses. These critics further contend that conditioning in

---

[4] Mrs. Gribbin tossed her bedraggled manuscript on the sand and motioned that I should put more wood on the fire. As I laid the driftwood on the embers, I asked her what role she thought computers might play in clarifying human thinking in, say, 10 years. For a moment, she looked as though she would ignore my question, but then she answered another one – one I hadn't asked. She said that these thinking machines aren't really threats, that they won't replace us. She said that's because they feel nothing. They don't give a hoot; they don't have emotion. But, she continued, despite their lack of feeling, the day is at hand when computers will act as though they really care, and many people will be fooled, and many will have the living begory scared out of them as a result. And then she started to read the manuscript again, and I turned the recorder back on.

Table 12.2 **Key words associated with theorists and their theories**

Mainly behaviorist positions

Watson	Guthrie	Thorndike	Hull	Skinner
Behaviorism	Contiguity	Law of effect	Habit strength	Operant
Classical conditioning	One-shot learning	Satisfiers	Hypothetico-deductive	Respondent
Reflexes	Habits	Annoyers	Reaction potential	Schedules
Environmentalism	Threshold	Stamping in	Drive	Extinction
Contiguity	Fatigue	Stamping out	Goal reactions	Rats
	Incompatible stimuli	Trial and error	Habit families	Shaping
	Movement-produced stimuli	Connectionism	Intervening variables	Superstition
			Fractional antedating goal responses	Behavior modification

Transition / **Mainly cognitive positions**

Hebb	Tolman	Gestaltists	Bruner	Piaget	Vygotsky	Bandura	Information-processing models
Cell assembly	Purposive	Perception	Categorizing	Equilibration	Culture	Imitation	Wetware
Phase sequence	Molar	Wholes	Concept	Assimilation	Language	Social learning	Hardware
Hebb rule	Intention	Closure	formation	Accommodation	Social speech	Behavior	Software
Mediating	Expectancy	Prägnanz	Attributes	Sensorimotor	Inner speech	control systems	Neural networks
processes	Sign–	Insight	Coding	Concrete	Egocentric speech	Personal agency	Parallel processing
Neurophysiology	significate	Behavioral	systems	operations	Zone of proximal	Reciprocal	Symbolic models
Arousal	Place	field	Strategies	Formal	development	determinism	Connectionist
	learning		Narratives	operations	Scaffolding	Self-efficacy	models
				Logic			Artificial
				Conservation			intelligence
							Deep Learning

Summary, Synthesis, and Integration

		Behaviorism			
Watson	**Thorndike**	**Guthrie**	**Hull**		**Skinner**
US → UR	1) $S_1 → R_1$ (pleasant)	$S_1 → R_1$	$_sE_R = {_sH_R} × D × V × K$		R + S_1 → reinforcement
CS → ?	2) $S_1 → R_1$	$S_1 → R_1$			
CS + US → UR					
CS + US → UR					↓
CS → CR	1) $S_2 → R_2$ (unpleasant)	$S_1 → R_1$			$S_1 → R_X$
	2) $S_2 →$				

	Transition		Cognitivism		
Hebb	**Tolman**	**Gestaltists**	**Bruner**	**Piaget**	**Information processing**

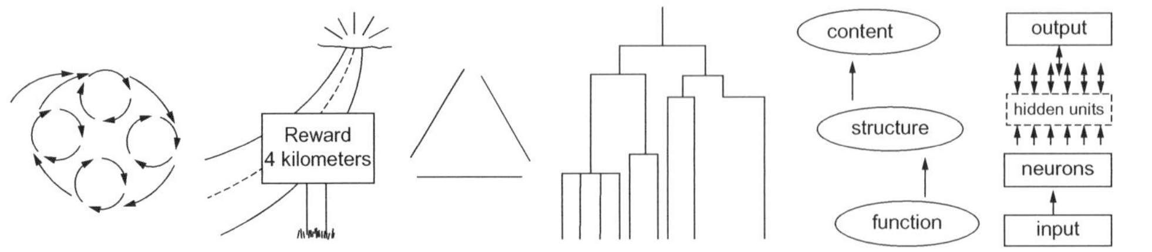

Figure 12.1 Diagrammatic and symbolic representations of the key concepts of each of the preceding 11 chapters.

all its varieties leaves much human behavior unexplained. Some also react negatively to the use of animals in studies whose results are then generalized to human behavior. Others are appalled and frightened at the thought of applying a science of human behavior to shape and control thought and action.

In their own defense, behaviorists maintain that only by dealing with those aspects of human functioning that are clearly measurable and definable can valid and reliable conclusions be reached. Behaviorists point in scorn at the often chaotic, jargon-laden, and confused nature of more "mentalistic" psychologies. They ask what images, feelings, schemata, and operations are and of what value these might be in developing a science of behavior.

Clearly, behaviorism stresses objectivity and loses some relevance in doing so. Nevertheless, the approach has generated a great deal of applicable research and theory and continues to have a tremendous influence on the development of learning theory. Much of the current emphasis on experimentation and scientific rigor stems from the work of people such as Guthrie, Watson, and Hull. Emphasis on the practical applicability of theory owes much to the work of Thorndike. And Skinner's contribution to a practical science of behavior can hardly be overestimated.

A Transition: Evolutionary Psychology and Early Cognitivism

Early behaviorists were certain that their theories, or others based like theirs on objective scientific data, would be widely applicable. If you can condition a rat to press a lever, a dolphin to throw a ball, or a horse to genuflect, then surely you can teach any animal and – why not? – any person to do whatever.

Not so. Even among animals, a number of apparently simple behaviors can be conditioned only with great difficulty or not at all. Certain biological constraints appear to govern much of what animals learn. Thus, pigs reinforced for depositing wooden "nickels" into a piggy bank often appear to prefer rooting around with them, even if doing so means going hungry. This and related observations, argue a group of psychologists, suggest very strongly that psychology should pay more attention to biology. Sociobiology, an attempt to provide a genetic explanation for social behavior, was one result of this emphasis. Sociobiology has now largely given way to what is termed *evolutionary psychology*.

An important contribution of evolutionary psychology has been to focus attention on the biological roots of human behavior. Related to this, increasing numbers of psychologists are looking at the role of the human brain in learning and behavior. One of the pioneers of this emphasis is Hebb.

The proposal for a theory advanced by Hebb is admittedly based on neurophysiological speculation as well as fact. Some critics argue that such an approach is not likely to lead to any new discoveries about learning or to anything more than an explanation of what is already known or suspected about behavior. Of course, the opposite argument can also be advanced. It can be countered that not all of Hebb's proposal is based on speculation, that there are sources of information about human neurology that are distinct from psychological experimentation, and that a great deal of new information about human neural activity is rapidly leading to a better understanding of learning and behavior. Neural network models of the new connectionism are highly compatible with Hebb's speculation and owe him an important debt. In addition, some of Hebb's notions concerning arousal have contributed significantly to current theories of motivation.

Hebb, a neobehaviorist, retained a commitment to the need to preserve the objective, scientific nature of psychological investigation. But he also responded to the need to include inferences about profoundly important mental processes such as thinking and imagining, thus serving as a transition from behaviorism to cognitivism.

Tolman, another neobehaviorist, also gave behaviorism a new twist by acknowledging the role of purpose. Many of the first generation of cognitivists were followers of Tolman.

The first psychological theories clearly identified with modern cognitivism were those of the Gestalt psychologists: Köhler, Wertheimer, and Koffka. Unlike behaviorists such as Thorndike, who believed that learning and problem solving occur through trial and error, the Gestaltists thought people learn through insight. Accordingly, their main concerns were with cognitive topics such as insight, perception, and problem solving. These theories are sometimes criticized for being vague. At the same time, however, they have contributed significantly to counseling practice as well as to the subsequent development of cognitive theories.

Cognitivism

Critics of cognitive approaches to human learning sometimes base their objections on the cognitivists' often less precise and more subjective approach to information gathering and to theorizing. The extensive use of jargon by many contemporary cognitivists and the seeming lack of agreement among different positions have also caused confusion and criticism.

Bruner and Piaget have been criticized because their terminology is sometimes confusing and because the metaphors they use are often obscure and impractical. Piaget has also been much

Summary, Synthesis, and Integration

criticized for his imprecise experimental methods, his nonrepresentative samples, the extremely small numbers of participants in most of his studies, the lack of statistical analysis in his early work, and for his tendency to overgeneralize and overtheorize from his data. And Vygotsky has been criticized for his lack of precision and for the global and all-encompassing nature of his theorizing.

Cognitive theorists sometimes counter these criticisms by pointing out that they are dealing with topics that are more relevant to human behavior than are questions relating only to stimuli, responses, and response consequences, and investigating these topics sometimes requires making inferences from relatively limited data.

Bruner, Piaget, and Vygotsky continue to have tremendous influence on child rearing and especially on practices in schools. Piaget is largely responsible for converting a generation of teachers, parents, and child care workers into fascinated observers of children and their development. And in recent decades, Vygotsky's theorizing has enjoyed increasing popularity among educators.

AN INTEGRATION

Historically, the search in learning theory has been for one best way of explaining human behavior – a search clearly based on the assumption that there is one best explanation. But what if there isn't? What if psychology assumes that because there are many different kinds of human learning, there is a need for many different explanations?

Several theorists have made just that assumption, and the resulting theories are typically an integration of various concepts that have traditionally been associated with separate positions. Among these thinkers is Jerome Bruner. Aspects of his theorizing can be viewed as a highly useful synthesis of many of the theories discussed earlier in this book.

Jerome Bruner: Models of the Learner

Learning theories, claims Bruner (1985), are really models of the learner. If we look at the various theories of learning that have been proposed, we get glimpses of the models of the human learner that underlie them.

Tabula Rasa

One of the oldest models of the learner is that of the *tabula rasa* ("blank slate"). This view is premised on the notion that the human is born with no prior knowledge, few inclinations, and no thoughts, although perhaps a few reflexes. All are equal at birth, says the model: Experience subsequently writes its messages on the slate, gradually molding the infant into the child, the adolescent, and eventually the adult, accounting for all the eventual differences among people.

The tabula rasa model is sometimes illustrated with the empty-vessel metaphor. The infant's mind, says this metaphor, is like a vessel that is completely empty at birth and that has the same capacity as every other infant's vessel. In time, the waters of experience are poured slowly into the vessel, and in the end, some vessels end up fuller than others. Some leak pretty badly.

The tabula rasa model is clearly reflected in the theories of the behaviorists, who undertook to discover and explain the rules by which experience writes its messages or pours its waters – namely, the rules of classical and operant conditioning. When Watson insisted he could make what he wanted of a dozen healthy infants, it was because he firmly believed all infants to be equal at birth and equally susceptible to the influences of experience.[5]

Hypothesis Generator

Some theorists objected to the mechanistic view of the learner presented by the tabula rasa model. Human learners are not so passive, these theorists argued; learners aren't simply pushed this way and that by the stimuli, the rewards, and the punishments that experience holds in store for them. Rather, they are characterized by intentionality. They choose experiences and, perhaps more important, interpret them through their own notions about the world (their own personal hypotheses).

Hull's antedating goal responses provide an early glimpse, albeit a carefully behavioristic one, of the learner as a **hypothesis generator** (as characterized by the ability to make predictions – to *hypothesize* – and to base intentions, expectations, and behavior on these predictions). Tolman's purposive behaviorism provides an even clearer view of behavior driven by intention rather than simply by external events.

Nativism

The complexity of what the infant and the child have to learn and the ease and rapidity with which they learn it suggest yet another model – one that views the human learner not as a blank slate but as possessing a mind characterized by previously built-in constraints and capabilities. **Nativism** holds that the mind is already shaped by important tendencies before any learning occurs. Bruner argues that the infant's mind is not the "blooming, buzzing confusion" that James had thought. Rather, it is remarkably sophisticated and well prepared to become the highly complex, culture-using and culture-producing mind of the adult (Bruner, 2000).

Nativistic models are central to the work of ethologists, who study and try to understand the behavior of organisms in natural situations. Imprinted behaviors such as the "following" response of young goslings, ethologists explain, are clear evidence of a prewired neurology

---

[5] I want you to tell your superintelligent readers, said Old Lady Gribbin somewhat imperiously, that it's a bit of a caricature, a misleading exaggeration, to suggest that most behaviorists adopted this tabula rasa model. Although it's true that aspects of the tabula rasa model are reflected in behaviorists' belief in the conditionability of humans, even the first of the behaviorists, Watson, accepted that infants are born with simple reflexes – hence, not entirely blank. Similarly, Skinner's Darwinian metaphor (the survival of reinforced responses) appeals to the importance of the organism's inherited behavioral repertoire.

448 | **Summary, Synthesis, and Integration**

that constrains and determines behavior. Much the same model underlies psychologists' discovery that some behaviors are more easily conditioned than others, as well as socio-biologists' belief that a wealth of important social behaviors are genetically preprogrammed.

The theories of the Gestalt psychologists also reflect this nativistic model remarkably closely. Thus, the tendency to perceive wholes rather than parts, to see the best form possible, and to look for patterns and similarities all illustrate wired-in tendencies. Similarly, Chomsky (1972) argues that humans have built-in neurological tendencies relating to language, and these explain how easily and quickly infants acquire language.

Constructivism

The world is not found or discovered, claim psychologists such as Bruner, Piaget, and Vygotsky; rather, it is constructed. The resulting model, *constructivism*, is a model of the learner as a builder of knowledge. It holds that through interactions with the world, children discover how to make meaning out of experience. Thus do children progressively discover rules that govern relationships among events, objects, and phenomena of the real world as well as rules for abstracting significance and for generating concepts. The constructivist learner is a self-motivated, mastery-oriented learner, driven by a need to know, to organize, to understand, to build meaning. Even adults continue to strive to build meaning and, perhaps far more than the child, to understand the significance of their lives. To this end, they tell themselves stories, personal narratives. And they struggle to understand the beginnings, the middles, and, yes, the ends of these stories to make sense of them and, by so doing, make sense of their own lives (Bruner, 2002).

Bruner's description of the learner as one who sifts through the data of experience to form concepts and to organize elaborate mental structures corresponding to the world is a construct-ivist model. The same is true of Piaget's view of the learner as assimilating and accommodating in order to invent and build progressively more advanced representations and systems of rules for dealing with the world.

Novice-to-Expert Model

A more recent model of the learner, says Bruner (1985), is one that is less concerned with theory than with the practical business of taking learners who are novices and making experts out of them. One approach suggested by this **novice-to-expert** model is to analyze experts and novices, describe the differences between them, and then devise ways of making the novice more like the expert. The novice-to-expert model is evident in information-processing approaches that use computers to simulate aspects of learning and thinking. For example, connectionism tries to mimic with computer-based neural networks the functioning of the human mind. In other words, in its creation of intelligent machines, it tries to create expert systems. These systems have the capacity to produce their own solutions for extremely complex problems. And, even now in the early stages of their development, they are better than humans

Table 12.3 **Models of the learner**

Model	Identifying belief	Theories reflecting the model*
Tabula rasa	The learner is an empty vessel waiting to be filled; a blank slate waiting for experience's messages.	Watson, Guthrie, Pavlov, Skinner, Thorndike
Hypothesis generator	The learner is characterized by intentionality and evaluates experiences through personal expectations, anticipations, and suppositions.	Tolman, Hull
Nativism	The learner is born with some biological, inherited constraints and predispositions that make learning some things (such as language) highly probable and others (such as tracking down and finding by following streams of odorous molecules) far less likely.	Ethologists, sociobiologists, Gestalt psychologists
Constructivism	The learner invents rules, discovers concepts, and builds representations of the world.	Piaget, Bruner, Vygotsky, Bandura
Novice-to-expert	The learner is a novice in specific domains and becomes more expert as differences between expert and novice functioning are eliminated.	Information-processing models, connectionist (neural network) models, artificial intelligence

* Note that most theories also include elements of other models.
Based in part on Bruner (1985).

at recognizing faces in enormous crowds, at playing difficult games like chess and Go, at answering complex questions extremely rapidly and accurately, at foreseeing consequences that result from complex interactions of a bewildering assortment of factors, even at driving vehicles.

These five models of the human learner are summarized in Table 12.3.

A LAST WORD

As this book makes clear, there have historically been a variety of different explanations of learning and, hence, a variety of different models of the learner. Through much of history, the notion has lingered that one model and one group of theories must be more correct, more useful, better than the others. "It was the vanity of a preceding generation," says Bruner, "to think

450 | **Summary, Synthesis, and Integration**

that the battle over learning theories would eventuate in one winning over all the others"
(1985, p. 8).

None has clearly won over all the others, perhaps because there isn't one kind of learning.
In the end, the most useful models may well prove to be those that recognize this most clearly
and allow for all the various kinds of learning possible in the wealth of circumstances under
which learning takes place. Such a model would recognize that the strength of the human
learner lies in the enormous range of competencies and adaptations possible.

Ideally, the human learner is flexible rather than rigid, open rather than closed, inventive
rather than receptive, changing rather than fixed, and poetic rather than prosaic. Models of the
learner and resulting theories should reflect this.

Main Point Chapter Summary

1. There appears to be a human need to simplify, to bring order out of chaos, to invent theory.
   One problem in summarizing learning theory is to simplify without lying.
2. The major divisions in learning theory reflect different concerns and different approaches
   to data gathering and science building. Behaviorists are primarily concerned with objective, observable events (stimuli, responses, reinforcers); cognitivists are more concerned
   with mental processes (thinking, problem solving, perception, decision making).[6]
3. Pavlov (*classical conditioning*), Watson (*environmentalism*), Guthrie (*one-shot learning*),
   Thorndike (*law of effect*), Hull (*hypothetico-deductive system*), and Skinner (*operant
   conditioning*) are behaviorists. Evolutionary psychologists, and psychologists such as
   Hebb (*cell assemblies and the Hebb rule*) and Tolman (*purposive behaviorism*), represent
   the beginning of a transition between behaviorism and cognitivism. Gestalt psychology
   (*the whole is greater than the sum of its parts*) reflects early attempts to develop cognitively
   based theories. Bruner (*categorization*), Piaget (*assimilation and accommodation*),
   Vygotsky (*zone of proximal development*), and theorists whose models are computer-
   based are cognitive psychologists.
4. Studying memory is another way of studying learning. Motivation looks at the causes and
   reasons for behavior and behavior change. Memory models are primarily cognitive; models
   of motivation include behaviorist approaches (needs, drives) and cognitive approaches
   (attributions, self-concepts, need for achievement, expectancy–value theory).
5. Social learning theory deals mainly with how we learn socially appropriate ways of
   behaving. Bandura's theory of social learning presents an important and highly integrative
   account of learning through observation.

---

[6] You should point out to your readers, said Mrs. Gribbin, that this statement implies a false dichotomy: cognitivists on the
one hand, who believe that learning takes place inside the head; and behaviorists on the other, who, by implication, must
believe that learning takes place elsewhere. In fact, none of the theorists discussed in this entire book would deny that
learning takes place inside the head. The point is that the cognitive emphasis has been shifting toward events inside the
head. In contrast, behaviorists have considered it more fruitful to deal with events outside the head.

Main Point Chapter Summary | 451

6. Machine learning models have led to the development of connectionist models (neural networks) that underlie artificial intelligence. It has resulted in machines that are better than humans at pattern recognition, intricate games, and complex predictions. What they will look like in the future remains unclear.

7. Major criticisms of behaviorism have to do with its mechanization of humans and its failure to account for mental events such as thinking, feeling, and understanding. Major criticisms of cognitivism relate to its less precise and more subjective approach and to its use of technical terms that are not always clearly defined.

8. Both behaviorist and cognitive models continue to influence psychological theory and practice, as do the more biologically based orientations. Major contributions of behaviorist approaches include an important assortment of therapies and suggestions for treating behavior problems and emotional disorders, as well as for changing behavior in classrooms.

9. Bruner describes five models of the learner, which are reflected in different learning theories: tabula rasa (empty vessel, behavioristic), hypothesis generator (intention and prediction; Tolman, Hull), nativism (prewired constraints and predispositions; ethologists, Gestaltists), constructivism (invention and building of cognitive representations; Piaget, Bruner, Vygotsky, Bandura), and novice-to-expert (computer simulation, information-processing models, neural networks, artificial intelligence).

10. No one has yet won the battle of the learning theories. However, except for minor skirmishes among radical factions, the battle has largely been abandoned following the recognition that there isn't just one kind of learning and that there is not likely to be just one kind of explanation.

LEFRANÇOIS'S EPILOGUE

Mrs. Gribbin is gone. "Where are you going?" I shouted as she trudged through the snow toward the beaver dam, Schrödinger dogging her heels. "Where are you from?" I yelled when she didn't answer my first question.

"I'll be back," she shouted an answer to a different question. Right! I've heard that before.

Suddenly a large old poplar tree came crashing down not far from the old lady. "You see that?" she cried. "You hear it? Here's a question for you to think about. 'If a tree falls in the forest and no one is around to hear it, does it make a sound?'" I'd heard that one before too.

"You want me to think about that?" I bellowed, incredulous.

"First," she yelled, "what I want you to do is Google Schrödinger's cat."

"What?" I shouted back. But she said no more. Instead, she pulled something from her pocket and hung it on a branch of the fallen tree. When she was done, Schrödinger darted in front of her, vanishing into the woods, almost as if he knew where the old lady was going. She waved once without turning around, and then she too disappeared. I haven't seen either of them since.

What Mrs. Gribbin had hung in the tree on the northwest quarter of Section 15, Township 48, Range 23, west of the 4th Meridian, was a flag just like the other two I already have folded up in one of the three shoeboxes under my bed back home. I have the new one on the wall here, in this tiny room where they're keeping me. You can see an image of it in the tiny cloud on the front cover.

The colors have faded, but you can still see the pig rampant on the right side of the escutcheon, facing the turkey glissant in some unexplained personal interaction. Both are on a field of flowers that look suspiciously like dandelions. Kongor's undershorts boasted the same design, said my aunt Lucy. How did she know?

The inscription on the flag, *fronti nulla fides*, is now barely legible, but its meaning is burned forever in my brain. "The forehead is never faithful" is the literal Latin-to-English translation. What it actually means is "You can't judge a book by its cover." Which is true.

Nor can you judge a book by its author or an author by his or her book.

"Tell that to the judge," said my grandmother. Then she added, "Good luck, anyways."

Yeah. Sure. Thanks.

Lefrançois's Epilogue | 453

Kongor. Not a real good photo but, what the hey, that was many decades ago

Kro thought himself an adventurous eater. But he was deathly afraid of wild mushrooms.

The Old Man always managed to hide when there was a camera around. All we ever got were long-distance shots.

Lefrançois's Epilogue

None of us ever got a photo of the Old Woman's face. She had thought she would move into this cabin until she saw mine.

The Professor caught in a rare candid moment. He had apparently forgotten about the motion sensitive, infrared camera that I had placed on the corner of the bush cabin.

Mrs. Gribbin and . . . I could have sworn Schrödinger, the cat, was in the photo when I first looked at it! She always turned her back whenever she saw a camera.

GLOSSARY

Absolute threshold The lowest level of stimulus intensity that can be detected at least 50 percent of the time. Absolute thresholds vary for different individuals depending on their sensitivity to different kinds of stimulation.

Accommodation Modification of an activity or ability in the face of environmental demands. In Piaget's description of development, assimilation and accommodation are the means by which individuals interact with and adapt to the world. (See *assimilation*.)

Acetylcholine A neurotransmitter present in the peripheral as well as the central nervous system; involved in voluntary activity as well as in physiological functions (such as heart and respiration rate). Also involved in the central nervous system in activities relating to learning and memory.

Action potential A pulse-like electrical discharge along a neuron. Sequences of linked action potentials are the basis for the transmission of neural messages.

Adaptation Changes in an organism in response to the environment. Such changes are assumed to facilitate interaction with that environment. Adaptation plays a central role in Piaget's theory. (See *assimilation*; *accommodation*.)

Agentic perspective An orientation, described by Bandura, that emphasizes the extent to which people are authors (agents) of their own actions rather than simply experiencing that which happens to them. Evident in the use of intentionality, forethought, self-reactiveness, and self-reflectiveness.

Agonist An agent or drug that enhances the activity of some naturally occurring substance. For example, cocaine is a dopamine agonist in that it appears to stimulate the activity of dopamine.

Algorithm A strategy or rule that leads to a correct solution for a problem. Simple mathematical problems are solved through algorithms. (See *heuristic*.)

Alpha waves Brain waves associated with restful but waking states of consciousness. Characteristically deep, regular waves. (See *beta waves*.)

Altruism	Selflessness. In an evolutionary sense, a powerful tendency to do things that increase the probability that other genetically related individuals will survive, even when doing these things poses serious risk to the actor.
Amnesia	A partial or total loss of memory. May often be associated with head injury or disease resulting in brain impairment.
Amygdala	A small structure in the limbic system (part of the forebrain) that is involved in emotion and aggression and that plays an important role in the processing and storage of memories that have to do with emotion.
Analog computer	A computer that, in contrast with a digital computer, represents variables as changing in a continuous rather than discrete fashion.
Anthropomorphism	The tendency to imbue inanimate objects, animals, and gods with human characteristics and feelings.
Aphasia	Loss of the ability to produce speech or to understand language as a result of brain injury. Sometimes manifested in loss of ability to read or write. May have a variety of causes, the most common of which is a cerebral stroke.
ARCS model of motivation	A model that provides suggestions for designing and implementing instructional strategies to foster and maintain high motivation, based on four elements: **A**ttention, **R**elevance, **C**onfidence, and **S**atisfaction.
Arousal	As a physiological concept, refers to changes in functions such as heart rate, respiration rate, electrical activity in the cortex, and electrical conductivity of the skin. As a psychological concept, refers to degree of alertness, awareness, vigilance, or wakefulness. Arousal varies from very low (coma or sleep) to very high (panic or high anxiety).
Arousal function	In Hebb's and Hull's theories, the motivating function of a stimulus. That aspect of the stimulus that relates to attention or alertness. (See *cue function*.)
Arousal theory	A motivational theory that looks at how intensity of motivation is related to physiological changes. (See *arousal*.)
Artificial intelligence (AI)	Describes models, procedures, devices, or mechanisms intended to simulate or duplicate some of the intelligent functions of human mental activity.
Assimilation	The act of incorporating objects or aspects of objects into previously learned activities. In a sense, to assimilate is to ingest or to use for something previously learned. (See *accommodation*.)
Associative shifting	A Thorndikean concept that describes a process whereby a response is gradually shifted to a situation entirely different from that in which it was learned. One way of doing this is to change the initial stimulus very gradually (a process called *fading*).

Glossary

Assumption	A belief important in reasoning; accepted as fact but often unprovable.
Attention	A state of the reacting organism that implies a narrowing and focusing of perception associated with awareness. A selection and emphasis of that to which the organism responds.
Attention-deficit hyperactivity disorder (ADHD)	A disorder marked by excessive general activity for a child's age, attention problems, high impulsivity, and low frustration tolerance. Also termed *hyperactivity*.
Attitude	A prevailing and consistent tendency to react in a certain way. Attitudes can be positive or negative and are important motivational forces.
Attribute	A characteristic of an object; a quality or value. (See *criterial attribute, intension, extension, category*.)
Attribution theory	A theory that looks for regularities in the ways in which people attribute things that happen to certain internal or external causes.
Autoshaping	Refers to responses that are learned in experimental situations even though they are not necessary to obtain reinforcement. Autoshaped behaviors (such as pecking in pigeons) often appear to be part of the organism's repertoire of "natural" behaviors typically linked with food, mates, or survival.
Aversion therapy	A therapy in which an undesirable behavior is paired with stimuli associated with nausea or illness (using drugs or radiation, for example). Sometimes used to treat addictions (alcohol, nicotine, drugs, sexual perversions) or to modify other undesirable habits.
Aversive control	The control of human behavior through the use of noxious (unpleasant) stimuli in contrast to techniques of positive control, which generally use positive reinforcement.
Avoidance learning	A conditioning phenomenon usually involving aversive (unpleasant) stimulation. The organism learns to avoid situations associated with specific unpleasant circumstances. (See *escape learning*.)
Axon	An elongated, trunk-like extension of a neuron. Neural impulses are ordinarily transmitted from the cell body outward along the axon.
Back-propagation rule	A type of neural network model in which the system uses information about the appropriateness of its output to adjust the weightings of the connections among intervening units.
Backward pairing	In classical conditioning, the presentation of the US before the CS. (See *delayed pairing; trace pairing; simultaneous pairing*.)
Behavior management	The deliberate and systematic application of psychological principles in attempts to change behavior. Behavior management programs are often based on behaviorist principles. (See *behavior modification; behavior therapy*.)

Glossary 459

Behavior modification   The deliberate application of operant conditioning principles in an effort to change behavior. Also used as a general term for therapies using any of a variety of learning principles. (See *behavior therapy*; *behavior management*.)

Behavior therapy   The systematic application of Pavlovian procedures and ideas in an effort to change behavior. Also used as a general term for therapies using other varieties of learning principles. (See *behavior modification*; *behavior management*.)

Behavioral field   A Gestalt concept defined in terms of the individual's personal perception of reality; also called the *psychological field*.

Behaviorism   A general term for approaches to theories of learning concerned primarily with the observable components of behavior such as stimuli and responses.

Belief   The acceptance of an idea as being accurate or truthful. Beliefs are often highly personal and highly resistant to change. (See *law*; *principle*; *theory*.)

Beta waves   Characteristically shallow, rapid brain waves associated with alertness. (See *alpha waves*.)

Biofeedback   The information we obtain about our biological functioning. Also refers to procedures whereby individuals are given information about their physiological functioning so they can achieve control over aspects of this functioning.

Biological constraints   Limitations on learning that result from biological factors rather than from experience.

Black box   Could be the squarish, blackish box (alluded to in Chapter 8) in which grandfathers keep their family jewels. In psychology, more likely to be a metaphor for the mind, implying its unknown (unknowable?) nature – a metaphor embraced by "radical" behaviorists who refrain from speculating about mental processes.

Blocked repetition   A learning technique where the learner practices a skill or repeats information continually, attempting to learn it in a single block of time. See *spaced repetition*; *interleaving*.

Blocking   A phenomenon in classical conditioning in which conditioning to a specific stimulus becomes difficult or impossible because of prior conditioning to another stimulus.

Brain-based education   The application of teaching/learning principles based on knowledge about how the brain functions.

Brain stem   The collection of brain structures that joins the brain to the spinal cord.

Bubba psychology   An expression for folk beliefs in psychology; also referred to as naïve or implicit theories. Bubba means grandmother.

Capability	Possessing the mental and physical ability to execute a behavior. Being able to do something.
Categorization	A Brunerian concept referring to the process of identifying objects or events on the basis of the attributes they share with other instances. (See *category*.)
Category	A term Bruner used to describe a grouping of related objects or events. In this sense, a category is both a concept (or class) and a percept. Bruner also defines it as a rule for classifying things as equivalent. (See *coding system, extension, attribute, intension*.)
Causes	Agents or forces that produce an effect or a result. Causes are one aspect of motivation. (See *reasons; motivation*.)
Cell assembly	A hypothetical structure in Hebb's theory, consisting of a circuit of neurons that reactivate one another. Corresponds to relatively simple sensory input. (See *phase sequence*.)
Central executive system	In Baddeley's model of working memory, that which is concerned with regulating the flow of information from sensory storage, processing it for long-term storage, and retrieving it from long-term storage. (See *working memory; phonological loop; visual-spatial sketch pad; episodic buffer*.)
Central nervous system (CNS)	The brain and the spinal cord.
Cerebellum	Literally "little brain," this structure is located at the bottom rear of the brain, attached to the brain stem. It controls rapid and habitual movements and coordinates motor activity.
Cerebral cortex	The one-eighth-inch thick outer covering of the cerebrum. Its four major divisions found on each side of the brain, the cerebral lobes, are implicated in sensation, hearing, language, speech, and higher thought processes.
Cerebrum	The largest, most complex, and most highly developed part of the human brain relative to the brains of nonhuman animals. Its outer covering, the cerebral cortex, is centrally involved in higher mental functioning.
Chaining	A Skinnerian explanation for the linking of sequences of responses through the action of discriminative stimuli that act as secondary reinforcers. According to Skinner, most behaviors involve chains.
Chunking	A memory process whereby related items are grouped together into more easily remembered "chunks" – for example, a prefix and four digits for a phone number rather than seven unrelated numbers.
Classical conditioning	Involves the repeated pairing of two stimuli so a previously neutral (conditioned) stimulus eventually elicits a response (conditioned response; CR) similar to that originally elicited by a nonneutral

	(unconditioned; US) stimulus. Originally described by Pavlov. (See *conditioning*; *operant conditioning*.)
Closure	A Gestalt principle referring to our tendency to perceive incomplete patterns as complete. (See *continuity*; *prägnanz*; *proximity*; *similarity*.)
Cocktail party phenomenon	An expression to describe sensory memory, the fleeting and unconscious availability for processing of stimuli to which the individual is not paying attention.
Coding system	A Brunerian concept referring to a hierarchical arrangement of related categories.
Cognitions	To cognize is to know. Cognition refers to knowing, understanding, problem solving, and related intellectual processes. The word *cognitions* refers to things that are known.
Cognitive architecture	A term used in cognitive research to refer to abstract, symbolic descriptions of the human cognitive processing system. Cognitive architecture includes all the systems and processes assumed to be necessary for perception, thinking, problem solving, and other cognitive activity.
Cognitive dissonance	A state of conflict involving beliefs, behaviors, or expectations. Festinger argued that cognitive dissonance is an important motive for behavior.
Cognitive map	Tolman's term for a mental representation of a physical environment in which goals are located as well as an internal representation of relationships between behavior and goals.
Cognitive strategies	The processes involved in learning and remembering. Cognitive strategies include procedures for identifying problems, selecting approaches to their solution, monitoring progress in solving problems, and using feedback.
Cognitive structure	A term used in reference to the content of mind – in effect, the individual's mental representations, which include knowledge of things as well as knowledge of how to do things. Defined by Piaget as comprising mental representations and actions.
Cognitivism	A general term for approaches to theories of learning concerned with such intellectual events as problem solving, information processing, thinking, and imagining.
Collective efficacy	The belief members of a group share about their ability to influence events to attain common goals.
Combined schedule	A combination of various types of schedules of reinforcement.
Common sense	Widely held beliefs that seem intuitively correct. Sometimes they are correct; sometimes not. (See *bubba psychology*.)
Compensation	A logical rule relating to the fact that certain changes can compensate for opposing changes, thereby negating their effect.

Computer literacy	The minimal skills required for effective interaction with computers. Does not require knowing how a computer functions or how to program computers.
Computer simulation	Attempts to develop computer systems capable of mimicking the intelligent functioning of humans (including errors and biases). In computer simulation, the emphasis is on process; in contrast, the field of artificial intelligence emphasizes the outcome. (See *artificial intelligence*.)
Concept	An abstraction or representation of the common properties of events, objects, or experiences; an idea or notion.
Conceptual change movement	A discovery-oriented movement in education, highly compatible with Bruner's theory, where the emphasis is on fostering discovery and mental reorganization rather than simply increasing the number of facts and procedures learned.
Concrete operations	The third of Piaget's four major stages, lasting from age 7 or 8 to approximately age 11 or 12 and characterized largely by the child's ability to deal with concrete or easily imagined problems and objects.
Concurrent schedule of reinforcement	A situation in which two or more different reinforcement schedules, each typically related to a different behavior, are presented concurrently (at the same time).
Conditioned emotional reactions (CERs)	A largely unavoidable emotional reaction associated with a conditioned stimulus, acquired through repeated exposure to specific emotion-related situations.
Conditioned response (CR)	A response elicited by a conditioned stimulus. In some obvious ways, a conditioned response resembles but is not identical to its corresponding unconditioned response.
Conditioned stimulus (CS)	A stimulus that initially does not elicit any response (or that elicits a global, orienting response) but, as a function of being paired with an unconditioned stimulus and its response, acquires the capability of eliciting that same response. For example, a stimulus that is always present at the time of a fear reaction may become a conditioned stimulus for fear.
Conditioning	A type of learning describable in terms of changing relationships between stimuli, between responses, or between stimuli and responses. (See *classical conditioning*; *operant conditioning*.)
Connectionism	Thorndike's term for his theory of learning, based on the notion that learning is the formation of connections between stimuli and responses.
Connectionist model	Label for neural network models of human cognitive processing made possible by parallel processing computers. Such models recognize unconscious, automatic, implicit, nonsymbolic

learning. They are based not on the application of previously determined rules but, rather, on the generation (learning) of new rules. The basic metaphor is that of cognitive processing involving complex arrangements and modifications of connections among neural units. (See *symbolic models*; *neural network*.)

Conservation A Piagetian term for the realization that certain quantitative attributes of objects remain unchanged unless something is added to or taken away from them. Characteristics of objects such as mass, number, area, and volume are capable of being conserved.

Constructivism A general term for student-centered approaches to teaching such as discovery-oriented approaches, reciprocal learning, or cooperative instruction – so called because of their assumption that learners should build (construct) knowledge for themselves. (See *direct instruction*.)

Contiguity The occurrence of events both simultaneously and in the same space. Contiguity is often used to explain classical conditioning.

Contingency A consequence or outcome of a behavior. Positive and negative contingencies define the various kinds of reinforcement and punishment. Contingency implies dependency. Events are said to be contingent when the occurrence of one depends on the occurrence of the other. For example, daylight is contingent on sunrise; good grades are contingent on studying (or intelligence, or good luck, or what have you).

Continuity A Gestalt principle evident in our tendency to perceive patterns as continuous. (See *closure*; *prägnanz*; *proximity*; *similarity*.)

Continuous reinforcement A reinforcement schedule in which every correct response is followed by a reinforcer.

Contrapreparedness In learning theory, describes learning that the organism finds very difficult, or even impossible, to acquire. (See *preparedness*.)

Control group In an experiment, a group comprising individuals as similar to the experimental group as possible except that they are not exposed to an experimental treatment. (See *experimental group*.)

Corporal punishment Punishment that uses physical force to inflict pain.

Counterconditioning A behavior modification technique (similar to Guthrie's threshold technique or his method of incompatible stimuli) in which stimuli associated with an undesirable response are presented below threshold or at times when the undesirable response is unlikely to occur. The object is to condition a desirable response to replace the undesirable one. (See also *systematic desensitization*, which is one form of counterconditioning.)

Criterial attribute An expression Bruner uses to describe the characteristics of objects, events, or experiences that define their membership in a

	category – in other words, that are essential to their being what they are.
Critical period	A period in development during which exposure to appropriate experiences or stimuli will bring about imprinting. (See *imprinting*.)
Cue-dependent forgetting	Forgetting due to the unavailability of appropriate cues for recall. Illustrated by retrieval-cue failure. (See *retrieval-cue failure*; *trace-dependent forgetting*.)
Cue function	In Hebb's and Hull's theories, the message function of a stimulus; the aspect of the stimulus that tells the organism how it should react. (See *arousal function*.)
Culture	The sum total of the attainments and accumulated customs, beliefs, and mores of a group. Human cultures are typically marked by shared languages, spiritual beliefs, habits, and so forth.
Cumulative recording	A graphical representation of a number of responses over time (hence, of rate of responding), Skinner used this widely in his investigations of bar-pressing and key-pecking.
Decay theory	An explanation for loss of information in short-term memory based on the notion that the physiological effects of stimulation fade. Similar to fading in connection with forgetting in long-term memory. (See *fading*.)
Declarative memory	Explicit, conscious long-term memory, in contrast with implicit memory. Declarative memory may be either semantic or episodic. (See *explicit memory*.)
Deductive	A type of reasoning that involves making inferences from general principles.
Deep learning	Algorithms (instructions regarding rules and procedures) used in machine learning designed to allow machines to process data and make decisions much as might an intelligent human.
Deferred imitation	The ability to imitate people or events in their absence. Piaget assumes that deferred imitation is crucial in the development of language abilities.
Delayed pairing	In classical conditioning, the presentation of the CS before the US, with both ending simultaneously. (See *backward pairing*; *simultaneous pairing*; *trace pairing*.)
Dendrite	Hair-like tendrils found on a neuron's cell body. Their function is to receive impulses.
Dependent variable	The variable (measurement, outcome, behavior) that reflects the assumed effects of manipulations of the independent variable(s) in an experiment. The *then* part of the if–then equation implicit in an experimental hypothesis. (See *independent variable*.)
Determinism	The belief that all things have causes rooted in antecedent events. In psychology, refers to the belief that all human behaviors are

	caused by preceding events and conditions, and not by the exercise of free will.
Differential reinforcement of successive approximations	The procedure of reinforcing only some responses and not others. Differential reinforcement is used in the shaping of complex behaviors. (See *shaping*.)
Differential threshold	(See *just noticeable difference [JND]*.)
Digital computer	A computer that, in contrast with an analog computer, represents variables through values that change discretely (one or zero, for example). A digital computer can be programmed to process as though it were an analog computer.
Direct instruction	A phrase used to describe teacher-directed approaches to teaching – in contrast with more student-centered approaches, such as reciprocal teaching and cooperative learning, which are often described as *constructivist* approaches. (See *constructivism*; *constructivist approaches*.)
Direct reinforcement	Reinforcement that occurs as a direct consequence of a behavior, such as getting paid to work. (See *vicarious reinforcement*.)
Direct teaching	A relatively authoritarian approach to teaching where teachers are considered the primary source of information. (See *constructivism*.)
Discovery learning	The acquisition of new information or knowledge largely because of the learner's own efforts. Discovery learning is often associated with Bruner and is contrasted with reception learning. (See *reception learning*.)
Discrimination	Making different responses in closely related situations, thus providing evidence of discriminating among the stimuli (also referred to as stimulus discrimination). The opposite of generalization. (See *generalization*.)
Discriminative stimulus (S^D)	Skinner's term for the features of a situation that an organism can discriminate to distinguish between occasions that might be reinforced or not reinforced.
Disinhibitory effect	Involves engaging in a previously inhibited, deviant behavior as a result of observing a model. The inhibitory effect involves refraining from a deviant behavior. (See *inhibitory effect*.)
Displacement theory	Miller's belief that there are a limited number of "slots" in short-term memory (seven plus or minus two) and that incoming information displaces older information.
Dispositions	Attitudes or inclinations. Changes in disposition are often involved in learning.
Distortion theory	A theory of forgetting that recognizes that what is remembered is often changed or reconstructed.

Dominant hemisphere	The hemisphere that controls speech and language. In the majority of people, the left hemisphere is dominant and the right is *non-dominant*.
Dopamine	A brain chemical involved in neural transmission. Dopaminergic cells (those that use dopamine for transmission) are found in at least one of the pleasure centers of the brain as well as in some areas that control physical movement. Loss of dopamine in areas involved in physical movement results in Parkinson's disease. Excessive dopamine activity in the pleasure centers, such as might result from the intake of cocaine and from rewards such as food and drink, lead to reactions of pleasure.
Double-blind procedure	An investigation where neither subjects nor investigators know who members of experimental and control groups are. (See *single-blind procedure*.)
Drive (D)	The tendency to behave that is brought about by an unsatisfied need (for example, the need for food is associated with a hunger drive). A central concept in Hull's theory.
Dualism	Descartes's belief that the mind and the body are fundamentally different and distinct substances. The body is material and therefore machine-like; the mind is immaterial and therefore godlike.
Dystopian	Relating to conditions marked by intense suffering and injustice. A state where existence is miserable, dehumanized, and wretched.
Egocentric speech	Vygotsky's intermediate stage of language development, common between ages three and seven, during which children often talk to themselves in an apparent effort to control their own behavior. (See *inner speech*; *social speech*.)
Egocentrism	A way of functioning characterized by an inability to assume the viewpoint of others. A child's early thinking is largely egocentric.
Elaboration	A memory strategy involving forming new associations. To elaborate is to link with other ideas or images.
Electrodermal response	A measure of skin resistance to an electrical current (also termed *galvanic skin response*). Skin conductivity increases with increasing arousal – and increasing perspiration.
Electroencephalogram (EEG)	An instrument used to measure electrical activity in the brain.
Eliciting effect	Imitative behavior in which the observer does not copy the model's responses but simply behaves in a related manner. (See *inhibitory effect*; *modeling effect*.)
Emotion	A synonym of *feeling*. A cognitive and physiological state describable with words such as *anxious*, *angry*, *sad*, *confused*, *cautious*, *lonely*, and a huge number of similar terms.

Enactive representation   A phrase Bruner used to describe how young children tend to represent their world in terms of sensations and actions (hence, enactive). (See *iconic representation*; *symbolic representation*.)

Engram   A permanent change in the brain presumed to underlie memory.

Entity theory   Dweck's label for the belief that ability is a fixed, unchanging entity. Associated with performance goals – that is, with doing well to be judged positively by others. (See *incremental theory*; *mastery goal*; *performance goal*.)

Episodic buffer   The component in Baddeley's model of working memory that integrates and makes sense of the functioning of the *slave systems* associated with phonological and visual-spatial information. (See *central executive system*, *phonological loop*, *visual-spatial sketch pad*.)

Episodic memory   A type of declarative, autobiographical (conscious, long-term) memory consisting of knowledge about personal experiences tied to specific times and places.

Epistemology   A branch of philosophy concerned with questions related to the nature of knowledge and of knowing.

Eponym   A person after whom something is named, such as a sandwich being named after the Earl of Sandwich or sideburns being named after the man with the strange hairstyle, Ambrose Burnside, or the Skinner box being named after Skinner.

Equilibration   A Piagetian term for the process by which people maintain a balance between assimilation (using old learning) and accommodation (changing behavior; learning new things). Equilibration is essential for adaptation and cognitive growth.

Escape learning   A conditioning phenomenon whereby the organism learns the means of escaping from a situation, usually following the presentation of aversive (unpleasant) stimulation. (See *avoidance learning*.)

Ethology   The study of organisms in their natural habitats. The science of animal behavior.

Eudemonic   (Also spelled *eudaimonic*). Describes an orientation that defines well-being in terms of the degree to which a person is fully functioning (fully actualized, in Maslow's terms). Often contrasted with *hedonism*, which defines well-being in terms of more immediate and worldlier outcomes viewed as pleasant. (See *psychological hedonism*.)

Eugenics   A form of genetic engineering that selects specific individuals for reproduction. Although widely accepted and practiced with animals, the concept raises many serious moral and ethical issues when applied to humans.

Glossary

Event-related field (ERF) — A measure of magnetic fields at the scalp related to neural activity typically associated with specific stimuli, detected by means of *magnetic encephalograms* (MEGs). Highly useful for studying brain functioning.

Event-related potential (ERP) — A measure of electrical activity in identifiable areas of the brain, corresponding to specific stimuli, often detected through use of *electroencephalograms* (EEGs), typically used in studies of ERPs.

Evolutionary psychology — An approach in psychology defined by its attention to biology and genetics as sources of explanation for human learning and behavior. Branches of evolutionary psychology are sometimes considered to include sociobiology and behavior genetics.

Exemplar model — A concept learning model that assumes that people learn and remember the best examples of a concept and then compare new instances with these examples. (See *prototype model.*)

Expectancy–value theory — A cognitive approach to motivation that describes decision making as involving a sort of mental calculus where the most important factors are expectancy of success (feelings of self-efficacy) on the one hand and the values and costs associated with the various options on the other.

Experiment — A deliberately controlled arrangement of circumstances under which a phenomenon is observed.

Experimental analysis of behavior — A phrase typically associated with Skinner's system. Reflects radical behaviorism's emphasis on the objective analysis of the variables involved in behavior: specifically, what the organism does, the circumstances under which the action occurs, and the consequences of the action (whether behavior occurs again under similar circumstances). (See *radical behaviorism.*)

Experimental group — In an experiment, the group of participants who are exposed to a treatment. (See *control group.*)

Explicit learning — Learning that is deliberate, conscious, and verbalizable. (See *implicit learning*).

Explicit memory — Also termed *declarative memory*. Explicit, conscious long-term memory, in contrast with implicit memory. Explicit memory may be either semantic or episodic. (See *episodic memory*; *semantic memory.*)

Extension — In concept formation, the term used to signify the class to which related objects or ideas belong. (Bruner uses the term *category* for *class* or *extension*) (See *category*; *attribute*; *intension.*)

Exteroceptive stimulation — Relates to sensations associated with external stimuli and involving the senses of vision, hearing, taste, and smell. (See *proprioceptive stimulation.*)

Glossary | 469

Extinction	In classical conditioning, the cessation of a response following repeated presentations of the CS without the US. In operant conditioning, the cessation of a response following the withdrawal of reinforcement.
Extinction rate	In Hull's system, the number of responses that would occur before the cessation of a response following withdrawal of reinforcement.
Extrinsic motive	A motive associated with external sources of reinforcement such as food, money, high grades, praise, and so on.
Extroverts	A term used to describe individuals who are predominantly oriented toward the outside rather than the inside. Principal characteristics of extroverts include concern with and involvement in social activities. Those who are outgoing and sociable.
Fading	A conditioning technique in which certain characteristics of stimuli are gradually faded out, eventually resulting in discriminations that did not originally exist.
Fading theory	The belief that inability to recall in long-term memory increases with the passage of time as memory "traces" fade.
False memory syndrome	Label sometimes used to describe the possibility that a memory, especially of a highly traumatic event, may be a memory of something that has not actually occurred.
Fatigue technique	One of Guthrie's methods for replacing habits; involves the repeated presentation of the stimuli that lead to the undesirable habit so the organism, eventually fatigued, emits (and learns) a different response. (See *method of incompatible stimuli*; *threshold technique*.)
Feedback	In machine systems, feedback is information about the effects of an action, often used to modify and adjust that action. In education, feedback is a two-way process where learners and teachers receive information about the results of actions and use that information to adjust their behaviors.
Fitness	A measure of the reproductive success of a variation in a trait. Traits that become more common through generations are said to have a higher degree of fitness. (See *inclusive fitness*.)
Fixed schedule	A type of intermittent schedule of reinforcement in which reinforcement occurs at fixed intervals of time (an interval schedule) or after a specified number of trials (a ratio schedule). (See *continuous reinforcement*; *interval schedule*; *ratio schedule*.)
Flashbulb memories	Unusually vivid and durable recollections of the details surrounding a personally significant, highly emotional event.
Folk knowledge	Widely held beliefs about the characteristics of people and the meanings of their behaviors and about the principles underlying natural phenomena.

Glossary

Forgetting	Loss from memory over time. May involve inability to retrieve or might involve actual loss of whatever traces or changes define storage. Contrasted with extinction, which occurs as a result of cessation of reinforcement. (See *memory*; *extinction*.)
Formal operations	The last of Piaget's four major stages. It begins around age 11 or 12 and lasts until age 14 or 15. It is characterized by the child's increasing ability to use logical thought processes.
Fractional antedating goal response (r_G)	One of a collection of related responses made by an organism before the actual goal response.
Frontal lobe	Frontal part of the cerebral cortex; centrally involved in higher thought processes. (See *occipital lobe*; *temporal lobe*; *parietal lobe*.)
Functional magnetic resonance imaging (fMRI)	A diagnostic imaging technique that detects extremely subtle changes in magnetic fields in the human body, allowing technicians to view real-time, computer-enhanced images of soft tissue. Used extensively to diagnose disease as well as to study neural activity in the brain. (See *Functional magnetic resonance spectrography [fMRS]*.)
Functional magnetic resonance spectrography (fMRS)	Allows detection of specific chemicals in the active brain using the same equipment as fMRI, but different computer software. (See *Functional magnetic resonance imaging [fMRI]*.)
Functionalism	An early American movement in psychology associated with William James. In contrast with structuralism, it urged that psychology look at the purpose of mental activity rather than at its structure. (See *structuralism*.)
Fuzzy logic	A logic that is relativistic, considers a variety of factors, and has a not entirely predictable probability of being correct. Characteristic of parallel processing-based connectionist models.
Generalization	The transference of a response from one stimulus to a similar stimulus (stimulus generalization) or the transference of a similar response for another response in the face of a single stimulus (response generalization). Also called *transfer*. (See *discrimination*.)
Generalized reinforcer	Any of a number of powerful, learned reinforcers that are reinforcing for a large variety of behaviors in many situations (behavioral consequences such as praise, prestige, money, fame, etc.).
Gestalt	A German word meaning whole or configuration. Describes an approach to psychology concerned with the perception of wholes, with insight, and with awareness. Gestalt psychology is a forerunner of contemporary cognitive psychology.
Gestation	Prenatal development; the period of time between conception and birth.

Grandmother cell	A neuron that is thought to be activated by a single complex stimulus. The notion of grandmother cells reflects a belief that memories may be *localized* in specific neurons or neural connections rather than spread out over a network of neurons, as in a parallel distributed processing system.
Guided mastery therapy	An approach to therapy based largely on social/cognitive theory, where the therapist attempts to boost relevant feelings of self-efficacy. Widely used in the treatment of phobias.
Habit strength ($_sH_r$)	A behaviorist Hullian concept. The strength of the bond between a specific stimulus and response, reflecting how often the two have been paired and reinforced in the past.
Habit	Highly predictable sequences of responses. In Guthrie's system, a combination of stimulus–response bonds that becomes stereotyped and expected.
Habit-family hierarchy	Hull's expression for a collection of habits (stimulus–response links) that are related because they share common goals.
Habituation	A highly common form of learning in which an organism's responses to stimulation gradually diminish or cease altogether. Most often occurs following mild, repetitive stimulation. (See *sensitization*.)
Hardware	The physical components of a computer, including monitors, controllers, keyboards, chips, cards, circuits, drives, printers, and so on. (See *software*; *wetware*.)
Hawthorne effect	A label for the observation that the behavior of research participants may change simply as a function of knowing they are being observed.
Hebb rule	Hebb's supposition that the repeated cofiring of two related neurons would lead to a permanent change in the strength of the synapse (connection) between them.
Heuristic	A problem-solving approach that serves as a guide for solving a problem, or for learning or discovering. Heuristic approaches often lead to a speculative rather than a definitely correct solution. A theory with high heuristic value suggests new avenues of research, new relationships, and new findings. (See *algorithm*.)
Higher mental processes	A general phrase to indicate unobservable processes that occur in the "mind" (for want of a more precise term). What we normally think of as "thinking."
Higher-order conditioning	A phenomenon in conditioning, where a conditioned stimulus takes on the role of an unconditioned stimulus. Thus, a dog conditioned to salivate to a tone may subsequently learn to salivate to another stimulus, such as a light, that has been paired with the tone but never with food. (See *second-order conditioning*.)

Glossary

Hippocampus	A limbic system structure in the forebrain, which is involved in learning and memory.
Holistic education	A comprehensive term for educational approaches that attempt to remedy what is seen as the failure of traditional education to educate the whole brain. Advocates of holistic education believe that the right hemisphere, speculatively linked with music, art, and emotion, is neglected by curricula that stress reason, logic, language, science, and mathematics.
Homunculus	Literally, a little man or dwarf. Term used for the hypothetical entity assumed by the ancient Greeks to be the cause of human behavior.
Hypothalamus	A small structure deep within the brain near the top of the brain stem involved in a variety of bodily functions, including the functioning of the endocrine glands.
Hypothesis	An educated guess, often based on theory, which can be tested. A prediction based on partial evidence of some effect, process, or phenomenon, which must then be verified experimentally.
Hypothesis generator	A model that has at its core the notion that the learner is characterized by intentionality and by the ability to generate hypotheses (suppositions or predictions) and to interpret experience in the light of these hypotheses.
Hypothetico-deductive system	A theoretical system consisting of general laws from which subsidiary principles can be derived and tested. Hull's learning theory is hypothetico-deductive.
Iconic representation	A Brunerian stage in the development of the child's representation of the world characterized by a representation of the world in terms of relatively concrete mental images (icons). (See *enactive representation*; *symbolic representation*.)
Id	One of three levels of the human personality, according to Freudian theory. The id includes all the instinctual urges that humans inherit. These are the source of all human motives.
Identity	A logical rule that specifies that certain activities leave objects or situations unchanged.
Idiot savant	Literally, a wise idiot. Used to describe individuals remarkably endowed in some highly specific ability, such as remembering long strings of numbers, but severely handicapped in others. The term *autistic savant* is now preferred.
Imitation	Copying behavior. To imitate a person's behavior is simply to use that person's behavior as a pattern. Bandura and Walters describe three different effects of imitation. (See *eliciting effect*; *inhibitory effect*; *modeling effect*.)
Implicit learning	Unconscious learning; not represented in symbols or analyzable with rules.

Glossary | 473

Implicit memory	Also termed *nondeclarative* or *procedural memory*. Refers to unconscious, inexpressible effects of experience, such as might be manifested in acquired motor skills or in classical conditioning.
Imprinting	Unlearned, instinct-like behaviors that are not present at birth but that become part of an animal's repertoire after exposure to a suitable stimulus during a critical period. The "following" behavior of young ducks, geese, and chickens is an example.
Incentive motivation	General term for the branch of motivational research concerned with how goals are valued by the individual – that is, with the different incentives associated with different goals.
Inclusive fitness	In sociobiology, refers to the fitness of genetically related groups relative to their likelihood of procreation and survival.
Incremental theory	Dweck's label for the belief that ability is malleable and can be increased through work and effort. The theory is associated with mastery goals – that is, with goals aimed at increasing personal competence. (See *entity theory*; *mastery goal*; *performance goal*.)
Independent variable	The variable that is manipulated in an experiment to see if it causes changes in the dependent variable. The *if* part of the if–then equation implicit in an experiment. (See *dependent variable*.)
Inductive	A type of reasoning that proceeds from particular instances to a general conclusion.
Information processing (IP)	Relates to how information is modified (or processed), resulting in knowledge, perception, or behavior. A dominant model of the cognitive approaches, it makes extensive use of computer metaphors.
Inhibitory conditioning	Edwin Guthrie's term for learning a response that interferes with another behavior. Inhibitory conditioning is illustrated by procedures for breaking habits. (See *fatigue technique*; *threshold technique*; *method of incompatible stimuli*.)
Inhibitory effect	The type of imitative behavior that results either in the suppression (inhibition) or appearance (disinhibition) of previously acquired deviant behavior. (See *eliciting effect*; *modeling effect*.)
Inner speech	Vygotsky's final stage in the development of speech, attained at around age seven and characterized by silent "self-talk," the stream-of-consciousness flow of verbalizations that give direction and substance to our thinking and behavior. Inner speech is involved in all higher mental functioning. (See *egocentric speech*; *social speech*.)
Input variables	Hull's phrase for the complex of stimuli to which an organism responds. Characteristics of input variables include intensity of the stimulus, the motivational state of the organism, the amount

	of work involved in responding, and the amount of associated reward.
Insight	The perception of relationships among elements of a problem situation. A problem-solving method that contrasts strongly with trial and error. The cornerstone of Gestalt psychology.
Instinctive drift	Refers to the tendency of organisms to revert to instinctual, unlearned behaviors.
Instincts	Complex, species-specific, relatively unmodifiable patterns of behaviors, such as migration or nesting in some birds and animals. Less complex, automatic inherited behaviors are usually termed *reflexes*.
Instrumental learning	The learning of voluntary responses as a function of their consequences. Associated with Thorndike's learning theory and sometimes used interchangeably with operant conditioning. (See *operant conditioning*.)
Intellectual style	A general term meant to include learning styles, personality styles, behavioral differences, and other apparent preferences that affect how the individual thinks, acts, and learns. (See *learning styles*.)
Intelligent tutor system (ITS)	A computer-based learning system that takes into account the individual learner's strengths and weaknesses and modifies its presentations accordingly.
Intension	Term used in logic referring to the collection of characteristics (*attributes*) that serve to identify things that belong to a given class or category.
Interference theory	The belief that previous learning might interfere with retention in short-term memory. (See *proactive interference*; *retroactive interference*.)
Interleaving	A highly effective learning technique involving alternating periods of practice or repetition of one skill or task with repetition and rehearsal of a second unrelated task. See *blocked repetition*; *spaced repetition*.
Intermittent reinforcement	A schedule of reinforcement that does not present a reinforcer for all correct responses. (See *interval schedule*; *ratio schedule*.)
Internalization	A Piagetian concept referring to the processes by which activities, objects, and events in the real world become represented mentally.
Interoceptive conditioning	The conditioning of actions involving glands or involuntary muscles, such as vasoconstriction or dilation.
Interval schedule	An intermittent schedule of reinforcement that is based on the passage of time. (See *fixed schedule*; *random schedule*.)
Intervening variables	Hull's phrase for the complex of assumed variables that intervene between the presentation of a stimulus and the occurrence of a response. Include the organism's habits, expectations of reward,

Glossary 475

and other factors related to previous responses in similar situations.

Interviews Data gathering method wherein investigators question participants.

Intrinsic motive A motive associated with internal sources of reinforcement, such as satisfaction and feelings of competence and worth.

Introspection A once-popular method of psychological investigation involving careful self-examination followed by an attempt to arrive at laws and principles that explain the introspector's own behavior and can be generalized to others.

Introverts A term used to describe individuals who turn inward rather than outward. Such individuals tend to be more interested in their internal states and less interested in externally oriented, social activities. Those who are sober, reserved, and withdrawn.

Intuitive thinking One of the substages of Piaget's preoperational thought, beginning around age four and lasting until age seven or eight. Marked by the child's ability to solve many problems intuitively and by the inability to respond correctly in the face of misleading perceptual features of problems.

Jennifer Aniston neuron Name given to a single, specific neuron associated with the recognition of a person (such as Jennifer Aniston) or a concept. Also called a *concept cell.*

Just noticeable difference (JND) The least amount of change in stimulation intensity that can be detected 50 percent of the time.

Latent Not evident; present but hidden; potential. Latent learning involves changes in capabilities or attitudes that are not immediately apparent in performance.

Latent inhibition Describes the observation that unreinforced pre-exposure to a conditioning stimulus reduces the likelihood that it will be associated with a subsequent conditioned response.

Lateralization A term that refers to the division of functions and capabilities between the two hemispheres of the brain.

Law A statement whose accuracy is beyond reasonable doubt. (See *belief*; *principle.*)

Law of effect A Thorndikean law of learning stating that the *satisfying* or *annoying* effect of a response leads to its being learned (stamped in) or not learned (stamped out).

Law of exercise One of Thorndike's laws of learning; basic to his pre-1930s system but essentially repudiated later. It maintained that the more frequently, recently, and vigorously a connection was exercised, the stronger it would be.

Law of multiple responses Law based on Thorndike's observation that learning involves the emission of a variety of responses (multiple responses) until one

	is reinforced. Because of this law, Thorndike's theory is often referred to as a theory of trial-and-error learning.
Law of prepotency of elements	A Thorndikean law of learning stating that people tend to respond to the most striking of the various elements that make up a stimulus situation.
Law of readiness	A Thorndikean law of learning stating that certain types of learning are impossible or difficult unless the learner is ready. In this context, readiness refers to maturational level, previous learning, motivational factors, and other characteristics of the individual that relate to learning.
Law of response by analogy	An analogy is typically an explanation, comparison, or illustration based on similarity. In Thorndike's system, response by analogy refers to responses that occur because of similarities between two situations. (See *theory of identical elements*.)
Law of set or attitude	A Thorndikean law of learning that recognizes that we are often predisposed to respond in certain ways as a result of our experiences and previously learned attitudes.
Learning	All relatively permanent changes in behavior that result from experience but that are not caused by fatigue, maturation, drugs, injury, or disease.
Learning styles	Label given to the learner's habitual or preferred approach to learning. Refers to a characteristic way of processing or acquiring information. (See *intellectual styles*.)
Learning theory	A systematic attempt to explain and understand how behavior changes. The phrase *behavior theory* is used synonymously.
Level of processing	Craik and Lockhart's suggestion that remembering is largely a function of the nature and extent of processing of material to be remembered. At the level of sensory storage, little or no processing occurs, and forgetting occurs almost immediately. Material in long-term storage has been encoded (processed) for meaning and may be retained indefinitely.
Leveling	In Gestalt theory, a tendency to smooth out peculiarities in a perceptual pattern. Also applies to learning and remembering.
Libido	A general Freudian term denoting sexual urges. The libido is assumed to be the source of energy for sexual urges, which are the most important force in human motivation.
Likert scale	A widely used scale in psychological research, where respondents indicate their level of agreement with a statement.
Limbic system	A grouping of brain structures located beneath the cerebral cortex, associated mainly with emotion, memory, reinforcement, and punishment.

Locus of control	Rotter's expression for an individual's tendency to attribute responsibility for behavior and its outcomes to external sources (for example, the individual blames others for failure) or internal sources (for example, the individual accepts full responsibility for successes and failures).
Logical construct	Also termed *hypothetical construct*. A label for assumed or invented entities that cannot be observed and whose existence cannot be proven. In scientific theories, logical constructs follow from observations and are postulated as attempts to explain observations.
Long-term depression (LTD)	A neurological change defined by a lasting decline in the strength of the connection between two neurons (a decline in synaptic strength).
Long-term memory (LTM)	A type of memory whereby, with continued rehearsal and recoding of sensory input (processing in terms of meaning, for example), material will be available for recall over a long period.
Long-term potentiation (LTP)	A lasting neurological change defined by an increase in the responsiveness of neurons.
Magazine training	The process of teaching an organism about the reward available in an experimental conditioning chamber so conditioning of some specific operant can occur.
Magnetoencephalogram (MEG)	A recording of magnetic fields that correspond to electrical activity of the brain. MEG recordings are obtained at the scalp by means of a magnetoencephalograph to yield event-related fields (ERFs).
Malware	Malicious software designed to surreptitiously enter a computer to profit its creator, wreak harm on the infected computer, or both. Malware includes viruses, worms, spyware, etc.
Mastery goal	A goal directed toward increasing one's personal competence. (See *entity theory*; *incremental theory*; *performance goal*.)
Matching law	An expression of Herrnstein's observation that in a choice situation, an organism's responses tend to be guided by the probability of reinforcement.
Maturation	The process of normal physical and psychological development. Maturation is defined as occurring independently of particular experiences.
Mechanistic behaviorism	Expression sometimes used to describe early behaviorist theories. Denotes a concern with the machine-like, predictable aspects of behavior and a refusal to consider mentalistic explanations for behavior.
Medial forebrain bundle	Group of nerve fibers in the limbic system associated with reinforcement.

Glossary

Memory	The ability to retain and retrieve recollections of past events and information. The information processing system involved in encoding, storing, and retrieving information. (See *forgetting*.)
Meta-analysis	A research procedure in which the results of many studies that have examined the same questions are reviewed and analyzed in an attempt to reach conclusions that are more generally valid.
Metaneeds	Maslow's term for higher needs (concerned with psychological and self-related functions rather than with biology). These include "needs" to know truth, beauty, and justice and to self-actualize.
Method of incompatible stimuli	One of Guthrie's techniques for breaking habits, involving presenting the stimulus complex associated with an unwanted habit in conjunction with other stimuli that lead to a response incompatible with the habit. (See *fatigue technique*; *threshold technique*.)
Méthode clinique	Piaget's experimental method, an interview technique in which questions are determined largely by the subject's responses. Its flexibility distinguishes it from ordinary interview techniques.
Millisecond	One-thousandth of a second. Hence, 1000 milliseconds equals 1 second.
Mind	Human consciousness; based in the brain and evident in thought, perception, feelings, imagination, and other mental processes. Our consciousness of *self*.
Mind–body problem	A general expression for questions related to the relationship between the body and the mind.
Mnemonic devices	Systematic aids to remembering, such as rhymes, acrostics, or visual imagery systems.
Mnemonist	Professional memorizer.
Modal model of memory	A general model of memory, the first version of which was proposed by Atkinson and Shiffrin in 1968. Describes memory in terms of three types of storage: sensory, working (short-term), and long-term.
Model	A representation, usually abstract, of some phenomenon or system. Alternatively, a pattern for behavior that can be copied by someone.
Modeling effect	The type of imitative behavior that involves learning a novel response. (See *eliciting effect*; *inhibitory effect*.)
Moore's law	The largely correct 1965 prediction that the computing capacity of a silicon chip would double every two years. Not really a law but simply a historical trend.
Mores	The established social conventions and customs of a group often considered essential to its identification and preservation as a distinct cultural group.

Moro reflex	The generalized startle reaction of a newborn infant. It typically involves throwing out the arms and feet symmetrically following sudden loss of support.
Motivation	The causes of behavior. The conscious or unconscious forces that lead to certain acts. (See *causes*; *reasons*.)
Movement-produced stimuli (MPS)	In Guthrie's system, proprioceptive (internal) stimulation that results from actions of muscles, glands, and tendons.
Nanosecond	One-thousand-millionth of a second – being one-billionth of a second. Hence, one billion nanoseconds equals one second.
Narratives	Literally, stories that transmit the details of an occurrence or of a series of events; a form of retelling. In psychology, personal narratives retell the story of our lives either to ourselves or to others. In Bruner's theory, narratives play a fundamental role in the construction of personal reality and meaning.
Nativism	A model that reflects the belief that the learner is born with biological and neurological constraints and predispositions that shape reactions to the world and that facilitate certain types of learning and behavior (such as imprinting in geese or learning language in people).
Nature–nurture controversy	A very old argument in psychology about whether genetics (nature) or environment (nurture) is more responsible for determining development. Also called the *heredity–environment question*.
Need	Ordinarily refers to a lack or deficit in the human organism. Needs may be either unlearned (termed *basic* or *physiological* – for example, the need for food or water) or learned (termed *psychological* – for example, the need for prestige or money).
Need for achievement	Expression for a personality characteristic evident in an individual's apparent need to achieve success (to accomplish, to do well, to win, to gain) and to avoid failure.
Negative reinforcement	An increase in the probability that a response will recur following the elimination or removal of a condition as a consequence(s) of the behavior. Ordinarily, negative reinforcement is the effect of a noxious stimulus that is removed as a result of a specific response. (See *punishment*.)
Negative reinforcer	An event that has the effect of increasing the probability of occurrence of the response that immediately precedes it. Negative reinforcement ordinarily takes the form of an unpleasant stimulus that is removed as a result of a specific response.
Negative transfer	The interference of previous learning with new learning or with problem solving, creative endeavors, or other related behaviors. (See *positive transfer*.)

Glossary

Neobehaviorist	A label Hull used to emphasize that, unlike the earlier behaviorists, he did not limit his theory to observable stimuli and responses but also considered what occurs between the presentation of a stimulus and the occurrence of a response.
Nerve	Bundle of neurons.
Nervous system	The part of the body that is composed of neurons. Its major components are the brain and the spinal cord (the central nervous system), and receptor systems associated with major senses, as well as effector systems associated with functioning of muscles and glands (the peripheral nervous system).
Net reaction potential	In Hull's system, the result of subtracting the tendency not to respond (called *inhibitory potential*) from the tendency to respond (called *reaction potential*).
Neural network	A connectionist model of brain functioning premised on the functioning of the parallel processing computer. Neural networks are complex arrangements of units that activate each other and modify their patterns of connections. In this model, meaning resides in patterns within the network, and responses are also determined by patterns.
Neurofeedback	A form of biofeedback in which participants are given information about their neurological functioning. Typically involves specific information about electrical activity in the brain. (See *biofeedback*.)
Neurogenesis	The process by which new nerve cells (neurons) are formed.
Neuron	A single nerve cell; the basic building block of the human nervous system. Neurons consist of four main parts: cell body, nucleus, dendrites, and axon.
Neurotransmitters	Naturally produced chemicals that are released by nerve cells and whose function it is to initiate or facilitate transmission of messages among neurons. The number of known neurotransmitters approaches 100, the best known of which are serotonin, dopamine, norepinephrine, and acetylcholine.
Nocebo effect	A sort of reverse placebo effect, where a person's belief in probable negative consequences, say of a treatment or a diagnosis, increases the likelihood of gloomy outcomes.
Nominal fallacy	The assumption that naming something explains it.
Nondeclarative memory	Also termed *implicit* or *procedural memory*, refers to unconscious, nonverbalizable effects of experience, such as might be manifested in acquired motor skills or in classical conditioning.
Nonsense syllables	Meaningless but *readable* combinations of letters and vowels usually consisting of a single syllable, such as *lar*, *vor*, or *kev*; often used in studies of memory.

Glossary | 481

Norepinephrine	A neurotransmitter linked with arousal, memory, and learning. Also called *noradrenaline*. Anomalies in the functioning of the norepinephrine system may be linked to some manifestations of depression.
Normalizing	A Gestalt principle describing the tendency for memories to change so they become closer to other related memories.
Novice-to-expert	An information-processing model of the learner reflecting the view that the differences between those who can (experts) and those who cannot (novices) can be determined and used to make novices more like experts. Less general and more domain-specific than other models.
Object concept	Piaget's expression for the child's understanding that the world is composed of objects that continue to exist apart from his or her perception of them.
Observational learning	A term used synonymously with the expression "learning through imitation." (See *imitation*.)
Occam's razor	Also called the *law of parsimony*. A principle, attributed to William of Occam, which holds that unless it is absolutely necessary, things that cannot be proven to exist should not be assumed to be real. Typically interpreted to mean that the simplest of competing explanations is preferable.
Occipital lobe	Part of the cerebral cortex located at the rear of the brain; importantly involved in vision. (See *frontal lobe*; *temporal lobe*; *parietal lobe*.)
Operant	Skinner's term for a response not elicited by any known or obvious stimulus. Most significant human behaviors appear to be operants (for example, writing a text or going for a walk).
Operant conditioning	The process of changing behavior by manipulating its consequences. Most of Skinner's work investigates the principles of operant conditioning. (See *classical conditioning*; *conditioning*.)
Operation	A Piagetian term referring to a thought process. An operation is an action that has been internalized in the sense that it can be "thought" and is reversible in the sense that it can be "unthought."
Operational definition	A definition that describes a variable by precise actions (operations) that can be observed and measured.
Organization	A memory strategy involving grouping items to be remembered in terms of similarities and differences.
Orienting reflex (OR)	The initial response of humans and other organisms to novel stimulation. Components of the orienting response include changes in electrical activity in the brain, in respiration and heart

	rate, and in conductivity of the skin to electricity. The orienting reflex is an alerting response.
Output variables	Hull's phrase for what the organism does (that is, the response). Output variables include response latency, response amplitude, and the number of responses required before extinction.
Overjustification hypothesis	The belief that providing substantial extrinsic rewards for an activity that is initially intrinsically motivated can have the effect of undermining intrinsic motivation.
Paradigm	A pattern or model. A theoretical, philosophical, or scientific framework that guides investigations, theories, and conclusions.
Parallel processing	Describes computer processing where several functions are carried out simultaneously and are related to common sets of input and output. Parallel processing is the basis for connectionist models and simulations of human thinking and underlies artificial intelligence.
Paranormal phenomena	Referring to experiences that lie outside the ordinary senses – that are *beyond normal*. Phenomena that are inconsistent with the world as we understand it through science. (See *pseudoscience*.)
Parietal lobe	Cerebral lobes located just above the temporal lobes, between the frontal and occipital lobes. The parietal lobes are involved in sensation. (See *occipital lobe*; *temporal lobe*; *frontal lobe*.)
Parsimonious	Avoiding excessive and confusing detail and complexity. Parsimonious theories explain all important relationships in the simplest, briefest manner possible.
Pedology	A Soviet discipline of child development, very popular in the Soviet Union in the 1930s, that used Western tests for psychoassessment. Vygotsky and Luria were pedologists. In the mid-1930s, the Soviet government decreed that pedology was a "bourgeois pseudoscience" and ordered that it should no longer be written about, researched, or even discussed, wiping out all pedology centers and putting all pedologists out of work.
Percept	A term Bruner used to refer to the effect of sensory experiences. In Bruner's system, percepts are equivalent to concepts. (See *concept*.)
Perception	Becoming aware of the meaning of that which is sensed. Interpreting and giving meaning to sensation.
Performance	Actual behavior. The act of completing a task or function. Often used as evidence that learning has occurred, although learning can also be latent (potential) rather than evident in performance.
Performance goal	A goal directed toward performing well rather than toward mastering a subject and increasing one's competence. (See *entity theory*; *incremental theory*; *mastery goal*.)

Glossary | 483

Periventricular tract	Group of nerve fibers in the limbic system associated with punishment.
Personalized System of Instruction (PSI)	A *mastery learning* instructional approach in which material is broken down into small units, learners progress through this material at their own pace, tests are given frequently, and progress depends on mastery as revealed in performance on the tests.
Phase sequence	In Hebb's system, an integrated arrangement of related cell assemblies. Corresponds to a concept or percept. (See *cell assembly*.)
Phonological loop	In Baddeley's model of working memory, one of the slave systems responsible for maintaining verbal information, such as words or numbers, in consciousness. (See *central executive system*; *episodic buffer*; *visual-spatial sketch pad*.)
Physiological needs	Basic biological needs, such as the need for food and water.
Pineal gland	A small, reddish, conical organ found near the base of the brain. It produces *melatonin*, involved in sleep regulation.
Placebo	A substance such as a drug, or a procedure, that has no therapeutic effect. Sometimes used to calm or please a patient, or to determine whether a treatment has a real effect.
Placebo effect	Describes the frequently observed beneficial effects of a treatment or substance that is known to have no intrinsic beneficial effects. The placebo effect is generally attributed to the patient's belief in the effectiveness of the treatment.
Pleasure center	Term Olds and Milner used to describe the part of the brain thought to be involved in reinforcement – specifically, a part of the hypothalamus that includes a group of nerve fibers known as the medial forebrain bundle located in the limbic system (a part of the brain that includes the hypothalamus and the thalamus, among other structures).
Pop psychology	*Popular* psychology, gleaned largely from magazines, television, and social media. Purports to be the real thing, but is largely *pseudopsychology*.
Population	Collections of individuals (or objects or situations) with similar characteristics. For example, the population of all first-grade children in North America. (See *sample*.)
Positive control	The control of human behavior through the presentation of pleasant stimuli. This is in contrast to techniques of aversive control, which generally use negative reinforcement and punishment.
Positive reinforcement	An increase in the probability that a response will recur as a result of a positive consequence(s) resulting from that behavior (that is, as a result of the addition of something). Usually is the effect of a pleasant stimulus (reward) that results from a specific response.

Glossary

Positive reinforcer An event added to a situation immediately after a response has occurred that increases the probability that the response will recur. Usually takes the form of a pleasant stimulus (reward) that results from a specific response.

Positive transfer A situation where previous learning is helpful in situations requiring new learning, problem solving, creative production, and related activities. (See *negative transfer*.)

Positron emission tomography (PET) An imaging technique used extensively in medicine and in physiological and neurological research. Records changes in blood flow by detecting the distribution of radioactive particles injected in the bloodstream.

Prägnanz A German word meaning "good form." An overriding Gestalt principle that maintains that what we perceive (and think) tends to take the best possible form, where *best* usually refers to a principle such as closure, continuity, similarity, or proximity. (See *closure*; *continuity*; *similarity*; *proximity*.)

Preconceptual thinking The first substage in the period of preoperational thought, beginning around age two and lasting until age four. It is so called because the child has not yet developed the ability to classify.

Premack principle The recognition that behaviors that are chosen frequently by an individual and that are therefore favored may be used to reinforce other, less frequently chosen behaviors (for example, "You can watch television when you've finished your homework").

Preoperational thinking The second of Piaget's four major stages, lasting from around age two to age seven or eight, characterized by certain weaknesses in the child's logic. It consists of two substages: intuitive thinking and preconceptual thinking. (See *intuitive thinking*; *preconceptual thinking*.)

Preparedness Describes learning situations where, for a given organism, biology has made certain kinds of learning exceptionally likely and easy. (See *contrapreparedness*.)

Primary reinforcer An event that is reinforcing in the absence of any learning. Stimuli such as food and drink are primary reinforcers because, presumably, an organism does not have to learn that they're pleasant.

Principle A statement relating to some uniformity or predictability. Principles are far more open to doubt than are laws but are more reliable than beliefs. (See *belief*; *law*; *theory*.)

Principle of belongingness Thorndike's belief that certain responses are easier to learn because, for cultural or logical reasons, they seem to go with (belong with) certain stimuli.

Proactive interference The interference of earlier learning with the retention of subsequent learning. (See *retroactive interference*.)

Productive thinking	Wertheimer's expression for the type of thinking that results from insight rather than from rote learning. Often used as a synonym for *creative thinking*.
Programmed instruction	An instructional procedure based on Skinnerian principles. It presents information systematically in small steps, often via computers or in the form of a workbook, requires frequent learner responses, and offers immediate reinforcement by providing the learner with information about the correctness of responses.
Progressive ratio (PR) schedule	An operant conditioning schedule of reinforcement where the ratio of correct responses required for reinforcement increases systematically during an experimental session.
Propositional thinking	A Piagetian label for the thinking of the formal-operations child. A proposition is a statement that can be true or false; hence, propositional thinking is the ability to think about abstract, hypothetical states of affairs.
Proprioceptive stimulation	Refers to internal sensations (relating to what's termed *kinesthetic sensation*), such as those associated with movements of muscles. (See *exteroceptive stimulation*.)
Prototype model	An original model that serves as a basis for other models. In concept learning, a prototype is an abstraction of the most average or representative features of a concept, to which new instances can be compared. (See *exemplar model*.)
Proximity	A Gestalt principle manifested in the tendency to perceive elements that are close together as being related. (See *closure*; *continuity*; *prägnanz*; *similarity*.)
Pseudoscience	Literally, false or fake science. Approaches or beliefs that purport to be scientific but that violate the rules and approaches of science. (See *science*.)
Psychological hedonism	Describes goals that focus on happiness and are premised on pleasure attainment and pain avoidance.
Psychological needs	Human needs other than those dealing with basic physical requirements such as food, sex, water, and temperature regulation (physiological needs). Psychological needs described by Maslow include the need to belong, to feel safe, to love and be loved, to maintain a high opinion of oneself, and to self-actualize. (See *self-actualization*.)
Psychology	The science that examines human thought and behavior (and also that of other animals). Also often defined as the science that studies the mind and mental processes.
Psychophysics	The measurement of physical stimuli and their effects.
Psychotherapy	A very general term for the variety of techniques used to alleviate mental disorders and emotional problems. Usually restricted to

Glossary

	procedures undertaken by psychiatrists, psychologists, and other specially trained individuals.
Punishment	Involves either the presentation of an unpleasant stimulus or the withdrawal of a pleasant stimulus as a consequence of behavior. Punishment should not be confused with negative reinforcement. (See *negative reinforcement*.)
Purposive behaviorism	Tolman's label for his theory, meant to underline his belief that the behavior of even nonhuman animals is purposeful (goal-directed) rather than simply a mindless reaction to stimuli, rewards, and punishments.
Questionnaires	Data gathering devices consisting of lists of predetermined questions to which subjects respond.
Radical behaviorism	Label applied by Skinner to distinguish his behaviorism from other behaviorist positions less insistent on not making inferences about mental states. In this sense, radical means root: Radical behaviorism maintains that the "root" (or origin) of psychological knowledge is observable behavior.
Random	Where the outcome cannot be predicted; attributable solely to chance. In a randomly selected sample, every member has the same probability of being selected.
Random schedule	Also called *variable schedule*; a type of intermittent schedule of reinforcement. It may be of either the interval or the ratio variety and is characterized by the presentation of rewards at random intervals or on random trials. Although fixed and random schedules may be based on the same intervals or on the same ratios, one can predict when a reward will occur under a fixed schedule, whereas it's impossible to do so under a random schedule.
Rate of learning	A measure of the amount of time or number of trials required to learn a correct response.
Ratio schedule	An intermittent schedule of reinforcement that is based on a proportion of correct responses. (See *fixed schedule*; *random schedule*.)
Reaction potential (sEr)	In Hull's system, the probability that stimulus conditions will lead to a response. Reaction potential is a combined function of specific intervening variables that reflect the individual's history as well as present stimulus conditions.
Reaction threshold (sLr)	In Hull's system, the magnitude of net reaction potential required before a response occurs.
Reasons	Explanations for or defenses of an action. In psychology, reasons are often treated as motives. (See *causes*; *motivation*.)
Reception learning	The type of learning that involves primarily instruction or tuition rather than the learner's own efforts. Often associated with Ausubel, reception learning usually involves expository or didactic teaching methods. (See *discovery learning*.)

Reciprocal determinism	Bandura's notion that personal characteristics, behavior, and the environment all affect each other reciprocally – that individuals are both products and producers of their environments. (See *triadic reciprocal determinism.*)
Reductio ad absurdum	A Latin phrase meaning, literally, reduced to the absurd. Refers to an argument in which a case is disproven by following its implications to an absurd conclusion.
Reductionist	Term used to describe theories that try to understand a process or a phenomenon by reducing it to its smallest components.
Reflex	A simple, unlearned stimulus–response link, such as salivating in response to food in one's mouth or blinking in response to air blowing into one's eye.
Refractory period	A brief period after firing during which a neuron is "discharged" and is incapable of firing again.
Rehearsal	A memory strategy involving simple repetition. The principal means of maintaining items in short-term memory.
Reinforcement	The effect of a reinforcer; specifically, to increase the probability that a response will occur. (See *negative reinforcement; positive reinforcement.*)
Reinforcer	An event associated with a response that changes the probability of that response occurring again. (See *reinforcement.*)
Repression theory	A theory of forgetting based on the notion that unpleasant, anxiety-provoking experiences might be blocked from consciousness in a self-protective move.
Reprimands	A mild form of punishment involving indications of disapproval – usually verbal but sometimes consisting of gestures (such as shaking one's head to indicate no).
Rescorla–Wagner model	A model based on the notion that contiguity is neither sufficient nor necessary to explain classical conditioning. Instead, it holds that what is learned in classical conditioning are relations among events (expectancies).
Respondent	Skinner's term for a response that, unlike an operant, is elicited by a known, specific stimulus. Unconditioned responses are examples of respondents. (See *unconditioned response.*)
Response amplitude (A)	In Hull's system, the physical strength of a response.
Response cost	A mild form of punishment in which tangible reinforcers that have been given for good behavior are taken away for misbehavior. Response-cost systems are often used in systematic behavior management programs.
Response latency $(_st_r)$	Time lag between the presentation of a stimulus and the appearance of a response.
Resting potential	Describes the state of a neuron when it is not transmitting impulses or being stimulated, but is electrically and chemically ready to do so.

Glossary

Reticular formation   The upper portion of the brain stem that appears to be importantly involved in the physiological arousal of the cortex and in the control of sleeping and waking. Forms part of the midbrain.

Retrieval cues   Stimuli such as sounds, words, locations, smells, and so on, that facilitate recall (that *remind* the individual of something).

Retrieval-cue failure   Inability to remember because of the unavailability of appropriate cues (as opposed to changes in memory "traces").

Retroactive interference   The interference of subsequently learned material with the retention of previously learned material. (See *proactive interference.*)

Reversibility   A logical property manifested in the ability to reverse or undo activity in either an empirical or a conceptual sense. An idea is said to be reversible when a child realizes the logical consequences of an opposite action.

Sample   A subset of a population. A representative selection of individuals with similar characteristics drawn from a larger group. (See *population.*)

Sapir–Whorf hypothesis   In its *strong* form, the belief that language is essential for thought and that different languages lead people to think and behave differently. In a weaker form, the belief that language *limits* but does not *determine* thought.

Scaffolding   A Vygotskian concept to describe the various types of support that teachers and parents need to provide for children if they are to learn. Scaffolding often takes the form of directions, suggestions, and other forms of verbal assistance and is most effective if it involves tasks within the child's zone of proximal development. (See *zone of proximal development.*)

Schedule of reinforcement   The timing and frequency of presentation of reinforcement to organisms. (See *continuous reinforcement*; *intermittent reinforcement.*)

Schema   The label Piaget used to describe a unit in cognitive structure. In one sense, a schema is an activity together with whatever biology or neurology might underlie that activity. In another sense, a schema may be thought of as an idea or a concept.

Science   An approach and an attitude toward knowledge that emphasizes objectivity, precision, and replicability. Also, one of several related bodies of knowledge.

Secondary reinforcer   An event that becomes reinforcing as a result of being paired with other reinforcers.

Second-order conditioning   In classical conditioning, the forming of associations between the CS and other stimuli that take the place of the US (typically other stimuli that have been paired with the US).

Self-actualization	The process or act of becoming oneself, developing one's potential, of achieving an awareness of one's identity, or of self-fulfillment. The term is central in humanistic psychology.
Self-determination theory	Deci and Ryan's cognitive theory of motivation, based on the assumption that people need to be self-determined, to feel autonomous and competent, and to develop close relations with others. The theory is highly compatible with attribution theory.
Self-efficacy	Judgments we make about how effective we are in given situations. Judgments of self-efficacy are important in determining an individual's choice of activities and in influencing the amount of interest and effort expended. (See *collective efficacy*.)
Self-referent thought	A thought that pertains to the self. Self-referent thought concerns our own mental processes (for example, thoughts that evaluate our abilities or monitor our progress in solving problems).
Self-regulated learner	Describes learners who are autonomous and self-directed in that they set their own goals, devise and apply strategies to reach them, evaluate their strategies and actions as these are being applied, and modify both goals and strategies when necessary.
Semantic memory	A type of declarative (conscious, long-term) memory consisting of stable knowledge about the world, principles, rules and procedures, and other verbalizable aspects of knowledge, including language.
Sensitization	A common form of learning in which an organism's response to stimulation increases in intensity. Most often occurs following intense stimulation. (See *habituation*.)
Sensorimotor intelligence	The first stage of development in Piaget's classification. It lasts from birth to approximately age two and is so called because children understand their world during that period primarily in terms of their activities in it and sensations of it.
Sensory deprivation	Refers to experiments in which subjects are kept in conditions of unvarying sensory stimulation over long periods.
Sensory memory	The fleeting, largely unconscious effect of stimuli such as a sound, a taste, or a sight. (See *working memory*; *long term memory*.)
Serial processing	Describes the functioning of computers that carried out a single operation at a time. Prior to 2005, personal computers were almost invariably serial processors. Now the vast majority have more than one *core* and can therefore carry out different, parallel operations simultaneously. (See *parallel processing*.)
Serotonin	A neurotransmitter, the bulk of which is found in the gut where it regulates intestinal activity. Also importantly implicated in human emotion as well as in cognitive activity. Too low levels of serotonin may be associated with depression.

Glossary

Set	A tendency to respond or perceive in a predetermined way.
Shaping	A technique for training animals and people to perform behaviors not previously in their repertoires. It involves reinforcing responses that are progressively closer approximations to the desired behavior. Also called the method of successive approximations or the method of differential reinforcement of successive approximations.
Sharpening	In Gestalt psychology, a tendency, evident with the passage of time, to exaggerate the most distinctive features of a memory.
Short-term memory	The *working memory* stage in which material is available for recall for a matter of seconds. It defines immediate consciousness. (See *working memory*.)
Significant	In research, refers to findings that would not be expected to occur by chance alone more than a small percentage of the time (for example, 5 percent or 1 percent).
Sign-tracking	Describes the tendency of organisms to respond to *signs* related to survival, eating, mating, and other genetically programmed tendencies. May lead to learning labeled *autoshaping*. (See *autoshaping*.)
Similarity	A Gestalt principle recognizing our tendency to perceive similar items as though they belonged together. (See *closure*; *continuity*; *prägnanz*; *proximity*.)
Simultaneous pairing	The presentation of CS and US at exactly the same time in classical conditioning. (See *backward pairing*; *delayed pairing*; *trace pairing*.)
Single-blind procedure	An experimental procedure where either the subjects or the investigator aren't aware of who are members of the experimental group and who are members of the control group. (See *double-blind procedure*.)
Skinner box	One of various experimental environments Skinner used in his investigations of operant conditioning. The typical Skinner box is a cage-like structure equipped with a lever and a food tray attached to a food-delivering mechanism. It allows the investigator to study operants (for example, bar-pressing) and the relationship between an operant and reinforcement.
Social cognitive theory	A label for Bandura's theory, which explains social learning through imitation using the principles of operant conditioning while recognizing the importance of cognitive activities such as imagining, symbolizing, and anticipating.
Social learning	The acquisition of patterns of behavior that conform to social expectations; learning what is acceptable and what is not acceptable in a given culture. Also, learning that involves interaction among individuals.

Glossary 491

Social speech	In Vygotsky's theorizing, the most primitive stage of language development, evident before age three, during which the child expresses simple thoughts and emotions out loud. The function of social speech is to control the behavior of others. (See *egocentric speech*; *inner speech*.)
Socialization	The complex process of learning both those behaviors that are appropriate within a given culture and those that are less appropriate. The primary agents of socialization are home, school, and peer groups.
Sociobiology	A discipline that applies the findings of biology, anthropology, and ethology to the understanding of human social behavior. Sociobiology looks for biological explanations for behavior.
Socioeconomic status (SES)	Relative position on a scale that reflects such factors as education, income, type of occupation, social status, and so on.
Software	Computer instructions or programs. (See *hardware*; *wetware*.)
Soma	Label for the cell body of a neuron. The main part of the neuron, containing the nucleus.
Spaced repetition	A learning technique where the learner repeats a skill or rehearses a grouping of information for a while, leaves it, returns to it, leaves it again, returns, and so on. See *blocked repetition*; *interleaving*.
Spontaneous recovery	The apparently spontaneous reappearance of a response that had previously been extinguished. (See *extinction*.)
Spread of effect	Thorndike's observation that rewards sometimes strengthen connections between a stimulus and a specific response and between the stimulus and other closely related responses.
SQ3R method	A study technique, especially valuable for textbook material and lecture notes, that requires the learner to *survey*, *question*, *read*, *recite*, and *review* key content.
Stimulus discrimination	(See *discrimination*.)
Stimulus generalization	(See *generalization*.)
Stimulus-intensity dynamism (V)	Hull's label for the effect of stimulus intensity on the individual. In general, the more intense a stimulus, the higher the probability of a response.
Structuralism	The first "school" in psychology, associated with Wilhelm Wundt, based on the notion that the mind can be best understood by analyzing its elements (looking at its component structure) using introspection. Studied such "elements" of consciousness as sensations, feelings, and images. (See *functionalism*.)
Sucking reflex	The automatic sucking response of a newborn child when the mouth area is stimulated.
Superstitious schedule	A kind of fixed interval schedule of reinforcement where reinforcement occurs after a fixed time interval no matter what

492 | **Glossary**

the organism is doing, sometimes leading to bizarre and unpredictable behaviors.

Surveys A collection of observations based on a sample (often large) representing some population.

Symbol shock A rare condition among students exposed to an overwhelming assortment of abstract symbols, the symptoms of which are bizarre and indescribable. There is no cheap cure.

Symbolic model In Bandura's theory of observational learning, a model other than a real-life person. For example, books, television, technological media, and written instructions are important symbolic models. In the computer-based study of human cognitive processes, a representation of human cognitive activities in terms of symbols such as language that can be programmed into software designed to investigate and perhaps to duplicate cognitive functioning. (See *connectionist model*.)

Symbolic representation In Bruner's system, the final stage in the development of a child's representation of the world. Symbolic representation uses arbitrary symbols such as language. (See *enactive representation*; *iconic representation*.)

Sympathetic nervous system Part of the nervous system that instigates the physiological responses associated with emotion.

Synapse A bridge or junction between neurons; a space between neurons that can be crossed by an electrical impulse.

Synaptic cleft Label for the space between terminal boutons (*synaptic knobs*) at the ends of axons and the dendrites or cell bodies of adjoining neurons.

Synaptic knobs Also called *terminal boutons*, slight enlargements on the wispy branches at the ends of axons.

Systematic desensitization A therapeutic approach designed to replace undesirable responses with those that are more desirable through conditioning. (See also *counterconditioning*.)

Tabula rasa Literally, blank slate. A model of the learner based on the assumption that people are born equal, each with no prior learning, inclinations, or thoughts and ready to be shaped by experience, like identical blank slates ready to be written on.

Taste aversion A powerful disinclination toward eating or drinking certain substances. Taste aversions are easily learned, often after a single exposure, are highly resistant to extinction, and demonstrate biological constraints.

Temporal lobe Cerebral structure located on either side of the cerebrum, associated primarily with speech, language, and hearing. (See *occipital lobe*; *frontal lobe*; *parietal lobe*.)

Terminal bouton	Also called synaptic knobs, these are slight enlargements on the hair-like branches at the ends of axons.
Testing effect	A phrase used to describe the observation that testing has long-term beneficial effects on learning and memory.
Thalamus	A tiny structure at the base of the brain that serves as the major relay center for incoming sensory stimulation.
Theory	A body of information pertaining to a specific topic, a method of acquiring or dealing with information, or a set of explanations for related phenomena.
Theory of identical elements	A Thorndikean theory that holds that similar stimuli are related because two situations possess a number of identical elements, and these identical elements lead to transfer of responses from one situation to another.
Theory of natural selection	Darwin's notion that variations that provide species with a survival and reproductive edge tend to become more common through succeeding generations.
Threshold technique	A method for breaking habits described by Guthrie in which the stimulus complex associated with an undesirable habit is presented in such mild form that the habit is not elicited. Stimulus intensity is gradually increased. (See *fatigue technique*; *method of incompatible stimuli.*)
Time-in	A reinforcement procedure sometimes used in combination with time-out procedures. Time-in involves *including* children and exposing them to reinforcers, such as praise and physical contact (in contrast with *time-out*, which involves excluding and not reinforcing). (See *time-out.*)
Time-out	A procedure in which students are removed from situations in which they might ordinarily be rewarded. Time-out procedures are widely used in classroom management.
Token	Something indicative of something else. In behavior management programs, token reinforcement systems involve using objects such as disks or point tallies that are themselves worthless but can later be exchanged for more meaningful reinforcement.
Trace pairing	In classical conditioning, the presentation and termination of the CS before the US so there is a time lag between the two. (See *backward pairing*; *delayed pairing*; *simultaneous pairing.*)
Trace-dependent forgetting	Forgetting related to actual changes in presumed neurological memory traces. Illustrated by forgetting due to brain injury or gradual forgetting with the passage of time. (See *cue-dependent forgetting.*)
Trait	A distinguishing feature of personality. A personal quality describable in terms of a trait name such as kind, generous, impulsive, mean, etc.

Transductive	The type of reasoning that proceeds from particular to particular rather than from particular to general or from general to particular. One example of transductive reasoning is the following: Cows give milk, and goats give milk; therefore, goats are cows.
Transfer	A general term for the application of old learning to a new situation. Also termed *generalization*. (See *generalization*.)
Triadic reciprocal determinism	Label used by Bandura to emphasize that the reciprocal interactions between person and environment also include the person's behavior. All three influence and change each other. (See *reciprocal determinism*.)
Trial and error	Thorndikean explanation for learning based on the idea that when placed in a problem situation, an individual will emit a number of responses but will eventually learn the correct one as a result of reinforcement. Trial-and-error explanations for learning are sometimes contrasted with insight explanations.
Turing test	The assumption that if thing A duplicates exactly thing B's functions, then thing A must have the same qualities as thing B.
Umami	Considered to be one of the five distinct tastes humans can distinguish (the others are sweet, sour, salt, and bitter). It is sometimes described as *meaty* or *savory* and is evident in the flavor of monosodium glutamate.
Unconditioned response (UR)	A response that is elicited by an unconditioned stimulus.
Unconditioned stimulus (US)	A stimulus that elicits a response before learning. All stimuli that are capable of eliciting reflexive behaviors are examples of unconditioned stimuli. For example, food is an unconditioned stimulus for the response of salivation.
Variable	A property, measurement, or characteristic that can vary from one situation to another. In psychological investigations, qualities such as intelligence, sex, personality, age, and so on, can be important variables.
Vicarious reinforcement	Reinforcement that results from observing someone else being reinforced. In imitative behavior, observers often act as though they are being reinforced when in fact they are not, but they think that the model is.
Virtual reality (VR)	A computer-based simulation that typically involves a number of sensory systems (such as bodily sensations, visual images, and auditory signals) in order to produce a sensation of realism.
Visual-spatial sketch pad	One of the slave systems in Baddeley's model of working memory. Concerned with processing material that is primarily visual or spatial. (See *central executive system*; *phonological loop*; *episodic buffer*; *working memory*.)

Vygotsky blocks	A set of 22 wooden blocks of different colors, heights, shapes, and horizontal area (size). Used to study the development of thought and language.
Weber's law	Just noticeable differences (JNDs) require proportionally greater increases as stimulus intensity increases.
Wetware	The brain's neurons and their interconnections. Corresponds to hardware in the computer metaphor. (See *hardware*; *software*.)
Working memory	(or *short-term memory*) Baddeley's model describing how information is processed in short-term memory by means of a control system (central executive system) and systems that maintain verbal material (phonological loop) and visual material (visual-spatial sketch pad). (See *central executive system*; *phonological loop*; *visual-spatial sketch pad*.)
Yerkes–Dodson law	States that the effectiveness of performance is an inverted U-shaped function of arousal, such that very low and very high levels of arousal are associated with least effective behavior.
Zeitgeist	A German word meaning the spirit of the times. Refers to the defining intellectual, political, or cultural characteristics of a historical period.
Zone of proximal development	(also called the *zone of proximal growth*) Vygotsky's phrase for the individual's current potential for further intellectual development.

REFERENCES

Abravanel, E., & Ferguson, S. A. (1998). Observational learning and the use of retrieval information during the second and third years. *Journal of Genetic Psychology, 159*, 455–476.

Addis, D. R., Barense, M., & Duarte, A. (2015). *The Wiley handbook on the cognitive neuroscience of memory.* New York: Wiley-Blackwell.

Aetna (2018). Chemical aversive conditioning for alcohol. Retrieved October 11, 2018, from www.aetna.com/cpb/medical/data/800_899/0896.html

Ahrens, L. M., Pauli, P., Reif, A., Muhlberger, A., Langs, G., Aalderink, T., & Wieser, M. J. (2016). Fear conditioning and stimulus generalization in patients with social anxiety disorder. *Journal of Anxiety Disorders, 44*, 36–46. doi:10.1016/j.janxdis.2016.10.003.

Akera, A. (2017). Bringing radical behaviorism to revolutionary Brazil and back: Fred Keller's Personalized System of Instruction and Cold War engineering education. *Journal of the History of the Behavioral Sciences, 53*(4), 364–382.

Alam, M. J., Kitamura, T., Saitoh, Y., Ohkawa, N., Kondo, T., & Inokuchi, K. (2018). Adult neurogenesis conserves hippocampal memory capacity. *The Journal of Neuroscience. 38*(31), 6854–6863.

Alcock, J. (2001). *The triumph of sociobiology.* Oxford: Oxford University Press.

Alferink, L. A., Critchfield, T. S., Hitt, J. L., & Higgins, W. J. (2009). Generality of the matching law as a descriptor of shot selection in basketball. *Journal of Applied Behavior Analysis, 42*(3), 595–608.

Allman, W. F. (1989). *Apprentices of wonder: Inside the neural network revolution.* New York: Bantam.

Alvarez, T. A., & Fiez, J. A. (2018). Current perspectives on the cerebellum and reading development. *Neuroscience and Biobehavioral Reviews, 92*, 55–66.

Alves, C. A., Lopes, E. L., & Hernandez, J. M. (2017). It makes me feel so good: An experimental study of the placebo effect generated by brands. *Journal of International Consumer Marketing, 29*(4), 223–238.

American Psychological Association (2012). *APA guidelines for ethical conduct in the care and use of nonhuman animals in research.* Washington, DC: American Psychological Association. Retrieved September 27, 2018, from www.apa.org/science/leadership/care/care-animal-guidelines.pdf.

American Psychological Association (2016). Ethical principles of psychologists and code of conduct. Retrieved September 27, 2018, from www.apa.org/ethics/code.

Amsel, A. (1989). *Behaviorism, neobehaviorism, and cognitivism in learning theory: Historical and contemporary perspectives.* Hillsdale, NJ: Erlbaum.

Amsel, A. (1992). B. F. Skinner and the cognitive revolution. *Journal of Behavior Therapy and Experimental Psychiatry, 23*, 67–70.

Anderson, C. A., Bushman, B. J., Bartholow, B. D., Cantor, J., Christakis, D., Coyne, S. M., ..., Ybarra, M. (2017). Screen violence and youth behavior. *Pediatrics, 140*(5, Supp. 2), S142–S147.

Andersson, G., Waara, J., Jonsson, U., Malmaeus, F., Carlbring, P., & Ost, L. G. (2013). Internet-based exposure treatment versus one-session exposure treatment of snake phobia: A randomized controlled trial. *Cognitive Behaviour Therapy, 42*(4), 284–291.

Animal Behaviour (2012). Guidelines for the treatment of animals in behavioural research and teaching. *Animal Behaviour, 83*, 301–309. Retrieved September 27, 2018, from www.elsevier.com/__data/promis_misc/ASAB2006.pdf.

Annerback, E. M., Svedin, C. G., & Gustafsson, P. A., (2010). Characteristic features of severe child physical abuse: A multi-informant approach. *Journal of Family Violence*, *25*(2), 165–172.

Anscombe, E., & Geach, P. T. (Eds.). (1954). *Descartes: Philosophical writings*. New York: Thomas Nelson.

Aoun, J. (2018). *Robot-proof: Higher education in the age of artificial intelligence*. Cambridge, MA: MIT Press.

Ardila, A. (2016). L.S. Vygotsky in the 21st century. *Psychology in Russia: State of the Art*, *9*(4), 4–15.

Arluke, A. (2012). Bystander apathy in animal abuse cases: Exploring barriers to child and adolescent intervention. *Anthrozoos*, *25*(1), 5–23.

Arnone, D., Horder, J., Cowen, P. J., & Harmer, C. J. (2009). Early effects of mirtazapine on emotional processing. *Psychopharmacology*, *203*(4), 685–691.

Artino A. R. Jr. (2007). Bandura, Ross, and Ross: Observational learning and the Bobo doll. Online submission. (ERIC Document Reproduction Service No. ED499095)

Ashmore, M., & Brown, S. D. (2010). On changing one's mind twice: The strange credibility of retracting recovered memories. In J. Haaken & P. Reavey (Eds.), *Memory matters: Contexts for understanding sexual abuse recollections* (pp. 17–40). New York: Routledge.

Atkinson, J. W., & Shiffrin, R. M. (1968). Human memory: A proposed system and its control processes. In K. W. Spence & J. T. Spence (Eds.), *The psychology of learning and motivation* (Vol. 2, pp. 89–195). New York: Academic Press.

Aubrey, C. (1993). An investigation of the mathematical knowledge and competencies which young children bring into school. *British Educational Research Journal*, *19*, 27–41.

Auer, M., & Griffiths, M. D. (2018). Cognitive dissonance, personalized feedback, and online gambling behavior: An exploratory study using objective tracking data and subjective self-report. *International Journal of Mental Health and Addiction*, *16*(3), 631–641.

Austad, C. S., & Gendron, M. S. (2018). Biofeedback: Using the power of the mind–body connection, technology, and business in psychotherapies of the future. *Professional Psychology: Research and Practice*, *49*(4), 264–273.

Ausubel, D. P. (1977). The facilitation of meaningful verbal learning in the classroom. *Educational Psychologist*, *12*, 162–178.

Ausubel, D. P., & Robinson, F. G. (1969). *School learning: An introduction to educational psychology*. New York: Holt, Rinehart and Winston.

Babskie, E., Powell, D. N., & Metzger, A. (2017). Variability in parenting self-efficacy across prudential adolescent behaviors. *Parenting: Science and Practice*, *17*(4), 242–261.

Baddeley, A. D. (1997). *Human memory: Theory and practice* (rev. ed.). Hove: Psychology Press.

Baddeley, A. D. (2000). Short-term and working memory. In E. Tulving & F. I. M. Craik (Eds.), *The Oxford handbook of memory* (pp. 77–92). New York: Oxford University Press.

Baddeley, A. D. (2002). Is working memory still working? *European Psychologist*, *7*, 85–97.

Baddeley, A. D. (2007). *Working memory, thought, and action*. New York: Oxford University Press.

Baddeley, A. D., & Hitch, G. J. (1974). Working memory. In G. Bower (Ed.), *The psychology of learning and motivation* (Vol. 8, pp. 47–89). New York: Academic Press.

Baillargeon, R. (1987). Object permanence in 3½- and 4½-month-old infants. *Developmental Psychology*, *23*, 655–664.

Baillargeon, R. (1993). The object concept revisited. In C. Granrud (Ed.), *Visual perception and cognition in infancy: Carnegie-Mellon Symposia on Cognition* (Vol. 23, pp. 265–315). Hillsdale, NJ: Erlbaum.

Bakhtadze, S., Beridze, M., Geladze, N., Khachapuridze, N., & Bornstein, N. (2016). Effect of EEG biofeedback on cognitive flexibility in children with attention deficit hyperactivity disorder with and without epilepsy. *Applied Psychophysiology and Biofeedback*, *41*(1), 71–79

Bakhurst, D., & Shanker, S. G. (2001). Introduction: Bruner's way. In D. Bakhurst & S. G. Shanker (Eds.), *Jerome Bruner: Language, culture, self* (pp. 167–183). Thousand Oaks, CA: Sage.

References

Ball, C., Huang, K. T., Cotten, S. R., & Rikard, R. V. (2017). Pressurizing the STEM pipeline: An expectancy-value theory analysis of youths' STEM attitudes. *Journal of Science Education and Technology, 26*(4), 372–382.

Bandin, C. V. (2017). Towards a notion of resistance in gestalt therapy. *Gestalt Review, 21*(3), 242–258.

Bandura, A. (1969). *Principles of behavior modification*. New York: Holt, Rinehart and Winston.

Bandura, A. (1977). *Social learning theory*. Englewood Cliffs, NJ: Prentice Hall.

Bandura, A. (1981). Self-referent thought: A developmental analysis of self-efficacy. In J. H. Flavell & L. Ross (Eds.), *Social cognitive development: Frontiers and possible futures* (pp. 200–239). Cambridge: Cambridge University Press.

Bandura, A. (1986). *Social foundations of thought and action: A social cognitive theory*. Englewood Cliffs, NJ: Prentice Hall.

Bandura, A. (1991). Social cognitive theory of self-regulation. *Organizational Behavior and Human Performance, 50*, 248–287.

Bandura, A. (1993). Perceived self-efficacy in cognitive development and functioning. *Educational Psychologist, 28*, 117–148.

Bandura, A. (1995). Exercise of personal and collective efficacy in changing societies. In A. Bandura (Ed.), *Self-efficacy in changing societies* (pp. 1–45). New York: Cambridge University Press.

Bandura, A. (1997). *Self-efficacy: The exercise of control*. New York: W. H. Freeman.

Bandura, A. (2001). Social cognitive theory: An agentic perspective. *Annual Review of Psychology, 52*, 1–26.

Bandura, A. (2006). Guide for constructing self-efficacy scales. In F. Pajares & T. Urdan (Eds.), *Self-efficacy beliefs of adolescents* (pp. 307–337). Charlotte, NC: Information Age Publishing.

Bandura, A. (2007). Albert Bandura. In G. Lindzey & W. M. Runyan (Eds.), *A history of psychology in autobiography*, (Vol. 9, pp. 43–75). Washington, DC: American Psychological Association.

Bandura, A. (2008a). Reconstrual of "free will" from the agentic perspective of social cognitive theory. In J. Baer, J. C. Kaufman, & R. F. Baumeister (Eds.), *Are we free? Psychology and free will* (pp. 86–127). New York: Oxford University Press.

Bandura, A. (2008b). An agentic perspective on positive psychology. In S. J. Lopez (Ed.), *Positive psychology: Exploring the best in people, Vol 1: Discovering human strengths* (pp. 167–196). Westport, CT: Praeger Publishers/Greenwood Publishing Group.

Bandura, A., & Walters, R. (1963). *Social learning and personality development*. New York: Holt, Rinehart and Winston.

Bandura, A., Ross, D., & Ross, S. A. (1961). Transmission of aggression through imitation of aggressive models. *Journal of Abnormal and Social Psychology, 63*, 575–582.

Barbagallo, G., Nistico, R., Vescio, B., Cerasa, A., Olivadese, G., Nigro, S., . . ., Quattrone, A. (2018). The placebo effect on resting tremor in Parkinson's disease: An electrophysiological study. *Parkinsonism & Related Disorders, 52*, 17–23.

Baretta, D., Greco, A., & Steca, P. (2017). Understanding performance in risky sport: The role of self-efficacy beliefs and sensation seeking in competitive freediving. *Personality and Individual Differences, 117*, 161–165.

Barnard, C. W., Wolfe, H. D., & Graveline, D. E. (1962). Sensory deprivation under null gravity conditions. *American Journal of Psychiatry, 118*, 92–125.

Barnes, B. R. (2010). The Hawthorne Effect in community trials in developing countries. *International Journal of Social Research Methodology: Theory & Practice, 13*(4), 357–370.

Barrett, L., Dunbar, R., & Lycett, J. (2002). *Human evolutionary psychology*. New York: Palgrave.

Barry, R. J., De Blasio, F. M., Bernat, E. M., & Steiner, G. Z. (2015). Event-related EEG time–frequency PCA and the orienting reflex to auditory stimuli. *Psychophysiology, 52*(4), 555–561.

Barry, R. J., MacDonald, B., De Blasio, F. M., & Steiner, G. Z. (2013). Linking components of event-related potentials and autonomic measures of the orienting reflex. *International Journal of Psychophysiology, 89* (3), 366–373.

Barth, B., Mayer, K., Strehl, U., Fallgatter, A. J., & Ehlis, A. C. (2017). EMG biofeedback training in adult attention-deficit/hyperactivity disorder: An active (control) training? *Behavioural Brain Research, 329*, 58–66.

Bartolotti, J., Bradley, K., Hernandez, A. E., & Marian, V. (2017). Neural signatures of second language learning and control. *Neuropsychologia, 98*, 130–138. Retrieved October 23, 2018, from www.ncbi.nlm .nih.gov/pmc/articles/PMC5055847.

Beach, F. A. (1959). Clark Leonard Hull 1884–1952. In *Biographical Memoirs, 27* (pp. 121–141). Washington, DC: National Academy of Sciences.

Belzak, W. C. M., Yoon Y. S., Thrash, T. M., & Wadsworth, L. M. (2017). Beyond hedonic and eudaimonic well-being: Inspiration and the self-transcendence tradition. In M. D. Robinson & M. Eid (Eds.), *The happy mind: Cognitive contributions to well-being* (pp. 117–138). Cham: Springer International Publishing.

Benjafield, J. G. (1996). *A history of psychology*. Boston, MA: Allyn & Bacon.

Bensemann, J., Lobb, B., Podlesnik, C. A., & Elliffe, D. (2015). Steady-state choice between four alternatives obeys the constant-ratio rule. *Journal of the Experimental Analysis of Behavior, 104*(1), 7–19.

Bensley, D. A., & Lilienfeld, S. O. (2017). Psychological misconceptions: Recent scientific advances and unresolved issues. *Current Directions in Psychological Science, 26*(4), 377–382.

Berlyne, D. E. (1960). *Conflict, arousal, and curiosity*. New York: McGraw-Hill.

Berlyne, D. E. (1965). *Structure and direction in thinking*. New York: Wiley.

Berlyne, D. E. (1966). Curiosity and exploration. *Science, 153*, 25–33.

Bernard, L. L. (1924). *Instinct: A study in social psychology*. New York: Holt, Rinehart and Winston.

Bernstein, I. L., & Webster, M. M. (1980). Learned taste aversion in humans. *Physiology & Behavior, 25*, 363–366.

Best, J. (2012). *IBM Watson: The inside story of how the Jeopardy-winning supercomputer was born, and what it wants to do next*. Tech Republic. Retrieved December 7, 2018, from www.techrepublic.com/article/ibm-watson-the-inside-story-of-how-the-jeopardy-winning-supercomputer-was-born-and-what-it-wants-to-do-next.

Best, J. (2014). IBM's Watson unit racks up less than $100m in three years – despite $1Bn hopes. Topic Enterprise Software. Retrieved December 7, 2018, from www.zdnet.com/article/ibms-watson-unit-racks-up-less-than-100m-in-three-years-despite-1bn-hopes.

Beversdorf, D. Q., Roos, R. P., Hauser, W. A., Lennon, V. A., & Mehler, M. F. (2015). Animal extremists' threats to neurologic research continue: Neuroreality II. *Neurology, 85*(8), 730–734.

Bevins, R. A. (2009). Altering the motivational function of nicotine through conditioning processes. In R. A. Bevins & A. R. Caggiula (Eds.), *The motivational impact of nicotine and its role in tobacco use* (pp. 111–129). New York: Springer Science.

Bexton, W. H., Heron, W., & Scott, T. H. (1954). Effects of decreased variation in the sensory environment. *Canadian Journal of Psychology, 8*, 70–76.

Bijou, S. W., & Sturges, P. S. (1959). Positive reinforcers for experimental studies with children: Consumables and manipulatables. *Child Development, 30*, 151–170.

Bitterman, M. E. (2006). Classical conditioning since Pavlov. *Review of General Psychology, 10*(4), 365–376.

Blackwell, L. S., Trzesniewski, K. H., & Dweck, C. S. (2007). Implicit theories of intelligence predict achievement across an adolescent transition: A longitudinal study and an intervention. *Child Development, 78*(1), 246–263.

Blakemore, S. J., & Frith, U. (2005). *The learning brain: Lessons for education*. New York: Wiley-Blackwell.

Blumenstein, B., & Orbach, I. (2014). Biofeedback for sport and performance enhancement. *Psychology, Health Psychology*. Retrieved October 15, 2018, from www.oxfordhandbooks.com/view/10.1093/oxfordhb/9780199935291.001.0001/oxfordhb-9780199935291-e-001.

Blumenstein, B., & Orbach, I. (2018). Periodization of biofeedback training: New trends in athletic preparation. In F. Chiappelli (Ed.), *Advances in psychobiology* (pp. 49–62). Hauppauge, NY: Nova Biomedical Books.

References

Bolles, R. C. (1970). Species-specific defense reactions and avoidance learning. *Psychological Review*, *77*, 32–48.

Bolles, R. C. (1979). *Learning theory* (2nd ed.). New York: Holt, Rinehart and Winston.

Bond, T. G., & Parkinson, K. (2010). Children's understanding of area concepts: Development, curriculum and educational achievement. *Journal of Applied Measurement*, *11*(1), 60–77.

Boring, E. G. (1950). *A history of experimental psychology* (2nd ed.). New York: Appleton-Century-Crofts.

Bowers, J. S. (2010). More on grandmother cells and the biological implausibility of PDP models of cognition: A reply to Plaut and McClelland (2010) and Quian Quiroga and Kreiman (2010). *Psychological Review*, *117*(1), 300–306.

Bowlby, J. (1982). *Attachment and loss: Vol. 1. Attachment* (2nd ed.). London: Hogarth.

Bowles, N. (2018, October 26). A dark consensus about screens and kids begins to emerge in Silicon Valley. *New York Times*. Retrieved October 28, 2018, from www.nytimes.com/2018/10/26/style/phones-children-silicon-valley.html.

Bowman, C. R., & Zeithamova, D. (2018). Abstract memory representations in the ventromedial prefrontal cortex and hippocampus support concept generalization. *The Journal of Neuroscience*, *38*(10), 2605–2614.

Bradley, C., Joyce, N., & Garcia-Larrea, L. (2016). Adaptation in human somatosensory cortex as a model of sensory memory construction: A study using high-density EEG. *Brain Structure & Function*, *221*(1), 421–431.

Brandon, T. H. (2001). Behavioral tobacco cessation treatments: Yesterday's news or tomorrow's headlines? *Journal of Clinical Oncology*, *19*(18S), 64s–68s.

Bransford, J. D., Brown, A. L., & Cocking, R. R. (Eds.). (2000). *How people learn: Brain, mind, experience, and school*. Washington, DC: National Academy Press.

Bray, E. E., MacLean, E. L., & Hare, B. A. (2015). Increasing arousal enhances inhibitory control in calm but not excitable dogs. *Animal Cognition*, *18*(6), 1317–1329.

Brehm, J. W., & Cohen, A. R. (1962). *Explorations in cognitive dissonance*. New York: Wiley.

Brehm, J. W., & Self, E. A. (1989). The intensity of motivation. *Annual Review of Psychology*, *40*, 109–131.

Breland, K., & Breland, M. (1951). A field of applied animal psychology. *American Psychologist*, *6*, 202–204.

Breland, K., & Breland, M. (1961). The misbehavior of organisms. *American Psychologist*, *16*, 681–684.

Breland, K., & Breland, M. (1966). *Animal behavior*. New York: Macmillan.

Briskin-Luchinsky, V., Levy, R., Halfon, M., & Susswein, A. J. (2018). Molecular correlates of separate components of training that contribute to long-term memory formation after learning that food is inedible in *Aplysia*. *Learning & Memory*, *25*(2), 90–99.

Broadbent, D. E. (1952). Speaking and listening simultaneously. *Journal of Experimental Psychology*, *43*, 267–273.

Bronfenbrenner, U. (1989). Ecological systems theory. In R. Vasta (Ed.), *Annals of child development* (Vol. 6, pp. 187–249). Greenwich, CT: JAI Press.

Brooks, R. A. (2002). *Flesh and machines: How robots will change us*. New York: Pantheon Books.

Broster, L. S., Jenkins, S. L., Holmes, S. D., Edwards, M. G., Jicha, G. A., & Jiang, Y. (2018). Electrophysiological repetition effects in persons with mild cognitive impairment depend upon working memory demand. *Neuropsychologia*, *117*, 13–25.

Brown, P. C., Roediger, H. L. III, & McDaniel, M. A. (2014). *Making it stick: The science of successful learning*. Cambridge, MA: The Belknap Press of Harvard University Press.

Brown, R. E. (2016). Hebb and Cattell: The genesis of the theory of fluid and crystallized intelligence. *Frontiers in Human Neuroscience*, *10*. Retrieved October 16, 2018, from www.frontiersin.org/articles/10.3389/fnhum.2016.00606/full.

Brown, R. E., & Milner, P. M. (2004). The legacy of Donald O. Hebb: More than the Hebb synapse. *Nature Reviews Neuroscience*, *4*, 1013–1019.

Bruner, J. S. (1957a). On going beyond the information given. In J. S. Bruner, E. Brunswik, L. Festinger, F. Heider, K. F. Muenzinger, C. E. Osgood, & D. Rapaport, (Eds.), *Contemporary approaches to cognition* (pp. 41–69). Cambridge, MA: Harvard University Press.

Bruner, J. S. (1957b). On perceptual readiness. *Psychological Review, 64*, 123–152.

Bruner, J. S. (1964). The course of cognitive growth. *American Psychologist, 19*, 15.

Bruner, J. S. (1966). *Toward a theory of instruction*. Cambridge, MA: Harvard University Press.

Bruner, J. S. (1983). *In search of mind: Essays in autobiography*. New York: Harper & Row.

Bruner, J. S. (1985). Models of the learner. *Educational Researcher, 14*, 5–8.

Bruner, J. S. (1986). *Actual minds, possible worlds*. Cambridge, MA: Harvard University Press.

Bruner, J. S. (1990a). *Acts of meaning*. Cambridge, MA: Harvard University Press.

Bruner, J. S. (1990b). Metaphors of consciousness and cognition in the history of psychology. In D. E. Leary (Ed.), *Metaphors in the history of psychology* (pp. 230–238). New York: Cambridge University Press.

Bruner, J. S. (1990c). *The proper study of man*. Cambridge, MA: Harvard University Press.

Bruner, J. S. (1991). The narrative construction of reality. *Critical Inquiry, 18*(1), 1–21.

Bruner, J. S. (1996a). Frames for thinking: Ways of making meaning. In D. R. Olson & N. Torrance (Eds.), *Modes of thought: Explorations in culture and cognition* (pp. 93–105). New York: Cambridge University Press.

Bruner, J. S. (1996b). *The culture of education*. Cambridge, MA: Harvard University Press.

Bruner, J. S. (1997a). Celebrating divergence: Piaget and Vygotsky. *Human Development, 40*, 63–73.

Bruner, J. S. (1997b). Comment on "Beyond competence." *Cognitive Development, 12*, 341–343.

Bruner, J. S. (1997c). A narrative model of self-construction. In J. G. Snodgrass & R. L. Thompson (Eds.), *The self across psychology: Self-recognition, self-awareness, and the self-concept* (pp. 145–161). New York: The New York Academy of Sciences.

Bruner, J. S. (1997d). Will the cognitive revolutions ever stop? In D. M. Johnson & C. E. Erneling (Eds.), *The future of the cognitive revolution* (pp. 279–292). New York: Oxford University Press.

Bruner, J. S. (2000). Human infancy and the beginnings of human competence. In J. A. Bargh & D. K. Apsley (Eds.), *Unraveling the complexities of social life: A festschrift in honor of Robert B. Zajonc*. Washington, DC: American Psychological Association.

Bruner, J. S. (2002). *Making stories: Law, literature, life*. New York: Farrar, Straus and Giroux.

Bruner, J. S. (2004). Life as narrative. *Social Research, 71*(3), 691–710.

Bruner, J. S., Goodnow, J. J., & Austin, G. A. (1956). *A study of thinking*. New York: Wiley.

Bruno, N., Uccelli, S., Viviani, E., & de'Sperati, C. (2016). Both vision-for-perception and vision-for-action follow Weber's law at small object sizes, but violate it at larger sizes. *Neuropsychologia, 91*, 327–334.

Bryant, R A., Baker, M. T., Mintz, J., Barth, J., Young-McCaughan, S., Creasy, B., . . ., Peterson, A. L. (2015). The role of posttraumatic stress in acute postconcussive symptoms following blast injury in combat. *Psychotherapy and Psychosomatics, 84*(2), 120–121.

Bryant, R. A., Creamer, M., O'Donnell, M., Silove, D., Clark, C. R., & McFarlane, A. C. (2009). Post-traumatic amnesia and the nature of post-traumatic stress disorder after mild traumatic brain injury. *Journal of the International Neuropsychological Society, 15*(6), 862–867.

Buckley, K. W. (1994). Misbehaviorism: The case of John B. Watson's dismissal from Johns Hopkins University. In J. T. Todd & E. K. Morris (Eds.), *Modern perspectives on John B. Watson and classical behaviorism* (pp. 37–63). Westport, CT: Greenwood Press.

Bull, P. N., Tippett, L. J., & Addis, D. R. (2015). Decision making in healthy participants on the Iowa Gambling Task: New insights from an operant approach. *Frontiers in Psychology, 6*. Retrieved October 9, 2018, from www.frontiersin.org/articles/10.3389/fpsyg.2015.00185/full.

Buller, D. J. (2008). Four fallacies of pop evolutionary psychology. *Scientific American, 300*, 74–81.

Burgos, J. E. (2015). Misbehavior in a neural network model. *International Journal of Comparative Psychology, 28*, Retrieved October 12, 2018, from https://cloudfront.escholarship.org/dist/prd/content/qt3vb500tv/qt3vb500tv.pdf?t=pf7jgy.

References

Burgos, J. E. (2016). Antidualism and antimentalism in radical behaviorism. *Behavior and Philosophy*, *43*, 1–37.

Burnham, J. C. (1994). John B. Watson: Interviewee, professional figure, symbol. In J. T. Todd & E. K. Morris (Eds.), *Modern perspectives on John B. Watson and classical behaviorism* (pp. 65–73). Westport, CT: Greenwood Press.

Burns, J. D., & Malone, J. C., Jr. (1992). The influence of "preparedness" on autoshaping, schedule performance, and choice. *Journal of the Experimental Analysis of Behavior*, *58*, 399–413.

Buxton, C. E. (1940). Latent learning and the goal gradient hypothesis. *Duke University: Contributions to Psychological Theory*, 2. [Special issue]

Caldwell, Y. T., & Steffen, P. R. (2018). Adding HRV biofeedback to psychotherapy increases heart rate variability and improves the treatment of major depressive disorder. *International Journal of Psychophysiology*, *131*, 96–101.

Cameron, J., & Pierce, W. D. (1994). Reinforcement, reward, and intrinsic motivation: A meta-analysis. *Review of Educational Research*, *64*, 363–423.

Campbell, F. A., & Ramey, C. T. (1990). The relationship between Piagetian cognitive development, mental test performance, and academic achievement in high-risk students with and without early educational intervention. *Intelligence*, *14*, 293–308.

Campbell, K., Chen, Y. J., Shenoy, S., & Cunningham, A. E. (2018). Preschool children's early writing: Repeated measures reveal growing but variable trajectories. *Reading and Writing*, *32*(4), 939–961.

Capa, R. L., Audiffren, M., & Ragot, S. (2008). The effects of achievement motivation, task difficulty, and goal difficulty on physiological, behavioral, and subjective effort. *Psychophysiology*, *45*(5), 859–868.

Carroll, J. B. (Ed.). (1997 [1956]). *Language, thought, and reality: Selected writings of Benjamin Lee Whorf*. Cambridge, MA: Technology Press of Massachusetts Institute of Technology.

Castine, B. R., Albein-Urios, N., Lozano-Rojas, O., Martinez-Gonzalez, J. M., Hohwy, J., & Verdejo-Garcia, A. (2018). Self-awareness deficits associated with lower treatment motivation in cocaine addiction. *The American Journal of Drug and Alcohol Abuse*. Retrieved October 13, 2018, from www.tandfonline.com/doi/full/10.1080/00952990.2018.1511725.

Cavanaugh, J. M., Giapponi, C., & Golden T. D. (2016). Digital technology and student cognitive development: The neuroscience of the university classroom. *Journal of Management Education*, *40*(4), 374–397.

Cellan-Jones, R. (2014). Stephen Hawking warns artificial intelligence could end mankind. *Technology*, Retrieved October 31, 2018, from www.bbc.com/news/technology-30290540.

Cermak, L. S., & Craik, F. I. (Eds.). (1979). *Levels of processing in human memory*. Hillsdale, NJ: Erlbaum.

Charest-Girard, C., & Parent, V. (2018). Training of the working memory: Effects on the performance in mathematics. *Canadian Journal of Experimental Psychology/Revue Canadienne de psychologie experimentale*, *72*(2), 127–139. [In French]

Charles, E. P., & Rivera, S. M. (2009). Object permanence and method of disappearance: Looking measures further contradict reaching measures. *Developmental Science*, *12*(6), 991–1006.

Chen, A. (2018). A pioneering scientist explains "deep learning." *The Verge*. Retrieved October 28, 2018, from www.theverge.com/2018/10/16/17985168/deep-learning-revolution-terrence-sejnowski-artificial-intelligence-technology.

Cherdieu, M., Versace, R., Rey, A. E., Vallet, G. T., & Mazza, S. (2018). Sleep on your memory traces: How sleep effects can be explained by Act-In, a functional memory model. *Sleep Medicine Reviews*, *39*, 155–163.

Cherry, K. (2018a). How many neurons are in the brain? Retrieved October 13, 2018, from www.verywellmind.com/how-many-neurons-are-in-the-brain-2794889.

Cherry, K. (2018b). The 10 percent of brain myth. Retrieved September 25, 2018, from www.verywellmind.com/10-percent-of-brain-myth-2794882.

Cheruvalath, R., & Tripathi, M. (2015). Secondary school teachers' perception of corporal punishment: A case study in India. *The Clearing House: A Journal of Educational Strategies, Issues and Ideas*, *88*(4), 127–132.

Chessbase News. (2006). Kramnik vs Deep Fritz: Computer wins match by 4:2. Retrieved May 7, 2010, from www.chessbase.com/newsdetail.asp?newsid=3524.

Chesworth, R., Brown, R. M., Kim, J. H., Ledent, C., & Lawrence, A. J. (2016). Adenosine 2A receptors modulate reward behaviours for methamphetamine. *Addiction Biology, 21*(2), 407–421.

Chiandetti, C., Avella, S., Fongaro, E., & Cerri, F. (2016). Can clicker training facilitate conditioning in dogs? *Applied Animal Behaviour Science, 184*, 109–116. Retrieved October 9, 2018, from https://pdfs.semanticscholar.org/621d/6a0d331a4c51789a16122707a83b2c85ecab.pdf.

Child Trends (2018). Attitudes toward spanking. Retrieved October 10, 2018, from www.childtrends.org/indicators/attitudes-toward-spanking.

Chin, E. C. H., Williams, M. W., Taylor, J. E., & Harvey, S. T. (2017). The influence of negative affect on test anxiety and academic performance: An examination of the tripartite model of emotions. *Learning and Individual Differences, 54*, 1–8.

Chiocca, E. M. (2017). American parents' attitudes and beliefs about corporal punishment: An integrative literature review. *Journal of Pediatric Health Care, 31*(3), 372–383.

Chomsky, N. (1972). *Language and mind* (rev. ed.). New York: Harcourt Brace Jovanovich.

Church, B. A., Rice, C. L., Dovgopoly, A., Lopata, C. J., Thomeer, M. L., Nelson, A., & Mercado, E. III (2015). Learning, plasticity, and atypical generalization in children with autism. *Psychonomic Bulletin & Review, 22*(5), 1342–1348.

Clarke, D. O. (2005). From philosopher to psychologist: The early career of Edwin Ray Guthrie, Jr. *History of Psychology, 8*, 235–254.

Clarke, W. F. (2010). Little utopias. *Journal of Psychiatric and Mental Health Nursing, 17*(1), 73–78.

Claro, S. Paunesku, D., & Dweck, C. S. (2016). Growth mindsets tempers the effects of poverty on academic achievement. *Proceedings of the National Academy of Sciences of the United States of America*, 113(31), 8664–8668.

Cole, S. O. (2002). Evolutionary psychology: Sexual ethics and our embodied nature. *Journal of Psychology & Theology, 30*, 112–116.

Coleman, S. R. (2007). Pavlov and the equivalence of associability in classical conditioning. *Journal of Mind and Behavior, 28*(2), 115–133.

Collins, H. M. (2008). Response to Selinger on Dreyfus. *Phenomenology and the Cognitive Sciences, 7*(2), 309–311.

Colombo, M., & Hayne, H. (2010). Episodic memory: Comparative and developmental issues. In M. S. Blumberg, J. H. Freeman, & S. R. Robinson (Eds.), *Oxford handbook of developmental behavioral neuroscience* (pp. 617–636). New York: Oxford University Press.

Coltheart, M. (2017). Grandmother cells and the distinction between local and distributed representation. *Language, Cognition and Neuroscience, 32*(3), 350–358.

Cooper, J. (2012). Cognitive dissonance: Revisiting Festinger's end of the world study. In J. R. Smith, & S. A. Haslam (Eds.), *Social psychology: Revisiting the classic studies*, (pp. 42–56). Thousand Oaks, CA: Sage.

Cooper, J., Feldman, L. A., & Blackman, S. F. (2018). Influencing Republicans' and Democrats' attitudes toward Obamacare: Effects of imagined vicarious cognitive dissonance on political attitudes. *The Journal of Social Psychology*. Retrieved October 25, 2018, from https://doi.org/10.1080/00224545.2018.1465023.

Corballis, M. C. (2007). The dual-brain myth. In S. Della Sala (Ed.), *Tall tales about the mind and brain: Separating fact from fiction* (pp. 291–313). New York: Oxford.

Cosmides, L., & Tooby, J. (1997). Evolutionary psychology: A primer. Retrieved June 1, 2010, from www.psych.ucsb.edu/research/cep/primer.html.

Covington, M. V. (2000). Goal theory, motivation, and school achievement: An integrative review. *Annual Review of Psychology, 51*, 171–200.

Cowley, G. (1989, March). How the mind was designed. *Newsweek, 113*, 56–58.

Craik, F. I. M. (2002). Levels of processing: Past, present . . . and future? *Memory, 10*, 305–318.

Craik, F. I. M., & Lockhart, R. S. (1972). Levels of processing: A framework for memory research. *Journal of Verbal Learning and Verbal Behavior, 11*, 671–684.

References

Crespi, L. (1942). Quantitative variation of incentive and performance in the white rat. *American Journal of Psychology, 55*, 467–517.

Crews, F. C. (2017). *Freud: The making of an illusion.* New York: Metropolitan Books, Henry Holt and Company.

Dagnall, N., Denovan, A., Drinkwater, K., Parker, A., & Clough, P. J. (2017). Urban legends and paranormal beliefs: The role of reality testing and schizotypy. *Frontiers in Psychology, 8.* Retrieved September 25, 2018, from https://doi.org/10.3389/fpsyg.2017.00942.

Darley, J. M., & Latané, B. (1968). Bystander intervention in emergencies: Diffusion of responsibility. *Journal of Personality and Social Psychology, 8*, 377–383.

Darwin, C. (1859/1962). *The origin of species by means of natural selection, or the preservation of favoured races in the struggle for life.* New York: Collier.

Darwin, C. (1871). *The descent of man and selection in relation to sex* (Vols. 1 and 2). London: John Murray.

Darwin, C. (1872). *The expression of emotions in man and animals.* London: John Murray.

Davydov, V. V. (1995). The influence of L. S. Vygotsky on education theory, research, and practice. *Educational Researcher, 24*, 12–21.

Deason, R. G., Strong, J. V., Tat, M. J., Simmons-Stern, N. R., & Budson, A. E. (2018). Explicit and implicit memory for music in healthy older adults and patients with mild Alzheimer's disease. *Journal of Clinical and Experimental Neuropsychology*, 1–12. doi:10.1080/13803395.2018.1510904.

de Bruijn, M. J., & Bender, M. (2018). Olfactory cues are more effective than visual cues in experimentally triggering autobiographical memories. *Memory, 26*(4), 547–558.

Deci, E. L., & Flaste, R. (1995). *Why we do what we do: The dynamics of personal autonomy.* New York: G. P. Putnam's Sons.

Deci, E. L., & Ryan, R. M. (2008). Facilitating optimal motivation and psychological well-being across life's domains. *Canadian Psychology, 49*, 14–23.

DeLancey, C. (2002). *Passionate engines: What emotions reveal about mind and artificial intelligence.* New York: Oxford University Press.

Delay, E. D., & Kondoh, T. (2015). Dried bonito dashi: Taste qualities evaluated using conditioned taste aversion methods in wild-type and T1R1 knockout mice. *Chemical Senses, 40*(2), 125–140.

Delius, J. D. (1992). Categorical discrimination of objects and pictures by pigeons. *Animal Learning and Behavior, 20*, 301–311.

Demorest, A. P., & Siegel, P. F. (1996). Personal influences on professional work: An empirical case study of B. F. Skinner. *Journal of Personality, 64*, 243–261.

Denizet, M., Cotter, L., Lledo, P. M., & Lazarini, F. (2017). Sensory deprivation increases phagocytosis of adult-born neurons by activated microglia in the olfactory bulb. *Brain, Behavior, and Immunity, 60*, 38–43.

Dennis, A. (2018). The strange survival and apparent resurgence of sociobiology. *History of the Human Sciences, 31*(1), 19–35.

Dever, B. V. (2016). Using the expectancy-value theory of motivation to predict behavioral and emotional risk among high school students. *School Psychology Review, 45*(4), 417–433.

Dewsbury, D. A. (2002). The Chicago five: A family group of integrative psychobiologists. *History of Psychology, 5*, 16–37.

Diamond, S. (2001). Wundt before Leipzig. In R. W. Rieber & D. K. Robinson (Eds.), *Wilhelm Wundt in history: The making of a scientific psychology* (pp. 1–63). New York: Kluwer Academic/Plenum.

Dickman, S. J. (2002). Dimensions of arousal: Wakefulness and vigor. *Human Factors, 44*, 429–442.

DiClemente, D. F., & Hantula, D. A. (2000). John Broadus Watson, I-O psychologist. *The Industrial-Organizational Psychologist, 37*(4), 47–55.

Didion, J. (1979). *The white album.* New York: Simon & Schuster.

Digdon, N., Powell, R. A., & Smithson, C. (2014). Watson's alleged Little Albert scandal: Historical breakthrough or new Watson myth? *Revista de Historia de la Psicologia, 35*(1), 47–60.

Dindo, M., Whiten, A., & de Waal, F. B. M. (2009). Social facilitation of exploratory foraging behavior in Capuchin monkeys (*Cebus apella*). *American Journal of Primatology, 71*(5), 419–426.

Ding, N., & Simon, J. Z. (2012). Neural coding of continuous speech in auditory cortex during monaural and dichotic listening. *Journal of Neurophysiology, 107*(1), 78–89.

Dittrich, A., Strapasson, B. A., da Silveira, J. M., & Abreu, P. R. (2009). On observation as a methodological procedure in behavior analysis: Logical positivism, operationism and radical behaviorism. *Psicologia: Teoria e Pesquisa, 25*(2), 179–187.

Djalal, F. M., Storms, G., Ameel, E., & Heyman, T. (2017). Feature taxonomy: What type of features do children associate with categories and how do they fare in predicting category judgments? *Acta Psychologica, 178*, 114–123.

Dolcos, F., Katsumi, Y., Weymar, M., Moore, M., Tsukiura, T., & Dolcos, S. (2017). Emerging directions in emotional episodic memory. *Frontiers in Psychology*, 8, Retrieved October 21, 2018, from www .frontiersin.org/articles/10.3389/fpsyg.2017.01867/full.

Domingos, P. (2018). *The master algorithm: How the quest for the ultimate learning machine will remake our world*. New York: Basic Books.

Domjan, M. (2018). *The essentials of conditioning and learning* (4th ed.). Washington, DC: American Psychological Association.

Dos Santos Fringe, J. J. (2018). Promoting holistic learning for the development of competences in Mozambique. *Tuning Journal for Higher Education, 5*(2), 19–43.

Doyle, W. (1986). Classroom organization and management. In M. C. Wittrock (Ed.), *Handbook of research on teaching* (3rd ed., pp. 392–431). New York: Macmillan.

Draaisma, D. (2000). *Metaphors of memory: A history of ideas about the mind*. (P. Vincent, trans.). New York: Cambridge University Press.

Drayton, A. K., Byrd, M. R., Albright, J. J., Nelson, E. M., Andersen, M. N., & Morris, N. K. (2017). Deconstructing the time-out: What do mothers understand about a common disciplinary procedure? *Child & Family Behavior Therapy, 39*(2), 91–107.

Dumas, R., & Luminet, O. (2016). Emotional context, rehearsal and memories: The mutual contributions and possible integration of flashbulb memory and eyewitness identification research. In C. Stone & L. Bietti (Eds.), *Contextualizing human memory: An interdisciplinary approach to understanding how individuals and groups remember the past* (pp. 37–65). New York: Routledge.

Dunlosky, J., Rawson, K. A., Marsh, E. J., Nathan, M. J., & Willingham, D. T. (2013). Improving students' learning with effective learning techniques: Promising directions from cognitive and educational psychology. *Psychological Science in the Public Interest, 14*(1), 4–58. Retrieved October 23, 2018, from http://journals.sagepub.com/doi/10.1177/1529100612453266.

Durmaz, A. A., Karaca, E., Demkow, U., Toruner, G., Schoumans, J., & Cogulu, O. (2015). Evolution of genetic techniques: Past, present, and beyond, *BioMed Research International*, 2015. Retrieved October 4, 2018, from https://doi.org/10.1155/2015/461524.

Dweck, C. S. (1986). Motivational processes affecting learning. *American Psychologist, 41*, 1040–1048.

Dweck, C. S. (1999). Caution: Praise can be dangerous. *American Educator, 23*(1), 4–9.

Dweck, C. S. (2002a). The development of ability conceptions. In A. Wigfield & J. S. Eccles (Eds.), *Development of achievement motivation* (pp. 57–88). San Diego, CA: Academic Press.

Dweck, C. S. (2002b). Beliefs that make smart people dumb. In R. J. Sternberg (Ed.), *Why smart people can be so stupid* (pp. 24–41). New Haven, CT: Yale University Press.

Dweck, C. S. (2006). *Mindset: The new psychology of success*. New York: Random House.

Dweck, C. S., & Grant, H. (2008). Self-theories, goals, and meaning. In J. Y. Shah & W. I. Gardner (Eds.), *Handbook of motivation science* (pp. 408–416). New York: Guilford Press.

Dweck, C. S., & Master, A. (2008). Self-theories motivate self-regulated learning. In D. H. Schunk & B. J. Zimmerman (Eds.), *Motivation and self-regulated learning: Theory, research, and applications* (pp. 31–51). Mahwah, NJ: Lawrence Erlbaum.

References

Dweck, C. S., & Yeager, D. S. (2018). Mindsets change the imagined and actual future. In G. Oettingen, A. T. Sevincer, & P. Gollwitzer, (Eds.), *The psychology of thinking about the future* (pp. 362–376). New York: Guilford Press.

Ebbinghaus, H. (1885/1964). *Memory* (H. A. Ruger & C. E. Busenius, trans.). New York: Dover.

Eby, C. M., & Greer, R. D. (2017). Effects of social reinforcement on the emission of tacts by preschoolers. *Behavioral Development Bulletin*, *22*(1), 23–43.

Eccles, J. S., & Wigfield, A. (2002). Motivational beliefs, values, and goals. *Annual Review of Psychology*, *53*, 109–132.

Ellonen, N., Lucas, S., Tindberg, Y., & Janson, S. (2017). Parents' self-reported use of corporal punishment and other humiliating upbringing practices in Finland and Sweden: A comparative study. *Child Abuse Review*, *26*(4), 289–304.

Ellonen, N., Peltonen, K., Poso, T., & Janson, S. (2017). A multifaceted risk analysis of fathers' self-reported physical violence toward their children. *Aggressive Behavior*, *43*(4), 317–328.

Ellsworth, R. M., & Walker, R. S. (2015). Sociobiology of lethal violence in small-scale societies. In M. DeLisi, & M. G. Vaughn, (Eds.), *The Routledge international handbook of biosocial criminology.* (pp. 57–74). New York: Routledge/Taylor & Francis Group.

Encyclopædia Britannica (2010a). Edward C. Tolman. Retrieved April 30, 2010, from www.britannica.com/EBchecked/topic/598668/Edward-C-Tolman.

Encyclopædia Britannica (2010b). Horst Köhler. Retrieved April 30, 2010, from www.britannica.com/EBchecked/topic/711087/Horst-Kohler.

Encyclopædia Britannica (2010c). Kurt Koffka. Retrieved April 30, 2010, from www.britannica.com/EBchecked/topic/320995/Kurt-Koffka.

Encyclopædia Britannica (2010d). Max Wertheimer. Retrieved April 30, 2010, from www.britannica.com/EBchecked/topic/639896/Max-Wertheimer.

Encyclopædia Britannica (2010e). Wolfgang Köhler. Retrieved April 30, 2010, from www.britannica.com/EBchecked/topic/321102/Wolfgang-Kohler.

Epstein, R. A., Patai, E. Z., Julian, J. B., & Spiers, H. J. (2017). The cognitive map in humans: Spatial navigation and beyond. *Nature Neuroscience*, *20*(11), 1504–1513.

Eriksen, B. C., Bergmann, S., & Mjølnerød, O. K. (1987). Effect of anal electrostimulation with the 'Incontan' device in women with urinary incontinence. *British Journal of Obstetrics and Gynaecology*, *94*(2), 147–156.

Evans, R. I. (1989). *Albert Bandura: The man and his ideas – a dialogue*. New York: Praeger.

Ewen, R. B. (2010). *An introduction to theories of personality* (7th ed.). New York: Psychology Press.

Eysenck, H. J. (1982). Neobehavioristic (S–R) theory. In G. T. Wilson & C. M. Franks (Eds.), *Contemporary behavior therapy: Conceptual and empirical foundations* (pp. 205–276). New York: Guilford.

Fahmy, S. R., & Gaafar, K. (2016). Establishing the first institutional animal care and use committee in Egypt. *Philosophy, Ethics, and Humanities in Medicine*, *11*, 1–6. Retrieved September 27, 2018, from www.pubfacts.com/detail/27060909/Establishing-the-first-institutional-animal-care-and-use-committee-in-Egypt.

False Memory Syndrome Foundation (2018). Memory and reality. Retrieved October 2018, from www.fmsonline.org.

Farmer-Dougan, V., & Alferink, L. A. (2013). Brain development, early childhood, and brain-based education: A critical analysis. In L. H. Wasserman & D. Zambo, Debby (Eds.), *Early childhood and neuroscience: Links to development and learning*, (pp. 55–76). New York: Springer Science + Business Media.

Farran, D. C., Wilson, S. J., Meador, D., Norvell, J., & Nesbitt, K. (2015). Experimental evaluation of the Tools of the Mind Pre-K Curriculum. Peabody Research Institute. Retrieved October 20, 2018, from https://my.vanderbilt.edu/toolsofthemindevaluation/files/2011/12/Tools-Technical-Report-Final-September-2015.pdf.

Fechner, G. (1860 [1966]). *Elements of psychophysics* (Vol. 1; H. E. Adler, trans.). New York: Holt, Rinehart and Winston.

Fenton, A. (2018). Decisional authority and animal research subjects. In K. Andrews and J. Beck (Eds.), *The Routledge handbook of philosophy of animal minds* (pp. 475–484). New York: Routledge.

Ferguson, B., & Waxman, S. (2017). Linking language and categorization in infancy. *Journal of Child Language*, *3*, 527–552.

Ferrari, P. F., Paukner, A., Ruggiero, A., Darcey, L., Unbehagen, S., & Suomi, S. J. (2009). Interindividual differences in neonatal imitation and the development of action chains in rhesus macaques. *Child Development*, *80*(4), 1057–1068.

Festinger, L. A. (1957). *A theory of cognitive dissonance.* Stanford, CA: Stanford University Press. .

Festinger, L. A. (1962, October). Cognitive dissonance. *Scientific American*, *207*, 93–106.

Flake, J. K., Barron, K. E., Hulleman, C., McCoach, B. D., & Welsh, M. E. (2015). Measuring cost: The forgotten component of expectancy-value theory. *Contemporary Educational Psychology*, *41*, 232–244.

Flavell, J. H. (1985). *Cognitive development* (2nd ed.). Englewood Cliffs, NJ: Prentice Hall.

Floridi, L., Taddeo, M., & Turilli, M. (2009). Turing's imitation game: Still an impossible challenge for all machines and some judges – an evaluation of the 2008 Loebner Contest. *Minds and Machines*, *19*(1), 145–150.

Follette, W. C., & Davis, D. (2009). Clinical practice and the issue of repressed memories: Avoiding an ice patch on the slippery slope. In W. O'Donohue & S. R. Graybar (Eds.), *Handbook of contemporary psychotherapy: Toward an improved understanding of effective psychotherapy* (pp. 47–73). Thousand Oaks, CA: Sage.

Folmer, A. S., Cole, D. A., Sigal, A. B., Benbow, L. D., Satterwhite, L. F., Swygert, K. E., & Ciesla, J. A. (2008). Age-related changes in children's understanding of effort and ability: Implications for attribution theory and motivation. *Journal of Experimental Child Psychology*, *99*(2), 114–134.

Fox, J. A., & Fridel, E. E. (2017). Gender differences in patterns and trends in U.S. homicides, 1976–2015. *Violence and Gender*, 4(2). Retrieved October 14, 2018, from www.liebertpub.com/doi/full/10.1089/vio.2017.0016.

Fraser, J., & Yasnitsky, A. (2016). Deconstructing Vygotsky's victimization narrative: A re-examination of the "Stalinist suppression" of Vygotskian theory. In A. Yasnitsky & R. van der Veer, (Eds.), *Revisionist revolution in Vygotsky studies*, (pp. 50–69). New York: Routledge.

Freeman, D. (1983). *Margaret Mead and Samoa: The making and unmaking of an anthropological myth.* Boston, MA: Harvard University Press.

Fridlund, A. J., Beck, H. P., Goldie, W. D., & Irons, G. (2012). Little Albert: A neurologically impaired child. *History of Psychology*, *15*(4), 302–327.

Fugazza, C., & Miklosi, A. (2015). Social learning in dog training: The effectiveness of the do as I do method compared to shaping/clicker training. *Applied Animal Behaviour Science*, *171*, 146–151. Retrieved October 9, 2018, from www.appliedanimalbehaviour.com/article/S0168-1591(15)00236-1/fulltext.

Fugazza, C., Pogany, A., & Miklosi, A. (2016). Spatial generalization of imitation in dogs (*Canis familiaris*). *Journal of Comparative Psychology*, *30*(3), 249–258.

Fuson, K. C. (2009). Avoiding misinterpretations of Piaget and Vygotsky: Mathematical teaching without learning, learning without teaching, or helpful learning-path teaching? *Cognitive Development*, *24*(4), 343–361.

Gabler, I. C., & Schroeder, M. (2003). *Constructivist methods for the secondary classroom.* Boston, MA: Allyn & Bacon.

Galanter, M. (2009). Review of spiritual evolution: A scientific defense of faith. *The American Journal of Psychiatry*, *166*(2), 239–240.

Gale Group. (2001). Bruner, Jerome S. (1915–). In *Gale encyclopedia of psychology*. Retrieved May 3, 2010, from www.findarticles.com/cf_dls/g2699/0000/2699000048/print.jhtml.

Gallo, A., Duchatelle, E., Elkhessaimi, A., Le Pape, G., & Desportes, J.-P. (1995). Topographic analysis of the rat's bar behaviour in the Skinner box. *Behavioural Processes*, *33*, 319–328.

Galton, F. (1870). *Hereditary genesis: An inquiry into its laws and consequences.* New York: Appleton.

References

Ganel, T. (2015). Weber's law in grasping. *Journal of Vision*, 8. Retrieved October 1, 2018, from https://jov.arvojournals.org/article.aspx?articleid=2346728.

Garcia, J., & Koelling, R. A. (1966). Relation of cue to consequence in avoidance learning. *Psychonomic Science, 4*, 123–124.

Gardner, H. (1987). *The mind's new science: A history of the cognitive revolution.* New York: Basic Books.

Geary, D. C. (2007). Educating the evolved mind: Conceptual foundations for an evolutionary educational psychology. In J. S. Carlson & J. R. Levin (Eds.), *Educating the evolved mind: Conceptual foundations for an evolutionary educational psychology* (pp. 1–100). Charlotte, NC: Information Age Publishing.

Gelman, R., Meck, E., & Merkin, S. (1986). Young children's numerical competence. *Cognitive Development, 1*, 1–29.

Gentile, B. F., & Miller, B. O. (2009). *Foundations of psychological thought: A history of psychology.* Thousand Oaks, CA: Sage.

Gershoff, E. T., & Font, S. A. (2016). Corporal punishment in U.S. schools: Prevalence, disparities in use, and status in State and Federal policy. *Social Policy Report, 2016, 30*(1). Retrieved October 10, 2018, from www.ncbi.nlm.nih.gov/pmc/articles/PMC5766273.

Ghiglieri, V., & Calabresi, P. (2017). Environmental enrichment repairs structural and functional plasticity in the hippocampus. In L. Petrosini (Ed.), *Neurobiological and psychological aspects of brain recovery*, (pp. 55–77). Cham: Springer.

Gibbons, F. X., Eggleston, T. J., & Benthin, A. C. (1997). Cognitive reactions to smoking relapse: The reciprocal relation between dissonance and self-esteem. *Journal of Personality and Social Psychology, 72*, 184–195.

Giles, O. T., Shire, K. A., Hill, L. J. B., Mushtaq, F., Waterman, A., Holt, R. J., . . . Mon-Williams, M. (2018). Hitting the target: Mathematical attainment in children is related to interceptive-timing ability. *Psychological Science, 29*(8), 1334–1345.

Gillen, J. (2000). Versions of Vygotsky. *British Journal of Educational Studies, 48*(2), 183–198.

Gilovich, T. (1991). *How we know what isn't so: The fallibility of human reason in everyday life.* New York: The Free Press.

Godec, C. J. (1983). Clinical application of Pavlov conditioning reflexes in treatment of urinary incontinence. *Urology, 22*(4), 397–400.

Goldblum, N. (2001). *The brain-shaped mind: What the brain can tell us about the mind.* New York: Cambridge University Press.

Goldman, W. P., & Seamon, J. G. (1992). Very long-term memory for odors: Retention of odor–name associations. *American Journal of Psychology, 105*, 549–563.

Goodwin, C. J. (2010). *Annotated readings in the history of modern psychology.* Hoboken, NJ: Wiley.

Gotzsche, C. R., & Woldbye, D. P. D. (2016). The role of NPY in learning and memory. *Neuropeptides, 55*, 79–89. doi:10.1016/j.npep.2015.09.010.

Gould, S. J. (2002a). *I have landed: The end of a beginning in natural history.* New York: Harmony Books.

Gould, S. J. (2002b). *The structure of evolutionary theory.* Cambridge, MA: Belknap Press of Harvard University Press.

Greenhoot, A. F., & Tsethlikai, M. (2009). Repressed and recovered memories during childhood and adolescence. In K. Kuehnle & M. Connell (Eds.), *The evaluation of child sexual abuse allegations: A comprehensive guide to assessment and testimony* (pp. 203–244). Hoboken, NJ: Wiley.

Greenwald, J. D & Shafritz, K. M. (2018). An integrative neuroscience framework for the treatment of chronic pain: From cellular alterations to behavior. *Frontiers in Integrative Neuroscience, 12*(18). doi:10.3389/fnint.2018.00018. eCollection 2018.

Griffee, K., Stroebel, S. S., O'Keefe, S. L., Harper-Dorton, K. V., Beard, K. W., Young, D. H., . . . Kuo, S. Y. (2017). Sexual imprinting of offspring on their parents and siblings. *Cogent Psychology, 4*(1). Retrieved October 24, 2018, from www.cogentoa.com/article/10.1080/23311908.2017.1307632.

Griffin, A. S., & Galef, B. G., Jr. (2005). Social learning about predators: Does timing matter? *Animal Behaviour, 69*(3), 669–678.

Griffin, P. (2017). Assessing and teaching 21st century skills: Collaborative problem solving as a case study. In A. A. von Davier, M. Zhu, & P. Kyllonen (Eds.), *Innovative assessment of collaboration.* (pp. 113–134). Cham: Springer.

Griggs, R. A. (2014). The continuing saga of Little Albert in introductory psychology textbooks. *Teaching of Psychology, 41*(4), 309–317.

Griggs, R. A. (2015). Psychology's lost boy: Will the real Little Albert please stand up?. *Teaching of Psychology, 42*(1), 14–18.

Gross, C. G., (2002). Genealogy of the "grandmother cell." *Neuroscientist, 8*(5), 512–518.

Grow, W. A. (2018). The cerebral cortex. In D. E. Haines & G. A. Mihailoff (Eds.), *Fundamental neuroscience for basic and clinical applications* (5th ed.; pp. 468–479). Philadelphia, PA: Elsevier.

Grusec, J. E. (Ed.). (2006). *Handbook of socialization.* New York: Guilford Publications.

Gunderson, K. (1964). The imitation game. *Mind*, New Series, *73*(260), 234–245.

Gunturkun, O., Koenen, C., Iovine, F., Garland, A., & Pusch, R. (2018). The neuroscience of perceptual categorization in pigeons: A mechanistic hypothesis. *Learning & Behavior, 46*(3), 229–241.

Guthrie, E. R. (1935). *The psychology of learning.* New York: Harper.

Guthrie, E. R. (1952). *The psychology of learning* (rev. ed.). New York: Harper.

Guthrie, E. R., & Horton, G. P. (1946). *Cats in a puzzle box.* New York: Rinehart.

Guthrie, E. R., & Powers, F. F. (1950). *Educational psychology.* New York: Ronald Press.

Hacklander, R. P. M., & Bermeitinger, C. (2017). Olfactory context-dependent memory and the effects of affective congruency. *Chemical Senses, 42*(9), 777–788.

Hagen, E. H. (2016). Evolutionary psychology and its critics. In D. M. Buss (Ed.), *The handbook of evolutionary psychology: Foundations* (Vol. 1, 2nd ed.; pp. 136–160). Hoboken, NJ: Wiley.

Haggbloom, S. J., Warnick, R., Warnick, J. E., Yarbrough, G. L., Borecky, C. M., Powell, J. L., III, . . . Monte, E. (2002). The 100 most eminent psychologists of the 20th century. *Review of General Psychology, 6*(2), 139–152.

Hahn, N., Jansen, P., & Heil, M. (2010). Preschoolers' mental rotation: Sex differences in hemispheric asymmetry. *Journal of Cognitive Neuroscience, 22*(6), 1244–1250.

Hailwood, J. M., Heath, C. J., Robbins, T. W., Saksida, L. M., & Bussey, T. J. (2018). Validation and optimisation of a touchscreen progressive ratio test of motivation in male rats. *Psychopharmacology, 235*(9), 2739–2753.

Haimovitz, K., & Dweck, C. S. (2017). The origins of children's growth and fixed mindsets: New research and a new proposal. *Child Development, 88*(6), 1849–1859.

Haines, D. E., & Terrell, A. C. (2018). Orientation to the structure and imaging of the central nervous system. In D. E. Haines & G. A. Mihailoff (Eds.), *Fundamental neuroscience for basic and clinical applications* (5th ed.; pp. 3–14). Philadelphia, PA: Elsevier.

Hajek, P., & Stead, L. F. (2004). Aversive smoking for smoking cessation. *Cochrane Database of Systematic Reviews, 3*, CD00546. doi:10.1002/14651858.CD000546.pub2

Hamilton, W. D. (1970). Selfish and spiteful behaviour in an evolutionary model. *Nature, 228*, 1218–1220.

Hamilton, W. D. (1971). Geometry for the selfish herd. *Journal of Theoretical Biology, 31*, 295–311.

Hamilton, W. D. (1972). Altruism and related phenomena, mainly in social insects. *Annual Review of Ecology and Systematics, 3*, 193–232.

Hampton, J. A., & Passanisi, A. (2016). When intensions do not map onto extensions: Individual differences in conceptualization. *Journal of Experimental Psychology: Learning, Memory, and Cognition, 42*(4), 505–523.

Harnish, R. M. (2002). *Minds, brains, computers: An historical introduction to the foundations of cognitive science.* Malden, MA: Blackwell.

Harpaz, Y. (2003). Human cognition in the human brain. Retrieved May 12, 2010, from http://human-brain .org.

Harre, R. (2015). How Bruner foresaw a future that has yet to be achieved. In G. Marsico (Ed.), *Jerome S. Bruner beyond 100: Cultivating possibilities* (pp. 87–91). Cham: Springer.

References

Harris, B. (1979). Whatever happened to little Albert? *American Psychologist, 34*, 151–160.

Harris M., & Reynolds, B. (2015). A pilot study of home-based smoking cessation programs for rural, Appalachian, pregnant smokers. *Journal of Obstetric, Gynecologic, & Neonatal Nursing: Clinical Scholarship for the Care of Women, Childbearing Families, & Newborns, 44*(2), 236–245.

Harter, S. (2006). Developmental and individual difference perspectives on self-esteem. In D. K. Mroczek & T. D. Little (Eds.), *Handbook of personality development* (pp. 311–334). Mahwah, NJ: Lawrence Erlbaum.

Harter, S. (2012). *The construction of the self* (2nd ed.). New York: Guilford Press.

Harter, S. (2018). Susan Harter self-report instruments. University of Denver. Retrieved October 26, 2018, from https://portfolio.du.edu/SusanHarter.

Haste, H., & Gardner, H. (2017). Jerome S. Bruner (1915–2016). *American Psychologist, 72*(7), 707–708.

Hattie, J. (2009). *Visible learning: A synthesis of over 800 meta-analyses relating to achievement.* New York: Routledge.

Hattie, J. (2012). *Visible learning for teachers: Maximizing impact on learning.* New York: Routledge.

Hattie, J. (2015a). The applicability of Visible Learning to higher education. *Scholarship of Teaching and Learning in Psychology, 1*(1), 79–91.

Hattie, J. (2015b), What works best in education: The politics of collaborative expertise. Retrieved October 23, 2018, from www.pearson.com/content/dam/one-dot-com/one-dot-com/global/standalone/hattie/files/150526_ExpertiseWEB_V1.pdf.

Hays, R. (Ed.). (1962). Psychology of the scientist: IV. Passages from the "idea books" of Clark L. Hull. *Perceptual and Motor Skills, 15*, 807–882.

Hazen, N. L., Allen, S. D., Christopher, C. H., Umemura, T., & Jacobvitz, D. B. (2015). Very extensive nonmaternal care predicts mother–infant attachment disorganization: Convergent evidence from two samples. *Development and Psychopathology, 27*(3), 649–661.

Hebb, D. O. (1949). *The organization of behavior.* New York: Wiley.

Hebb, D. O. (1958). *A textbook of psychology* (1st ed.). Philadelphia, PA: Saunders.

Hebb, D. O. (1960). The American revolution. *American Psychologist, 15*, 735–745.

Hebb, D. O. (1966). *A textbook of psychology* (2nd ed.). Philadelphia, PA: Saunders.

Hebb, D. O. (1972). *A textbook of psychology* (3rd ed.). Philadelphia, PA: Saunders.

Hebb, D. O. (1980). D. O. Hebb. In G. Lindzey (Ed.), *A history of psychology in autobiography* (Vol. 7, pp. 273–309). San Francisco, CA: Freeman.

Hebe, H. N. (2017). Towards a theory-driven integration of environmental education: The application of Piaget and Vygotsky in Grade R. *International Journal of Environmental and Science Education, 12*(6), 1525–1545.

Hellmann, D. R., Stiller, A., Glaubitz, C., & Kliem, S. (2018). (Why) do victims become perpetrators? Intergenerational transmission of parental violence in a representative German sample. *Journal of Family Psychology, 32*(2), 282–288.

Herculano-Houzel, S. (2009). The human brain in numbers: A linearly scaled-up primate brain. *Frontiers of Human Neuroscience, 3*(31). Retrieved October 13, 2018, from www.frontiersin.org/articles/10.3389/neuro.09.031.2009/full.

Hernandez-Orallo, J. (2017). *The measure of all minds: Evaluating natural and artificial intelligence.* New York: Cambridge University Press.

Heron, W. (1957, January). The pathology of boredom. *Scientific American, 196*, 52–56.

Herrnstein, R. J. (1974). Formal properties of the matching law. *Journal of the Experimental Analysis of Behavior, 21*(1), 159–164.

Herrnstein, R. J. (1997). *The matching law: Papers in psychology and economics* (R. J. Herrnstein, H. Rachlin & D. I. Laibson, eds.). New York: Russell Sage.

Herrnstein, R. J., Loveland, D. H., & Cable, C. (1976). Natural concepts in the pigeon. *Journal of Experimental Psychology: Animal Behavior Processes, 2*, 285–302.

Higgins, I., Stringer, S., & Schnupp, J. (2017). Unsupervised learning of temporal features for word categorization in a spiking neural network model of the auditory brain. *PLoS One, 12*(8). Retrieved October 16, 2018, from https://journals.plos.org/plosone/article?id=10.1371/journal.pone.0180174.

Hilbig, B. E. & Moshagen, M. (2014). Generalized outcome-based strategy classification: Comparing deterministic and probabilistic choice models. *Psychonomic Bulletin & Revie, 21*(6), 1431–1433.

Hipolito, L., Wilson-Poe, A., Campos-Jurado, Y., Zhong, E., Gonzalez-Romero, J., Virag, L., . . . Moron, J. A. (2015). Inflammatory pain promotes increased opioid self-administration: Role of dysregulated ventral tegmental area micro opioid receptors. *The Journal of Neuroscience, 35*(35), 12217–12231.

Hirst, W., & Phelps, E. A. (2016). Flashbulb memories. *Current Directions in Psychological Science, 25*(1), 36–41.

Hirst, W., Phelps, E. A., Meksin, R., Vaidya, C. J., Johnson, M. K.,Mitchell, K. J., . . . Olsson, A. (2015). A ten-year follow-up of a study of memory for the attack of September 11, 2001: Flashbulb memories and memories for flashbulb events. *Journal of Experimental Psychology: General, 144*(3), 604–623.

Hoffart, A. (2016). Cognitive models for panic disorder with agoraphobia: A study of disaggregated within-person effects. *Journal of Consulting and Clinical Psychology, 84*(9), 839–844.

Holland, S. K., Vannest, J., Mecoli, M., Jacola, L. M., Tillema, J. M., Karunanayaka, P. R., . . . Byars, A. (2007). Functional MRI of language lateralization during development in children. *International Journal of Audiology, 46*, 533–551.

Holman, D., & Spivey, M. J. (2016). Connectionist models of bilingual word reading. In R. R. Heredia, J. Altarriba, & A. B. Cieslicka (Eds.). *Methods in bilingual reading comprehension research* (pp. 213–229). New York: Springer.

Holyoak, R. J., & Spellman, B. A. (1993). Thinking. *Annual Review of Psychology, 44*, 265–315.

Homa, D. (2008). Long-term memory. In N. J. Salkind (Ed.), *Encyclopedia of educational psychology* (Vol. 2, pp. 620–624). Thousand Oaks, CA: Sage.

Houston, F. (2018). Gestalt in a changing world. In R. House, D. Kalisch, & J. Maidman (Eds.), *Humanistic psychology: Current trends and future prospects* (pp. 245–250). New York: Routledge.

Hull, C. L. (1933). *Hypnosis and suggestibility: An experimental approach.* New York: Appleton-Century-Crofts.

Hull, C. L. (1943). *Principles of behavior.* New York: Appleton-Century-Crofts.

Hull, C. L. (1951). *Essentials of behavior.* New Haven, CT: Yale University Press.

Hull, C. L. (1952). *A behavior system.* New Haven, CT: Yale University Press.

Hunt, M. M. (2007). *The story of psychology.* New York: Anchor Books.

Hutter, S. A., & Wilson, A. I. (2018). A novel role for the hippocampus in category learning. *The Journal of Neuroscience, 38*(31), 6803–6805.

IBM (2018). Real answers to your AI questions. Retrieved December 7, 2018, from www.ibm.com/watson/think-2018.

ICGA Tournaments. (2018). Tournaments between computer programs. Retrieved October 29, 2018, from www.grappa.univ-lille3.fr/icga/game.php?id=1.

Iliescu, B. F., & Dannemiller, J. L. (2008). Brain–behavior relationships in early visual development. In C. A. Nelson & M. Luciana (Eds.), *Handbook of developmental cognitive neuroscience* (2nd ed.; pp. 127–145). Cambridge, MA: MIT Press.

Inhelder, B. (1982). Outlook. In S. Modgil & C. Modgil (Eds.), *Jean Piaget: Consensus and controversy* (pp. 401–417). London: Praeger.

Inhelder, B., & Piaget, J. (1958). *The growth of logical thinking from childhood to adolescence.* New York: Basic Books.

Iordan, M. C., Greene, M. R., Beck, D. M., & Fei-Fei, L. (2016). Typicality sharpens category representations in object-selective cortex. *NeuroImage, 134*, 170–179.

Iyer, L. R., Doboli, S., Minai, A. A., Brown, V. R., Levine, D. S., & Paulus, P. B. (2009). Neural dynamics of idea generation and the effects of priming. *Neural Networks, 22*(5–6), 674–686.

Jagadeesh, B. (2009). Recognizing grandmother. *Nature Neuroscience, 12*(9), 1083–1085.

References

Jäkel, F., Singh, M., Wichmann, F. A., & Herzog, M. H. (2016). An overview of quantitative approaches in Gestalt perception. *Vision Research, 126*, 3–8.

James, W. (1890 [1950]). *Principles of psychology* (Vol. 1). New York: Holt.

Jean Piaget Society. (2010). Retrieved May 5, 2010, from www.piaget.org.

Jean Piaget Society. (2018). A brief biography of Jean Piaget. Retrieved October 19, 2018, from www.piaget .org/aboutPiaget.html.

Jerlhag, E. (2018). GLP-1 signaling and alcohol-mediated behaviors; preclinical and clinical evidence. *Neuropharmacology, 136*(Part B), 343–349.

Joffe, A. R., Bara, M., Anton, N., & Nobis, N. (2016). The ethics of animal research: A survey of the public and scientists in North America. *BMC Medical Ethics, 17*. Retrieved September 27, 2018, from https://bmcmedethics.biomedcentral.com/articles/10.1186/s12910-016-0100-x.

Johanson, D. J., & Shreeve, J. (1989). *Lucy's child*. New York: Morrow.

Johnson, D. W., & Johnson, R. T. (1994). *Learning together and alone: Cooperative, competitive, and individualistic learning* (4th ed.). Boston, MA: Allyn & Bacon.

Johnson, G. (1992). *In the palaces of memory: How we build the worlds inside our heads*. New York: Vintage.

Johnson, M. K., Bransford, J. D., & Solomon, S. (1973). Memory for tacit implications of sentences. *Journal of Experimental Psychology, 98*, 203–205.

Johnson, S. (2004). *Mind wide open: Your brain and the neuroscience of everyday life*. New York: Scribner.

Johnson, S. B., Riis, J. L., & Noble, K. G. (2016). State of the art review: Poverty and the developing brain. *Pediatrics, 137*(4), 1–16.

Johnston, J. M. (2013). *Radical behaviorism for ABA practitioners*. Cornwall on Hudson, NY: Sloan publishing.

Joiner, T. E., Buchman-Schmitt, J. M., Chu, C., & Hom, M. A. (2017). A sociobiological extension of the interpersonal theory of suicide. *Crisis: The Journal of Crisis Intervention and Suicide Prevention, 38*(2), 69–72.

Jonason, P. K. I. (2017). The grand challenges for evolutionary psychology: Survival challenges for a discipline. *Frontiers in Psychology, 8*. doi:10.3389/fpsyg.2017.01727.

Joncich, G. (1968). *The sane positivist: A biography of Edward L. Thorndike*. Middleton, CT: Wesleyan University Press.

Jones, M. C. (1974). Albert, Peter, and John B. Watson. *American Psychologist, 29*, 581–583.

Kalat, J. W. (2016). *Biological psychology* (12th ed.). Belmont, CA: Cengage/Thomson/Wadsworth.

Kamil, A. C., & Mauldin, J. E. (1988). A comparative ecological approach to the study of learning. In R. C. Bolles & M. D. Beecher (Eds.), *Evolution and learning* (pp. 117–133). Hillsdale, NJ: Lawrence Erlbaum.

Kamin, L. J. (1968). "Attention-like" processes in classical conditioning. In M. R. Jones (Ed.), *Miami symposium on the prediction of behavior: Aversive stimulation* (pp. 9–33). Miami, FL: University of Miami Press.

Kamin, L. J. (1969). Predictability, surprise, attention and conditioning. In B. A. Campbell & R. M. Church (Eds.), *Punishment and aversive behavior* (pp. 279–296). New York: Appleton-Century-Crofts.

Kaneda, K. (2018). Neuroplasticity in cholinergic neurons of the laterodorsal tegmental nucleus contributes to the development of cocaine addiction. *European Journal of Neuroscience*. Retrieved October 2013, from https://onlinelibrary.wiley.com/doi/full/10.1111/ejn.13962.

Karadottir, R. T., & Kuo, C. T. (2018). Neuronal activity-dependent control of postnatal neurogenesis and gliogenesis. *Annual Review of Neuroscience, 41*, 139–161.

Keith, J. R., Rapgay, L., Theodore, D., Schwartz, J. M., & Ross, J. L. (2015). An assessment of an automated EEG biofeedback system for attention deficits in a substance use disorders residential treatment setting. *Psychology of Addictive Behaviors, 29*(1), 17–25.

Keith-Lucas, T., & Guttman, N. (1975). Robust single trial delayed backward conditioning. *Journal of Comparative and Physiological Psychology, 88*, 468–476.

Keller, F. S. (1968). Good-bye teacher . . .. *Journal of Applied Behavior Analysis, 1*(1), 79–89.

Keller, F. S. (1969). *Learning: Reinforcement theory* (2nd ed.). New York: Random House.

Keller, J. M. (2010). *Motivational design for learning and performance: The ARCS model approach*. New York: Springer.

Kelley, H. H. (1992). Common-sense psychology and scientific psychology. *Annual Review of Psychology*, *43*, 1–23.

Kellogg, D. (2017). Thinking of feeling: Hasan, Vygotsky, and some ruminations on the development of narrative sensibility in children. *Language and Education*, *31*(4), 374–387.

Kempen, E., Kasambala, J., Christie, L., Symington, E., Jooste, L., & Van Eeden, T. (2017). Expectancy-value theory contributes to understanding consumer attitudes towards cow's milk alternatives and variants. *International Journal of Consumer Studies*, *41*(3), 245–252.

Kenrick, D. T., Maner, J. K., Butner, J., Li, N. P., & Becker, D. V. (2002). Dynamical evolutionary psychology: Mapping the domains of the new interactionist paradigm. *Personality and Social Psychology Review*, *6*, 347–356.

Keri, S. (2003). The cognitive neuroscience of category learning. *Brain Research Reviews*, *43*, 85–109.

Kerz, E., Wiechmann, D., & Riedel, F. B. (2017). Implicit learning in the crowd: Investigating the role of awareness in the acquisition of L2 knowledge. *Studies in Second Language Acquisition*, *39*(4), 711–734.

Khng, K. H. (2017). A better state-of-mind: Deep breathing reduces state anxiety and enhances test performance through regulating test cognitions in children. *Cognition and Emotion*, *31*(7), 1502–1510.

Killeen, P. R. (2003). Complex dynamic processes in sign tracking with an omission contingency (negative automaintenance). *Journal of Experimental Psychology: Animal Behavior Processes*, *29*, 49–60.

Killeen, P. R., Posadas-Sanchez, D., Johansen, E. B., & Thraikill, E. A. (2009). Progressive ratio schedules of reinforcement. *Journal of Experimental Psychology: Animal Behavior Processes*, *35*(1), 35–50.

Kim, W. S., Fu, Y., Dobson-Stone, C., Hsiao, J. H. T., Shang, K., Hallupp, M., . . . Kwok, J. B. J. (2018). Effect of fluvoxamine on amyloid-beta peptide generation and memory. *Journal of Alzheimer's Disease*, *62*(4), 1777–1787.

Kincheloe, J. L., & Horn, R. A., Jr. (Eds.). (2007). *The Praeger handbook of education and psychology*. Westport, CT: Praeger.

King, A. R., Ratzak, A., Ballantyne, S., Knutson, S., Russell, T. D., Pogalz, C. R., & Breen, C. M. (2018). Differentiating corporal punishment from physical abuse in the prediction of lifetime aggression. *Aggressive Behavior*, *44*, 306–315. Retrieved October 10, 2018, from https://onlinelibrary.wiley.com/doi/epdf/10.1002/ab.21753.

Klein, R. G. (2017). Language and human evolution. *Journal of Neurolinguistics*, *43*(Part B), 204–221.

Knight, R. G., & O'Hagan, K. (2009). Autobiographical memory in long-term survivors of severe traumatic brain injury. *Journal of Clinical and Experimental Neuropsychology*, *31*(5), 575–583.

Knight, W. (2018). A plan to advance AI by exploring the minds of children. *MIT Technology Review*. Retrieved October 28, 2018, from www.technologyreview.com/s/612002/a-plan-to-advance-ai-by-exploring-the-minds-of-children.

Koffka, K. (1922). Perception: An introduction to Gestalt theory. *Psychological Bulletin*, *19*, 531–585.

Koffka, K. (1925). *The growth of the mind*. New York: Harcourt, Brace & World.

Koffka, K. (1935). *Principles of Gestalt psychology*. New York: Harcourt, Brace & World.

Köhler, W. (1925). *The mentality of the apes*. New York: Harcourt, Brace & World.

Köhler, W. (1929). *Gestalt psychology*. New York: Liveright.

Köhler, W. (1969). *The task of Gestalt psychology*. Princeton, NJ: Princeton University Press.

Kolb, B., Harker, S., & Gibb, R. (2017). Principles of plasticity in the developing brain. *Developmental Medicine & Child Neurology*, *59*(12), 1218–1223.

Koriat, A., Goldsmith, M., & Pansky, A. (2000). Toward a psychology of memory accuracy. *Annual Review of Psychology*, *51*, 481–537.

Kozulin, A. (1990). *Vygotsky's psychology: A biography of ideas*. Cambridge, MA: Harvard University Press.

Krech, D., Rosenzweig, M., & Bennett, E. L. (1960). Effects of environmental complexity and training on brain chemistry. *Journal of Comparative and Physiological Psychology*, *53*, 509–519.

References

Krech, D., Rosenzweig, M., & Bennett, E. L. (1962). Relations between brain chemistry and problem-solving among rats in enriched and impoverished environments. *Journal of Comparative and Physiological Psychology, 55*, 801–807.

Krech, D., Rosenzweig, M., & Bennett, E. L. (1966). Environmental impoverishment, social isolation, and changes in brain chemistry and anatomy. *Physiology and Behavior, 1*, 99–104.

Kuhn, T. S. (1962). *The structure of scientific revolutions.* Chicago, IL: University of Chicago Press.

Kuriscak, E., Marsalek, P., Stroffek, J., & Toth, P. G. (2015). Biological context of Hebb learning in artificial neural networks, a review. *Neurocomputing: An International Journal, 152*, 27–35.

Kwok, D. W. S., & Boakes, R. A. (2015). Taste aversion learning despite long delays: How best explained? *International Journal of Comparative Psychology, 28*, 1–15.

Kwok, D. W. S., Sun, Q., & Boakes, R. A. (2016). Mediated overshadowing and potentiation of long-delay taste aversion learning: Two versus six cue-taste pairings. *Journal of Experimental Psychology: Animal Learning and Cognition, 42*(1), 106–115.

Laczo, J., Vlcek, K., Vyhnalek, M., Vajnerova, O., Ort, M., Holmerova, I., . . . Hort, J. (2009). Spatial navigation testing discriminates two types of amnestic mild cognitive impairment. *Behavioural Brain Research, 202*(2), 252–259.

Lambert, E. B., & Clyde, M. (2003). Putting Vygotsky to the test. In D. E. Lytle (Ed.), *Play and educational theory and practice: Play and culture studies* (Vol. 5; pp. 59–98). Westport, CT: Praeger.

Lana, R. E. (2002). The behavior analytic approach to language and thought. *Journal of Mind & Behavior, 23*, 31–49.

Lanciano, T., Curci, A., Matera, G., & Sartori, G. (2018). Measuring the flashbulb-like nature of memories for private events: The flashbulb memory checklist. *Memory, 26*(8), 1053–1064.

Laney, C., & Loftus, E. F. (2010). Truth in emotional memories. In B. H. Bornstein & R. L. Wiener (Eds.), *Emotion and the law: Psychological perspectives* (pp. 157–183). New York: Springer.

Lantolf, J. P. (2003). Vygotsky's psychology-philosophy: A metaphor for language theory and learning. *Modern Language Journal, 87*, 137–138.

Lashley, K. S. (1924). Studies of cerebral function in learning. *Archives of Neurological Psychiatry, 12*, 249–276.

Lavigne, K. M., Rapin, L. A., Metzak, P. D., Whitman, J. C., Jung, K., Dohen, M., . . . Woodward, T. S. (2015). Left-dominant temporal-frontal hypercoupling in schizophrenia patients with hallucinations during speech perception. *Schizophrenia Bulletin, 41*(1), 259–267.

Leahey, T. H. (2000). *A history of modern psychology.* Englewood Cliffs, NJ: Prentice Hall.

Leäo, M. F. F. C., Laurenti, C., & Haydu, V. B. (2016). Darwinism, radical behaviorism, and the role of variation in Skinnerian explaining behavior. *Behavior Analysis: Research and Practice, 16*(1), 1–11.

Leclerc, G., Lefrançois, R., Dube, M., Hebert, R., & Gaulin, P. (1998). The self-actualization concept: A content validation. *Journal of Social Behavior and Personality, 13*, 69–84.

Lefrançois, G. R. (2018). *Psychology for teaching* (2nd ed.). San Diego, CA: Bridgepoint Education.

Lehar, S. (2003). *The world in your head: A Gestalt view of the mechanism of conscious experience.* Mahwah, NJ: Erlbaum.

Lehrer, P. M., & Gevirtz, R. (2014). Heart rate variability biofeedback: How and why does it work? *Frontiers of Psychology, 5*. Retrieved October 15, 2018, from www.ncbi.nlm.nih.gov/pmc/articles/PMC4104929.

Leopold, T. (2017). A professor built an AI teaching assistant for his courses – and it could shape the future of education. *Backchannel.* Retrieved December 17, 2018, from www.businessinsider.com/a-professor-built-an-ai-teaching-assistant-for-his-courses-and-it-could-shape-the-future-of-education-2017-3.

Lepper, M. R. (1981). Intrinsic and extrinsic motivation in children: Detrimental effects of superfluous social controls. In W. A. Collins (Ed.), *Aspects of the development of competence: The Minnesota symposium on child psychology* (Vol. 14, pp. 155–213). Hillsdale, NJ: Lawrence Erlbaum.

Lepper, M. R., & Greene, D. (1975). Turning play into work: Effects of adult surveillance and extrinsic rewards on children's intrinsic motivation. *Journal of Personality and Social Psychology, 31*, 479–486.

Leslie, J. C. (2006). Herbert Spencer's contributions to behavior analysis: A retrospective review of *Principles of Psychology*. *Journal of the Experimental Analysis of Behavior*, *86*, 123–129.

Letourneau, E. J., & O'Donohue, W. (1997). Classical conditioning of female sexual arousal. *Archives of Sexual Behavior*, *26*, 63–78.

Li, X. (2002). Connectionist learning: A comparison of neural networks and an optical thin-film multilayer model. *Connection Science: Journal of Neural Computing, Artificial Intelligence & Cognitive Research*, *14*, 49–63.

Lilly, J. C. (1972). *The center of the cyclone: An autobiography of inner space*. New York: Julian.

Lin, J. Y., Arthurs, J., & Reilly, S. (2017). Conditioned taste aversions: From poisons to pain to drugs of abuse. *Psychonomic Bulletin & Review*, *24*(2), 335–351.

Linderholm, T. (2006). Reading with purpose. *Journal of College Reading and Learning*, *36*(2), 70–80.

Linnenbrink-Garcia, L., Wormington, S. V., Snyder, K. E., Riggsbee, J., Perez, T., Ben-Eliyahu, A., & Hill, N. E. (2018). Multiple pathways to success: An examination of integrative motivational profiles among upper elementary and college students. *Journal of Educational Psychology*, *110*(7), 1026–1048.

Lodish, H. F., Berk, A., Kaiser; C. A., Bretscher, A., Ploegh, H., Amon, A., & Martin, K. C. (2016). *Molecular cell biology* (8th ed.). New York: W. H. Freeman.

Loftus, E. F. (1979). *Eyewitness testimony*. Cambridge, MA: Harvard University Press.

Loftus, E. F. (1997). Creating false memories. *Scientific American*, *227*(3), 70–75.

Loftus, E. F. (2007). Memory distortions: Problems solved and unsolved. In M. Garry & H. Hayne (Eds.), *Do justice and let the sky fall: Elizabeth Loftus and her contributions to science, law, and academic freedom* (pp. 1–14). Mahwah, NJ: Lawrence Erlbaum.

Loftus, E. F., & Cahill, L. (2007). Memory distortion: From misinformation to rich false memory. In J. S. Nairne (Ed.), *The foundations of remembering: Essays in honor of Henry L. Roediger, III* (pp. 413–425). New York: Psychology Press.

Loftus, E. F., Feldman, J., & Dashiell, R. (1995). The reality of illusory memories. In D. L. Schacter, J. T. Coyle, G. D. Fischbach, M. M. Mesulam, & L. E. Sullivan (Eds.), *Memory distortion: How minds, brains and societies reconstruct the past* (pp. 47–68). Cambridge, MA: Harvard University Press.

Lombardi, M. G., Fadda, L., Serra, L., Di Paola, M., Caltagirone, C., & Carlesimo, G. A. (2016). Recollection and familiarity components of recognition: Effect of side of mesio-temporal damage. *Neurocase*, *22*(1), 1–11.

Lorenz, K. (1952). *King Solomon's ring*. London: Methuen.

Lorusso, M. L., Burigo, M., Borsa, V., & Molteni, M. (2015). Processing sentences with literal versus figurative use of verbs: An ERP study with children with language impairments, nonverbal impairments, and typical development. *Behavioural Neurology*, *2015*, Retrieved October 21, 2018, from www.hindawi.com/journals/bn/2015/475271.

Losos, J. B., & Lenski, R. E. (Eds.). (2017) *How evolution shapes our lives: Essays on biology and society*. Princeton, NJ: Princeton University Press.

Lourenco, O., & Machado, A. (1996). In defense of Piaget's theory: A reply to 10 common criticisms. *Psychological Review*, *103*, 143–164.

Luria, A. R. (1968). *The mind of a mnemonist*. New York: Avon.

Lyons-Ruth, K., Pechtel, P., Yoon, S. A., Anderson, C. M., & Teicher, M. H. (2016). Disorganized attachment in infancy predicts greater amygdala volume in adulthood. *Behavioural Brain Research*, *308*, 83–93.

Macfarlane, D. A. (1930). The role of kinesthesis in maze learning. *University of California Publications in Psychology*, *4*, 277–305.

Macmillan, M. (2008). Phineas Gage: Unravelling the myth. *The Psychologist*, *21*(9), 828–831.

Maehler, C., & Schuchardt, K. (2016). Working memory in children with specific learning disorders and/or attention deficits. *Learning and Individual Differences*, *49*, 341–347.

Magidson, J. F., Roberts, B. W., Collado-Rodriguez, A., & Lejuez, C. W. (2014). Theory-driven intervention for changing personality: Expectancy value theory, behavioral activation, and conscientiousness. *Developmental Psychology*, *50*(5), 1442–1450.

References

Magro, L. O., Attout, L., Majerus, S., & Szmalec, A. (2018). Short- and long-term memory determinants of novel word form learning. *Cognitive Development, 47*, 146–157.

Mahr, J. B., & Csibra, G. (2018). Why do we remember? The communicative function of episodic memory. *Behavioral and Brain Sciences, 41*. Retrieved October 21, 2018, from www.yorku.ca/mar/Mar%20&%20Spreng%202018%20BBS%20Commentary.pdf.

Malak, M. S., Sharma, U., & Deppeler, J. M. (2015). "Can I really teach without my magic cane?" Teachers' responses to the banning of corporal punishment. *International Journal of Inclusive Education, 19*(12), 1325–1341.

Malone, J. C., Jr., & Cruchon, N. M. (2001). Radical behaviorism and the rest of psychology: A review/précis of Skinner's About Behaviorism. *Behavior & Philosophy, 29*, 31–57.

Manassa, R. P., McCormick, M. I., Dixson, D. L., Ferrari, M. C. O., & Chivers, D. P. (2014). Social learning of predators by coral reef fish: Does observer number influence acquisition of information? *Behavioral Ecology and Sociobiology, 68*(8), 1237–1244.

Manrique, H. M., & Walker, M. J. (2017). *Early evolution of human memory: Great apes, tool-making, and cognition*. Cham: Palgrave Macmillan.

Manuel, A. L., & Schnider, A. (2016). Differential processing of immediately repeated verbal and non-verbal stimuli: An evoked-potential study. *European Journal of Neuroscience, 43*(1), 89–97.

Markman, A. B., & Gentner, D. (2001). Thinking. *Annual Review of Psychology, 52*, 223–247.

Marsh, A. A. (2016). Neural, cognitive, and evolutionary foundations of human altruism. *WIREs Cognitive Science, 7*(1), 59–71.

Marsico, G. (Ed.). (2015). Jerome S. Bruner beyond 100: Cultivating possibilities. *Cultural Psychology of Education* (Vol. 2). Cham: Springer.

Marsico, G. (2017). Jerome S. Bruner: Manifesto for the future of education/Jerome S. Bruner: Manifiesto por el futuro de la educación. Infancia y Aprendizaje. *Journal for the Study of Education and Development, 40*(4), 754–781.

Martens, B. K., & Hiralall, A. S. (1997). Scripted sequences of teacher interaction: A versatile, low-impact procedure for increasing appropriate behavior in a nursery school. *Behavior Modification, 21*, 308–323.

Martí, E., & Rodríguez, C. (Eds.). (2012). *After Piaget*. Piscataway, NJ: Transaction Publishers.

Martinez-Marti, M. L., & Ruch, W. (2017). Character strengths predict resilience over and above positive affect, self-efficacy, optimism, social support, self-esteem, and life satisfaction. *The Journal of Positive Psychology, 12*(2), 110–119.

Martinie, M. A., Milland, L., & Olive, T. (2013). Some theoretical considerations on attitude, arousal and affect during cognitive dissonance. *Social and Personality Psychology Compass, 7*(9), 680–688.

Maslow, A. H. (1970). *Motivation and personality* (2nd ed.). New York: Harper & Row.

Mason, O. J., & Brady, F. (2009). The psychotomimetic effects of short-term sensory deprivation. *Journal of Nervous and Mental Disease, 197*(10), 783–785.

Mayo Clinic (2018). Serotonin and norepinephrine reuptake inhibitors (SNRIs). Retrieved October 15, 2018, from www.mayoclinic.org/diseases-conditions/depression/in-depth/antidepressants/art-20044970.

McAdams, D. P. (1984). Love, power, and images of the self. In C. Z. Malatesta & C. E. Izard (Eds.), *Emotion in adult development* (pp. 159–174). Beverly Hills, CA: Sage.

McClelland, J. L., & Rumelhart, D. E. (Eds.). (1986). *Parallel distributed processing: Explorations in the microstructure of cognition* (Vol. 2). Cambridge, MA: Bradford/MIT Press.

McConnell, J. V. (1962). Memory transfer through cannibalism in planarians. *Journal of Neuropsychiatry, 3* (Suppl. 1), 542–548.

McConnell, J. V. (1976). Worm-breeding with tongue in cheek and the confessions of a scientist hoist by his own petard. *UNESCO Courier, 32*, 12–15.

McDougall, W. (1908). *An introduction to social psychology*. London: Methuen.

McDowell, J. J., Caron, M. L., Kulubekova, S., & Berg, J. P. (2008). A computational theory of selection by consequences applied to concurrent schedules. *Journal of the Experimental Analysis of Behavior, 90*(3), 387–403.

McGrath, A. (2017). Dealing with dissonance: A review of cognitive dissonance reduction. *Social and Personality Psychology Compass, 11*(12), 1–17.

McKeachie, W. J. (1997). McConnell: Mischievous but not malevolent? *American Psychologist, 52*, 269.

Mead, H. K., Beauchaine, T. P., & Shannon, K. E. (2010). Neurobiological adaptations to violence across development. *Development and Psychopathology, 22*(1), 1–22.

Mead, M. (1935). *Sex and temperament in three primitive societies.* New York: Morrow.

Meadows, S. (2018). *Understanding child development: Psychological perspectives and applications.* New York: Routledge.

Medin, D. L., Lynch, E. B., & Solomon, K. O. (2000). Are there kinds of concepts? *Annual Review of Psychology, 51*, 121–147.

Meltzoff, A. N., & Moore, M. K. (1989). Imitation in newborn infants: Exploring the range of gestures imitated and the underlying mechanisms. *Developmental Psychology, 25*, 954–962.

Mendonca, A., Felgueiras, H., Verdelho, A., Camara, S., Grilo, C., Maroco, J., ... Guerreiro, M. (2018). Memory complaints in amnestic mild cognitive impairment: More prospective or retrospective? *International Journal of Geriatric Psychiatry.* Retrieved October 21, 2018, from https://onlinelibrary.wiley.com/doi/epdf/10.1002/gps.5005.

Mervis, C. B., & Rosch, E. (1981). Categorization of natural objects. *Annual Review of Psychology, 32*, 89–115.

Mihailoff, G. A., Haines, D. E., & May, P. J. (2018). The midbrain. In D. E. Haines & G. A. Mihailoff (Eds.), *Fundamental neuroscience for basic and clinical applications* (5th ed.; pp. 183–194). Philadelphia, PA: Elsevier.

Milkman, H. B., & Sunderwirth, S. G. (2010). *Craving for ecstasy and natural highs: A positive approach to mood alteration.* Thousand Oaks, CA: Sage.

Milkowski, M. (2018). From computer metaphor to computational modeling: The evolution of computationalism. *Minds and Machines: Journal for Artificial Intelligence, Philosophy and Cognitive Science, 28*(3), 515–541.

Miller, G. A. (1956). The magical number seven, plus or minus two: Some limits on our capacity for processing information. *Psychological Review, 63*, 81–97.

Miller, H. C., Rayburn-Reeves, R., & Zentall, T. R. (2009). Imitation and emulation by dogs using a bidirectional control procedure. *Behavioural Processes, 80*(2), 109–114.

Miller, M. (2013). Artificial intelligence, our final invention? *Washington Post.* Retrieved October 31, 2018, from https://wapo.st/2ZIs9zE.

Miller, N. E. (1951). Learnable drives and rewards. In S. S. Stevens (Ed.), *Handbook of experimental psychology* (pp. 435–472). New York: Wiley.

Miller, N. E. (1969). Learning of visceral and glandular responses. *Science, 163*, 434–445.

Miller, N. E., & Carmona, A. (1967). Modification of a visceral response, salivation in thirsty dogs, by instrumental training with water reward. *Journal of Comparative and Physiological Psychology, 63*, 1–6.

Miller, N. E., & Dollard, J. C. (1941). *Social learning and imitation.* New Haven, CT: Yale University Press.

Miller, W. R., & Atencio, D. J. (2008). Free will as a proportion of variance. In J. Baer, J. C. Kaufman, & R. F. Baumeister (Eds.), *Are we free? Psychology and free will* (pp. 275–295). New York: Oxford University Press.

Mills, J. A. (1998). *Control: A history of behavioral psychology.* New York: New York University Press.

Milshtein-Parush, H., Frere, S., Regev, L., Lahav, C., Benbenishty, A., Ben-Eliyahu, S., ... Slutsky, I. (2017). Sensory deprivation triggers synaptic and intrinsic plasticity in the hippocampus. *Cerebral Cortex, 27*(6), 3457–3470.

Mironenko, I. A. (2009). "Great ideas" in Russian psychology: Personality impact on psychophysiological functions and causal approach to self-determination. *Psychology in Russia: State of the Art, 2*, 225–238.

MIT Technology Review (2018). Machine learning predicts world cup winner. *Data Science.* Retrieved October 31, 2018, from www.datascience.us/machine-learning-predicts-world-cup-winner.

Modgil, S., & Modgil, C. (Eds.). (1982). *Jean Piaget: Consensus and controversy.* London: Praeger.

References

Mohl, J. C. (2012). Seeing the future by looking at the past: Comment on Kirsch et al. *Contemporary Hypnosis & Integrative Therapy, 29*(2), 169–174.

Mohring, W., Libertus, M. E., & Bertin, E. (2012). Speed discrimination in 6- and 10-month-old infants follows Weber's law. *Journal of Experimental Child Psychology, 111*(3), 405–418.

Moll, L. C. (2014). *L.S. Vygotsky and education*. New York: Routledge.

Moore, J. (2010). Philosophy of science, with special consideration given to behaviorism as the philosophy of the science of behavior. *The Psychological Record, 60*(1), 137–150.

Moray, N. (1959). Attention in dichotic listening: Affective cues and influence of instruction. *Quarterly Journal of Experimental Psychology, 11*, 56–60.

Moreno, M., & Giralt, E. (2015). Three valuable peptides from bee and wasp venoms for therapeutic and biotechnological use: Melitin, apamin and mastoparan. *Toxins (Basel), 7*(4), 1126–1150.

Morgado, L. (2003). The role of representation in Piagetian theory: Changes over time. In T. Brown & L. Smith (Eds.), *Reductionism and the development of knowledge* (pp. 159–175). Mahwah, NJ: Lawrence Erlbaum.

Morvan, C., & O'Connor, A. (2017). *An analysis of Leon Festinger's A theory of cognitive dissonance*. New York: Routledge.

Mozur, P. (2018). Inside China's dystopian dreams: A.I., shame and lots of cameras. *New York Times*. Retrieved October 28, 2018, from www.nytimes.com/2018/07/08/business/china-surveillance-technology.html.

Mueller, C. M., & Dweck, C. S. (1998). Praise for intelligence can undermine children's motivation and performance. *Journal of Personality and Social Psychology, 75*, 33–52.

Mukherjee, S., & Sahay, A. (2018). Nocebo effects from negative product information: When information hurts, paying money could heal. *Journal of Consumer Marketing, 35*(1), 32–39.

Muller, U., Ten Eycke, K., & Baker, L. (2015). Piaget's theory of intelligence. In S. Goldstein, D. Princiotta, & J. Naglieri (Eds.), *Handbook of intelligence: Evolutionary theory, historical perspective, and current concepts* (pp. 137–151). New York: Springer.

Murchison, C. (Ed.). (1936). *A history of psychology in autobiography* (Vol. 3). Worcester, MA: Clark University Press.

Nakajima, S. (2018). Effect of water temperature on swimming-based taste aversion learning in rats. *Learning and Motivation, 63*, 91–97.

Nakajima, S., Ogai, T., & Sasaki, A. (2018). Relapse of conditioned taste aversion in rats exposed to constant and graded extinction treatments. *Learning and Motivation, 63*, 11–19.

Nasser, H. M., Lafferty, D. S., Lesser, E. N., Bacharach, S. Z., & Calu, D. J. (2018). Disconnection of basolateral amygdala and insular cortex disrupts conditioned approach in Pavlovian lever autoshaping. *Neurobiology of Learning and Memory, 147*, 35–45.

National Institute on Drug Abuse (2018). What is cocaine. Retrieved October 13, 2013, from www.drugabuse.gov/publications/research-reports/cocaine/what-cocaine.

Navakatikyan, M. A., Murrell, P., Bensemann, J., Davison, M., & Elliffe, D. (2013). Law of effect models and choice between many alternatives. *Journal of the Experimental Analysis of Behavior, 100*(2), 222–256.

Navarra, R. L., & Waterhouse, B. D. (2018) Considering noradrenergically mediated facilitation of sensory signal processing as a component of psychostimulant-induced performance enhancement. *Brain Research*. Retrieved October 15, 2018, from www.ncbi.nlm.nih.gov/pubmed/29935154.

Neisser, U. (1976). *Cognition and reality: Principles and implications of cognitive psychology*. San Francisco, CA: Freeman.

Neruda, P. (1972). *The captain's verses*. New York: New Directions.

Nestler, E. J. (2016). Reflections on: "A general role for adaptations in G-Proteins and the cyclic AMP system in mediating the chronic actions of morphine and cocaine on neuronal function". *Brain Research, 1645*, 71–74.

New World Encyclopedia (2018a). Lev Vygotsky. Retrieved October 19, 2018, from www.newworldencyclopedia.org/entry/Lev_Vygotsky.

New World Encyclopedia (2018b). Clark L. Hull. Retrieved April 12, 2010, from www.newworldencyclopedia.org/entry/Clark_L._Hull?oldid=680368.

Newell, A. (1973). Artificial intelligence and the concept of mind. In R. C. Schank & C. M. Colby (Eds.), *Computer models of thought and language* (pp. 1–60). San Francisco, CA: Freeman.

Newell, A., & Simon, H. A. (1972). *Human problem solving.* Englewood Cliffs, NJ: Prentice Hall.

Newell, A., Shaw, J. C., & Simon, H. A. (1958). Elements of a theory of human problem-solving. *Psychological Review, 65,* 151–166.

Nguyen, M. A. (2017). Liberal education and the connection with Vygotsky's theory of the zone of proximal development. *Cultural-Historical Psychology, 13*(1), 89–104. [In Russian]

Nicolai, J., Moshagen, M., & Demmel, R. (2018). A test of expectancy-value theory in predicting alcohol consumption. *Addiction Research & Theory, 26*(2), 133–142.

Ninness, C., Ninness, S. K., Rumph, M., & Lawson, D. (2018). The emergence of stimulus relations: Human and computer learning. *Perspectives on Behavior Science, 41*(1), 121–154. Retrieved October 31, 2018, from https://link.springer.com/article/10.1007/s40614-017-0125-6.

Norcross, J. C., & Tomcho, T. J. (1994). Great books in psychology: Three studies in search of a consensus. *Teaching of Psychology, 21,* 86–90.

Nordvik, J. E., Walle, K. M., Nyberg, C. K., Fjell, A. M., Walhovd, K. B., Westlye, L. T., & Tornas, S. (2014). Bridging the gap between clinical neuroscience and cognitive rehabilitation: The role of cognitive training, models of neuroplasticity and advanced neuroimaging in future brain injury rehabilitation. *Neuro-Rehabilitation, 34*(1), 81–85.

Nosofsky, R. M., Sanders, C. A., & McDaniel, M. A. (2018). Tests of an exemplar-memory model of classification learning in a high-dimensional natural-science category domain. *Journal of Experimental Psychology: General, 147*(3), 328–353.

Nucci, L., & Turiel, E. (2001). Message from the Jean Piaget Society. *Cognitive Development, 16,* 657–658.

O'Brien, K. S., Kolt, G. S., Weber, A., & Hunter, J. A. (2010). Alcohol consumption in sport: The influence of sporting idols, friends and normative drinking practices. *Drug and Alcohol Review.* Retrieved May 17, 2010, from www3.interscience.wiley.com/cgi-bin/fulltext/123358202/PDFSTART.

Obukhova, L. F. (2016). On account of the 120th birthday anniversary of L.S. Vygotsky and J. Piaget. *Cultural-Historical Psychology, 12*(3), 226–231.

Ocumpaugh, J., San Pedro, M. O., Lai, H. Y., Baker, R. S., & Borgen, F. (2016). Middle school engagement with mathematics software and later interest and self-efficacy for STEM careers. *Journal of Science Education and Technology, 25*(6), 877–887.

O'Donohue, W., & Ferguson, K. E. (2001). *The psychology of B. F. Skinner.* Thousand Oaks, CA: Sage.

O'Leary, K. D., Kaufman, K. F., Kass, R. E., & Drabman, R. S. (1970). The effects of loud and soft reprimands on the behavior of disruptive students. *Exceptional Children, 37,* 145–155.

O'Neil, W. M. (1991). In what sense do Tolman's intervening variables intervene? *Australian Journal of Psychology, 43,* 159–162.

Oesterdiekhoff, G. W. (2016). Child and ancient man: How to define their commonalities and differences. *The American Journal of Psychology, 129*(3), 295–312.

Olds, J. (1956). Pleasure centers in the brain. *Scientific American, 195,* 105–116.

Olds, J., & Milner, P. (1954). Positive reinforcement produced by electrical stimulation of septal area and other regions of rat brain. *Journal of Comparative and Physiological Psychology, 47,* 419–427.

Oscar-Berman, N., & Blum, K. (2016). Reward dependence and reward deficiency. In V. Jagaroo & S. L. Santangelo (Eds.), *Neurophenotypes: Advancing psychiatry and neuropsychology in the "OMICS" era.* (pp. 193–211). New York: Springer.

Oswick, C., Keenoy, T., & Grant, D. (2002). Metaphor and analogical reasoning in organization theory: Beyond orthodoxy. *Academy of Management Review, 27,* 294–303.

Öttl, A., & Behne, D. M. (2016). Experience-based probabilities modulate expectations in a gender-coded artificial language. *Frontiers in Psychology, 7.* Retrieved October 29, 2018, from www.ncbi.nlm.nih.gov/pmc/articles/PMC4993866.

References

Öttl, A., & Behne, D. M. (2017). Assessing the formation of experience-based gender expectations in an implicit learning scenario. *Frontiers in Psychology*, 8. Retrieved October 29, 2018, from www.ncbi.nlm.nih.gov/pmc/articles/PMC5594219.

Overmier, J., & Meyers-Manor, J. (2015). Alerts for assessing biological constraints on learning. *International Journal of Comparative Psychology*, 28. Retrieved October 12, 2018, from https://escholarship.org/uc/item/8tk8h8c4.

Paasch, V., Leibowitz, L., Accardo, J., & Slifer, L. (2016). Preparing children with autism spectrum disorders for overnight sleep studies: A case series. *Clinical Practice in Pediatric Psychology*, *4*(2), 153–163.

Paiva, R. C., Ferreira, M. S., & Frade, M. M. (2017). Intelligent tutorial system based on personalized system of instruction to teach or remind mathematical concepts. *Journal of Computer Assisted Learning*, *33*(4), 370–381.

Pajares, F. (2004). Albert Bandura: Biographical sketch. Retrieved May 16, 2010, from http://des.emory.edu/mfp/bandurabio.html.

Pan, S. C. (2015). The interleaving effect: Mixing it up boosts learning. *Scientific American*. Retrieved October 23, 2018, from www.scientificamerican.com/article/the-interleaving-effect-mixing-it-up-boosts-learning.

Paolini, C. I., & Oiberman, A. J. (2017). Age of object permanence acquisition in Argentine infants. *Acta Psiquiatrica y Psicologica de America Latina*, *63*(3), 163–173. [In Spanish]

Paradis, E., & Sutkin, G. (2017). Beyond a good story: From Hawthorne effect to reactivity in health professions education research. *Medical Education*, *51*(1), 31–39.

Pascal, B. (1820). *Pensées de Blaise Pascal*. Paris: Ledentu, Libraire, quai des Augustins.

Pass, S. (2007). When constructivists Jean Piaget and Lev Vygotsky were pedagogical collaborators: A viewpoint from a study of their communications. *Journal of Constructivist Psychology*, *20*, 277–282.

Paul, D. B., & Blumenthal, A. L. (1989). On the trail of Little Albert. *Psychological Record*, *39*, 547–553.

Pear, J. J. (2007). *A historical and contemporary look at psychological systems*. Mahwah, NJ: Lawrence Erlbaum.

Penfield, W. (1969). Consciousness, memory and man's conditioned reflexes. In K. H. Pribram (Ed.), *On the biology of learning* (pp. 129–168). New York: Harcourt Brace Jovanovich.

Perez, L., Patel, U., Rivota, M., Calin-Jageman, I. E., & Calin-Jageman, R. J. (2018). Savings memory is accompanied by transcriptional changes that persist beyond the decay of recall. *Learning & Memory*, *25*(1), 45–48.

Perinat, A. (2007). La teoría histórico-cultural de Vygotsky: Algunas acotaciones a su origen y su alcance. *Revista de Historia de la Psicología*, *28*, 19–25.

Perry, R. E., Blair, C., & Sullivan, R. M. (2017). Neurobiology of infant attachment: Attachment despite adversity and parental programming of emotionality. *Current Opinion in Psychology*, *17*, 1–6.

Peterson, L. R., & Peterson, N. J. (1959). Short-term retention of individual verbal items. *Journal of Experimental Psychology*, *58*, 193–198.

Piaget, J. (1926). *The language and thought of the child*. New York: Harcourt, Brace & World.

Piaget, J. (1929). *The child's conception of the world*. New York: Harcourt, Brace & World.

Piaget, J. (1930). *The child's conception of physical causality*. London: Kegan Paul.

Piaget, J. (1932). *The moral judgment of the child*. London: Kegan Paul.

Piaget, J. (1946). *Le développement de la notion de temps chez l'enfant*. Paris: Presses Universitaires de France.

Piaget, J. (1950). *The psychology of intelligence*. New York: Harcourt, Brace & World.

Piaget, J. (1951). *Play, dreams and imitation in childhood*. New York: Norton.

Piaget, J. (1961). *On the development of memory and identity*. Worcester, MA: Clark University Press.

Piaget, J. (1972). Intellectual development from adolescence to adulthood. *Human Development*, *15*, 1–12.

Piaget, J. (1976). *The grasp of consciousness*. Cambridge, MA: Harvard University Press.

Piaget, J. (1980). *Les formes élémentaires de la dialectique*. Paris: Gallimard.

Piaget, J. (2001). *Studies in reflecting abstraction*. (R. Campbell, ed. and trans.). Hove: Psychology Press.

Piaget, J., & Inhelder, B. (1941). *Le développement des quantités chez l'enfant*. Neuchatel: Délachaux et Niestlé.

Piaget, J., & Inhelder, B. (1956). *The child's conception of space*. New York: Norton.

Piskorowski, R. A., & Chevaleyre, V. (2018). Memory circuits: CA2. *Current Opinion in Neurobiology, 52*, 54–59.

Plancher, G., Boyer, H., Lemaire, B., & Portrat, S. (2017). Under which conditions can older participants maintain information in working memory? *Experimental Aging Research, 43*(5), 409–429.

Plato. (428–348 BC). *Republic 5*. (1993 translation and introduction by S. Halliwell). Warminster: Aris & Phillips.

Plebanek, D. J., & Sloutsky, V. M. (2018). Selective attention, filtering, and the development of working memory. *Developmental Science*. Retrieved October 21, 2018, from https://onlinelibrary.wiley.com/doi/full/10.1111/desc.12727.

Plenge, M., Curio, E., & Witte, K. (2000). Sexual imprinting supports the evolution of novel male traits by transference of a preference for the colour red. *Behaviour, 137*, 741–758.

Polak, J., Sedlackova, K., Nacar, D., Landova, E., & Frynta, D. (2016). Fear the serpent: A psychometric study of snake phobia. *Psychiatry Research, 242*, 163–168. doi:10.1016/j.psychres.2016.05.024.

Poos, J. M., Jiskoot, L. C., Papma, J. M., van Swieten, J. C., & van den Berg, E. (2018). Meta-analytic review of memory impairment in behavioral variant frontotemporal dementia. *Journal of the International Neuropsychological Society, 24*(6), 593–605.

Pope, L., & Harvey, J. (2015). The impact of incentives on intrinsic and extrinsic motives for fitness-center attendance in college first-year students. *American Journal of Health Promotion, 29*(3), 192–199.

Postma, A., Morel, S. G., Slot, M. E., Oudman, E., & Kessels, R. P. C. (2018). Forgetting the new locations of one's keys: Spatial-memory interference in Korsakoff's amnesia. *Experimental Brain Research, 236*(7), 1861–1868.

Powell, G. L., Bonadonna, J. P., Vannan, A., Xu, K., Mach, R. H., Luedtke, R., & Neisewander, J. L. (2018). Dopamine D3 receptor partial agonist LS-3-134 attenuates cocaine-motivated behaviors. *Pharmacology, Biochemistry and Behavior, 171*, 46–53.

Powell, R. A, Digdon, N., Harris, B., & Smithson, C. (2014). Correcting the record on Watson, Rayner, and Little Albert: Albert Barger as "Psychology's lost boy". *American Psychologist, 69*(6), 600–611.

Premack, D. (1965). Reinforcement theory. In D. Levine (Ed.), *Nebraska symposium on motivation* (Vol. 13, pp. 123–180). Lincoln, NE: University of Nebraska Press.

Prensky, M. (2016). *Education to better their world: Unleashing the power of 21st-century kids*. New York: Teachers College Press.

Prytula, R. E., Oster, G. D., & Davis, S. F. (1977). The "rat rabbit" problem: What did John B. Watson really do? *Teaching of Psychology, 4*, 44–46.

Quiroga, R. Q. (2017). *The forgetting machine: Memory, perception, and the "Jennifer Aniston Neuron."* Dallas, TX: BenBella Books.

Quiroga, R. Q., & Kreiman, F. (2010a). Postscript: About grandmother cells and Jennifer Aniston neurons. *Psychological Review, 117*(1), 297–299.

Quiroga, R. Q., & Kreiman, G. (2010b). Measuring sparseness in the brain: Comment on Bowers (2009). *Psychological Review, 117*(1), 291–297.

Quiroga, R. Q., Reddy, L., Kreiman, G., Koch, C., & Fried, I. (2005). Invariant visual representation by single neurons in the human brain. *Nature, 435*(7045), 1102–1107.

Ramanoel, S., Hoyau, E., Kauffmann, L., Renard, F., Pichat, C., Boudiaf, N., . . . Baciu, M. (2018). Gray matter volume and cognitive performance during normal aging: A voxel-based morphometry study. *Frontiers in Aging Neuroscience, 10*. Retrieved October 21, 2018, from http://dx.doi.org/10.3389/fnagi.2018.00235.

Ramsay, J. R. (2010). Neurofeedback and neurocognitive training. In J. R. Ramsay (Ed.), *Nonmedication treatments for adult ADHD: Evaluating impact on daily functioning and well-being* (pp. 109–129). Washington, DC: American Psychological Association.

Raphael, B. (1976). *The thinking computer: Mind inside matter*. San Francisco, CA: Freeman.

Ratner, C., & Silva, D. N. H. (Eds.). (2017). *Vygotsky and Marx: Toward a Marxist psychology*. New York: Routledge.

References

Rayner, R. (1930). I am the mother of a behaviorist's sons. *Parents Magazine, 5*, 16–18.

Rebecca Glatt, A., St. John, S.J., Lu, L., & Boughter, J.D. Jr.(2016). Temporal and qualitative dynamics of conditioned taste aversions in C57BL/6J and DBA/2J mice self-administering LiCl. *Physiology & Behavior, 153*, 97–108.

Rebellon, C.J., & Straus, M. (2017). Corporal punishment and adult antisocial behavior: A comparison of dyadic concordance types and an evaluation of mediating mechanisms in Asia, Europe, and North America. *International Journal of Behavioral Development, 41*(4), 503–513.

Reese, E.P. (1966). *The analysis of human operant behavior.* Dubuque, IA: Brown.

Reilly, D., Neumann, D.L., & Andrews, G. (2016). Sex and sex-role differences in specific cognitive abilities. *Intelligence, 54*, 147–158.

Rescorla, M. (2009). Chrysippus' dog as a case study in non-linguistic cognition. In R.W. Lurz (Ed.), *The philosophy of animal mind* (pp. 52–71). New York: Cambridge University Press.

Rescorla, R.A. (1980). *Pavlovian second-order conditioning: Studies in associative learning.* Hillsdale, NJ: Lawrence Erlbaum.

Rescorla, R.A. (1988). Pavlovian conditioning: It's not what you think it is. *American Psychologist, 43*, 151–160.

Rescorla, R.A., & Holland, P.C. (1976). Some behavioral approaches to the study of learning. In M.R. Rosenzweig & E.L. Bennet (Eds.), *Neuromechanisms of learning and memory.* Boston, MA: MIT Press.

Revusky, S. (2009). Chemical aversion treatment of alcoholism. In S. Reilly & T.R. Schachtman (Eds.), *Conditioned taste aversion: Behavioral and neural processes* (pp. 445–472). New York: Oxford University Press.

Richardson, J.H. (2017). Inside the race to hack the human brain. *Wired.* Retrieved October 28, 2018, from www.wired.com/story/inside-the-race-to-build-a-brain-machine-interface.

Richardson, R.C. (2017). Evolutionary psychology. In J.B. Losos & R.E. Lenski (Eds.), *How evolution shapes our lives: Essays on biology and society,* (pp. 77–90). Princeton, NJ: Princeton University Press.

Rieber, R.W., & Robinson, D.K. (Eds.) (2001). *Wilhelm Wundt in history: The making of a scientific psychology.* New York: Kluwer Academic/Plenum.

Riesen, A.H., Chow, K.L., Semmes, J., & Nissen, H.W. (1951). Chimpanzee vision after four conditions of light deprivation. *American Psychologist, 6*, 282.

Rilling, M. (1996). The mystery of the vanished citations: James McConnell's forgotten 1960s quest for planarian learning, a biochemical engram, and celebrity. *American Psychologist, 51*, 589–598.

Robertson, R., Garcia, Y., & Garcia, J. (1988). Darwin was a learning theorist. In R.C. Bolles & M.D. Beecher (Eds.), *Evolution and learning* (pp. 17–38). Hillsdale, NJ: Lawrence Erlbaum.

Robin, J., & Moscovitch, M. (2017). Familiar real-world spatial cues provide memory benefits in older and younger adults. *Psychology and Aging, 32*(3), 210–219.

Roethlisberger, S.J., & Dickson, W.J. (1939). *Management and the worker.* Cambridge, MA: Harvard University Press.

Rogers, C.R., & Skinner, B.F. (1956). Some issues concerning the control of human behavior: A symposium. *Science, 124*, 1057–1066.

Romanes, G.J. (1883). *Animal intelligence.* New York: D. Appleton. Reissued as Robinson, D.W. (Ed.). (1977). *Animal intelligence: George John Romanes.* Washington, DC: University Publications of America.

Rosch, E. (1973). Natural categories. *Cognitive Psychology, 4*, 328–350.

Rosch, E. (1977). Human categorization. In N. Warren (Ed.), *Advances in cross-cultural psychology* (Vol. 1; pp. 1–72). London: Academic Press.

Rose, N.S., Myerson, J., Roediger, H.L., III, & Hale, S. (2010). Similarities and differences between working memory and long-term memory: Evidence from the levels-of-processing span task. *Journal of Experimental Psychology: Learning, Memory, and Cognition, 36*(2), 471–483.

Rotter, J.B. (1954). *Social learning and clinical psychology.* Englewood Cliffs, NJ: Prentice Hall.

Rowan, J. (1998). Maslow amended. *Journal of Humanistic Psychology, 38*, 81–92.

Rozeske, R. R., & Herry, C. (2018). Neuronal coding mechanisms mediating fear behavior. *Current Opinion in Neurobiology*, *52*, 60–64.

Rozin, P., & Kalat, J. W. (1971). Specific hungers and poison avoidance as adaptive specializations of learning. *Psychological Review*, *78*, 459–486.

Rubin, R. D., & Cohen, N. J. (2017). Memory, relational representations, and the long reach of the hippocampus. In D. E. Hannula & M. Duff (Eds.), *The hippocampus from cells to systems: Structure, connectivity, and functional contributions to memory and flexible cognition*, (pp. 337–366). Cham: Springer.

Ruck, N. (2016). Controversies on evolutionism: On the construction of scientific boundaries in public and internal scientific controversies about evolutionary psychology and sociobiology. *Theory & Psychology*, *26*(6), 691–705.

Runegaard, A. H., Jensen, K. L., Wortwein, F., & Gether, U. (2018). Initial rewarding effects of cocaine and amphetamine assessed in a day using the single-exposure place preference protocol. *European Journal of Neuroscience*. Retrieved October 15, 2018, from https://onlinelibrary.wiley.com/doi/full/10.1111/ejn.14082.

Ryan, R. M., & Deci, E. L. (2008). Self-determination theory and the role of basic psychological needs in personality and the organization of behavior. In O. P. John, R. W. Robins, & L. A. Pervin (Eds.), *Handbook of personality psychology: Theory and research* (3rd ed.; pp. 654–678). New York: Guilford Press.

Rymal, A. M., & Ste-Marie, D. M. (2017). Imagery ability moderates the effectiveness of video self modeling on gymnastics performance. *Journal of Applied Sport Psychology*, *29*(3), 304–322.

Sabbatini, R. M. E. (2010). Are there differences between the brains of males and females? Retrieved June 2, 2010, from www.cerebromente.org.br/n11/mente/eisntein/cerebro-homens.html.

Sahakian, W. S. (1981). *Psychology of learning: Systems, models, and theories* (2nd ed.). Chicago, IL: Markham.

Sale, A. (Ed.). (2016). *Environmental experience and plasticity of the developing brain*. New York: Wiley-Blackwell.

Samelson, F. (1980). J. B. Watson's Little Albert, Cyril Burt's twins, and the need for a critical science. *American Psychologist*, *35*, 619–625.

Samoilov, V. O, & Zayas, V. (Trans.). (2007). Ivan Petrovich Pavlov (1849–1936). *Journal of the History of the Neurosciences*, *16*, 74–89.

Santiago-Delefosse, M. J., & Delefosse, J. M. O. (2002). Spielrein, Piaget and Vygotsky: Three positions on child thought and language. *Theory & Psychology*, *12*, 723–747.

Sapir, E. (1921). *Language: An introduction to the study of speech*. New York: Harcourt, Brace and Company.

Sato, N., Fujishita, C., & Yamagishi, A. (2018). To take or not to take the shortcut: Flexible spatial behaviour of rats based on cognitive map in a lattice maze. *Behavioural Processes*, *151*, 39–43.

Scheuermann, C., & Zand, B. (2018). Pedro Domingos on the arms race in artificial intelligence. *Spiegel Online*. Retrieved October 28, 2018, from http://bit.ly/2VaumVR.

Schultz, D. P. (1965). *Sensory restriction: Effects on behavior*. New York: Academic Press.

Schulze, K., Vargha-Khadem, F., & Mishkin, M. (2018). Phonological working memory and FOXP2. *Neuropsychologia*, *108*, 147–152.

Schuman, D. L., & Killian, M. O. (2018). Pilot study of a single session heart rate variability biofeedback intervention on veterans' posttraumatic stress symptoms. *Applied Psychophysiology and Biofeedback*. doi: 10.1007/s10484-018-9415-3.

Sclafani, V., Paukner, A., Suomi, S. J., & Ferrari, P. F. (2015). Imitation promotes affiliation in infant macaques at risk for impaired social behaviors. *Developmental Science*, *18*(4), 614–621.

Scott, W. D., & Cervone, D. (2008). Self-efficacy interventions: Guided mastery therapy. In W. T. O'Donohue & J. E. Fisher (Eds.), *Cognitive behavior therapy: Applying empirically supported techniques in your practice* (2nd ed.; pp. 390–395). Hoboken, NJ: Wiley.

Searle, J. (1980). Minds, brains, and programs. *Behavioral and Brain Sciences*, *3*, 417–424.

References

Searle, John R. (1984 [2008]). Can computers think? In W. G. Lycan & J. J. Prinz (Eds.), *Mind and cognition: An anthology* (3rd ed.; pp. 213–219). Malden, MA: Blackwell.

Sejnowski, T. J. (2018). *The deep learning revolution*. Cambridge, MA: MIT Press.

Sejnowski, T. J., & Delbruck, T. (2012). The language of the brain. *Scientific American, 307*(4), 54–59.

Sejnowski, T. J., & Rosenberg, C. R. (1987). Parallel networks that learn to pronounce English text. *Complex Systems, 1*, 145–168.

Seligman, M. E. P. (1975). *Helplessness: On depression, development, and death*. San Francisco, CA: Freeman.

Seligman, M. E. P., & Hager, J. L. (1972). *Biological boundaries of learning*. New York: Appleton-Century-Crofts.

Seung, H. S. (2000). Half a century of Hebb. *Nature Neuroscience, 3*, 1166.

Shanks, N. (2002). *Animals and science: A guide to the debates*. Santa Barbara, CA: ABC-Clio.

Shapiro, B. B. (2018). Subtherapeutic doses of SSRI antidepressants demonstrate considerable serotonin transporter occupancy: Implications for tapering SSRIs. *Psychopharmacology, 235*(9), 2779–2781.

Shaw, J. (2016). *The memory illusion: Remembering, forgetting and the science of false memory*. London: Random House.

Sheehy, A. F. (2003). *Fifty key thinkers in psychology*. New York: Routledge.

Shell, D. F., & Husman, J. (2008). Control, motivation, affect, and strategic self-regulation in the college classroom: A multidimensional phenomenon. *Journal of Educational Psychology, 100*(2), 443–459.

Sherwood, C. C., & Gomez-Robles, A. (2017). Brain plasticity and human evolution. *Annual Review of Anthropology, 46*, 399–419.

Shotter, J. (2001). Towards a third revolution in psychology: From inner mental representations to dialogically structured social practices. In D. Bakhurst & S. G. Shanker (Eds.), *Jerome Bruner: Language, culture, self* (pp. 167–183). Thousand Oaks, CA: Sage.

Shtark, M. B., Kozlova, L. I., Bezmaternykh, D. D., Mel'nikov, M. Y., Savelov, A. A., & Sokhadze, E. M. (2018). Neuroimaging study of alpha and beta EEG biofeedback effects on neural networks. *Applied Psychophysiology and Biofeedback, 43*(2), 169–178.

Siegel, P. F. (1996). The meaning of behaviorism for B. F. Skinner. *Psychoanalytic Psychology, 13*, 343–365.

Siep, N., Tonnaer, F., van de Ven, V., Arntz, S., Raine, A., & Cima, M. (2018). Anger provocation increases limbic and decreases medial prefrontal cortex connectivity with the left amygdala in reactive aggressive violent offenders. *Brain Imaging and Behavior*. Retrieved October 13, 2018, from https://link.springer.com/article/10.1007/s11682-018-9945-6.

Simon, A. (2018). Will evolutionary psychology become extinct? Evolutionary psychology as the Leaning Tower of Pisa. *Journal of Human Behavior in the Social Environment*. Retrieved October 12, 2018, from www.tandfonline.com/doi/full/10.1080/10911359.2018.1482810?scroll=top&needAccess=true.

Sirera Miralles, C. (2015). Enlightened paternalism: The prohibition of corporal punishment in Spanish public schools in the nineteenth century. *History of Education, 44*(2), 156–170.

Skinner, B. F. (1938). *The behavior of organisms: An experimental analysis*. New York: Appleton-Century-Crofts.

Skinner, B. F. (1948). *Walden two*. New York: Macmillan.

Skinner, B. F. (1950). Are theories of learning necessary? *Psychological Review, 57*, 193–216.

Skinner, B. F. (1951, December). How to teach animals. *Scientific American, 185*, 26–29.

Skinner, B. F. (1953). *Science and human behavior*. New York: Macmillan.

Skinner, B. F. (1957). *Verbal behavior*. New York: Appleton-Century-Crofts.

Skinner, B. F. (1961). *Cumulative record* (rev. ed.). New York: Appleton-Century-Crofts.

Skinner, B. F. (1969). *Contingencies of reinforcement: A theoretical analysis*. New York: Appleton-Century-Crofts.

Skinner, B. F. (1971). *Beyond freedom and dignity*. New York: Knopf.

Skinner, B. F. (1973). Answers for my critics. In H. Wheeler (Ed.), *Beyond the punitive society; operant conditioning: Social and political aspects* (pp. 256–266). San Francisco, CA: Freeman.

Skinner, B. F. (1976). *Particulars of my life*. New York: Knopf.

Skinner, B. F. (1979). *The shaping of a behaviorist*. New York: Knopf.

Skinner, B. F. (1983). *A matter of consequences*. New York: Knopf.

Skinner, B. F. (1986). Why I am not a cognitive psychologist. In T. J. Knapp & L. C. Robertson (Eds.), *Approaches to cognition: Contrasts and controversies* (pp. 79–90). Hillsdale, NJ: Lawrence Erlbaum.

Skinner, B. F. (1989). *Recent issues in the analysis of behavior*. Columbus, OH: Merrill.

Skinner, B. F. (1996). Some responses to the stimulus "Pavlov." *Integrative Physiological and Behavioral Science, 31*, 254–257.

Slater, L. (2004). *Opening Skinner's Box: Great Psychological Experiments of the Twentieth Century*. London: Bloomsbury.

Smedley, E. B., & Smith, K. S. (2018). Evidence of structure and persistence in motivational attraction to serial Pavlovian cues. *Learning & Memory, 25*(2), 78–89.

Smith, J. C. (2010). *Pseudoscience and extraordinary claims of the paranormal: A critical thinker's toolkit*. New York: Wiley.

Smith, L. (1997). Jean Piaget. In N. Sheehy, A. Chapman., & W. Conroy (Eds.). *Biographical dictionary of psychology*. London: Routledge.

Smith, L. D. (1990). Metaphors of knowledge and behavior in the behaviorist tradition. In D. E. Leary (Ed.), *Metaphors in the history of psychology* (pp. 239–266). New York: Cambridge University Press.

Snopes (2010). The ten-percent myth. Retrieved May 19, 2010, from www.snopes.com/science/stats/10percent.asp.

Solari, N., & Hangya, B. (2018). Cholinergic modulation of spatial learning, memory and navigation. *European Journal of Neuroscience, 48*(5), 2199–2230.

Solomon, T., Plamondon, A., O'Hara, A., Finch, H., Goco, G., Chaban, P., . . . Tannock, R. (2018). A cluster randomized-controlled trial of the impact of the tools of the mind curriculum on self-regulation in Canadian preschoolers. *Frontiers in Psychology, 8*. doi:10.3389/fpsyg.2017.02366.eCollection 2017.

Sonderegger, T. B. (1970). Intracranial stimulation and maternal behavior. APA Convention Proceedings, 78th meeting, pp. 245–246.

Sonnier, I. L. (1995). Nurturing hemispheric preference through affective education. *Journal of Instructional Psychology, 22*, 182–185.

Sousa, D. A. (2017). *How the brain learns* (5th ed.). Thousand Oaks, CA: Corwin Press.

Spilt, J. L., Leflot, G., Onghena, P., & Colpin, H. (2016). Use of praise and reprimands as critical ingredients of teacher behavior management: Effects on children's development in the context of a teacher-mediated classroom intervention. *Prevention Science, 17*(6), 732–742.

Squire, L. R. (1987). *Memory and brain*. New York: Oxford University Press.

Squire, L. R., Knowlton, B., & Musen, G. (1993). The structure and organization of memory. *Annual Review of Psychology, 44*, 453–495.

Staddon, J. E. R. (2014). On choice and the law of effect. *International Journal of Comparative Psychology, 27*(4), 569–564.

Stagner, R. (1988). *A history of psychological theories*. New York: Macmillan.

Stamoulis, C., Vanderwert, R., Zeanah, C. H., Fox, N., & Nelson, C. A. (2017). Neuronal networks in the developing brain are adversely modulated by early psychosocial neglect. *Journal of Neurophysiology, 118*(4), 2275–2288.

Stapleton, K., & Wilson, J. (2017). Telling the story: Meaning making in a community narrative. *Journal of Pragmatics, 108*, 60–80.

Sternberg, R. J., & Ben-Zeev, T. (2001). *Complex cognition: The psychology of human thought*. New York: Oxford University Press.

Subiaul, F., Renner, E., & Krajkowksi, E. (2016). The comparative study of imitation mechanisms in non-human primates. In S. Obhi & E. Cross (Eds.), *Shared representations: Sensorimotor foundations of social life* (pp. 109–135). New York: Cambridge University Press.

Swanson, H. L., Kudo, M. F., & Van Horn, M. L. (2018). Does the structure of working memory in EL children vary across age and two language systems? *Memory*. Retrieved October 21, 2018, from www.tandfonline.com/doi/full/10.1080/09658211.2018.1496264.

References

Talarico, J. M., & Rubin D. C. (2003). Confidence, not consistency, characterizes flashbulb memories. *Psychological Science, 14*(5), 455–461.

Talarico, J. M., & Rubin D. C. (2007). Flashbulb memories are special after all; in phenomenology, not accuracy. *Applied Cognitive Psychology, 21*(5), 557–578.

Tanford, S., & Montgomery, R. (2015). The effects of social influence and cognitive dissonance on travel purchase decisions. *Journal of Travel Research, 54*(5), 596–610.

Tay, P. K. C., & Yang, H. (2017). Angry faces are more resistant to forgetting than are happy faces: Directed forgetting effects on the identity of emotional faces. *Journal of Cognitive Psychology, 29*(7), 855–865.

Taylor, C. A., Fleckman, J. M., & Lee, S. J. (2017). Attitudes, beliefs, and perceived norms about corporal punishment and related training needs among members of the "American Professional Society on the Abuse of Children". *Child Abuse & Neglect, 71*, 56–68.

Taylor, C. B., Fitzsimmons-Craft, E. E., & Goel, N. J. (2018). Prevention: Current status and underlying theory. In W. W. Agras & A. Robinson, (Eds.), *The Oxford handbook of eating disorders* (2nd ed.; pp. 247–270). New York: Oxford University Press.

Templeton, A. R. (2017). The future of human evolution. In J. B. Losos & R. E. Lenski (Eds.), *How evolution shapes our lives: Essays on biology and society* (pp. 362–379). Princeton, NJ: Princeton University Press.

Teng, C., Cheng, Y., Wang, C., Ren, Y., Xu, W., & Xu, J. (2018). Aging-related changes of EEG synchronization during a visual working memory task. *Cognitive Neurodynamics*. Retrieved October 21, 2018, from http://link-springer-com-443.webvpn.jxutcm.edu.cn/article/10.1007%2Fs11571-018-9500-6#citeas.

Thomas, R. K. (1997). Correcting some Pavloviana regarding "Pavlov's bell" and Pavlov's "mugging." *American Journal of Psychology, 110*, 115–125.

Thomas, R. K. (2007). Recurring errors among recent history of psychology textbooks. *American Journal of Psychology, 120*(3), 477–495.

Thomas, R. M. (2005). *Comparing theories of child development* (6th ed.). Belmont, CA: Cengage/Wadsworth.

Thompson, T. (2014). Review of radical behaviorism for ABA practitioners. *The Psychological Record, 64*(1), 133–138.

Thomsen, M., Fink-Jensen, A., Woldbye, D. P. D., Wortwein, G., Sager, T. N., Holm, R., . . . Caine, S. B. (2008). Effects of acute and chronic aripiprazole treatment on choice between cocaine self-administration and food under a concurrent schedule of reinforcement in rats. *Psychopharmacology, 201*(1), 43–53.

Thorndike, E. L. (1898). Animal intelligence: An experimental study of the associative processes in animals. *Psychological Review Monograph Supplement, 2*(8).

Thorndike, E. L. (1911). *Animal intelligence: Experimental studies.* New York: Hafner (facsimile of 1911 edition; published in 1965).

Thorndike, E. L. (1913–1914). *Educational psychology* (Vols. 1–3). New York: Teachers College Press.

Thorndike, E. L. (1913a). *Educational psychology: Vol. 1: The psychology of learning.* New York: Teachers College Press.

Thorndike, E. L. (1913b). *Educational psychology: Vol. 2: The original nature of man.* New York: Teachers College Press.

Thorndike, E. L. (1922). *The psychology of arithmetic.* New York: Macmillan.

Thorndike, E. L. (1923). The influence of first year Latin upon the ability to read English. *School and Society, 17*, 165–168.

Thorndike, E. L. (1931). *Human learning.* Cambridge, MA: MIT Press.

Thorndike, E. L. (1935). *The psychology of wants, interests, and attitudes.* New York: Appleton-Century-Crofts.

Thorndike, E. L. (1936 [1949]). *Selected writings from a connectionist's psychology.* New York: Appleton-Century-Crofts.

Thurschwell, P. (2009). *Sigmund Freud.* Florence, KY: Taylor and Francis.

Tinklepaugh, O. L. (1928). An experimental study of representative factors in monkeys. *Journal of Comparative Psychology, 8*, 197–236.

Titova, L., & Sheldon, K. M. (2018). Why do I feel this way? Attributional assessment of happiness and unhappiness. *The Journal of Positive Psychology.* doi:10.1080/17439760.2018.1519081.

Todd, J. T., & Morris, E. K. (Eds.). (1994). *Modern perspectives on John B. Watson and classical behaviorism.* Westport, CT: Greenwood Press.

Tokuhama-Espinosa, T. (2014). *Making classrooms better: 50 practical applications of mind, brain, and education science.* New York: W.W. Norton.

Tolman, E. C. (1932). *Purposive behavior in animals and men.* Berkeley, CA: University of California Press.

Tolman, E. C. (1951). *Collected papers in psychology.* Berkeley, CA: University of California Press.

Tolman, E. C. (1952). Autobiography. In E. G. Boring, H. S. Langfeld, H. Werner, & R. M. Yerkes (Eds.), *A history of psychology in autobiography* (Vol. 4; pp. 323–339). Worcester, MA: Clark University Press.

Tolman, E. C. (1959). Principles of purposive behavior. In S. Koch (Ed.), *Psychology: A study of a science* (Vol. 2; pp. 92–157). New York: McGraw-Hill.

Tolman, E. C. (1967). *Purposive behavior in animals and men.* New York: Appleton-Century-Crofts.

Tolman, E. C., & Honzik, C. H. (1930). Insight in rats. *University of California Publications in Psychology, 4,* 215–232.

Tolman, E. C., Ritchie, B. F., & Kalish, D. (1946). Studies in spatial learning: II. Place learning versus response learning. *Journal of Experimental Psychology, 36,* 221–229.

Top Chess Engine Championship, (2018). Retrieved October 29, 2018, from http://tcec.chessdom.com.

Toulmin, S. (1978). The Mozart of psychology. *New York Review of Books, 25,* 51–57.

Tramoni-Negre, E., Lambert, I., Bartolomei, F., & Felician, O. (2017). Long-term memory deficits in temporal lobe epilepsy. *Revue Neurologique, 173*(7–8), 490–497.

Trivers, R. (2002). *Natural selection and social theory: Selected papers of Robert Trivers.* New York: Oxford University Press.

Trivers, R. L. (1974). Parent–offspring conflict. *American Zoologist, 14,* 249–264.

Tropea, D., Capsoni, S., Tongiorgi, E., Giannotta, S., Cattaneo, A., & Domenici, L. (2001). Mismatch between BDNF mRNA and protein expression in the developing visual cortex: The role of visual experience. *European Journal of Neuroscience, 13,* 709–721.

Tuchina, O. D., Agibalova, T. V., Shustov, D. I., Shustova, S. A., Buzik, O. Z., & Petrosyan, Yu. E. (2018). Use of the placebo effect in the psychotherapy of narcology patients: Therapeutic and ethical aspects. *Neuroscience and Behavioral Physiology, 48*(4), 392–398.

Tulving, E. (1974). Cue-dependent forgetting. *American Scientist, 62,* 74–82.

Tulving, E. (1989). Remembering and knowing the past. *American Scientist, 77,* 361–367.

Tulving, E. (2002). Episodic memory: From mind to brain. *Annual Review of Psychology, 53,* 1–25.

Tulving, E., Schacter, D. L., McLachlan, D. R., & Moscovitch, M. (1988). Priming of semantic autobiographical memory: A case study of retrograde amnesia. *Brain and Cognition, 8,* 3–20.

Turing, A. M. (1950). Computing machinery and intelligence. *Mind, 59,* 433–460.

Turnwald, A., & Wollherr, D. (2018). Human-like motion planning based on game theoretic decision making. *International Journal of Social Robotics.* Retrieved October 31, 2018, from www.springerprofessional.de/en/human-like-motion-planning-based-on-game-theoretic-decision-maki/15947046.

Ueno, R., & Taniuchi, T. (2016). Using operant conditioning to train a persistent nose-poke response by pigs. *Japanese Journal of Behavior Analysis, 30*(2), 127–136.

Uswatte, G., & Taub, W. (2010). You can teach an old dog new tricks: Harnessing neuroplasticity after brain injury in older adults. In P. S. Fry & C. L. Keyes (Eds.), *New frontiers in resilient aging: Life-strengths and well-being in late life* (pp. 104–129). New York: Cambridge University Press.

Uttal, W. R. (2002). *A behaviorist looks at form recognition.* Mahwah, NJ: Lawrence Erlbaum.

Valentova, J. V., Bartova, K., Sterbova, Z., & Varella, M. A. C. (2017a). Influence of sexual orientation, population, homogamy, and imprinting-like effect on preferences and choices for female buttock size, breast size and shape, and WHR. *Personality and Individual Differences, 104,* 313–319.

Valentova, J. V., Varella, M. A. C., Bartova, K., Sterbova, Z., & Dixson, B. J. W. (2017b). Mate preferences and choices for facial and body hair in heterosexual women and homosexual men: Influence of sex, population, homogamy, and imprinting-like effect. *Evolution and Human Behavior, 38* (2), 241–248.

References

van der Locht, M., van Dam, K., & Chiaburu, D. S. (2013). Getting the most of management training: The role of identical elements for training transfer. *Personnel Review*, *42*(4), 422–439.

van der Veer, R. (1996). Vygotsky and Piaget: A collective monologue. *Human Development*, *39*, 237–242.

Veraksa, N., Shiyan, O., Shiyan, I., Pramling, N., & Pramling-Samuelsson, I. (2016). Communication between teacher and child in early child education: Vygotskian theory and educational practice. *Infancia y Aprendizaje/Journal for the Study of Education and Development*, *39*(2), 221–243.

Versaggi, C. L., King, C. P., & Meyer, P. J. (2016). The tendency to sign-track predicts cue-induced reinstatement during nicotine self-administration, and is enhanced by nicotine but not ethanol. *Psychopharmacology*, *233*(15–16), 2985–2997.

Vincent, J. (2017). Artificial intelligence isn't as clever as we think, but that doesn't stop it being a threat. *The Verge*. Retrieved October 28, 2018, from www.theverge.com/2017/12/1/16723238/ai-artificial-intelligence-progress-index.

Vitterso, J. (Ed.). (2016). *Handbook of eudaimonic well-being*. Cham: Springer.

Vogel, J. J., Bowers, C. A., & Vogel, D. S. (2003). Cerebral lateralization of spatial abilities: A meta-analysis. *Brain & Cognition*, *52*, 197–204.

von der Embse, N. P., Schultz, B. K., & Draughn, J. D. (2015). Readying students to test: The influence of fear and efficacy appeals on anxiety and test performance. *School Psychology International*, *36*(6), 620–637.

Vrooman, J. R. (1970). *René Descartes: A biography*. New York: G. P. Putnam's Sons.

Vygotsky, L. (1962). *Thought and language* (E. Hamsman & G. Vankan, Eds. and trans.). Cambridge, MA: MIT Press.

Vygotsky, L. S. (1978). *Mind in society*. Cambridge, MA: Harvard University Press.

Vygotsky, L. (1987). The historical meaning of the crisis in psychology: A methodological investigation. In *The collected works of Vygotsky* (R. Van Der Veer, trans.) (pp. 233–343). New York: Plenum. (Original work published 1927.)

Vygotsky, L. S. (1997). The problem of the development of higher mental functions. In R. W. Rieber (Ed.), *Collected works of L. S. Vygotsky: Vol. 4: The history of the development of higher mental functions* (pp. 83–96). New York: Plenum. (Original work published in 1960.)

Wagman, M. (2002). *Problem-solving process in humans and computers: Theory and research in psychology and artificial intelligence*. Westport, CT: Praeger.

Waldrop, M. M. (1992). *Complexity: The emerging science at the edge of order and chaos*. New York: Simon & Schuster.

Walters, R. H., & Llewellyn, T. E. (1963). Enhancement of punitiveness by visual and audiovisual displays. *Canadian Journal of Psychology*, *17*, 244–255.

Walters, R. H., Llewellyn, T. E., & Acker, W. (1962). Enhancement of punitive behavior by audiovisual displays. *Science*, *136*, 872–873.

Wang, C. C., Chai, S. C., & Holahan, M. R. (2010). Effect of stimulus pre-exposure on inhibitory avoidance retrieval-associated changes in the phosphorylated form of the extracellular signal-regulated kinase-1 and -2 (pERK1/2). *Neurobiology of Learning and Memory*, *93*(1), 66–76.

Warneken, F., & Tomasello, M. (2014). Extrinsic rewards undermine altruistic tendencies in 20-month-olds. *Motivation Science*, *1*(S), 43–48. Retrieved October 25, 2018, from www.eva.mpg.de/psycho/pdf/Publications_2014_PDF/Warneken_Extrinsic_MotivationSci_2014.pdf.

Warwick, K., & Shah, H. (2016). Can machines think? A report on Turing Test experiments at the royal society. *Journal of Experimental & Theoretical Artificial Intelligence*, *28*(6), 989–1007.

Watanabe, S. (2010). Pigeons can discriminate "good" and "bad" paintings by children. *Animal Cognition*, *13*(1), 75–85.

Watson, J. B. (1913). Psychology as the behaviorist views it. *Psychological Review*, *20*, 158–177.

Watson, J. B. (1914). *Behavior: An introduction to comparative psychology*. New York: Holt.

Watson, J. B. (1916). The place of the conditioned-reflex in psychology. *Psychological Review*, *23*, 89–116.

Watson, J. B. (1928). *The ways of behaviorism*. New York: Harper.

Watson, J. B. (1930). *Behaviorism* (2nd ed.). Chicago, IL: University of Chicago Press.

Watson, J. B., & Rayner, R. (1920). Conditioned emotional reactions. *Journal of Experimental Psychology, 3*, 1–14.

Watson, R. I. (1971). *The great psychologists* (3rd ed.). Philadelphia, PA: Lippincott.

Waxman, S. R., & Lidz, J. L. (2006). Early word learning. In D. Kuhn, R. S. Siegler, W. Damon, & R. M. Lerner (Eds.), *Handbook of child psychology: Vol. 2: Cognition, perception, and language* (6th ed.; pp. 299–335). Hoboken, NJ: Wiley.

Webster, R. K., Weinman, J., & Rubin, G. J. (2018). Explaining all without causing unnecessary harm: Is there scope for positively framing medical risk information? *Patient Education and Counseling*. Retrieved September 27, 2018, from https://doi.org/10.1016/j.pec.2018.09.014.

Webster, S., & Coleman, S. R. (1992). Contributions to the history of psychology: LXXXVI. Hull and his critics: The reception of Clark L. Hull's behavior theory, 1943–1960. *Psychological Reports, 70*, 1063–1071.

Weiner, B. (1980). *Human motivation*. New York: Holt Rinehart.

Weiner, B. (1986). *An attributional theory of motivation and emotion*. New York: Springer.

Weiner, B. (1992). *Human motivation: Metaphors, theories and research*. Newbury Park, CA: Sage.

Weiner, B. (2008). Reflections on the history of attribution theory and research: People, personalities, publications, problems. *Social Psychology, 39*(3), 151–156.

Weiner, I., & Arad, M. (2009). Using the pharmacology of latent inhibition to model domains of pathology in schizophrenia and their treatment. *Behavioural Brain Research, 204*(2), 369–386.

Wertheimer, M. (1959). *Productive thinking* (rev. ed.). New York: Harper & Row.

Westby, G. (1966). Psychology today: Problems and directions. *Bulletin of the British Psychological Society, 19*(65), 1–19.

Westermann, G., & Monaghan, P. (2017). Connectionist modeling. In B. Hopkins, E. Geangu, & S. Linkenauger (Eds.), *The Cambridge encyclopedia of child development* (2nd ed.; pp. 170–176). New York: Cambridge University Press.

Wheeler, R. L., & Gabbert, F. (2017). Using self-generated cues to facilitate recall: A narrative review. *Frontiers in Psychology, 8*, doi:10.3389/fpsyg.2017.01830.

Whishaw, I. Q., Faraji, J., Mirza Agha, B., Kuntz, J. R., Metz, G. A. S., & Mohajerani, M. H. (2018). A mouse's spontaneous eating repertoire aids performance on laboratory skilled reaching tasks: A motoric example of instinctual drift with an ethological description of the withdraw movements in freely-moving and head-fixed mice. *Behavioural Brain Research, 337*, 80–90. doi:10.1016/j.bbr.2017.09.044.

Whitehead, A. N., & Russell, B. (1925). *Principia mathematica* (Vol. 1; 2nd ed.). Cambridge: Cambridge University Press.

Whyte, G., Saks, A. M., & Hook, S. (1997). When success breeds failure: The role of self-efficacy in escalating commitment to a losing course of action. *Journal of Organizational Behavior, 18*, 415–432.

Wierenga, L. M., Oranje, B., & Durston, S. (2017). Brain and behavioral development. In B. Hopkins, E. Geangu, & S. Linkenauger, (Eds.), *The Cambridge encyclopedia of child development* (2nd ed.; pp. 565–575). New York: Cambridge University Press.

Wigfield, A., Tonks, S., & Klauda, S. L. (2009). Expectancy-value theory. In K. R. Wenzel & A. Wigfield (Eds.), *Handbook of motivation at school* (pp. 55–75). New York: Routledge.

Wilcoxon, H. C., Dragoin, W. B., & Kral, P. A. (1971). Illness-induced aversions in rat and quail: Relative salience of visual and gustatory cues. *Science, 171*, 826–828.

Williams, J. M., Gandhi, K. K., Lu, S. E., Steinberg, M. L., & Benowitz, N. L. (2013). Rapid smoking may not be aversive in schizophrenia. *Nicotine & Tobacco Research, 15*(1), 262–266.

Williams, T., & Williams, K. (2010). Self-efficacy and performance in mathematics: Reciprocal determinism in 33 nations. *Journal of Educational Psychology, 102*(2), 453–466.

Williamson, R. A., & Gonsiorowski, A. (2017). Imitation. In B. Hopkins, E. Geangu, & S. Linkenauger (Eds.), *The Cambridge encyclopedia of child development* (2nd ed.; pp. 310–315). New York: Cambridge University Press.

Willis, M.A., & Haines, D.E. (2018). The limbic system. In D.E. Haines & G.A. Mihailoff (Eds.), *Fundamental neuroscience for basic and clinical applications* (5th ed.; pp. 457–467). Philadelphia, PA: Elsevier.

Willmarth, E.K. (2015). Foreword to the special issue: Rediscovering Jay Haley's contributions to hypnosis. *International Journal of Clinical and Experimental Hypnosis, 63*(4), 373–375.

Wilmer, H.H., Sherman, L.E., & Chein, J.M. (2017). Smartphones and cognition: A review of research exploring the links between mobile technology habits and cognitive functioning. *Frontiers in Psychology.* Retrieved November 1, 2018, from www.ncbi.nlm.nih.gov/pmc/articles/PMC5403814.

Wilson, E.O. (1975). *Sociobiology: The new synthesis.* Cambridge, MA: Belknap.

Wilson, E.O. (1976). Academic vigilantism and the political significance of sociobiology. *Bio-Science, 183,* 187–190.

Windholz, G. (1996a). Hypnosis and inhibition as viewed by Heidenhain and Pavlov. *Integrative Physiological and Behavioral Science, 31,* 155–162.

Windholz, G. (1996b). Pavlov's conceptualization of paranoia within the theory of higher nervous activity. *History of Psychiatry, 7,* 159–166.

Windholz, G. (1997). Ivan P. Pavlov: An overview of his life and psychological work. *American Psychologist, 52,* 941–946.

Wolpe, J. (1958). *Psychotherapy by reciprocal inhibition.* Stanford, CA: Stanford University Press.

Woodiwiss, J. (2010). "Alternative memories" and the construction of a sexual abuse narrative. In J. Haaken & P. Reavey (Eds.), *Memory matters: Contexts for understanding sexual abuse recollections* (pp. 105–127). New York: Routledge.

Woodworth, R.S. (1952). Edward Lee Thorndike, 1874–1949. In *Biographical Memoirs, 27* (pp. 209–237). Washington, DC: National Academy of Sciences.

Woodworth, R.S., & Sheehan, M.R. (1964). *Contemporary schools of psychology* (3rd ed.). New York: Ronald Press.

Workman, L., Chilvers, L., Yeomans, H., & Taylor, S. (2006). Development of cerebral lateralisation for recognition of emotions in chimeric faces in children aged 5 to 11. *Laterality: Asymmetries of Body, Brain and Cognition, 11,* 493–507.

Wright, R. (1994). *The moral animal: Evolutionary psychology and everyday life.* New York: Pantheon.

Wrigley. (2017). Benefits of chewing gum. Retrieved October 14, 2018, from www.wrigley.com/global/benefits-of-chewing.aspx?utm_source=gumisgood.com&utm_medium=domain&utm_content=boc&utm_campaign=wrigley.

Wu, F., & Fan, W. (2017). Academic procrastination in linking motivation and achievement-related behaviours: A perspective of expectancy-value theory. *Educational Psychology, 37*(6), 695–711.

Wulf, S. (1938). Tendencies and figural variations. In W.D. Ellis (Ed.), *A source book of Gestalt psychology* (pp. 136–148). New York: Harcourt, Brace & World. (Original work published 1922.)

Xie, W., & Zhang, W. (2017). Negative emotion enhances mnemonic precision and subjective feelings of remembering in visual long-term memory. *Cognition, 166,* 73–83. Retrieved October 22, 2018, from http://bit.ly/2ZQ7GZV.

Yamagishi, N. (2008). Investigation of attention mechanisms using brain imaging techniques. *Japanese Psychological Review, 51*(2), 347–355.

Yeager, D., Romero, C., Paunesku, D., Hulleman, C.S., Schneider, B., Hinojosa, C., . . . Dweck, C. (2016). Using design thinking to improve psychological interventions: The case of the growth mindset during the transition to high school. *Journal of Educational Psychology.* Retrieved October 25, 2018, from www.ncbi.nlm.nih.gov/pmc/articles/PMC4981081.

Yeates, J.W., & Reed, B. (2015). Animal research through a lens: Transparency on animal research. *Journal of Medical Ethics: Journal of the Institute of Medical Ethics, 41*(7), 504–505.

Yerkes, R.M., & Dodson, J.D. (1908). The relationship of strength of stimulus to rapidity of habit formation. *Journal of Comparative Neurological Psychology, 18,* 459–482.

Yin, G.-H., Fang, Y.-H., & Zhang, J.-J. (2016). Working memory deficits in Alzheimer's disease. *Chinese Journal of Clinical Psychology*, *24*(1), 144–148. [In Chinese]

Zeaman, D. (1949). Response latency as a function of amount of reinforcement. *Journal of Experimental Psychology*, *39*, 466–483.

Zhang, L. (2017). *The value of intellectual styles*. Cambridge: Cambridge University Press.

Zhang, L., & Sternberg, R. J. (2006). *The nature of intellectual styles*. Mahwah, NJ: Lawrence Erlbaum.

Zhang, Q., van Vugt, M., Borst, J. P., & Anderson, J. R. (2018). Mapping working memory retrieval in space and in time: A combined electroencephalography and electrocorticography approach. *NeuroImage*, *174*, 472–484.

Zimmerman, B. J. (2001). Theories of self-regulated learning and academic achievement: An overview and analysis. In B. J. Zimmerman & D. H. Schunk (Eds), *Self-regulated learning and academic achievement: Theoretical perspectives* (pp. 1–37). Mahwah, NJ: Lawrence Erlbaum.

Zimmerman, B. J. (2008). Goal setting: A key proactive source of academic self-regulation. In D. H. Schunk & B. J. Zimmerman (Eds.), *Motivation and self-regulated learning: Theory, research, and applications* (pp. 267–295). Mahwah, NJ: Lawrence Erlbaum.

Zimmerman, B. J., & Schunk, D. H. (2003). Albert Bandura: The scholar and his contributions to educational psychology. In B. J. Zimmerman & D. H. Schunk (Eds.), *Educational psychology: A century of contributions* (pp. 431–457). Mahwah, NJ: Lawrence Erlbaum.

Zubek, J. P. (1969). *Sensory deprivation: Fifteen years of research*. New York: Appleton-Century-Crofts.

Zubek, J. P., & Wilgosh, L. (1963). Prolonged immobilization of the body: Changes in performance in the electroencephalogram. *Science*, *140*, 306–308.

Zulkiply, N., & Burt, J. S. (2013). The exemplar interleaving effect in inductive learning: Moderation by the difficulty of category discriminations. *Memory & Cognition*, *41*(1), 16–27.

NAME INDEX

Abravanel, F., 372
Accardo, J., 148
Acker, W., 379
Addis, D.R., 134, 307
Ahrens, L.M., 53
Akera, A., 150
Alam, M.J., 13
Alcock, J., 175
Alferink, L.A., 134, 188
Allman, W.F., 399, 417
Alvarez, T.A., 182
Alves, C.A., 24
Ameel, E., 250
American Psychological Association, 25–27
Amsel, A., 213, 256
Anderson, C.A., 378, 419
Anderson, J.R., 314
Andersson, G., 53
Andrews, G., 186
Annerback, E.M., 145
Anscombe, E., 6
Anton, N., 25
Aoun, J., 421
Arad, M., 160
Ardila, A., 278
Arluke, A., 12
Arthurs, J., 158, 160
Artino, A.R., 370, 391
Association for the Study of Animal Behavior, 26
Atencio, D.J., 387
Atkinson, J.W., 294
Aubrey, C., 275
Audiffren, M., 352
Austad, C.S., 189
Austin, G.A., 254
Ausubel, D.P., 257
Avella, S., 137

Babskie, E., 354
Baddeley, A.D., 297–301
Baillargeon, R., 274
Baker, L., 263
Bakhtadze, S., 190
Ball, C., 358

Bandin, C.V., 232
Bandura, A., 353–356, 370
Bara, M., 25
Barbagallo, G., 24
Barense, M., 307
Baretta, D., 354
Barnard, C.W., 341
Barnes, B.R., 23
Barrett, L., 164
Barry, R.J., 329
Barth, B., 190
Bartolomei, F., 314
Bartolotti, J., 318
Beach, F.A., 97
Beauchaine, T.P., 170
Beck, H.P., 60
Becker, D.V., 169
Behne, D.M., 404
Belzak, W.C., 337
Bennett, E.l., 186, 312
Bensemann, J., 88, 134
Bensley, D.A., 12
Benthin, A.C., 345
Ben-Zeev, T., 412
Bergmann, S., 48
Berlyne, D.E., 334
Bermeitinger, C., 302
Bertin, E., 42
Best, J., 418
Beverdorf, D.Q., 26
Bevins, R.A., 64
Bexton, W.H., 341
Bijou, S.w., 143
Bitterman, M.E., 54
Blackman, S.F., 344
Blackwell, L.S., 350
Blair, C., 332
Blakemore, S.J., 187
Blum, K., 181
Blumenstein, B., 190
Blumenthal, A.I., 59
Boakes, R.A., 157–158
Bolles, R.C., 169, 176
Bond, T.G., 269
Boring, E.G., 41, 223
Borsa, V., 314

Borst, J.P., 314
Bouchter, J.D., 158
Bowers, C.A., 185, 419
Bowlby, J., 330–331
Bowman, C.R., 254
Boyer, H., 318
Bradley, C., 296
Bradley, K., 318
Brady, F., 341
Brandon, T.H., 65
Bransford, J.D., 317
Bray, E.E., 339
Brehm, J.W., 343
Breland, K., 167–169
Breland, M., 167–169
Briskin-Luchinsky, V., 205
Broadbent, D.E., 295
Bronfenbrenner, U., 279
Broster, L.S., 307
Brown, P.C., 320–321
Brown, R.E., 212
Bruner, J.S., 232, 241, 244, 278, 417, 448
Bruno, N., 42
Bryant, R.A., 316
Buchman-Schmidt, J.M., 175
Buckley, K.W., 56
Budson, A.E., 307
Bull, P.N., 134
Buller, D.J., 172–173
Burgos, J.E., 114, 170
Burigo, M., 314
Burnham, J.C., 56
Burns, J.D., 169
Burt, J.S., 320
Bussey, T.J., 130
Butner, J., 169
Buxton, C.E., 9, 218

Cable, C., 241, 253
Cahill, L., 317
Cameron, J., 348
Campbell, K., 282
Capa, R.L., 352
Carmona, A., 189
Carroll, J.B., 280

Name Index

Castine, B.R., 181
Cavanaugh, J.M., 420
Cellan-Jones, R., 410
Cermak, L.S., 301
Cerri, F., 137
Cervone, D., 390
Chai, S.C., 160
Charest-Girard, C., 301
Charles, E.P., 275
Chein, J.M., 420
Chen, A., 412
Chen, Y.J., 282
Cherdieu, M., 318
Cherry, K., 13, 178, 188
Chessbase News, 402
Chevaleyre, V., 183
Chiaburu, D.S., 90–91
Chiandetti, C., 137
Chin, E.C.H., 339
Chiocca, E.M., 145
Chomsky, N., 170, 370, 448
Chu, C., 175
Church, B.A., 418
Clarke, O., 67–68, 151
Claro, S., 352
Clough, P.J., 11
Clyde, M., 284
Cohen, A.R., 343
Cohen, N.J., 314
Cole, S.O., 175
Coleman, S.R., 48, 108
Collins, H.M., 414
Colpin, H., 146
Coltheart, M., 419
Cooper, J., 344
Corballis, M.C., 185
Cosmides, L., 172
Cotton, S.R., 358
Covington, M.V., 332
Cowley, G., 170
Craik, F.I.M., 301
Crespi, L., 101
Crews, F.C., 330
Cruchon, N.M., 151
Csibra, G., 302
Cunningham, A.E., 282
Curci, A., 304
Curio, E., 330

Dagnall, N., 11
Dannemiller, J.L., 186
Darley, J.M., 12
Dashiell, R., 317
Davis, D., 318
Davis, S.F., 61
Davison, M., 88
Davydov, V.V., 279

de Waal, F.B.M., 86, 372
Deason, R.G., 307
Deci, E.L., 348, 357–358
Delbruck, T., 399
Demmel, R., 358
Demorest, A.P., 115
Denizet, M., 342
Dennis, A., 173
Denovan, A., 11
de'Sperati, C., 42
Desportes, J.-P, 119
Dever, B.V., 358
Dewsbury, D.A., 199
Diamond, S., 41
Dickman, S.J., 338
Dickson, W.J., 23
DiClemente, D.F., 56
Digdon, N., 60
Dindo, M., 86, 372
Ding, N., 296
Djalal, F.M., 250
Dodson, J.D., 339
Dolcos, F., 314
Dollard, J.C., 370
Domingos, P., 416
Domjan, M., 318
Doyle, W., 389
Draaisma, D., 290
Drabman, R.S., 146
Dragonin, W.B., 159
Draughn, J.D., 339
Drayton, A.K., 146, 389
Drinkwater, K., 11
Duarte, A., 307
Dube, M., 336
Duchatelle, E., 119
Dumas, R., 304
Dunbar, R., 164
Dunlosky, J., 320
Durmaz, A.A., 63
Durston, S., 186
Dweck, C.S., 350–352, 361–362

Ebbinghaus, H., 291, 293
Eby, C.M., 148
Eccles, J.S., 356–357
Eggleston, T.J., 345
Elkessaimi, A., 119
Elliffe, D., 88, 134
Ellonen, N., 145
Ellsworth, R.M., 175
Epstein, R.A., 205
Eriksen, B.C., 48
Euler, Leonard, 290
Evans, R.I., 369–370, 376, 378, 380
Ewen, R., 116
Eysenck, H.J., 61

Fahmy, S.R., 26
False Memory Syndrome Foundation, 318
Fan, W., 358
Fang, Y.-h, 301
Farmer-Dugan, V., 188
Farrar, D.C., 282
Feldman, J., 317
Feldman, L.A., 344
Felician, O., 314
Fenton, A., 25
Ferguson, B., 252
Ferguson, K.E., 115, 149, 151
Ferguson, S.A., 372
Ferrari, P.F., 86, 372
Ferreira, M.S., 150
Festinger, L.A., 342, 344–345
Fiez, J.A., 182
Fitzsimmons-Craft, E.E., 346
Flake, J.K., 357
Flaste, R., 357
Flavell, J.H., 260–261
Fleckman, J.M., 145
Floridi, L., 414
Follette, W.C., 318
Folmer, A.S., 350
Fongaro, E., 137
Fox, J.A., 186
Frade, M.M., 150
Fraser, J., 284
Freeman, D., 24
Fridel, E.E., 186
Fridlund, A.J., 60
Fried, I., 313
Frith, U., 187
Fugazza, C., 85, 137
Fujishita, C., 205
Fuson, K.C., 274

Gaafar, K., 26
Gabbert, F., 319
Gabler, I.C., 257
Galanter, M., 175
Gale Group, 246
Galef, B.G., 51
Gallo, A., 119
Ganel, T., 42
Garcia, J., 159, 164
Garcia, Y., 164
Garcia-Larria, L., 296
Gardner, H., 246
Gaulin, P., 336
Geach, P.T., 6
Geary, D.C., 171–172
Gelman, R., 275
Gendron, M.S., 189
Gether, U., 202

Name Index

Gevirtz, R., 189
Giapponi, C., 420
Gibb, R., 160
Gibbons, F.X., 345
Giles, O.T., 274
Gillen, J., 284
Gilovich, T., 60
Glaubitz, C., 145
Goel, N.J., 346
Golden, T.D., 420
Goldie, W.D., 60
Goldman, W.P., 302
Goldsmith, M., 304
Gomez-Roblas, A., 170
Gonsiorowski, A., 262
Goodnow, J.J., 254
Goodwin, C.J., 116
Gotzsche, C.R., 314
Gould, S.J., 175
Grant, D., 289
Graveline, D.E., 341
Greco, A., 354
Greene, D., 347–348
Greenhoot, A.F., 318
Greenwald, J.D., 207
Greer, R.D., 148
Griffee, K., 331
Griffin, A.S., 51
Griffin, P., 283
Gross, C.G., 313
Grow, W.A., 183
Grusec, J.E., 386
Gunturkun, O., 253
Gustafsson, P.A., 145
Guttman, N., 50

Hacklander, R.P.M., 302
Hagen, E.H., 165
Hager, E.H., 169
Haggbloom, S.J., 392
Hahn, N., 186
Hailwood, J.M., 130
Haimovitz, K., 352
Haines, D.E., 180, 182–183
Hajek, P., 65
Halfon, M., 205
Hamilton, W.D., 174
Hampton, J.A., 249
Hangya, B., 202
Hantula, D.A., 56
Hare, B.A., 339
Harker, S., 160
Harre, R., 255
Harris, B., 60–61
Harris, M., 159
Harter, S., 354–355
Harvey, J., 348
Harvey, S.T., 339

Haste, H., 246
Hattie, J., 321–322
Hauser, W.A., 26
Hayman, T., 250
Heath, C.J., 130
Hebe, H.N., 274, 284
Heil, M., 186
Hellmann, D.R., 145
Herbert, R., 336
Herculano-Houzel, S., 178
Hernandez, A.E., 318
Hernandez, J.M., 24
Hernandez-Orallo, J., 414
Heron, W., 341
Herrnstein, R.J., 134, 241, 253
Herry, C., 183
Higgins, I., 205
Hiralall, A.S., 389
Hirst, W., 304–305
Holahan, M.R., 160
Holland, S.K., 185
Holman, D., 418
Holyoak, R.J., 231
Hom, M.A., 175
Homa, D., 319
Honzik, C.H., 216
Hook, S., 354
Horn, R.A., 97, 116, 246, 259, 278
Horton, G.P., 67
Houston, F., 232
Huang, K.T., 358
Hunt, M.M., 116, 171
Husman, J., 362
Hutter, S.A., 254

Iliescu, B.F., 186
Inhelder, B., 270, 275, 304
Irons, G., 60

Jäkel, F., 231–232
Jansen, P., 186
Janson, S., 145
Jean Piaget Society, 259, 276
Jensen, K.L., 202
Jerlhag, E., 202
Jiskoot, L.C., 301
Joffe, A.R., 25
Johansen, E.B., 132
Johanson, D.J., 245
Johnson, G., 288, 312, 426
Johnson, M.K., 317
Johnson, S.B., 187
Johnston, J.M., 150
Joiner, T.E., 175
Jonason, P.K., 175
Jones, M.C., 61
Joyce, N., 296
Julian, J.B., 205

Kalat, J.W., 181
Kalish, D., 217
Kamil, A.C., 166
Kamin, L.J., 160–162
Kaneda, K., 181, 202
Karadottir, R.T., 13
Kass, R.E., 146
Kaufman, K.F., 146
Keenoy, T., 289
Keith, J.R., 190
Keith-Lucas, T., 50
Keller, F.S., 48, 150
Keller, J.M., 363
Kellogg, D., 284
Kempen, E., 358
Kenrick, D.T., 169
Keri, S., 253
Khng, K.H., 339
Killeen, P.R., 132, 183
Killian, M.O., 189
Kim, W.S., 203
Kincheloe, J.L., 97, 116, 246, 259, 278
King, A.R., 145, 202
King, C.P., 166
Klein, R.G., 171
Kliem, S., 145
Knight, R.G., 316
Knight, W., 416–417
Knowlton, B., 306
Koch, C., 313
Koelling, R.A., 159
Kolb, B., 160
Koriat, A., 304
Kozulin, A., 278
Krajkowksi, E., 85, 372
Kral, P.A., 159
Krech, D., 186, 312
Kreiman, G., 313, 419
Kudo, M.F., 301
Kuhn, T.S., 13
Kuo, C.T., 13
Kuriscak, E., 417
Kwok, D,W.S., 157–158

Laczo, J., 314
Lambert, E.B., 284
Lambert, J., 314
Lancciano,T., 304
Laney, C., 317
Lantolf, J.P., 284
Lashley, K., 179, 311
Latané, B., 12
Lawson, D., 409
le Pape, G., 119
Leahey, T.H., 97
Leclerc, G., 336
Lee, S.J., 145
Leflot, G., 146

Lefrançois, G.R., 54, 231, 257, 305, 336
Lehrer, P.M., 189
Leibowitz, L., 148
Lemaire, B., 318
Lennon, V.A., 26
Lenski, R.E., 170
Leopold, T., 418
Lepper, M.R., 347–348
Leslie, J.C., 88
Letourneau, E.J., 48
Levy, R., 205
Li, N.P., 169
Libertus, M.E., 42
Lidz, J.L., 252
Lilienfeld, S.O., 12
Lilly, J.C., 341
Lin, J.Y., 158, 160
Linderholm, T., 304
Linnenbrink-Garcia, L., 327
Llewellyn, T.E., 379
Lobb, B., 134
Lockhart, R.S., 301
Lodish, H.F., 206
Loftus, E.F., 317
Lombardi, M.G., 314
Lopes, E.L., 24
Lorenz, K., 330
Lorusso, M.L., 314
Losos, J.B., 170
Lourenco, O., 275
Loveland, D.H., 241, 253
Lu, L., 158
Lucas, S., 145
Luminet, O., 304
Luria, A.R., 22, 290
Lycett, J., 164
Lynch, E.B., 252
Lyons-Ruth, K., 332

Macfarlane, D.A., 218
Machado, A., 275
MacLean, E.L., 339
Macmillan, M., 178
Magidson, J.F., 358
Mahr, J.B., 302
Malone, J.C., 151, 169
Manassa, R.P., 51
Maner, J.K., 169
Manrique, H.M., 308
Manuel, A.L., 314
Marian, V., 318
Marisco, G., 257
Marsalek, P., 417
Marsh, A.A., 174
Martens, B.K., 389
Martí, E., 276
Martinez-Marti, M.I., 390

Martinie, M.A., 329
Maslow, A.H., 336–337
Mason, O.J., 341
Master, A., 362
Matera, G., 304
Mauldin, J.E., 166
May, P.J., 180
Mayo Clinic, 202
McAdams, D.P., 255
McClelland, J.L., 405
McConnell, J.V., 312
McDaniel, M.A., 254, 320–321
McDougall, W., 329
McDowell, J.J., 108
McGrath, A., 329
McKeachie, W.J., 312
McLachlan, D.R., 307
Mead, H.K., 170
Meadows, S., 265
Meck, E., 275
Medin, D.L., 252
Mehler, M.F., 26
Meltzoff, A.N., 262
Mendonca, A., 314
Merkin, S., 275
Mervis, C.B., 252
Metzger, A., 354
Meyer, P.J., 166
Meyers-Manor, J., 169
Mihailoff, G.A., 180
Miklosi, A., 85, 137
Milkman, H.B., 332
Milkowski, M., 397
Milland, L., 329
Miller, G.A., 298, 381–382
Miller, H.C., 86
Miller, M., 415
Miller, N.E., 189, 370
Miller, W.R., 387
Mills, J., 58, 68, 77, 108, 149–151
Milner, P., 180
Milshtein-Parush, H., 342
Mironenko, I.A., 277
Mishkin, M., 301
Mjølnerød, O.K., 48
Modgil, C., 275
Modgil, S., 275
Mohl, J.C., 108
Mohring, W., 42
Moll, L.C., 284
Molteni, M., 314
Monaghan, P., 409
Moore, M.K., 262
Moray, N., 295
Moreno, M., 203
Morgado, L., 275
Morris, E.K., 56
Morvan, C., 343–344

Moscovitch, M., 304, 307
Moshagen, M., 358
Mozur, P., 416
Muelller, C.M., 352
Mukherjee, S., 24
Muller, U., 263
Murchison, C., 55
Murrell, P., 88
Musen, G., 306

Nakajima, S., 157–158
Nasser, H.M., 183
Navakatikyan, M.A., 88
Navarra, R.L., 202
Neisser, U., 296
Neruda, P., 232
Nestler, E.J., 181
Neumann, D.L., 186
New World Encyclopedia, 278
Newell, A., 400–401
Nguyen, M.A., 283
Nicolai, J., 358
Ninness, C., 406, 409
Ninness, S.K., 409
Nobis, N., 25
Noble, K.G., 187
Nordvik, J.E., 185
Nosofsky, R.M., 254
Nucci, L., 259

O'Brien, K.S., 373
Obukhova, L.F., 276
O'Connor, A., 343–344
Ocumpaugh, J., 354
O'Donohue, W., 48, 115, 149, 151
Oesterdiekhoff, G.W., 275
Ogai, T., 158
O'Hagan, K., 316
Oiberman, A.J., 275
Olds, J., 179–180
O'Leary, K.D., 146
Olive, T., 329
O'Neil, W.M., 220
Onghena, P., 146
Oranje, B., 186
Orback, I., 190
Oscar-Berman, N., 181
Oster, G.D., 61
Oswick, C., 289
Ötti, A., 404
Overmier, J., 169

Paasch, V., 148
Paiva, R.C., 150
Pajares, F., 370
Pan, S.C., 320
Pansky, A., 304
Paolini, C.I., 275

Name Index

Papma, J.M., 301
Paradis, E., 23
Parent, V., 301
Parker, A., 11
Parkinson, K., 269
Pascal, B., 412, 430
Pass, S., 276
Passanisi, A., 249
Patal, E.Z., 205
Paukner, A., 86, 372
Paul, D.B., 59
Paunesko, D., 352
Peltnen, K., 145
Penfield, W., 311
Perez, L., 205
Perinat, A., 279
Perry, R.E., 332
Peterson, L.R., 297
Peterson, N.J., 297
Phelps, E.A., 304
Pierce, W.D., 348
Piskorowski, R.A., 183
Plancher, G., 318
Plebanek, D.J., 298
Plenge, M., 330
Pogany, A., 85
Polak, J., 46
Polesnik, C.A., 134
Poos, J.M., 301
Pope, L., 348
Portrat, S., 318
Posadas-Sanchez, D., 132
Poso, T., 145
Postma, A., 318
Powell, D.N., 354
Powell, G.L., 130
Powell, R.A., 60
Powers, F.F., 68, 136
Premack, D., 144
Prensky, M., 419
Prytula, R.E., 61

Quiroga, R.Q., 313, 419

Ragot, S., 352
Ramanoel, S., 316
Ramsay, J.R., 190
Raphael, B., 411
Ratner, C., 279
Rayburn-Reeves, R., 86
Rayner, R., 56, 59
Rebecca Glatt, A., 158
Rebellon, C.J., 145
Reddy, L., 313
Reed, B., 26
Reese, E.P., 139
Reilly, S., 158, 160

Reilly,D., 186
Renner, E., 85, 372
Rescoria, R.A., 162–163, 176, 218
Revusky, S., 159
Reynolds, B., 159
Richardson, R.C., 165, 416
Rieber, R.W., 41
Riesen, A.H., 186
Riis, J.L., 187
Rikard, R.V., 358
Rilling, M., 312
Ritchie, B.F., 217
Rivera, S.M., 275
Robbins, T.W., 130
Robertson, R., 164
Robin, J., 304
Robinson, D.K., 41
Robinson, F.G., 257
Rodríguez, C., 276
Roediger, H.L., 320–321
Roethlisberger, S.J., 23
Rogers, C.R., 359
Roos, R.P., 26
Rosch, E., 252, 254
Rose, N.S., 301
Rosenberg, C.R., 407–409
Rosenzweig, M., 186, 312
Ross, D., 377
Ross, S.A., 377
Rotter, J.B., 349
Rowan, J., 337
Rozeske, R.R., 183
Rubin, D.C., 305
Rubin, G.J., 24
Rubin, R.D., 314
Ruch, W., 390
Ruck, N., 175
Rumelhart, D.E., 405
Rumph, M., 409
Runegaard, A.H., 202
Russell, B., 401
Ryan, R.M., 348, 358
Rymal, A.M., 373

Sabbatini, R.M.E., 186
Sahakian, W.S., 215, 223
Sahay, A., 24
Saks, A.M., 354
Saksida, L.M., 130
Sale, A., 187
Samelson, F., 61
Samoilov, V.O., 44
Sanders, C.A., 254
Sapir, E., 280
Sartori, G., 304
Sasaki, A., 158
Sato, N., 205

Schacter, D.L., 307
Scheuermann, C., 416
Schnider, A., 314
Schnupp, J., 205
Schroeder, M., 257
Schultz, B.K., 339
Schultz, D.P., 341
Schulze, K., 301
Schuman, D.L., 189
Schunk, D.H., 370
Sclafani, V., 86, 372
Scott, T.H., 341
Scott, W.D., 390
Seamon, J.G., 302
Sejnowski, T.J., 399, 407–410, 415
Seligman, M.E.P., 169
Seung, H.S., 200
Shafritz, K.M., 207
Shah, H., 414
Shanks, N., 397
Shannon, K.E., 170
Shapiro, B.B., 203
Shaw, J., 318, 400
Sheehan, M.R., 215, 223
Sheehy, A.F., 370
Sheldon, K.M., 350
Shell, D.E., 362
Sheny, S., 282
Sherman, L.E., 420
Sherwood, C.C., 170
Shiffrin, R.M., 294
Shotter, J., 256
Shreeve, J., 245
Shtark, M.B., 190
Siegel, P.F., 115
Siep, N., 183
Silva, D.N.H., 279
Simmons-Stern, N.R., 307
Simon, A., 175
Simon, H.A., 400–401
Simon, J.Z., 296
Slater, L., 119
Slifer, L., 148
Sloutsky, V.M., 298
Smedley, E.B., 166
Smith, J.C., 16
Smith, K.S., 166
Smith, L., 259
Smith, L.D., 233
Smithson, C., 60
Solari, N., 202
Solomon, K.O., 252
Solomon, S., 317
Solomon, T., 282
Sonderegger, T.B., 180
Sonnier, I.L., 185

Sousa, D.A., 61, 184, 186, 206, 296, 301
Spellman, B.A., 231
Spiers, H.J., 205
Spilt, J.L., 146
Spivey, M.J., 418
Squire, L.R., 306, 312
St. John, S.J., 158
Staddon, J.F.R., 88
Stagner, R., 64
Stamoulis, C., 160
Stapleton, K., 255
Stead, L.F., 65
Steca, P., 354
Ste-Marie, D.M., 373
Sternberg, R.J., 78, 412
Stiller, A., 145
Storms, G., 250
Straus, M., 145
Stringer, S., 205
Stroffek, J., 417
Strong, J.V., 307
Sturges, P.S., 143
Subiaul, F., 85, 372
Sullivan, R.M., 332
Sun, Q., 158
Sunderwirth, S.G., 332
Suomi, S.J., 86, 372
Susswein, A.J., 205
Sutkin, G., 23
Svein, C.G., 145
Swanson, H.L., 301

Taddeo, M., 414
Talarico, J.M., 305
Taniuchi, T., 136
Tat, M.J., 307
Taub, W., 185
Tay, P.K.C., 302
Taylor, C.A., 145
Taylor, C.B., 346
Taylor, J.I., 339
Templeton, A.R., 172
Ten Eycke, K., 263
Teng, C., 298
Terrell, A.C., 182–183
Thomas, R.K., 44
Thomas, R.M., 13
Thompson, T., 149
Thraikill, E.A., 132
Thurschwell, P., 330
Tindberg, Y., 145
Tinklepaugh, O.L., 217, 242
Tippett, L.J., 134
Titova, L., 350
Todd, J.T., 56
Tomasello, M., 348

Tooby, J., 172
Toth, P.G., 417
Toulmin, S., 278
Tramoni-Negre, E., 314
Trivers, R., 174
Tropea, D., 160
Trzesniewski, K.H., 350
Tsethlika, M., 318
Tuchina, O.D., 24
Tulving, E., 292, 307–308, 319
Turiel, E., 259
Turilli, M., 414
Turning, A.M., 412
Turnwald, A., 414

Uccelli, S., 42
Ueno, R., 136
Uswatte, G., 185
Uttal, W.R., 213

Valentova, J.V., 331
van Dam, K., 90–91
van den Berg, E., 301
van der Locht, M., 90–91
Van der Veer, R., 276
Van Horn, M.L., 301
van Swieten, J.C., 301
van Vugt, M., 314
Vargha-Khadem, F., 301
Veraksa, N., 284
Versaggi, C.L., 166
Vincent, J., 399, 410
Vitterso, J., 332
Viviani, E., 42
Vogel, D.S., 185
Vogel, J.J., 185
von der Embse, N.P., 339
Vrooman, J.R., 6

Walker, M.J., 308
Walker, R.S., 175
Walters, R., 370, 375–376, 379
Wang, C.C., 160
Warneken, F., 348
Warwick, K., 414
Watanabe, S., 53, 242
Waterhouse, B.D., 202
Watson, R.I., 44
Waxman, S.R., 252
Webster, R.K., 24
Webster, S., 108
Weiner, B., 349, 353, 355
Weiner, I., 160
Weinman, J., 24
Westby, G., 113
Westermann, G., 409

Wheeler, R.L., 319
Whishaw, I.Q., 168
Whitehead, A.N., 401
Whiten, A., 86, 372
Whyte, G., 354
Wierenga, L.M., 186
Wigfield, A., 356
Wilcoxon, H.C., 159
Wilgosh, L., 341
Williams, J.M., 65
Williams, K., 354
Williams, M.W., 339
Williams, T., 354
Williamson, R.A., 262
Willis, M.A., 180
Willmarth, E.K., 108
Wilmer, H.H., 420
Wilson, A.I., 254
Wilson, E.O., 174
Wilson, J., 255
Windholz, G., 42–44
Witte, K., 330
Woldbye, D.P.D., 314
Wolfe, H.D., 341
Wolherr, D., 414
Wolpe, J., 53, 76
Woodiwiss, J., 317
Woodworth, R.S., 215, 223
Workman, L., 185
Wortwein, F., 202
Wright, R., 176
Wu, F., 358
Wulf, S., 227

Xie, W., 304

Yamagishi, A., 205, 313
Yang, H., 302
Yasnitsky, A., 284
Yeager, D., 351–352
Yeates, J.W., 26
Yerkes, R.M., 339
Yin, G.-H., 301

Zand, B., 416
Zayas, V., 44
Zeaman, D., 335
Zeithamova, D., 254
Zentall, T.R., 86
Zhang, J.-j, 301
Zhang, L., 78
Zhang, Q., 78, 314
Zhang, W., 304
Zimmerman, B.J., 359, 370
Zubek, J.P., 341
Zulkiply, N., 320

SUBJECT INDEX

absolute threshold, 40
abstract relations (cognitive), 271
accommodation, 260–261, *See also*
    assimilation, adaptation
acetylcholine, 202
achievement need, 352–353
acquisition (classical conditioning), 51
action potential, 201
adaptation, 260–261, *See also*
    assimilation, accommodation
agentic perspective, 383–388
agonist, 181
alcoholism, 159
algorithm, 402, 405, *See also* heuristic
    value
alpha waves, 338, *See also* beta waves
altruism, 174–175
amygdala, 183, 314
analog computer, 457
animal intelligence
    Darwin on, 82
    Thorndike on, 83–86
annoyers, 88, 95
anthropomorphism, 82
aphasia, 183
Aplysia, 205–207
ARCS model of motivation, 363
Aristotle, 5
arousal, 338, 342
arousal function, 340, *See also* cue
    function
arousal theory, 210–211, 340–342
artificial intelligence (AI). *See also*
    computer simulation
    defined, 410, 441–442
    educational implications of, 419–421
    history of, 410–411
    recent developments in, 415–416
    thinking in, 411–413
    Turing test, 412–415
assimilation, 261, *See also* adaptation,
    accommodation
associations (learning), 209, 310
associative shifting, 91
assumption, 14
attention, 210, 297, 372–373

attention-deficit hyperactivity disorder
    (ADHD), 202
attitude, 344
attribute, 249, 353–356, *See also*
    intension, extension, criterial
    attributes, category
attribution theory, 349–350
autistic savant, 472, *See also* idiot
    savant
autobiographical memories. *See*
    episodic memory
autonomic response classical
    conditioning, 189
autoshaping, 165–166, *See also*
    sign-tracking
aversive contingencies applications,
    144–147
aversive control, 142
avoidance learning, 124, *See also*
    escape learning
axon, 201

Babinski reflex, 47, 328
back-propagation rule, 408–409
backward pairing. *See also* trace
    pairing, simultaneous pairing,
    delayed pairing
    biological predispositions for, 50–51
    defined, 49–50
Bacon, Frances, 10
Bandura, Albert
    agentic perspective, 383–388
    applications of social cognitivism,
        388–391
    appraisal of social cognitivism,
        391–392
    biography, 369–370
    control systems in social
        cognitivism, 380–383
    observational learning and, 371
    operant conditioning, 374–380
    overview of social cognitivism,
        371–374
behavior
    learning and potential changes in, 8–9
    prediction of, 359

behavior control, 359–360
behavior management, 148, *See also*
    behavior therapy, behavior
    modification
behavior modification, 64–65, 144,
    148, *See also* behavior therapy,
    behavior management
behavior theory. *See* learning theory
behavior therapy, 148, *See also*
    behavior modification, behavior
    management
behavioral field, 228–229, *See also*
    psychological field
behaviorism
    basic beliefs of, 57–58, 432
    behavior modification and, 64–65
    conditioned emotional reactions,
        58–59, 61
    counterconditioning in, 60–61
    defined, 28
    environmentalism in, 62–63
    higher learning and, 63
    practical applications of, 63–65
    revolution in, 65–66
    strengths and weaknesses of,
        442–444
    transfer in, 60–62
    versus cognitivism, 242–243
behaviorism, early
    evolutionary psychology and,
        164–191
    Guthrie and one-shot learning law,
        66–77
    Pavlov and classical conditioning,
        42–54
    psychophysics and, 39–42
    taste aversion in, 156–164
    theory evaluation of, 78
    Watson and, 54–66
behaviorism, effects of
    Hull and hypothetico-deductive
        system, 96–108
    Thorndike and connectionism, 83–95
behaviorism, radical, 113–151
behaviorism, transition to cognitivism
    Gestalt psychology, 47–48

Subject Index 539

Hebb's theory, 197–213
mechanistic behaviorism, 214
metaphors, 232–233
neobehaviorism, 213
Tolman's purposive behaviorism,
214–221, 435–436
behavioristic manifesto, 57
belief. *See also* theory, principle
bubba and pop psychology and,
11–12
common sense and pseudoscience,
16
false, 12
and scientific theory, 11
beta waves, 338, *See also* alpha waves
Beyond Freedom and Dignity
(Skinner), 149, 387
biased sampling, 23–24
biofeedback, 189–191, *See also*
neurofeedback
biological constraints, 169–170
black box, 395
blocked repetition, 320, *See also*
spaced repetition, interleaving
blocked-path study, 216–217
blocking, 160–161
brain
ablations, 179
advantages of, 246
biofeedback and neurofeedback in,
189–191
chemicals and addiction, 180–181
cognitivism and, 245
computer and, 396–400
electrical stimulation of, 179–180
experience and, 186–187
functions, 178
imaging techniques, 181
injuries, 179
misconceptions about role and
functioning of, 13
neurons in, 178
pineal gland in, 7
sex differences in, 185–186
brain components
amygdala, 183
cerebellum, 182
cerebral cortex, 183
cerebrum, 183
frontal lobe, 183
hemispheres, 184–185
hippocampus, 183
hypothalamus, 182
limbic system, 183
for memory, 314
occipital lobe, 184
parietal lobe, 184

reticular formation, 182
temporal lobes, 184
thalamus, 183
brain imaging
event-related fields, 312–314
event-related potential, 312–314
brain stem, 179
brain-based education, 187–189
Bruner, Jerome Seymour
biography, 245–246
brain evolution and, 245
categorization, 248–250
coding systems and, 250–251
constructivism, 254–257, 437
hypothesis generator, 447
on mind evolution, 246–248
novice-to-expert model, 448–449
strengths and weaknesses of learner
model, 446–449
symbolic representation, 248
tabula rasa doctrine, 446–447
bubba psychology, 11–12, *See also*
common sense

capability (learning), 8
Cartesian. *See* Descartes, René
castigation, 124–125
categorization, 248–250
category. *See also* intension, extension,
coding system, attribute
abstraction of, 253–254
attributes of, 249–250
boundaries, 253
decision making in, 250
neurobiology of, 253
rules for, 249–250
causes, 327, *See also* reasons,
motivation
cell assembly, 203, 205, 207–208, *See
also* phase sequence
central executive system, 299, *See also*
working memory, visual-spatial
sketch pad, phonological loop,
episodic buffer
central nervous system (CNS)
acetylcholine in, 202
components of, 200–201
dopamine and, 202
neural transmission in, 201
norepinephrine in, 202
serotonin in, 203
synapses in, 203
cerebellum, 182
cerebral cortex, 183
cerebrum, 183
chaining, 137–138
chunking, 298

classical conditioning. *See also* operant
conditioning, conditioning
autonomic responses, 189
backward pairing in, 50–51
contiguity and reinforcement in,
49–50
educational implications of, 54
emotional learning and, 64
extinction and recovery in, 52–53
generalization and discrimination
in, 53
higher-order conditioning, 53
and one-shot learning, 69–70
operant conditioning and, 117–118
overview of, 44–47, 431
reflexive behaviors, 47–48, 329
in social cognitive theory, 375–376
taste aversion and, 156–159
classification, 270
closure, 225, *See also* similarity,
proximity, prägnanz, continuity
cocktail party phenomenon, 295
coding system, 250–251, *See also*
category
cognitions, 215
cognitive architecture, 405
cognitive dissonance, 342–346, 349
cognitive map, 217
cognitive revolution, 256
cognitive strategies, 461
cognitive structure, 263–264
cognitivism
brain advantages, 246
categorization in, 248–250
coding systems in, 250–251
constructivism, 254–257
defined, 28, 214, 241–242
educational implications of, 257
and Gestalt, 230, 436
metaphors and, 233
mind evolution in, 246–248
principal beliefs of, 243–244
research in, 252–254
strengths and weaknesses of,
445–446
symbolic representation in, 248
versus behaviorism, 242–243
cognitivism, developmental
adaptation, 260–261
cognitive structure, 264
criticisms of, 274–276
equilibration, 261
imitation, 262–263
in learning theory, 446–449
intelligence, 263
méthode clinique, 259–260
play, 262

Subject Index

cognitivism, developmental (cont.)
  stage theory, 264–272
cognitivism, social
  agentic perspective, 383–388
  applications of, 388–391
  appraisal of, 284, 391–392
  control systems in, 380–383
  culture role in, 278–279
  language and thought in, 279–280
  languages stages, 281–282
  motivation and, 342–346
  observational learning and, 371
  operant conditioning in, 374–380
  overview of, 371–374
  scaffolding in, 283–284
  Vygotsky blocks, 280
  zone of proximal development,
    282–283
collective efficacy, 385–386, *See also*
  self-efficacy
combined schedule, 126
common sense, 16, *See also* bubba
  psychology
comparison group. *See* control group
compensation, 270
computer literacy, 422
computer simulation, 410, *See also*
  artificial intelligence
computers
  brain and, 396–400
  chess masters and, 401–403
  fuzzy logic, 403
  serial and parallel processing,
    399–400
  thinking in, 411–415
concept. *See also* percept
  abstraction of, 253–254
  boundaries in, 253
  developments in, 252
  formation, 252
  neurobiology of, 253
concept cell. *See* Jennifer Aniston
  neuron
conceptual change movement, 462
concrete operations, 269–271
concurrent schedule of reinforcement,
  133–134
conditioned emotional reactions,
  58–59, 375–376
conditioned response (CR), 44–46
conditioned stimulus (CS)
  defined, 44–46
  urination and, 48
conditioning. *See also* operant
  conditioning, classical
  conditioning
  higher-order, 53, 163–164

inhibitory, 73
interoceptive, 48
second-order, 53
connectionism
  defined, 88
  law of effect, 88–89, 92–93
  law of exercise, 88, 92
  law of multiple responses, 90
  law of prepotency of elements, 90
  law of readiness, 90
  law of response by analogy, 90–91
  law of set or attitude, 90
  principle of belongingness, 94
  spread of effect, 94
  summary of, 94–95
connectionist model, 400, 403–405,
  417–419, *See also* symbolic
  models, neural network
consciousness, 198, 228, 297
conservation, 267, 269–270
constructivism, 172, 231, 254–257,
  448, *See also* direct teaching,
  direct instruction
consummatory responses, 105
contiguity
  and one-shot learning, 72–77
  reinforcement and, 86–87
  through movement-produced
    stimuli, 70
contingency
  and contiguity, 49–50
  operant contingency and, 122
continuity. *See also* similarity,
  proximity, prägnanz, closure
  and contingency, 49–50
  defined, 49
continuous reinforcement, 126, *See
  also* schedule of reinforcement,
  fixed schedule
contrapreparedness, 51, *See also*
  preparedness
control group, 20, *See also*
  experimental group
corporal punishment, 144
counterconditioning, 60–61, 76, 148,
  See also systemic desensitization,
  synaptic knobs
Cousin Renault study, 76–77
criterial attributes, 249–250, *See also*
  attribute
critical period, 330, *See also*
  imprinting
cue function, 340, *See also* arousal
  function
cue-dependent forgetting, 319, *See
  also* trace-dependent forgetting,
  retrieval-cue failure

culture, 246, 256, 278–279, 368
cumulative recording, 128

Darwin, Charles
  animal intelligence, 82
  functionalism and, 27–28
  natural selection, 108, 164, 447
  Skinner and, 119
decay fading, 316, *See also* fading
declarative memory. *See also* explicit
  memory
  defined, 306–307
  models of, 308–311
  physiological evidence for, 307
deductive reasoning, 266
deep learning, 415
deferred imitation, 263
delayed pairing, 49–50, *See also* trace
  pairing, simultaneous pairing,
  backward pairing
dendrites, 201
dependent variable, 18–20, *See also*
  independent variable
Descartes, René, 6–7
Descent of Man, The (Darwin), 164
determinism
  defined, 10
  scientific theory and, 14
developmental stage theory (cognitive)
  concrete operations, 269–271
  criticisms of, 274–276
  educational implications,
    273–274
  formal operations, 271–272
  maturation, 273
  preoperational thinking, 265–266
  sensorimotor intelligence, 318
  summary of, 264, 272
differential reinforcement of
  successive approximations, 136,
  See also shaping
differential threshold, 41
digital computer, 405
direct instruction, 172, 255, *See also*
  constructivism
direct reinforcement, 375, *See also*
  vicarious reinforcement
direct teaching, 231, *See also*
  constructivism
discovery learning, 257, *See also*
  reception learning
discrimination, 139–140, *See also*
  generalization
discriminative stimulus, 120
disinhibitory effect, 378–379, *See also*
  inhibitory effect
displacement theory, 465

Subject Index 541

disposition
  and latent learning, 9
  and learning, 8
dissonance theory, 342–346, 349
distortion theory, 317
do-as-I-do training, 137
dominant hemisphere, 185
dopamine, 180–181, 202
double-blind procedure, 24, *See also* single-blind procedure
drive, 100–101, 333
drive-reduction theory, 100, 333
dualism, 7

early behaviorism
  evaluation of early theories of, 78
  Guthrie and one-shot learning law, 66–77
  Pavlov and classical conditioning, 42–54
  psychophysics and, 39–42
  Watson and, 54–66
educational implications
  artificial intelligence, 419–421
  behaviorism, 63
  brain-based education, 187–188
  classical conditioning, 54
  cognitivism, 257
  evolutionary psychology, 22
  Gestalt, 230–231
  Hebb rule, 210–211
  memory and learning, 319–322
  motivation theory, 359–363
  Piaget's theory, 273–274
  purposive behaviorism, 219
  Thorndike and Hull, 108–109
Educational Psychology (Thorndike), 87
egocentric speech, 281, *See also* social speech, inner speech
egocentrism, 267
elaboration, 466
electrodermal response, 338
electroencephalogram (EEG), 181
eliciting effect, 380, *See also* modeling effect, inhibitory effect, imitation
emotion
  long-term memory and, 304
  motivation and, 338
enactive representation, 247–248, *See also* symbolic representation, iconic representation
end of the world study, 345
engram, 311–312
entity theory, 350–351, *See also* performance goal, mastery goal, incremental theory

episodic buffer, 299, *See also* visual-spatial sketch pad, phonological loop, central executive system
episodic memory, 307–308, *See also* explicit memory
epistemology, 5
eponym, 119
equilibration, 261
escape learning, 124, *See also* avoidance learning
ethology, 173
eudemonic orientation, 336–337, *See also* psychological hedonism
eugenics, 62
Euler, Leonard, 290
event-related field (ERF), 181, 312–314
event-related potential (ERP), 181, 312–314, 329
evolutionary psychology
  appraisal of, 175–176
  autoshaping and, 165–166
  biological constraints of, 169–170
  and brain evolution, 170
  defining characteristics, 164–165, 434–435
  instinctive drift and, 167–168
  learning implications, 171–172
  pop evolutionary psychology and, 172–173
  sociobiology and, 173–175
  strengths and weaknesses of, 444–445
excitatory potential. *See* reaction potential
exemplar model, 254, *See also* prototype model
expectancy–value theory, 356–358
expectations study, 217
experiment
  defined, 17
  in scientific method, 18–20
experimental analysis of behavior, 117, 125, *See also* radical behaviorism
experimental group, 20, *See also* control group
experimenter bias, 23–24
explicit learning, 405, *See also* implicit learning
explicit memory, 306–311, *See also* semantic memory, episodic memory, declarative memory
Expression of the Emotions in Man and Animals, The (Darwin), 164
extension, 249, *See also* intension, category, attribute

exteroceptive stimulation, 70, *See also* proprioceptive stimulation
extinction. *See also* spontaneous recovery, forgetting
  in classical conditioning, 52–53
  forgetting and, 131
  in one-shot learning, 71–72
  in operant conditioning, 148–149
extinction rate, 103, 129–130
extrinsic motive, 347
extroverts, 469

fact, 21
fading, 139, *See also* decay fading
fading theory, 316
fake truth, 11
false memory syndrome, 317–318
False Memory Syndrome Foundation, 318
fatigue technique, 73, *See also* threshold technique, method of incompatible stimuli, inhibitory conditioning
Fechner, Gustav Theodor, 39–42
feedback (learning), 321–322
fitness, 174, *See also* inclusive fitness
fixed schedule, 126, *See also* ratio schedule, interval schedule, continuous reinforcement
flashbulb memories, 304–305
folk knowledge, 11–12, 171
forgetting. *See also* memory, extinction
  brain injury and, 316
  defined, 292
  distortion theory, 317
  extinction and, 131
  fading theory, 316
  false memory syndrome, 317–318
  interference theory, 318
  repression theory, 317–318
  retrieval-cue failure, 319
formal operations, 271–272
fractional antedating goal response, 105–106
free will, 10
Freud, Sigmund, 330
frontal lobe, 183, *See also* temporal lobe, parietal lobe, occipital lobe
functional magnetic resonance imaging (fMRI), 181, 292, *See also* functional magnetic resonance spectrography
functional magnetic resonance spectrography (fMRS), 181, *See also* functional magnetic resonance imaging

Subject Index

functionalism, 27–28, 431, structuralism

fuzzy logic, 403

Gage, Phineas, 178

Galton, Francis, 62

galvanic skin response. *See* electrodermal response

gender brain differences, 185–186

General Problem Solver (computer program), 401

generalization, 139–140, *See also* discrimination

generalized reinforcer, 125

Gestalt
  appraisal of, 231–232
  background of, 221
  behavioral field in, 228–229
  defined, 224–225, 436
  educational implications of, 230–231
  founders of, 222–223
  insight and, 223–224
  leveling in, 227
  and modern cognitivism, 230
  nativism and, 447–448
  normalizing in, 228
  prägnanz, 225
  principle of closure in, 225
  principle of continuity in, 226
  principle of proximity in, 226
  principle of similarity in, 226
  sharpening in, 227

Gestalt Psychology (Köhler), 222

gestation, 206

grandmother cell, 313, 419

guided mastery therapy, 390

Guthrie, Edwin R.
  biography, 66–68
  on extinction, 71–72
  on habits, 70–71
  law of one-shot learning, 68–70, 432
  movement-produced stimuli (MPS), 70
  on shaping, 136
  one-shot learning practical applications, 72–77
  reward and punishment, 72

habit, 70–73

habit strength, 100

habit-family hierarchy, 106

habituation, 206, *See also* sensitization

hardware, 397, *See also* wetware, software

Hawthorne effect, 23

Hebb rule
  appraisal of, 211–213

central nervous system in, 200–205

higher mental processes and, 197–200

main assumptions of, 203–205, 435

mediating processes, 207–210

as neurological basis for learning, 205–206, 417

reactivity and plasticity in, 206–207

set and attention, 210

Hebb, Donald Olding
  arousal theory, 340–342
  biography, 199–200
  need/drive theory and, 334
  pseudo-behavioristic viewpoint of, 200, 435

Heisenberg uncertainty principle, 312

heredity–environment question, 479, *See also* nature–nurture controversy

heuristic problem solving, 14, *See also* higher mental processes

heuristic value, 14, *See also* algorithm

higher mental processes, 197–200, *See also* thinking, heuristic problem solving

higher-order conditioning, 53, 163–164, *See also* second-order conditioning

hippocampus, 183, 314

holistic education, 185

homunculus, 113

Hull, Clark L.
  biography, 96–97
  fractional antedating goal response, 105–106
  habit-family hierarchy, 106
  hypothetico-deductive system appraisal, 107–108
  hypothetico-deductive system components, 97–98
  hypothetico-deductive system summary, 98–105, 433
  mediating processes and, 198
  metaphors and, 233
  Pavlov and, 98
  postulates of, 96
  summary equation, 103–105

hyperactivity. *See* attention-deficit hyperactivity disorder

hypothalamus, 182

hypotheses
  defined, 10
  in scientific method, 17

hypothesis generator, 447

hypothetico-deductive system
  appraisal of, 107–108
  defined, 96

Gestalt and, 231

main components of, 97–98

overview of, 96–97

summary of, 98–105, 433

ICGA Tournaments, 402

iconic representation, 247–248, *See also* symbolic representation, enactive representation

id, 330

idealism, 6

identity, 270

idiot savant, 290, *See also* autistic savant

if–then statements, 10–11, 20

imitation. *See also* observational learning, modeling effect, inhibitory effect, eliciting effect
  learning by, 85–86
  and learning social behaviors, 370
  models and, 371–372
  in social cognitive theory, 374–380

immaterialism, 7

implicit learning, 403–405, *See also* explicit learning

implicit memory, 291–292, 306–307

implicit psychology, 11–12

imprinting, 330–332, *See also* critical period

incentive motivation, 101–102, 335–336

inclusive fitness, 174–175, *See also* fitness

incremental theory, 350–351, *See also* performance goal, mastery goal, entity theory

independent variable, 18–20, *See also* dependent variable

inductive reasoning, 266

information processing (IP)
  as cognitive psychology metaphor, 243
  connectionist models for, 400, 406–409
  defined, 397
  symbolic models for, 400–403

informed consent principle, 27

inhibitory conditioning, 73, *See also* threshold technique, method of incompatible stimuli, fatigue technique

inhibitory effect, 378–379, *See also* modeling effect, imitation, eliciting effect, disinhibitory effect

inner speech, 281, *See also* social speech, egocentric speech

Subject Index 543

input variable, 97, 99
insight, 223–224
insight problem solving, 84
instinctive drift, 167–168
instincts, 329–330
instrumental learning, 89, *See also* operant conditioning
intellectual limitations, 14
intellectual style, 78, *See also* learning style
intelligence
    entity and incremental theories of, 350–351
    goals and beliefs about, 361–362
    mindsets about, 351–352
intelligent tutor system (ITS), 420
intension, 249–250, *See also* extension, category, attribute
interactive dualism, 7
interference theory, 318, *See also* retroactive interference, proactive interference
interleaving, 320–321, *See also* spaced repetition, blocked repetition
intermittent reinforcement, 126, *See also* schedule of reinforcement, ratio schedule, interval schedule
internalization, 262
interoceptive conditioning, 48
interval schedule, 126, *See also* random schedule, intermittent reinforcement, fixed schedule
intervening variables, 97, 99–103
interviews (scientific method), 17
intrinsic motive, 346–348
introspection, 27
introverts, 475
intuitive thinking, 267–268, *See also* preoperational thinking

James, William
    functionalism and, 27–28, 39
    on instincts, 329
Jennifer Aniston neuron, 313, 419
just noticeable difference (JND), 41

Koffka, Kurt
    on behavioral field, 228–229
    biography, 222–223
    on declarative memory, 308
    prägnanz, 225
Köhler, Wolfgang
    biography, 221–223
    on Gestalt, 231
    on insight, 223–224
    insight problem solving, 84

Lake of Constance (story), 228–229
language development (social cognitivism)
    implicit learning in, 405
    interference theory, 318
    stages of, 281–282
latent, 475
latent inhibition, 159–160
latent learning, 9
latent learning study, 218
lateralization, 185
law of effect, 88–89, 92–93, 157, 432–433
law of exercise, 92
law of multiple responses, 90
law of one-shot learning
    basic beliefs of, 68–70, 432
    extinction and, 71–72
    habits and, 70–71
    movement-produced stimuli in, 70
    reward and punishment, 72
law of prepotency of elements, 90
law of readiness, 90
law of response by analogy, 90–91, *See also* theory of identical elements
law of set or attitude, 90
laws (scientific), 11
learning
    definition of, 7–9
    latent, 9
    misconception about, 12–13
learning by ideas, 93–94
learning style, 12, 78, *See also* intellectual style
learning theory
    classification of, 28–29
    key words associated with, 443
    strengths and weaknesses of, 442–446
    structuralism and functionalism in, 27–28
    summary table of, 428–430
level of processing, 301
leveling, 227
libido, 330
Likert scale, 354
limbic system, 180, 183
limited capacity, 297–298
Little Albert study, 58–62
Locke, John, 62
locus of control, 349
Logic Theorist (computer program), 400–401
logical constructs, 107
long-term depression (LTD), 207

long-term memory (LTM). *See also* sensory memory
    defined, 302
    flashbulb memories and, 304–305
    generative nature of, 296–303
    stability of, 302
    understanding and, 303–304
long-term memory categories
    declarative memory, 306–311
    nondeclarative memory, 306
long-term potentiation (LTP), 207

machine learning
    brain and, 396–400
    chess masters and, 401–403
    fuzzy logic, 403
    serial and parallel processing, 399–400
    summary of, 441–442
    thinking in, 411–415
Machine Learning Predicts World Cup Winner, 410
magazine training, 128–129
magnetoencephalogram (MEG), 181, 313
malware, 397
mastery goal, 350–351, *See also* performance goal, incremental theory, entity theory
mastery goals, 350
matching law, 133–134
materialism
    defined, 6
    versus immaterialism, 7
maturation, 273
Mead, Margaret, 23–24
mechanistic behaviorism, 214
medial forebrain bundle, 180
mediating processes, 207–210
memory. *See also* forgetting
    and the brain, 184
    brain imaging and, 312–314
    defined, 290
    differences between long and short-term, 305
    educational applications, 319–322
    forgetting and, 315–319
    Gestalt of, 226–228
    implicit, 291–292
    level of processing, 301
    long-term, 302–311
    maze learning and, 220
    metaphors, 289–293
    modal model, 294–305
    and nominal fallacy, 22
    physiology of, 311–315
    principle of belongingness and, 94

Subject Index

memory (cont.)
  research on early, 292–293
  storage and retrieval, 292
  working, 296–301
memory metaphors, 295
Mentality of the Apes, The (Köhler), 221, 223
meta-analysis, 321
metaneeds, 336
metaphors
  in cognitive psychology, 232–233, 243
  computer, 397–398
  memory, 289–293, 295
Metaphors of Memory (Draaisma), 289
method of incompatible stimuli, 74, *See also* threshold technique, inhibitory conditioning, fatigue technique
méthode clinique, 259–260
millisecond, 478
mind
  in classical philosophy, 5–6
  in cognitivism, 247
  consciousness and, 27
mind–body problem, 6–7
mnemonic devices, 122
mnemonist, 22
modal model of memory, 294–305
model
  defined, 371
  types, 371–372
modeling effect, 376–378, *See also* inhibitory effect, imitation, eliciting effect
Moore's law, 410
mores, 368
Moro reflex, 47, 328
motivation. *See also* reasons, causes
  applications of, 359–363
  arousal function, 338–342
  attribution theory and, 349–353
  biological causes for, 328–332
  and changes in disposition, 8
  cognitive dissonance theory and, 342–346
  defined, 327, 439–440
  in social cognitive theory, 374
  intrinsic and extrinsic, 346–348
  Maslow's hierarchy, 336–337
  need/drive theory and, 332–335
  psychological hedonism and, 332
movement-produced stimuli (MPS), 70

naive psychology, 12
nanosecond, 399
narratives, 255–256

nativism, 447–448
natural selection, 108, 164
nature–nurture controversy, 62–63, *See also* heredity environment question
need
  and drive, 100
  for stimulation, 340–342
need for achievement, 352–353
negative reinforcement, 122–124, 147, *See also* punishment
negative reinforcer, 124
negative transfer, 62, *See also* positive transfer
neobehaviorist, 98, 213
nerve, 200
nervous system, 200, 328–332, 396–400
net reaction potential, 104
NETtalk, 407–409
neural network, 405–409, *See also* connectionist model
neurofeedback, 189, *See also* biofeedback
neurogenesis, 13, 188
neuron
  defined, 178, 200
  misconceptions, 13
neurotransmitters, 201
nocebo effect, 24
nominal fallacy, 22
nondeclarative memory, 306–307
nonsense syllables, 293
norepinephrine, 202
normalizing principle, 228
no-treatment group. *See* control group
novice-to-expert model, 448–449

object concept, 264
observational learning. *See also* imitation
  applications of, 388–389
  learning social behaviors and, 370
  in scientific method, 17
Occam's razor, 14
occipital lobe, 184, *See also* temporal lobe, parietal lobe, frontal lobe
On the Origin of Species (Darwin), 164
operant, 481
operant conditioning. *See also* instrumental learning, conditioning, classical conditioning
  appraisal of, 149–151
  aversive contingencies applications, 144–147
  behavior management, 148

chaining, 137–138
counterconditioning, 148
defined, 89, 118, 374–380, 433–434
discriminative stimulus and, 120
everyday life reinforcement schedules, 135–139
extinction, 148–149
generalization and discrimination, 138–140
individual differences, 140–141
positive contingencies, 142–144
prevalence of, 118
punishment and, 122–125, 144–147
reinforcement in, 120–122
reinforcement schedules, 126–134
and respondent learning, 117–118
operant conditioning chamber, 119
operant learning, 120
operants, 117
operation, 268
operational definition, 18
organization (Gestalt), 224
Organization of Behavior, The (Hebb), 200
orienting reflex (OR), 328
output variables, 97, 103
overjustification hypothesis, 348

paradigm, 255
parallel processing, 400, *See also* serial processing
paranormal phenomena, 16, *See also* pseudoscience
parietal lobe, 184, *See also* temporal lobe, occipital lobe, frontal lobe
parsimonious theories, 14
participants in psychological research
  animals, 25–26
  ethics of, 24–25
  humans, 26–27
Pavlov, Ivan Petrovich
  backward pairing, 50–51
  biography, 42–44
  classical conditioning, 44–47, 431
  classical conditioning educational implications, 54
  classical conditioning findings, 51–53
  Hull and, 98
  learning explanations, 49–50
  reflexive behaviors, 47–48
  Skinner and, 119, 137
Pavlovian conditioning. *See* classical conditioning
pedology, 278
percept, 249, *See also* concept
perception, 482

Subject Index

performance (learning), 8
performance goal, 350–351, *See also*
  mastery goal, incremental theory,
  entity theory
performance goals, 350
periventricular tract, 180
personal narratives, 255
personalized system of instruction
  (PSI), 150
phase sequence, 204–205, *See also* cell
  assembly
phobias, 158
phonological loop, 299, *See also*
  working memory, visual-spatial
  sketch pad, episodic buffer,
  central executive system
physiological needs, 333–334
Piaget, Jean
  adaptation, 260–261
  biography, 258–259
  cognitive structure, 264
  equilibration, 261
  intelligence, 263
  long-term memory and
    understanding, 304
  maturation, 273
  méthode clinique, 259–260
  play, 262
  stage theory, 264–272, 437–438
pineal gland, 7
place learning study, 217–218
placebo, 24
placebo effect, 24
plasticity, 206–207
Plato, 5–6
play, 262
pleasure center, 180
pop evolutionary psychology,
  172–173
pop psychology, 11–12
population, 20, *See also* sample
positive control, 142
positive reinforcement, 122, 124, 148
positive reinforcer, 124
positive transfer, 61–62, *See also*
  negative transfer
positron emission tomography (PET),
  181
postulates, 96
prägnanz, 225, *See also* similarity,
  proximity, continuity, closure
preconceptual thinking, 265–266,
  See also preoperational thinking
Premack principle, 144
preoperational thinking, 265–266,
  See also preconceptual thinking,
  intuitive thinking

preparedness, 50, *See also*
  contrapreparedness
primary reinforcer, 125
Principia Mathematica, 401
principle, 11, *See also* theory, belief
principle of belongingness, 94
principle of continuity, 226
Principles of Behavior (Hull), 97
Principles of Gestalt Psychology
  (Koffka), 222
proactive interference, 293, *See also*
  retroactive interference,
  interference theory
productive thinking, 230
programmed instruction, 150
progressive ratio schedule, 130
propositional thinking, 272
proprioceptive stimulation, 70, *See
  also* exteroceptive stimulation
prototype model, 254, *See also*
  exemplar model
proximity, 226, *See also* similarity,
  prägnanz, continuity, closure
pseudoscience, 16, *See also* science,
  paranormal phenomena
psychological field. *See* behavioral
  field
psychological hedonism, 332, *See also*
  eudemonic orientation
psychological needs, 333–334, *See
  also* self-actualization
psychological research
  evaluation and scientific method,
    20–24
  participants, 24–27
psychology
  defined, 5
  natural selection and, 164
  Skinner and, 116
Psychology of Learning, The (Guthrie),
  68
psychophysics, 39–42
psychotherapy, 148–149
punishment. *See also* negative
  reinforcement
  corporal, 144
  defined, 122
  in law of one-shot learning, 72
  negative reinforcement versus, 123
  operant conditioning case against,
    144–146
  operant conditioning case for,
    146–147
  presentation, 124–125
  in social cognitive theory, 379
  versus positive reinforcement,
    148

purposive behaviorism
  appraisal of, 220–221
  blocked-path study of, 216–217
  defined, 218
  educational implications of, 219
  expectations study of, 217
  latent learning study, 218
  place learning study of, 217–218
  tenets of, 214–215, 435–436
puzzle boxes, 83–84

questionnaires (scientific), 17

radical behaviorism. *See also*
  experimental analysis of behavior
  as antitheory, 113–115
  defined, 113, 214
  overview of, 114–120
random sampling, 20
random schedule, 126, *See also* ratio
  schedule, interval schedule
rapid smoking, 64–65, 159
rate of learning, 130
ratio schedule, 126, 132–133, *See also*
  random schedule, intermittent
  reinforcement, fixed schedule
reaction potential, 102–103
reaction threshold, 103
reactivity, 206–207
reasons, 327, *See also* motivation, causes
reception learning, 257, *See also*
  discovery learning
reciprocal determinism, 354, 386–388,
  See also triadic reciprocal
  determinism
reductio ad absurdum, 413–415
reductionist theories, 214
reflex
  defined, 46
  motivation and, 328–329
reflexive behaviors, 47–48
refractory period, 201
rehearsal, 487
reinforcement
  concurrent schedules of, 133–134
  contiguity and, 86–87
  continuous, 126
  defined, 49, 120
  in everyday life, 135–139
  generalized, 125
  intermittent, 126
  and natural selection, 108
  negative, 122–123, 147
  operant conditioning and, 120–122
  positive, 122, 124
  primary, 125
  schedules of, 125–133

Subject Index

reinforcement (cont.)
 secondary, 125
 in social cognitive theory, 375
 spread of effect and, 94
reinforcer, 120
relational thinking, 223–224
repetition, 69
repression theory, 317–318
reprimands, 146
reproductive thinkers, 230
Rescoria–Wagner model, 161–162
respondent, 117–118, *See also*
 unconditioned response
response amplitude, 103
response cost, 487
response latency, 103
responses (behaviorist), 28
resting potential, 201
reticular formation, 182, 340
retrieval cues, 319
retrieval-cue failure, 319, *See also* cue-
 dependent forgetting
retroactive interference, 293, *See also*
 proactive interference,
 interference theory
reversibility, 270
reward (one-shot learning), 72
Russell's paradox, 68

sample. *See also* population
 and group representation, 22
 in scientific method, 20
samples of convenience, 20, 22
Sapir–Whorf hypothesis, 280
satisfiers, 88, 95
scaffolding, 283–284, *See also* zone of
 proximal development
schedule of reinforcement, 125–133,
 See also intermittent
 reinforcement, continuous
 reinforcement
schema, 261
science. *See also* pseudoscience
 defined, 16
 and psychological research
 evaluation, 20–24
scientific method steps, 16–20
scientific theory
 characteristics of good, 13–15
 components of, 10–11
 defined, 10
 purposes of, 13
secondary reinforcer, 125
second-order conditioning, 53, *See*
 also higher-order conditioning
self-actualization, 336–337, *See also*
 psychological needs

self-determination theory, 358
self-efficacy, 353–356, 380, 385, *See*
 also collective efficacy
self-referent thought, 380
self-regulated learner, 358
semantic memory, 307–308, *See also*
 explicit memory
sensitization, 206, *See also* habituation
sensorimotor intelligence, 318
sensory deprivation, 340–342
sensory memory, 295–296, *See also*
 working memory, long-term
 memory
serial processing, 399–400, *See also*
 parallel processing
seriation, 270
serotonin, 203
set, 210
shaping. *See also* differential
 reinforcement of successive
 approximations
 chaining and, 138
 defined, 136
 verbal instructions and, 139
sharpening, 227
short-term memory. *See* working
 memory
signal learning, 46
significant findings, 17
sign-tracking, 166, *See also*
 autoshaping
similarity, 226, *See also* proximity,
 prägnanz, continuity, closure
simultaneous pairing, 49–50, *See also*
 trace pairing, delayed pairing,
 backward pairing
Singer, Edgar Arthur, 68
single-blind procedure, 24, *See also*
 double-blind procedure
Skinner box, 119, 137, 143
Skinner, B.F.
 biography, 115–116, 119
 on free will, 387
 metaphors and, 233
 on motivation, 359
 natural selection and, 164
 and operant conditioning, 433–434
 Pavlov and, 137
 and physiology of learning, 200
 radical behaviorism, 214
Skinner, B.F. and operant conditioning
 appraisal of, 149–151
 aversive contingencies applications,
 144–147
 behavior management, 148
 chaining, 137–138
 counterconditioning, 148

defined, 89, 118
discriminative stimulus and, 120
everyday life reinforcement
 schedules, 135–139
extinction, 148–149
generalization and discrimination,
 138–140
individual differences, 140–141
positive contingencies, 142–144
prevalence of, 118
punishment and, 122–125, 144–147
reinforcement in, 120–122
reinforcement schedules, 126–134
and respondent learning, 117–118
social cognitive theory
 agentic perspective, 383–388
 applications of, 388–391
 appraisal of, 391–392
 control systems in, 380–383
 observational learning and, 371
 operant conditioning in, 374–380
 overview of, 371–374
social learning, 368, 440–441
social speech, 281, *See also* inner
 speech, egocentric speech
socialization, 368
sociobiology
 defined, 173
 inclusive fitness and altruism,
 174–175
 instincts, 330
 reaction to, 175
socioeconomic status (SES), 187
software, 397, *See also* wetware,
 hardware
soma, 201
soul, 7
spaced repetition, 320, *See also*
 interleaving, blocked repetition
Spielrein, Sabrina, 260
spontaneous recovery, 52, 131, *See*
 also extinction
spread of effect, 94
SQ3R method, 491
stamping in/out (connections), 88, 119
stepping reflex, 47
stimulation need, 340–342
stimuli
 as input variable, 99
 scientific psychology, 28
stimulus discrimination, 53
stimulus generalization, 53
stimulus generation. *See* transfer
stimulus substitution, 91
stimulus-intensity dynamism (V), 101
structuralism, 27, 430, *See also*
 functionalism

Study of Thinking, A (Bruner), 254
subjects (sampling), 23
sucking reflex, 47
suicide, 175
superstitious schedule, 127–128
surveys, 17
swimming reflex, 47
symbol shock, 103
symbolic models, 371, 400–403, *See also* connectionist model
symbolic representation, 248, *See also* iconic representation, enactive representation
sympathetic nervous system, 338
synapse, 203
synaptic cleft, 201
synaptic knobs, 201, *See also* terminal boutons, counterconditioning
systemic desensitization, 53, *See also* counterconditioning

tabula rasa doctrine, 62, 165, 446–447
taste aversion
  blocking, 160–163
  classical conditioning and, 156–159
  defined, 48, 156
  latent inhibition and, 159–160
  selectivity in, 159
teacher importance, 321–322
temporal lobe, 184, 314, *See also* parietal lobe, occipital lobe, frontal lobe
terminal boutons, 201, *See also* synaptic knobs
Terminal Notes: Foresight, Foreknowledge, Expectancy and Purpose (Hull), 105
testing effect, 321
Textbook of Psychology, A (Hebb), 200
thalamus, 183
theory, 493, *See also* principle, belief
theory of identical elements, 90–91, *See also* law of response by analogy
theory of natural selection, 108, 164
thinking. *See also* higher mental processes
  computers and, 401–403
  higher mental processes and, 198
  logical thought and narratives in, 255
  mediation as, 209–210

third-order conditioning. *See* higher-order conditioning
Thorndike, Edward L.
  on animal intelligence, 83–86
  associative shifting, 91
  biography, 86–87
  law of effect, 88–89, 92–93, 432–433
  law of exercise, 88, 92
  law of multiple responses, 90
  law of prepotency of elements, 90
  law of readiness, 90
  law of response by analogy, 90–91
  law of set or attitude, 90
  natural selection and, 164
  principle of belongingness, 94
  Skinner and, 119
  spread of effect, 94
  summary of, 94–95
Thought and Language (Vygotsky), 278
threshold technique, 39–42, 73, *See also* method of incompatible stimuli, inhibitory conditioning, fatigue technique
time-in procedure, 146, *See also* time-out procedure
time-out procedure, 389, *See also* time-in procedure
Titchener, Edward Bradford, 40
toe grasp, 47
token, 493
Tolman, Edward Chace
  biography, 214–215
  metaphors and, 233
  need/drive theory and, 334
  purposive behaviorism, 214–221, 435–436
  Skinner and, 113
Top Chess Engine Championship, 403
trace-dependent forgetting, 319. *See also* cue-dependent forgetting
trace pairing. *See also* simultaneous pairing, delayed pairing, backward pairing
  defined, 49–50
  taste aversion and, 158
trait, 141
transductive reasoning, 266
transfer. *See* generalization
triadic reciprocal determinism, 387, *See also* reciprocal determinism

trial and error learning, 224
trial and error problem solving, 84
tribalism, 386
Turing test, 412–415

umami, 158
unconditioned response, 44–46, *See also* respondent
unconditioned stimulus (US), 44–46

variable, 18
verbal instructions, 139
vicarious reinforcement, 375, *See also* direct reinforcement
virtual reality (VR), 372, 420
visual-spatial sketch pad, 299, *See also* working memory, phonological loop, episodic buffer, central executive system
Vygotsky blocks, 280
Vygotsky, Lev
  biography, 277–278
  culture and language concepts of, 438

Walden Two (Skinner), 151
Watson, John B.
  behaviorism and, 57–58, 63–66, 432
  biography, 54–56
  environmentalism and, 62–63
  individual differences, 140
  learning explanation, 58
  Little Albert study, 58–62
  on higher learning, 63
Weber's law, 42
Wertheimer, Max, 222–223, 230
wetware, 397, *See also* software, hardware
working memory, 296–301, *See also* visual-spatial sketch pad, short-term memory, sensory memory, phonological loop, central executive system
Wundt, Wilhelm
  absolute threshold, 40
  structuralism and, 27, 39

Yerkes–Dodson law, 338–340

zeitgeist, 64
zone of proximal development, 282–283, *See also* scaffolding